THE SOCIAL VALUE OF THE FINANCIAL SECTOR

Too Big to Fail or Just Too Big?

World Scientific Studies in International Economics

(ISSN: 1793-3641)

Vol. 22 International Trade Policy Formation: Theory and Politics
by Wolfgang Mayer (University of Cincinnati, USA)

Vol. 23 Priorities and Pathways in Services Reform:
Part I — Quantitative Studies
edited by Philippa Dee (Australian National University, Australia)

Vol. 24 Globalizing Information: The Economics of International Technology Trade
by Keith E Maskus (University of Colorado at Boulder, USA)

Vol. 25 Priorities and Pathways in Services Reform: Part II — Political Economy Studies
edited by Christopher Findlay (University of Adelaide, Australia)

Vol. 26 World Trade Organization and International Trade Law: Antidumping, Subsidies and Trade Agreements
by Gary N Horlick (Law Offices of Gary N Horlick, USA & University of Bern, Switzerland)

Vol. 27 European Economic Integration, WTO Membership, Immigration and Offshoring
by Wilhelm Kohler (University of Tübingen, Germany)

Vol. 28 Services Trade Reform: Making Sense of It
by Philippa Dee (Australian National University, Australia)

Vol. 29 The Social Value of the Financial Sector: Too Big to Fail or Just Too Big?
edited by Viral V Acharya (New York University, USA & Centre for Economic Policy (CEPR), UK), Thorsten Beck (Tilburg University, The Netherlands & Centre for Economic Policy (CEPR), UK), Douglas D Evanoff (Federal Reserve Bank of Chicago, USA), George G Kaufman (Loyola University Chicago, USA), & Richard Portes (London Business School, UK & Centre for Economic Policy (CEPR), UK)

Vol. 30 The Role of Central Banks in Financial Stability: How Has It Changed?
edited by Douglas D Evanoff (Federal Reserve Bank of Chicago, USA), Cornelia Holthausen (European Central Bank, Germany), George G Kaufman (Loyola University Chicago, USA) & Manfred Kremer (European Central Bank, Germany)

The complete list of the published volumes in the series can be found at
http://www.worldscientific.com/series/wssie

29 World Scientific Studies in International Economics

THE SOCIAL VALUE OF THE FINANCIAL SECTOR

Too Big to Fail or Just Too Big?

Editors

Viral V Acharya

New York University, USA & Centre for Economic Policy (CEPR), UK

Thorsten Beck

Tilburg University, The Netherlands & Centre for Economic Policy (CEPR), UK

Douglas D Evanoff

Federal Reserve Bank of Chicago, USA

George G Kaufman

Loyola University Chicago, USA

Richard Portes

London Business School , UK & Centre for Economic Policy (CEPR), UK

World Scientific

NEW JERSEY • LONDON • SINGAPORE • BEIJING • SHANGHAI • HONG KONG • TAIPEI • CHENNAI

Published by

World Scientific Publishing Co. Pte. Ltd.
5 Toh Tuck Link, Singapore 596224
USA office: 27 Warren Street, Suite 401-402, Hackensack, NJ 07601
UK office: 57 Shelton Street, Covent Garden, London WC2H 9HE

Library of Congress Cataloging-in-Publication Data
Acharya, Viral V.
The social value of the financial sector : too big to fail or just too big? / by Viral V Acharya (New York University, USA & Centre for Economic Policy (CEPR), UK), Thorsten Beck (Centre for Economic Policy (CEPR), UK & Tilburg University, The Netherlands), Douglas D Evanoff (Federal Reserve Bank of Chicago, USA), George G Kaufman (Loyola University Chicago, USA) & Richard Portes (Centre for Economic Policy (CEPR), UK & London Business School , UK).
pages cm. -- (World scientific studies in international economics, ISSN 1793-3641 ; 29)
Includes bibliographical references and index.
ISBN 978-9814520287
1. Financial institutions. 2. Financial institutions--Government policy. 3. Banks and banking. 4. Social policy. I. Title.
HG173.A224 2013
332.1--dc23

2013027960

British Library Cataloguing-in-Publication Data
A catalogue record for this book is available from the British Library.

Cover Illustration by Ping Homeric.

In-house Editors: Sandhya Venkatesh/Dipasri Sardar

Typeset by Stallion Press
Email: enquiries@stallionpress.com

Printed in Singapore by World Scientific Printers.

Preface

The large-scale damage inflicted on the economies of countries throughout the world by the financial crisis of 2007 to, at least, 2010, has ignited widespread re-evaluation of the net social benefits derived from large and growing domestic and international financial sectors. These sectors tended to expand much faster before the crisis than did their national GDPs. For example, the aggregate on-balance-sheet dollar size of the 11 major types of US financial institutions included in the Federal Reserve's flow of funds data more than doubled from 1.27% of GDP in 1970 to 2.85% of GDP in 2007.

A large number of empirical research studies have provided evidence that deeper and more efficient financial systems are associated in the longer run with higher and more rapid economic growth. But periodically, the system crashes, and the larger the system, the deeper and broader the damage. Does the damage partially, totally, or more than totally offset the gains realized from the financial sector during noncrisis periods? We typically think of market distortions, and resulting adverse welfare effects, from having financial institutions that are too-big-to-fail. However, it may be that in certain cases, the financial sector is simply too big, resulting in inefficiencies and generating societal welfare losses. If this is the case, how can public policy do something about it?

These were some of the major questions addressed by participants at the Fifteenth Annual Federal Reserve Bank of Chicago International Banking Conference, cosponsored with the Centre for Economic Policy Research (CEPR) in London. The conference was held in Chicago on November 15–16, 2012. Some 175 participants, representing policymakers, financial regulators, financial practitioners, researchers, and academics from some 30 countries participated. Specific topics discussed included the costs and benefits of the current financial industry structure, social benefits from financial industry innovation, effects of regulation on societal welfare, the financial situation and resulting economic activity across countries, and the potential benefits and costs associated with the breaking up of large banks.

This volume includes the papers presented at the Chicago conference, including the keynote addresses by leading experts in the field. The publication of the papers in this volume is intended to disseminate the conference ideas, analyses, and conclusions to a wider audience. Hopefully, that broader distribution will generate additional discussion, serve as the basis for further analyses, and be used to guide public policy.

Acknowledgments

Both the conference held at the Federal Reserve Bank of Chicago, November 15–16, 2012, and this volume represent a joint effort of the Federal Reserve Bank of Chicago and the Centre for Economic Policy Research (CEPR). Various people at each institution contributed to the effort. The five editors served as the principal organizers of the conference program and would like to thank all the people who contributed their time and energy to the effort. At the risk of omitting some people, we would like to thank Julia Baker, John Dixon, Ella Dukes, Ping Homeric, and Rita Molloy. Special mention should be accorded Kathryn Moran, who managed the Chicago Fed's web effort; Sandy Schneider, who expertly managed the conference administration; as well as Helen O'D. Koshy and Sheila Mangler, who had primary responsibility for preparing the manuscripts for this book.

Contents

PART I

KEYNOTE ADDRESSES

A Ferment of Regulatory Proposals

Charles A. E. Goodhart*

London School of Economics

A Simpler Approach?

The financial crisis has spawned a ferment of ideas for improving regulation. As with most fermentation, some rather odd notions have bubbled up to the surface. One such is that there was a golden era in the past, between World War II and the 1970s, when banking was simple, straightforward, and trustworthy; banking crises were nonexistent; and, as an ordinary depositor, one could actually talk personally to one's bank manager, either face to face or over the phone.

Actually in my country, the UK, those conditions were primarily achieved by direct controls over both the amount of bank lending to the private sector, and often its direction between sectors, and by a rigorous suppression of competition in the financial sector. All parts of finance were cartelized, and rates were set via such central cartels, all with the vocal encouragement of the authorities. You could, indeed, talk to your bank manager, but he (there were no "shes") was programmed to say "no."

From the late 1960s onward, a small group of us in the Bank of England, led by John Fforde but including Eddie George and Andrew Crockett, campaigned to end this tightly controlled system, and in 1971 we succeeded with the publication of "Competition and Credit Control." The competition-easing aspect worked fine, but during the subsequent 1972–1973 boom the credit control left much to be desired, not least because of political constraints over the flexible use of the interest rate weapon.

---

*Charles Goodhart is Emeritus Professor of Banking and Finance in the Financial Markets Group at the London School of Economics.

More recently, interest rates have been predicated to the primary need to achieve an inflation target, and that, once again, has meant that, during a contemporaneous housing boom, interest rates could not be, or at any rate were not, used to stabilize credit and asset price expansion. This has led to proposals for other instruments of control, in particular via macroprudential regulatory control. There is, however, a problem here. If regulation is to be effective, it must have the effect of preventing the regulated from doing what they want to do. So they will attempt to avoid it. Usually they succeed, though perhaps only after a time. As Ed Kane has argued, there is a dialectic in the regulatory process: Crisis leads to regulation, which begets avoidance and erosion, which begets crisis, and so on ad infinitum. Let me coin an aphorism, "If regulation is simple, it will be simple to avoid it." The Basel I risk buckets were simple, and they were simply avoided, for example, via securitization.

Indeed this suggests a second dialectic. We start with a simple regulatory proposal. The regulated then find some fairly easy ways around it. This leads to a more complicated and lengthy second round of regulations to prevent or mitigate such avoidance measures. These more complicated measures in themselves then open up further ways of trying to avoid such regulations, which, in turn, leads to a vastly more complex third stage of countervailing measures. At this point the regulations run into hundreds of pages, and no one is quite sure quite how they operate, if they operate effectively at all. At this juncture the cry goes up that we must revert to a simpler system. This proposal has obvious advantages, and so we start on yet another cycle.

Incidentally I have never owned, and have rarely seen, a dog that could catch frisbee, which, as you may recall, was the title of Andy Haldane's much-quoted paper at the latest Jackson Hole Conference, arguing for more simplicity in regulation. Perhaps that was because my dogs took after their owner in being resolutely nonmathematical. Indeed, my cairn terriers would have regarded chasing plastic Frisbees rather than flesh-and-blood squirrels as below their dignity.

Almost all regulatory structures, on their own, can be avoided and manipulated. The direction and channeling of the recent crisis was considerably influenced by regulatory arbitrage between US banks, which were subject to an overall leverage limit but not to Basel II, and US broker–dealers and European banks, which were subject to Basel II but not to a simple leverage ratio. What happened, unsurprisingly, was that the Basel II banks gorged on supposedly low-risk leverage expansion, while the US banks took on the riskier tranches of MBS, and indeed suffered higher losses per unit of assets than their European counterparts.

In my view, the Europeans came off worst in this exchange, partly because risk weighting is inherently defective. The riskiness of an asset is *not* constant over time, but context dependent, even more so in the face of innovation. Moreover, the risk weights adopted are inevitably somewhat subject to political interference involving the exercise of national interest, as witnessed by the long saga of what risk weight to attach to the government bonds of other states. Governments, as well as private sector agents, can be subject to conflicts of interest. Thus, I personally am sorry that Basel III still places much more emphasis on risk-weighted ratios than on a simpler leverage ratio, with the latter being so permissive, at 33 to 1, that it is hardly more than a back-up minimal protection; though I would just note, *en passant*, that the central banks themselves are not now practicing what they preach in this respect. I hesitate to calculate their own leverage ratios in case I might scare someone.

I would prefer to shift the regulatory balance more toward the simpler overall leverage ratio, but to believe that *by itself* would suffice is to forget my prior aphorism. Simple leverage ratios can be overcome by taking on riskier assets, by accounting tricks, and by disintermediating over the boundary between what is included and what excluded in both the numerator and denominator. I would certainly not go so far as to promote a theory about the conservation of risk, but nevertheless much regulation has more influence on the locus where risk becomes concentrated rather than its overall extent. Nevertheless, the greater reliance in the US on simpler leverage ratios did help to limit the size, and hence the potential damage from the financial sector here, in contrast to Europe.

It has now become fashionable in economics to switch our similes from physics to epidemiology and ecology. In that vein, let me note that when a dangerous condition is resistant to a single antidote, it can often be treated by a cocktail of drugs. In the field of regulation that means that we should not aim to rely on a single approach, but use both risk-weighted *and* overall simple leverage ratios, belt and braces.

How to Get from Here to There

There are many who might claim that this issue of how to design the regulatory approach, i.e., risk-weighted, or simple leverage, or both, or something else again, is a second-order problem. The first-order problem was, instead, that the required amount of loss-absorbing equity capital, and available liquid assets, was just too low. Waving our Modigliani–Miller theorem in the air, we triumphantly demonstrate that the equilibrium interest rate spreads would not be much higher, whereas safety would be greatly enhanced, if normal equity ratios were raised by some sizable multiple over its pre-2008 starting point. Moreover, unless the standard, normally maintained, equilibrium ratio is much higher, how could the authorities possibly *lower* required ratios during periods of economic and financial stress, which is exactly what countercyclical macroprudential policy would imply that you *should* do.

Well okay, but such very much higher ratios have two consequential implications. First, they should not be treated, as they have been in the past, as reputational lower limits. They must be part of a usable buffer. That implies devising a ladder of sanctions as banks start to eat into such a large buffer, and on the need to make a conscious decision on where the bottom, acceptable limit, beyond which intervention and resolution should occur, is taken to be. Basel III has made a start in this direction, with the conservation range between 7% and 4.5% of core tier 1 equity, with banks in this range being restricted in their payouts to shareholders and management. But much more needs to be done to change ideas, presentation, and semantics to shift from treating all regulatory ratios as minimums to having many of them seen as norms.

But what is more immediately important is that the Modigliani–Miller analysis represents a comparison of static equilibrium states and has relatively little bearing on the dynamic process of shifting from state 1 to state 2. Indeed, several of our best economists who have been most prominent in defending Modigliani–Miller from the assault of bankers, for example, Anat Admati and Martin Hellwig, have been equally vocal in warning that the dynamic process of trying to move toward a much higher equilibrium capital ratio is fraught with difficulty and danger.

A combination of debt overhang, miserable price to book equity value ratios, and bank executives whose wealth is largely tied up with their own bank's equity valuation means that banks will prefer deleveraging to making new equity issues. The more that regulators force up required ratios now, the worse will be deleveraging. Some answer that it is the market, not regulators, who demand higher bank equity ratios. Up to a point, but remember that so long as such ratios are treated as reputational minimums, what the market will demand is satisfactory buffers, or margins, *above* such regulatory ratios, whereas the latter are set by the regulatory authorities. To some extent the strong incentive at present *not* to issue more equity capital can be partially met by setting regulatory requirements, for the time being at least, in absolute rather than in ratio format, and using limitations on payouts to shareholders and bank executives as a sanction, or incentive, to get from here to there. In all such respects the actions on this front taken in the US have been much, much better than those in Europe.

Let me next draw your attention to an important recent British development related to the current Funding for Lending Scheme, or FLS. In economics, especially microeconomics, we are well aware of the important distinction between marginal and average. We can, and perhaps should, make that same distinction in regulation. Thus, under the FLS, *additional* lending to the UK private sector enjoys a waiver of risk-weighted CARs, while for other assets CARs have been greatly increased. Thus, by divorcing marginal from average regulatory requirements we can, to some extent, influence portfolio distribution separately from average safety requirements. I have advocated doing the same trick with commercial bank reserves at the central bank by lowering marginal returns, relative to the average returns on such reserves. One concern that I do have is that such schemes could be used to reinforce national financial protectionism by privileging lending at home rather than abroad. Another concern could be that regulatory instruments, which should be primarily about systemic safety, could then be increasingly employed for other macroeconomic purposes. But, that said, it is generally better to have more instruments rather than fewer.

A More Structural Approach

So there are undoubtedly difficulties in moving at all rapidly to a world in which the norm would be for banks to maintain substantially higher capital (and liquidity) ratios than in the recent past. Moreover, the ease of avoiding simple regulations suggests that we will have to maintain complex belt-and-braces combinations of risk-weighted and simpler leverage ratios. Even then, many would back clever bank employees to circumvent whatever the regulators think up. In this context there is a growing bandwagon toward a much more dirigiste approach to financial intermediation, constraining what banks can do, and what they are not permitted to do, a more structural approach. Let me repeat: I saw this latter kind of systemic structural approach personally when I started back in the 1960s and 1970s, and I did not much like it then. No doubt my views are colored by my personal experience.

Perhaps the leading example of this approach is to be found in the recommendation to separate retail and wholesale banking, as advanced by the British Independent Commission on Banking, the Vickers Report, and taken on in a marginally different guise by the recent Liikanen Report. It is far from clear to me why this separate subsidiarization under a single holding company should make for greater safety. Moreover, the bets that sank our banks were primarily about lending on property, commercial as well as residential. Such property-related loans are the bread and butter of retail banking. One of my legal colleagues in the UK has quipped that the effect of the separation will be to protect the safer wholesale bank from the risky retail outlet.

Moreover, with reinforced deposit insurance in place, and the availability of bridge banks, and good bank/bad bank mechanisms, the adverse externalities of allowing a retail bank to be closed and liquidated are, I would guess, considerably less than those arising from the closure of a similar-sized wholesale bank. The latter are likely to be far more interconnected, and their liquidation would, I expect, have a far more widespread and devastating effect on asset prices and the financial system more generally. The limitation of the public sector's bailout safety net to the retail subsidiaries of banks strikes me as owing more to real-politik than to economic analysis.

Apart from the 1981–1982 LDC loan crisis, all the recent periods of severe financial stress in the UK, 1973–1975, 1991–1992, and 2008–2009, have all been connected with property price bubbles and busts. The adoption of the Vickers Report will not prevent the next banking crisis in the UK, which I forecast will probably occur around 2026–2027, (note the 16-year gaps between each of the last three cases). Several of the more radical structuralists, such as Larry Kotlikoff in the US or John Kay in the UK tend to concur, and to advocate that retail banks get forcibly transformed into "narrow" banks, holding only short-dated or cash claims on the public sector.

But narrow bank deposits would have a low return. If one were to allow broad, wholesale banks to compete by offering transactions related, short-dated deposits, there would be a hugely procyclical stampede of such deposits out of broad banks into narrow banks during busts, and in the opposite direction during good times. Our radical structuralists have, however, thought of this, and would respond by *preventing* broad banks from offering any transactions-related, or short-dated deposits. Such broad banks could only be financed by equity or by long-dated deposits with significant penalties for early withdrawal. They would be made run-proof by diktat.

Such a system with narrow banks holding only cash-type assets, and all other finance done through the equivalent of investment trusts would, indeed, be safe. But it would also be inflexible and inefficient. Banks currently make promises to potential borrowers that they will be prepared to lend to them in future, in the form of facilities and overdrafts, at a time of the borrower's choosing without the bank having first already obtained the funding necessary to pay out to the borrower. It can do so because the bank in turn has, often short-term, lines of credit in wholesale markets, holds liquid assets, and at a pinch can also borrow from the central bank. Under the radical structural reforms, the investment banks would be left entirely reliant on their buffer reservoir of liquid assets for flexibility, or alternatively on the public sector providing the marginal funding. Either this buffer would have to expand a lot, which would both reduce the volume and raise the cost of the residual loans to the private sector, or potential private sector borrowers would have to queue until the broad banks had the funds in hand to lend on.

Overall the need for narrow banks to hold public sector debt and for broad banks to rely on a liquid assets buffer, presumably largely also of public sector debt, would privilege sales of public sector debt, relative to private sector debt, the hallmark of a repressed financial system. Indeed one aspect of Michael Kumhof's "Chicago Plan Revisited" is that it helps to resolve the problem of financing an over-large public sector debt.

That was more or less exactly how the banking system worked in the UK and Europe before liberalization. Admittedly the constraint was direct controls over bank lending rather than the narrow bank/investment bank set up, but the effects would be much the same. Certainly it was safer; but I did not like it then and I would not like it now. Let us try the belt-and-braces approach to capital adequacy first, moving much more carefully toward a much higher norm for equity ratios, before turning back toward radical restructuring.

Progress and Priorities for Financial Reform

Mary John Miller*

US Department of the Treasury

Introduction

Good afternoon. Thank you, David, for that kind introduction, and thanks for inviting me to be part of the Federal Reserve Bank of Chicago's Fifteenth Annual International Banking Conference. It is a pleasure to join this distinguished group of leaders in academia, government, and financial markets from around the world. Events like these, which promote public and private sector collaboration, help officials like me rise above my daily work and focus on the broader issues that affect our economy and markets. I look forward engaging with you further during question and answer period following my remarks.

As Under Secretary for Domestic Finance at the Treasury Department, I look for ways that we can work together on many of our country's most pressing economic challenges. I am very engaged in monitoring the economy and markets, managing our national debt, advancing housing finance reform, and overseeing the wind-down of our TARP investments. I also have another day job — I call it financial regulatory reform.

Just consider one high-profile example: the Volcker rule, which will restrict banking entities' ability to engage in proprietary trading and limit their investments in certain funds. Over the last two years, Treasury has been working closely with the five independent regulatory agencies responsible for writing the rule.

We received more than 18,000 comment letters, representing a wide range of views, on the proposed rule. We've gained additional insights

* Mary John Miller serves as the Under Secretary for Domestic Finance at the US Department of the Treasury.

from dozens of meetings with investor advocates, industry officials, and other market participants. Our goal is to achieve a strong and consistent rule, although the process is not as easy or simple as many of us would like.

Still, I'm pleased to report that we are making steady progress on the Volcker rule, and perhaps just as importantly, on the dozens of other rules introduced by the Dodd–Frank Act. Indeed, about 9 out of 10 rules scheduled to be in place have been either proposed or finalized — and we anticipate even more will take shape next year.

That should leave consumers, businesses, and other market participants with greater clarity and certainty, which is critical to strengthening our financial markets and instilling the confidence necessary for robust economic growth.

And that is why I want to take advantage of this opportunity to review some of the progress that we have made over the last four years and focus on some of the key areas that still need to be addressed.

A Stronger Financial System: Public and Private Reforms

Today, it is all too easy for us to forget that only four years ago we were in the middle of the worst financial crisis since the Great Depression. Housing prices plunged nearly 30% — the first nationwide decline in over 70 years. Our credit markets were frozen. And many of our financial institutions were so weak that they threatened the stability of the entire financial system.

However, thanks to the combined actions of our regulators, lawmakers, and officials from both parties, we were able to rebuild confidence, restore credit, and begin getting our economy back on track. Through novel liquidity facilities, guarantees, capital support programs, and intervention in the housing market, our government prevented a far more severe outcome.

Four years ago, almost no one anticipated recovering the crisis-related investments we made in our banking institutions or in AIG. Earning a return was an even more distant prospect. But thanks to the Treasury's Office of Financial Stability (OFS), we have been carefully unwinding our outstanding investments in ways that are beneficial to both taxpayers and markets.

Although these measures were necessary to rescue our financial system and to begin repairing the damage, we recognized early on that they were not a substitute for meaningful, long-term reform. We needed to make consumers safer, our financial institutions more resilient, and our markets more transparent. We also needed to empower our regulators with new legal and risk management tools to make sure that taxpayers would not be in a position to bear the costs of these firms' mistakes.

So, we enacted a package of critical reforms as part of the Dodd–Frank Act. We set up several new institutions, such as the Consumer Financial Protection Bureau (CFPB), the Financial Stability Oversight Council (FSOC), and the Office of Financial Research (OFR). New practices, such as annual stress tests and the use of living wills, were introduced to strengthen our financial institutions and make sure that our firms and regulatory agencies would be better prepared for the next financial storm. Meanwhile, we have worked with our international counterparts to coordinate our efforts globally through the G-20, the Financial Stability Board, and other forums.

At the same time, the private sector has been changing many practices on its own. We have seen financial markets and institutions adapt to a new environment, not just in anticipation of financial reform but in recognition that the old way of doing business would no longer work.

As a result of all these efforts, financial institutions have bolstered their level and quality of capital. US banks have raised their private capital levels to approximately $1 trillion, up 75 percent from $578 billion three years ago. Our financial institutions are also less reliant on the so-called shadow banking system for funding. Bank balance sheets are more liquid and transparent. These developments have made our financial system safer and stronger — and better able to support lending and economic growth.

In fact, one of the most encouraging signs has been the vast improvement in the credit markets. Four years ago, the credit markets were so deeply frozen that even the highest-quality issuers were unable to roll over their short-term debt. Short-term funding market yields were over 400 basis points higher than the Fed's policy rates. Major industrial corporations were highly constrained in their ability to issue commercial paper. In mid-September 2008, nearly $300 billion left prime money market funds in just one week.

Today, nearly all of the credit pipes of our financial system have reopened and, outside of the banking sector, credit spreads have largely returned to their pre-crisis levels. Short-term funding rates are clustered near 30 basis points, with secured financial transactions playing a more important role. And while we need to do more to restore credit availability, I am encouraged that consumers, businesses, and municipal governments are taking advantage of today's historically low interest rates.

Our financial markets are also becoming safer and stronger. For example, most swaps trading activity will increasingly move onto clearing houses and trading facilities over the next few years. Much of this can be attributed to the Dodd–Frank Act, which created a comprehensive regulatory framework for over-the-counter (OTC) derivatives. In fact, market participants have started to implement many of these changes in advance of full implementation of these new rules.

In particular, we have seen significant growth in centrally cleared interest rate swaps and credit default swaps. This year, central counter parties (CCPs) have started to accept new types of derivatives to clear, including energy swaps and new index products. These changes will reduce the risk that a default spreads across counter parties and will also enhance investor protection through increased disclosure. In addition to increased transparency and credit risk mitigation, firms can start to benefit from the possibility of netting offsetting contracts that trade through CCPs.

Our financial market infrastructure has also been bolstered by the development of trade repositories and a new supervisory framework over financial market utilities (FMUs). Under Title VII of the Dodd–Frank Act, trade repositories for each asset class will give regulators a more comprehensive understanding of the size, makeup, and distribution of exposure in the swap markets. In turn, this additional level of oversight should help mitigate the possibility of outsized risks building up in our financial system without anyone noticing.

Our payment, clearing, and settlement systems will also be strengthened by enhanced federal oversight. In July, the FSOC designated eight systemically important FMUs, subjecting them to heightened supervision and new risk-management standards. As we encourage more of these entities to handle higher volumes and manage risk throughout the system, supervisors should ensure they are adequately capitalized and subject to strong oversight and heightened risk-management practices.

More and more, I'm convinced that the concrete steps that we have taken to strengthen the foundation of our financial system are starting to pay dividends for stronger economic growth. We reversed a staggering 8.9% decline in economic output in the fourth quarter of 2008 and have posted 13 straight quarters of GDP growth. This helped create more than 5 million private sector jobs since the trough of the labor market in February 2010, including more than 500,000 in the manufacturing sector.

We have also seen the stock market more than double since the low point of early 2009. Indeed, its performance over the last four years stands out when compared to the major equity market indices in Europe and Asia.

And in many parts of the country, the housing market is coming back to life. Today, fewer borrowers are falling behind on their mortgage payments, and foreclosures in many areas are falling. And most recently, home sales, housing starts, and home prices have all improved on a national level.

As a long-time investor before I joined Treasury, I will be the first to acknowledge that these market developments are open to many different interpretations. We should never rely on one measure either to assess our progress or the challenges ahead. Indeed, resolution of the impending fiscal cliff as well as the ongoing uncertainty regarding the European debt crisis represent two pressing concerns. I believe, however, that the healing of the financial and housing markets over the last few years at least partially reflects a much stronger financial system — one that is better able to withstand economic stress and set us on a course for greater prosperity.

Looking Ahead

We still have more work to do. So, over the next few minutes, I would like to set out a few key near-term priorities. There are four areas that strike me as particularly important:

- Completing the Dodd–Frank Act mortgage-finance related rules in order to reinvigorate the private lending market;
- Reforming the short-term funding markets to improve investor confidence and reduce the risk of unnecessary market volatility;
- Delivering a set of derivatives rules that can be efficiently implemented and serve as a leading global standard; and
- Finalizing the Basel capital rules to help banks expand their lending activities with more confidence.

Let me provide more detail on each.

First, we must bring more clarity to the housing market by finalizing the mortgage finance rules required by the Dodd–Frank Act. This is critical to helping us bring more private investors back into the mortgage market to take credit risk, minimize taxpayer exposure by reducing the government's footprint, and improve access to mortgage credit — all priorities of the President and the Treasury Secretary.

In the coming weeks, we expect the CFPB to finalize the qualified mortgage rule, also known as QM. We expect this rule to provide a clear and standard definition for what qualifies as a quality mortgage for both lenders and borrowers. Once the QM rule is completed, it will be important to finalize the asset-backed securities risk retention rule, another rule in Dodd–Frank that affects mortgages and includes the qualified residential mortgage definition.

Once finalized, these rules should help enhance lender clarity at the point of mortgage origination. The rules should also improve investor confidence in the underlying credit characteristics of the loans investors might purchase in the secondary market. This, in turn, can help restart a more robust private securitization market for mortgages.

Reopening this market on a stronger footing is absolutely critical for achieving mortgage finance reform. Furthermore, private capital will expand access to mortgage credit, particularly to first-time homebuyers and those who are working to rebuild their credit in the aftermath of the crisis. That is why we remain committed to a future system where private markets — subject to strong oversight and standards for consumer and investor protection — will be the primary source of mortgage credit and bear the burden for losses.

Second, we must address the structural vulnerabilities of the short-term funding markets, including money market funds, so they do not put the health of our broader financial system at risk.

Indeed, money market funds provide a significant source of short-term funding for financial institutions, businesses, and governments. They are an important cash-management vehicle for both institutional and retail investors. However, the crisis demonstrated that money market funds are susceptible to runs and can be a source of financial instability with serious implications for broader financial markets and the economy.

To reduce this risk, we need to adopt reforms that strengthen money market funds' loss absorption capacity and reduce the risk of destabilizing investor runs. This week, the FSOC released for public comment its proposed recommendations for reform. We look forward to hearing from a range of market participants over the next few months as the FSOC process moves ahead.

We must also continue to improve the safety and soundness of our repurchase markets, which underpin another crucial source of short-term funding. Market participants and regulators need to complete the work of the Tri-Party Repo Infrastructure Reform Task Force. We need to finalize a framework that reduces reliance on intraday credit, adopts appropriate haircuts on less-liquid collateral, and improves the operational systems technology in tri-party repo. Deep and liquid repo markets are important for financial markets to operate efficiently, but they can also introduce risks to financial stability if they are not appropriately managed and monitored.

Third, we must be focused on completing derivatives rules that work domestically and internationally. Our reforms should be guided by the key pillars of derivatives market reform noted earlier: (i) trades should be cleared where appropriate and subject to a strong margin regime, (ii) the most standard derivatives should move to trade execution platforms, and (iii) we should develop prudential regulations of large dealers and large market participants and provide enhanced disclosure to the public and regulators. In the near term, we will work with the market regulators to help adopt rules that are driven by these core principles.

The derivatives market is global and highly mobile, and as a result one regulator or one jurisdiction cannot effectively enact reforms alone. We strongly support efforts by US market regulators to align their rules on transactions that are subject to regulation under the Dodd–Frank Act. To provide certainty to global market participants, many of whom are hedging risks that are integral to their core operations, the US market regulators should strive to establish consistent standards that apply to cross-border transactions of similar types. We also support our regulators' work with their international counterparts to develop robust frameworks for effective substituted compliance wherever appropriate while always keeping in mind the notes of regulatory arbitrage and the need for transparency. US market regulators should also continue to work with their foreign peers to develop consistent frameworks to avoid unnecessary and unproductive conflicts that inhibit the development of coordinated global rules. This will help increase confidence in markets.

Finally, it is important for the banking regulators to finalize the regulations implementing the new Basel III standards for capital and liquidity. Having clear, final rules will give banking institutions the clarity and confidence to expand their lending activities. This past June, the Federal Reserve, OCC, and FDIC jointly issued the final market risk capital rules and also issued three notices of proposed rulemaking (NPRs) that would help implement the new Basel capital rules as well as certain aspects of the Dodd–Frank Act. Regulators are now reviewing the nearly 1,500 comment letters on the three NPRs as they work toward completing the rulemaking process.

As many of you know, these regulations were expected to be phased in starting January 2013 through January 2019. However, earlier this month, the banking agencies formally announced they do not expect the proposed rules to become effective on January 1, 2013. They also offered some assurance that institutions will have time for transition after the rules take effect.

In the meantime, our banking agencies should work closely with their international counterparts toward Basel III implementation. Currently, only eight of the 27 Basel committee members have issued final Basel III regulations. US banking regulators should be mindful of divergences with their international peers, which may lead to regulatory arbitrage and uncertainty on the part of firms trying to manage capital resources. In addition, we encourage our international counterpart to implement the Basel III leverage ratio to ensure that there is a simple backstep against excessive note and to promote a level playing field.

In Treasury's conversations with community banks and with our colleagues at the regulatory agencies, it has become clear that the standards established in Basel III may have different implications for different types of institutions. While we strongly believe that finalizing the regulations is critically important for certainty and planning, we also believe there are merits to considering alternative, simpler approaches to rules that apply to community banks. For example, prudent mortgage lending by institutions like community banks and savings associations are critical to many communities. Our rules should recognize the important roles these institutions play.

Why It Matters

Why am I so intent on laying out these priorities? Because finalizing the mortgage finance rules, derivatives regulations, and the Basel capital rules as well as protecting short-term funding markets are not just goals unto themselves. Clarity engenders confidence in our financial system, and it is a crucial ingredient for job creation and economic growth. That is why it is so important that we press forward with financial reform.

I recognize that this is not easy. Reform is hard. Memories of the financial crisis fade. And we have some tough assignments ahead that require coordination not just among banking and market regulators, but also with our international counterparts. The term "level playing field" is often invoked, but is hard to achieve in practice. While we strive for simplicity in our reform efforts, we must recognize that we have a complex and globally interconnected financial system.

But I think the importance of getting the rules right goes directly to the theme of this conference, and more broadly, the work that we do at the Treasury Department every day. Quite simply, our financial policies matter because of the critical role that financial institutions and markets play in our everyday lives.

- They matter for the small business seeking to borrow funds to hire and expand.
- They matter for families seeking to send their children to college or purchase a home.
- They matter to governments that must finance public services.
- And they matter for workers who are investing for retirement.

We've made significant progress since the crisis four years ago. Our financial system is better off. But we still must complete the charge that we laid out in 2009. If we get reform right, we will not only continue to strengthen our financial system but bolster the prospects for a stronger recovery in the months and years ahead.

PART II

DESCRIPTION AND MEASUREMENT OF THE FINANCIAL SYSTEM

What Is Meaningful Banking Reform, Why Is It So Necessary ... and So Unlikely?

Charles W. Calomiris*
Columbia Business School
and
National Bureau of Economic Research

The Problem

Reform or repression: That is fast becoming the choice. On one hand, there is evidence that large, global, universal banks have played a unique and productive role as providers of financial services. It is worth preserving the unique capacities of those global banks, if possible. For example, Great Britain's Big Bang of 1986 — which not only reformed its securities trading, but also ushered in a new era of global universal banking — was associated with a boom in securities offerings and trading and also produced a tripling of the ratio of bank credit to GDP from 1986 to 1990 (Calomiris and Haber, 2013, Chapter 5, Figure 5.4). The new global universal banks offered a rich and unique array of financial services for their global corporate clients, and unique geographical reach, which made banks useful not only for credit, hedging, and securities offerings, but also for strategic advice about managing the financial structure and global operations of clients.

It is just as clear, however, that unless meaningful reforms are undertaken — which result in proper risk management practices and the end of too-big-to-fail bailouts — eventually, the political tide will turn against global universal banking. The social costs of bailing out global

*Charles W. Calomiris is the Henry Kaufman Professor of Financial Institutions at Columbia Business School and Research Associate of the National Bureau of Economic Research.

banks — especially in countries like Great Britain and Switzerland, whose banking systems are enormous relative to their GDP — are simply too great to be tolerated.

The 2007–2009 financial crisis was the most disruptive global banking crisis since the Depression, but it was not a unique event. Over the past three decades, the world has experienced a global pandemic of banking instability. Over 100 major banking crises have occurred worldwide, with bailout costs that average about 16% of GDP, and forgone GDP costs resulting from the recessions that coincided with those credit collapses of roughly the same amount. This is unprecedented. For example, during the prior wave of financial globalization, from 1874 to 1913, there were only five country-episodes of significant banking system insolvency in the world, with much smaller resolution costs as a share of GDP. Those episodes (in Argentina, Australia, Brazil, Italy, and Norway) reflected unusual policy choices that encouraged or subsidized banking system risk; what was rare historically has become the norm (Calomiris and Haber, 2013, Chapter 1).

The exceptionalism of the current era of banking instability gives cause for hope about the physical possibility of reform to succeed; it shows that banking systems are not inherently prone to disaster. But the exceptionalism of the current era also gives cause for pessimism: The new era of banking instability reflects a pervasive change in the politics of banking that will be hard to reverse.

The key political decision driving instability has been the protection of banks' liabilities by governments. Once governments protect banks — through a combination of explicit deposit insurance, lender of last resort assistance, and ad hoc bailouts — bank debt holders have little incentive to monitor banks' risks or to withhold funding as the result of increases in the riskiness of bank debts. In principle, prudential regulation, enforced by regulators and supervisors, can replace market discipline, and thereby prevent banks from taking excessive risks, by imposing minimum capital ratio and cash ratio requirements and other prudential rules. In practice, however, regulators and supervisors generally have not proven equal to the task.

How and Why Regulatory Discipline Fails

In the decades leading up to the recent banking crisis, regulators and supervisors consistently failed in three key areas: (1) they did not measure banks' risks credibly or accurately, or set sufficient minimum equity capital buffers in accordance with those risks so that banks would be able to absorb potential portfolio losses reliably; (2) they failed to enforce even the inadequate capital requirements that they did impose because supervisors consistently failed to identify bank losses as they mounted, and thus allowed banks to overstate their levels of capital; and (3) they failed to design or enforce intervention protocols for timely resolution of the affairs of weakened banks to limit the exposure of taxpayers to protecting the liabilities of feeble, "too-big-to-fail" banks.

The failures of prudential bank regulation have been visible for decades and have motivated many regulatory reform proposals by financial economists. There are credible solutions to the key policy challenges that the government faces. For the most part, my proposed solutions to those problems are not new; they have been known and advocated by financial economists for quite some time. The failure to prevent the crisis was not a failure of thinking, but a failure of will on the part of our political system. Our politicians and regulators have found it expedient to offer hidden subsidies for risk-taking to bankers and bank borrowers through the combination of safety net protection and ineffectual prudential regulation. Attempts to identify and rein in those subsidies have been defeated politically time and time again.

Will proposed reforms in response to the crisis this time be effective? Will reformers succeed in implementing changes in the rules of the game that would reduce the chance of a repeat of the recent crisis? The experience with post-crisis reforms in financial history offers, at best, a mixed record of responses (see Calomiris, 2010; 2011a); overall, it is fair to say that there is lots of cause for pessimism for a simple reason: Politicians don't really have strong incentives to solve the problems of banking regulation; they have strong incentives only to pretend to do so.

The typical post-crisis response gives the appearance of diligence, as politicians and regulators assemble a laundry list of the things that went wrong in the crisis — typically defined with reference to the specific symptoms of poor policies, not the deeper incentive problems that policy errors have produced. That laundry list then gives rise to a new, more complex set of regulatory initiatives, and these laws and rules are advertised as preventing a recurrence of the problems.

Deficiencies are supposedly remedied by ever-more complex sets of rules for measuring risk — by the granting of increased supervisory discretion to a variety of new government officials with varying mandates, by scores of new research initiatives pursued by increasingly fragmented research and supervisory divisions at central banks and supervisory agencies, and by the creation of new international study groups. Is it too cynical to see this exponential increase in complexity of rules, and of the regulatory and supervisory authorities charged with designing and enforcing them, as purposely designed to reduce accountability by dividing responsibility and by making the regulatory process less comprehensible to outsiders? I don't think so.

The implicit theory behind these sorts of initiatives, to the extent that there is a theory, is that the recent crisis happened because regulatory standards were not quite complex enough, because the extensive discretionary authority of bank supervisors was not great enough, and because rules and regulations prohibiting or discouraging specific practices were not sufficiently extensive.

This theory is demonstrably false. At the core of the recent financial crisis — and the many that preceded it around the world in the past three decades — have been basic incentive problems in the rules of the game set by the government. The pre-2007 environment was one in which regulatory complexity was unprecedented, supervisory enforcement was virtually nonexistent, and private risk-taking at public expense was virtually unlimited. This is the environment that has produced the most unstable three decades of global banking history, and the most severe financial crisis in the US since the Great Depression.

The need is not for more complex rules, and more supervisory discretion, but rather, for *rules that are meaningful in measuring and limiting risk, hard for market participants to circumvent, and credibly enforced by supervisors.* These qualities are best achieved by constructing *simpler* rules that are grounded in an understanding of the *incentive problems of market participants and supervisors/regulators.* At the heart of the failure of regulatory discipline has been the failure to address the basic incentive problems of market participants — which benefit by gaming the system to increase the amount of risk they take at taxpayers' expense — and supervisors and regulators — who are subject to acute short-term political pressures to keep credit flowing and long-term political pressures to favor the interests of particular borrowers and lenders.

Most recently, these influences have been clearly visible — almost comically — in the new liquidity standards proposed under the Basel III rules. Ironically, cash requirements are a centuries-old prudential tool that has been used, and continues to be used, in some countries, to great effect. Rather than follow hundreds of years of countless precedents by imposing a simple requirement that banks hold a substantial amount of cash assets (clearly and narrowly defined) in proportion to some observable quantity (e.g., total debt, total deposits, total assets, or total risk-weighted assets), the Basel Committee devised two complicated formulas for liquidity requirements. In each formula, the numerator (which defines liquid assets) includes noncash assets, and the denominator requires judgment about the liquidity risk associated with various categories of bank liabilities. Not only does this standard have potentially undesirable adverse consequences (by discouraging bank liquidity creation), but its complexity renders the enforcement of the standard opaque and therefore unaccountable. Then, in reaction to industry complaints that this ill-advised standard would have adverse consequences for the supply of lending, its implementation was postponed until 2019.

The keys to effective prudential regulatory reform are, first, recognizing the core incentive problems that encourage excessive risk-taking and ineffective prudential regulation and supervision, and, second, designing reforms that are "incentive-robust" — that is, reforms that are likely not to be undermined by the self-seeking regulatory arbitrage of market participants, or the self-seeking avoidance of the recognition of problems by supervisors. The primary challenge is not devising effective ideas for reform, but rather, building a political coalition that will support the implementation of such ideas.

Some Specific Ideas

The first overarching reform that I would propose is a procedural one. Any economist or policymaker who puts forth a regulatory reform proposal should have to explain, within that proposed reform, why market participants will find it difficult to circumvent the reform, and why regulators and supervisors will have personal incentives to enforce it in a manner that will make it effective. Until our conversation of regulation takes these incentive problems seriously, progress will be impossible.

I have also developed numerous specific incentive-robust reform proposals that meet these criteria. These proposals would simplify the regulatory structure, make it transparent and therefore accountable, and focus attention on the key challenges of bank risk measurement, bank capital measurement, and the timely enforcement of regulatory standards that ensure banks will continuously maintain adequate capital and cash relative to their risk (for the details of these proposals, and explanations of why they would promote effective management of risk, see Calomiris, 2011b; 2012; Calomiris and Herring, 2012). Rather than beginning by pretending that incentive problems on the part of market participants and regulators and supervisors do not exist (as in the Basel system), my proposals begin by taking those incentive problems seriously and trying to devise rules that are robust in spite of them.

These proposals include seven prudential reforms, which I summarize in Table 1: (1) the reform of the regulatory use of ratings that would quantify the meaning of debt ratings and hold nationally recognized statistical rating organizations (NRSROs) accountable financially for egregious inaccuracy in forecasting the probability of default of rated debts; (2) the use of observable loan interest rate spreads as forecasts of nonperforming loans for purposes of budgeting capital to absorb loan default risk; (3) the establishment of a transparent and simple contingent capital (CoCo) requirement that incentivizes large banks to replace lost capital in a timely way (rather than disguise losses and avoid replacing lost capital); (4) the setting of simple cash requirements for banks (this would not resemble the complicated and poorly conceived new "liquidity" requirements created by the Basel III process); (5) the creation of a simple macroprudential rule to govern the variation in capital requirements over time, which would trigger changes only under clearly extreme circumstances, based on objective, observable criteria; (6) a reform of resolution procedures for large financial institutions that would require a pre-specified minimum "haircut" on unsecured creditors whenever the resolution authority employs taxpayer funds in the resolution (i.e., whenever there is a departure from the enforcement of strict priority in the resolution process); and (7) the establishment, as part of the "living wills" of global financial institutions that govern their prospective

Table 1. A program for incentive-robust regulatory reform.

1. Use observable "total loan cost spreads" (which combine information from loan interest rates and amortized loan fees) to measure the risk weights applied to loans when setting minimum capital requirements on those loans. For loans with initial "teaser" rates, the maximum loan spread during the life of the loan would be used to measure risk.

2. Reform the use of credit ratings of debt instruments to require NRSROs to predict the probability of default, rather than give letter grades, and hold NRSROs accountable for accuracy using "sit outs." Specifically, for each class of rated debt (e.g., credit card securitized debts) BBB would be defined as an estimate of a 2% five-year PD, and A as an estimate of a 1% five-year PD. If a five-year moving average of actual PD for the rated BBB instruments in this class exceeds 4%, then the NRSRO will have a six-month "sit out" in rating that class of debts. If a five-year moving average of actual PD for the rated A instruments in this class exceeds 2%, then the NRSRO will have a six-month "sit out" in rating that class of debts.

3. Establish a minimum uninsured CoCo requirement for large banks (a specially designed class of debt called contingent capital), which improves risk management and capital raising incentives. If designed properly (with sufficient conversion dilution risk), CoCos would incentivize timely recapitalization of bank to avoid dilutive conversion of CoCos. A combination of common equity and a CoCo requirement can achieve more than a common equity requirement alone, and at a lower social cost. The CoCo requirement would: (1) set a high, and observable, market-based trigger (voluntary equity issuance would occur above the trigger, which would be far above the bank failure point); (2) conversion would be dilutive (to encourage banks to avoid triggering conversion through the voluntary issuance of equity to replace lost capital); (3) the required amount of CoCos issued by banks would be large (sufficient to encourage banks to avoid dilution through the alternative of voluntary issuance); and (4) qualified CoCo holders would be restricted to nonbank institutional investors.

4. Require banks to maintain cash reserves greater than 20% of outstanding liabilities (excluding capital), remunerated at the federal funds rate. These reserves must be held at their central bank on a continuous basis.

5. Vary capital required over time using a simple dual threshold model of credit growth and asset price growth. When both annual banking system credit growth, and either annual stock price or real estate price growth, exceed pre-established limits, raise minimum capital ratio requirements on banks by a pre-specified amount. Regulators would not be required to do so unconditionally, but would face an "enforce or explain" mandate to do so. Similarly, in recessions, capital standards would be temporarily relaxed by a pre-specified amount, for a pre-specified period, also subject to an "enforce or explain" mandate.

6. Establish a clearly stated division of responsibilities internationally in the resolution of bank operations, assets, and liabilities. This entails an agreement among regulatory authorities internationally as to which country will have authority to resolve which

(*Continued*)

Table 1. (*Continued*)

subsidiaries, branches, and corporate entities. This implies a clear division of responsibility with respect to the disposition of all assets and liabilities.

7. All bank debts that are not explicitly insured by a government agency are subject to a bailout limit. Specifically, if a government provides resources in support of any uninsured debt holders, those debt holders must bear a minimum 10% "haircut," implying a loss of at least 10% of the face value of the debt.

resolution, of clearly demarcated lines of legal and regulatory jurisdiction ("ring fencing") over the disposition of all the assets and liabilities within a bank.

This program of reform would be effective in addressing the real challenges that have threatened our financial system for decades, and continue to threaten it. Indeed, as discussed in Calomiris (2011b; 2012) and Calomiris and Herring (2012), if these standards had been in place prior to the recent crisis, it is highly unlikely that the crisis of 2007–2009 would have produced widespread banking distress or the collapse of interbank markets. If the high contractual interest rates of subprime mortgages had been used to gauge their risks (rather than the optimistic risk models of bankers), much more capital would have been required of subprime mortgages. If ratings agencies rating CDOs and subprime CDS had faced strong incentives to be honest in their appraisal of risk, then the bank capital required against those holdings would also have been much higher. If the proposed CoCos requirement had been in place, banks would have restored much more of their lost capital long before the collapse of September 2008. Higher cash reserve requirements, combined with higher capital resulting from the CoCos requirement, would have improved risk management prior to the crisis and would have avoided the extreme problems of counterparty risk and market illiquidity that plagued the system after Lehman's collapse in 2008.

That is not to say that any of these seven specific ideas is perfect. Each of them, in isolation, works imperfectly, and will not always fully achieve its desired outcomes. That can be said of all rules — especially simple ones. The combination of these simple and credible reforms, however, will be very unlikely to fail to achieve its overarching goal of improved risk management, as the individual rules will act together as a sort of "belt and suspenders" for prudential risk management. At a minimum, it is clear that these proposals, taken together, would constitute a substantial improvement over the current hopelessly complex and ineffectual prudential regulatory system.

It is also beyond doubt that there are ways to improve upon and add to this list of seven ideas. One idea that I think is particularly deserving of detailed examination is to require that different lines of bank business (e.g., trading) be placed in separate subsidiaries, and that these subsidiaries be required to satisfy separate prudential and corporate governance standards, in addition to those imposed on the parent bank. Furthermore, for a trading subsidiary, it would be beneficial to subject it to *margin requirements* that are sufficient to ensure that it cannot produce losses that could substantially affect the parent institution (see the related discussion in Acharya, Adler, and Richardson, 2012).

A credible approach to reform would not only limit banking distress, but also avoid much of the collateral damage to banking business that comes from the many hundreds of pages of complex, costly, and misguided mandates that typically substitute for credible reform. Furthermore, because this approach would be effective, it would succeed in forestalling the destruction of global universal banking. As I argued at the beginning of this essay, ultimately, risk management in the banking system either will be subjected to real reform, or financial repression will inevitably result as a means of avoiding the insuperable costs of bailouts.

Unfortunately, I am not optimistic about the prospects for meaningful reform. Politically powerful market participants (borrowers and lenders) are short-sighted — more interested in the next few years of benefits they can extract than in the long-term efficiency of the banking system. Politicians almost universally hate simple regulatory criteria, based on observable measures, precisely because such regulatory standards work by removing the discretionary control that politicians, bankers, and regulators enjoy, and abuse, over the enforcement of regulatory standards. Overcoming these political challenges will require more than good economic thinking; real political leadership, guided by politicians who possess sufficient character and courage to place long-term national interests ahead of short-term political convenience, will be needed. Such individuals are in short supply. And postponing reforms even for a few years (in the interest of aiding global economic recovery) substantially increases the risk that financial repression, rather than reform, will be the long-term solution to our banking system problems.

References

Acharya, V. B. Adler and M. Richardson (2012). "A proposal to resolve the distress of large and complex financial institutions," New York University Stern School. Available at http://www.ise.ac.uk/fmg/events/conferences/past-conferences/2011/DBWorkshop14Mar2011/13Acharyaetal.pdf.

Calomiris, C. W. (2010). "The political lessons of Depression-era banking reform," *Oxford Review of Economic Policy*, Vol. 26, Autumn, pp. 540–560.

Calomiris, C. W. (2011a). "Banking crises and the rules of the game," in *Monetary and Banking History: Essays in Honour of Forrest Capie*, Nicholas Crafts, Terry Mills, and Geoffrey Wood (eds.), Oxford, UK: Routledge, pp. 39–72.

Calomiris, C. W. (2011b). "An incentive-robust programme for financial reform," *The Manchester School*, Supplement, 2011, *Journal of Financial Perspectives*, pp. 39–72.

Calomiris, C. W. (2012). "Getting the right mix of capital and cash requirements in prudential bank regulation," *Journal of Applied Corporate Finance*, Vol. 24, Winter, pp. 33–41.

Calomiris, C. W. and S. Haber (2013). *Fragile By Design: Banking Crises, Scarce Credit and Political Bargains*, Princeton, NJ: Princeton University Press, forthcoming.

Calomiris, C. W. and R. J. Herring (2012). "Why and how to design a contingent convertible debt requirement," in *Rocky Times: New Perspectives on Financial Stability*, Yasuyuki Fuchita, Richard J. Herring, and Robert E. Litan (eds.), Washington, DC: Brookings Institution Press, pp. 117–162.

The Great Leveraging

Alan M. Taylor*
University of California, Davis
National Bureau of Economic Research
and
Center for Economic Policy Research

An intellectual as much as an economic crash, the 2007–2008 global financial crisis has thrown macroeconomic theory and policymaking into wreckage-sorting mode yet again. What will be picked up and what discarded during this time around remains an unsettled question. While a useful result can be hoped for, theory alone can only take us so far. This paper starts from the premise that economic history is the only laboratory we have at our disposal for the study of many serious macroeconomic questions. In economics, as in any other scientific pursuit, empirical evidence is the ultimate arbiter of whether any particular model bears a useful relation to reality.

The Great Leveraging: Five Facts and Five Lessons for Policymakers

What can history tell us about the relationship between the evolution of the private credit system, the occurrences of financial crises, linkages to the global economy, and macroeconomic performance? All of these are key

*The author gratefully acknowledges financial support through a grant from the Institute for New Economic Thinking (INET) administered by the University of Virginia. An earlier draft of this paper was presented at the BIS Annual Conference, Lucerne, June 21–22, 2012. For helpful comments, the author is grateful to conference participants, and especially to his discussants, Barry Eichengreen and Y. Venugopal Reddy. This chapter draws on recent work with collaborators, whom the author thanks; but the views expressed are those of the author alone, and the responsibility for interpretation, and any and all errors, are his.

issues at the center of the current macroeconomic and financial economic crisis and remain an ongoing focus of researchers and policymakers.

This paper's title, "The Great Leveraging," comes from a simple observation — we live in a world that is more financialized than ever before. It is simple, at least, when you take the trouble to look at long-run data: Over a couple of decades, and compared to more than a century of modern finance capitalism, the so-called advanced countries shifted recently to an economic framework with a banking system (judged by aggregate bank balance sheets or private bank loans) that is larger, relative to GDP, than anything we have ever seen in the past (Schularick and Taylor, 2012).

On that dimension, at least, this time is different. One implication is that we are, in some sense, having an out-of-sample experience. For an economist or a policymaker, this may be as disorienting as an out-of-body experience is for a normal person. But in taking a look at the same questions over the very long run, I will argue that, in many important respects, the causes and consequences of today's crisis are by no means unusual relative to prior experience, although they represent a very extreme version of phenomena we have seen many times before. This, I hope, offers some modest reassurance — which is to say that, although we have an extreme draw, we are not operating in a strange economic world, but rather in an environment that should be quite recognizable, and which is, indeed, all too familiar to the macroeconomic historian.

A wide range of work in a long tradition has deeply shaped what historians know today and fundamentally shapes the perspective I present below. Macroeconomic history is a work in progress, and a rather counter cyclical one at that, but it is reassuring to note a new surge of interest in issues of macroeconomic and financial history. There are many others working in this field, more each year, and judging by current events, the need for us all to produce insightful research is not receding.

All that said, it is not at all clear that the historical record and its implications for the present critical moment are fully and widely appreciated, so it is worth putting forward a summary of several essential issues that bear consideration not only by researchers, but, perhaps more importantly, by the policymakers currently at the helm. To respect constraints of space, I organize my discussion of these issues into 10 key points: Five facts and five lessons for policymakers.

Fact 1. Crises: Almost Forgotten, Now They're Back

The first fact is that in the last 60 years, until 2008, we had all but forgotten about financial crises in the "advanced" countries. And this was, arguably, for good reasons — as for two or three generations, going back to the Great Depression, very few such crises had occurred, and absolutely *none at all* occurred from World War 2 (WW2) until the 1970s. This we knew from the work of Bordo *et al.* (2001), and more recent extensions and refinements to the historical data by Reinhart and Rogoff (2009) only serve to reinforce this message (Fig. 1).

Thus, even as emerging markets began to experience financial crises at an increased frequency in the 1970s, 1980s, and especially 1990s, the risks in advanced countries appeared much smaller. There were some advanced-country crises: A few of them were "systemic" and quite painful macroeconomically, as in Scandinavia and especially Japan; others, like the US savings and loan crisis, involved non-negligible fiscal costs but appeared to have limited macroeconomic consequences. With the benefit of hindsight, naturally, we can say that this period of history amounted to nothing so

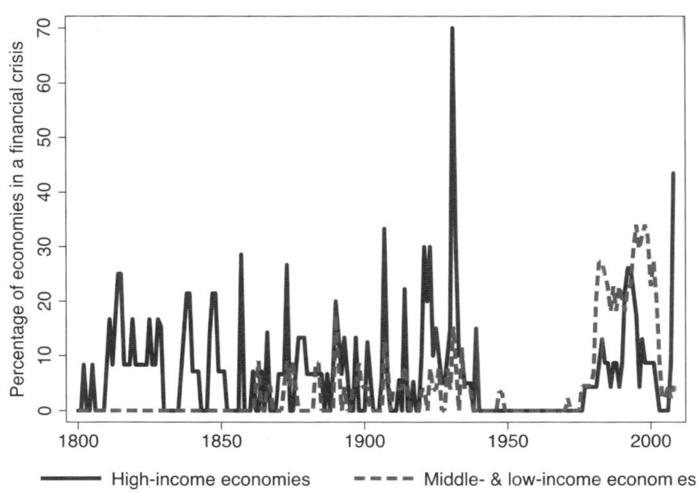

Fig. 1. The frequency of banking crises.

Note: The chart shows the percentage of economies in each subgroup that were in a financial crisis in each year in the period 1800 to 2008.
Source: Data from Qian, Reinhart, and Rogoff (2010).

much as an opportunity, albeit a self-created one, for advanced countries to lull themselves into a false sense of security.

Having dragged their macroeconomies out of the doldrums of the Depression and the ravages of war, and having built elaborate, and at times repressive, systems of financial regulation and supervision, these countries rode for three decades on favorable tailwinds. A glorious 30-year phase of high growth, partly technological and partly simple catch-up, provided expanding real resources. Modest but positive inflation allowed nominal resources to grow even faster and debts to inflate away gently but nontrivially, especially at long horizons. And finally, the post-war financial system was, for a long time, carrying low leverage, arising from a mixture of its own technology, historically conditioned preferences informed by the disaster of the 1930s, as well as the constraints imposed by authorities. Such a framework simply could not generate the kind of credit boom-and-bust cycles that had recurrently derailed economies every decade or two from the beginnings of modern finance capitalism circa 1800 up until the epic collapse and recalibration of the world economy after the 1930s. Though still attended to by those with any eye to history (see, e.g., Kindleberger, 1978) or more lately to the emerging world (see e.g., Kaminsky and Reinhart, 1999), the contemplation of macrofinancial crisis risks was naïvely ignored by most modern macroeconomists and policymakers.

However, it remains an open question, and an object of current and future research for many of us, to pin down exactly why that period from the 1940s to the 1970s was so unusually quiescent, with no financial crises at all. And also, more importantly, to ask the question at what price, if any, such tranquility was bought. Up until the crisis of 2008, the consensus view was that financial development — meaning more finance, or more M2, or more loans relative to GDP, as well as more financial instruments — all of these were an unalloyed good thing.

That premise is, as of now at least, not so easily taken for granted, and firm empirical evidence for the proposition remains elusive. Earlier work emphasizing potential benefits (e.g., King and Levine, 1993; Rajan and Zingales, 1998; Levine, 2005) has been joined by new work pointing to potentially offsetting costs or risks (e.g., Rajan, 2006; Arcand, Berkes and Panizza, 2012).

One way to frame the skeptical view in the context of the historical data might be as follows: How was it that the advanced economies could enjoy

Les Trente Glorieuses up to 1975 despite having such small, repressed, and less innovative financial systems, as compared to the era since? What can we infer from the fact that those olden times mobilized and allocated high volumes of saving to support rapid rates of economic growth yet without inculcating instability, as compared to today's financial systems?

The specification problem is of course quite serious here: What indeed is the counterfactual? Would post-1970s growth have been even slower had limitations on the financial system been maintained or expanded? Would the previous epoch have been even more glorious had banks been allowed or encouraged to lever up and take risks even sooner than they were?

Moreover, is it really just a question about the financial system anyway — after all, many other things were different in the 1950s and the 1960s, including pervasive fixed exchange rates resting on a foundation of capital controls. The Bretton Woods-style resolution of the trilemma was so different from what we see today at the moment of writing (i.e., setting aside potential imminent developments in the Eurozone periphery). It is an important question whether that set of constraints on the external finance was a supporting or even dominating factor in preserving financial stability as compared to the many and varied internal restrictions on domestic finance previously noted. We shall return later to this issue, when we examine the links between capital flows, credit, and crises.

This is a deep and challenging research agenda that will keep us, and our successors, busy for quite a while, but I will try to expand on this point as it is a central question as policymakers contemplate the tradeoffs inherent in any new designs for the world's macrofinancial architecture.

Fact 2. Consequences: Crises are Depressing and Deflationary

Perhaps because financial crises were almost forgotten, so too was much of the accumulated historical evidence showing that the consequences of crises for the economy could be profound and very damaging indeed compared to the normal experience in garden-variety downturns. And just as interest in this kind of evidence was waning, so too did the attention of theory turn away from mechanisms that incorporated monetary and financial phenomena and their implications for the real economy in times of crisis. For example, the analysis of phenomena such as panics, deflation, flight-to-safety, liquidity traps, fiscal policies, etc., with notable exceptions, has only returned to the forefront of research prominence in the wake of the events of 2008. A return to a careful empirical evaluation of the history of financial crises is long overdue and may better support the development of theory going forward.

To summarize, I draw on some of my recent and ongoing collaborative work. This is evidence-based macroeconomics, and uses data from 14 advanced countries over 140 years of history to analyze what goes on before, during, and after financial crises. Some of the work is causal analysis and other work looks at consequences using an event study framework, an approach that is now being widely used to establish long-run stylized facts by others working in this field (Almunia *et al.*, 2010; Reinhart and Rogoff, 2009).

A new ingredient in our work, however, is the inclusion of data, not just on the dates of sovereign and financial crises and on levels of public debt, but also the collection and compilation of data on levels of private credit, which is to say the amount of loans and the size of balance sheets of the banking system (see Schularick and Taylor, 2012; Jordá, Schularick, and Taylor, 2011a, 2011b). This is highly relevant to current concerns, such as the question of whether financial crises tend to ultimately stem in large part from fiscal problems (a potentially plausible argument for Greece) or more typically reflect excesses in the private sector due to credit booms (the more agreed-upon narrative for catastrophic cases like Ireland or Spain, as well as in other less-distressed economies still affected by credit hangovers).

Can history speak to these issues? The current crisis is but a small sample, yet by drawing together episodes across time and space we can mitigate the "rare event" problem for this phenomenon and thereby seek tighter inference. Figure 2 pulls together some evidence along these lines and compares what happens before and after in a typical normal recession (i.e., without an associated financial crisis) with what happens in financial crises. Here we show the effects on real GDP growth per capita, real investment per capita, and the rate of inflation.

The evidence sends a clear message. Recessions might be painful, but they tend to be even more painful when combined with financial crises, and we already know that post-2008 experience will not overturn this conclusion. The impact on investment is also very strong: Financial crises lead to strong setbacks in capital formation compared to what happens in normal

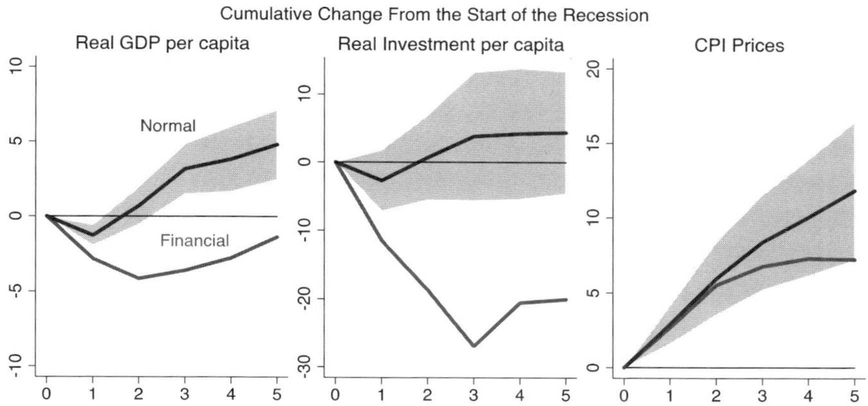

Fig. 2. Trend changes in recessions: Normal recessions, financial crisis recessions, and global crisis recessions.

Note: Paths shown are cumulative impacts in percent. Results from a conditional local-projection model. Sample of 14 advanced countries, 1870–2008. Dark solid line = normal recession path with 95% confidence interval; Light solid line = financial recession.
Source: Jordà, Schularick, and Taylor (2011b).

recessions. Finally, inflation generally falls in recessions, but the downdraft is stronger in financial crisis times.

Fact 3. Extreme Leverage: Size of the Banking Sector Is Unprecedented

Given these findings, a third fact is very much worth discussing, as it is central to the argument. It is the fact that, looking back over the long sweep of history, the financial sector in the world's advanced economies is now larger than it ever has been. The increase in size has been dramatic since the 1980s; after that date, compared with what had been the norm for more than a century, the banks almost doubled in size relative to GDP measured by loan activity, and almost tripled measured by total balance sheet size.

This fact is displayed in Fig. 3, which shows the following three variables: bank loans (aggregate to the nonfinancial sector), bank balance sheets (all inclusive, including interbank lending), and broad money (typically M2), all relative to GDP. The sample, again, is the 14 advanced countries, and the graph shows year effects, that is to say averages for each period for the cross section, which serves to isolate the global trends in these variable, while also smoothing out cross-country variation (Schularick and Taylor, 2012).

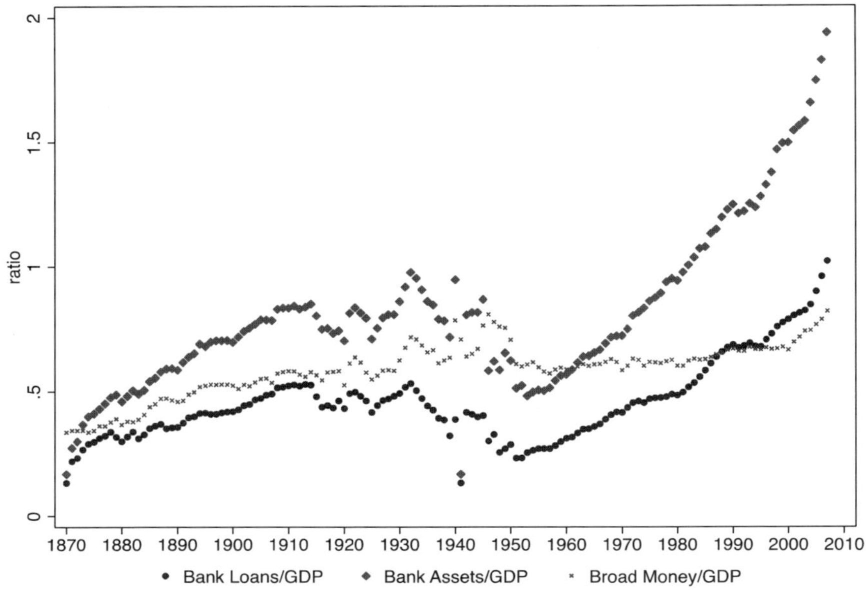

Fig. 3. The size of the banking sector relative to GDP: Loans, assets, and broad money in 14 advanced countries.

Note: The sample period is 1870–2008. Bank loans are loans by banks in aggregate to the nonfinancial sector, excluding interbank lending and foreign currency lending. Bank assets are equal to the total balance sheet size of all banks in aggregate. Broad money is M2 or a proxy thereof.

Source: Data and more detailed definitions can be found in Schularick and Taylor (2012).

The behavior of these variables up to the 1970s would be almost as any economic historian would have predicted, and the trends are, in particular, consistent which the predominant monetarist view associated with Friedman and Schwartz (1963). In that "money view," the fluctuations in the monetary liabilities of the banking sector are a very good proxy for what is happening on the asset side of the banks' balance sheet, and the levels and changes in both broad money and credit move together almost hand in hand. We can refer to this first period from 1870 to the 1970s as the "Age of Money" and apart from the Great Depression and subsequent years of financial repression in the 1940s and 1950s, the ratio of loans to money was more or less stable. Loans to GDP hovered in a range around 0.4 to 0.5, with broad money to GDP sitting a little higher at an average of about 0.6 to 0.7.

From the 1970s, this picture changed dramatically, and we entered what might be called the "Age of Credit." Although broad money relative to GDP remained almost flat at around 0.7 (rising a little only in the 2000s), the asset side of banks' balance sheets exploded. Loans to GDP doubled from 0.5 to 1.0 and assets to GDP tripled from about 0.7 to roughly 2. The decoupling of loans from broad money reflected the rise of nonmonetary liabilities on bank balance sheets, such as wholesale funding. The even faster expansion of bank assets reflected this too, plus the rise in more interbank lending. Along the way risk also increased, as the banks' asset mix put an ever-diminishing weight on safe assets (government securities), a fraction which was down to virtually zero in the 2000s, after starting at 60–70% in 1950.

Both trends went along with increased leverage as conventionally measured, or as measured here by the leverage of loans relative to the stable funding base provided by deposits, which by the post-war period had been insured to try to prevent runs. However, in the end, the banking system, insured against one type of run, can be seen to have endogenously switched over time to alternative funding sources, like wholesale, which had no such insurance, at least explicitly.

These trends highlight important changes in the modern financial landscape in the last 30 or 40 years, and suggest that much more attention be given to how and why those changes took place, and with what beneficial (or harmful) effects. For example, one hypothesis would be that banks' risk tolerance changed over time, as they rebuilt their enterprises after the ravages of the Depression and WW2. Another would be that binding regulations were gradually relaxed as a result of financial liberalizations from the 1970s onward, allowing banks to push further out along the volume/leverage/risk frontiers. The impact of Lender of Last Resort and deposit insurance — the moral hazard argument — could also play a role, whereby the authorities, trying to avert one problem after the 1930s, created a new problem down the road as an unintended consequence.

Two further points deserve mention. The first is that we can compare private debt creation via the banks with public debt creation. The trends since 1945 are striking and show an almost complete inversion. The scale

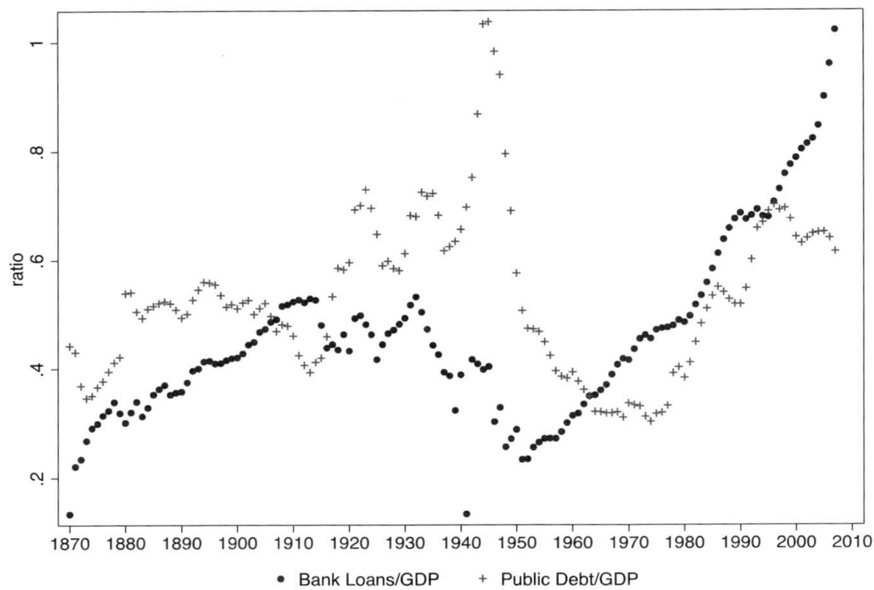

Fig. 4. Private (bank) loans versus public (sovereign) debt, 14 advanced countries.

Note: The sample period is 1870–2008.
Source: Bank loans are loans by banks in aggregate to the nonfinancial sector, excluding interbank lending and foreign currency lending based on Schularick and Taylor (2012). Public debt is total sovereign debt outstanding based on Reinhart and Rogoff (2009). See Jordà, Schularick, and Taylor (forthcoming).

of the increase in the balance sheets in the banking sector has effectively flipped the main credit risk nexus, measured by debt magnitude, from the sovereign side to the banking side. After the war, banks were cautious and had few loans to the private sector on their books, but most of the sovereigns naturally had very large debts after the conflict. But by the 1990s and 2000s — and even after substantial post-crisis increases in average public debt in advanced countries — the reverse now holds true, as seen in Fig. 4. It is private debts on bank balance sheets that far outweigh public debts on sovereign balance sheets.

One can surely find exceptions (like Greece, which is not in our sample) but the data suggest that recent Irish or Spanish tribulations are much more indicative of the dangers that lurk, hopefully in a more contained fashion, in the balance sheets of almost every advanced nation. There is much more private debt out there than public debt, and this can only change rapidly if there is sudden debt shifting (as the pollution of Irish and Spanish sovereign credit shows).

The other point to stress is that the phenomena under discussion are not just a result of trends in a few countries, for example, the Anglo-Saxons. Figure 5 shows country trends over the long run, and the run up in credit in the post-war period is evident across the board. The UK and US saw large expansions, but so too did Australia and Canada, Germany and France, and Scandinavia and Switzerland. They may not be quite at peak Icelandic levels, but all the advanced countries now have banking sector balance sheets that are a multiple, and in some cases, quite a large multiple, of national GDP.

Fact 4. Global Asymmetry: EMs Buy Insurance, DMs Sell It

Moving from a focus on financial structures to financial flows, the last two key facts focus on aspects of the global financial system, which mark the last two decades as one of the most unusual epochs ever witnessed in economic history. Here again, this time is quite different when it comes to the emergence of global imbalances on the scale we have seen. To grasp their causes and consequences, we will again need a historical perspective to figure out why the flows emerged, what form they took, and to understand when and how those forces might eventually unravel.

In the 1990s, the global financial system changed fundamentally for two linked reasons: emerging markets (EMs) joined developed markets (DMs) in an integrated global economy (globalization), but with very different economic fundamentals (asymmetry). Globalization allowed EMs to expand their external balance sheets, to admit both net and gross flows, either inward or outward. Which of these would dominate? The neoclassical prediction once held sway. To quote H. Ross Perot, many expected a giant sucking sound: a flow of investment "downhill" from rich to poor countries. In the end, the opposite seemed to happen: a net flow "uphill" from poor to rich. But a focus on net flows obscures crucial information in the structure of capital flows in the post-1990 financially globalized world.

First, *private capital has been flowing downhill* all the time and in substantial quantities. Here, in the area where private incentives for investment

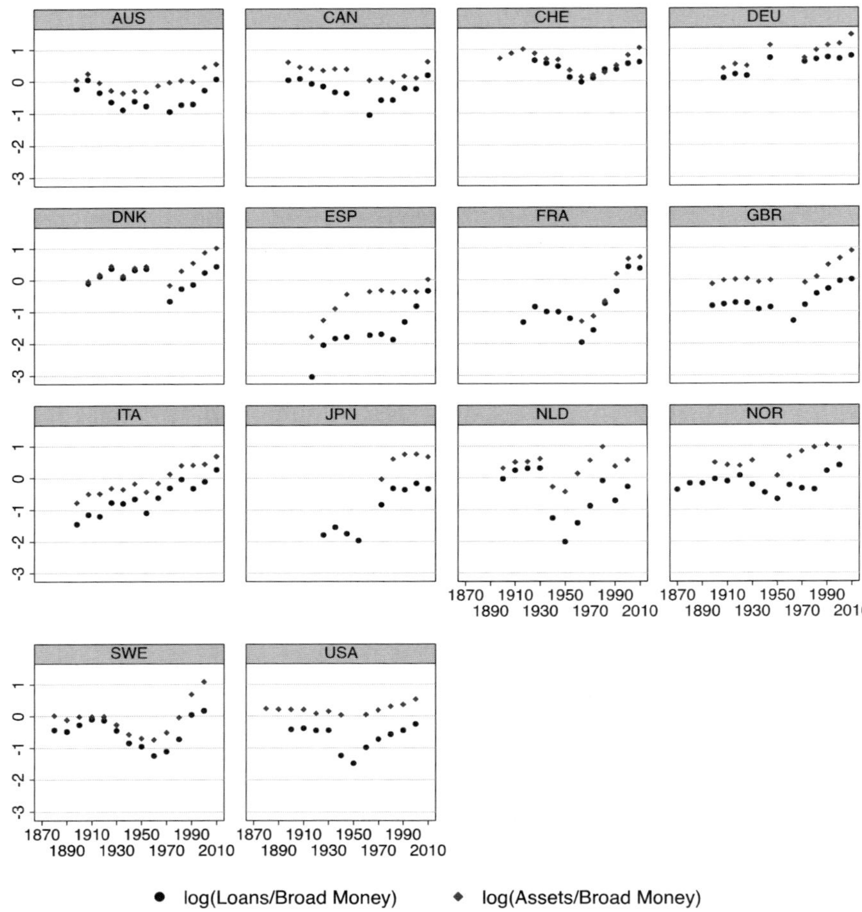

Fig. 5. Long-run trends by country.

Note: Bank loans are loans by banks in aggregate to the nonfinancial sector, excluding interbank lending and foreign currency lending. Bank assets are equal to the total balance sheet size of all banks in aggregate. Broad money is M2 or a proxy thereof.
Source: Data and more detailed definitions can be found in Schularick and Taylor (2012).

actually matter, there is no paradox, no puzzle of uphill flows at all. Private investors have moved capital from rich to poor countries all along, just as standard economic theory would predict. Second, and especially after the Asian crises of the late 1990s, *official capital has been flowing uphill* from EM to DM, but at an even greater rate, sufficient on net to more than offset the private capital flows from DM to EM. These official flows are principally driven by what we might call the "Great Reserve Accumulation" (in the region of $10 trillion in EMs, after a brief run down in the crisis) plus a smaller but rapidly growing component in sovereign wealth funds (where the data are more opaque, but the totals may now be above $4 trillion).

An extended discussion appears in Pradhan and Taylor (2011a), but Fig. 6 shows some key facts. Note that we have never seen anything like the Great Reserve Accumulation at any time in previous economic history. There were episodes during the gold standard where a country would, for idiosyncratic reasons, feel a need to expand or replenish reserves. But that system was able to run on low reserve levels on average, at least in the advanced countries of that time. Episodes such as the Argentine

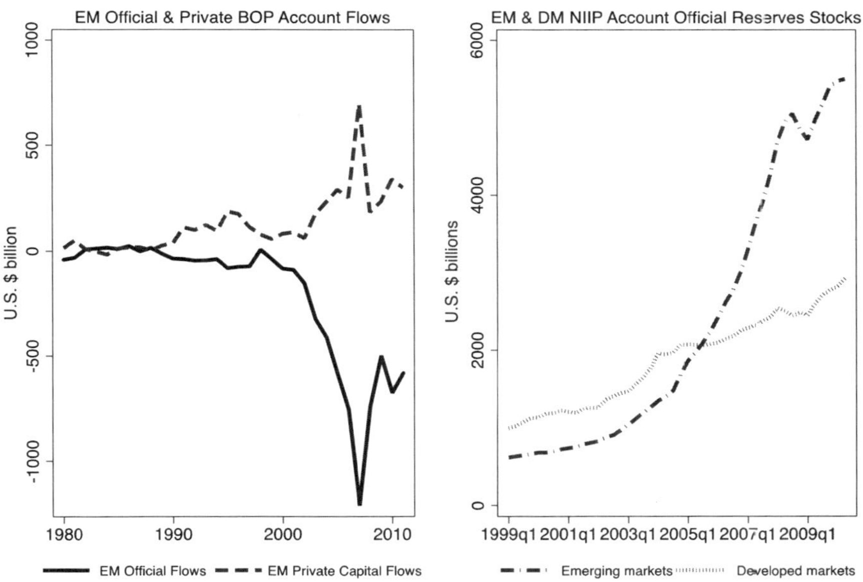

Fig. 6. Private and official capital, stocks and flows, emerging markets (EMs), and developed markets (DMs).

Note: The left panel shows EM financial account BOP data for official reserve flows and private (nonreserve) financial flows; negative = capital outflow. The right panel shows EM and DM NIIP data for stock of official reserves.
Source: Data from IMF; see Pradhan and Taylor (2011a).

gold accumulation of the 1890s or the French hoarding in the 1920s were relatively rare. And it was a zero-sum game, given inelastic supply at most times: On the whole, one country's gain in gold reserves had to be another's loss.

Now we live in a fiat world, and the reserve unit is the US dollar, plus maybe one or two other currencies, vying for a secondary role. (No doubt the plan was that the euro would be vying for a primary role right now, but the current fiasco has probably delayed that and may yet destroy the possibility altogether.) And unlike gold, these paper reserves can be created at will. Although therein lies a problem because if the demand grows too far or too fast (as it could do given the possibility divergent EM and DM growth rates), or if the supply of creditworthy reserve issuers contracts (from overissuance in the case of several DMs, plus the risk of euro collapse) then, in the Triffin sense, this game cannot go on forever.

I interpret these trends as a result of insurance motives in the EMs, particularly after the painful EM crises of the 1990s made clear to EM policymakers that the risk of currency crises, financial crises, and sovereign crises were extremely high for them, a fact that was only amplified by the associated and well-known political risks that could befall you when one or more of those events took place on your watch. Without insurance, a sudden stop, or perhaps more seriously, a sudden flight, could leave your economy and polity in ruins, and entirely dependent on the kindness of strangers — and given multiple equilibriums, such fates may or may not be entirely deserved. In recent collaborative work, I have argued that it is the potential flight of liquid liabilities in quasi-fixed exchange rate systems that drives the remarkable, and ex post successful, reserve hoarding of EM countries in recent years (Obstfeld, Shambaugh, and Taylor, 2009; 2010).

Without market access, and absent reserves, a crisis meant that you had to go looking for credit, at the IMF or elsewhere. As Korea and other countries learned then (and as Greece, Ireland, Spain, and others know now) such liquidity may arrive in the end, but it could be too little too late, and it will almost always come on terms that are stringent and humiliating. The only feasible alterative for now is self-insurance, absent some large, global, international risk pooling entity. (But as the Eurozone example suggests, the latter may be a fantastical idea for the foreseeable future; even at the level of Europe, a political project with over 50 years of groundwork and a deep historical sense of destiny, even ideas for limited forms of international risk sharing, via full banking union or common bonds, face resistance.)

In this way, ironically, EM policymakers have taken on board, with greater gusto than many might have expected, the kind of advice on prudence and fiscal rectitude handed out decades ago by the DMs: moving to more countercyclical policies over the cycle and building up buffer stocks over the longer run (Frankel, Végh, and Vuletin, 2011). Many DMs have done the opposite, piling up gross debits and, if anything, undoing automatic stabilizers and practicing austerity during downturns.

One might marvel that, on these dimensions, the world has to some degree turned upside down, but on reflection, this is in large part a manifestation, perhaps unanticipated, of the underlying deeper asymmetries that financial globalization has brought to the surface. A natural question then, is, how long will this last? Is this a permanent switch to a new state of affairs? Will the urge to hoard persist in the EMs, and will this ultimately be a self-defeating force that will run up against the constraint that there can never be an infinitely elastic supply of safe assets?

Fact 5. Savings Glut: Short-Run Panic versus Long-Run Demography

The data show that we have been living through a spectacular and never before witnessed structural shift in gross and net flows, and thus stocks, with marked differences between private and official behavior. The risk assets are almost all on the private side; the safe assets on the official side. And the official flows have shown little sign of diminution yet, with every signal in the market suggesting that growth of demand is outstripping supply, e.g., US 10-year yields at all-time lows (under 1.5% of late), and the Swiss curve turning negative out to the 5-year tenure. So what happens next? Are we going to be in savings glut mode forever? Is cheap capital here to stay? I think there are three reasons to be wary of simply extrapolating the recent past here, as argued in Pradhan and Taylor (2011b).

One is simply to note that some of the demand for safe assets is probably panic augmented, even though the trend in real yields goes back over a decade, beyond the crisis. Historical experience shows that real and nominal yields always fall in times of fear, and this time is no exception. When (Or do we say, if?) normality resumes, as in every previous cycle, the reversal of the flight-to-safety trade will start to undo the relentless downward pressure on the yields of safe sovereigns. Investors will put capital to work in risk assets, and the hoarding will stop. In this larger than normal cycle, the postponement of investment has been of a more extreme form in magnitude and duration, so the rebound, when it comes, could be sharp. (The moment is hard to predict, given the special circumstances of deleveraging plus the failure of policymakers, and Eurozone policymakers in particular, to take decisive measures to end the depression in the developed world.)

Second, there is reason to doubt that the stocks, and hence, flows, of EM reserve assets will expand ad infinitum at the same rate. The EMs were painfully short of reserves in the 1990s, as events revealed. So, to some extent, the last 10 to 15 years have been about a step change, building up from a low toward an adequate level of reserves. Once something deemed adequate has been reached, the catch-up may be nearly complete, and future accumulation only needs to keep pace with the growth in the size of the EM economies. That force too may also be subject to slowdown in the longer terms as the forces of economic convergence wane, and the development gap continues to close.

Lastly, when we think about the deep determinants of real yields, there are other more fundamental forces at work in the medium run, and the key one is demography. For many decades, first DMs and then EMs have experienced major demographic tailwinds. The boomer cohorts in the DM world gave a boost to savings worldwide, and this trend was augmented by the start of a massive demographic transition in the EM countries. But looking forward, these forces are now starting to abate and will soon go into reverse as shown in Fig. 7.

The DM world now faces a demographic tailwind as the boomers retire, and in the EM world, aging populations are set to grow as the demographic transition winds down. Substantial heterogeneity lies behind these averages, of course, but these patterns presage major changes in the saving–investment balance going forward.

Summing Up the Facts: What Is Happening?

At first glance, the historical record appears to present us with a rather inconvenient truth, namely that financial crises might just be an

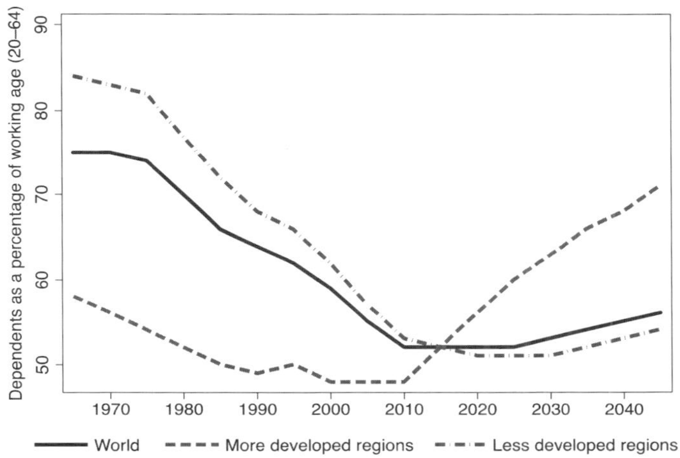

Fig. 7. Long-run demographic trends, dependents per 100 working age.

Note: The dependency ratio is the population of ages 0–19 and 65 + divided by the working age population of ages 20–64.
Source: Data from UN Population Statistics; see Pradhan and Taylor (2011b).

occupational hazard, a simple fact of life, in modern finance capitalism. However, one major exception was the era 1950–1970, which witnessed tighter domestic financial regulation and external capital controls. This was a period of low credit growth, with very little in the way of financial innovation. But it was also still a period of very high investment, savings, and real growth for the advanced economies.

This period did not last, thanks to a series of unfortunate events. Starting in the 1980s, it gave way to a less regulated and more risk-hungry world, reflected above in the rapid growth of bank lending. By the 1990s, with a firmer low-inflation nominal anchor, the entry of high-saving, self-insuring emerging economies took the world down a path of ever lower nominal and real rates. Ostensibly a good thing for the consenting adults involved (who could object to cheaper capital?), but in hindsight, we see that not every private project funded by this glut of funds was, ex post, worthwhile from a risk–reward point of view. In this respect, a historian might reflect that we have traversed back to not only the good aspects of integration seen in the first era of globalization, but also its not so good aspects, namely increased financial fragility, despite all we had supposedly learned along the way.

Will anything change? On some level, probably not. The EM economies have seen their reserve accumulation strategies pay off handsomely, as they avoided the worst of the crisis and bounced back strongly. The hunger for safe assets may well grow for some time, and joined with persistent deleveraging and precautionary motives in the DM world, we are unlikely to see change in a hurry. Real rates will be low for some time. And with that as a backdrop, plus the ongoing deflationary forces amplified by the shift to cash and cash-like safe instruments, safe sovereigns will be able to fund themselves for a time at the low or even negative rates we now see.

They might be well advised to grab that opportunity while they can. Over a longer time, frame adjustments will, and indeed must, occur. As an accounting device, the long-run budget constraint alone tells us that one can no more borrow for ever than save forever, and historical experience tells us that at some point, those limits do get breached. Demographic shifts will start to put a drag on savings, and the world's investment drought, intensified by the near-disappearance of DM net capital formation in 2008–2009, will leave a large overhang of unmet investment requirements.

Yet even if a new more or less steady state makes its presence felt in the long run, its nature and stability, and the path we take from here to there, are highly contingent on what steps policymakers take in the short run. Thus, the remainder of this paper turns from the macroeconomic and financial facts that we can see in past and present, to the lessons we can draw for policy in the future.

Lesson 1: Past Private Credit Growth Does Contain Valuable Predictive Information About Likelihood of a Crisis

The first point makes use of new evidence and new methods, but builds on important precursors. Indeed any work in this area stands on the shoulders of the BIS, and especially Borio and White (2004), whose warnings at Jackson Hole and elsewhere went unheeded by those who should have known better. Bolstering arguments can be found in Eichengreen and Mitchener (2004) on the origins of the Great Depression as "a credit boom gone wrong."

A more formal approach can confirm that, over the course of history, credit growth turns out to contain valuable predictive information about the likelihood of a financial crisis event (Schularick and Taylor, 2012). To see this in the historical data, we used a simple classification test, standard in clinical and other applications in hard sciences. We stay agnostic about the policymaker's utility function, but given current information x, we just ask whether our classifier (a model signal $f(x)$ and a fixed threshold c) can generate something better than the null (a coin toss) in sorting the binary crisis event data.

To proceed with inference, we can chart true positives against true negatives in the unit box, for all thresholds c, and create a correct classification frontier (CCF). A classifier is informative if its CCF is above the null CFF of a coin toss which lies on the diagonal, i.e., generates "more truth." Formally, the area under the curve (AUC) should exceed 0.5 for the null to be rejected, and inference on families of AUCs turns out to be simple (they are asymptotically normal). In what follows, we adopt a null of country-fixed-effects, which captures the unconditional likelihood of a crisis in one country versus another.

A key result is shown in Fig. 8, which covers 14 advanced countries for the period 1870 to 2008. We group predictions from the pre-WW2 and post-WW2 models in Schularick and Taylor (2012), where it is in the post-war period that the distinctions between money and credit are starkest. For reference, the area under the curve or AUC for the credit-based model (five-year lagged moving average of the change in loans to GDP ratio) is 0.750; but the broad money-based model is not all that informative with an AUC of 0.686. The credit model AUC is higher and significantly different from the country-fixed effects null, whereas the money model AUC is not.

Similar results hold for the pre-war and post-war samples, and robustness checks confirm the results with controls for macroeconomic conditions, asset prices, and other specifications (e.g., multiple lags of annual credit growth). In a nutshell, credit matters, and it matters more than broad money, as a useful predictor of financial crisis events. Unfortunately, such indicators were not widely used — or if used, not heeded — by central banks and financial stability authorities prior to the crisis. Even the ECB's monetary pillar was largely dormant, and one could argue that a focus on money rather then credit was the wrong kind of pillar anyway.

If history is a guide, then it is surely welcome that we should finally see, as we already do, interest among macroprudential authorities in including

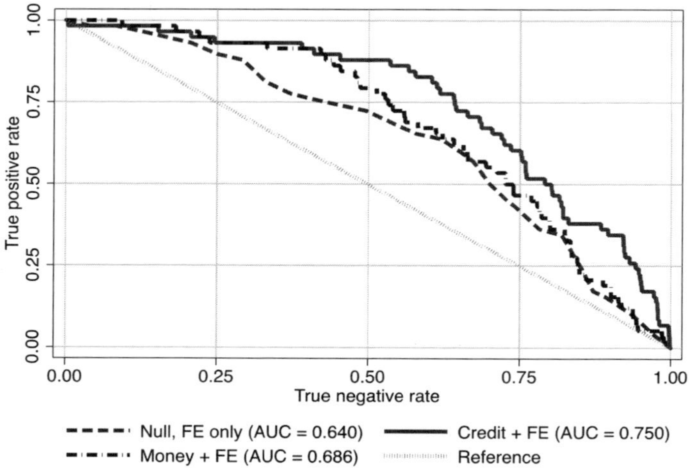

Fig. 8. Using lagged credit growth as a classifier to forecast financial crises: The correct classification frontier.

Note: See Schularick and Taylor (2012). In this chart, for all models, the predictions from the pre-war and post-war country-fixed-effects logit models of Schularick and Taylor (2012) are combined to give a crisis prediction for the full sample 1870–2008 and 14 advanced countries. War years are omitted. Schularick and Taylor (2012) show that the models using credit and broad money differ significantly between the two eras, with the predictive value of credit outstripping that of broad money after WW2. The "Null" is the model with country-fixed-effects only and no other regressors. The "Money" model uses a five-year lagged moving average of the change in broad money to GDP ratio. The "Credit" model uses five-year lagged moving average of the change in loans to GDP ratio. The chart shows the correct classification frontiers (akin to ROC curves) and inference is based on a χ^2 test of the area under the curve, AUC, which would be 0.5 under the "Reference" null of no information.

some form of "excessive credit" indicators into the set of inputs that will be considered going forward. Assessing exactly how to form reliable indicators, and more importantly how one should act upon them, will remain an important goal for research in the foreseeable future.

Lesson 2: As Symptoms of Financial Crises, External Imbalances Are a Distraction, and so Are Public Debts

But with the correct classification test apparatus, we can do much more than analyze which variables may contain useful predictive information about financial crisis risk. We can also seek to find out which variables do not. In the current debate over the origins of the crisis, a couple of candidate variables cry out for such scrutiny.

The first comes from those worried about the risks from *global imbalances* — according to this view, excessive external current account deficits could amplify or spillover into the risk of a financial crisis. The second comes from those worried about *fiscal excess* — according to that view, rising public sector debt levels could be an important risk trigger for financial crisis. However, neither of these hypotheses follows unambiguously from theory, and each rests on a number of assumptions. So these hypotheses are not *a priori* valid; they are empirically testable propositions, and, as such, ideal candidates for the statistical framework we have at our disposal.

So what do the historical data say? Have current account deficits or rising public debt levels contributed anything to the elevation of financial crisis probabilities? Drawing on ongoing work (Jordà, Schularick, and Taylor, forthcoming), Fig. 9 provides an answer, by taking our existing and quite successful forecast model based on credit and running it against rival models with a different variable added: In the upper panel, it is the five-year lagged moving average of the change in the current account to GDP ratio, and in the lower panel, it is the five-year lagged moving average of the change in the public debt to GDP ratio. Each model can be run with credit, the other variable, both or neither (the null being fixed-effects only, again).

The question is, do any of these other variables add any information at all, either relative to the null or relative to the credit-based model, when they are added in the classifier, as judged by a positive and statistically significant increase in the area under the CCF? And the answer in both cases is very clearly no.

Adding the current account slightly improves on the country-fixed-effects null (AUC rises from 0.641 to 0.685, $p = 0.02$), but credit does much better (AUC rises to 0.750, $p = 0.00$). Once credit is in the model, adding the current account on top achieves little (AUC of 0.767). After a moment's thought, this result perhaps should not come as too much of a surprise. There are clearly cases of countries today, and certainly in the past, where current account deficits have gone hand in hand with credit booms and, ultimately, financial crises — the Eurozone periphery comes to mind. But by the same token, there have been cases today of current account-surplus countries ending up in financial distress. Why?

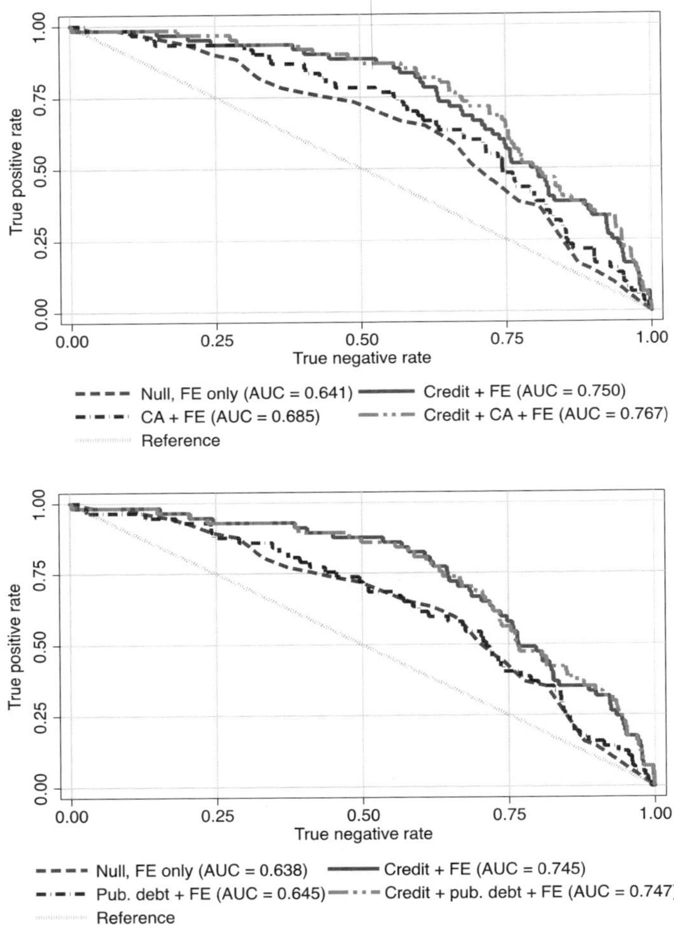

Fig. 9. Using lagged credit growth plus current accounts or public debts as a classifier to forecast financial crises: The correct classification frontier.

Note: See Fig. 8 and Jordà, Schularick, and Taylor (2011a and forthcoming). In the upper panel, "CA" uses a five-year lagged moving average of change in the current account to GDP ratio. In the lower panel, "Pub. debt" uses a five-year lagged moving average of change in the public debt to GDP ratio. Relative either to the "Null" or the "Credit" model, the addition of "CA" or "Pub. Debt" does not significantly improve the classifier. In this chart, for all models, the predictions of the pre-war and post-war country-fixed-effects logit models are combined as in Fig. 8.

Credit booms and busts can be driven just as easily by domestic savings as foreign saving. Gross stocks and flows can often be delinked from net flows across border, so balance sheets can expand even if no net cross border flows are recorded. Finally, at a disaggregated level, current account gross and net flows can be composed of a widely varying mix of bank, debt, equity, FDI, and other claims, and each type has very different risk characteristics, with bank and debt flows being the ones at risk of rollover risk (stops, flight). Recent evidence points to all of these factors playing a role in the current crisis, globally, within the Eurozone, and away, that should push future analysis beyond the narrow and simplistic "global imbalance" framework which all too often dominated discussions in the last decade.[1]

Historical evidence backs this idea of an important distinction between current account flows and the behavior of credit. Suppose we look back over history since 1870 and compute correlations in the aforementioned 14-country advanced-economy datasets between external inflows (current account, % of GDP) and the change in aggregate credit (change in bank loans, % of GDP). If we divide the panel into 20-year periods from 1870, excluding the two world wars, the answer is that over the long run the correlation has been essentially zero. Only in one period, 1870 to 1889, was there a significant negative correlation between the current account and changes in bank lending, which is not surprising, since this was a peak period of

[1]See, for example, Lane (2012) and Obstfeld (2012) for suggestions as to the way ahead. Past policy misdirection is acutely observed in the self-flagellating IMF (2011) postmortem into the global financial crisis, *viz.*: "For much of the period [2004–2007] the IMF was drawing the membership's attention to the risk that a disorderly unwinding of global imbalances [and inflation].... The IMF gave too little consideration to deteriorating financial sector balance sheets, financial regulatory issues, to the possible links between monetary policy and the global imbalances, and to the credit boom and emerging asset bubbles. It did not discuss macro-prudential approaches that might have helped address the evolving risks. Even as late as April 2007, the IMF's banner message was one of continued optimism...benign global environment...positive near-term outlook and fundamentally sound financial market conditions. Only after the eruption of financial turbulence did the IMF take a more cautionary tone.... The lack of a coherent macro-financial storyline to underpin the laundry list of risks...created an impression that the IMF was warning only about global imbalances and inflation. This was the message heard by authorities, other stakeholders, and most staff interviewed for this evaluation.... Confirmation bias...may explain staff's focus on the IMF's primary concern — global imbalances and a disorderly dollar decline — as the key risk to global stability, largely ignoring evidence pointing to other risks."

settler economy capitalism with large capital flows out of high-saving core economies. In one later period, the post-war years 1949– 1968, there was a positive correlation: High-saving economies were in current account surplus but also expanding credit rapidly. Apart from these periods, and on average, the correlation was zero.

Thus, compared to credit conditions, the horse race shows that current accounts seem to perform poorly in a head-to-head contest to explain the incidence of crises.

A similar exercise can be undertaken for public debt, by adding the change in public debt to GDP ratios as a crisis predictor, as shown in the second panel of Fig. 9. This might as well be a one-horse race. The public debt variable clearly has no benefit as a predictor even as compared to the country-fixed-effects null (AUC of 0.645 versus 0.638, $p = 0.45$). Thus, the idea that financial cries have their roots in fiscal problems is not supported over the long sweep of history. Some cases may of course exist — like Greece today — but these have been the exception not the rule. In general — like Ireland and Spain today — financial crises can be traced back to developments in the financial sector itself, namely excess credit.

Over 140 years, there has been no systematic correlation of financial crises with either prior current account deficits or prior growth in public debt levels. Private credit has always been the only useful and reliable predictive factor.

Lesson 3: After a Credit Boom, Expect a More Painful "Normal Recession" as Well as a More Painful "Financial Crisis Recession"

As far as they go, these results may be somewhat provocative, but could be downplayed. If boom–bust cycles of credit were occasionally responsible for rare, but still quite painful, financial crises, that might be a useful finding. But from a policymaking standpoint, it would be like a doctor faced with a test for a very rare disease. If the treatment is painful, in any utility-weighted decision, the incentive to act will be downweighted for two reasons: The cost of a false positive and the infrequency of positive outcomes overall.

Thus, in more recent collaborative work, we sought to address the relevance of the credit cycle, not just for the rare events known as "financial crises" but for all recessions of any form (Jordà, Schularick, and

Taylor, 2011b). To do this, we classify all recession events in all countries, and classify them as normal recessions or financial crisis recessions based on coincidence (± 2 years) with a crisis event. This takes our sample size way up, and brings into view recession events that are far more frequent than financial crises. In just under 140 years for 14 countries, we observe over 200 recessions of all kinds (normal and financial).

The question we wanted to ask here was: Are the echoes of credit booms during the expansion phase only manifested in the likelihood of a financial crisis taking place in subsequent years, a zero-one binary outcome? Or is there a more generalized echo of a credit boom, whereby more leverage in the expansion years can be traced to weaker economic performance in the subsequent recession phase?

Figure 10 sums up what appears to be a clear answer, one that is robust to many different controls, samples, and specifications, some of which we shall see in a moment. The bottom line here is that our earlier argument that credit booms matter as a financial crisis risk factor is a rather narrow conclusion, and that a more general and worrying correlation is evident.

During any business cycle, whether ending in a financial crisis recession or just a normal recession, there is a very strong relationship between the growth of credit (relative to GDP) on the upswing, and the depth of the subsequent collapse in GDP on the downswing.

The import of these results is broader and applies to recessions, not just crises. Following credit should not only interest financial policymakers or macroprudential powers who are mainly concerned with averting a low-probability crisis or tail event. It should also concern central bankers and other policymakers who are concerned with overall macroeconomic stability at business-cycle frequencies, that is, even in more typical cycles when crises are averted and the economy suffers only a "normal" recession (see, e.g., Drehmann *et al.*, 2011; Turner, 2011).

History matters, in a very important way: In recessions following bigger credit build-ups, our research shows that an "unconditioned" policy forecast would be prone to optimistically biased errors, whereas under a properly "conditioned" policy, allowance is made for that fact that economic outcomes are systematically worse the larger has been the prior credit boom. If such a finding were ever to have any applicability, it might be in the present circumstances.

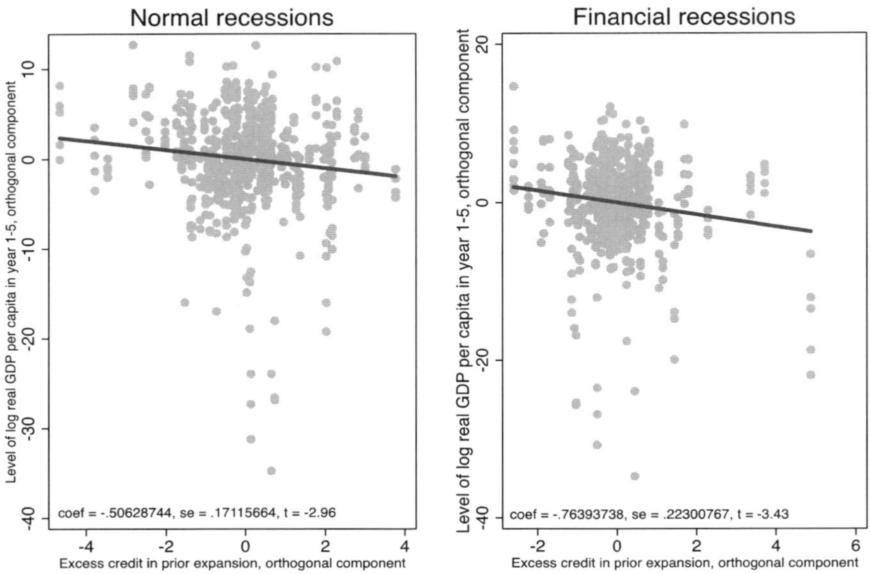

Fig. 10. "Excess" credit growth in expansion and the intensity of recession.

Source: Based on the data in Jordà, Schularick, and Taylor (2011b). The charts show simple added- variable plots (partial scatters) between the deviation of the level of log real GDP per capita in recession/recovery years 1–5 after a normal or financial peak, and the annual rate of change of credit-to-GDP in the prior expansion. The left chart shows financial crisis recessions only, the right chart normal recessions only. In the underlying regression, additional control variables include five-year time fixed effects interacted with normal and financial recession dummies. Both partial correlations are statistically significant at the 1% level.

The importance of such findings is apparent. The results challenge the view held by some economists that credit is an epiphenomenon: Something driven by real fundamentals, but not an interesting or important economic driver in its own right. In a naïve view, high- and low-levels of credit-to-GDP growth in expansion phases might occur, with credit intensity levels given by disturbances around some mean; these might be followed by weak or harsh recession phases, or even financial crises, with these outcomes also distributed around some mean. But, after properly conditioning the cyclical data, it is not clear why there should still be a systematic link between the two, which is what we actually tend to see in the historical data. In closing, we take a closer look at other patterns which strengthen this point.

***Lesson 4: In a Financial Crisis with Large Run-Up in Private Sector Credit, Mark Down Growth/Inflation** More*

The final two lessons take off from the preceding idea of conditioning recession path outcomes on economic conditions seen at the pre-recession peak or in the prior expansion phase, but in what follows we can expand the modeling framework using local projection methods to ask two questions of contemporary salience (Jordà, Schularick, and Taylor, 2011b).

First, we ask: How are macroeconomic characteristics of the recession path related to expansion phase credit build up? In Fig. 11, we show *cumulative impacts* from a local-projection estimation cumulated over 5 years after a recession peak for our sample of 14 countries for 1870 to 2008. The experiment is to compute the marginal treatment effect on each path of an extra unit (here + 1 s.d.) in the rate of change of the loan to GDP ratio during the prior expansion. For reference, actual observed average rate of change during expansions is + 0.25 percentage points per year just before normal recessions (s.d. = 2), and about + 1.25 percentage points per year (s.d. = 2.5) before financial recessions.

In Figure 11, the dark solid path is that for a normal recession under the average excess credit expansion in the prior expansion (with shaded

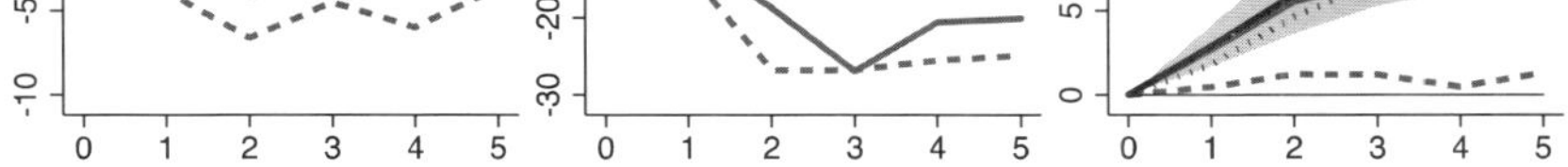

Fig. 11. "Excess" credit growth and the paths of normal and financial recessions.

Note: Paths shown are cumulative impacts in percent. Results from a conditional local-projection model. Sample of 14 advanced countries, 1870–2008. Solid lines = recession paths with 0% pa excess growth of credit in prior expansion measured by rate of change of loans to GDP ratio percentage points per year; dark solid line = normal recession with 95% confidence interval; light solid line = financial recession. Dashed lines show perturbations to forecast when excess credit measure rises by + 1, + 2 or + 3 percentage points per year.
Source: Jordà, Schularick, and Taylor (2011b).

95% confidence interval). The dark dotted path is for a normal recession under the marginal treatment with an increase of 1 s.d. in excess credit in the prior expansion. The light solid and dashed lines show the path in a financial crisis recession when excess credit at its mean, and mean +1 s.d., respectively, in the prior expansion.

Important inferences quickly follow from this chart based on over a century of experiences. First, unsurprisingly, excess credit generally makes matters worse, but especially so in a financial crisis, with lower output and investment and inflation. The working paper also documents slower lending, lower interest rates, and a sharper move to current account surplus for that case — characteristics that are highly noteworthy in the context of the present weak recovery in crisis-hit countries from the 2008 financial shock.

The point is simply that from an empirical point of view, a credit boom and a financial crisis together appear to be a very potent mix that correlate with abnormally severe downward pressures on growth, prices, and capital formation for sustained periods. A "normalization" of the economy on all these dimensions just takes much longer under such a scenario. It is easy to see how policymakers, if they happened to be ignorant of such factors, might carelessly wander into unduly optimistic forecasts or premature policy actions, putting at risk a very fragile recovery path.

Lesson 5: In a Financial Crisis with Large Public Debt, and Large Run-up in Private Sector Credit Mark Down your Forecast Even More

The final lesson builds on the last one. Now we can add the much-debated fiscal policy dimension to the analysis. Such is the flexibility of the local projection framework that it can be easily used to generate forecasts adapted to discrete bins corresponding to various conditioning events, or it can be used with a continuous conditioning variable to see how outcomes vary over some meaningful range of conditions. The question we focus on here is how the fiscal health of the government ex ante, at the start of the recession, might shape the subsequent recession path.

Figure 12, from work in progress (Jordà, Schularick, and Taylor, forthcoming), studies the impact of a similar marginal treatment as in the last exercise (here +1% per year of extra loan to GDP growth during the

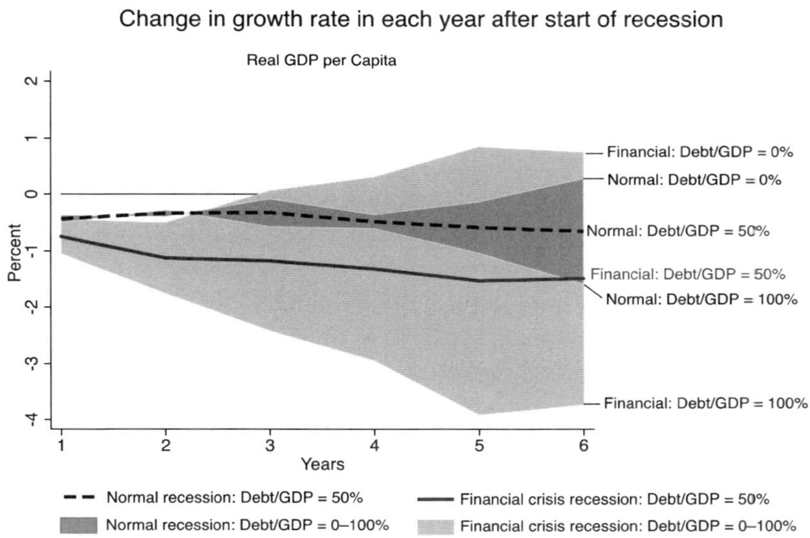

Fig. 12. "Excess" credit growth and the paths of real GDP in normal and financial recession contingent on initial public debt levels.

Note: Paths shown are dynamic impacts at each date, not cumulative. Results from a conditional local-projection model. Sample of 14 advanced countries, 1870–2008. Zero = recession path with 0% pa excess growth of credit in prior expansion measured by loans to GDP. Dashed and solid paths: normal and financial recession paths, at +1% pa excess credit growth in prior expansion when country starts recession with initial public debt to GDP ratio of 50%. Dark and light gray fans: deviation from these last two respective paths as starts recession with initial public debt to GDP ratio varying from 0% to 100%.
Source: Jordà, Schularick, and Taylor (forthcoming).

prior expansion), but here the fan chart shows dynamic impacts (in this case, *noncumulative*) with forecast paths for varying levels of public debt to GDP at the recession onset, where the range goes from 0% to 100% across the fan (shaded), with a central forecast (dashed and solid lines) at the 50% public debt to GDP level. The exercise is revealing. For brevity, we examine here just the results for the GDP path.

First, look at normal recessions (dashed line, dark shaded fan). Extra credit growth in the prior expansion is correlated with mild drag in the recession, say 50–75 bps in the central case, but the effect is small, and does not vary all that much when we condition on public debt to GDP levels (the dark fan is not that wide).

Now look at financial crisis recessions (solid line, light shaded fan). Extra credit growth in the prior expansion is correlated with much larger drag, almost twice as large at 100–150 bps, and the impact is very sensitive to public debt to GDP levels going in (the light fan is very wide). At public debt to GDP levels near 100%, a sort of tailspin emerges after a financial crisis, and the rate of growth craters down from the reference levels by 400 bps at the end of the window. (Recall, effects in Fig. 11 are shown as noncumulative.)

In terms of historical resonance, these results have a deep ring to them as we contemplate the current crisis. Exposure to a credit boom can make recessions painful, but when combined with an adverse fiscal position at the onset of the crash, economies are perhaps even more vulnerable. Such empirical evidence would suggest that even if the stakes are lower in normal recessions, countries with more "fiscal space" are better able to withstand a financial crisis, perhaps by having room to offer stabilizing support to their economy — or at least dodge austerity, whether "voluntary" or "involuntary."

Summing Up: What Next for Macroeconomics and Policy?

In many old-fashioned macroeconomic models and policy frameworks, the key issues at the core of the crisis were frequently simplified to the point of unrecognizability, or else assumed away altogether: for example, banks, financial crises, defaults, lenders of last resort, safe assets, credit, leverage, debt-deflation, central banking (beyond simple targets and policy rules), and even money itself, to name a few.

For observers with a longer perspective, however, such matters were far from irrelevant, and surely not merely epiphenomena. Instead, they seemed so to be so systematically important and have such recurrent patterns across the broad sweep of economic history that it was hard to see how they could be placed to one side.

If a better empirical foundation is to be found, then what features of the real world should new and better models and policymaking pay heed to? If something beneficial can be said to have come out of the crisis, it has at least reignited interest in crucial macrofinancial issues.

With a focus on banking systems and credit, this paper has summarized some new historical evidence on the evolution of a key part of the global financial system, its workings, and its fragility. Arguably, empirical research is now ahead of theory, but the two will need to work together.

For researchers, constructing models consistent with the evidence, as well as strengthening and expanding the evidence itself, is a major challenge for the future. For policymakers, unfortunately, the challenge is right now, and first and foremost it is to understand, based on these and other empirical observations emerging from the historical laboratory, the peculiar nature of the fiercely depressing and deflationary spiral in which the advanced world now finds itself — and, once they grasp that, to then figure out what to do about it.

References

Almunia, M., A. Bénétrix, B. Eichengreen, K. H. O'Rourke and G. Rua (2010). "From Great Depression to Great Credit Crisis: Similarities, differences and lessons," *Economic Policy*, Vol. 25, No. 62, April, pp. 219–252.

Arcand, J.-L., E. Berkes and U. Panizza (2012). "Too much finance?" International Monetary Fund Working Paper No. WP/12/161, June.

Bordo, M., B. Eichengreen, D. Klingebiel and M. S. Martinez-Peria (2001). "Is the crisis problem growing more severe?" *Economic Policy*, Vol. 16, No. 32, April, pp. 51–82.

Borio, C. and W. R. White (2004). "Whither monetary and financial stability? The implications of evolving policy regimes," in *Monetary Policy and Uncertainty: Adapting to a Changing Economy, Proceedings of the 2003 Jackson Hole Economic Policy Symposium*, Jackson Hole, WY, August 28–30, pp. 131–211.

Drehmann, M., C. Borio and K. Tsatsaronis (2011). "Anchoring countercyclical capital buffers: The role of credit aggregates," *International Journal of Central Banking*, Vol. 7, No. 4, December, pp. 189–240.

Eichengreen, B. and K. James Mitchener (2004). "The Great Depression as a credit boom gone wrong," *Research in Economic History*, Vol. 22, pp. 183–237.

Frankel, J. A., C. A. Végh and G. Vuletin (2011). "On graduation from fiscal procyclicality," National Bureau of Economic Research Working Paper No. 17619.

Friedman, M. and A. Jacobson Schwartz (1963). *A Monetary History of the United States, 1867–1960*, Princeton, NJ: Princeton University Press.

International Monetary Fund (2011). "IMF performance in the run-up to the financial and economic crisis: IMF surveillance in 2004–07." Report, Washington, DC: International Monetary Fund.

Jordà, Ò., M. Schularick and A. M. Taylor (2011a). "Financial crises, credit booms, and external imbalances: 140 years of lessons," *IMF Economic Review*, Vol. 59, No. 2, June, pp. 340–378.

Jordà, Ò., M. Schularick and A. M. Taylor (2011b). "When credit bites back: Leverage, business cycles, and crises," National Bureau of Economic Research Working Paper No. 17621.

Jordà, Ò., M. Schularick and A. M. Taylor, "Sovereigns versus banks: Crises, causes, and consequences," forthcoming.

Kaminsky, G. L. and C. M. Reinhart (1999). "The twin crises: The causes of banking and balance-of-payments problems," *American Economic Review*, Vol. 89, No. 3, June, pp. 473–500.

Kindleberger, C. P. (1978). *Manias, Panics, and Crashes: A History of Financial Crises*, New York: Basic Books.

King, R. G. and R. Levine (1993). "Finance and growth: Schumpeter might be right." *Quarterly Journal of Economics*, Vol. 108, No. 3, August, pp. 717–737.

Lane, P. R. (2012). "Financial globalisation and the crisis." BIS Working Papers 397, Bank for International Settlements.

Levine, R. (2005). "Finance and growth: Theory and evidence," in *Handbook of Economic Growth*, Philippe Aghion and Steven N. Durlauf (eds.), Vol. 1B, Amsterdam: Elsevier/North-Holland, pp. 865–934.

Obstfeld, M. (2012). "Does the current account still matter?" *American Economic Review*, Vol. 102, No. 3, May, pp. 1–23.

Obstfeld, M., J. C. Shambaugh and A. M. Taylor (2009). "Financial instability, reserves, and central bank swap lines in the panic of 2008," *American Economic Review*, Vol. 99, No. 2, May, pp. 480–486.

Obstfeld, M., J. C. Shambaugh and A. M. Taylor (2010). "Financial stability, the trilemma, and international reserves," *American Economic Journal: Macroeconomics*, Vol. 2, No. 2, pp. 57–94.

Pradhan, M. and A. M. Taylor (2011a). "The great rebalancing," *Emerging Issues*, Morgan Stanley, February 18.

Pradhan, M. and A. M. Taylor (2011b). "Are EMs the new DMs?" *Emerging Issues*, Morgan Stanley, May 4.

Qian, R., C. M. Reinhart, K. S. Rogoff (2011). "On graduation from default, inflation and banking crises: elusive or illusion?" NBER Macroeconomics Annual 2010, Vol. 25, pp. 1–36.

Reinhart, C. M. and K. S. Rogoff (2009). *This Time is Different: Eight Centuries of Financial Folly*, Princeton, NJ: Princeton University Press.

Rajan, R. G. (2006). "Has financial development made the world riskier?" in *The Greenspan Era: Lessons for the Future. Proceedings of the 2005 Jackson Hole Economic Policy Symposium*, Jackson Hole, WY, August 25–27, pp. 313–369.

Rajan, R. G. and L. Zingales (1998). "Financial dependence and growth," *American Economic Review*, Vol. 88, No. 3, June, pp. 559–586.

Schularick, M. and A. M. Taylor (2012). "Credit booms gone bust: monetary policy, leverage cycles, and financial crises, 1870–2008." *American Economic Review*, Vol. 102, No. 2, April, pp. 1029–1061.

Turner, A. (2011). "Debt and deleveraging: Long term and short term challenges." Speech at the Presidential Lecture, Centre for Financial Studies, Frankfurt, Germany, November 21. Available at: http://www.fsa.gov.uk/library/communication/speeches/2011/1121_at.shtml.

Finance and Economic Development in a Model with Credit Rationing

Jean-Louis Arcand*
Graduate Institute, Geneva, Switzerland

Enrico Berkes
Northwestern University, Chicago

Ugo Panizza
Graduate Institute, Geneva, Switzerland

Introduction

Bagehot (1873) and Schumpeter (1911) were among the first to point out that finance plays a key role for economic development. Empirical work by Goldsmith (1969) confirmed the presence of a correlation between finance and economic development but could not establish whether the link between these two variables was causal. Successive work by King and Levine (1993); Levine, Loayza, and Beck (2000); Beck, Levine, and Loayza (2000); and Rajan and Zingales (1998) provided convincing evidence that financial development has a causal effect on economic growth. There is now an enormous literature showing that finance does indeed play a positive role in promoting economic development and, while recent research has shown that not all types of credit are the same (with enterprise credit

*Jean Louis Arcand is affiliated with the Graduate Institute, Geneva, Switzerland, Enrico Berkes is affiliated with the Northwestern University, Chicago and Ugo Panizza is affiliated with the Graduate Institute, Geneva, Switzerland. The views expressed in this paper are the authors' only and need not reflect, and should not be represented as, the views of any of the institutions that the authors are affiliated with.

being the driver of growth, Beck *et al.*, 2008), most economists now believe in such a causal link (Levine, 2005).[1]

It is, however, possible that there is a threshold above which finance starts having negative returns and that the current crisis was caused by financial sectors that were "too large" compared to the size of the domestic economy. Proponents of this view include Martin Wolf, who noted that there might be something wrong with a situation in which "instead of being a servant, finance had become the economy's master" (Wolf, 2009); two former chief economists of the International Monetary Fund (Rajan, 2005; Johnson, 2009), who wrote influential articles on the potential dangers of large financial sectors; and a recent World Bank report (De La Torre *et al.*, 2011). Along similar lines, Tobin (1984) suggested that a large financial sector may lead to a suboptimal allocation of talents and to private returns that are much larger than social returns (for evidence in this direction, see Philippon and Reshef, 2008). In Arcand *et al.* (2012) we show that these claims have an empirical backing and that the marginal effect of financial development on economic growth becomes negative when credit to the private sector reaches 100% of GDP. In that paper, we show that our results are not driven only by volatility, banking crises, or poor institutions.

In a simple model without credit rationing and with exogenous probability of default, it is easy to show that the presence of a bank bailout will generate a level of credit that is greater than the social optimum. In this paper, we show that the results hold more generally when we allow for credit rationing and endogenize the probability of default. A paper which is closely related to our work is De Gregorio and Guidotti (1995), who develop a model in which the presence of a government bailout and a poor regulatory framework lead to suboptimal screening and excessive lending.

The Economics 101 Model

We set the stage with the simplest textbook model. Consider an economy in which entrepreneurs who cannot post collateral produce by borrowing from competitive banks which, in turn, borrow abroad at an exogenous interest rate R and lend at a rate $r \geq R$. In such a setup, the capital stock K

[1]There are, however, also papers that challenge this view (for a review, see Panizza, 2012).

is equal to the size of the financial sector. Entrepreneurs are successful with probability π and unsuccessful with probability $1-\pi$. The representative entrepreneur has the following production function:

$$Y = \begin{cases} AF(K) & \text{with probability } \pi \\ \delta K & \text{with probability } (1-\pi) \end{cases} \tag{1}$$

with $F' > 0$, $F'' < 0$ and $\delta < (1+R)$ (i.e., failed projects have negative residual value).[2]

A social planner interested in maximizing the country's value added $V = \pi AF(K) + (1-\pi)\delta K - (1+R)K$ would choose the level of capital that satisfies the first order condition:

$$F'(K^{SP}) = \frac{(1+R)-(1-\pi)\delta}{\pi A}. \tag{2}$$

Let us now consider the decentralized equilibrium. When the project is successful, banks are paid back in full and get $(1+r)K$. When the project is not successful, they receive the residual value of the project and potentially a bailout: $(1+\gamma)\delta K$ ($\gamma \geq 0$ is the bailout; we assume that $(1+\gamma)\delta K \leq (1+r)K$).[3] Competitive banks choose the interest rate that satisfies the zero-profit condition $(1+r)\pi + (1-\pi)(1+\gamma)\delta = (1+R)$, yielding:

$$r = \frac{(1+R)-(1-\pi)(1+\gamma)\delta - \pi}{\pi}. \tag{3}$$

Given limited liability, a firm's expected profits are given by $P = \pi[AF(K) - (1+r)K]$, with FOC $F' = \frac{(1+r)}{A}$. Using (3), we obtain:

$$F'(K^*) = \frac{(1+R)-(1-\pi)(1+\gamma)\delta}{A\pi}. \tag{4}$$

Without distortions (i.e., with $\gamma = 0$), the decentralized equilibrium is equal to the social optimum (with $\gamma = 0$, $F'(K^*) = F'(K^{SP})$). In the presence of a bailout ($\gamma > 0$), we find that the capital stock (and total credit) in the decentralized equilibrium is larger than the socially optimal level of capital.

---

[2]The results would not change if the production function were to include labor, with perfectly inelastic labor supply.

[3]In the next section, we also allow for imperfect creditor rights and discuss what happens when γ is negative.

The Credit Rationing Model

We now check whether the Economics 101 result can be replicated in a model with credit rationing and endogenous default probability. In particular, we consider a simple economy where production takes place in two sectors, and where individuals supply labor inelastically and never save.

Given our zero-saving assumption, firms finance investment by borrowing abroad at the exogenous interest rate R (as in the Economics 101 model). The only role of the competitive financial sector is to screen projects and use its screening technology to intermediate foreign loans.[4]

We assume that the economy consists of two sectors. The first sector is composed of a large number of established competitive firms with a standard constant returns to scale technology: $y_c = F(K, L)$ (with $F_K > 0, F_L > 0, F_{KK} < 0$, and $F_{LL} < 0$). As output is nonstochastic, we assume that established firms can post collateral, guaranteeing that they will always repay their loans. Since loans to these firms carry no risk, the competitive banking sector will charge them an interest rate $r_c = R$ (with $F_K = r_c$, and $F_L = w$; where w is the wage rate). At this stage, the only reason for introducing this sector is to generate resources for the bailout. In the concluding section, we also discuss how the second sector could be used to build a model that links the size of the financial sector to economic growth.

Next, we build on Stiglitz and Weiss's (1981) credit rationing model and assume that the second sector is composed of monopolistic new entrants with the following stochastic production function:

$$y = \theta\sqrt{D}, \tag{5}$$

where D is the firm's stock of debt and θ is a random variable distributed according to the uniform density over $[0, N]$.[5] Given stochastic production, loans to firms in this sector are risky and the banks will charge an interest rate $r > R$.

Total production is given by $Y = y_c + y$ and GNP is equal to $Y - (1+R)(K + D)$, where $K + D$ is the size of the financial sector.

---

[4]We rule out any concerns related to the behavior of the exchange rate by assuming a common currency. We also assume, without loss of generality, no cost associated with screening projects.

[5]We choose a specific functional form because it is impossible to obtain a closed-form solution with a generic production function.

Social Planner

The optimal size of the financial sector is equal to the level of investment that maximizes domestic value added. Since the contribution to domestic value added of the traditional sector is fully determined by the exogenous labor supply and foreign interest rate, we only consider the innovative sector. The social planner's problem is:

$$\max_D \frac{1}{N}\int_0^N \theta\sqrt{D}d\theta - (1+R)D. \tag{6}$$

The solution to this problem yields a level of debt and investment that maximizes social welfare, and which is equal to:

$$D^{**} = \frac{N^2}{16(1+R)^2}. \tag{7}$$

The optimal level of debt is a negative function of the cost of funds R, and a positive function of productivity which, in turn, is determined by the upper bound of the distribution of θ.

Decentralized Equilibrium

Because of limited liability and the assumption that entrepreneurs have no equity capital, the profit of the representative entrepreneur is given by: $\pi = \max\left\{\theta\sqrt{D} - (1+r)D, 0\right\}$. Given the uniform distribution of θ, this yields an expected profit of:

$$E(\pi) = \frac{1}{N}\int_{\theta^*}^N [\theta\sqrt{D} - (1+r)D]d\theta, \tag{8}$$

where $\theta^* = (1+r)\sqrt{D}$ is the threshold level of the realization of the random variable above which the entrepreneur makes positive profits and is able to repay the loan. Performing the integration we obtain:

$$E(\pi) = \frac{\sqrt{D}}{2N}[(1+r)\sqrt{D} - N]^2. \tag{9}$$

In order to use Equation (9) to find the level of debt that maximizes profit, we need to solve for the endogenous lending rate r. Given our assumption of a competitive banking system, this is the rate that equates a lender's expected profits, $E(L)$, to zero.

$E(L)$ is composed of three elements: (i) full debt repayment times the probability that the project will be successful; (ii) the recovery value times the probability that the investment will be unsuccessful; and (iii) the cost of funds. Formally:

$$E(L) = \frac{1}{N}\int_{\theta^*}^{N}(1+r)Dd\theta + \frac{1}{N}\int_{0}^{\theta^*}[\theta\sqrt{D} + \gamma((1+r)D - \theta\sqrt{D})]d\theta - (1+R)D. \quad (10)$$

The term in the first integral is the repayment if the investment is successful, while the term in the second integral measures what the lenders will recover in case of default; the third term in Equation (10) is the cost of lending. If $\gamma \neq 0$, the recovery value in case of default is different from the residual value of the defaulted project. As in the Economics 101 model, the parameter γ is crucial in our story because it introduces a wedge between the socially optimal level of debt and the market equilibrium. We will show that when $\gamma < 0$, the financial system is too small with respect to the social optimum, and when $\gamma > 0$, the financial system is too big with respect to the social optimum.

We can think of γ as a combination of the strength of creditors' rights (c) and government bailout (b) in case of default. To fix ideas, assume that $\gamma = (c + b - 1)$, with $0 \leq c \leq 1$ and $0 \leq b < 2$.[6] In this setting, $c = 1$ denotes a situation with perfect creditor rights (lenders can recover the whole residual value of the failed investment project) and $c < 1$ denotes a situation in which lenders can only recover a fraction of the failed investment project. Similarly, $b = 0$ denotes a situation in which the government never bails out lenders, and $b > 0$ denotes a situation in which the government offers a (possibly partial) bailout. We assume that the bailout is financed with a lump-sum tax on the first sector.

[6] In order to avoid negative payments or payments which are greater than the original loan, it is also necessary to impose a joint constraint on c and b such that their sum guarantees that $-\frac{\theta\sqrt{D}}{(1+r)D-\theta\sqrt{D}} \leq \gamma < 1$ (we use a strict inequality, $\gamma < 1$, for technical reasons). Note that in case of default the denominator of the lower bound is always positive and $-\frac{\theta\sqrt{D}}{(1+r)D-\theta\sqrt{D}} > -1$.

Consider, for instance, the case of a country with no creditor rights and no bailout. In this case, creditors will receive no payments in case of default: $(\theta\sqrt{D} + \gamma[(1 + r)D - \theta\sqrt{D}]) = 0$ and $\gamma = -\frac{\theta\sqrt{D}}{(1+r)D-\theta\sqrt{D}} < 0$. With perfect creditor rights ($c = 1$) and no bailout ($b = 0$), instead, we get $\gamma = 0$, and the bank will receive all the residual value of the failed investment project (i.e., $\theta\sqrt{D}$). Note that the presence of a positive bailout ($b > 0$) is a necessary but not sufficient condition for $\gamma > 0$. With a positive bailout ($b > 0$), creditors could receive either less than the recovery value (if $b < 1 - c$) or more than the recovery value (if $b > 1 - c$).

Performing the integration in Equation (10), we obtain:

$$E(L) = \frac{D[2N(r - R) + (1 + r)^2(\gamma - 1)\sqrt{D}]}{2N}. \tag{11}$$

Competitive lenders will choose the interest rate that sets expected profits equal to zero. Equation (11) is a quadratic in r and admits two solutions:

$$r_1^* = \frac{N + \sqrt{\psi}}{\sqrt{D}(1 - \gamma)} - 1; \quad r_2^* = \frac{N - \sqrt{\psi}}{\sqrt{D}(1 - \gamma)} - 1, \tag{12}$$

where $\psi = N[N - 2\sqrt{D}(1 + R)(1 - \gamma)]$. For the time being we will assume that $\psi > 0$: we will later show that this condition holds in practice.[7] With $\psi > 0$ it is always true that $r_1^* > r_2^*$.

Since lenders are indifferent between interest rates (they always make zero profits), we pick the one that makes the borrower better off (any lender who charges a different interest rate would lose all customers). By substituting the expressions in (12) into (9) we obtain:

$$E(\pi_1) = \sqrt{D}\frac{[\sqrt{\psi} + N\gamma]^2}{2N(\gamma - 1)^2}; \quad E(\pi_2) = \sqrt{D}\frac{[\sqrt{\psi} - N\gamma]^2}{2N(\gamma - 1)^2}. \tag{13}$$

Since $\psi > 0$, $E(\pi_1) > E(\pi_2)$ if $\gamma > 0$ and $E(\pi_1) < E(\pi_2)$ if $\gamma < 0$ (if $\gamma = 0$, $E(\pi_1) = E(\pi_2)$). Whenever $\gamma > 0$, borrowers will prefer the higher interest rate, and when $\gamma < 0$, borrowers will prefer the lower interest rate. The intuition for this is simple: Inspection of Equation (9) reveals that $E(\pi)$ is quadratic (and U-shaped) in r. It is therefore not surprising that a

[7]Our assumption that $\gamma < 1$ is necessary to guarantee that the denominators in the interest rate equations are nonzero.

higher level of the interest rate is entirely compatible with higher borrower welfare.[8]

We can now maximize $E(\pi_1)$ and $E(\pi_2)$ with respect to D and solve for the optimal amount of debt. Let us start with the case in which $\gamma > 0$ and expected profits are given by $E(\pi_1)$. In this case, the FOC is given by:

$$\frac{\partial E(\pi_1)}{\partial D} = \frac{[\sqrt{\psi} + N\gamma][N - 4\sqrt{D}(1+R)(1-\gamma) + \gamma\sqrt{\psi}]}{4\sqrt{D}\sqrt{\psi}(\gamma - 1)^2} = 0. \quad (14)$$

Given our previous assumptions, when $\gamma > 0$, the first term in square brackets in the numerator and the denominator of (14) are both always positive. Therefore, we can find the optimal value of D by setting the second term in square brackets in the numerator equal to zero. This yields two solutions:

$$D^*_{11} = \frac{N^2[8 + \gamma^4 - \gamma(4 - \gamma^2)\sqrt{8 + \gamma^2}]}{128(1+R)^2(\gamma - 1)^2};$$

$$D^*_{12} = \frac{N^2[8 + \gamma^4 + \gamma(4 - \gamma^2)\sqrt{8 + \gamma^2}]}{128(1+R)^2(\gamma - 1)^2}. \quad (15)$$

Since $0 < \gamma < 1$, $\gamma(4 - \gamma^2) > 0$, and $D^*_{12} > D^*_{11}$.

At this point, we can substitute D^*_{11} and D^*_{12} into ψ and, after some tedious algebra, show that they satisfy the condition that $\psi > 0$. It is also easy to show that $\frac{\partial^2 E(\pi_1)}{\partial D^2} < 0$, and therefore that our solution satisfies the second-order condition for a maximum.[9] The appendix shows that when $\gamma > 0$, expected profits are always higher with D^*_{12}, and therefore the borrower always prefers the solution with a higher level of credit.

Summing up, with $\gamma = 0$ the decentralized equilibrium is equal to the social optimum ($D^*_{11} = D^*_{12} = D^{**}$ where D^{**} was given in Equation (7)), but for positive values of γ, we find that credit is always above the social optimum ($D^*_{12} > D^{**}$). The presence of a bailout leads to too much risk-taking and to a financial sector that is larger than the social optimum (this does not necessarily mean that bailouts are never desirable; more on this below).

---

[8]In turn, the U-shape of $E(\pi)$ in (9) stems from the linearity in θ of the integrand in Equation (8), combined with the limited liability assumption.

[9]Let $A = [\sqrt{\psi} + N\gamma]$; $B = [\psi/N + \gamma\sqrt{\psi}]$; and $C = (4\sqrt{D}\sqrt{\psi}(\gamma - 1)^2)$. Then $\frac{\partial^2 E(\pi_1)}{\partial D^2} = \frac{(A\frac{\partial B}{\partial D} + B\frac{\partial A}{\partial D})C - \frac{\partial C}{\partial D}AB}{C^2}$. Given that at D^*, B is equal to zero, the SOC simplifies to $\frac{\partial^2 E(\pi_1)}{\partial D^2} = \frac{A}{C}\frac{\partial B}{\partial D}$. Since $A > 0$, $C > 0$, and $\frac{\partial B}{\partial D} < 0$, we get that $\frac{\partial^2 E(\pi_1)}{\partial D^2} < 0$.

We now consider the case with $\gamma < 0$. In this case, $E(\pi_2) > E(\pi_1)$ and the borrowers will choose the lower interest rate r_2^*. Taking the first-order condition, we obtain:

$$\frac{\partial E(\pi_2)}{\partial D} = \frac{[\sqrt{\psi} - N\gamma][N - 4\sqrt{D}(1+R)(1-\gamma) - \gamma\sqrt{\psi}]}{4\sqrt{D}\sqrt{\psi}(\gamma-1)^2} = 0. \quad (16)$$

Since $\gamma < 0$, the first expression in square brackets in the numerator is always positive (and so is the denominator). We can thus find that value of D that maximizes profits by setting the second term in the numerator equal to zero. As this term is equal to the one considered earlier (in Equation (14)), we obtain the same solutions: $D_{21}^* = D_{11}^*$ and $D_{22}^* = D_{12}^*$. However, γ is now negative and $D_{21}^* > D_{22}^*$. The appendix shows that with $\gamma < 0$, borrowers always prefer D_{21}^* (again, with $\gamma = 0$ we get $D_{21}^* = D_{22}^* = D^{**}$).

We can now use the expressions in (15) to fully describe the size of the financial sector under positive and negative values of γ.

$$D^* = \begin{cases} \dfrac{N^2[8+\gamma^4-\gamma(4-\gamma^2)\sqrt{8+\gamma^2}]}{128(1+R)^2(\gamma-1)^2} & \text{if } \gamma < 0, \\ \dfrac{N^2}{16(1+R)^2} & \text{if } \gamma = 0, \\ \dfrac{N^2[8+\gamma^4+\gamma(4-\gamma^2)\sqrt{8+\gamma^2}]}{128(1+R)^2(\gamma-1)^2} & \text{if } \gamma > 0. \end{cases} \quad (17)$$

It is easy to show that when $\gamma > 0$, there is always "too much" finance ($D^* > D^{**}$ because $\gamma^4 + \gamma(4-\gamma^2)\sqrt{8+\gamma^2} > 0$ and $(\gamma-1)^2 < 1$).

With $\gamma < 0$, the comparison between D^* and D^{**} is more complicated because γ increases both the numerator and the denominator of D^*(with $\gamma < 0$, $\gamma^4 - \gamma(4-\gamma^2)\sqrt{8+\gamma^2} > 0$ and $(\gamma-1)^2 > 1$). We can, however, plot the D^*/D^{**} ratio for $\gamma \in [-1, 1)$ and show that when $-1 \leq \gamma < 0$, it is always true that $D^*/D^{**} < 1$ and when $0 < \gamma < 1$, it is always true that $D^*/D^{**} > 1$ (Fig. 1). Therefore, when $\gamma < 0$, the financial system is always too small with respect to the social optimum ($D^* < D^{**}$).

Equation (17) shows that bailouts are not necessarily a bad idea. The optimal bailout rule is $b = 1 - c$. Only with perfect creditors' rights ($c = 1$) are bailouts never desirable. If $c < 1$ and the bailout is financed with lump-sum taxes, society will be indifferent between setting $b = 1 - c$ and

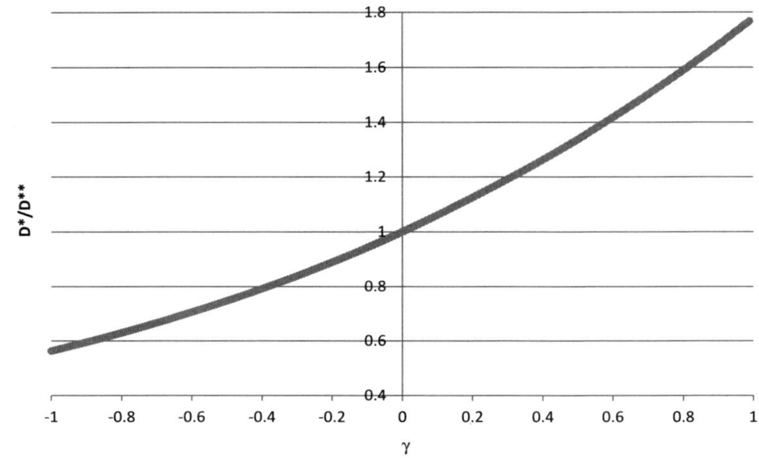

Fig. 1. The optimal level of debt. This figure plots D^*/D^{**} for $\gamma \in [-1.1)$. It shows that when $\gamma > 0$, D^* is always greater than D^{**} and when $\gamma < 0$, it is always true that $D^* < D^{**}$.

a reform that improves creditors' rights. Improving creditors' rights will be the preferred option only if the bailout is financed with a distortionary tax.

Note, however, that Fig. 1 shows that D^*/D^{**} is generally an increasing and convex function of γ. Thus, for any pair of γs with $|\gamma_i| = |\gamma_j|$ and $\gamma_i < 0$, $\gamma_j > 0$, the deviation from the social optimum is always larger when γ is positive. Therefore, in the presence of uncertainty on the value of c, policymakers should be conservative in offering bailouts because the costs of overshooting are larger than those of undershooting. This result would be strengthened if we were to assume that the bailout is financed with distortionary taxes.

However, it is straightforward to use our model to show that, under certain conditions, a distortionary tax on the second sector can restore the social optimum. In particular, if $\gamma > 0$ and $c = 1$, a Pigouvian tax equal to the cost of the potential bailout will make entrepreneurs internalize the cost of overborrowing and lead them to choose D^{**}. This is a result similar to that of Jeanne and Korinek's (2010) model of credit booms and busts.

Conclusions

In this paper, we develop a model with endogenous default probability and credit rationing and show that the presence of a bailout leads to a financial system which is "too large" with respect to the social optimum.

Within the model of this paper, there are three factors that determine the size of the financial sector: The productivity parameter N, the exogenous interest rate R, and the distortion γ. Therefore, countries with large financial sectors do not necessarily have "too much finance." However, if the size of the financial sector is positively correlated with its political and lobbying power, γ could become endogenous, leading to a situation in which countries that have a naturally large financial sector (because of high N) also end up having too much finance. This is the implicit message of Johnson (2009). We think that the model developed in this paper could serve as a building block for a political economy model aimed at endogenizing γ.

It is also worth noting that while this paper looks at the relationship between financial development and the *level* of income, most of the literature concentrates on the relationship between finance and economic growth. While a full dynamic specification is well beyond the scope of this paper, we think that our simple approach could also be used as a building block for a model that describes the relationship between financial development and economic growth. A possible avenue would be to make the number of firms that operate in the traditional sector a function of the number of surviving firms in the innovative sector. In such a setup, policies that maximize the number of surviving firms should also maximize growth.

References

Arcand, J. L., E. Berkes and U. Panizza (2012). "Too much finance?" International Monetary Fund Working Paper No. 12/161.

Bagehot, W. (1873). *Lombard Street: A Description of the Money Market*, History of Economic Thought Books, McMaster University Archive for the History of Economic Thought.

Beck, T., R. Levine and N. Loayza (2000). "Finance and the sources of growth," *Journal of Financial Economics*, Vol. 58, No. 1–2, pp. 261–300.

Beck, T., B. Buyukkarabacak, F. Rioja and N. Valev (2008). "Who gets the credit and does it matter? Household vs. firm lending across countries," The World Bank Policy Research Working Paper No. 4661.

De la Torre, A., A. Ize and S. Schmukler (2011). *Financial Development in Latin America and the Caribbean: The Road Ahead*, Report. Washington, DC: The World Bank.

De Gregorio, J. and P. Guidotti (1995). "Financial development and economic growth," *World Development*, Vol. 23, No. 3, pp. 433–448.

Goldsmith, R. W. (1969). *Financial Structure and Development*, New Haven, CT: Yale University Press.

Jeanne, O. and A. Korinek (2010). "Excessive volatility in capital flows: A Pigouvian taxation approach," Peterson Institute for International Economics, working paper series, No. WP10-5.

Johnson, S. (2009). "The quiet coup," *The Atlantic*, May 1, 2009.

King, R. G. and R. Levine (1993). "Finance and growth: Schumpeter might be right," *The Quarterly Journal of Economics*, Vol. 108, No. 3, pp. 717–737.

Levine, R. (2005). "Finance and growth: Theory and evidence," in *Handbook of Economic Growth*, Vol. 1, P. Aghion, and S., Durlauf (eds.), Amsterdam: Elsevier/North-Holland, Chapter 12, pp. 865–834.

Levine, R., N. Loayza and T. Beck (2000). "Financial intermediation and growth: Causality and causes," *Journal of Monetary Economics*, Vol. 46, No. 1, pp. 31–77.

Panizza, U. (2012). "Finance and economic development," *International Development Policy*, pp. 141–160.

Philippon, T. and A. Reshef (2008). "Wages and human capital in the U.S. financial industry: 1909–2006," New York University Mimeo.

Rajan, R. G. and L. Zingales (1998). "Financial dependence and growth," *American Economic Review*, Vol. 88, No. 3, pp. 559–586.

Rajan, R. G. (2005). "Has financial development made the world riskier?" in *Proceedings of the Federal Reserve Bank of Kansas City's 2005 Jackson Hole Conference*, Jackson Hole, WY.

Schumpeter, J. A. (1911). *A Theory of Economic Development*, Cambridge, MA: Harvard University Press.

Stiglitz, J. and A. Weiss (1981). "Credit rationing in markets with imperfect information," *American Economic Review*, Vol. 71, No. 3, pp. 393–410.

Tobin, J. (1984). "On the efficiency of the financial system," *Lloyds Bank Review*, Vol. 153, pp. 1–15.

Wolf, M. (2009). "Why dealing with the huge debt overhang is so hard," *Financial Times*, January 27.

Appendix A

A.1 Proof that when $\gamma > 0$, the firm will choose D^*_{12} (and when $\gamma < 0$, the firm will choose D^*_{21})

By substituting D^*_{11} and D^*_{12} into $E(\pi_1)$, we get:

$$E(\pi_1(D^*_{11})) = \frac{N^2\phi_1(4\gamma - 2\sqrt{2}\phi_1)^2}{256\sqrt{2}(1+R)(\gamma-1)^2}$$

$$E(\pi_1(D^*_{12})) = \frac{N^2\phi_2(4\gamma - 2\sqrt{2}\phi_2)^2}{256\sqrt{2}(1+R)(\gamma-1)^2}$$

$$\phi_1 = \sqrt{8+\gamma^4 - \gamma(4-\gamma^2)\sqrt{8+\gamma^2}} \quad \text{and}$$

$$\phi_2 = \sqrt{8+\gamma^4 + \gamma(4-\gamma^2)\sqrt{8+\gamma^2}}.$$

Considering the positive roots, we have $sign(\phi_2 - \phi_1) = sign(\gamma)$. Let us now write:

$$\frac{E(\pi_1(D^*_{11}))}{E(\pi_1(D^*_{12}))} = \frac{\phi_1(4\gamma - 2\sqrt{2}\phi_1)^2}{\phi_2(4\gamma - 2\sqrt{2}\phi_2)^2} = \varphi(\gamma)$$

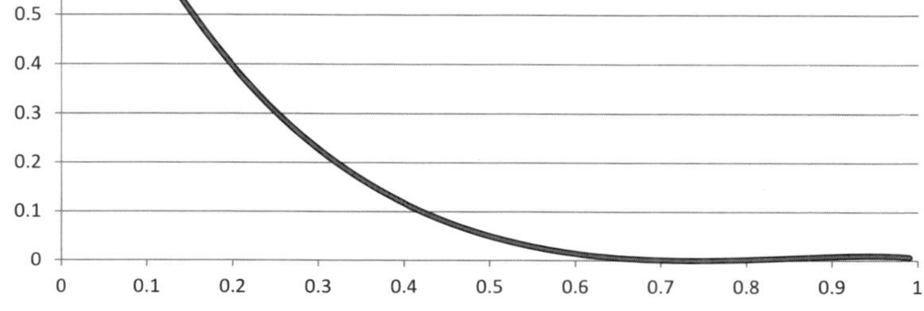

Fig. 2. $\boldsymbol{\phi(\gamma) = \frac{E(\pi_1(D^*_{11}))}{E(\pi_1(D^*_{12}))}}$ **for $\boldsymbol{\gamma \in (0,1)}$. The figure shows that, for $\boldsymbol{\gamma>0, \phi(\gamma) < 1}$. Therefore, the entrepreneur will always chooses $\boldsymbol{D^*_{12}}$.**

Figure 2 plots $\varphi(\gamma)$ for $\gamma \in (0, 1)$. It shows that $\varphi(\gamma)$ is always smaller than one, indicating that profits are always higher with D^*_{12}.

Given that $E(\pi_2(D^*_{21})) = E(\pi_1(D^*_{12}))$ and $E(\pi_1(D^*_{11})) = E(\pi_2(D^*_{22}))$, it is always true that when $\gamma < 0$, $\frac{E(\pi_2(D^*_{21}))}{E(\pi_2(D^*_{22}))} > 1$ and that the borrower will always prefer D^*_{21} over D^*_{22}.

Too Much Finance, Too Much Credit? Comments on Papers by Calomiris, Arcand–Berkes–Panizza, and Taylor

Eugene N. White*
Rutgers University
and
National Bureau of Economic Research

The papers in this session treat different aspects of the unfinished business of reforming the financial system. Charles Calomiris offers a bold multi-point plan for reform, whose underlying theme is that we do not need more complex rules and more supervisory discretion but simpler rules that limit measurable risk and are easier to enforce. From his vantage point, there are four important components to supervision: regulation, measurement, supervision, and incentives for stake holders. It is hard to disagree with most of his assessment, but I would push his argument one step further and propose that there is too much emphasis currently on the development of more and more instruments of regulation, measurement, and supervision, and not enough on creating the incentives for stake holders to control excessive risk-taking. It is within this framework that my comments are offered.

The papers by Jean-Louis Arcand, Enrico Berkes, and Ugo Panizza and Alan Taylor propose new measures to identify an excessive expansion of the financial system. We are more concerned than ever about measurement because of a general belief that during the last crisis, regulators failed to act promptly to contain system-threatening risk for one of three

---

* The author is Professor of Economics at Rutgers University and a Research Associate of the National Bureau of Economic Research.

reasons: (1) they lacked enough information or the right information, (2) they lacked adequate resources to obtain the needed information, or (3) they lacked the right incentives or were limited by politics to take the necessary corrective actions. If more measurement is to contribute to these information or incentive deficiencies, it needs to meet certain criteria, including whether the costs of collection are worth the benefits it brings and whether it serves as a useful guide for policy.

Arcand, Berkes, and Panizza's provocatively titled paper, "Too Much Finance," builds on the common perception that too much of the economy's scarce resources have been devoted to the financial sector. How can we determine what is excessive? How can it be measured? As we now know, thanks to the many contributions to the finance and growth literature (King and Levine, 1993; Beck and Levine, 2004), finance is an important contributor to economic growth. Very generally, these studies show that greater finance depth in the past is positively related to future growth. The authors argue that relationship, which has been treated linearly, gives the mistaken impression that more finance must always be better. Using the ratio of private credit to GDP (PC/GDP), as a measure of financial depth, they add squared term for this ratio to pick up the possibility that, at some point, finance might not add to growth. As financial regulation and supervision, bank capital, strength of private monitoring, and the general "quality" of government may condition how finance affects growth, they include variables for these factors and interact them with PC/GDP. They use existing indices for these variables, so that all aspects of the quality of government or financial regulation can be condensed into a variable that ranges from zero to one. While the coefficients on the variables of interest generally have the correct signs, the more interesting question is, obviously, when will there be too much finance. In the simplest case, when PC/GDP reaches 70%, it no longer has a positive effect on growth; and when it hits 110%, the effect is negative and significant. However, when the control factors are taken into consideration, there appears to be little consistency. To identify the potential magnitude of their effects, the authors divide countries into "strict" and "weak." For example, for countries with strong bank supervision, PC/GDP has no positive effect at 81% and turns negative and significant at 105%. For nations with weak supervision, there is no positive effect at 82% but it never turns negatively significant. For countries with strict and weak capital requirements, PC/GDP has no positive effect at 58% and 105%, but they never significantly detract from growth. In countries with strict and weak private monitoring, finance has a negative effect on growth at 64% and 77%. While we might think better monitoring by the government and private sector puts the brakes on the financial sector, there is no clear evidence here; and the authors conclude that the "vanishing effect" cannot be attributed to these factors. This conclusion about the potency of these factors is, perhaps, too easily dismissed given the limited and imprecise nature of how they are measured.

It would be interesting to see what countries had a financial sector so large that it placed a drag on the economy. This exercise might also provide some insight into what the regressions are actually telling us. For the US, in the early 1980s, PC/GDP reached over 125% — well over the limits to a positive contribution to growth according to Arcand, Berkes, and Panizza — and continued ever upward. Does this mean that Congress should have intervened to limit its growth from that point onward? If the safe number were 70%, then the only time after 1920 when PC/GDP was below it would be during the Great Depression and its aftermath. All of this has bearing on whether a broad ratio like this can convey any timely information for policy makers. Even if this measure were refined and estimates were tighter, it is not clear to me that there is a policy takeaway.

Taylor's paper, "The Great Leveraging," attributes the primary responsibility for financial crises to credit booms. Figure 3 in his paper is particularly eye-catching, with his two measures of credit soaring upward after 1960, while his measure for money seeming almost quiescent. Taylor proposes to find threshold values for predicting when a financial crisis is likely to occur, using two measures of the magnitude of a credit boom, bank assets to GDP (BA/GDP), and bank loans to GDP (BL/GDP). This exercise is carried out using a 5-year lagged moving average for three variables for 14 countries, from 1870 to 2008. The method that Taylor employs is "a simple classification test, standard in clinical and other applications in the hard sciences." While this approach might seem to be useful for provide policy makers with a forecasting tool, we need to know more about its performance in this paper. What are the Type-I and Type-II errors? What is the trade-off? What were the misclassifications? The last question points to another feature of Taylor's exercise: All crises are treated equally. Apparently, the

1974 Secondary Banking Crisis in the UK was treated the same as the 1933 banking panic in the US — events of very different scale and character. The depth and duration of a crisis, whether it was a liquidity event or a solvency event is not a feature of this test, even though it matters vitally for the policy response.

Given that we still have not escaped from the effects of the 2008 crisis, the spectacular rise in BA/GDP and BL/GDP in Fig. 3 would certainly seem to indict excessive growth of credit, but there are no alternative hypotheses to explain the rise of these ratios. However, there are two contenders: (1) financial innovation, including technological changes and improvements in financial management (including diversification) and (2) policy regimes. I have taken the liberty of using his Fig. 3 to show how these factors might account for the movement of the ratios. For the first explanation, there is a clear upward trend before 1914. The two World Wars and the Great Depression hit private credit hard and may have sent it off its trajectory, to which it gradually returned in the post-war era. If explanation (1) were true, then extrapolating a trend line in Fig. 3 for the pre-1914 era suggests that we have only recently moved back to trend. Although Taylor's empirical exercise includes 14 countries for 1870 to 2008, there are generally three policy regimes for these years (Grossman, 2010). The 1870–1913 period is what I have called the era of prudent banking. In general, regulation and supervision were light, and the incentives for bank stake holders were generally well aligned. In many countries, shareholders faced some form of extended liability beyond limited liability, and there was no deposit insurance for depositors, forcing both groups to more closely monitor banks. Directors met very frequently, and officers often had to post bonds. Although bank failures occurred, they were never deeply insolvent, yielding small losses to their creditors (White, 2013). There was no socialization of risk in banking. The era of financial repression (1914–1970, very roughly the end point) saw a great increase in regulation and supervision. Notable were the controls on entry, pricing, and products. Competition was greatly reduced, and banks were restricted from taking risks. In many countries, bank portfolios were stuffed with government bonds. At the same time, there were the beginnings of a gradual weakening of incentives for the stake holders. The final period, the era of imprudent banking, began in the 1970s and still continues. It was a period of partial de-regulation. It important to emphasize that it was partial because as many regulations that constrained competition and risk-taking were eased, while deposit insurance programs were adopted and expanded and Too-Big-to-Fail became accepted in most countries. In response to crises, ever more complex regulations were added and a greater burden was placed on supervision for preventing crises. The risk in banking was socialized as the risk-controlling incentives for stake holders continued to diminish. This periodization by regime gives a very different interpretation to figures like Fig. 3. It is not that there is simply too much finance but the laws, regulations, and other policies have induced banks to take more and more risk. This interpretation emphasizes that more important than downsizing an "excessively" large financial sector, is the correction of the distorting incentives.

Charles Calomiris' recommendations for reforming the financial system move in that direction. Some key features of his program include the end to subsidizing mortgage default risk and Too-Big-to-Fail. He also calls for an improvement in prudential supervision to produce credible measurements of ex ante risk and ex post losses. One area that I believe deserves more attention is providing the stake holders with better incentives. Like many other proposals, Calomiris is vague on this issue. He criticizes "poorly designed compensation systems" and writes: "The key to avoiding these sorts of problems [like the subprime mortgage backed securities] is to establish a healthy risk management culture. Such a culture rewards long-term performance of portfolios not just short-term growth." The question is how is it to be achieved? If it is not government regulation, then policies that govern and reward the behavior by employees have to be influenced incentives given by policy to shareholders, directors, and creditors to influence management. Calomiris acknowledges this: "While risk managers, acting in the interest of their stockholders, are the first line of defense against imprudent investing, prudential supervision and regulation is the second line of defense." He recommends that macroprudential regulation should be structured "so it is time-varying in response to economic and financial conditions." However, Calomiris' paper does not address the question of what are appropriate expectations for supervision. As in other reform proposals, there is a belief that with more information and more resources, prudential supervision will be able to identify problems and correct them in a timely fashion.

The problem with this hopeful scenario is that personnel, resources, and surveillance of the banking system by regulatory agencies have grown since the 1970s, and yet crises are larger. The failure to understand the limits of what supervision can accomplish in a financial system where there are large incentives to take risk can be seen in the public's reaction to 2012 multibillion-dollar trading loss at JPMorgan Chase. Shock spread when it was revealed that there were roughly 40 bank examiners from the Federal Reserve Bank of New York and 70 from the Office of the Comptroller of the Currency embedded in the bank and yet they failed to identify the problem (Silver-Greenberg and Protess, 2012, p. 1). But, this may not be surprising, as JPMorgan Chase is a vast and complex organization, with approximately 262,000 employees and perhaps as many divisions as regulators.

In discussions of the causes of excess risk-taking or financial crises, the far-reaching consequences of distorting incentives are under appreciated, certainly for their effects on the labor market and apparent inability to foster "a healthy risk management culture." In the general labor market, the multiple incentives to take risk from deposit insurance, Too-Big-to-Fail, subsidization of housing, and other policies, result in attracting risk-taking individuals to the financial industry. In a recent paper, Philippon and Reschef (2012) detailed the relative wage for the financial industry to the nonfinancial sector in the US. They find that before the Great Depression, the wage for the financial industry was about 50% higher. This plunged during the era of financial repression to near equality and after 1980 gradually recovered its 50% premium. In a regression analysis, controlling for education, skills, and employment risk, Philippon and Reschef found that compensation of financial industry employees for the years 1990–2006 was too high to be sustainable with labor market equilibrium. Their findings underline the need to address the underlying causes of risk-taking, rather than trying to regulate outcomes. If they are not addressed, there is little alternative to increasingly complex regulatory and supervisory interventions.

References

Beck, T. and R. Levine (2004). "Stock markets, banks, and growth: Panel evidence," *Journal of Banking and Finance*, Vol. 28, March, pp. 423–442.

Grossman, R. S. (2010). *Unsettled Account: The Evolution of Banking in the Industrialized World Since 1800*, Princeton, NJ: Princeton University Press.

King, R. G. and R. Levine (1993). "Finance and growth: Schumpeter might be right," *Quarterly Journal of Economics*, Vol. 108, August, pp. 717–737.

Philippon, T. and A. Reschef (2012). "Wages and human capital in the U.S. finance industry: 1900–2006," *Quarterly Journal of Economics*, Vol. 127(4), November, pp. 1551–1609.

Silver-Greenberg, J. and B. Protess (2012). "Bank regulators under scrutiny in JPMorgan Loss," *New York Times*, May 25, p. 1.

White, E. N. (2013). "To establish a more effective supervision of banking: How the birth of the Fed altered bank supervision," in *The Origins, History and Future of the Federal Reserve: A Return to Jekyll Island*, M. D. Bordo and W. Roberds (eds.), Cambridge: Cambridge University Press, 2013, pp. 7–54.

PART III

SOCIAL BENEFITS AND COSTS OF THE CURRENT FINANCIAL SYSTEM

Bank Regulatory Reforms and Racial Wage Discrimination

Ross Levine*
Haas School of Business
University of California, Berkeley
The Milken Institute
National Bureau of Economic Research

Alexey Levkov
Federal Reserve Bank of Boston

Yona Rubinstein
London School of Economics
CEPR and IZA

Introduction

Banks influence economic opportunities directly and indirectly. Banks directly shape economic opportunities by determining who has access to credit. They influence who can start a business and who cannot, who can expand a business, and who is credit constrained (Levine, 1997, 2005; Demirgüç-Kunt and Levine, 2009). Banks also indirectly affect economic opportunities by shaping the economic environment in which people — even people who never use a bank — work and search for work. For example, more efficient banks can lower entry barriers facing nonfinancial firms, spurring product market competition and affecting the

*Ross Levine is affiliated with the Haos School of Business at the University of California, Berkeley; the Milken Institute; and the National Bureau of Economic Research. Alexey Levkov is affiliated with the Federal Reserve Bank of Boston. Yona Rubinstein is affiliated with the London School of Economics, the CEPR, and IZA. The views expressed here are solely those of the authors and do not necessarily reflect official positions of the Federal Reserve Bank of Boston or the Federal Reserve System.

demand for labor. Beck, Levine, and Levkov (2010) show that an exogenous increase in competition among US banks reduced income inequality among salaried workers in nonfinancial industries by disproportionately increasing the demand for lower-skilled workers. Thus, banks can influence the economic opportunities of people who never use banking services to start a business.

Based on our analyses in Levine, Levkov, and Rubinstein (2013), this paper contributes to research on how banks influence economic opportunities by assessing the impact of bank regulatory reforms on racial discrimination in labor markets. Research documents that black workers earn about 20% less than their white counterparts after controlling for differences in education, experience, and other characteristics. These lower wages not only define the economic opportunities of the workers themselves but also shape the opportunities available to the workers' children and hence to future generations. In this paper, we examine whether US bank deregulation indirectly influenced racial wage discrimination by altering the relative demand for black workers. More specifically, we ask whether US bank regulatory reforms that enhanced the competitiveness of the banking industry (a) reduced the manifestation of racial prejudices on the demand for labor, (b) boosted the wages of black workers toward those of equally productive white counterparts, and hence (c) expanded the economic opportunities of black workers and their families.

To address these questions, we build on two lines of research. First, Becker's (1957) theory of racial discrimination provides a natural framework for understanding and evaluating the indirect mechanisms through which banks influence labor markets and hence racial discrimination. Becker argues that taste-based discrimination, the disutility that employers attach to hiring black workers, can create a gap between the wages of equally productive white and black workers and that intensified product market competition will erode this gap. More specifically, Becker argues that, with lower entry barriers, firms with weaker racial prejudices can initiate profitable operations by hiring equally productive black workers at lower wage rates than their white counterparts, boosting the relative demand for black workers and reducing the racial wage gap. From this perspective, an intensification of competition in labor markets does not alter racial prejudices; rather, an increase in competition for labor among firms reduces the manifestation of those prejudices on the labor market outcomes of workers.

The second line of research that is crucial for assessing the impact of banks on racial discrimination emphasizes that more competitive, efficient banks spur competition in nonfinancial sectors. Black and Strahan (2002), Cetorelli and Strahan (2006), and Kerr and Nanda (2009) show that the deregulation of geographic restrictions on the establishment of bank branches and subsidiaries improved the functioning of the US banking industry, lowered entry barriers facing nonfinancial industries, and intensified product and labor market competition in these nonfinancial industries. In particular, from the mid-1970s to 1994, individual US states relaxed restrictions on the entry of banks from other states and the branching of banks within states, which intensified competition, boosted bank efficiency, and enhanced the effectiveness of credit allocation (Jayaratne and Strahan, 1998; Hubbard and Palia, 1995). These improvements in the banking industry lowered barriers to the entry of new firms within nonfinancial industries, intensifying competition throughout the economy. Critically, this research does not just show that bank deregulation enhanced the efficiency of the banking sector. It shows that more efficient banks boosted the contestability and competitiveness of nonfinancial industries.

Combining these two lines of research, Levine, Levkov, and Rubinstein (2013) argue that if racial prejudices create a racial wage gap, then Becker's (1957) theory of racial discrimination predicts that bank deregulation that intensifies product and labor market competition will reduce the manifestation of those racial prejudices on wages, boosting the relative wages of black workers. Thus, a deregulatory-induced improvement in the banking system will boost blacks' relative wages and enhance their economic opportunities in economies where racial prejudices were repressing blacks' wages. From this perspective, more competitive, efficient banks can expand the economic opportunities of a historically repressed group by altering labor market conditions.

By rigorously linking the analyses to Becker's (1957) theory of discrimination, our research better identifies how banks indirectly influence racial discrimination through their effects on labor markets. Becker's model implies that financial regulation that intensifies product market competition will reduce racial discrimination in states with a sufficiently high degree of racial prejudice. According to this theory, competition will not boost blacks' relative wages in states in which racial prejudices were not depressing blacks' relative wages. This is tested explicitly by differentiating states by their degree of racial prejudice. From the 1970 US Census, Levine, Levkov, and Rubinstein (2013) compute the predicted rate of racial intermarriage based on individual and state characteristics. The difference between the predicted rate of intermarriage that would emerge with no racial biases and the actual rate — the racial bias index — is used as a proxy for the state's degree of racial prejudice. Although imperfect, this racial bias index captures marriage decisions made far before the period of bank deregulation. Furthermore, as shown in Levine, Levkov, and Rubinstein (2013), the results are robust to using survey-based measures of racial attitudes from Charles and Guryan (2008).

The results from Levine, Levkov, and Rubinstein (2013) illustrated below are striking: Bank deregulation that intensified competition among nonfinancial firms substantially reduced racial wage discrimination by reducing the manifestation of racial prejudices on blacks' relative wages. Moreover, consistent with Becker's (1957) theory of racial discrimination, bank deregulation increased blacks' relative wage rates only in "economies," i.e., US states, where racial prejudices had been depressing blacks' wages. Specifically, in states with above-the-median level of the racial bias index, bank deregulation eliminated about one-third of the initial racial wage gap after five years. But, in states with below-the-median level of the racial bias index, the intensification of product market competition triggered by bank deregulation had little impact on the relative wages of black workers. Thus, while bank deregulation boosted the intensity of competition among nonfinancial firms in both high- and low-racial-bias states, there is a positive association between blacks' relative wages and bank deregulation only in high-racial-bias states. These results are fully consistent with Becker's theory of racial discrimination, using bank deregulation as an exogenous source of variation in product market competition.

Several sensitivity tests confirm these findings. First, blacks' wages rise relative to comparable white workers within the same occupation and industry. Second, bank deregulation boosted blacks' relative wages in particular, not the relative wages of comparatively low-income workers in general. Third, the results hold after accounting for state and year fixed effects, which controls for all national influences, as well as state-specific factors. Fourth, as demonstrated by Levine and Rubinstein (2013), the results are stronger for bank-dependent industries: Bank deregulation boosted blacks' relative wages only in industries that rely heavily on bank financing, within high-racial-bias states. The results imply that competition boosts blacks' relative wages by eroding the adverse effects of racial prejudices on the relative demand for black workers.

Banks, and hence bank regulations, exert a powerful influence on economic opportunities. Beyond making loans or selling other financial services directly to a few people, banks can influence product and labor markets and therefore indirectly influence the economic lives of virtually all workers. As illustrated below, regulatory changes that intensified competition among banks also boosted product market competition among nonfinancial firms and increased the relative demand for a historically repressed group in the US. Financial deregulation reduced racial inequality by diminishing the impact of racial bigotry on labor market opportunities.

Bank Deregulation and Competition in Nonfinancial Industries

A considerable body of evidence highlights the validity of treating US bank deregulation from the mid-1970s through the mid-1990s as an exogenous source of variation in the competitiveness and efficiency of the US banking industry. Geographic restrictions on banking protected local banks from competition for much of the 20th century. This created a powerful lobby for maintaining those restrictions. By the 1970s, however, several technological innovations (discussed by Levine, Levkov, and Rubinstein (2013) and others) lowered the costs of using distant banks. This reduced the value of lobbying for the maintenance of regulations, restricting the geographic expansion of banks both within states and across state boundaries. As these lobbing efforts weakened, states deregulated geographic restrictions on banking between the mid-1970s and 1994, when the Riegle–Neal Act essentially eliminated them. Research also indicates that the forces driving the state-specific timing of the removal of these geographic restrictions were exogenous to competition in the nonfinancial sector and the racial wage gap. The timing of deregulation was not shaped by new firm formation (Black and Strahan, 2002; Kerr and Nanda, 2009), the degree of earnings inequality (Beck, Levine, and Levkov, 2010), the nature of labor unions (Levkov, 2010), or the racial wage gap (Levine, Levkov, and Rubinstein, 2013). Levine, Levkov, and Rubinstein (2013) provide the dates when each state removed regulatory limits on intrastate branching and interstate banking.

Deregulation increased competition within the banking sector. Intrastate deregulation allowed banks to open branches across markets within a state. Interstate deregulation allowed banks to purchase, and in some cases, open new subsidiaries in other states. Bank deregulation reduced interest rates on loans, raised them on deposits, lowered overhead costs, and shrank the proportion of bad loans (Jayaratne and Strahan, 1998).

Furthermore, by enhancing the efficiency of the banking industry, bank deregulation reduced entry barriers facing nonfinancial sectors firms, which intensified competition throughout the economy. Black and Strahan (2002) show that deregulation helped entrepreneurs start new businesses, with the rate of new incorporations per capita in a state increasing by six percentage points following deregulation. Kerr and Nanda (2009) show that deregulation both increased the number of new start-ups and the rate of firm exit, suggesting that bank deregulation increased contestability and competition within nonfinancial industries.

Blacks' Relative Wages and the Racial Bias Index

Since Levine, Levkov, and Rubinstein (2013) provide extensive details on the construction of the relative wages of black workers and the racial bias index, here we simply summarize these data. The US *Current Population Survey* (CPS) provides data on wages and worker traits. We start in survey year 1977 because that is when the CPS reports information on each person's state of residence. We restrict the sample to non-Hispanic white and black civilian males aged between 18 and 65 years.

We define the relative wage rate of a black worker, i, in state s, during year t (R_{ist}) as the difference between the wage rate that a white worker with identical experience and educational traits would earn in the same industry and occupation and the black worker's actual wage rate. To construct R_{ist}, we run Mincerian wage regressions for all white workers where the regressors are years of completed education, potential experience, dummy variables for occupation, industry, and state, and where we run these regressions separately for each year, so that the estimated coefficients on education, experience, and the dummy variables vary over time. We then use these estimated coefficients along with the actual traits of each black worker to compute the wage rate that a white worker with identical traits would earn on average. Finally, the difference between this estimated wage rate of a white worker with identical traits as a black worker and the black worker's actual wage is our estimate of the relative wage rate of each black worker, R_{ist}.

We also develop a measure of the degree of racial prejudice in each state. Recall, that one implication of Becker's (1957) theory is that an intensification of competition will only boost blacks' relative wages in economies in which racial prejudices materially influence labor markets. If racial prejudices do not repress the relative wages of black workers, then intensified competition will not boost blacks' relative wages within the confines of Becker's (1957) theory.

To examine this prediction, we construct a racial bias index for each state based on racial intermarriage in 1970. The racial bias index equals the difference between the rate of intermarriage that would exist if married people were randomly matched and the actual intermarriage rate. Larger values of the racial bias index indicate that intermarriage occurs less in practice than if marriage pairings were random. We interpret larger values as indicating greater racial bias. As shown in Levine, Levkov, and Rubinstein (2013), we obtain the same results discussed below when using (1) a racial bias index that accounts for education and age in forming a "predicted" intermarriage rate or (2) subjective, survey measures of racial attitudes.

Armed with this racial bias index, we assess whether an intensification of competition influences blacks' relative wages in states with higher values of the racial bias index. For simplicity, we illustrate the findings using the median. Thus, we define states with above-the-median value of the racial bias index as high-racial-bias states and states with below-the-median value as low-racial-bias states.

Results

Prerequisites

Our empirical strategy assumes that racial inequality did not affect the timing of bank deregulation across the US. Figure 1 validates this

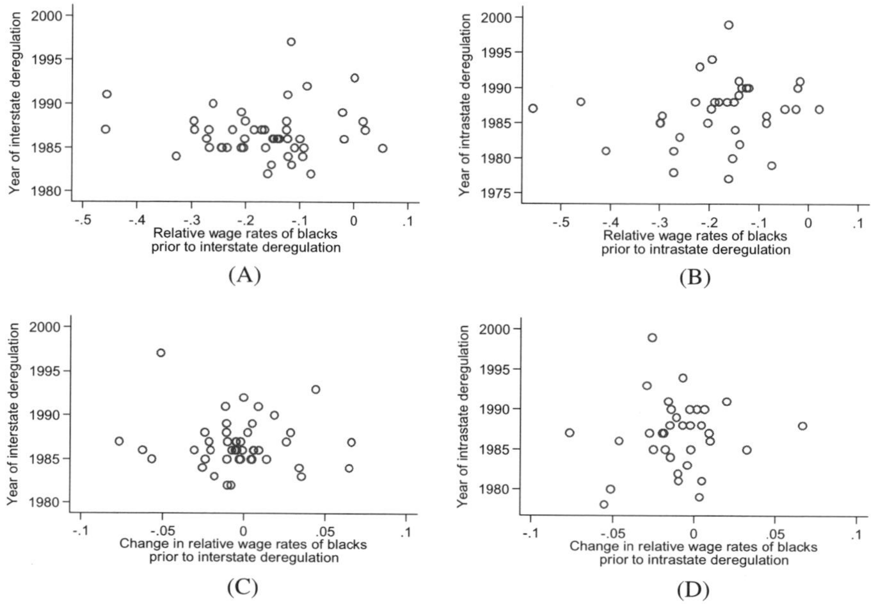

Fig. 1. Trends and innovations in the relative wage rates of blacks prior to bank deregulation.

Note: Figures 1(A) and 1(B) plot the year of bank deregulation against the average black-white wage differential prior to deregulation. In Fig. 1(A), we consider years prior to interstate deregulation. In Fig. 1(B), we consider years prior to intrastate deregulation. Figures 1(C) and 1(D) plot the year of bank deregulation against the change in the black-white wage differential prior to deregulation. In Fig. 1(C), we consider years prior to interstate deregulation. In Fig. 1(D), we consider years prior to intrastate deregulation.

assumption, as neither the level of blacks' relative wages before deregulation (Panel A) nor the rate of change in blacks' relative wages before deregulation (Panel C) predict the timing of interstate bank deregulation. Similarly, Panels B and D show that neither the level nor the rate of change in blacks' relative wages predicts the timing of intrastate bank branch deregulation.

The empirical strategy also assumes that bank deregulation intensified competition among firms in nonfinancial industries. As discussed in Sec. 1, a substantial body of research demonstrates that bank deregulation spurred the entry of new, nonfinancial corporations. Levine, Levkov, and Rubinstein (2013) provide additional evidence on the dynamics between deregulation and competition. Here, Fig. 2 illustrates the link between interstate and intrastate bank deregulation and subsequent rates of new incorporations.

Figure 2 shows that bank deregulation increases the rate of new incorporations. Specifically, Fig. 2 depicts the year-by-year relationship between the natural logarithm of new incorporations in state s during year t (N_{st}) and both forms of bank deregulation. The figure starts nine years before each form of deregulation and traces out the relationships until nine years after each form of deregulation. Year zero is the year that each particular state started removing inter- and intrastate banking restrictions respectively. We omit this year from the figure. We control for state and year fixed effects, so that the figures provide a picture of the relationship between bank deregulation and the rate of new incorporations for the average state.

Figure 2 illustrates three key points. First, interstate and intrastate boost the rate of new incorporations, suggesting that these forms of bank deregulation intensified competition among firms in nonfinancial industries. Second, there is a dynamic relationship: The impact of bank deregulation on competition among nonfinancial firms emerges over at least five years. Thus, we should also expect the impact of bank deregulation on the relative wages of black workers to also emerge dynamically. Third, bank deregulation boosted competition in high- and low-racial-bias states, though the marginal impact of intrastate deregulation on the rate of new incorporations in low-racial-bias states is less pronounced than in high-racial-bias states. Thus, we can test whether an exogenous intensification of competition only boosts blacks' relative wages in high racial bias states.

The Impact of Deregulation on Blacks' Relative Wages

In this section, we examine the dynamic relationship between bank deregulation and the relative wages of black workers. As with the figures relating bank deregulation to new incorporations, we trace out the year-by-year relationship between deregulation and blacks' relative wages using the same procedure employed to create Fig. 2.

Consistent with our approach of using Becker's (1957) theory of racial discrimination, we separately examine the impact of bank deregulation on blacks' relative wages in states with above-the-median value of the racial

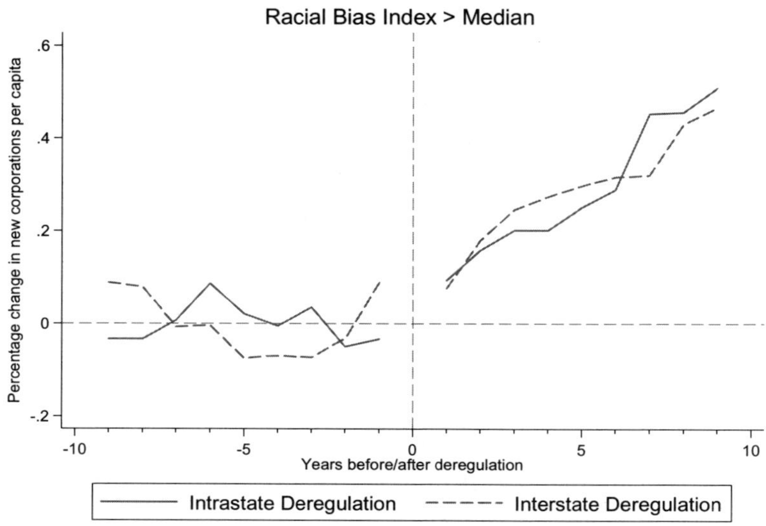
Racial Bias Index > Median
Percentage change in new corporations per capita
.6
.4
.2
0
-.2
-10
-5
0
5
10
Years before/after deregulation
Intrastate Deregulation
Interstate Deregulation

(A)

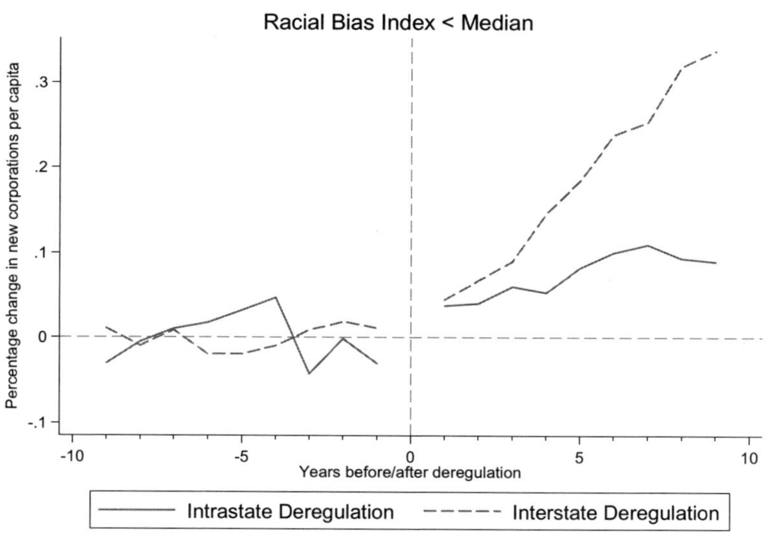
Racial Bias Index < Median
Percentage change in new corporations per capita
.3
.2
.1
0
-.1
-10
-5
0
5
10
Years before/after deregulation
Intrastate Deregulation
Interstate Deregulation

(B)

←

Fig. 2. The impact of deregulation on entry of firms.

Source: Data on new corporations per capita are taken from Black and Strahan (2002). Dates of intrastate and interstate deregulations are taken from Kroszner and Strahan (1999).

Note: The figures plot the impact of interstate and intrastate bank deregulations on log new corporations per capita. The upper figure is for states with racial bias index above the median. The lower figure is for state with racial bias index below the median. We consider an 18-year window spanning from 9 years before deregulations until 9 years after deregulations. The solid lines represent the impact of intrastate deregulation on log new per capita. The dashed lines represent the impact of interstate deregulation on log new corporations per capita. Specifically, we report estimated coefficients from the following regression:

$$Y_{st} = \alpha + \beta_1 \text{Intra}_{-9} + \gamma_1 \text{Inter}_{-9} + \beta_2 \text{Intra}_{-8} + \gamma_2 \text{Inter}_{-8} + \cdots + \beta_{18} \text{Intra}_{+9} + \gamma_{18} \text{Inter}_{+9} + \delta_s + \delta_t + \varepsilon_{st}$$

Y_{st} is log new corporations per capita in state s and year t. Intra_{-j} equals one for states in the jth year before intrastate deregulation and equals zero otherwise. Intra_{+k} equals one for states in the kth year after intrastate deregulation and equals zero otherwise. Similarly, Inter_{-j} equals one in states in the jth year before interstate deregulation and equals zero otherwise. Inter_{+k} equals one in states in the kth year after interstate deregulation and equals zero otherwise. δ_s and δ_t are state and year fixed effects, respectively. We exclude the year of intrastate and interstate deregulation, thus estimating the dynamic effect of deregulation on log new corporations per capita relative to the corresponding year of deregulation. We de-trend the coefficients by prior trends and normalize their average prior to deregulation to be zero. The estimates are weighted by the number of black workers.

bias index and in states with below-the-median value. In Panel A of Fig. 3, the subsample includes states with above the median values of the racial bias index. Panel B reports the dynamic relation between the relative wage rates of black workers and bank deregulation for the subsample of states with below-the-median values. The dashed line depicts the evolving impact of interstate bank deregulation on blacks' relative wages. The solid line illustrates the dynamic relationship between intrastate bank branch deregulation and blacks' relative wages.

Figure 3 illustrates two major messages emerging from the more formal analyses presented in Levine, Levkov, and Rubinstein (2013). First and foremost, interstate and intrastate bank deregulation exert a much bigger impact on blacks' relative wages in high-racial-bias states than in states with below the median values of the racial bias index. Following interstate bank deregulation, blacks' relative wages rise over time in high-racial-bias

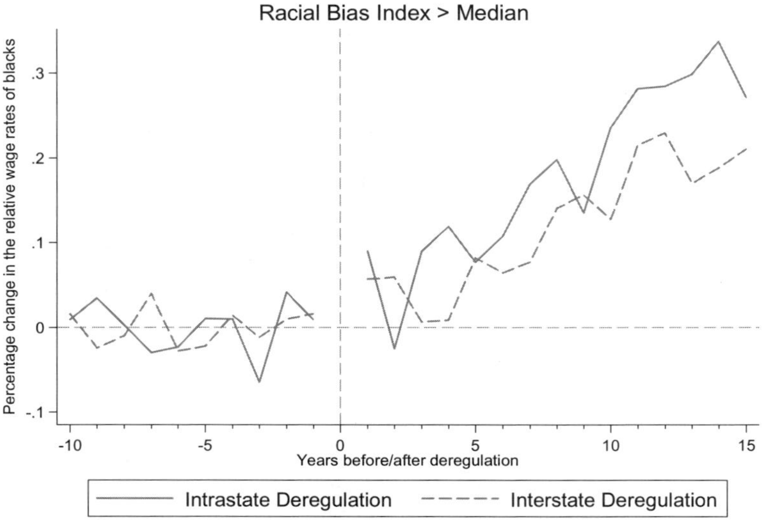
Racial Bias Index > Median
Percentage change in the relative wage rates of blacks
.3
.2
.1
0
-.1
-10
-5
0
5
10
15
Years before/after deregulation
Intrastate Deregulation
Interstate Deregulation

(A)

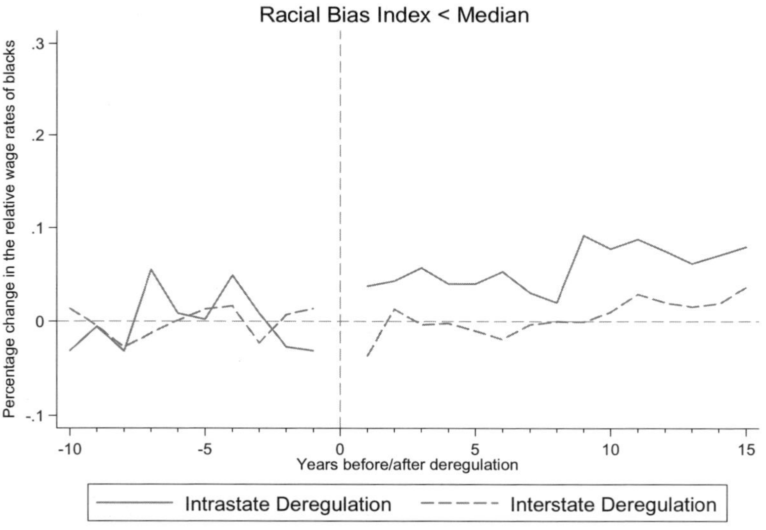
Racial Bias Index < Median
Percentage change in the relative wage rates of blacks
.3
.2
.1
0
-.1
-10
-5
0
5
10
15
Years before/after deregulation
Intrastate Deregulation
Interstate Deregulation

(B)

←

Fig. 3. The impact of deregulation on the relative wage rates of blacks.

Note: The figures plot the impact of interstate and intrastate bank deregulations on the relative wage rates of blacks. The upper figure is for states with racial bias index above the median. The lower figure is for state with racial bias index below the median. We consider a 25-year window, spanning from 10 years before deregulation until 15 years after deregulation. The solid lines represent the impact of intrastate deregulation on the relative wage rates of blacks. The dashed lines represent the impact of interstate deregulation on the relative wage rates of blacks. Specifically, we report estimated coefficients from the following regression:

$$\hat{R}^B_{ist} = \alpha + \beta_1 D^{-10}_{st} + \beta_2 D^{-9}_{st} + \cdots + \beta_{25} D^{+15}_{st} + \delta_s + \delta_t + v_{ist}.$$

The D's equal zero, except as follows: D_{-j} equals one for states in the jth year before deregulation, while D_{+j} equals one for states in the jth year after deregulation. We exclude the year of deregulation, thus estimating the dynamic effect of deregulation on the relative wage rates of blacks relative to the year of deregulation. We de-trend the coefficients by prior trends and normalize their average prior to deregulation to be zero. The estimates are weighted by the number of black workers.

states. But, the relative wages of blacks do not rise after interstate bank deregulation in states with below-the-median values of the racial bias index. Besides being fully consistent with Becker's theory of racial discrimination, these results are fully consistent with the view that bank regulatory reforms that spurred competition among banks — and hence among nonfinancial firms — reduced the adverse manifestation of racial prejudices on the economic opportunities of black Americans.

Second, the impact of deregulation on blacks' relative wages grows over time in a manner that is fully consistent with the dynamic relationship between deregulation and competition among nonfinancial firms. As illustrated in Figs. 2 and 3, both competition among nonfinancial firms and blacks' relative wages rose in the five years following deregulation, as predicted by Becker's view of competition and racial discrimination. These findings indicate that bank regulatory reforms that intensified competition reduced racial inequality.

Extensions

Several extensions of these analyses confirm the finding that banking policies that encouraged competition reduced racial inequality in America. First, while Figs. 2 and 3 illustrate the close relationship between bank deregulation, competition, and blacks' relative wages, they do not formally use bank deregulation as an instrumental variable to identify exogenous sources of variation in competition among firms in nonfinancial industries and then trace the effects through to blacks' relative wages. Thus, while the figures are illustrative, they do not provide direct evidence on the underlying causal mechanisms. Levine, Levkov, and Rubinstein (2013) provide these assessments and also demonstrate the validity of the identification strategy. They confirm the message from Figs. 2 and 3: Bank regulatory reforms that intensified competition both among banks and firms in financial industries reduced the manifestation of racial prejudices on blacks' relative wages.

Second, a major potential concern is whether deregulation boosted blacks' relative wages or the relative wages of lower-income workers. We know from Beck, Levine, and Levkov (2010) that bank deregulation exerts a disproportionately positive impact on the poor. We also know that blacks are on average comparatively poor. Thus, our current analyses could reflect this income distributional effect, rather than the impact of bank deregulation and competition on blacks in particular.

In extensions reported in Levine, Levkov, and Rubinstein (2013), however, we argue that these concerns are invalid. First, recall that bank deregulation boosted blacks' relative wages only in high racial bias states, but bank deregulation boosted the relative incomes of lower income workers in all states. This suggests that our results do not simply reflect the tightening of the distribution of income.

Second, and most directly, we perform a rank analysis and compare the change in blacks' relative wages with those of comparable whites across the full distribution of relative wage rates. If deregulation is simply helping the poor, we should not see that blacks converge toward whites at each point in the wage distribution. But, as shown in Fig. 4, the results show that bank deregulation, and the accompanying boost in competition in nonfinancial industries, disproportionately helped black workers across the full distribution of wages in high-racial-bias states. Figure 4 shows the rank plot for the high-racial-bias states, and for the sample of states with below-the-median level of the racial bias index. The solid and dashed lines represent the location of blacks within the conditional log hourly wage distribution of whites before and after deregulation, respectively. The

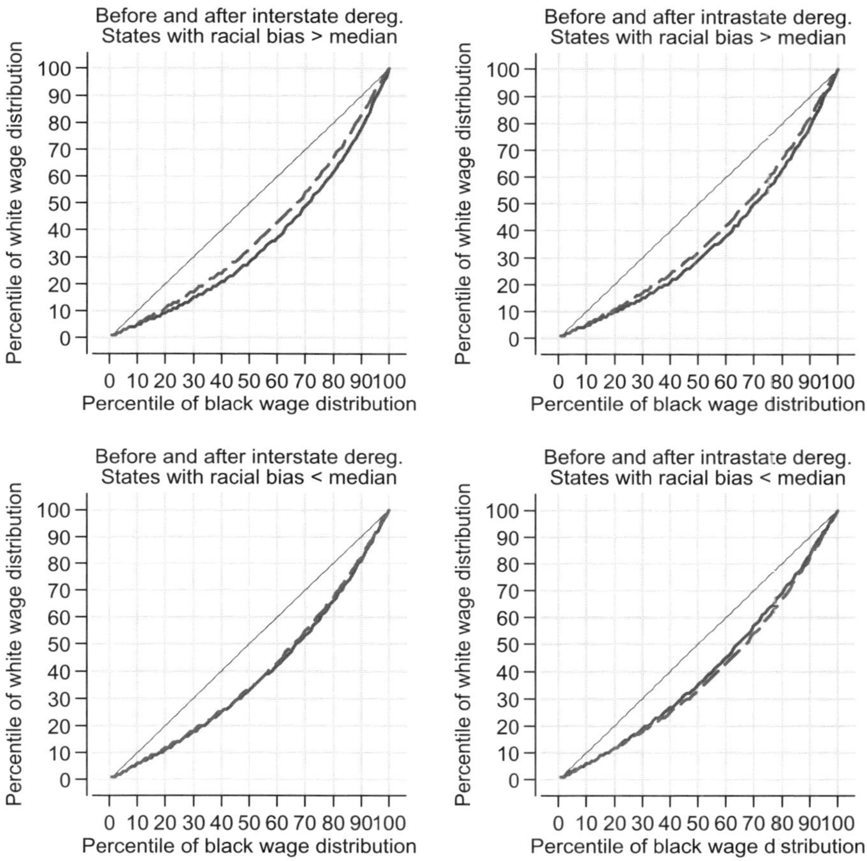

Fig. 4. The location of blacks in the white wage distribution before and after deregulation.

Note: The figures provide rank analyses and compare the change in black workers' relative wages with those of comparable whites across the full distribution of wage rates, before and after bank deregulation. The results in the plots were obtained using the following procedure: First, we calculate residuals for black and white workers from Equation (7) in Levine, Levkov, and Rubinstein (2013). We keep 100 black workers, each corresponding to a different percentile of black workers' relative log hourly wage distribution. Next, we calculate their position in the white workers' log hourly wage distribution. We repeat this procedure before (solid line) and after (dashed line) inter- and intrastate deregulations. The upper figures refer to states with racial bias index above the median. The lower figures refer to states with racial bias index below the median. We use sampling weights in all estimations.

median black among the high-racial-bias states, for example, corresponds to the 28th percentile white worker prior to deregulation and the 32nd percentile white work after deregulation. The median black, therefore, gained four ranks in the white wage distribution as a result of deregulation, but only in high racial bias states. Consistent with the earlier results, there is little change in relative wage rates in the low-racial-bias states. These results suggest that deregulation exerted a particularly pronounced effect on black workers.

Conclusions

In this paper, we find that US bank regulatory reforms that enhanced competition among nonfinancial firms reduced the manifestation of racial prejudices on the demand for labor and raised the wages of black workers toward those of equally productive white workers. Our research emphasizes the role of indirect channels. We do not find that banks reduced racial inequality by lending more to African Americans. Rather, we find that bank regulatory reforms that fostered competition reduced the adverse effects of racial bigotry on labor markets, expanding the economic opportunities of a historically repressed group.

Our analyses indicate that banking reforms — and hence banks — shape the economic environment in which people work and search for work (Beck, Levine, and Levkov, 2010; Levine, Levkov, and Rubinstein, 2013; Levine and Rubinstein, 2013; and Levkov, 2010). By affecting the barriers facing the entry of new nonfinancial firms, banks influence product market competition and hence the demand for labor in nonfinancial sectors. This highlights the powerful influence of banks on the economic opportunities of virtually all individuals, including people with no entrepreneurial tendencies.

References

Beck, T., R. Levine and A. Levkov (2010). "Big bad banks? The winners and losers from bank deregulation in the United States," *Journal of Finance*, Vol. 65, pp. 1637–1667.

Becker, G. S. (1957). *The Economics of Discrimination*, Chicago: University of Chicago Press.

Black, S. E. and P. E. Strahan (2002). "Entrepreneurship and bank credit availability," *Journal of Finance*, Vol. 57, December, pp. 2807–2832.

Blau, P. M. (1977). *Inequality and Heterogeneity*, New York: Free Press.

Cetorelli, N. and P. E. Strahan (2006). "Finance as a barrier to entry: Bank competition and industry structure in local U.S. markets," *Journal of Finance*, Vol. 61, February, pp. 437–461.

Charles, K. K. and J. Guryan (2008). "Prejudice and the economics of discrimination," *Journal of Political Economy*, Vol. 116, pp. 773–809.

Demirgüç-Kunt, A. and R. Levine (2009). "Finance and inequality: Theory and evidence," *Annual Review of Financial Economics*, Vol. 1, December, pp. 287–318.

Hubbard, G. R. and D. Palia (1995). "Executive pay and performance: Evidence from the U.S. banking industry," *Journal of Financial Economics*, Vol. 39, September, pp. 105–130.

Jayaratne, J. and P. E. Strahan (1998). "Entry restrictions, industry evolution, and dynamic efficiency: Evidence from commercial banking," *Journal of Law and Economics*, Vol. 41, April, pp. 239–273.

Kerr, W. and R. Nanda, (2009), "Democratizing entry: Banking deregulations, financing constraints, and entrepreneurship," *Journal of Financial Economics*, Vol. 94, October, pp. 124–149.

Kroszner, R. and P. E. Strahan (1999). "What drives deregulation? Economics and politics of the relaxation of bank branching deregulation," *Quarterly Journal of Economics*, Vol. 114, November, pp. 1437–1467.

Levine, R. (1997). "Financial development and economic growth: Views and agenda," *Journal of Economic Literature.*

Levine, R. (2005). "Finance and growth: Theory and evidence," in *Handbook of Economic Growth*, Philippe Aghion and Steven Durlauf (eds.), Amsterdam: Elsevier/North-Holland.

Levine, R., A. Levkov and Y. Rubinstein (2013). "Bank deregulation and racial inequality in America," *Critical Finance Review*, forthcoming.

Levine, R. and Y. Rubinstein (2013). "Competition and racial discrimination," University of California, Berkeley, Haas School of Business, mimeo.

Levkov, A. (2010). "Branching of banks and union decline," Federal Reserve Bank of Boston, working paper, No. QAU10-7.

Finance: Economic Lifeblood or Toxin?

Marco Pagano*
University of Naples Federico II,
EIEF
and
CSEF

Introduction

MBA or PhD students in their first asset-pricing classes are typically presented with a picture of finance as an efficient allocation machine that puts capital to its best possible use and allows people to share all kinds of risks efficiently. But nowadays, when they walk out of their classroom, these same students need to read no further than the front page of the *Financial Times* or the *Wall Street Journal* to see financial markets and intermediaries indicted as the culprits in an enormous misallocation of resources, as witnessed by the huge, vacant real-estate developments in the US, Ireland, and Spain; the massive losses of the banks that funded them; and crippling tax bills for the taxpayers to bail them out. The media also routinely describe banks and security markets as the sources of risk, not efficient devices for trading and sharing the risks of production and natural events.

*Marco Pagano is Professor of Economics at the University of Naples Federico II, President of the Einaudi Institute for Economics and Finance, and Director of the Centre for Studies in Economics and Finance at the Centre for Economic Policy Research (CEPR).
The author has benefited from comments by Claudio Borio, Jerry Caprio, Andrew Ellul, Tullio Jappelli, Giorgio Questa, Lucio Sarno, David Thesmar, and participants at the 2012 CEPR–Federal Reserve Bank of Chicago's 15th Annual International Banking Conference, "The Social Value of the Financial Sector: Too Big to Fail or Just too Big?;" the Inaugural CEPR–Modena Conference, "Growth in Mature Economies;" and the presentation of the 2012 Henry Thornton Lecture, Cass School of Business, City University of London. He thanks Viral Acharya and Robert Capellini (NYU–Stern) for providing measures of systemic risk, and Alessio Piccolo for outstanding research assistance. He acknowledges financial support from EIEF and the ERC (FINLAB project no. 295709).

Such contrasting attitudes toward financial markets have been present in the writings of economists for decades, with both sides fighting for the hearts and minds of generations of students and colleagues. What makes the contrast more strident today is the increased visibility of finance and the enormous scale of the current crisis (though not even these are entirely novel features, looking back at the role of finance in the Great Depression).

Economists have long seen banks and securities markets as the source of the economy's lifeblood; or, more specifically, as essential prerequisites for economic growth. For instance, John Hicks (1969) argued that what had made the Industrial Revolution possible was not technical progress *per se* but the development of liquid capital markets. "According to Hicks, the products manufactured during the first decades of the Industrial Revolution had been invented much earlier. Thus, technological innovation did not spark sustained growth. Many of the existing innovations, however, required large injections and long-run commitments of capital. The critical new ingredient that ignited growth in 18th-century England was capital market liquidity" (Levine, 1997, p. 692).[1] As we shall see below, the view that finance promotes growth is supported by a vast and solid body of research work.

However, more critical voices have also been raised among economists, at least since Keynes (1936), who warned that financial markets can produce inefficient investment decisions, in that they may encourage short-term speculation rather than sound investment choices based on firms' long-term prospects: "If I am allowed to appropriate the term speculation for the activity of forecasting the psychology of the market, and the term enterprise for the activity of forecasting the prospective yield of assets over their whole life, it is by no means always the case that speculation predominates over enterprise. As the organization of investment markets improves, the risk of the predominance of speculation does however increase.... These

[1] Rousseau and Sylla (2005) show that the same applies to the early stages of US industrialization: "Establishment of the nation's modern financial structure predated by three decades the transportation improvements and widespread use of water- and steam-powered machinery that are thought to have triggered modernization" (p. 1). They provide econometric evidence that measures of banking and equity market activity preceded investment and business incorporations from 1790 to 1850, and therefore support the hypothesis of "finance-led" growth.

tendencies are a scarcely avoidable outcome of our having successfully organized 'liquid' investment markets. It is usually agreed that casinos should, in the public interest, be inaccessible and expensive. And perhaps the same is true of Stock Exchanges" (pp. 158–159). Keynes' viewpoint was echoed by a platoon of later researchers, including Hyman Minsky, who argued in the 1960s and 1970s that credit markets are inherently prone to boom–bust cycles driven by the irrational expectations of bankers and investors, and Robert Shiller, who, since the 1980s, has argued that stock and housing prices are often propelled by fads, causing bubbles and crashes. The recurrent financial crises of recent decades, culminating in the subprime crisis in the US and the euro-area debt crisis, have led an increasing number of economists to see that, in some circumstances, the operation of financial markets poses a severe threat to economic activity — generating massive misallocation of resources and bubble-driven expansions followed by drastic deleveraging and slumps.

Economists have generally ascribed this dysfunctional behavior of financial markets to one of two root causes. Some hold that bubbles and crashes are caused by investors being guided by irrational (or not wholly rational) beliefs. This "behavioral finance" school is essentially a derivation of the Keynes–Minsky–Shiller line of thought. Others argue that the problem has to do with the incentives to bankers, asset managers, and investors resulting from their contractual relationships, and even more from misguided regulation and monetary policy. For instance, the excessive credit boom and deterioration of lending standards in the run-up to the recent crisis has been blamed on the rise of an unregulated shadow banking system via securitizations (Adrian and Shin, 2010), on very lax monetary policy (Dell'Ariccia, Igan, and Laeven, 2012; Maddaloni and Peydró, 2011), and on the expectation of government bailouts (Fahri and Tirole, 2012). Of course, this thesis raises the question of why policy makers should choose policies that work such perverse incentive effects on the financial markets. That is, it carries implications for the political economy of financial regulation.

Yet while our view may be dominated at present by instances of the dysfunctional behavior of the financial markets, we cannot forget the volumes of evidence of their positive effect on growth and the allocation of investment. What is essential, then, is to understand when and why finance may cease to be the "lifeblood" of the economy and turn into a "toxin."

This paper is a first step in this direction. The thesis is that the metamorphosis will occur when finance gets "too large" in relation to the underlying economy.

In the initial phase of economic development, as in Britain during the Industrial Revolution and in many of today's developing countries, advances in the financial system typically benefit real economic activity. In these periods, firms are typically subject to binding financing constraints, therefore, removing institutional barriers to financial development makes external finance available and spurs real economic growth. For instance, reforms that improve the enforcement of credit contracts or allow the entry of better-managed banks will result in the growth of credit, output, and employment. Such reforms are likely to be associated with better selection of borrowers, hence fewer insolvencies.

However, as the availability of external finance expands, the fraction of financially constrained firms decreases, so that additional improvements in access to finance produce decreasing increments to output and employment. Indeed, when firms are no longer financially constrained, further increases in credit are unwarranted. Yet, at this point, financial regulation or monetary policy may still induce banks to expand credit beyond the funding needs of solvent firms and households, possibly by creating the expectation that banks will be bailed out if they become insolvent. Beyond some critical credit/GDP ratio threshold, therefore, we should find that further increases in external financing produce no significant expansion of real economic activity but cause a deterioration in credit quality and possibly even systemic instability.

Section 2 of this paper sets this idea of a nonlinear relationship between financial development and real economic activity against the backdrop of the literature. After a brief summary of the extensive work on finance and growth, I review some recent inquiries into why financial markets may become both "hypertrophic" and economically dysfunctional. Section 3 presents evidence on this nonlinear pattern, looking at how financial development relates first to economic growth and then to bank solvency and systemic instability. Section 4 concludes by asking why regulation should ever let the dark side of financial development emerge rather than contain it within bounds that ensure positive effects. In other words, we venture into the political economy of financial regulatory failure.

A Mixed Record: The Literature

Despite economists' notorious inability to agree on much of anything,[2] in the last two decades, the idea that credit and security market development is conducive to economic growth has gained a broad and solid consensus, buttressed by an impressive body of evidence based on disparate data sets. But the recurring crises of the last decade have prompted a reconsideration, with a growing awareness that, in some situations, financial development may be far in excess of the needs of the real economy, producing severe misallocation of resources and needless volatility in output and employment. This section contrasts the glowing portrait of finance in most of the earlier academic literature (Sec. 2.1) with the darker side that has received more attention lately (Sec. 2.2).

The Bright Side

The real economic effects of financial development have been the subject of substantial research, in terms of the breadth of financial markets and their efficiency in allocating capital. This work has identified a number of sources of financial development. Liberalization may allow the entry of new, perhaps more sophisticated intermediaries, resulting in cheaper and more abundant finance. Stronger legal protection for creditors or shareholders may reduce moral hazard in lending and equity capital issuance, easing the financial constraints on firms. In these cases, financial development increases the amount of external funding available to firms, facilitating business start-ups and expansion. Financial development can also foster growth by allocating capital more efficiently, channeling resources to the more promising projects and thus boosting aggregate productivity.[3]

The correlation between indicators of financial development and of economic growth is well established, at least since Goldsmith (1969). But, of course, correlation does not establish causality. To determine whether

[2] In Winston Churchill's words: "If you put two economists in a room, you get two opinions, unless one of them is Lord Keynes, in which case you get three opinions."

[3] Pagano (1993) provides a simple framework capturing the effects of financial development both on the rate of capital accumulation and efficiency of its allocation and briefly reviews the theoretical foundations of both effects, as well as the early empirical literature on finance and growth. For a more up-to-date review of this literature, see Levine (2005).

financial development is cause or effect of growth, researchers have used econometric techniques and identification strategies to control for the possible effect of growth on financial development, using three types of data: country-level, industry-level, and firm-level.

Using country-level data, King and Levine (1993a, 1993b) relate economic growth rates to measures of lagged financial development in 80 countries. All their indicators of economic performance are positively associated with the predetermined component of financial development, defined as the size of the financial sector at the beginning of the sample period. However, the use of predetermined variables to measure financial development overcomes the problem of endogeneity only in part. An omitted common variable could still determine both long-run growth and the initial level of financial development, generating a spurious correlation. Accordingly, researchers have sought instruments that are unquestionably exogenous. One choice has been a type of legal system, which La Porta, Lopez-de-Silanes, and Shleifer (1998) show to be correlated with the size of a country's financial market. Legal systems can be considered as exogenous because they were created centuries ago and spread mainly through occupation and colonialism. Beck, Levine, and Loayza (2000a) use legal origin as an instrument for financial development, and again find that the size of the financial sector is positively correlated with the growth of per capita GDP and of total factor productivity — a result corroborated and extended by other studies, including Beck, Levine, and Loayza (2000b) and Demirgüç-Kunt and Levine (2001).

Another strand of inquiry relies on industry-level data to address causality, on the hypothesis that financial market development should be more beneficial to the growth of industries that are more dependent on external finance. Rajan and Zingales (1998) construct their test by first identifying each industry's need for external finance from US data (positing that the US financial system is highly developed) and then interact this industry-level "external dependence" variable with a country-level measure of financial development. This interacted variable is then included in a regression for industry-level growth, where its coefficient should capture the severity of constraints on growth due to degree of financial development, using fixed effects to control for time-invariant country and sector characteristics. Applying this approach to industry-level data for a large sample of countries in the 1980s, they find that measures of financial development do indeed affect economic growth disproportionately in externally dependent industries.

Further evidence on the nexus between finance and growth comes from firm-level data. Guiso, Sapienza, and Zingales (2004) find that, in Italy, local financial development, as measured by self-reported information on households' access to credit, is positively correlated with an individual's probability of starting a business, the ratio of new firms to the population, the growth rate of firms over and above internally financed growth, and per capita GDP. They control for the potential endogeneity of financial development by instrumenting their indicator with bank branch density as determined by regulation in 1936. Guiso *et al.* (2004) apply the Rajan–Zingales approach to data for companies in the EU and in Central and Eastern Europe, producing firm-level estimates consistent with industry-level studies and finding that financial development fosters the growth of smaller firms in particular. Firm-level data have also been used to gauge the impact of financial development on market entry for small businesses. Aghion, Fally, and Scarpetta (2007), applying the Rajan–Zingales approach to firm-level data in 16 industrial and emerging economies, find that financial development encourages entry by small firms in the sectors that are most dependent on external finance. And Klapper, Laeven, and Rajan (2006) show that in Europe financial development favors entry in the sectors that are relatively dependent on external finance.

A particularly convincing way of addressing the issue of causality exploits the "quasi-natural experiments" offered by specific (and arguably exogenous) changes in financial market regulation. For instance, Jayaratne and Strahan (1996) document that the relaxation of the geographical restrictions on bank expansion in the US between the 1970s and the early 1990s was associated with faster local growth. Dehejia and Lleras-Muney (2007) document the same relationship with earlier data, showing that changes in state-level banking regulation between 1900 and 1940 were also associated with higher growth. Bertrand, Schoar, and Thesmar (2007) find that the deregulation of the French credit market triggered by the Banking Act of 1985 was associated with greater asset and job reallocation at the industry level and better allocation of capital across firms: Banks became less willing to bail out poorly performing firms, and firms in bank-dependent sectors became more likely to restructure.

Related evidence comes from stock market liberalizations, i.e., policies relaxing restrictions on share purchases by foreign investors. These policies are associated with an increase in liquidity, a jump in stock prices, a decline in the cost of equity capital, and an increase in private investment. For instance, in a sample of 11 developing countries that liberalized their stock markets, Henry (2000) finds that the growth rate of private investment was higher than the pre-liberalization median in nine countries one year after liberalization, in ten countries two years after, and in eight countries three years after. The average growth rate of private investment in the three years after liberalization exceeds the mean of Henry's sample by 22 percentage points. Similarly, Bekaert, Harvey, and Lundblad (2005) show that equity market liberalization is associated with a subsequent increment of about 1 percentage point in the average annual real economic growth rate, and that this effect is robust to controls for capital account liberalization and other simultaneous reforms. Effects of similar magnitude have been found at the sector level by Gupta and Yuan (2009), who show that industries that are more externally dependent and have better growth opportunities grow faster following liberalization.

The Dark Side

Several recent papers emphasize that, in the run-up to the subprime crisis, the US and several European countries featured not only housing and securities market bubbles but also an abnormal growth in private credit and the leverage of financial institutions. Indeed, the two phenomena — the asset price bubble and the overexpansion of credit — appear to have fed on each other, multiplying their effects. Researchers have identified three key reasons for this hypertrophy of finance: (i) the rise of an unregulated "shadow banking system" funded by securities markets and especially securitizations; (ii) lax monetary policy both in the US and in Europe, with abundant liquidity and very low interest rates, especially between 2002 and 2005; and (iii) the general expectation that in the face of widespread financial distress, government would bail out financial institutions with abundant liquidity and capital injections — as indeed is still happening in the US, in Europe, and now in China as well.

Shadow banks and securitization

The shadow banking sector has developed most extensively in the US. A good number of intermediaries managed to secure massive funding by issuing securities rather than taking customer deposits, and so theoretically were not eligible for central bank liquidity or public sector guarantees. As is explained by Pozsar *et al.* (2010), shadow banks may be finance companies, asset-backed commercial paper conduits, structured investment vehicles, credit hedge funds, money market mutual funds, securities lenders, limited-purpose finance companies, or even government-sponsored agencies such as Fannie Mae and Freddie Mac. The establishment of these shadow banks created a more direct link between asset prices and credit than had existed in commercial banking. Adrian and Shin (2010) point out that the rise in asset prices increased these intermediaries' net worth, with very large multipliers owing to their very high leverage, thus enabling them to expand their balance sheets: This put additional upward pressure on asset prices, further increasing net worth and expanding balance sheets. In other words, in the run-up to the crisis the asset price rises and the expansion of financial intermediaries' balance sheets fed on each other, leading to a bubble. The same process operated in reverse as soon as asset prices (starting with housing) started to decline in 2007.

Greenwood and Scharfstein (2012) documented that the enormous growth of the US financial industry in the last three decades — from 4.9% of GDP in 1980 to 7.9% in 2007 — was due mainly to the asset management sector and the household credit sector and was fueled precisely by the "shadow banking system" and the securitization process. This explains the results of Philippon (2008), who models the relationship between the financial sector and the real economy in an overlapping-generations setting, where people choose whether to work in banks or firms and banks can mitigate firms' financing constraints. When calibrated to US data, Philippon's model is quite a good fit with the evolution of the US financial sector over a century-and-a-half, except for the last decade, when it seriously underestimates its relative size. This erroneous prediction might well be due to the model's neglect of households' demand for financial services, as well as of the recent innovations in the US financial industry.

This oversizing of the US financial industry is accompanied by increasing remuneration of its employees. Philippon and Reshef (2008) find that the earnings gain is concentrated in asset management and investment banking, precisely the sectors most heavily involved in the shadow banking system. In these two sectors salaries, which in the early 1980s were aligned with those of other nonfarm workers, by 2007 were four times as high. Both of these phenomena — oversizing and overpay — could stem from the opacity of the relevant financial markets, as in the model of Bolton, Santos, and Scheinkmann (2012). Insofar as more opaque markets attract the employees who are most skilled at evaluating deals, they manage to skim off the best deals, taking them away from more transparent markets, and — again owing to their opacity — gain high rents. This results in very high salaries in the more opaque segments of the financial industry and the allocation of too much talent to information processing.

However, while it is undeniable that the securitization process that funded the shadow banks was very opaque, it may be argued that it featured too little, rather than too much, information processing. Investors in asset-backed securities (ABS) were given very scanty information on the underlying asset pools and risk characteristics of ABS payoffs, as is witnessed by their massive underpricing in the pre-crisis years. Pagano and Volpin (2012) argue that ABS issuance was made highly opaque deliberately in order to allow placement with a broad set of investors: Placing large amounts of ABS meant also marketing them to unsophisticated investors, who could not process the information necessary to price them properly. In fact, if such information had been released, it would have put them at a disadvantage *vis-à-vis* the "smart money" that can process it. This created an incentive for ABS issuers to negotiate a low degree of transparency with credit rating agencies — that is, relatively coarse and uninformative ratings. Ironically, the elimination of some price-relevant information served to expand the market and support prices in the ABS new issue market.[4]

[4]Di Maggio and Pagano (2012) show that issuers of complex securities may also prefer opaqueness in order to avoid giving a strategic advantage to sophisticated investors, which would depress the issue price: Once information is disclosed, unsophisticated investors will worry that if the asset has not already been bought by others, it could be because more

The extraordinary growth of shadow banking and securitizations before the crisis may have diminished the quality of financial information for two other reasons as well. First, the very growth of ABS issuance probably made it harder for credit rating agencies to resist opportunistic behavior, i.e., lowering their standards in order to attract issuers. In fact, there is evidence that the ratings actually assigned to CDOs were higher than would have resulted from the agencies' models. Griffin and Tang (2012), based on data from one major rating agency, report that by means of "adjustments" to its ratings, the agency increased the size of AAA-rated tranches on average by 12.1%, and that the CDOs on which the "adjustments" were larger performed worse subsequently. They conclude that if the agency had actually followed its model before April 2007, 91.2% of its AAA tranches would have been rated AA.[5] Second, apart from opportunism, before the crisis the agencies may have lowered their standards because they were overburdened by work. Bar-Isaac and Shapiro (2011) observe that the agencies "lacked adequate staff, motivation, and quality personnel just at the time when their business was booming the most" (p. 1), and could not expand their staff with talented employees in the face of keen competition from highly profitable investment banks.

Low Interest Rates and the Fall in Credit Standards

As mentioned above, in the pre-crisis period, shadow banks and securitizations gained especially great prominence in the US, but the hypertrophic growth of finance was not confined to the US financial system. To some extent, it also characterized Europe. In Ireland and Spain, the feedback loop between house prices and credit expansion was as evident and as violent as in the US. This underscores another factor that was at work in the period leading up to the crisis: very abundant liquidity (and low interest rates).

---

sophisticated investors, who can understand this information, have concluded that it is not worth buying. This drives down the price that unsophisticated investors are willing to pay; sophisticated investors, in turn, anticipating that the seller will have a hard time finding buyers among the unsophisticated, will offer a price below the no-disclosure level.

[5] See also Ashcraft, Goldsmith-Pinkham, and Vickery (2010) and Griffin and Tang (2010). For a survey of the failings of credit rating agencies during the crisis, see Pagano and Volpin (2010).

A substantial body of evidence indicates that the low interest rates encouraged banks to make larger and riskier bets in the "search for yield," both in lending business and in proprietary trading. Dell'Ariccia, Igan, and Laeven (2012) document that, prior to the subprime mortgage crisis, the rapid expansion of credit went hand-in-hand with declining lending standards. Standards dropped most sharply in the areas that experienced larger credit booms and house price increases, and in those where mortgage securitization was most common. Maddaloni and Peydró (2011) analyze the determinants of banks' lending standards in the euro area on the basis of the Eurosystem's quarterly Bank Lending Survey, whereby central banks gather information on the terms of credit for bank customers. After controlling for the improvement of borrowers' credit worthiness resulting from cheaper credit, they show that low short-term interest rates soften lending standards for businesses and households alike, especially if rates stay "too low for too long." They also find that securitization business and weak supervision amplify the impact of low short-term interest rates on the banks' risk-taking. Of course, the great challenge empirically is to determine whether low interest rates impact on the riskiness of loans by affecting the banks' supply of credit or the demand from firms and households. Jiménez *et al.* (2011) address this challenge by drawing data on loan contracts and applications from Spain's credit register since 1984, and using sophisticated panel data techniques to distinguish the changes due to the composition of credit supply from those arising from changes in demand. They find that a lower overnight interest rate induces less highly capitalized banks to expand credit to riskier firms, to decrease the frequency with which they terminate loans to risky firms, and to be more likely to extend longer and larger loans to risky new applicants.[6]

The reason why low interest rates may prompt banks to relax their lending standards and offer loans to riskier customers is well captured by the model of Acharya and Naqvi (2012), where moral hazard within banks induces excess risk-taking, which is exacerbated when bank liquidity is abundant. In their model, banks face random deposit withdrawals and, in the event of a liquidity shortfall, pay a cost, possibly because they are forced

[6]Ioannidou, Ongena, and Peydró (2009) also show that when the US federal funds rate is low, in dollarized Bolivia banks are more likely to extend loans with a subprime credit rating or loans to borrowers with a poor solvency record.

to hold "fire sales" of assets or to raise funds at penalty rates. Absent moral hazard, this penalty, together with the expected profits from the funding of projects, induces banks to choose a lending rate that properly reflects the risk of the projects. But if the loan officers' effort is unobservable, then it is optimal to tie their compensation to the amount of loans they make, and randomly carry out a costly audit to determine whether they have overlent and underpriced loans. The time-consistent audit policy is to audit the loan officer only when the liquidity shortfall is sufficiently large. So in times when the bank can count on abundant liquidity, loan officers will rationally anticipate a lenient policy of infrequent audits and will accordingly engage in excessive lending, i.e., charge an interest rate that underprices credit risk.

Systemic bailouts, excessive lending, and systemic risk

The research just discussed hypothesizes that policy affects the behavior of banks: Lax monetary policy encourages over lending and lower credit standards. Farhi and Tirole (2012) note that the causality may also be reversed. That is, policy itself may be captive to the choices of financial institutions, in that once they are collectively overexposed to risk after lending too much, the central bank has no option but to lower interest rates and expand liquidity in order to avert financial meltdown. And when they realize that policymakers are captive to their choices, banks have an incentive to engage in excessive lending, which generates systemic risk.

Consequently, Farhi and Tirole (2012) take the notion of moral hazard to the collective, or systemic, level. The incentive for excessive lending exists for banks collectively, not just individually; by the same token, each bank has the incentive to overlend, insofar as it expects others to do so. Put another way, the policymaker's expected response generates a strategic complementarity in banks' leverage decisions, which in turn makes monetary accommodation optimal, ex post. The final outcome is undesirable monetary accommodation, too much lending, and excessive risk-taking.

This model offers a number of additional insights. One is that banks have the incentive to choose risks correlated with those chosen by other banks, since in a crisis there is "safety in numbers." A crisis that involves many banks is more likely to induce an accommodating policy response than one that is narrowly circumscribed. Brown and Dinç (2011) document this "too-many-to-fail" effect in a study of bank failures in 21 emerging market countries in the 1990s, showing that governments are less likely to take over or close a failing bank when the entire banking system is weak, in the sense that other banks also have low capital ratios.

Another insight concerns the fact that an accommodating policy response "plants the seeds of a new crisis" by reinforcing expectations of similar responses in the future. This is reflected in the notion of "Greenspan put." The Fed's consistently accommodating response to crises under the chairmanship of Alan Greenspan (from 1987 to 1990) was perceived as a guarantee that plunging asset prices and widespread financial distress would always prompt the Fed to lower the federal funds rate and expand liquidity, and possibly also arrange bailouts of distressed institutions. And this is precisely what the Fed did following the 1987 stock market crash, during the 1994 Mexican crisis, the 1997 Asian crisis, the 1998 LTCM crisis, the 2000–2001 burst of the dotcom bubble, and then massively during the subprime crisis and continuing right down to the present, with interest rates down near zero and accommodating policy in the form of now open-ended quantitative easing.

Moreover, the single instance in which the Fed tried to break out of this accommodative pattern — the decision to let Lehman Brothers fail — bears witness to the disruptions provoked by deviating from the time-consistent equilibrium described by Farhi and Tirole (2012). That is, it highlights the great extent to which policy is hostage to banks' expectations. Of course, these insights go beyond monetary policy alone and can also apply to other accommodative policies, such as government bailouts and recapitalizations.

How can policymakers get "trapped" in an equilibrium of this kind, with excess lending by banks, recurrent systemic risk, and far too accommodating policy responses? I leave this issue for the final section. Now, I turn to some evidence on both the bright and the dark side of financial development, indicating when each tends to manifest itself.

The Nonlinear Effect of Financial Development: Some Evidence

This section explores whether the evidence is consistent with nonlinear real economic effects of financial development. Merging the insights from the two strands of literature surveyed in Section 2, I devise the working hypothesis that initially the expansion of the financial industry contributes to economic growth without endangering the solvency of banks and systemic stability. However, beyond a critical threshold, financial development makes no meaningful contribution to long-run growth, while it reduces bank solvency and creates systemic risk. Accordingly, I investigate two different types of evidence: One relevant to growth, the other to bank solvency and systemic stability.

Nonlinear Effect on Long-Run Growth

The approach I adopt follows Rajan and Zingales (1998). The assumption is that the impact of financial development on growth should be heterogeneous across industries, depending on their technological need for external finance. Because dependence on external finance is unobservable, here — as in Rajan and Zingales (1998) — it is proxied by the reliance on external finance of US listed companies in the Compustat database. The dependent variable is the average annual growth rate of real value added between 1970 and 2003, by sector and country. Denoting the dependent variable by Y, the baseline specification is:

$$Y_{jc} = \delta(FD_c \times ED_j) + \gamma SHARE_{jc}^{1970} + \mu_j + \mu_c + \varepsilon_{jc}, \qquad (1)$$

where the subscript c denotes countries and j sectors, FD_c is a country index of financial development as measured by the initial ratio of total credit and/or stock market capitalization to GDP, and ED_j is industry j's external finance requirement. The variable $SHARE_{jc}^{1970}$ denotes the industry's share of manufacturing Y_{cj} in 1970. Fixed sector and country effects are denoted by μ_j and μ_c, respectively, and ε_{jc} is the residual. Fixed effects are included in order to preclude a spurious correlation between finance and real variables due to unobserved heterogeneity in country or industry characteristics.

The coefficient δ in Equation (1) captures the effect of financial development on growth: It estimates the differential response of Y_{cj} to financial development in industries with different external finance requirements. A positive and significant estimate of δ is consistent with the thesis that financial development facilitates growth in the sectors that are relatively more dependent on external finance. To allow this effect to differ between countries with different degree of financial development, in Table 1

Table 1. Financial development and output growth.
The dependent variable is the percentage growth rate of value added in the relevant country and industry. The estimation period is 1970–2004. Industry's share in 1970 refers to total value added. Robust standard errors are reported in parentheses. The estimates are drawn from Table 1 in Pagano and Pica (2012).

Explanatory variable	All countries		OECD countries		Non-OECD countries	
Industry's share in 1970	−0.156*** (0.030)	−0.204*** (0.027)	−0.212*** (0.054)	−0.212*** (0.055)	−0.161*** (0.032)	−0.213*** (0.030)
External dependence × stock market capitalization (80–95)	0.026* (0.014)		−0.022 (0.018)		0.037** (0.016)	
External dependence × claims of banks other fin. inst. (80–95)		0.034** (0.016)		−0.011 (0.011)		0.091** (0.036)
Observations	1533	1637	628	628	905	1009
R^2	0.32	0.33	0.48	0.48	0.30	0.32

Note: *, ** and *** denote coefficients significant at the 10%, 5%, and 1% level, respectively.

Equation (1) is also estimated separately for OECD and non-OECD countries, since the data indicate that the latter are less financially developed.

The UNIDO INDSTAT3 2006 database used offers annual value-added data for 28 industries (three-digit codes) from 1970 to 2003.[7] That is, the sample does not cover the 2007–2009 financial crisis. Since indicators of financial development are not available for many countries, data for at most 63 countries are used. The US is excluded, being the benchmark country. Additional observations are lost due to missing data, which reduces the final sample somewhat.

Table 1 presents the estimates, drawn from Pagano and Pica (2012). For comparability with the literature, financial development is measured

[7]The 2006 release is used because later releases have more missing observations, particularly for developing countries.

by two indicators: the GDP ratios (1980–1995 average) of stock market capitalization and private credit. The estimates of δ in Table 1 show that, in the entire sample, a higher level of financial development is associated with faster growth of value added in the sectors that depend more heavily on external finance. But Table 1 also shows that, in the subsample of OECD countries, financial development has no significant impact on value-added growth: The estimates of δ are small and not significantly different from zero. For the non-OECD countries, by contrast, the estimates indicate that financial development does spur value added.[8] This suggests that the results for the whole sample are in fact driven by the non-OECD countries, where firms are more likely to be finance-constrained. The nonlinearity of the effect of financial development on growth also emerges from a specification (not reported for brevity) in which both the level of financial development and its square are present: Consistent with the forecast of nonlinear effects, the coefficient of the linear term is positive and that of the quadratic term is negative, and both are significantly different from zero if financial development is measured by private credit/GDP (while neither one is significantly different from zero if it is measured by stock market capitalization/GDP).[9]

Hence, the evidence that financial development benefits growth appears to come exclusively from the countries where financial development is at a relatively early stage, so that an expansion of the financial industry tends to be associated with an increase in local firms' access to finance. Beyond a certain point, that is, financial development does not appear to contribute significantly to real economic activity. Indeed, some recent works show that beyond a certain threshold it actually has a negative effect on growth. Arcand, Berkes, and Panizza (2012) produce country- and industry-level evidence that finance has a negative effect on output growth when credit to the private sector is more than 100% of GDP. Ductor and Grechyna (2011) find in OECD data that when financial-sector growth rate exceeds that of real-sector industries by 4.5 percentage points, the correlation turns negative and attribute this nonlinearity to financial crises.

[8] Similar results are obtained by re-estimating these regressions on the original data set used by Rajan and Zingales (1998). There, too, the correlation between financial development and growth obtains only for the non-OECD countries.

[9] Pagano and Pica (2012) document a similar nonlinear effect on employment growth.

Relatedly, there is evidence that financial development increases the sensitivity of output and employment to banking crises. Extending the Rajan–Zingales approach, Kroszner, Laeven, and Klingebiel (2007) find that, during banking crises, the sectors that depend heavily on external finance suffer sharper output contraction in countries with a higher degree of financial development, and Pagano and Pica (2012) find a similar result for employment. However, neither study covers the post-2007 recession. Accordingly, I now turn to evidence on the relationship between financial development and financial stability in which data from the recent crisis play a key role.

Nonlinear Effects on Bank Solvency and Systemic Stability

Besides affecting the long-run growth rate, financial development may affect the solvency of banks and the stability of the banking system. As argued above, insofar as an expansion in lending simply relieves the financial constraints on solvent firms, it need not lead to deterioration in credit quality. But if banks are awash with liquidity, they are likely to end up extending loans to bad risks or underpricing credit risk, as is implied by the model of Acharya and Naqvi (2012) and the evidence set out in Sec. 2.3. In this case, the expansion of credit will lead to bank distress, possibly even endangering systemic stability.

To explore the relationship between the credit worthiness of banks and the development of the credit market, I rely on the 2012 update of the Financial Structure Dataset constructed by Beck and Demirgüç-Kunt (2009) and Čihák, Demirgüç-Kunt, Feyen, and Levine (2012). It has data for 203 countries from 1960 through 2010. Creditworthiness is measured by banks' "Z-score," i.e., the sum of return on assets (ROA) and the equity/assets ratio, divided by the standard deviation of ROA, based on underlying bank-by-bank unconsolidated data from Bankscope. Unfortunately this variable is available only since 1997, at best. Credit market development is measured by the private credit issued by deposit money banks and other financial institutions, scaled by GDP.

The simple visual inspection of the data offers revealing insights. Figure 1 shows the two variables for selected countries where the credit/GDP ratio does not exceed the 50% threshold during the 1997–2010 sample

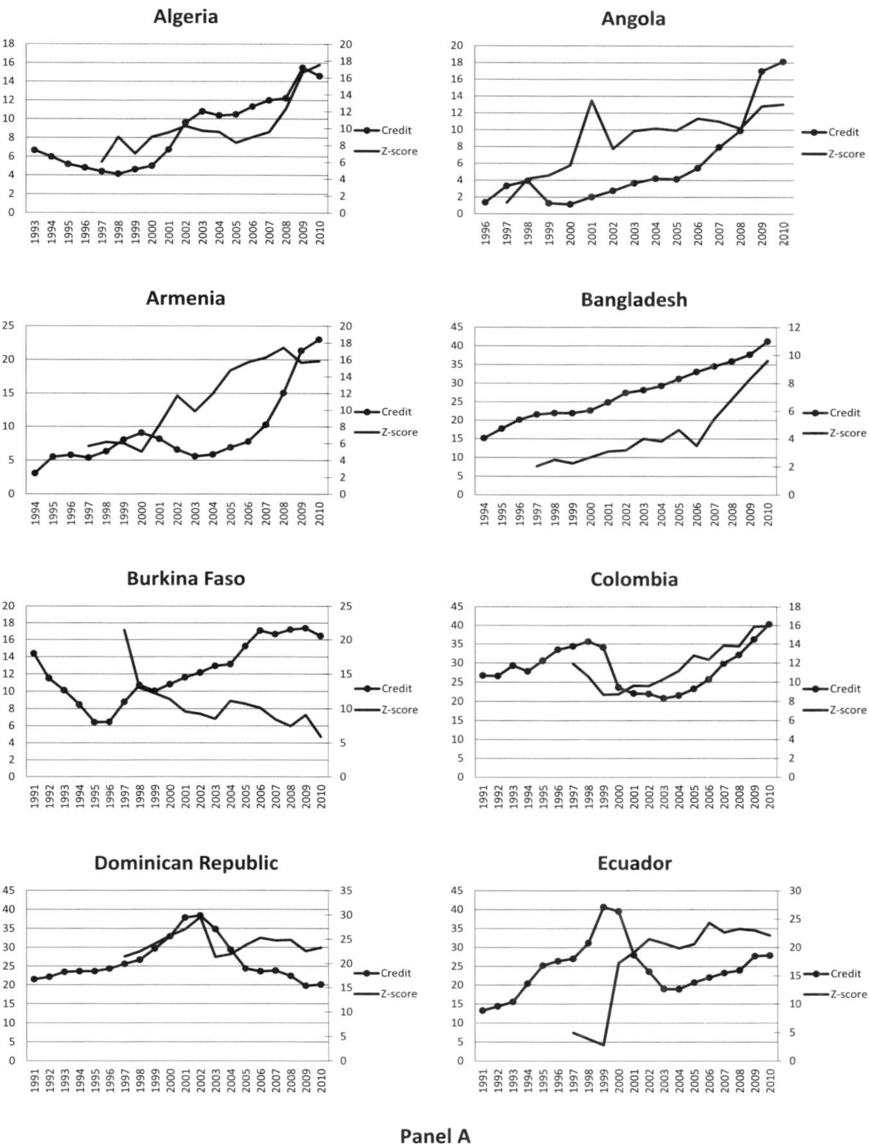

Fig. 1. Bank creditworthiness and credit/GDP in selected countries with credit/GDP < 50%.

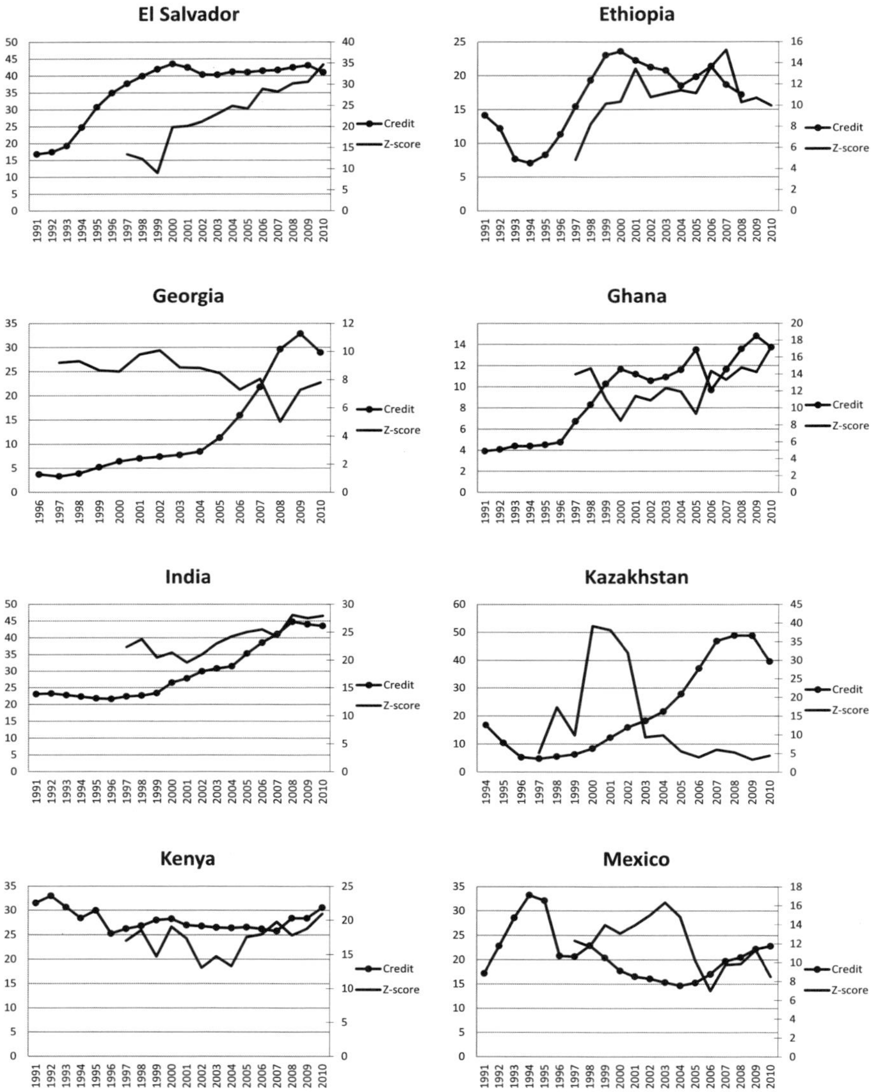

Panel B

Fig. 1. (*Continued*)

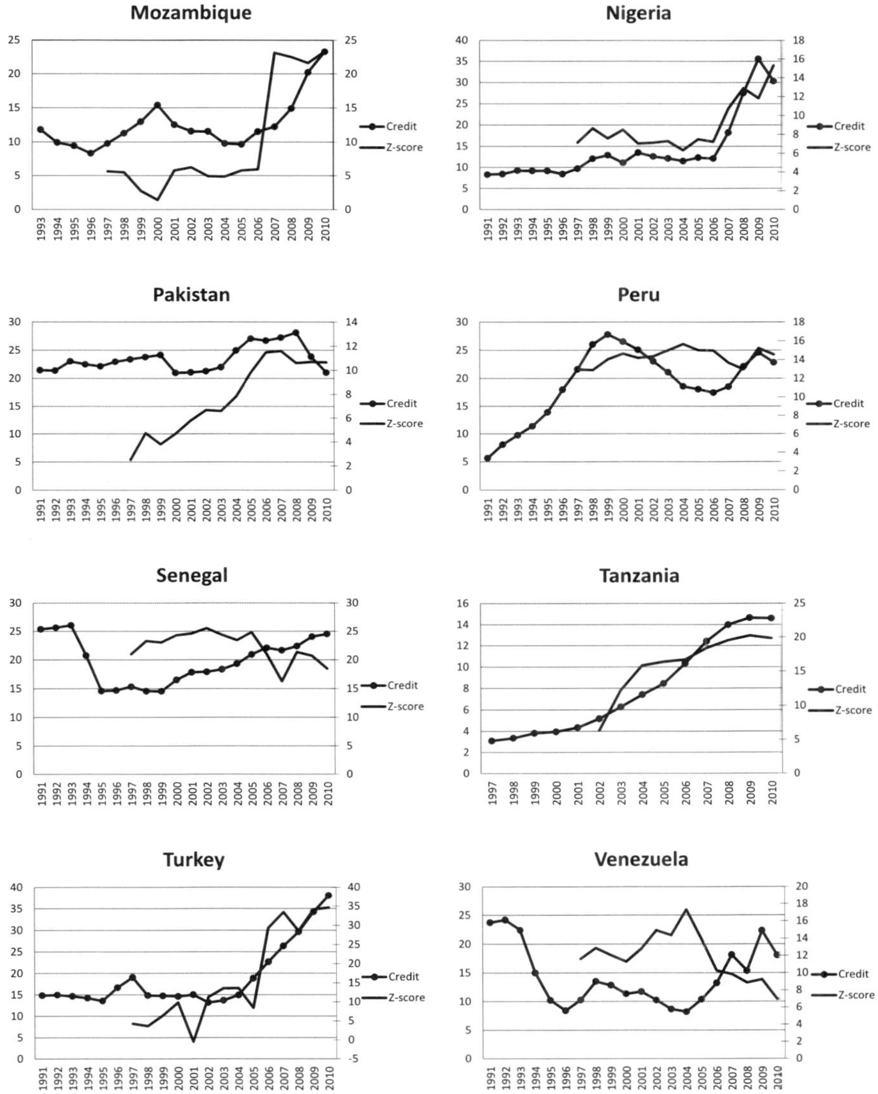

Panel C

Fig. 1. (*Continued*)

period. Almost all of the countries plotted in Fig. 1 are developing countries. In most of them, the two variables are positively correlated, although in some (Burkina Faso, Ecuador, Georgia, Kazakhstan, and Venezuela) the correlation is negative and in others (Ghana, Kenya, Mexico, and Senegal) it is unclear. This suggests that in countries at a relatively low level of financial development, credit expansion is not necessarily correlated with a deterioration in banks' creditworthiness. The positive correlation in many countries may stem from a rise in firms' growth and profitability, calling for an expansion in credit while simultaneously enabling banks to increase profits and strengthen their capital base.

A very different picture emerges from Fig. 2, which shows the same two variables for selected countries where the credit/GDP ratio exceeded the 50% threshold at least once during the sample period. In almost all of them (one clear exception being Australia) the correlation is negative. Interestingly, the correlation tends to turn negative in particular when the ratio crosses some quite high threshold (around 100% for Austria, Canada, Denmark, Germany, and United Kingdom; 70–80% for Belgium, Finland, France and Portugal; and 90% for Korea). The countries that experience the sharpest drop in the Z-score are those where the credit/GDP ratio increases most spectacularly, often to extraordinarily high levels: from 137% to 270% in Cyprus, from 26% to over 105% in Greece, from 41% to 272% in Iceland, from 64% to 238% in Ireland, from 78% to 210% in the Netherlands, and from 44% to 186% in Portugal. Other countries offer interesting counter-examples: Both the Czech Republic and Japan feature a sizable reduction in the credit/GDP ratio (respectively, from 70% to 30% between 1994 and 2003 and from over 230% to 170% between 1999 and 2010), while their banks' Z-scores improve enormously.

The visual impression is confirmed by the panel regressions of the Z-score on the previous year's credit/GDP ratio in Table 2. The explanatory variable is lagged in order to reduce potential reverse causation: In principle, lower bank creditworthiness may require an accommodating central bank stance, leading to a credit expansion. All the regressions include fixed country effects, to control for unobserved heterogeneity, and fixed year effects, to account for worldwide fluctuations in bank profitability, especially during the crisis.

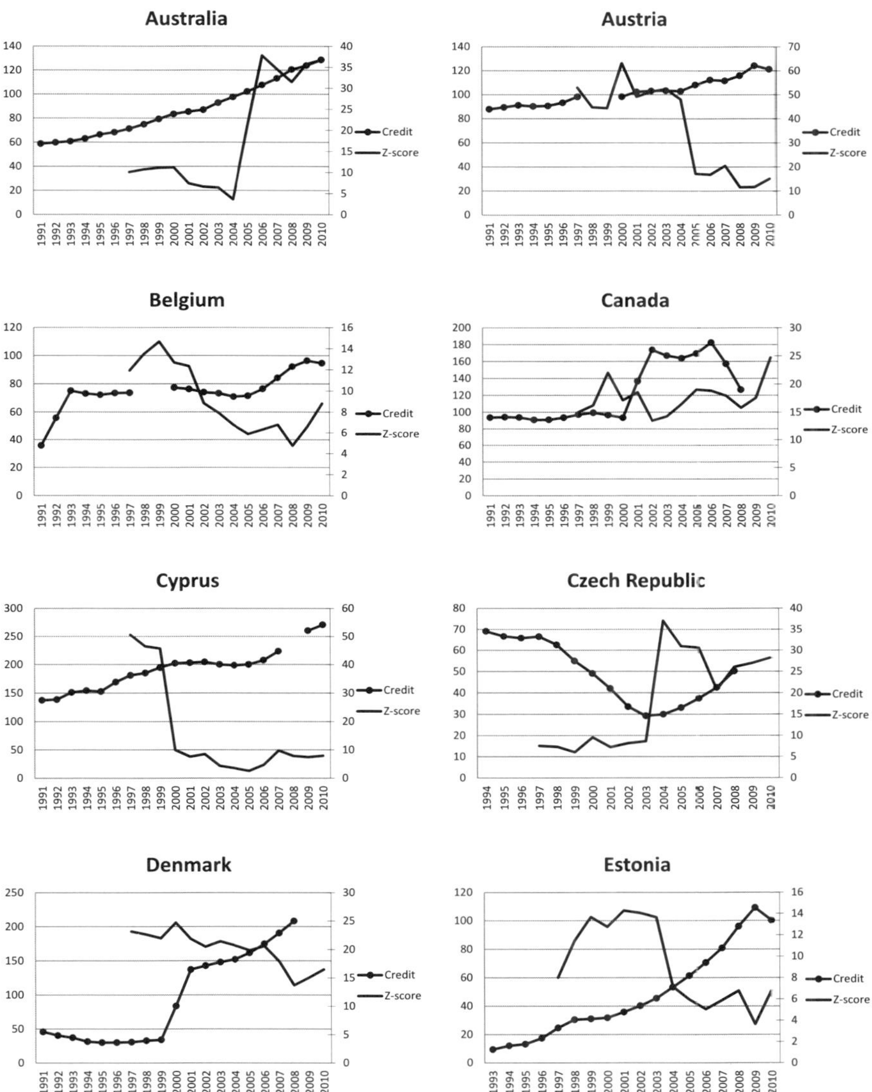

Panel A

Fig. 2. Bank creditworthiness and credit/GDP in selected countries with credit/GDP > 50%.

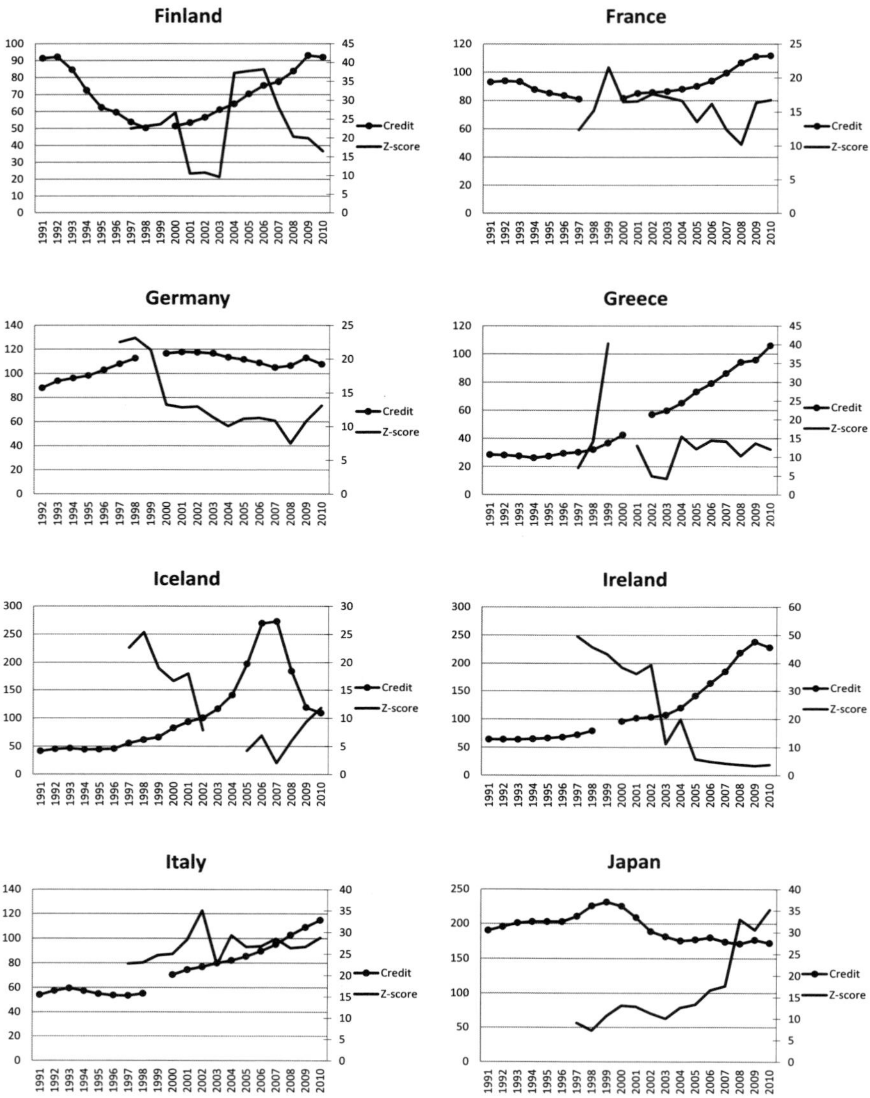

Panel B

Fig. 2. (*Continued*)

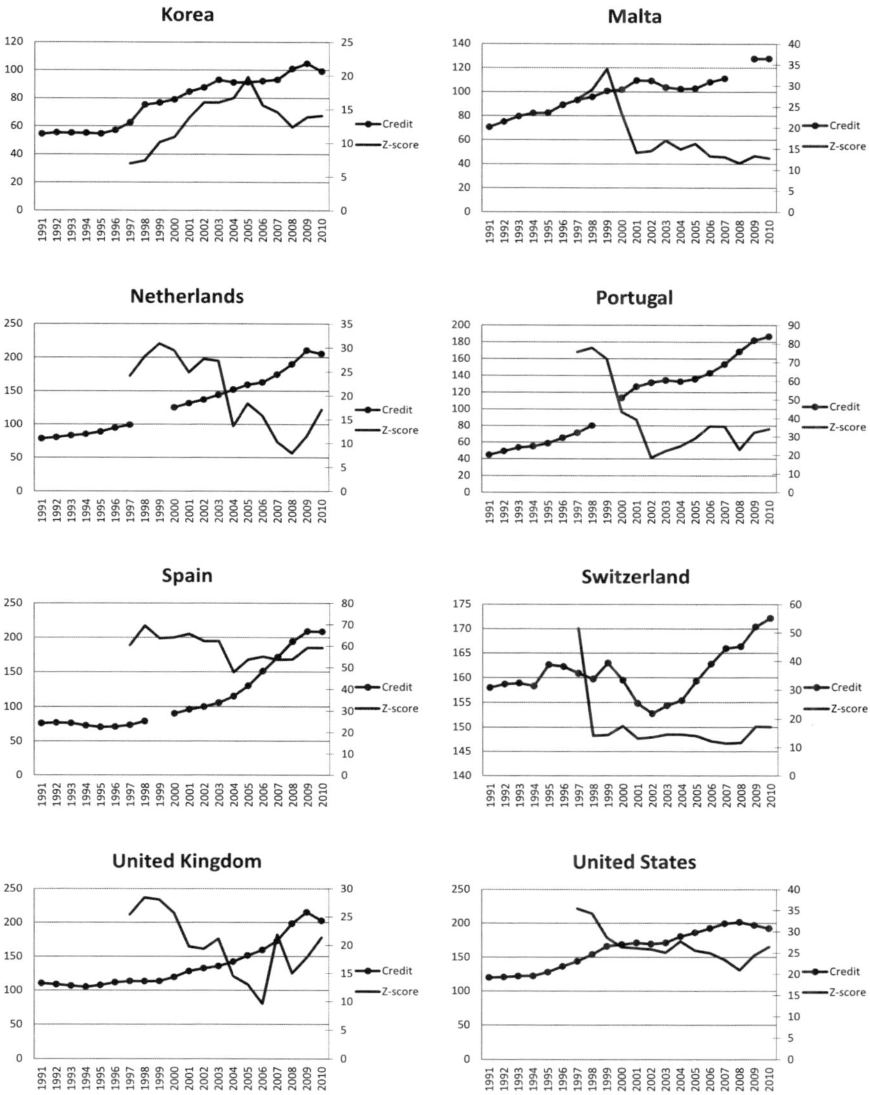

Panel C

Fig. 2. (*Continued*)

Table 2. Credit market size and creditworthiness of banks.
The dependent variable is the Z-score, estimated as the sum of banks' ROA and equity/assets ratio, divided by the standard deviation of ROA. Credit/GDP is the ratio to GDP of the private credit granted by deposit money banks and other financial institutions. All regressions include fixed-country effects and calendar-year effects. The maximum estimation period is 1997–2010 in all three regressions.

Explanatory variable	All countries	Countries with credit/GDP<50%	Countries with credit/GDP>50%
Credit/GDP	−0.111***	−0.055	−0.116***
	(0.014)	(0.055)	(0.014)
Observations	2,048	1,073	975
Countries	166	88	78
R^2	0.61	0.51	0.64

Note: *, ** and *** denote coefficients significant at the 10%, 5%, and 1% level, respectively.

The sample includes 166 countries, all the countries (except the non-market economies of North Korea, Laos, and Libya) for which the 2012 version of the Financial Structure Dataset has at least two observations for both variables. Due to missing observations for the dependent variable, the sample spans at most 1997 to 2010 (see Appendix 1 for the list of countries and number of observations). The coefficient of the credit/GDP variable is negative for the whole sample, but this result depends on the subsample of countries where the ratio is high; in the subsample of countries where it is below 50%, the coefficient is not significantly different from zero. The coefficient for the whole sample and for the subsample of more financially developed countries is economically significant. In the subsample of more financially developed countries, a one-standard-deviation increase in the credit/GDP ratio (49.6, which is not uncommon in these countries, as is shown by Fig. 2) is associated with a decrease of 5.75 in the Z-score, i.e., 28.6% of its subsample mean (20.1).

Table 3 uncovers a similar nonlinearity in the relationship between private credit and systemic stability. The measure of systemic risk is an estimate of the capital shortfall that banks are expected to incur in a financial crisis, based on work by Brownlees and Engle (2012) and Acharya, Engle, and Richardson (2012). Though produced from publicly available information, this estimate is conceptually similar to those obtained via

Table 3. Credit market size and systemic risk.
The dependent variable is an estimate of the capital shortfall that all the banks in a given country and year are expected to incur in a financial crisis, scaled by their total market capitalization. The estimate of the capital shortfall is based on Brownlees and Engle (2011) and Acharya, Engle, and Richardson (2012). The country-level values were produced by VLab at NYU and kindly provided by Viral Acharya and Robert Capellini. Credit/GDP is the ratio to GDP of private credit granted by deposit money banks and other financial institutions. All regressions include fixed-country effects and calendar-year effects. The maximum estimation period is 2000–11 in all three regressions.

Explanatory variable	All countries	Countries with credit/GDP<50%	Countries with credit/GDP>50%
Credit/GDP	0.009***	−0.024	0.0078**
	(0.003)	(0.033)	(0.002)
Observations	353	51	302
Countries	46	10	36
R^2	0.44	0.46	0.52

Note: *, ** and *** denote coefficients significant at the 10%, 5%, and 1% level, respectively.

stress tests by US and European regulators and takes into account the correlation between the value of each bank's assets and the financial sector aggregate in a crisis. The estimates are updated weekly by VLab and posted at http://vlab.stern.nyu.edu/welcome/risk. More precisely, the dependent variable is the sum of the capital shortfall of the banks in the VLab database for each country and year, scaled by their total stock market capitalization. The explanatory variables are the lagged credit/GDP ratio, country effects, and year effects, as in Table 2. The maximum estimation period is 2000–2011, since the VLab estimates are available for 2000–2012 and credit/GDP data only until 2011 (see Appendix 2 for the list of countries and number of observations).

In the entire sample, systemic risk is positively correlated with the credit/GDP ratio, jibing with the results of Table 2: A credit expansion is associated not only with less sound banks but also with a more unstable system. Again, however, the relationship is statistically significant only for the countries with high credit/GDP ratios. Interestingly, for this subsample the estimate in Table 3 predicts that a 1-standard-deviation increase in the ratio is associated with an increase in systemic risk of 0.362, which is 88%

of its subsample mean (0.412). In other words, it almost doubles systemic risk.[10]

Why Didn't Regulation Prevent Financial Hypertrophy?

As we saw in Section 2.2, a good deal of recent research has cited flaws in financial regulation and monetary policy as the cause of the excessive expansion of the financial sector in developed countries. Poor regulation is blamed chiefly for the unfettered growth of the shadow banking system, lax and accommodative monetary policy for banks' overexpansion of credit, and watered-down lending standards.

"Sins of Omission:" Neglecting Financial Innovation and Changing Incentives

Many of the regulatory failures are "sins of omission," lack of adaptation to fast-paced financial innovation with the growth of shadow banking and securitization. Some of the "sins" consisted in passive retention on tools that had once been effective but now, in the new market setting, were dysfunctional. An example is regulators' heavy reliance on credit ratings, which had been a reasonably good gauge of credit risk in corporate bond markets but were unsuited to the much more complex securities created by securitization. Nevertheless, prudential regulators simply reproduced the delegation of power to the rating agencies, as in the corporate bond sector.

Another example is LIBOR, the reference rate set by London-based banks in the unregulated Eurodollar market since the 1950s. Over the years, LIBOR eventually came to be the reference for an enormous volume of

[10]Some of the countries in the regressions of Tables 2 and 3 are offshore financial centers, which naturally tend to feature higher credit/GDP ratios. In principle, these countries may display a different relationship between the credit/GDP ratio and bank soundness or systemic stability. So for both Tables 2 and 3, I have estimated specifications that include an interaction variable allowing the slope coefficient of credit/GDP to differ between the countries classified by the IMF as offshore centers and the others. The results are qualitatively unchanged and are accordingly not reported. To test whether systemic stability is endangered not only by the level of credit but also by the speed at which it grows, I have also estimated specifications that include the lagged growth of credit/GDP among the explanatory variables; however, the coefficient of this variable is not statistically significant.

financial contracts and the derivative markets; thus the banks that took part in determining the rate were often parties to contracts indexed to LIBOR — a clear conflict of interest. Yet policymakers neglected the need to oversee the rate-setting process, until in June 2012, criminal investigations uncovered significant fraud and collusion in the banks' rate submissions.

The similarity between the two examples is that an indicator (be it a credit rating or a LIBOR rate submission) that is reliable in the context of a specific market does not serve in new, much broader, and more sophisticated markets, because the enormously higher stakes make conflicts of interest and fraudulent behavior far more likely — essentially, an incentive-based version of Goodhart's Law.[11] If regulation is not revised as the growth of the financial markets alters incentives and thus threatens the reliability of the indicator, then regulation itself ends up contributing to the dysfunctional behavior of the markets.

"Sins of Commission:" The Role of Politics

However, regulators have also made "sins of commission" to assist the over-expansion of the financial sector. In some cases, the flaws stemmed from regulations to correct some inefficiency. A prime example is the explicit and implicit guarantees provided to banks. Deposit insurance, for instance, was introduced to prevent bank runs but ultimately fostered excessive risk-taking by bank managers and more generally created an implicit subsidy to banks. The result was excess capacity (overbanking), which in turn induced banks to compete too aggressively in the search for yield.

Many regulatory "sins of commission" have been prompted by politics, whose role in planting the seeds of the recent crises has not been sufficiently recognized. For instance, in the US, the political determination to support widespread home ownership induced government-sponsored agencies such as Fanny Mae, Freddie Mac, and AIG to guarantee low-quality loans in the securitization process, which contributed enormously to the subprime mortgage boom and the house price bubble. The same can be said of the 2001 decision by the Federal Deposit Insurance Corporation (FDIC) to lower — drastically, from 8% to 1.6% — the capital requirement

[11]According to Goodhart's Law, when an economic indicator becomes an economic policy target it loses the information content that would qualify it to play that role.

on banks in respect of MBSs and most private sector CDOs (compared with the 4% requirement against mortgage loans and lower-rated mortgage securities), as well as of the 2004 SEC decision to exempt investment banks from capital regulations and entrust their risk monitoring to their own internal risk models. These decisions provided a huge inducement for banks both to securitize their loans and to invest in high-rated asset-backed and mortgage-backed securities. Similarly, in Europe, the decision by the EU Commission to exploit the "carve-out option" of Basel II regarding prudential ratios on sovereign debt permitted the assignment of zero risk weight to all euro-area sovereign debt. This encouraged EU banks to buy euro-area government bonds, especially those featuring high yields and high risk. While this undoubtedly facilitated national Treasuries in placing risky public debt, it also certainly increased the riskiness of euro-area banks (Acharya and Steffen, 2012).

One of the most spectacular cases of the role of politics in the overexpansion of finance before the bursting of the subprime bubble was that of Iceland. Benediktsdottir, Danielsson, and Zoega (2011) describe how politicians provided essential support to the incredible transformation of a tiny fishing and aluminum-producing economy into an international banking platform, just in time to be a protagonist in the debt expansion and asset price bubble of 2003–07 and the subsequent catastrophic collapse. They explain how politicians first privatized the banks by selling them to their cronies in business (who bought their stakes using funds borrowed from those very banks) and then together with these cronies dreamt up the plan to make Iceland an international financial marketplace. A crucial ingredient was the implicit sovereign support that the government gave to the banks' record borrowing in 2004–2005, which enabled them to access cheap, abundant international funding. No less important was the politicians' failure to equip their fledgling financial center with adequate supervisory authorities: The banks dwarfed the agencies that supposedly supervised them.

Another case in which regulators' failings were largely rooted in politics is that of Spain. The huge capital inflow into Spain prior to the crisis was mediated by a power bloc of managers of the savings banks (*cajas*), regional politicians, and real estate developers, reciprocally supporting each other with favors and easy credit. They channeled massive amounts of credit into real estate, generating the housing bubble and substantial bad loans. Cuñat and Garicano (2009) show that the *cajas* whose chief executives had no banking experience and no graduate education, but did have strong political connections, extended more loans to real estate developers and fared substantially worse both before and during the crisis. The close connection between politicians and the bank managers was also a factor in the slow and ineffective response of Spanish prudential supervisors to the crisis, and the protracted forbearance on bad loans to developers. As Luis Garicano (2012) puts it, "The main explanation for the supervisory failure of the Banco de España has to do with the political control of the *cajas* ...[T]he supervisor, confronted with powerful and well-connected ex-politicians decided to look the other way in the face of obvious building trouble. Indeed the political connection of the managers of the entities was a good predictor of brewing trouble."

The experience of Iceland and Spain underscores another important point: Namely, that credit-fueled asset bubbles can easily produce broad political consensus, well beyond the circle of politicians and financiers. Once the bubble has started, the consensus tends to stretch throughout the population — a feature common to other countries as well in the run-up to the crisis. Most of society seemed to profit from the bubble, not only bankers earning huge profits and bonuses, but also households reaping high returns on their assets and firms gaining from the boom in business — and of course politicians at the helm of governments basking in popularity. In 2008, Iceland ranked fourth in the world in per capita GDP!

What these patterns show is that politics is indeed a root cause of the hypertrophy of finance, and not just because of the capture of politicians by the banking lobby. The euphoria associated with the bubble creates vast political support, while the few who question its sustainability are seen as "spoilsports" and "party poopers," gadflies to be ignored — in the banks, in the political parties, and most likely even inside households. This is a point that applies to economy-wide bubbles very much in general. Once a bubble gets under way there is no constituency to stop it, because everyone simply tries to grab as much profit as possible as long as it lasts. The unfortunate implication is that the "dark side" of finance is entangled with a "dark side" of politics and society.

Appendix 1. Countries included in the regressions of Table 2.

Country	Number of observations	Country	Number of observations
Countries with credit/GDP < 50%			
Afghanistan	3	Macedonia, FYR	14
Albania	14	Madagascar	14
Algeria	14	Malawi	14
Angola	14	Mali	14
Argentina	14	Mauritania	5
Armenia	14	Mexico	14
Azerbaijan	14	Moldova	14
Bangladesh	14	Mongolia	12
Belarus	14	Mozambique	14
Benin	14	Myanmar	12
Bhutan	14	Namibia	8
Botswana	14	Nepal	14
Burkina Faso	14	Nicaragua	10
Burundi	14	Niger	14
Cambodia	11	Nigeria	14
Cameroon	14	Oman	8
Central African Republic	12	Pakistan	14
Chad	12	Papua New Guinea	12
Colombia	14	Paraguay	14
Congo, Dem. Rep.	9	Peru	14
Congo, Rep.	4	Poland	13
Costa Rica	14	Romania	14
Cote d'Ivoire	14	Russian Federation	14
Djibouti	10	Rwanda	10
Dominica	6	Samoa	14
Dominican Republic	14	Senegal	14
Ecuador	14	Serbia	12
El Salvador	14	Seychelles	8
Equatorial Guinea	7	Sierra Leone	14
Ethiopia	13	Sri Lanka	14
Gabon	14	St. Vincent and the Grenadines	3
Gambia, The	13	Sudan	14
Georgia	14	Suriname	14
Ghana	14	Swaziland	14
Guatemala	14	Syrian Arab Republic	12
Haiti	14	Tajikistan	6
India	14	Tanzania	9
Iraq	2	Togo	14

(*Continued*)

Appendix 1. (*Continued*)

Country	Number of observations	Country	Number of observations
Jamaica	13	Trinidad and Tobago	14
Kazakhstan	14	Turkey	14
Kenya	14	Uganda	14
Kyrgyz Republic	9	Venezuela, RB	14
Lesotho	12	Yemen, Rep.	9
Liberia	4	Zambia	14
Countries with credit GDP > 50%			
Antigua and Barbuda	8	Jordan	14
Aruba	7	Korea, Rep.	14
Australia	14	Kuwait	14
Austria	12	Latvia	13
Bahamas, The	14	Lithuania	14
Bahrain	7	Luxembourg	12
Barbados	14	Macao SAR, China	14
Belgium	12	Malaysia	14
Belize	12	Maldives	4
Bolivia	14	Malta	13
Bosnia and Herzegovina	3	Mauritius	14
Brazil	14	Montenegro	4
Brunei Darussalam	9	Morocco	14
Bulgaria	13	Netherlands	12
Canada	13	New Zealand	14
Cape Verde	11	Norway	11
Chile	13	Panama	14
China	14	Philippines	14
Croatia	14	Portugal	13
Cyprus	13	San Marino	6
Czech Republic	13	Saudi Arabia	14
Denmark	13	Singapore	14
Egypt, Arab Rep.	14	Slovak Republic	13
Estonia	14	Slovenia	13
Finland	13	South Africa	14
France	12	Spain	13
Germany	13	St. Kitts and Nevis	14
Greece	12	St. Lucia	14
Grenada	14	Sweden	13
Guyana	14	Switzerland	14
Honduras	14	Thailand	14

(*Continued*)

Appendix 1. (*Continued*)

Country	Number of observations	Country	Number of observations
Countries with credit GDP > 50%			
Hong Kong SAR, China	14	Tunisia	14
Hungary	13	Ukraine	14
Iceland	12	United Kingdom	14
Indonesia	14	United States	14
Ireland	13	Uruguay	14
Israel	14	Vanuatu	9
Italy	13	Vietnam	14
Japan	14	Zimbabwe	6

Appendix 2. Countries included in the regressions of Table 3.

Country	Number of observations	Country	Number of observations
Countries with credit/GDP<50%			
Argentina	8	Peru	3
India	12	Philippines	2
Indonesia	4	Poland	6
Kazakhstan	2	Russian Federation	2
Mexico	6	Turkey	6
Countries with credit/GDP>50%			
Australia	11	Korea, Rep.	12
Austria	10	Luxembourg	4
Belgium	11	Malaysia	12
Brazil	10	Malta	2
Canada	10	Mauritius	3
Chile	6	Netherlands	11
China	7	Norway	8
Cyprus	6	Portugal	5
Denmark	9	Saudi Arabia	2
Finland	7	Singapore	2
France	11	South Africa	12
Germany	11	Spain	5
Greece	11	Sweden	10
Hong Kong SAR, China	6	Switzerland	12
Ireland	6	Thailand	11
Israel	12	United Kingdom	11
Italy	10	United States	12
Japan	12	Vietnam	2

References

Acharya, V. and H. Naqvi (2012). "The seeds of a crisis: A theory of bank liquidity and risk taking over the business cycle," *Journal of Financial Economics*, Vol. 106, No. 2, pp. 349–366.

Acharya, V., R. Engle and M. Richardson (2012). "Capital shortfall: A new approach to ranking and regulating systemic risks," *American Economic Review Papers and Proceedings*, Vol. 102, No. 3, pp. 59–64.

Acharya, V. and S. Steffen (2012). "The 'greatest' carry trade ever? Understanding eurozone bank risks," New University Working Paper.

Adrian, T. and H. S. Shin (2010). "The changing nature of financial intermediation and the financial crisis of 2007–2009," *Annual Review of Economics*, Vol. 2, pp. 603–618.

Aghion, P., T. Fally and S. Scarpetta (2007). "Credit constraints as a barrier to the entry and post-entry growth of firms," *Economic Policy*, Vol. 22, No. 52, October, pp. 731–779.

Arcand, J. L., E. Berkes and U. Panizza (2012). "Too much finance?," International Monetary Fund, Working Paper No. WP/12/161.

Ashcraft, A. and P. Goldsmith-Pinkham and J. Vickery (2010). "MBS ratings and the mortgage credit boom," Federal Reserve Bank of New York Staff Report No. 449.

Bar-Isaac, H. and J. Shapiro (2011). "Credit ratings accuracy and analyst incentives," *American Economic Review Papers and Proceedings*, Vol. 101, No. 3, pp. 1–7.

Beck, T. and A. Demirgüç-Kunt (2009). "Financial institutions and markets across countries and over time: Data and analysis," World Bank Policy Research Working Paper No. 4943, May.

Beck, T., R. Levine and N. Loayza (2000a). "Financial intermediation and growth: Causality and causes," *Journal of Monetary Economics*, Vol. 46, No. 1, pp. 31–47.

Beck, T., R. Levine and N. Loayza (2000b). "Finance and the sources of growth," *Journal of Financial Economics*, Vol. 58, No. 1–2, October/November, pp. 261–300.

Bekaert, G., C. Harvey and C. Lundblad (2005). "Does financial liberalization spur growth?" *Journal of Financial Economics*, Vol. 77, pp. 3–55.

Benediktsdottir, S., J. Danielsson and G. Zoega (2011). "Lessons from a collapse of a financial system," *Economic Policy*, Vol. 26, No. 66, pp. 183–231.

Bertrand, M., A. Schoar and D. Thesmar (2007). "Banking deregulation and industry structure: Evidence from the French banking reforms of 1985," *Journal of Finance*, Vol. 62, No. 2, pp. 597–628.

Bolton, P., T. Santos and J. A. Scheinkman (2012). "Cream skimming in financial markets," Columbia University Working Paper.

Brown, C. O. and I. Serdar Dinç (2011). "Too many to fail? Evidence of regulatory forbearance when the banking sector is weak," *Review of Financial Studies*, Vol. 24, No. 4, pp. 1378–1405.

Brownlees, C. and R. Engle (2012). "Volatility, correlation and tails for systemic risk measurement," New York University Working Paper.

Čihák, M., A. Demirgüç-Kunt, E. Feyen and R. Levine (2012). "Benchmarking financial development around the world," World Bank Policy Research Working Paper No. 6175.

Cuñat, V. and L. Garicano (2009). "Did good cajas extend bad loans? The role of governance and human capital in cajas' portfolio decisions," FEDEA.

Dehejia, R. and A. Lleras-Muney (2007). "Financial development and pathways of growth: State branching and deposit insurance laws in the United States from 1900 to 1940," *Journal of Law and Economics*, Vol. 50, No. 2, 239–272.

Dell'Ariccia, G., D. Igan and L. Laeven (2012). "Credit booms and lending standards: Evidence from the subprime mortgage market," *Journal of Money, Credit and Banking*, Vol. 44, pp. 367–384.

Demirgüç-Kunt, A. and R. Levine (eds.) (2001). *Financial Structure and Economic Growth: A Cross-Country Comparison of Banks, Markets and Development*, MIT Press, Cambridge, MA.

Di Maggio, M. and M. Pagano (2012). "Financial disclosure and market transparency with costly information processing," University of Naples, Centre for Studies in Economics and Finance Working Paper No. 323; Einaudi Institute for Economics and Finance Working Paper No. 12–12.

Ductor, L. and D. Grechyna (2011). "Excess financial development and economic growth," Social Science Research Network Working Paper. Available at: http://ssrn.com/abstract=1997526.

Farhi, E. and J. Tirole (2012). "Collective moral hazard, maturity mismatch, and systemic bailouts," *American Economic Review*, Vol. 102, No. 1, pp. 60–93.

Garicano, L. (2012). "Five lessons from the Spanish cajas debacle for a new euro-wide supervisor," October 16. Available at: www.voxeu.org.

Goldsmith, R. W. (1969). *Financial Structure and Development*, Yale University Press, New Haven, CT.

Greenwood, R. and D. Scharfstein (2012). "The growth of modern finance," Harvard Business School, Working Paper.

Griffin, J. M. and D. Yongjun Tang (2010). "Did credit rating agencies make unbiased assumptions on CDOs?," *American Economic Review Papers and Proceedings*, Vol. 101, No. 3, pp. 125–130.

Griffin, J. M. and D. Yongjun Tang (2012). "Did subjectivity play a role in CDO credit ratings?" *Journal of Finance*, Vol. 67, No. 4, August, pp. 1293–1328.

Guiso, L., T. Jappelli, M. Padula and M. Pagano (2004). "Financial market integration and economic growth in the EU," *Economic Policy*, Vol. 19, No. 40, pp. 523–577.

Guiso, L., P. Sapienza and L. Zingales (2004). "Does local financial development matter?" *Quarterly Journal of Economics*, Vol. 119, No. 3, pp. 929–969.

Gupta, N. and K. Yuan (2009). "On the growth effect of stock market liberalizations," *Review of Financial Studies*, Vol. 22, No. 11, pp. 4715–4752.

Henry, P. B. (2000) "Do stock market liberalizations cause investment booms?" *Journal of Financial Economics*, Vol. 58, pp. 301–334.

Hicks, J. (1969). *A Theory of Economic History*, Clarendon Press, Oxford, UK.

Ioannidou, V., S. Ongena and J.-L. Peydró (2009). "Monetary policy, risk-taking and pricing: Evidence from a quasi-natural experiment," European Banking Center Discussion Paper No. 2009-04S.

Jayaratne, J. and P. Strahan (1996). "The finance-growth nexus: Evidence from bank branch deregulation," *Quarterly Journal of Economics*, Vol. 111, No. 3, pp. 639–670.

Jiménez, G., S. Ongena, J.-L. Peydró and J. Saurina (2011). "Hazardous times for monetary policy: What do 23 million loans say about the impact of monetary policy on credit risk-taking?" Tilburg University Working Paper.

Keynes, J. M. (1936). *The General Theory of Employment, Interest, and Money*, New York: Harcourt, Brace, and Co.

King, R. G. and R. Levine (1993a). "Finance and growth: Schumpeter may be right," *Quarterly Journal of Economics*, Vol. 108, No. 3, pp. 713–737.

King, Robert G. and Ross Levine 1993b, "Finance, entrepreneurship and growth," *Journal of Monetary Economics*, Vol. 32, No. 3, pp. 513–542.

Klapper, L., L. Laeven, and R. Rajan (2006). "Entry regulation as a barrier to entrepreneurship," *Journal of Financial Economics*, Vol. 82, No. 3, pp. 591–629.

Kroszner, R. S., L. Laeven and D. Klingebiel (2007). "Banking crises, financial dependence, and growth," *Journal of Financial Economics*, Vol. 84, pp. 187–228.

La Porta, R., F. Lopez-de-Silanes and A. Shleifer (1998). "Law and finance," *Journal of Political Economy*, Vol. 106, No. 6, pp. 1113–1155.

Levine, R. (1997). "Financial development and economic growth: Views and agenda," *Journal of Economic Literature*, Vol. 35, pp. 688–726.

Levine, R. (2005). "Finance and growth: Theory and evidence," in *Handbook of Economic Growth*, P. Aghion and S. Durlauf (eds.), Amsterdam: Elsevier Science.

Maddaloni, A. and J.-L. Peydró (2011). "Bank risk-taking, securitization, supervision, and low interest rates: Evidence from the euro area and U.S. lending standards," *Review of Financial Studies*, Vol. 24, pp. 2121–2165.

Pagano, M. (1993). "Financial markets and growth: An overview," *European Economic Review*, Vol. 37, No. 2/3, pp. 613–622.

Pagano, M. and G. Pica (2012). "Finance and employment," *Economic Policy*, Vol. 27, No. 69, pp. 7–55.

Pagano, M. and P. Volpin (2010). "Credit ratings failures and policy options," *Economic Policy*, Vol. 25, No. 62, pp. 403–431.

Pagano, M. and P. Volpin (2012). "Securitization, disclosure and liquidity," *Review of Financial Studies*, Vol. 25, No. 8, pp. 2417–2453.

Philippon, T. (2008). "The evolution of the US financial industry from 1860 to 2007: Theory and evidence," New York University, Stern School of Business Working Paper.

Philippon, T. and A. Reshef (2008). "Wages and human capital in the U.S. financial industry: 1909–2006," *Quarterly Journal of Economics*, Vol. 127, No. 4, November, pp. 1551–1609.

Pozsar, Z., T. Adrian, A. Ashcraft and H. Boesky (2010). "Shadow banking," Federal Reserve Bank of New York Staff Report No. 458, July, revised February 2012.

Rajan, R. G. and L. Zingales (1998). "Financial dependence and growth," *American Economic Review*, Vol. 88, 3, pp. 559–587.

Rousseau, P. L. and R. Sylla (2005). "Emerging financial markets and early US growth," *Explorations in Economic History*, Vol. 42, pp. 1–26.

Finance: Is Bigger Badder?

Gerard Caprio, Jr.*

Center for Development Economics Williams College

Last year, I was a discussant of a session at this conference on the social productivity of the financial sector, and those of us at that session — Ross Levine, Alex Popov, and Josh Lerner — must have really whet appetites for the subject, as it was decided to make that the theme of the conference this year. Further discussion is timely, as the questioning of the role of the contributions of the financial system, suggestions to break up banks — now coming even from several within the Federal Reserve System, with Governor Tarullo being the latest to weigh in — and suggestions on the need to cap the size of the financial sector or intervene with other restrictions have gained a new currency, one not seen since the 1930s. When Sandy Weil is suggesting the downsizing of banks, it is clear that the debate has shifted. Financial restraint has been urged before — Joe Stiglitz has been recommending that for most of his professional career — and financial repression, mild or not, is likely not only when the intellectual climate is accommodating, but even more important, when financing the government becomes onerous.

So is some financial restraint warranted, and if so, what form should it take? On the positive case for finance, what Marco Pagano calls the bright side, there is an impressive array of evidence, some of which Marco summarizes. In the literature on the contributions of finance to growth, there are now studies using aggregate, industry-level, and firm-level data, as well as individual case studies and the financial history literature, all of which support an important role for finance in stimulating development. So my only conclusion is that if people do not believe that finance has a positive

*Gerard Caprio, Jr., is the William Brough Professor of Economics and Chair of the Center for Development Economics at Williams College.

contribution to growth, then they must not put any weight on empirical studies. Although the methodologies of each of the above approaches can be criticized as having weaknesses, those weaknesses vary significantly across the different methodologies and data employed. And for me, if different approaches keep giving the same answer, then it is time to begin believing that answer. In addition to influencing growth, Thorsten Beck, Asli Demirgüç-Kunt, Ross, and others have shown that financial development tends to be pro-poor, that is, that the deepening of financial sector contributes to a reduction of inequality, fewer people living in poverty, and higher incomes for the poor. These findings, less than a decade old, were a surprise to many, who seemed to reason that, since they never saw a poor person coming out of a bank or, more generally, that poor people did not consume many of the services produced by the financial industry, finance must disproportionately benefit the rich, and perhaps only trickle down to the poor. This reasoning neglected that what the poor need most is not debt, but rather income, and that finance can contribute to job creation.

At last year's conference, I remarked that Ross Levine's paper on the contributions of finance omitted a very important one, namely his own work on the impact of finance in reducing racial discrimination in the labor markets. So I was particularly pleased this year to see that his paper focuses exclusively on this contribution. I am sure that many will want to ask questions about the data, the identification strategy, and so forth. What I would like to point out for the purpose of this session is that this benefit of finance, of which I am persuaded, is something that not only I had not anticipated, but I had never come across anyone in my career working on financial sector issues who had anticipated such an effect. The relevance of that point is that finance supplies a variety of services and that going back to the days of John Stuart Mill, finance was thought to only matter when it broke down. This became the intellectual justification for ignoring the financial sector, and for thinking that it was not "real," a distinction that still is embedded in most economists' vocabulary. So the fact that in the early 21st century we are still learning about the benefits of financial sector development should not be a surprise and should motivate us to be sure that in enacting reforms to limit crises, that we do not kill off the benefits of finance.

I also remind the reader that even though he did not advertise it in this paper, as noted in his presentation, Ross continues to espouse the functional approach to finance that he laid out in his 1997 *JEL* paper, and in my view it is an approach that we ignore at the peril of forgetting what finance does. In this approach, finance contributes to growth by mobilizing savings, allocating credit, monitoring (exerting corporate control), facilitating risk management, and easing the trading of goods and services. This reminder will be germane when we get to the dark side of finance, which both Marco Pagano and Romain Rancière discuss.

Romain agrees that finance helps growth by improving credit allocation, and that this single function is worth the normal (or one might say limited) crises that could occur from "time to time." Even though his liberalized regime has systemic bailout guarantees, only garden- variety (limited) crises occur in what I will call the good regulation state, and so he concludes that the benefits of finance outweigh it costs in this state. However, in the "bad" state in which it is possible to engage in unlimited leverage — in his model through the issuance of option-like instruments that pay off in default states — the costs of crises become enormous. One response is to prohibit such instruments. The problem I have with this approach is that in the recent crisis, credit default swaps played no role in the Icelandic, Irish, British, or Spanish crises. Also, I see risk rather as endogenous, arising from the incentives that determine how assets and instruments are used, and not as inherent in specific instruments. Moreover, most crises — and I believe that of 2007 — occurred less as a result of new financial instruments but rather from excessive leverage and absurdly weak credit standards, along with compensation focused on return without a consideration of risk. These features occurred while regulators sat and watched.

Marco Pagano's paper looks at how finance can be both economic lifeblood and a toxin, at different times. I have already discussed what he calls the "bright side" of finance. But Marco then focuses on the dark side of the force (sorry, of finance), and I commend him for his bravery given that we are in the heart of "freshwater" economics, where all the actors are rational, the bubbles (apologies for using this word within the Chicago city limits) are nonexistent, and all the children are above average. He says that the dark side is related to "an abnormal growth in private credit and in the leverage of financial institutions (p. 7)," and posits that the impact of finance on development is nonlinear. As Marco puts it, eventually the number of firms with external financing constraints declines to the point that further increases in credit no longer are warranted. Beyond some point, a hypertrophy of finance occurs, the ingredients for which are said to be an unregulated shadow banking system, easy monetary policy, and the widespread expectation of bailout. At least as far as this argument goes, Marco too is looking at finance as if it performed a single function, namely, credit provision.

I have several problems with the idea that there is some magic point beyond which finance can be said to be too large. First, I spent 18 years at the World Bank working on financial systems that were vastly smaller relative to GDP (and relative to any other sensible denominator), compared with that in high-income countries, and yet which blew up in financial crises. So I'm inherently skeptical about the idea that size somehow is a determining variable. Countries with banking sectors, and indeed entire financial systems, whose assets were on the order of 20% to 30% of GDP, suffered serious banking crises. Should we have drawn the line for banking systems at about 15% of GDP? To ask that question is to answer it.

Second, the term hypertrophy is popular in the medical field where it refers to the enlargement of the component organs or cells, and is contrasted with hyperplasia, which refers to an increase in the number of those components. When financial growth becomes excessive, it can easily happen through a growth in the size of the components, in their number, or both. Hyperplasia best described the state of the US financial system in the 30 years ending in 1920, when the number of banks mushroomed to 30,000, right before the failure of about half as many in the ensuing 15 years. It certainly was size that killed in 19th and early 20th century crises, but it was small size that killed, not large size. Moreover, the medical field specifically recognizes that some hypertrophy can be good. Ventricular hypertrophy, that is, the enlargement of the ventricles of the heart, can happen for good reasons — marathoners often have this condition, I'm told — as well as bad reasons, most commonly high blood pressure. So just as physicians are urged to go beyond looking at the surface conditions to find out what's going on underneath, economists by now, like physicians, should be guided by the principle of doing no harm and must be encouraged to look beyond mere size to try to figure out what is driving changes in the financial system.

Regarding the size of individual banks, we now have ample experience with Too Big to Fail that the cost of large individual banks is clear. But for the system as a whole, a recommendation to constrain its size is on shakier ground.

Third, I find myself more in agreement with Robert Shiller (2012) than with Paul Volcker on financial innovation, meaning that I not only recognize more than the ATM as a recent innovation (e.g., social impact bonds), but also am reluctant to take steps that could rule out future innovations. This in no way means that I am against regulation — and in fact, my take on the last crisis is "Regulation, what a good idea, why didn't we try some?" — but rather that I think that it is far too easy to come up with simple Jeffersonian rules on how to limit the growth of the financial sector: Rules that would hamstring our ability to deal with upcoming changes in the real economy. And before some say, "Wait a minute, Jeffersonian reasoning on the corrupting powers of finance looks a lot better post-crisis," let's remember that, had Thomas Jefferson succeeded in quashing the reforms of Alexander Hamilton, Katrina would have been a problem for the French authorities to deal with, that is, the Louisiana Purchase never would have happened (Sylla, 2008). More broadly, the restrictions that were in force in the US in the early 19th century limiting the branching of banks — which made the US financial system prone to crises — led to banks that were far too small to finance larger industrial corporations that started growing up around midcentury. Fortunately, no one was around to prevent the growth of capital markets, which took off and became far more deeply developed than in any other country relative to their banking system.

As Shiller has emphasized, there are still many risks that finance is not helping people in society address, and I have no idea how large the sector has to be or what it would need to look like in order to provide insurance against more macro risks. For example, to cover the risks of climate change, we might need a very large financial system to ensure sufficient risk diversification; Hurricane Sandy, which was impressive in the area it affected, might make one revise their priors upward. And it should be evident from the housing crash, which though national in scope varied significantly throughout the country, that Shiller's zip code insurance — protecting homeowners from the greatest risk that they face, namely that the value of their house will fall relative to those in other areas — should be a hot seller once sufficient data are available. And as someone teaching at a liberal arts college, I know that despite the great value of that education, the pressure to specialize early is intense. Insurance against the risk of picking a specialty whose relative wage declines also could improve welfare. What size financial system will we need to provide these services?

Lastly, the argument that finance is big enough might be very appealing to those who already have access to the financial system. I quite agree that we learned in the recent crisis, as other countries have learned in their own crises, that there can be some very bad ways of attempting to increase access to credit. Given the aforementioned evidence on the inequality reducing benefits of financial deepening, and given that the Gini coefficient in the US today is worse than in Russia in 1905, I am averse to measures that can reduce financial access to broader groups of society.

So when people start talking about overall limits on the financial sector relative to GDP, I get very nervous. I have heard no credible argument in the economics profession that would help draw that line. However, the suggestion that some limit on the size of the sector is appropriate, even though economics has no way to define those limits, is tantamount to a decision to leave it to the politicians. How well did the deposit insurance premium that was arrived during the 1930s (and copied by so many countries) or the 8% capital rule, another political compromise, work out for us?

Fortunately, Marco goes beyond the simple argument about the relationship of size with negative outcomes in the sector, and notes that both through sins of omission — regulation not being updated sufficiently to take account of innovation and changing incentives in markets — and sins of commission, by flaws in regulation as well as political interference, that regulation can contribute to crises. Here I could not agree more. I would just state it more strongly. The Basel system of risk weighting was a driver behind securitization and thus bears partial responsibility for the crisis that began in 2007; without risk weighting, it is unlikely that there would have been as much use for shadow banking and credit default swaps. The banks would not have lobbied the Fed to allow CDS because there would have been no gain from them. Also, as Marco notes, Basel's risk weighting encouraged lending to euro sovereigns and thus is a factor in the ongoing euro crisis. I understand, per my earlier comments on financial repression, that now is not a time when governments will want to make change rules that would make government debt less attractive, but from the standpoint of stability, ending risk weighting would further that goal. It would also dramatically reduce the complexity of regulation, which would help in several respects, not least of which would be in improving transparency. We might differ in the importance assigned to the role of regulatory omission via the lack of enforcement of regulations by regulators, which I would have stressed more, as I view as an important factor in most crises, that of 2007 in particular. Indeed, the common thread behind the crises in the US, Iceland, Ireland, and the UK, was regulators watching painfully obvious risks — NINJA loans in the US, banks doubling in size in about two years in Ireland, or even faster in Iceland as examples — and not using the powers that they had to stop them.

How should regulation adapt to changes in the financial system? We know that since the birth (or rebirth) of modern banking in the Middle Ages, finance has responded quickly to circumvent regulation. One method of response would be to have legislators annually reconsider financial regulation. This in my view would be a boon to financial sector lobbyists and a bane for society. The alternative, which is embedded in most countries' approach, is to give regulators some discretion to adapt, so that new legislation is not required so regularly. But if regulators are to be endowed with discretion and are regularly making regulatory decisions that side with the industry they are overseeing, then if we are to pretend that we wish to be a democracy with checks and balances, there is no alternative but coming up with a system by which to hold the regulators accountable.

Now I understand that one should always beware of the risk that authors tend to see the world through their writings, but it is warranted when the world keeps confirming one's views. Yes, this is a bit like the Rorschach test joke in which a patient keeps seeing sexual images in various inkblots and then blames the psychiatrist for the dirty pictures, true; but in the wake of the Morgan trading losses, the Libor scandal, banks lending to Iran or laundering money, credit card overcharges, wrongful foreclosures for military families, and other evidence of somnolent regulators, it should be increasingly clear that current models of regulation are not serving the public well. Jim Barth, Ross, and I argue in *The Guardians of Finance: Making Regulators Work for Us* that it is necessary to have a small agency overseeing regulators, getting access to all information that is available to the regulator, and regularly issuing a report on what are the key risks and what the regulator is doing about them. Otherwise, the time when taxpayers discover the under performance of regulators is when the bill comes due. We understand that such an agency, which we call the Sentinel, would need great expertise and would have to pay incredibly well, especially as it would only work if staff were not allowed to move to the private sector for a substantial length of time, if ever. But we also believe that just as instant replay in sports reduces home field advantage by reducing the psychological pressure on the referees to conform to the crowd, a Sentinel would produce more even-handed regulation instead of an approach that is biased in favor of the industry.

To conclude, the goal for society remains maximizing the benefits of finance while minimizing its costs. The benefits are considerable, some of which are still being discovered. Many will conclude that the solution depends on getting regulation right. But the change no one wants to discuss is how to get regulators to implement whatever rules are decided. Regulators are only humans and humans evidently applaud accountability for everyone but themselves. And the last thing that the financial services industry wants is to have regulators who act like pitbulls rather than pussycats. I also understand that the search for a bright line rule that is easily understandable and evident to all as a means of controlling banks is seductive, but I do not hold out much hope of finding one. As I indicated here, I would not support a rule that tries to limit overall financial sector size. What Marco and Romain's papers demonstrated to me is that the particular way in which we allowed finance to grow did not work — though I think that I knew that already — rather than that any kind of growth is bad. In my view, the benefits of finance arise from all of the functions that it provides, and that as we get more and better data sources, it is likely that the risk mitigation function will become even more important. Though it may be so for individual banks, as we will discuss in another session, for the financial system as a whole, bigger is not necessarily badder.

Lastly, I cannot let down the conference organizers. At past conferences here, I have often argued here that every conference should have a movie that illustrates its key themes or issues, with past choices being *A Wing and a Prayer* in 2006, *Jaws* in 2007, and for last year's reconsideration of the role of central banks, *Groundhog Day*. This year, one obvious choice is the movie *Back to the Future*, as the pendulum has swung back in the direction of greater financial repression. In that movie, Marty McFly, played by Michael J. Fox, has to travel back to the past to make sure that his parents got together in high school in order that the history in which he comes to exist is repeated. We need to revisit our past to understand what happened, but the goal should be the reverse: To abort the cycle of having a crisis, changing a few rules, and ignoring regulatory oversight. Until we are willing to change the basic framework of regulation, a repetition of this cycle is my version of the "doom loop." However, that suggests then that *Groundhog Day* should be a repeat theme for the conference!

References

Barth, J., G. Caprio, Jr. and R. Levine (2012). *The Guardians of Finance: Making Regulators Work for Us*, Cambridge, MA: MIT Press.

Levine, R. (1997). "Financial development and economic growth: Views and agenda," *Journal of Economic Literature*, Vol. 35, No. 2, June.

Shiller, R. (2012). *Finance and the Good Society*, Princeton, NJ: Princeton University Press.

Sylla, R. (2008). "The political economy of early U.S. financial development," in *Political Institutions and Financial Development*, S. Haber, D. C. North and B. R. Weingast (eds.), Stanford, CA: Stanford University Press.

PART IV

FINANCIAL INDUSTRY INNOVATION

A Proposal for the Resolution of Systemically Important Assets and Liabilities: The Case of the Repo Market*

Viral V. Acharya
Stern School of Business New York University
NBER and CEPR

T. Sabri Öncü
Centre for Advanced Financial Research and Learning, Reserve Bank of India
and
Stern School of Business New York University

One of the several regulatory failures behind the global financial crisis that started in 2007 has been the regulatory focus on individual rather than systemic risk of financial institutions. Focusing on systemically important assets and liabilities (SIALs) rather than individual financial institutions, we propose a set of resolution mechanisms, which is not only capable of inducing market discipline and mitigating moral hazard, but also capable of addressing the associated systemic risk, for instance, due to the risk of

*The material in this article was originally published in the *International Journal of Central Banking*, Volume 9, Supplement 1, January 2013. It is reprinted with permission with minor alterations to adhere to the style of World Scientific Ltd. The authors are deeply indebted to Barry Adler, Nouriel Roubini, and Matt Richardson for collaborations and discussions on earlier work on the issue of resolution mechanisms for systemically important financial firms. The authors are also grateful for discussions on the issues of safe harbor for repo contracts and repo-market related systemic risks with Rocco Huang, Antoine Martin, Enrico Perotti, and Mark Roe, and comments from discussants (Andrew Crockett and Ricardo Caballero) and participants at the Federal Reserve Board of Governors conference on "Central Banking: Before, During and After the Crisis." Last, but not least, we would like to thank George Kaufman for bringing the Glass proposal to our attention.

fire sales of collateral assets. Furthermore, because of our focus on SIALs, our proposed resolution mechanisms would be easier to implement at the global level compared to mechanisms that operate at the level of individual institutional forms. We, then, outline how our approach can be specialized to the repo market and propose a repo resolution authority for reforming this market.

Introduction

Systemic risk can be defined broadly as the expected losses from the risk that the failure of a significant part of the financial sector leads to a reduction in credit availability with the potential for adversely affecting the real economy.[1] There are at least two contesting views on the causes of systemic risk. In the so-called micro-prudential view, the systemic risk arises from contagion of the failure of a financial institution to the rest of the financial sector. As short- term creditors of an institution demand immediacy against its long-term assets ("run"), short- term creditors of inter-connected or similar institutions may demand such immediacy too. In contrast, in the so-called macro-prudential view, the systemic risk arises from the collective failure of many financial institutions because of their common risk factor exposures. In this view, when short-term creditors of an institution demand immediacy against long-term assets, there is a disruptive run only if other institutions are unable to acquire the long-term assets at fair values; in particular, if institutions have correlated exposures, then other institutions are potentially facing runs too and assets must be sold at fire-sale prices, resulting in disorderly liquidations, potential allocation inefficiencies and a general increase in the rate of return on savings (which can induce hoarding behavior and cut-back on real-sector lending).

Although these two views are not mutually exclusive, much of the regulatory reforms take one view or the other. In the micro-prudential regulations, the focus is on the systemically important financial institutions (SIFIs) whereas in the macro-prudential regulations, the focus is (also) on the risk of a crisis in the financial sector and its spillover to the economy at large. Taking the micro-prudential view, both the Dodd–Frank Wall Street

[1]This definition is based on Acharya *et al.* (2010b). See, for example, Kaufman and Scott (2003) for other definitions.

Regulation and Consumer Protection Act (DFA) signed into law by President Obama in July 2010 in the US and, internationally, Basel III focus on single financial institutions.

SIFIs consist of financial intermediaries that include not only commercial banks taking deposits and making loans but also investment banks, money market funds, mutual funds, insurance firms, and potentially, even hedge funds, whose failure poses a systemic risk to the financial system. This systemic risk can occur through multiple forms which include counterparty risk on other financial institutions, asset liquidations that can produce a depressing effect on asset prices, liquidity hoarding that raises funding costs in interbank markets even for safe firms, and an information contagion effect resulting in a significant reduction in overall market liquidity. Therefore, any mechanism set up by the regulators to deal with the insolvency of SIFIs must follow at least four basic principles (Acharya *et al.*, 2010a):

(1) The counterparty risk of the SIFIs must be contained through regulations including the imposition of capital requirements, margin rules, and limitation on risky investments *ex ante.*
(2) There needs to be a procedure for dealing with large amounts of illiquid assets whose forced sales can have a catastrophic effect on the financial system.
(3) The resolution mechanism should be able to identify insolvent institutions promptly as they can become pockets where financial resources of the economy can get trapped, potentially creating funding problems even for otherwise solvent firms.
(4) There must be well-defined rules for what happens to the liabilities of the financial institution when it fails, for otherwise, a run on most of the institution's liabilities will occur, potentially leading to a system-wide run.

Furthermore, since many SIFIs operate across borders (global SIFIs — G-SIFIs) and, as we have witnessed in the recent financial crisis, their failure can threaten the integrity of the entire global financial system, to the above four principles we must add:

(5) The national resolution mechanisms should be amenable to easy international coordination for the effective resolution of G-SIFIs.

When the collapse or near collapse of such financial institutions as Bear Stearns, Lehman Brothers, and AIG after the onset of the global financial crisis in 2007 revealed the inability of the existing resolution mechanisms to deal with the failure of SIFIs clear, the US was the first mover with the Dodd–Frank Act. To address the concerns about the inability of the existing resolution mechanisms to handle the failure of SIFIs, Title II of the DFA created the Orderly Liquidation Authority (OLA) as a new mechanism. However, as it is stated fairly clearly in Title II of the DFA, the OLA is not a resolution but liquidation mechanism.[2]

Putting aside the question of whether such liquidation — rather than a resolution — authority focusing on individual financial institutions is sufficient to achieve the DFA-stated goals of inducing market discipline and mitigating moral hazard, the question of whether the OLA can address the systemic risk associated with such systemically important markets as the sale and repurchase agreement ("repo") market or such systemically important sectors of small institutions as the money market mutual funds (MMMFs) remains debatable.[3] Although we discuss our concerns regarding the OLA in the next section in detail, let us give a simple example from September 2008 to illustrate how the OLA may fail in containing the systemic risk:

After the Lehman Brothers' bankruptcy filed on September 15, 2008, its outstanding debt collapsed in price almost immediately. Since one of the largest MMMFs, the Reserve Primary Fund, was highly exposed to Lehman Brothers' collapsing short-term debt, the next day its net asset value (NAV) fell below par. Since MMMFs offer stable NAV and investors can redeem anytime at par, an immediate run on the Reserve Primary Fund occurred, causing it to shut down.

This failure opened up the possibility that other MMMFs were similarly exposed, and a run on the MMMFs began. Since MMMFs are a primary source for the commercial paper market, this run opened up the possibility of capital shortfalls at many financial institutions that needed to roll

[2]HR 4173, Title II, "Orderly Liquidation Authority," Sec. 24, "Orderly Liquidation of Covered Financial Companies."

[3]See, Acharya *et al.* (2010a, 2011) for detailed discussions.

over commercial paper. Only after the government guaranteed the MMMF deposits 100%, the run came to a halt and the slide was stopped.

Under the OLA, if invoked as described in Title II of the DFA, the Reserve Primary Fund would have been placed into a receivership administered by the Federal Deposit Insurance Corporation (FDIC) to be liquidated (assuming that the Reserve Primary Fund — or the money market funds sector as a whole — were deemed systemically important by the Financial Stability Oversight Council, set up under the DFA). Although the FDIC could have borrowed from the Treasury to finance the liquidation, if the proceeds from liquidation were insufficient to repay the Treasury, the FDIC would have had to claw back from creditors any amounts received in excess of what they would have received in an ordinary liquidation.[4] Given that the investors of MMMFs were offered stable NAV and promised that they could redeem anytime at par, it is evident that a liquidation authority such as the OLA — which, with its focus on eliminating the moral hazard associated with the "too-big-to-fail" status, recovers from creditors any amounts received in excess of what they would have received in an ordinary liquidation — neither could have nor will have stopped the slide in such an episode.[5] An orderly liquidation of the assets of the Reserve Primary Fund was not even an issue then. Furthermore, neither was the Reserve Primary Fund "too-big-to-fail" despite its $64.8 billion worth of assets prior to its shut down nor was it even an SIFI on its own right. What was systemically important in September 2008 was the $3.5 trillion financial sector of MMMFs. The intervention had to be done at the sector level to avoid a possible collapse of the entire financial system.

Another problem associated with the OLA is that it does not apply to the foreign subsidiaries of the G-SIFIs. For example, when Lehman Brothers filed for Chapter 11 protection in September 2008, this action triggered well over 60 insolvency proceedings worldwide, some of which were particularly harmful to global financial stability (Acharya, Adler and Richardson, 2011).

[4] If there is any remaining shortfall, the FDIC can levy an assessment on all financial companies deemed an SIFI by the involved regulators.

[5] Had the MMMFs offered floating rather than stable NAV, there might not have been a run on the Reserve Primary Fund, entailing the system-wide run on all MMMFs, of course. However, in such a scenario, all MMMFs would be disintermediated by the bank money market accounts rapidly.

Even if the OLA existed at the time of the Lehman Brothers' insolvency, the assets and liabilities of its UK prime brokerage would have been resolved under the UK law. Although in response to the G20 call for action, the Financial Stability Board (FSB) issued recently a new international standard for resolution mechanisms "*so that any financial institution, whatever its size and complexity, can be resolved without disruption to the financial system and without taxpayer solvency support*",[6] it is still unclear how this new standard will be implemented in the US and can be reconciled with the OLA.

Furthermore, even the FSB issued a new international standard, described in its November 2011 "*Key Attributes*" document,[7] which focuses on individual financial institutions that are to be deemed globally systemically important, i.e., G-SIFI. To see why this might be a problem, take, for example, the re-hypothecation of hedge funds' assets held at Lehman's UK prime brokerage unit during the company's bankruptcy. The then UK Law (which was changed later) gave the ownership of these assets to Lehman's creditors. This led not only to runs on hedge funds but also to overall uncertainty about which assets at financial institutions were safe and which were not (Acharya, Adler, and Richardson, 2011). No resolution mechanism focusing on G-SIFIs, even if internationally coordinated as described in "*Key Attributes*," could have worked quickly enough to stop these effects.

Finally, while there were indeed runs on SIFIs in this and previous crises, there were also a large number of collective runs on relatively smaller financial institutions, especially in the so-called "shadow banking," such as on hedge funds, special purpose vehicles (conduits and SIVs), and, as discussed earlier, money market funds. For instance, the asset-backed commercial paper (ABCP) run on conduits and SIVs sponsored by commercial banks starting August 8, 2007 (see Acharya, Schnabl and Suarez, 2009) highlights that a collection of small institutions and an entire class of claims or markets can also be systemically important, i.e., their failure can lead to system-wide loss of financial intermediation.

With these in mind and taking the macro-prudential view, we propose an alternative set of resolution mechanisms, based on the insights of Acharya, Adler and Richardson (2011), which is not at the level of SIFIs

[6] See www.financialstabilityboard.org/press/pr_111104dd.pdf.
[7] See www.financialstabilityboard.org/publications/r_111104bb.pdf.

but at the level of SIALs of financial institutions, whether these institutions are deemed systemically important or not. Systemically important liabilities (SILs) can be defined broadly as those liabilities of highly leveraged entities that are assets of other highly leveraged entities and, therefore, when faced with haircuts in case of default, would trigger runs on other entities. Examples of SILs include deposits, repos, and over-the-counter (OTC) derivatives. Similarly, systemically important assets (SIAs) can be defined broadly as those assets that are either SILs of other highly leveraged entities or potentially illiquid, high-risk assets financed through SILs. Examples of SIAs include exposures to SIFIs, asset-backed commercial paper (ABCP), and risky repo collaterals such as mortgage-backed securities (MBSs). To the extent possible, the set of mechanisms should be expanded to cover as many classes of SIAs and SILs as possible.[8]

What we propose is that, instead of attempting the regulation of SIFIs (a "top-down" approach to regulating SIALs), prudential regulation be built in the form of a "bottom-up" approach — one that works at the level of the SIALs rather than at the level of the SIFI that owns them. Under the "bottom-up" approach, there would be an automatic stabilizer built for each SIAL. The automatic stabilizers could be in the form of government-provided but appropriately charged deposit insurance, centrally cleared SIALs with initial and variation margins or haircuts charged by a clearing-house or dedicated resolution authority for those SIALs, and in extreme cases, lender-of-last-resort from the central bank against eligible assets (but to avoid moral hazard, only to firms that pay a market-rate fee). This way, when an SIFI fails, it is not the orderly resolution of an individual SIFI that has to be effected, but rather the resolution of its various SIALs; the parts of its capital structure that are not systemically important would be resolved by market-determined contracts and relevant bankruptcy procedures. A particularly attractive feature of the "bottom-up" approach is that it requires no uniform institution-level insolvency process and therefore might be the simplest way of achieving international agreement on

[8]A detailed discussion of our approach, originally proposed by Acharya, Adler, and Richardson (2011), can be found in their document, whereas a detailed analysis of many reasons that warrant macro-prudential regulations rather than micro-prudential regulations can be found in Acharya (2011).

resolving the financial distress of G-SIFIs (as long as there is global agreement on resolution mechanisms for SIALs).

As a leading example of our approach, we propose a potential repo resolution authority for reforming the repo market and illustrate how our approach can be implemented for this particular class of SIALs.[9] A repurchase agreement — also known as a "sale and repurchase agreement," or more popularly as a repo — is a short-term transaction between two parties in which one party borrows cash from the other by pledging a financial security as collateral. One important feature of the US repo market is that all transactions that fall under the umbrella of repos are exempt from the automatic stay in bankruptcy and therefore all repo transactions can be liquidated following a bankruptcy filing. As is well known, the ongoing global financial crisis was triggered in the summer of 2007 essentially by a "run" on two Bear Stearns hedge funds speculating in the potentially illiquid subprime mortgages by borrowing short-term in the US repo market and eventually on Bear Stearns in March 2008. In the section titled "Repo Market and the Crisis of 2007–2009," we describe in detail, these "repo bank runs" and the role the fire-sale liquidation of the repo collaterals — that are exempt from the automatic stay — played in the ensuing systemic crisis.

Our proposal for resolving repo runs is to create a "Repo Resolution Authority" in each jurisdiction with significant repo transactions. The repo collaterals will, in general, not be exempt from bankruptcy of borrowing financial firms, except when the collateral is in the form of highest quality government or government-guaranteed bonds. All other repo collateral on defaulting repo transactions will be resolved by the repo resolution authority, which makes an immediate "liquidity" payment to repo financiers. The immediate payment is based on conservative assumptions (a "haircut") about the liquidation proceeds from the collateral. The realized proceeds will, in general, exceed or be smaller than the conservative payment and will be repatriated or clawed-back from repo financiers. In the process, however, the repo resolution authority takes on credit risk of the repo financiers. To manage this credit risk and to attenuate the moral hazard induced on part of repo financiers, the repo resolution authority would include as

[9]The proposal and discussion to follow elaborate on the initial case the authors made in Acharya and Öncü (2010).

eligible only relatively high-quality collateral; charge repo financiers an *ex ante* fee for the liquidity enhancement provided in case of default in a manner that is commensurate with the residual credit risk borne by the facility; require that eligible repo financiers meet pre- specified solvency criteria; and impose a concentration limit at the level of individual repo financiers, as well as on the financier's overall portfolio size.

In effect, the repo resolution authority does resemble a clearinghouse for repo contracts, in that it has the right to suspend automatic conversion of repo claims into liquidations of underlying collateral. It takes on the liquidation rights itself but ensures that its provision of liquidity to the market in case of default does not engender insolvency concerns. The repo financiers, which face participation criteria and haircuts in good times, would pass on the relevant costs to borrowers in the repo markets. Collateral that is not eligible for the repo resolution authority would remain outside of bankruptcy exemption as well as outside of the liquidity enhancement provided by the repo resolution authority; these contracts would thus be relatively subordinated in the capital structure of financial firms and could be subject to prudential capital requirements or minimum haircut/over-collateralization requirements (as with other parts of the capital structure of financial firms).

An important issue that our proposed resolution approach highlights is that of the desirability of granting unconditional liquidation rights ("safe harbor" provisions) to certain claims of creditors ("qualified financial contracts") of financial institutions. The advantage of granting such rights is to extend money-like immediacy properties to such claims and enhance the capacity of financial institutions to generate liquidity. The macro-prudential view of financial crises highlights, however, that in times of a substantial aggregate shock, the system may be rendered incapable of granting such immediacy to *all* creditors of financial institutions: not all demandable deposits can be paid off without resorting to bank failures and loss of relationship loans, or not all repo or derivative counter parties can be paid off without engaging in disorderly fire-sales and generating associated externalities.

Indeed, in much the same way that commercial bank clearinghouses in the pre-Federal Reserve era were forced to suspend conversion of immediacy of demandable deposits in order to stem bank runs, our proposal recommends that safe harbor provisions be conditionally suspended when there has been a sufficiently adverse common shock to the financial institutions. When such systemic exception is invoked on safe-harbor provisions, our resolution approach grants partial immediacy to the affected claims (through the repo resolution authority or the lender of last resort), but suspends immediacy of the remaining part, forcing them to bear long-run risk of the underlying collateral or assets backing the claims. The long- run risk is managed in an orderly manner by such suspension, making it clear that the clearinghouses, repo resolution authorities, and the lender of last resort must also be granted asset-liquidation rights in times of systemic crises. Equally importantly, since the management of such risk exposes these authorities to potential losses, they are also granted the rights to contain *a priori* the extent of immediacy granted by financial firms to their creditors.

We organize the rest of the paper as follows: In the second section, we describe some specific details of the DFA, and evaluate it with respect to the efficiency of the process and its ability to mitigate moral hazard and systemic risk. In the third section, we describe how the repo market came to play such an important role in securitized banking in the US, discuss its critical role in the form of runs in the crisis, and argue a case for reforming the repo market based on our analysis. We then outline in the fourth section, our proposed "Repo Resolution Authority" for such reform, and compare and contrast it with an interesting precedent, the Federal Government Liquidation Corporation proposed by Senator Glass in the early 1930s, in the fifth section. Finally, in the last section, we discuss how our proposed resolution mechanism for the repo market may be coordinated globally and present our concluding remarks.

The Dodd–Frank Resolution Mechanism for Nonbank SIFIs

A central objective of the DFA is to create a new resolution mechanism for nonbank SIFIs and bring them within the FDIC insurance model. Established in 1933, the FDIC is an independent federal agency of the US that insures deposits at its member banks and savings and loan institutions, currently up to $250,000 per depositor per institution. If a member institution fails, it is taken into receivership by the FDIC, which within a few days either facilitates a merger with another FDIC-insured institution or pays each depositor for the insured portion of their accounts at the closed institution and then liquidates the closed institution's assets. Since the Federal Deposit Insurance Reform Act of 2005 signed into law by President Bush in February 2006 and became effective March 31, 2006, the FDIC finances the liquidations from the Deposit Insurance Fund (DFI) to which member institutions pay an *ex ante* insurance fee based on the balance of insured deposits, as well as on the FDIC assessed risk the institution poses to the DFI.[10] And, if further funds are needed, the FDIC can draw on a line of credit with the US Treasury. Furthermore, the FDIC deposit insurance is backed by the *full faith and credit* of the US government, which means that the resources of the US government stand behind FDIC-insured depositors.

According to Sheila Bair (FDIC, 2011), the former chair of the FDIC, the DFA resolution mechanism has these basic elements:

(1) Title I: The establishment of the Financial Stability Oversight Council (FSOC), chaired by the Secretary of the Treasury and composed of members from the other financial regulatory agencies, with the responsibility of designating SIFIs or "covered companies" that will be subject to heightened supervision by the Federal Reserve Board of Governors (FRB);
(2) Title I: The requirement for the preparation of detailed resolution plans — often referred to as "living wills" — by covered companies to demonstrate that they are resolvable under the bankruptcy laws if they run into severe financial stress and provide valuable advance information that will assist in implementing their orderly liquidation, if necessary;
(3) Title II: The prohibition of bailouts of individual companies by providing an alternative to bankruptcy with the establishment of an OLA, which allows the FDIC to resolve nonbank financial companies by using many of the same trustee powers over systemic nonbank financial companies that it has long used to manage failed bank receiverships.

The DFA characterizes nonbank financial companies that can be covered under the OLA quite broadly. The companies eligible for covered financial company (CFC) designation include bank holding companies,

[10] For a history prior to 2006, see: http://www.fdic.gov/deposit/insurance/history.html.

nonbank financial companies supervised by the FRB, and any other company predominantly engaged in activities that the FRB determined financial in nature, as well as the US subsidiaries of these eligible companies. However, the DFA resolution mechanism is an iterative process: First comes the attempted resolution, as described in the living wills through the bankruptcy code in a manner that "*does not pose a systemic risk.*" If the attempt fails, then follows the "*orderly liquidation*" under the OLA, presumably avoiding the systemic risk and therefore the "*too-big-fail*" bailout of the SIFIs with the tax-payer funds. Or so goes the theory.

The above is one of the main problems associated with the new DFA resolution mechanism. Under the DFA resolution mechanism, a failed non-bank SIFI goes through normal bankruptcy or other applicable insolvency law first.[11] Only after the Secretary of the Treasury, upon recommendation by the FRB by a two-thirds vote and a similar vote by the FDIC (or, in some cases, other involved regulators), in consultation with the President, determines that the failed financial company should be subject to OLA and the board of directors of the CFC approves the Secretary of the Treasury's determination, the FDIC is appointed as receiver of the CFC. Otherwise, the Secretary of the Treasury files a petition with the US District Court for the District of Columbia seeking judicial review of his decision. If the District Court finds the Secretary's petition "arbitrary and capricious" within 24 hours, then the petition is denied. Otherwise, either through Court approval or, if the District Court does not make a determination within 24 hours of receipt of the petition, through operation of law, the petition is granted, and the FDIC is appointed as receiver of the CFC. If the FDIC is appointed as receiver of the CFC either through the first or the second of the above processes, then the board of directors of the CFC — as well

[11] We acknowledge at the outset that our discussion of the OLA is based on the Dodd–Frank Act's "letter of the law," whereas it is clear from its specific implementation that is currently underway that some of the criticisms we raise concerning OLA are being partly addressed. Since the implementation details are still evolving, our presentation of the OLA can be interpreted as a "straw man" representing the micro-prudential view of resolution authority, rather than simply as a criticism of the Dodd–Frank Act's vision of the OLA. We note, however, that most of the fixes under the OLA's implementation of concerns we raise also operate at the level of individual financial institutions, rather than taking a collective or macro-prudential view of the resolution authority (as we propose).

as other aggrieved parties — has 30 days to appeal the appointment of the FDIC as receiver.

There are at least two issues with the above: The first issue is that the regulators may wait too long to intervene and have no choice but to put the SIFI through the liquidation process. This is a very risky proposition in terms of systemic risk, as we describe below. The second issue is that, despite the commendable efforts to expedite the liquidation process, the procedure may not be sufficiently fast to contain the ensuing run on liabilities that can be pulled immediately. Because of these uncertainties underlying the OLA process, it is highly likely that (Acharya *et al.*, 2010a):

(1) Runs on these and other short-term liabilities of the institution will occur in anticipation of such determination, creating a self-fulfilling OLA event;
(2) Holders of the institution's longer-term debt and equity will try to sell their holdings in secondary markets, putting pressure on the financial firm's position in capital markets;
(3) Runs on similar financial firms may occur, essentially leading to the regulators having no choice but an OLA determination for a significant part of the financial sector.

While any insolvency procedure is subject to these problems, it is unclear how the DFA resolution mechanism will address them through the OLA.

Another problem associated with the DFA resolution mechanism is the Orderly Liquidation Fund (OLF) on which the FDIC will be authorized to draw as the receiver. In the originally proposed bill, this fund was to be financed *ex ante* by risk-based assessments of the CFCs in such a way that the more systemically important the CFC, the larger the assessment. In the signed law, however, this provision was dropped. Instead, the FDIC will borrow from the Treasury and will repay the borrowings from creditors who receive funds in the OLA process that are greater than what they would have received in normal liquidation under the bankruptcy code. And, if this *claw-back* is not sufficient, the FDIC will repay from *ex post* assessments on bank holding companies with total assets of $50 billion or more and on any nonbank SIFI.

Although the FDIC's use of the OLF is discretionary, let us suppose that the FDIC used the OLF to finance the failed CFC as intended by the

DFA. That is, the failed CFC is supplied with liquidity but a portion of its assets — presumably equal in value to the loans extended — is retained for the OLF. However, if the CFC has failed because the value of its assets is less than that of its obligations, unless it is subsidized in receivership, its counterparties will not be paid in full and hence the risk of contagion will remain. Therefore, the OLA might not contain the systemic risk that the failure of a large, interconnected SIFI might undermine the financial system.

Consequently, it might be expected that the FDIC as the receiver will not use the OLF to achieve an orderly liquidation of the assets of the failed CFC, but rather will use it to bailout the failed CFC creditors. That is, to prevent contagion, the FDIC might be expected to satisfy counterparty claims that could not be paid from the assets of the failed CFC even if the assets are liquidated in an "orderly" fashion. This very likely to materialize bailout expectation — a perceived insurance that covers the losses of the creditors — creates moral hazard, the very risk the DFA aims to eliminate.

If, on the other hand, the claw-back provision of the OLA is indeed credible and, as a result, the creditors become the *de facto* insurers, then the DFA would realign incentives, eliminating the potential moral hazard as intended. The question then remains whether the FDIC as the receiver can claw back the money paid to creditors in excess of what they would have received in normal liquidation under the bankruptcy code after the "orderly" liquidation. If the perception is that the receiver can, then the bailout will have no effect. Under this scenario, however, as soon as it is remotely perceived that a CFC will be subject to the OLA, a large-scale run on the SILs, i.e., SILs of the failed CFC and similar financial institutions will occur.

Furthermore, even after ignoring all of the problems discussed above, there remains the question of who picks up the bill if all else fails to repay the Treasury. The DFA answer to this question is the financial industry itself. But the DFA imposed *ex post* assessments require that even the prudent financial companies pay for the failure of the others. This would be a problem even from merely an *ex post* perspective as the costs to the financial system could be substantial and might weigh against the ability of the system to provide credit, creating an illiquid financial system the DFA is intended to avoid. From an *ex ante* perspective, the problem is even worse.

The DFA plan for even the healthy financial institutions to pay the creditors of failed CFCs creates a free rider problem. This encourages all financial institutions to take excessive risks, leading to an even more fragile financial system and hence increasing the likelihood of deep financial crises.

Yet another principal difficulty in writing insolvency law for SIFIs is the issue of how to treat their so-called qualified financial contracts (QFCs). In the US, under the current bankruptcy code, QFCs include forwards, swaps, repos, and other OTC derivative contracts, and are essential for the functioning of SIFIs. In fact, what differentiates SIFIs from other financial institutions is essentially their substantial presence in the market for QFCs. The QFCs are related to our notion of SIALs, and whether a QFC is an SIL or SIA depends on the position taken in the QFC, as well as on the market conditions. For example, a long position in a call option is an SIA irrespective of the market conditions while a long position in an interest rate swap — that is, a fixed-payer interest rate swap — may be either an SIL or SIA depending on the market conditions.

The current US bankruptcy code, enacted in 1978, initially provided a *safe harbor* from *automatic stay* and other bankruptcy provisions for commodity and forward contracts. In this context, *safe harbor* means exemption from bankruptcy proceeding, whereas *automatic stay* means an injunction issued automatically by the bankruptcy court upon the filing of a bankruptcy that prohibits collection against the debtor or the debtor's property. The *safe harbor clause* allows the counterparty to the failed financial institution to terminate the QFCs and take control of what it is owed from the assets of the failed institution. With the Bankruptcy Abuse Prevention and Consumer Protection Act (BAPCPA) enacted in 2005, the safe harbor exception has been broadly expanded to cover such QFCs as cross-netting provisions, credit default swaps, interest rate swaps, and margin loans among other arrangements, including repos. We discuss how the BAPCPA reform of 2005 affected the repos in detail in subsequent sections. An excellent discussion of the advantages and disadvantages of the safe harbor clauses for QFCs can be found in Tuckman (2010), and we briefly review these below. See also Edwards and Morrison (2004), Jackson (2009), Miller (2009), Faubus (2010), and Roe (2010), among others.

The original motivation for the safe harbor status of the QFCs in the bankruptcy code was to reduce the systemic risk in the financial system.

Because most QFCs are either hedged or used as hedges continually, tying up counterparty QFC positions in bankruptcy would unwind the hedges in place and lead to wide-scale risk exposures for leveraged institutions. Moreover, if the underlying collaterals are tied up, the loss in potential liquidity for the counterparty might also have serious consequences. Either of these problems, together with uncertainty about when the failed institution QFCs would be cleared, could cause the associated markets to freeze. Hence, the safe harbor status granted to the QFCs has some merit.

However, the reduction in systemic risk arising from QFCs avoiding the automatic stay and related provisions in bankruptcy is replaced by another form of systemic risk involving fire sales of QFCs and funding illiquidity spirals. For example, consider the repo agreements. Many repo financiers are MMMFs subject to restrictions on average maturity of their investments. When they face default on a repo of a long-term asset such as mortgage-backed security (MBS), their typically overnight role as a lender in a repo financing gets translated into being the holder of a long-term asset. As a result, the MMMFs as the repo financier may be forced to liquidate the asset upon failure of their repo counterparty. Similarly, counterparties of a failing firm in a derivative contract might need to terminate and replace the contract right away as it might be serving as a hedge of some financial risk. Then, as counterparties liquidate the repo collateral all at once, or terminate and replace their derivative positions simultaneously, with the large number of trades and multiple participants, money markets and derivatives markets can be destabilized. In the recent crisis, there was considerable concern that a bankruptcy of SIFIs like AIG, Merrill Lynch, or Citigroup would have forced large amounts of mortgage-backed derivatives to be sold on the marketplace. Given widespread exposure to these securities by other financial institutions, these losses would have caused a funding liquidity freeze, resulting in even more sales and losses and therefore leading to a death spiral of large parts of the financial system.

An equally strong argument against the safe harbor is the regulatory arbitrage it creates within the system: counterparties can build up large concentrated exposures without much consequence. Specifically, because most QFCs can be engineered to mimic an underlying asset, there exist at least two claims with essentially the same economic behavior. However, these essentially same claims may be subject to different rules and therefore may have different implications for *ex ante* risks. For example, consider again a repo against an AAA-rated MBS. If the MBS is held on the banking book of an SIFI, it gets treated as a long-term holding subject typically to capital requirement against potential credit risk for a year. If the MBS is instead on the trading book as an available-for-sale security that is being rolled overnight in repo markets, then it gets treated as being sold and repurchased each day, so that as far as its capital requirement concerned, it is subject to market risk for only one day.

This transformation of a long-term asset into an overnight asset is primarily because of the repo financier's right to take over the asset in case of failure of the repo counterparty. However, as explained above, in many cases, repo financiers themselves cannot own these assets in the long run and must liquidate them upon failure of their repo counterparty. Therefore, the migration of the MBS from the banking to trading book lowers the capital requirement against it throughout the financial system, since no institution is holding capital for a scenario where there is systemic illiquidity under which some institution — most likely an institution which incurred a huge illiquidity discount in the fire sale of the asset — must hold the asset for the long run.

Such distortions push counterparties toward designing complex products that can help shift assets from the banking to the trading book, which are then financed using short-term repos in the repo market, away from the monitoring of regulators and at substantially lower capital requirements. The effective outcome is tremendous liquidity in repo markets for these products in good times, with systemic stress and fragility when the products are anticipated to experience losses. The expansion of safe harbor to repo transactions with underlying mortgage- based assets in the Bankruptcy Act of 2005 has thus been cited as one of the reasons for the growth in mortgage-based derivatives over the period from 2005 to 2007.

The DFA essentially treats QFCs the same way the FDIC treats them in receiverships not covered by the Act. That is, at the end of the first business day after a receivership commences, counterparties would be able to exercise their rights against the CFC such as to terminate, net out, set off, and apply collateral with respect to all their QFCs. Therefore, although the provision of a safe harbor under the DFA is not identical to that of the bankruptcy code, QFCs still benefit from special protection. An exception is that, until the end of the first business day after commencement, the FDIC would be allowed to transfer all (and only all) of the QFCs between the CFC and a given counterparty. Although such exceptions to the safe harbor clause make some sense to the extent the systemic risk of financial institutions might vary from one situation to the next, a better approach would be (Acharya, Adler, and Richardson, 2011) as follows:

(1) QFCs that are liquid should keep the exemption. Liquid QFCs will cause less systemic risk in fire sales, yet still allow counterparties to manage their risk without the uncertainty generated by the bankruptcy of a SIFI. Moreover, in order to get the exemption, counterparties will have an incentive to trade in liquid QFCs.
(2) QFCs that are illiquid — or potentially illiquid (such as repo contracts on MBSs) — should be subject to the ordinary rules of bankruptcy, including the automatic stay. The systemic risk underlying fire sales would be avoided, especially given that complex, illiquid transactions are more difficult to unwind. Of course, this would come at the cost of general liquidity of the counterparties and impact their ability to manage risk. To the extent regulators impose capital and liquidity standards, QFCs subject to the stay should apply higher liquidity standards to the counterparty.

Lastly, as we discussed in the previous section at length, the DFA resolution mechanism is completely domestic. This is an important problem because many US SIFIs operate globally, so that they are G-SIFIs. Furthermore, many G-SIFIs incorporated in other countries operate in the US as well. If a G-SIFI operating in the US needs to be liquidated in an orderly manner, the DFA cannot specify how its SIALs in other countries will be resolved. The resolution of G-SIFIs requires an international arrangement. Although the Financial Stability Board — established by G7 in 1999 and re-established by G20 in 2009 to coordinate at the international level the work of national financial authorities and international standard setting bodies — issued a new international standard for resolution mechanisms in November 2011, as we mentioned earlier, no international resolution mechanism has yet been proposed by any international body. This leaves the global financial system still wide open to significant systemic risk that may result from a disorderly liquidation of SIALs somewhere in the world, thereby requiring "too-big-to-fail" or "too-many-to-fail" or "too-interconnected-fail" bailouts of SIFIs everywhere, even if the DFA resolution mechanism manages to avoid a disorderly liquidation of associated US-based SIALs in spite of the problems we pointed out above.

The US Repo Market

Recall that a repurchase agreement is a short-term transaction between two parties in which one party borrows cash from the other by pledging a financial security as collateral. In a repo transaction, the collateral provider enters into a "sale and repurchase agreement" or, in short, a *repo*. The cash provider enters into a "purchase and resale agreement," or, in short, a *reverse repo*. Hence, every repo is also a reverse repo and vice versa. The perspective depends on who is the seller and who is the purchaser.

The day the repo is initiated is called the sale date, and the day the repo is terminated is called the purchase date. The difference, if any, between the values of the collateral and loan is called the "haircut" or margin. The haircut, if any, is a protection against the counterparty risk in the transaction. In principle, either the cash or the collateral provider may be subject to a haircut. When the cash provider is subject to a haircut, then the haircut is the margin required by the collateral provider as protection against the potential value gain of the collateral in case the cash provider fails to deliver the collateral on the purchase date so that the collateral provider has to buy a substitute. When the collateral provider is subject to a haircut, then the haircut is the margin required by the cash provider as protection against the potential value loss of the collateral in case the collateral provider fails to come back, and the cash provider has to take ownership of the collateral, sell it and recover the loss.

In the US repo market, loans are mostly extended overnight — that is, they are one-day transactions. Overnight repos constitute about half of all repo transactions, and most of them are open, i.e., they roll over automatically until either party chooses to exit. Other repo transactions, called term repos, have terms longer than one day but shorter than one year, although the vast majority have maturities of three months or less. Participants in the repo market include commercial banks, investment banks, hedge funds, mutual funds, pension funds, money market funds, municipalities, corporations, and other owners of large amounts of idle cash, as well as the Fed and primary securities dealers.

The Fed participates in the repo market mainly to implement its monetary policy; primary securities dealers participate mostly to finance their market-making and risk management activities. On the other hand, owners of large amounts of idle cash engage in the repo market mainly for two reasons: (1) to get better interest rates in the repo market compared with deposits at commercial banks and (2) for insurance purposes; while large deposits at commercial banks are not insured, deposits at "repo banks" are secured by debt used as collateral.

Evolution of the US Repo Market

The repos were introduced to the US financial market by the Federal Reserve in 1917. Repos allowed the Fed to extend credit to its member banks, after a war-time tax on interest payments on commercial paper had made it difficult for banks to raise funds in the commercial paper market. Later in the 1920s, the New York Fed used repos secured with bankers' acceptances to extend credit to dealers to encourage the development of a liquid secondary market for acceptances. Repos fell from grace during the Great Depression after massive bank failures and low interest rates, only to make a comeback after the Treasury-Federal Reserve Accord of 1951 "that renewed emphasis on controlling inflation rather than keeping interest rates low" (Garbade, 2006).

Early repos in the US had two distinguishing features. First, accrued interest was excluded from the price of the repo securities. Second, even though the creditor could sell or deliver the repo securities to settle a prior sale at prices that included the accrued interest during the term of the repo, ownership of the repo securities rested with the debtor. These features had the following implications: (1) the repo securities were underpriced; (2) the creditor had to remit to the debtor any coupon payments on the repo securities during the term of the repo; and (3) in the event of a bankruptcy of the debtor, the repo securities were subject to automatic stay, that is, the creditor could not take ownership of the repo securities and sell them immediately.[12] These features remained intact until the early 1980s.

During the period of high inflation in the 1970s and early 1980s, rising short-term interest rates made repos a highly attractive short-term investment to holders of large amounts of idle cash. Increasing numbers of corporations, local and state governments, and at the encouragement of securities dealers, even school districts and other small creditors started depositing their idle cash in "repo banks" to earn interest rather than depositing money in commercial banks that did not pay interest on demand deposits. Furthermore, the US Treasury started borrowing heavily after 1974, eventually changing the status of the US from a creditor to a debtor nation and increasing the volume of marketable Treasury debt significantly. This led to a parallel growth in government securities dealers' positions and financing, and the repo market grew by leaps and bounds. Figure 1 depicts the size of the market from January 1970 to January 1986, as reported by the Federal Reserve Board.

The first important change to repo contracts came after the spectacular collapse of Drysdale Government Securities Inc. in 1982. Despite its limited equity, Drysdale had been acquiring substantial amounts of debt securities through reverse repos and at prices that excluded the accrued interest. Drysdale then short-sold these securities to third parties at prices that included the accrued interest. Drysdale used the surplus thus generated to raise more capital and to make interest payments to its reverse repo counterparties. However, when interest rates moved against Drysdale in

[12]However, there appears to have been some deliberate vagueness about this until a government securities dealer, Lombard-Wall, collapsed in 1982, and the Federal Bankruptcy Court of New York imposed an automatic stay on the repo securities that Lombard-Wall had used as collateral. See http://www.nytimes.com/1982/12/17/business/lombard-wall.html. This point had always been uncertain until the 1982 and 1984 amendments to Code 11 of the US Bankruptcy Code. In a "true sale," the buyer is not subject to the automatic stay. For instance, if an automobile dealer bought a car from GM the day before it filed for bankruptcy, it could resell the car without asking for permission of the court. However, if the deal were financed by GM, the dealer would need a court order to sell the car. The repo transactions are structured formally as a true sale, free of the automatic stay. The question was, and still is, whether courts would reclassify it as a secured transaction. Before 1982–1984, this would inflict the stay on the collateral taker. After 1982–1984, it would only affect the rights of a secured party, which are more limited than the rights of a buyer.

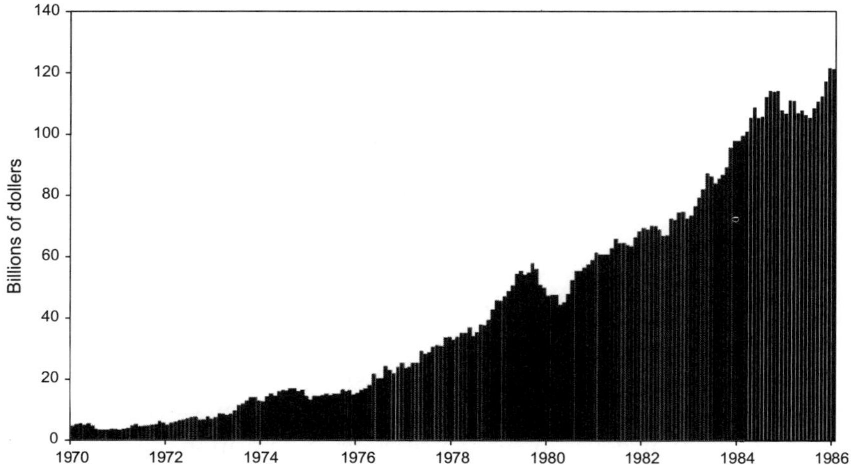

Fig. 1. Monthly averages of daily outstanding overnight and term repos, 1970–1986.

Source: Federal Reserve Board.

May 1982, the cumulative losses on its interest rate bets depleted its capital. On May 17, 1982, Drysdale failed to pay the interest on the securities it had borrowed. When that news hit the repo market, it came to a near halt, forcing the Fed to intervene as a lender of last resort to calm fears and prevent a collapse. This near collapse exposed the systemic risk associated with the exclusion of accrued interest, and therefore, largely at the encouragement of the Federal Reserve Bank of New York, inclusion of accrued interest in the invoice price of repo securities became standard market practice (for details, see Garbade, 2006).

The foundation for the second important change in repo contracts was laid when another government securities dealer, Lombard-Wall, with $2 billion in assets and comparable liabilities, collapsed three months later in August 1982. Prior to Lombard-Wall's August 12, 1982, filing with the Federal Bankruptcy Court of New York, there had been no precedent court case in which the question of whether repos were secured loans or independent sale and repurchase agreements was directly addressed. If repos were classified as sale and repurchase agreements, then creditors could take immediate possession of the repo securities; if, on the other hand, they were classified as secured loans, then repo securities would have been subject to automatic stay. On August 17, 1982, the Federal Bankruptcy Court of New York announced that Lombard-Wall's repos were secured loans and issued a restraining order prohibiting the sale of these repo securities. Although submissions by the Federal Reserve Bank of New York and several others argued that this decision would undermine the liquidity of the repo market, the court reaffirmed its decision a month later (Garbade, 2006). This removed the vagueness associated with whether repos were secured loans or independent sale and repurchase agreements. Despite this ruling, investment banks, mutual funds, and other large financial institutions favored the exception of repo securities from the application of automatic stay, although they seemed unwilling to write contracts that clearly stated that a repo was a pair of outright sale and repurchase transactions.[13]

Debates continued until another securities dealer, Lion Capital Group, collapsed in May 1984, and a bankruptcy court placed an automatic stay on Lion's repo securities.[14] Shortly thereafter, Congress ended the debates about the classification of repos by enacting the Bankruptcy Amendments and Federal Judgeship Act of 1984, exempting repos on Treasury and federal agency securities, as well as those on bank certificates of deposit and bankers' acceptances, from the application of automatic stay. Since then, repos on these securities have been exempt from automatic stay.

Dealer delivery failures in the 1980s also gave rise to the emergence of "tri-party repos," in which the counterparties used a third agent, called the tri-party agent, to manage the collateral. The tri-party agent ensured that the collateral pledged was sufficient and met eligibility requirements, and all parties agreed to use the collateral prices supplied by the tri-party agent. Today, there are only two tri-party agents in the US, called the "tri-party clearing banks": Bank of New York Mellon and J P Morgan Chase. Tri-party repos became popular partly because of these efficiency gains associated with the intermediation role of the clearing banks. Indeed, the efficiency gains, and the fact that so many institutions use it, are among the reasons the Federal Reserve uses the tri-party repo market to implement monetary policy (Copeland, Martin, and Walker, 2010). However, because

[13]Even if they did, a court would be free to reclassify them.

[14]"Lion Capital's Collapse Raises Issue of Unresolved Legal Status of 'Repos'," *Wall Street Journal*, May 8, 1984.

these two clearing banks have a huge amount of exposure on an intraday basis, regulators expressed concerns that fears of the financial health of a major dealer or clearing bank could quickly spread contagion throughout the market. Indeed, the Fed's decision to extend its lender of last resort support to the systemically important primary dealers during the recent financial crisis through the so-called "Primary Dealer Credit Facility" (PDCF) was partly a result of these concerns.

The "tri-party settlement" is one of two settlement methods used in the US.[15] The other is the "delivery versus payment" (DVP) method. For example, the Federal Reserve's reverse repos are settled via the DVP method, wherein securities are moved against simultaneous payment. The Federal Reserve sends collateral to the clearing bank of its reverse repo counterparty, triggering a simultaneous movement of money against the collateral on the sale date. On the purchase date, the counterparty sends the collateral back to the Fed, which triggers the simultaneous return of the counterparty's funds. Such repo transactions are called *bilateral repo* transactions. Dealers also use DVP repos to obtain funding. However, because DVP repos are not as convenient as tri-party repos, they are believed to represent a small share of dealer funding (Copeland, Martin, and Walker, 2010). There is also the GCF repo® market dealers use to exchange cash and general collateral with each other (Fleming and Garbade, 2003), as well as an interdealer repo market for less liquid collateral (Gorton and Metrick, 2009a, 2009b).

Although the repo market grew rapidly after the Bankruptcy Amendments and Federal Judgeship Act of 1984, until the mid-1990s, it remained confined mostly to US government debt, federal agency debt, corporate debt, and federal agency mortgage-backed securities. However, since the mid-1990s, it has grown to include a broad range of debt instruments as collateral: all types of private-label MBS, such as residential mortgage-backed securities (RMBS) and commercial mortgage-backed securities (CMBS); all types of asset-backed securities (ABS), such as automobile loans, credit cards, and student loans; and tranches of structured products such as collateralized mortgage obligations (CMOs), collateralized loan obligations

[15]See Copeland *et al.* (2012) for an excellent yet brief overview of the US Repo Market, as of June 25, 2012.

(CLOs), collateralized debt obligations (CDOs), and the like (see Gorton, 2009).

The last significant change to the repo contracting conventions came in 2005. In April 2005, Congress enacted the Bankruptcy Abuse Prevention and Consumer Protection Act of 2005 (BAPCPA), which took effect in October 2005. BAPCPA expanded the definition of repurchase agreements to include mortgage loans, mortgage-related securities, and interest from mortgage loans or mortgage-related securities. This meant that, as of October 2005, repo contracts on even MBS, CMOs, CMBS, and CDOs backed by mortgages and the like as collateral, became exempt from automatic stay. We summarize the milestones in the evolution of the US repo market in Box 1.

Furthermore, although repos collateralized by other financial securities such as corporate bonds, municipal loans, and equities are excluded from

Box 1. Timeline of important events in the US repo market.

1917	Federal Reserve introduces repos; accrued interest is excluded from the invoice price of repo securities and repo securities are subject to automatic stay.
1929	Use of repos declines with the onset of the Great Depression.
1951	Congress enacts the Treasury-Federal Reserve Accord of 1951 bringing repos back into favor.
1982	Accrued interest is included in the invoice prices of repo securities.
1984	Congress enacts the Bankruptcy Amendments and Federal Judgeship Act of 1984 to exempt repos on Treasury and federal agency securities, as well as on bank certificates of deposit and bankers' acceptances, from the application of automatic stay.
2005	Congress enacts the Bankruptcy Abuse Prevention and Consumer Protection Act of 2005 to expand the definition of repos to include mortgage loans, mortgage-related securities, or interest from mortgage loans or mortgage securities; all mortgage-related repo securities become exempt from the application of automatic stay.

the Bankruptcy Code definition of "repurchase agreements" and hence do not qualify for exemption from automatic stay for "repurchase agreements," since they qualify as "securities contracts," they are subject to safe harbor from automatic stay for the QFCs discussed in the previous section. To sum up, all transactions that fall under the umbrella of repos will likely be exempt from the automatic stay in bankruptcy either as "repos" or as "securities contracts" and therefore all repo transactions can be liquidated following a bankruptcy filing.

No official statistics of the actual size of the repo market have been collected since inclusion of almost all types of securitized debt as collateral was allowed in repo agreements. Therefore, there is no official information on the evolution of the size of the repo market over the past quarter of a century. Figure 2 depicts the evolution of financing by primary dealers in the US government securities market from 1996 through 2011 and offers a feel for the exponential growth of the repo market since the mid-1990s. Meanwhile, Fig. 3, reproduced from the FRBNY Task Force on Tri-Party Infrastructure White Paper (2010), shows the growth of the tri-party repo market from May 2002 through May 2010.

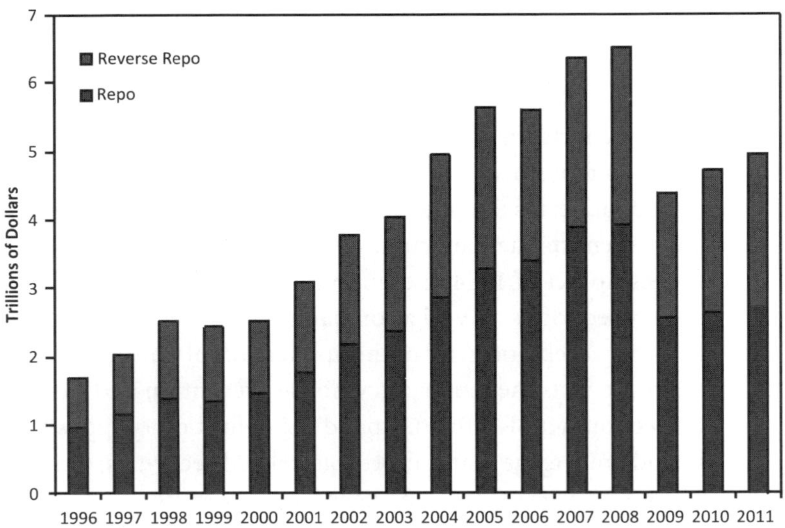

Fig. 2. Annual averages of daily financing by US government securities primary dealers.

Source: Securities Industry and Financial Markets Association.

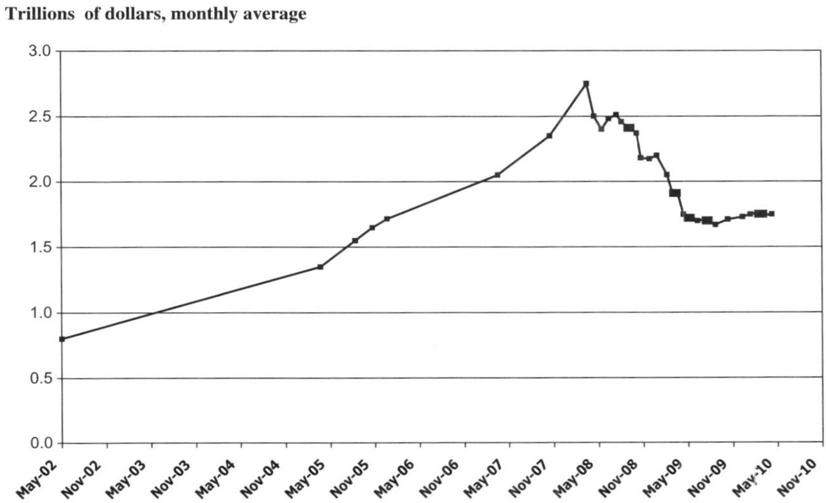

Fig. 3. Growth of tri-party repo market.

Source: FRBNY Task Force On Tri-Party Infrastructure White Paper (2010).

Repo Market and the Crisis of 2007–2009

The financial crisis of 2007–2009 was a crisis not only of the traditional banks but also of the shadow banks.[16] Unlike traditional banks, shadow banks did not have access to the safety nets designed to prevent wholesale runs on banks — deposit insurance and the central bank as the lender of last resort — until 2008. Although there was no wholesale run on the traditional banking system in this period, we effectively observed a run on shadow banks that led to the demise of a significant part of the shadow banking system. Since repo financing was the basis of most of the leveraged positions of the shadow banks, a large part of the run occurred in the repo market. Other important runs that occurred in this period were on mortgage lenders, asset-backed commercial

[16] A shadow bank is a nonbank financial institution that behaves like a bank, borrows short-term in rollover debt markets, leverages itself significantly, and lends and invests in longer-term in illiquid assets. Unlike banks, however, the shadow banks are much less regulated (Acharya and Öncü, 2010).

paper (ABCP) programs, structured investment vehicles (SIVs), and money market funds.

When the housing market changed course in the first quarter of 2006, the subprime mortgage market began to deteriorate. The first casualty of the continued weakness in the housing market was in the form of the collapse of two highly levered Bear Stearns hedge funds that invested in subprime mortgages on June 20, 2007. The collapse of these two hedge funds was indeed a run on a shadow bank in the repo market. The two funds (one of which at its peak was levered 10 times its equity) were speculating mostly in CDOs on subprime mortgages, borrowed funds in the repo market and pledged their CDOs as collateral.

With the deterioration of the subprime market in the first half of 2007, creditors began asking the two Bear Stearns funds to post more collateral to back the repos by mid-June 2007. When the funds failed to meet these margin calls, creditors, led by Merrill Lynch, threatened to declare the funds in default of repo agreements and seize the investments. In fact, on June 19, 2007, Merrill seized $850 million of the CDOs and tried to auction them. When Merrill was able to sell only about $100 million worth of CDOs, the illiquid nature and the declining value of subprime assets became evident. Bloomberg reported that at least seven other lenders, including Lehman Brothers and Deutsche Bank, also circulated lists of CDOs and other bonds that they were planning to sell. This shadow bank run and the systemic crisis that followed illustrate the significance of the exemption of repo securities from the application of automatic stay; had the repo securities been subject to automatic stay (or alternatives proposed below), the Bear Stearns funds could have filed for bankruptcy and the forced fire sale of their assets could have been avoided.

Eventually, the subprime mortgage decline became systemic. In early August 2007, a run ensued on the assets of three SIVs of BNP Paribas. On August 9, BNP Paribas suspended redemptions from these SIVs. BNP Paribas's SIVs were bankruptcy-remote entities financing their subprime holdings through the issuance of ABCPs that had essentially lost their liquidity and became non-tradable. The announcement of the suspension of redemptions by BNP Paribas gave rise to counterparty risk concerns and caused the ABCP market to freeze. This freeze coincided with the first major jump in the LIB-OIS spread. When fears of counterparty risk spread through markets, all short-term debt markets — including the repo market — froze, only to open after central banks injected massive amounts of liquidity into the system (see Acharya and Richardson, 2009).

Based on a dataset obtained from dealer banks, Gorton and Metrick (2009) studied the repo spreads and haircuts for various types of repo securities. The spreads and the haircuts reported in their work are only for dealers; non-dealer counterparties may have been subject to other spreads and haircuts. The repo spreads are the spreads between the three-month repo and the three-month OIS rates. Their results demonstrate clearly how a crisis that started in the subprime market spread like a wildfire to other types of comparable non-transparent securitized debt, such as automobile, credit cards, student loan asset-backed securities, as well as the high-credit-rated structured products, such as AAA- and AA-rated CLOs and CDOs.

As Gorton and Metrick claim, the increasing haircuts in the interdealer repo market may be interpreted as a run on shadow banks. Figure 4, reproduced from Gorton and Metrick (2009b), shows how that run evolved. The data they examine are the interdealer repo haircuts for the following asset classes: (1) A-AAA Auto/Credit card/Student loan ABS; (2) AA-AAA

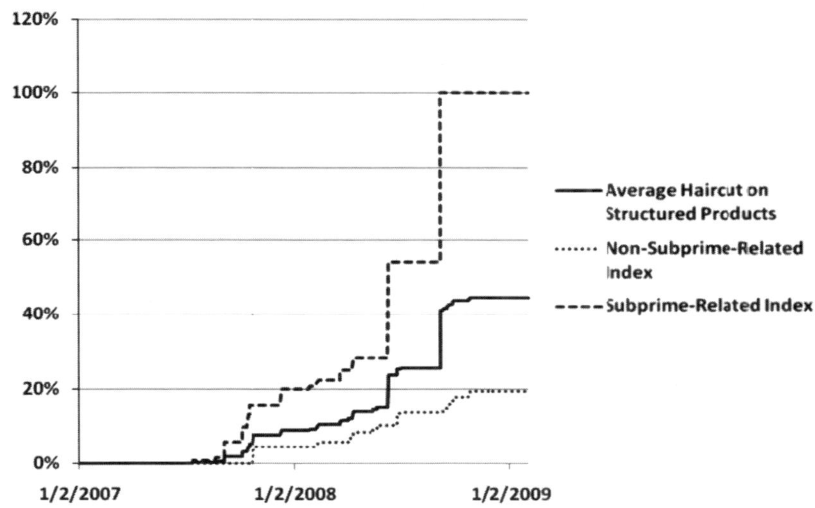

Fig. 4. Repo haircuts on different categories of structured products.

Source: Reproduced from Gorton and Metrick (2009b).

RMBS/CMBS; (3) <A RMBS/CMBS; (4) AA-AAA CLOs; (5) Unpriced ABS/MBS/all subprime; (6) AA-AAA CDOs; (7) Unpriced CLOs/CDOs (where "unpriced" means that the collateral does not have public pricing on either Reuters or Bloomberg). Of these, the categories (1)–(4) do not contain subprime mortgages and are labeled "Non-Subprime-Related" by Gorton and Metrick. In particular, the RMBS referred to in categories (2) and (3) are prime mortgages. The categories (5)–(7) are either directly subprime or contain subprime mortgages. CDOs, in particular, contain some subprime mortgages. Finally, using all seven categories, they also construct an equal-weighted average repo haircut index for structured bonds.

As can be seen from Fig. 4, the run on the shadow banking system in the interdealer repo market occurred in two phases. Although Bear Stearns's hedge funds were the first victims, it was BNP Paribas's suspension of redemptions on its three SIVs that triggered the first phase in August 2007. The failure of Bear Stearns in mid-March 2008 was the next phase of the run in the repo markets. It was not only the interdealer repo market for less liquid collateral that Gorton and Metrick (2009) studied where repo runs occurred. FRBNY White Paper (2010) states that "(a)t several points during the financial crisis of 2007–2009, the tri-party repo market took on particular importance in relation to the failures and near-failures of Countrywide Securities, Bear Stearns, and Lehman Brothers. The potential for the tri-party repo market to cease functioning, with impacts to securities firms, MMMFs, major banks involved in payment and settlements globally, and even to the liquidity of the US Treasury and Agency securities, has been cited by policy makers as a key concern behind aggressive interventions to contain the financial crisis."

Consider for instance the "run" on Bear Stearns.[17] As an intrinsic part of its business, Bear Stearns relied day-to-day on its ability to obtain short-term finance through secured borrowing. At this time, Bear was reported to be financing $85 billion of assets, primarily mortgage-backed securities (MBS), on the overnight market (Cohan, 2009). Beginning late

[17]The discussion that follows is based on the Securities and Exchange Commission press release on March 20, 2008, entitled, "Chairman Cox Letter to the Basel Committee in Support of New Guidance on Liquidity Management/." Available at: http://www.sec.gov/news/press/2008/2008-48.htm.

Monday, March 10, rumors spread about liquidity problems at Bear Stearns. Counterparties became unwilling to lend on customary terms. In particular, Federated and Fidelity — two money markets usually rolling over $5 billion each of repo financing to Bear — did not roll over. This unwillingness to fund on a secured basis placed enormous stress on the liquidity of Bear Stearns. On Tuesday, March 11, the holding company liquidity pool declined from $18.1 billion to $11.5 billion (see Fig. 5). On Thursday, March 13, Bear Stearns' liquidity pool fell sharply and continued to fall on Friday. In the end, the fear of repo financiers that they would be left with highly illiquid MBS collateral to sell in the market led to a "run" and the near failure of the firm and was eventually sold with assistance of the Federal Reserve to J P Morgan. In contrast to the smoothly rising haircuts in the bilateral repo market shown in Fig. 4, financing terms for Bear Stearns in the tri-party repo system did not rise dramatically, but it experienced a sudden freeze or a "run" from some of its largest repo financiers who feared acquiring the underlying collateral and fire-selling it in an illiquid market.

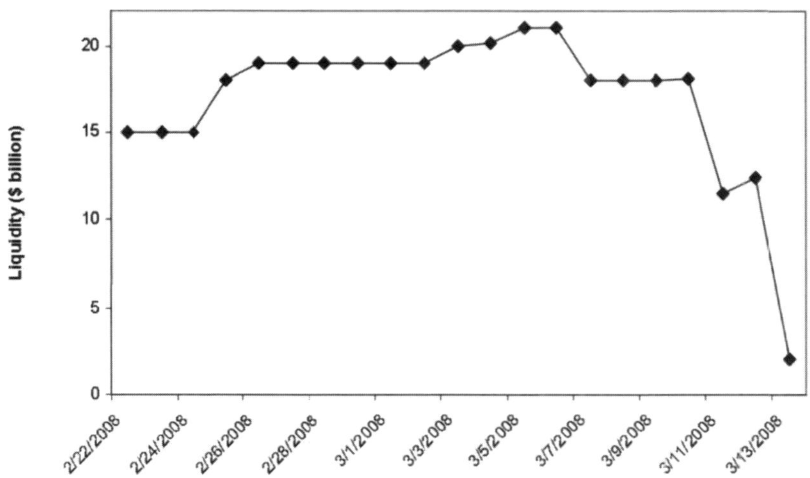

Fig. 5. Bear Stearns' liquidity pool just before its near failure.

Source: SEC Chairman Christopher Cox's letter to Basel Committee in support of New Guidance on Liquidity Management. Available at: http://www.sec.gov/news/press/2008/2008-48.htm.

After Bear Stearns collapsed in March 2008, the Fed introduced its most radical change in monetary policy since the Great Depression by extending its lender of last resort support to the systemically important primary dealers through the new Primary Dealer Credit Facility (PDCF). However, even this extension of the lender of last resort facility did not prevent the run on Lehman Brothers, as investors realized that this support was not unconditional and unlimited (see Acharya *et al.*, 2009).[18]

Indeed, using data collected by the FRBNY to document quantitative features of this market, Copeland, Martin, and Walker (2010) studied the tri-party repo market and demonstrated that haircuts in the tri-party repo market barely moved during the crisis. They found that both the level of haircuts and the amount of funding were surprisingly stable in this market during the period from July 2008 to early 2010 for which they had data.[19] Although the stability of the margins was in contrast to evidence from other repo markets, they provided evidence that "this apparent stability did not prevent the tri-party repo market from contributing to the problems experienced by Lehman Brothers, . . . The available evidence suggests that runs in the tri-party repo market may occur precipitously, more like traditional bank runs, rather than manifest themselves in the form of large increases in margins." Figure 6, reproduced from Copeland, Martin, and Walker (2010), provides a feel for the run on Lehman in the tri-party repo market they documented (see, Copeland, Martin, and Walker, 2010, for details).

With the Lehman bankruptcy on September 15, 2008, the repo market on even US government debt, federal agency debt, corporate debt, and federal agency mortgage-backed securities came to a near halt, and settlement fails of primary dealers skyrocketed. Table 1 shows a quarterly summary of the primary dealer settlement fails from the first quarter of 2007 to the last quarter of 2009. Figure 7 provides a quarterly summary of the effects of the

[18]While the largest haircut jump in Fig. 4 corresponds to the collapse of Lehman on September 15, 2008, the second largest jump, which came in the summer of 2008, corresponds to traditional bank runs on likely insolvent banking institutions, such as IndyMac, Washington Mutual, and Wachovia.

[19]This finding is also corroborated in Krishnamurthy, Nagel, and Orlov (2011), who also attribute the relative stability of the tri-party repo market to the substitute for repo funding provided by Fed-initiated liquidity facilities against illiquid collateral, especially following the collapse of Bear Stearns.

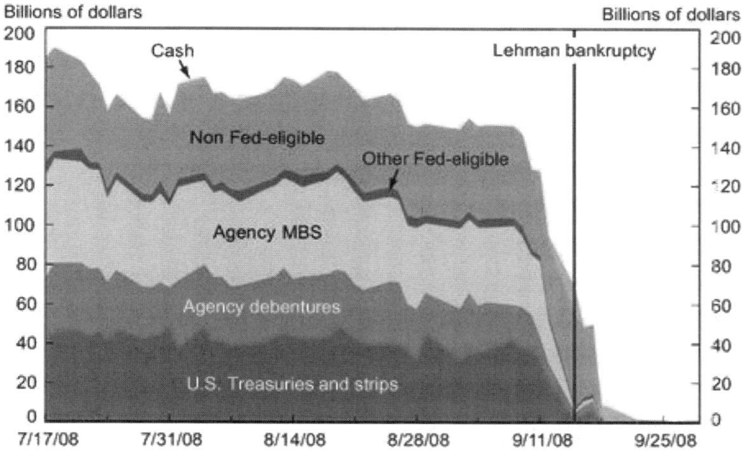

Fig. 6. Lehman Brothers' tri-party repo book by collateral type.

Source: Copeland, Martin, and Walker (2010).

Table 1. Settlement fails of US government securities primary dealers during the crisis, 2007–2009 ($ billions).

	Treasury		Agency		MBS		Corporate	
	Receive	Deliver	Receive	Deliver	Receive	Deliver	Receive	Deliver
2007								
Q1	738.1	586.8	91.2	76.6	474.6	473.8	356.1	404.2
Q2	726.8	528.3	117.7	118.2	595.8	617.7	498.0	572.9
Q3	834.4	549.7	239.5	231.7	805.6	819.7	822.9	884.3
Q4	1373.0	1085.4	202.8	192.5	757.8	686.8	488.4	547.5
2008								
Q1	3946.2	3835.7	234.7	221.8	1023.3	952.1	364.8	413.4
Q2	3762.9	3726.3	202.4	192.6	596.1	566.5	361.3	407.2
Q3	3077.4	2784	238.1	228.4	463.1	425.5	199.4	214.9
Q4	16824.6	16266.6	586.6	600.7	971.9	863.5	271.7	337.8
2009								
Q1	1442.9	1286	143.1	167.1	867.8	950.3	168.0	225.8
Q2	806.6	764.8	95.4	100.9	1078.9	1319.4	151.6	215.6
Q3	617.7	536.8	62.1	76.7	1283.9	1553.2	145.2	192.4
Q4	245.0	184.4	141.9	163.9	3128.6	3945.1	156.7	192.2

Source: Federal Reserve Bank of New York.

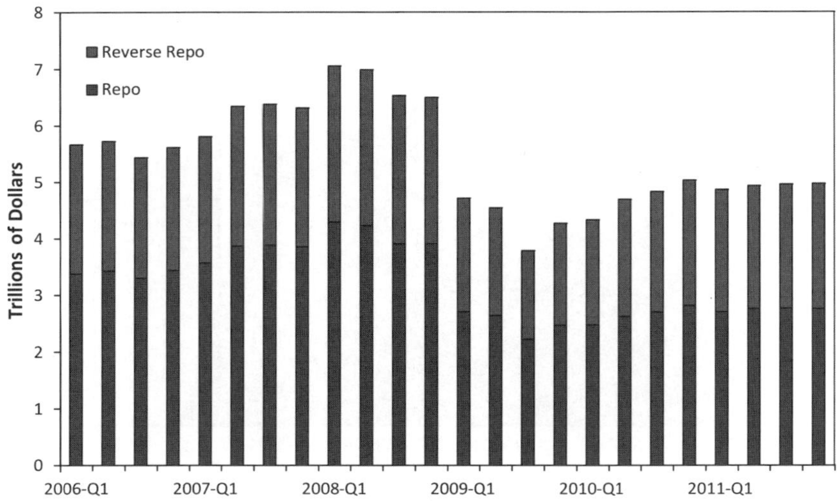

Fig. 7. Quarterly averages of daily financing by US government securities primary dealers, 2006–2011.

Source: Securities Industry and Financial Markets Association.

run on the repo market on the financing of primary dealers after Lehman's collapse. As shown, it was the borrowing ability of the primary dealers that went down significantly, not their lending ability. Since this may be interpreted as large withdrawals from the broker-dealer shadow banks in the repo market, Fig. 7 also illustrates the disappearing confidence in the shadow banking system and the severity of the run on shadow banks. When the Fed and the US government let Lehman collapse, the next in line for a run, Merrill Lynch, had to merge with Bank of America. Shortly thereafter, the two remaining independent broker-dealers, Morgan Stanley and Goldman Sachs, were forced to convert to bank holding companies and were formally put under supervision and regulation of the Federal Reserve. In fact, the entire Wall Street system of independent broker-dealers collapsed in a matter of seven months (see Acharya *et al.*, 2009).

A Case for Reforming the Repo Market

As Acharya and Krishnamurthy (2010) clarify, the primary issue with financing risky securities (such as mortgage-backed securities) through repo markets is that such financing is likely to freeze or experience stress in times of aggregate (economy- or financial sector-wide) stress, and on their own, financial firms do not have the incentive to internalize the costs of such a freeze or stress. By virtue of being secured and typically short-term financing arrangements, repo markets, by and large, function smoothly; in other words, repos usually get rolled over. When the underlying assets, such as Treasury or agency debt, are essentially safe, the repo financier is undeterred from rolling over the financing even in stressful times. Indeed, Treasury and agency debt might even experience a flight to safety in such times.

In contrast, if the underlying collateral is a mortgage-backed security and an economic downturn ensues, the risk of an already illiquid market for MBS gets compounded; this is because many financial institutions' portfolios are crowded with MBS or have lost capital. In this scenario, repo financiers run the real risk of being forced to sell their collateral in illiquid markets. The repo financier may respond by raising the required haircut or simply refusing to roll over. The resulting fall in repo financing ability against the collateral is perverse, as it sets up an adverse dynamic: The future buyers of assets anticipate that they are likely to face steep haircuts too and thus will not offer attractive prices for assets; in turn, the collateral's ability to be financed with repo today falls even further. A complete market freeze can arise as it did during the crisis of 2007–2009. Indeed, in his analysis of the failure of Bear Stearns, the Federal Reserve Chairman Ben Bernanke observed[20]:

> "[U]ntil recently, short-term repos had always been regarded as virtually risk-free instruments and thus largely immune to the type of rollover or withdrawal risks associated with short-term unsecured obligations. In March, rapidly unfolding events demonstrated that even repo markets could be severely disrupted when investors believe they might need to sell the underlying collateral in illiquid markets. Such forced asset sales can set up a particularly adverse dynamic, in which further substantial price declines fan investor concerns about counterparty credit risk, which then feed back in the form of intensifying funding pressures. . . [F]uture liquidity planning will have to take into account the possibility of a sudden loss of substantial amounts of secured financing."

[20]The quotes are based on Ben Bernanke's remarks to the Risk Transfer Mechanisms and Financial Stability Workshop at the Bank for International Settlements, May 29, 2008.

To summarize, unlike the liquidity risk that unsecured financing may become unavailable to a firm (a risk largely specific to the credit risk of the firm), the liquidity risk that secured repo financing may become unavailable to a firm is inherently a systemic risk, materializing in circumstances where other financial firms are also experiencing stress and the markets for assets held predominantly by the financial sector are rendered illiquid. This leads to the problem that, while in good times, financial firms may not fully internalize the costs imposed on the system by being excessively financed through short-term repo markets, in bad times, they charge excessively high haircuts on repo financing and do not internalize the pecuniary externalities imposed on other firms through the resulting fire sales of assets. Indeed, to support financial firms facing a repo freeze or to support the assets directly, the likely lender of last resort would only accentuate a problem that firms ignore in good times — namely, the systemic risk associated with repo financing. Viewed this way, in good times, there is a case for subjecting repo-financed risky securities to a capital charge — effectively a *regulatory haircut* — which takes into account the security's systemic risk and maturity mismatch relative to the repo tenor. Equally important, there is a case for a better design of the bankruptcy of a repo-financed debtor than simply granting its repo financier the full right to seize the collateral and liquidate it at will in an illiquid market.

Proposal for a Repo Resolution Authority

Although the DFA is completely silent about how to reform it, at least two attempts have been made to address weaknesses inherent in the repo market. The first of these attempts was made by the Committee on Payment and Settlement Systems (CPSS) of the Basel Committee on Banking Supervision, which undertakes specific studies in the field of payment and settlement systems. The CPSS commissioned a working group on repo market infrastructure "to investigate the extent to which the clearing and settlement infrastructure for repos contributed to the instability evident in some repo markets" in June 2009.[21] After a comprehensive survey of the clearing and settlement arrangements for repos in selected CPSS member

[21] See http://www.bis.org/cpss/index.htm.

countries, the working group published their report in September 2010.[22] Their conclusion was that it was worthwhile for the stakeholders in each market to review how the clearing and settlement arrangements for repos could be further strengthened.

The second of these attempts was made by the Tri-Party Repo Infrastructure Reform Task Force ("Task Force"), which was formed "to address weaknesses that became visible over the course of the recent financial crisis" in September 2009, under the auspices of the Payments Risk Committee, a private sector body sponsored by the Federal Reserve Bank of New York.[23] The Task Force published its final report with recommendations to strengthen the infrastructure supporting the tri-party repo market in May 2010.[24] The July 6, 2011, progress report of the Task Force indicated that, although progress had been made in regards to implementing the reforms recommended in May 2010, they were behind schedule and were continuing to develop the remaining steps to achieve their objectives.[25] The focus of the Task Force had primarily been on the issue of whether J P Morgan Chase and Bank of New York, the tri-party brokers, extend credit risk intra-day, how that risk could be mitigated or adequately capitalized, and other intra-day infrastructure issues. The Task Force released its final report on February 15, 2012, and reported that, despite significant accomplishments, their ultimate goal of the "practical elimination" of intra-day credit extension by the clearing banks was years away. Consequently, the Fed decided to explore additional policy options, including limitations on eligible collateral and a "facility to foster the orderly liquidation of collateral in the event of a dealer's default" (see, Tuckman, 2012a, for details).[26]

On balance, the macro-prudential issue of containing bank-style runs in the repo markets and the risk of fire-sale liquidations of illiquid collateral, such as mortgage-backed securities, has not been discussed substantially.

---

[22] See http://www.bis.org/publ/cpss91.htm.

[23] See http://www.newyorkfed.org/tripartyrepo/.

[24] See http://www.newyorkfed.org/banking/nyfrb_triparty_whitepaper.pdf.

[25] See http://www.newyorkfed.org/tripartyrepo/pdf/PR_110706.pdf.

[26] Interestingly, "limitations on eligible collateral and a facility to foster the orderly liquidation of collateral" were among the policy suggestions we also had made in an earlier work (see Archarya and Öncü, 2010).

On this macro-prudential issue, possible reforms of the repo market can be put into three categories:

(1) a full government-guarantee scheme for repo market liabilities;
(2) a full market-discipline scheme in which repo liabilities are not exempt from bankruptcy but subject to automatic stay as with secured borrowing contracts of non-financial firms; and
(3) a combination of the two. As we explain below, our preferred alternative is the combination but where guarantee extended is in the form of a temporary liquidity guarantee and its potential moral hazard consequences are controlled for.

At one extreme, some (most notably, Gorton, 2009) have suggested that repo financing is akin to demandable deposits in many ways and thus is similarly vulnerable to the information-sensitive panics when adverse information about underlying collateral (or counterparties) hits markets. His proposal is thus to treat repo financing in a similar way — that is, offer federal deposit insurance to the repo contracts, at least against securities that are relatively "safe," such as the super-senior tranches of securitization pools and "deposits" (technically savings) with the money market funds. Under this proposal, it is recognized that repo financing has the inherent systemic fragility akin to demandable deposits, and in all likelihood, the government would end up backing up repo counterparties were the fragility to materialize. Hence, by explicitly recognizing the guarantee upfront, it becomes possible to charge repo financiers for the guarantee. As with any insurance premium, the objective is not just only to collect fees for an *ex post* guarantee, but also get repo financiers to internalize the systemic fragility inherent in repo contracts.

At another extreme, others (most notably, Roe, 2009; Perotti, 2010) have proposed that repo financiers should not be allowed unrestricted access to collateral even in case of default of the counterparty. That is, there should be some sort of "automatic stay" on repo financiers' claims, and they should join the bankruptcy of the defaulting counterparty as a secured creditor, as in the case of corporate bankruptcies. The rationale for this is twofold: first, it prevents the systemic liquidity risk due to fire sales of the repo collateral by the financiers and avoids the adverse dynamic we highlighted before; and second, by exposing the repo financiers to credit risk of the counterparty (and not just that of the collateral), the financiers would subject the borrowers to much greater market discipline. In particular, financiers would opt for safer counterparties, all else being equal, or charge higher haircuts to riskier ones — either way, discriminating *ex ante* between safer and riskier borrowers.

The advantage of the government guarantee scheme is that it resolves virtually all *ex post* uncertainty by transferring the risk of repo contracts away from financiers to the government agency for an upfront fee. However, its disadvantages are more subtle and somewhat pernicious. The charging of FDIC premiums has been heavily influenced by the banking industry, and no premiums have historically been charged to most banks when the FDIC's reserve fund is capitalized above 1.25% to 1.35% of the insured deposits. This kind of a fee structure gives rise to a highly pro-cyclical risk-taking incentive, because, as far as the risk-return tradeoff is concerned, the risks are back-loaded. There is no guarantee that repo insurance premiums would work any differently. Perhaps, and somewhat more disturbingly, such a guarantee scheme effectively amounts to transferring the credit risk of virtually most parts of the securitization market to the government's balance sheet. While "conforming" mortgages in the US are already being backstopped by Fannie Mae and Freddie Mac, the proposed guarantee scheme would extend such a backstop to subprime securitized pools, corporate loans, automobile receivables, credit-card receivables, and so on. Due to its potential sovereign risk concerns in an environment of difficult fiscal position for the government, the idea of extending guarantees to practically all financial assets of the economy should be viewed with caution. Such caution would be even more necessary for governments other than the US, whose balance sheets are already heavily stretched.

On the other hand, the advantage of market discipline through the automatic stay approach is that it transfers the entire risk of the repo transaction to the repo financier — to some extent the risk of the collateral but also that of the borrower's ability to pay. This way, other than through *ex post* forbearance, private markets are allowed to function — bear and price risks — and thereby provide incentives to take account of relevant risk–return tradeoffs. There are, however, several countervailing issues that arise. First, since the primary issue with repo contracts is their systemic externality, it is unclear that private market outcomes would be necessarily efficient from a risk–return standpoint of the economy as a whole. Second, automatic stay introduces "basis risk" in the repo contract, since its eventual payoff is linked not just to the underlying asset but to the whole pool of assets of the borrower and the rest of its capital structure. In general, this may create sufficient *ex ante*, as well as *ex post*, uncertainty to reduce the financier's willingness to lend against certain assets to all types of borrowers. The result might be a significant reduction in *ex ante* liquidity in some parts of repo-financed securitized markets. Third, a rationale for the bankruptcy exemption of the repos has been that when the borrower defaults, counterparty risk transmission is reduced as far as the repo contract goes because it is protected from any spillover of the borrower's remaining risks and liabilities.

Given this relative assessment, our preferred approach is one that facilitates a ready winding down of the repo contracts as far as reasonable liquidity for repo financiers is concerned and at the same time eliminates disorderly fire sales of underlying assets. In particular, the approach consists of setting up a Repo Resolution Authority that meets the criteria (1)–(5) we laid out in the Introduction for resolution of SIALs. In case of default of a repo counterparty (the borrower), the repo resolution authority would ensure orderly resolution of its repo liabilities and also an orderly liquidation of the underlying collateral; in good times, the repo resolution authority would ensure that the services it provides at time of default are not contributing to excessive risk of defaults in the repo markets.

Specifically, instituting the repo resolution authority requires the following pieces:

(1) In case of default of a borrower, its repo counterparties on Treasuries, and perhaps agency-backed securities (assuming the agency-backed securities are effectively government backed), are "exempt from stay" and counterparties are allowed to take their collateral as under the current arrangements.
(2) However, repo counterparties on risky collateral, such as ABS and MBS, are subjected to a "stay" (or a suspension of conversion to immediacy) as with secured borrowing of non-financial firms.
(3) Immediately upon default, repo financiers of risky collateral are paid by a "repo resolution fund," a recovery amount that is based

on a conservative value assessment of the collateral.[27] Such a value assessment could be based on market intelligence, historical estimates, projected valuations obtained from a poll of dealers, etc. The important issue is that the assessment should be "conservative" and reflect reasonable haircuts that an asset liquidator would expect to incur when faced with asset liquidations. In particular, the conservative value could depend on the total size of repo liabilities of a borrower and/or on the total size of liabilities against a given type of collateral. The conservative recovery amount (or it schedule) should, however, be pre-determined and known to market participants.

(4) In case of default on repo backed by risky collateral, the underlying repo collateral is taken over by the repo resolution authority (which effectively has liquidation rights over the collateral) and liquidated in an orderly manner over a pre-specified period, say, not more than six months (but with some flexibility to deal with unexpected circumstances).

   (a) If the eventual recovery on the collateral is *greater* than the conservative estimate paid to the repo financiers (see step **3** above), then the time- value adjusted difference is paid eventually to the repo financiers.
   (b) Conversely, if the eventual recovery is *lower* than the conservative estimate paid to the repo financiers, the time-value adjusted difference is "clawed back" from the repo financiers. The claw-back feature would have to be explicitly legislated (as with the current mechanism used by FDIC to deal with uninsured depositors of failed FDIC-regulated banks).

(5) In effect, steps **3** and **4** resemble a lender of last resort (LOLR) operation, whereby risky collateral in times of a systemic crisis would be provided liquidity, albeit conservatively at a "haircut" or penalty rate. The operation is of the LOLR flavor since it suspends immediate

[27]The repo resolution fund could be dedicated to the repo resolution authority, or it is conceivable that it could simply be within the FDIC or the Federal Reserve. The fund should potentially be eligible for participating in the lender of last resort facilities of the central bank. If such participation is not clear *a priori*, uncertainty concerning it could lead to breakdown of our proposed resolution plan.

conversion to currency for repo financiers in the form of collateral liquidations and replaces it with an upfront but conservative payment by repo resolution fund at time of default, with rights to liquidation conferred upon the repo resolution authority and *not* on repo financiers.

(6) In case of an isolated default in the repo market, that is, default in a time when the underlying collateral market is reasonably liquid, the collateral liquidation by the repo resolution authority would be relatively swift, at close to fundamental or liquid collateral values, and effectively, the repo financiers will be repaid conservative amount plus the additional recovery within a few days. That is, in this case, an effective automatic stay on repo contracts would be just a couple of days.

(7) However, in case of clustered defaults of several counterparties in the repo market, e.g., because there is an aggregate shock such as a significant housing price decline or because the market for housing-related assets is weak due to overhang of other financial firms from holdings of similar assets, the collateral liquidation by the repo resolution authority could take time and not generate liquidation proceeds that are up to the conservative recovery payment made to repo financiers. This implies that:

    (a) The effective automatic stay on repo contracts would be more substantive, but in economic terms not as substantive as the asset liquidation period due to the conservative early payment made by the repo resolution fund.
    (b) Importantly, the claw-back feature would come in to play and repo financiers could be required in part to return the liquidity provided by the repo resolution fund (when the time-adjusted eventual recovery is lower than the conservative recovery payment made at the time of default).

(8) The claw-back possibility in **7b** above implies that the repo resolution authority takes on the credit risk of repo financiers, as well as of the underlying collateral. This credit risk is limited to the difference between realized recovery and the conservative estimate at the time of the borrower's bankruptcy, and linked to the credit quality of the repo financier. In particular, if the repo financier defaults in the period when

the repo resolution authority is liquidating the underlying collateral, then the repo resolution authority effectively becomes a creditor of the repo financier and may face losses in case of the repo financier's default. To manage this credit risk, the repo resolution authority should do the following:

(a) Include as eligible only relatively high-quality collateral, that is, certain highly risky securities such as pools backed by low-quality mortgages may be excluded from repo resolution authority altogether and repos with them as underlying collateral subject to the usual automatic stay as in case of secured borrowing by non-financial firms;
(b) charge repo financiers an *ex ante* fee for the lender of last resort or conservative liquidity payment facility, commensurate with the residual credit risk borne by the facility, in order to provide a financing for the repo resolution fund;
(c) require that eligible repo financiers for the lender of last resort facility provided by the repo resolution authority meet pre-specified solvency criteria (which should be based on a range of solvency metrics, including market capitalization and funding capacity, rather than just easily arbitraged and static risk-weight style rules on book value of equity); and
(d) impose a concentration limit at the level of individual repo financiers, as well as on the financier's overall portfolio size, recognizing that controls in (a)–(c) above may mitigate credit risk borne by the repo resolution authority but not eliminate it altogether.

A difficult design issue in proposing such resolution authority is to define the event of "default" of a repo borrower. One possibility is that given the ability of the authority to suspend conversion of immediacy of financiers, the borrower would itself have incentives to file for bankruptcy early, an option that currently would not give them the rights to stem runs from creditors who have safe harbor provisions. Another possibility is that recognizing the incentives of distressed firms to gamble for resurrection and to avoid filing for bankruptcy, the resolution authority could itself define adequate default triggers that would suspend conversion of repo contracts on specific collateral and take over the asset liquidation rights (as outlined above). As we explained above, in case of idiosyncratic distress of firms, the repo resolution authority would operate effectively like a safe-harbor provision making the full payment upon swift liquidation of collateral to other firms. However, in case of systemic distress, the repo resolution authority's ability to make partial immediate payments and liquidate collateral in due course would be most important. This suggests that the default trigger designed by the resolution authority would need to feature both firm-specific solvency and liquidity conditions as well as system-wide solvency and liquidity conditions.[28]

Thus, our preferred approach in the form of a repo resolution authority provides *ex post* liquidity to the repo market rather than a complete guarantee of underlying risks. This approach also charges *ex ante* for this liquidity facility and ensures that the risks undertaken by the market participants do not expose the taxpayers to losses beyond a certain size. That is, it makes an effort not to take on solvency risk while trying to address liquidity risk of repo markets. It combines the attractive features of full insurance and full market-discipline schemes, avoiding their weaknesses. Furthermore, in contrast to FDIC's recent proposal of a fixed haircut for all repo collateral, it allows the haircut to be determined differentially for different collateral classes and sub-classes based on conservative value assessments at the time of the borrower's bankruptcy. As highlighted in the Introduction, it attempts to address the systemic risks of both the repo runs and the market for underlying collateral, while containing the ex-ante risks created in the first place, and in a manner that can be harmonized internationally in a ready manner provided the various criteria in the schemes (**1**)–(**8**) above are agreed upon by large repo centers of the world, or at least that they all meet some minimum reasonable standards.

Our proposal has similarities to the approach to regulation shadow banking laid out in Gorton and Metrick (2010). Specifically, the idea of limiting access to the safe harbor or bankruptcy exemption clauses for specific types of collateral-backed repos is also a part of Gorton–Metrick

[28]The issue of whether the triggers should be based on book values of solvency and liquidity conditions or market values is an important and interesting one, raising the familiar trade-offs of the lagged and discretionary nature of book values against the timely but vulnerable (to manipulation and downward spiral) nature of market values.

approach. However, there are also differences. The Gorton–Metrick approach recommends government guarantee scheme, akin to deposit insurance, for liabilities of money market funds, whereas under our approach, once money market funds are subject to strict guidelines in repo market financing (and similarly in other SIALs), they would effectively be subject to solvency criteria similar to those for banks (and might not survive competition from banks in the first place). Further, while the primary risk-control in the Gorton–Metrick scheme is through restriction of eligible collateral for safe harbor provisions, safe harbor is, in principle, eliminated from our repo resolution authority and it just conditionally happens to be akin to safe harbor in some cases even for eligible collateral (when defaults are isolated as in (**6**) above).

Our proposal also has some similarities to the Federal Liquidity Options proposal of Tuckman (2012b), which recommends that central banks pre-sell liquidity options as the exclusive means of lending money to non-banking institutions in a crisis. The idea of reducing the risk of the lender of last resort through paid-for commitments, and thereby minimizing the ex-post socialization of residual risks, is in similar spirit as our proposal. The difference is that our approach also proposes a mechanism to manage the residual risks not backed by the lender of last resort (or the repo resolution authority) once the *ex ante* commitments have been met (payments beyond conservative haircuts are made with immediacy).

Finally, Bliss and Kaufman (2011) propose refinements of the OLA under the Dodd–Frank Act that would apply regular bankruptcy proceedings to failing financial firms but with advance payments to such firms upon failure ("modified debtor-in-possession (DIP) financing") and mandatory but limited haircuts to all "protected" (e.g., safe-harbored) creditors. Both of these refinements also feature in our proposal, as immediate liquidity provided by the repo resolution authority to claims in failure and the credit risk on underlying collateral being passed on to the claims in due course. The key distinguishing feature of our proposal is that it grants the rights to large-scale asset liquidations to the resolution authority in order to address the issue of disorderly bankruptcy or fire sales when the failure of an institution is not in isolation but is coincident with other regulations.

It is important to discuss what would happen to repo contracts on collateral that is not eligible under the repo resolution authority and its strict guidelines and requirements. This would constitute the hypothetical "shadow banking" in a world of repo resolution authorities. These repo contracts would not have access to safe harbor and would be perceived as ex-ante riskier and of lower liquidity by financiers. However, this would not necessarily guarantee that financiers internalize the externalities of runs in the shadow banking. To guard against this, the repo resolution authority should, on a periodic basis, assess if a class of repo claims has become large enough and the underlying collateral is suitable quality enough to be eligible for repo resolution authority's LOLR. If yes, they should be required by legislation to be moved out of shadow banking into the repo resolution authority. And, where the underlying collateral is not of adequate quality or the repo contract class sufficiently small in size, a minimum haircut (or over-collateralization) requirement should be imposed, akin to FDIC's proposed haircut on all repos, or a more risk-sensitive scheme, such as bank capital requirements. Ideally, the haircut scheme should be counter-cyclical and certainly not pro-cyclical (i.e., not provide too low or non-existent haircuts in good times, such as on MBS with low-quality mortgages or government bond repos where government credit risk is non-trivial as in the Eurozone since 2008).

Having highlighted the various benefits of our proposed approach, such as its flexibility in extending to new asset and liability classes over time and the difficulty of gaming it by the financial sector since it operates for all institutions participating in a given asset or liability class, we note that it does — like the Dodd–Frank Act and the OLA — rely on a certain amount of ability of the regulators to get things right. In particular, the approach relies on regulators to be able to estimate conservative values of collateral which necessitates (perhaps incentivizes) them to ensure sufficient transparency of prices in underlying asset markets in normal times. The approach also relies on adequate incentives for the resolution authority to adopt *ex ante* risk controls in the form of haircuts, concentration limits, and eligibility restrictions on collateral, among others. While the approach can be harmonized internationally in a relatively straightforward manner if such controls are harmonized, competition for market shares across borders can potentially put downward pressure on the adoption and the extent of these controls in practice. For this reason, besides the fact that the lenders of last resort such as central banks would ultimately have to step in when these authorities do not have adequate liquidity to make conservative payments, the lenders of last resort would need to act as watchdogs over our proposed resolution authorities, preventing a race to the bottom in their risk controls.

A Historical Precedent: The Glass Proposal

As Graeber (2011), and Reinhart and Rogoff (2009) documented, banking crises have been ubiquitous throughout recent history and one common problem to almost all has been the loss of liquidity to bank depositors. In the wake of one of these crises, namely, the banking panic of 1907, the National Monetary Commission of the US, established by the Congress in the Aldrich-Vreeland Act of 1908, prepared a 19-question questionnaire and mailed to various representatives of the US banking industry (Kaufman, 2004). One of the questions — the 18th — asked:[29]

> "*Would it be well, in your opinion, to change the existing laws so that liquidating banks could, in some way, arrange to pay depositors more rapidly? A careful examination of the assets of failed banks will show about how much dividend they can eventually pay, and considerable distress would be prevented if something approximating this amount could be paid to depositors without any delay.*"

As Kaufman (2004) reports, "(r)esponses were obtained from 85 respondents. Of these, 63, or some two-thirds, favored a change to pay depositors of closed banks more rapidly. This percent was the same among bankers and bank examiners, the two largest groups of respondents. Only 12 respondents, or 14%, were opposed to such a change and the remainder either skipped the question or were undecided."

As we mentioned in the beginning of the second section, a central objective of the DFA is to create a new resolution mechanism for nonbank SIFIs and bring them within the FDIC insurance model. In the wake of the next banking crisis after the panic of 1907, namely, in the early years of the Great Depression of 1929 and before the establishment of the FDIC in 1933, Senator Carter Glass — the then chairman of the Senate Banking Committee and a coauthor of the Federal Reserve Act of 1933 — proposed more rapid payment to depositors at failed banks as a superior alternative to deposit

[29] As quoted by Kaufman (2004), p. 243.

insurance, which he opposed (Kaufman, 2004). As quoted by Kaufman (2004), Willis and Chapman (1934, pp. 65–67) describe the objective of the Glass proposal as follows:

> "Recognizing that in bank failures the source of difficulty and loss is not primarily found in lack of assets, but ... that the resources of depositors are tied up and rendered unavailable for long periods ... liquidation power and not guaranty was demanded ... insuring an almost immediate settlement within a short time upon the basis of the estimated worth of the [failed] bank's assets ... This plan was considered by the [Banking] Committee entirely adequate to the protection of the bank depositor against most of the evils to which he had been subject, while leaving him still with a measure of individual responsibility for the protection of his claims through the selection of a well-qualified bank."

The Glass proposal called for the establishment of a Federal Government Liquidating Corporation (FGLC) to estimate a bank's recovery value immediately upon its failure, quickly sell the bank as a whole or in parts, and quickly pay the proceeds to the receiver for speedy disbursement to the depositors (Kaufman, 2004). Despite the differences, the similarities between our repo resolution proposal and the proposal of Senator Glass are astounding. Although we do not promote quickly selling the "repo banks" as a whole or in parts — except their highly liquid repo collaterals such as Treasuries, and perhaps agency-backed securities — for reasons we have argued at length, we also call for a liquidating agency (our repo resolution authority) to "*estimate a (repo) bank's recovery value immediately upon its failure, ... and quickly pay ... the receiver for speedy disbursement to the depositors (repo financiers).*" In the first regard, our repo resolution authority resembles the Orderly Liquidation Authority of the Dodd–Frank Act more than the Federal Government Liquidating Corporation that Senator Glass proposed, since we are concerned also with the orderly liquidation of potentially illiquid and risky repo collaterals such as the MBSs. In the second regard, our repo resolution authority resembles the FGLC of the Glass proposal more than the OLA of the Dodd–Frank Act because of our call for paying the repo financiers of risky repo collaterals a recovery amount that is based on a conservative value assessment of the collateral by a "repo resolution fund."

In the end, the Glass proposal was found too difficult to implement, primarily because many believed that it required more accurate estimates of the market value of the failed bank's assets than possible at the time (Kaufman, 2004). This is another similarity between our proposal and the Glass proposal. Many may argue that our proposal requires more accurate estimates of the market value of the risky and illiquid repo collaterals than possible at our time. Yet, the advantages of the scheme proposed by Senator Glass had also been seen by others.

For example, although it did not become operational, the Federal Reserve Bank of New York attempted to have depositors at failed banks receive the recovery value of their claims faster by requesting healthy member banks to buy the assets of failed banks and advance the proceeds to them for immediate distribution in 1931 (again see, Kaufman, 2004, and the references therein). And, in 1933, the New York State Banking Department was able to implement such an arrangement when it entered into agreements with Manufacturers Trust Co. and other large New York City commercial banks to serve as both liquidating and paying agents for a failed bank and partially assume the deposits of the bank up to an agreed percentage of paramount (Upham and Lamke, 1934). As quoted by Kaufman (2004), Charles Clough, comptroller of Manufacturers Trust, noted the advantages of this program as follows:

> "Three things were definitely accomplished. Business men, whose working capital was frozen, were given relief through the release of their bank balances, and at the same time, were given immediate substantial banking connections which would enable them to continue in business; apparent distress among depositors was relieved at once; and the entire process of liquidation was accomplished more expeditiously and economically than was thought possible."

Another example, which is also an important precedent that relates to our proposal for a repo resolution authority and inspired by the Glass proposal, is the Reconstruction Finance Corporation (RFC). The RFC was established by the Reconstruction Finance Corporation Act in 1932 and authorized to loan funds to banks closed for liquidation or reorganization to enable them to make quick partial payments to depositors. As Kaufman (2004) quotes from Jesse Jones, long-time chairman of the RFC, these loans — securitized by the failed banks' assets — would

> "*. . . make at least a part of the depositor's balance available to him, pending liquidation. . . . We endeavored to lend up to the probable liquidation value of their*

> *[the bank's] assets... The government could afford to wait; often the individual could not."*

The reason for the establishment of the RFC was that "(f)reezing deposits at these banks was viewed as decreasing purchasing power in the community and delaying recovery from the Depression (Kaufman, 2004)." Indeed, to avoid decreased purchasing power in the community and delayed recovery from the Depression, President Franklin Roosevelt suggested a deposit liquidation program "to stimulate and encourage liquidating agents of banks closed after January 1, 1933 to borrow funds from the RFC in order that funds may be made available to depositors as quickly as possible" (Upham and Lamke, 1934, pp. 168–169).

However, the RFC did not agree to operate in the suggested program directly. For this and other reasons, Roosevelt established a new liquidation board, i.e., the Deposit Liquidation Board (DLB) to lend to the failed banks. The DLB could borrow from the RFC using the assets of the failed banks as collateral, but it charged the banks a lower interest rate on the loans than the rate charged by the RFC (Kaufman, 2004). The DLB loaned on 80% of the liquidation value of the assets, but this liquidation value was determined not on the basis of the current book value of the failed bank's assets but on values that the RFC projected it could get in "an orderly liquidation period of three to five years in a recovering stock and bond market" (Olson, 1988, p. 75).

Although the volume of loans provided by the DLB increased rapidly in 1933, it was still considered by some as too little and too slow. A number of bills were introduced in Congress to have the Treasury or other federal agencies also advance funds to depositors at closed banks, but, despite gathering considerable support, none of the bills were enacted (Calomiris and White, 1994). Kaufman (2004) notes that "(a)uthority to provide such loans was, however, included in the Federal Deposit Insurance Act, although apparently not used to liquefy frozen uninsured deposits until 50 years later in 1983. With the sharp decline in the number of bank failures after 1934, legislative interest in liquefying deposits at failed banks diminished."

Concluding Remarks

Regulators and policymakers in the US and abroad have made rough sketches of proposals that would avoid bankruptcy proceedings for SIFIs.

One idea is that there should be provision of "contingent capital" or "co-co bonds," a (small) part of SIFI's liabilities that would convert to equity mechanically based on a firm-specific and/or system-specific trigger. Such conversion would provide the SIFI with some debt relief and thus some extra time to deal with its problems. A related idea is that of a "bail in" under which a SIFI's deterioration past a specified benchmark would trigger for some claims a pre-specified haircut or the elimination of some claims entirely, effectively writing down firm's liabilities to a predetermined extent. Bail-ins in particular are attractive if they can be enacted as part of an integrated capital structure, wherein SILs (such as swap agreements) are placed in high-priority tranches while ordinary bonds and equity are left to suffer conversion or elimination in the event that the firm would be unable to pay all of its obligations. Such a capital structure, enacted perhaps as part of a SIFI's living will — a plan of resolution required for the US firms by the DFA — could lend stability by providing certainty about where losses would rest in the event of a financial crisis.

What we propose, based on the insights of Acharya, Adler, and Richardson (2011), is that "top-down" (or institution-level) approaches such as contingent capital, bail-in, or living wills, be built on top of a "bottom-up" approach — one that works at the level of the SIALs rather than at the level of the SIFI that owns them. Under the bottom-up approach, there would be an automatic stabilizer built into each systemically significant part of an SIFI's capital structure. The automatic stabilizers could be in the form of government-provided but appropriately charged deposit insurance, centrally cleared SIALs with initial and variation margins or haircuts charged by a clearinghouse or dedicated resolution authority for those SIALs, and in extreme cases, lender-of-last-resort from the central bank against eligible assets (but to avoid moral hazard, only to firms that pay a market-rate fee). A particularly attractive feature of this "bottom-up" approach is that it requires no uniform institution-level insolvency process and therefore might be the simplest way of achieving international agreement on resolving the financial distress of G-SIFIs (as long as there is global agreement on resolution mechanisms for SIALs).

As an illustration of why such a bottom-up approach is needed, we note that the current financial legislation proposals are completely silent on how to reform the repo market in which financial firms borrow secured at a short-term maturity with rights for repo financiers in cases of most underlying collateral to be exempt from bankruptcy and liquidate the collateral in case of borrower's default. We believe this omission is a mistake in light of the systemic nature of the repo market and its structural weaknesses. As we mentioned, unlike the liquidity risk that unsecured financing may become unavailable to a firm, the liquidity risk that secured repo financing may become unavailable to a firm is inherently a systemic risk: The markets for the repo securities may become illiquid precisely when a large part of the financial sector is experiencing undercapitalization or funding stress.

Unless this systemic liquidity risk of repo market is resolved, the risk of a run on the repo market will remain. Our proposed solution is to set up a "Repo Resolution Authority" that maintains liquidity for repo markets in case of defaults, takes on the role of orderly liquidation of collateral, but controls its credit risk through ex-ante restrictions on qualifying collateral, qualifying repo financiers, concentration limits and minimum haircuts. Such a resolution mechanism addresses the externality of systemic risk of repo contracts on risky and potentially illiquid collaterals. And, such a mechanism can be exercised without overly compromising market discipline, market liquidity or taxpayer funds.

Interestingly, the Federal Reserve, the Bank of England, and the European Central Bank set up many facilities to halt a total financial collapse during the hay days of the ongoing global financial crisis. These have invariably been facilities set up for SIALs. For instance, the Fed's Term Auction Facility, which auctioned term loans to depository institutions, and the Primary Dealer Credit Facility, which provided overnight loans to primary dealers, were to lengthen the maturity of their SILs. The Fed's Asset-Backed Commercial Paper Money Market Mutual Fund Liquidity Facility and Term Asset-Backed Securities Loan Facility were to provide liquidity directly to borrowers holding systemically important assets. Stated differently, financial regulators around the globe were forced in the midst of a crisis to act on SIALs, rather than just on individual financial institutions holding them. Our key recommendation is to recognize the need for such action ahead of time and build the essential infrastructure to ensure that excessive risk-taking is discouraged and markets know that regulators have an orderly resolution plan.

Finally, although we have focused on the US repo markets, our discussion and proposed reforms apply to other countries as well. Repo markets exist around the globe, from China to Japan to Hungary to Turkey, to name but a few countries, although their histories are much shorter and their sizes much smaller than that of the US repo market. Many emerging countries' repo markets date back to the early 1990s. The largest repo market outside the US is the European repo market, which was established with the introduction of the Euro in 1999 and stood at €5.6 trillion based on the amount outstanding on December 9, 2009 (according to the survey conducted by the International Capital Market Association with 53 financial institutions located in 14 European countries, as well as the US and Japan). The European market is the only repo market outside the US where potentially illiquid financial assets are used as repo collateral, and therefore, our proposed reforms are also relevant to the European repo market. In other repo markets, the repo collateral generally represents government bonds issued by the sovereign states, so that in these markets, the repo financiers do not appear to run a substantial risk of being forced to sell their collateral in illiquid markets in the event of financial crises. This may change however, if potentially illiquid collateral were to become acceptable in repo transactions in these countries. Indeed, when sovereign credit risk is an issue, even the repo markets for government bonds may be vulnerable.

At any rate, leaving the repo markets out of the discussion of financial reforms is not an alternative; if these markets are not reformed and their participants not made to internalize the risk that large quantities of underlying repo collateral could be put up for liquidation in an illiquid market, then runs on the repo market will occur in the future, potentially leading to new systemic crises, in spite of the huge regulatory apparatus being built around financial firms on other fronts and markets.

References

Acharya, V. V. (2011). "Systemic Risk and Macro-Prudential Regulation," New York University, Stern School of Business Working Paper.

Acharya, V. V., B. Adler and M. Richardson (2011). "A proposal to resolve the distress of large and complex financial institutions," New York University, Stern School of Business Working Paper.

Acharya, V. V., B. Adler, M. Richardson and N. Roubini (2010). "Resolution authority," Chapter 8 in *Regulating Wall Street, The Dodd-Frank Act and the New Architecture of Global Finance*, V. V. Acharya *et al.* (eds.), New York University Stern School of Business; John Wiley & Sons.

Acharya, V. V., T. F. Cooley, M. Richardson and I. Walter (eds.) (2010). *Regulating Wall Street, The Dodd-Frank Act and the New Architecture of Global Finance*, New York University Stern School of Business; John Wiley & Sons.

Acharya, V. V., T. F. Cooley, M. Richardson and I. Walter (eds.) (2011). *Dodd-Frank: One Year On*. Available at: www.voxeu.org.

Acharya, V. V. and A. Krishnamurthy (2010). "Why bankers must bear the risk of 'too safe to fail' assets," *Financial Times*, March 17.

Acharya, V. V. and T. S. Öncü (2010). "The repurchase agreement (repo) market," Chapter 11 in *Regulating Wall Street, The Dodd-Frank Act and the New Architecture of Global Finance*, V. V. Acharya *et al.* (eds.), New York University Stern School of Business; John Wiley & Sons.

Acharya, V. V., L. H. Pedersen, T. Philippon and M. Richardson (2010). "Measuring systemic risk," New York University, Stern School of Business Working Paper.

Acharya, V. V. and M. Richardson (eds.) (2013). *Restoring Financial Stability: How to Repair a Failed System*, New York University Stern School of Business; John Wiley & Sons.

Acharya, V. V., P. Schnabl and G. Suarez (2009). "Securitization without risk transfer," *Journal of Financial Economics*, 107(3), pp. 515–536.

Basel Committee on Banking Supervision (2010). "BCBS-CGFS Working Group on Systemic Liquidity Risk," CGFS Report, June 2010.

Bliss, Robert and G. Kaufman (2011). "Resolving large, insolvent complex financial institutions: A better way," *The Banking Law Journal*, April, pp. 339–363.

Calomiris, C. W. and E. N. White (1994). "The origins of federal deposit insurance," in *The Regulated Economy*, C. Goldin and G. D. Libecop (eds.), Chicago: University of Chicago Press, pp. 145–188.

Cohan, W. D. (2009). *House of Cards: A Tale of Hubris and Wretched Excess on Wall Street*. New York: Knopf Doubleday.

Copeland, A., I. Davis, E. LeSuer and A. Martin (2012). "Mapping and sizing the U.S. repo market," *Liberty Street Economics*, The Federal Reserve Bank of New York, June 25, 2012.

Copeland, A., A. Martin and M. W. Walker (2010). "The tri-party repo market before the 2010 reforms," Federal Reserve Bank of New York Working Paper.

Edwards, F. and E. Morrison (2004). "Derivatives and the bankruptcy code: Why the special treatment?" Columbia Law and Economics Research Paper No. 258.

FDIC (2011). "The Meeting of the Systemic Resolution Advisory Committee of the Federal Deposit Insurance Corporation, Held in the Board Room, Federal Deposit Insurance Corporation Building," June 21.

FRBNY White Paper (2010). "Tri-Party Repo Infrastructure Reform," May 17.

Faubus, B. (2010). "Narrowing the bankruptcy safe harbor for derivatives to combat systemic risk," *Duke Law Journal*, Vol. 59, pp. 802–842.

Fleming, M. and K. D. Garbade (2003). "The repurchase agreement refined: GCF Repos®," *FRBNY Current Issues in Economics and Finance*, Vol. 9, No. 6, pp. 1–7.

Garbade, K. D. (2006). "The evolution of repo contracting conventions in the 1980s," *FRBNY Economic Policy Review*, May, pp. 27–42.

Gorton, G. (2009). "Slapped in the face by the invisible hand: Banking and the panic of 2007," The Federal Reserve Bank of Atlanta's 2009 Financial Markets Conference: Financial Innovation and Crisis, May 11–13.

Gorton, G. and A. Metrick (2009a). "Securitized banking and run on the repo," Yale ICF Working Paper No. 09-14.

Gorton, G. and A. Metrick (2009b). "Haircuts," Yale ICF Working Paper No. 09-15.

Gorton, G. and A. Metrick (2010). "Regulating the shadow banking system", Yale University Working Paper.

Graeber, D. (2011). *Debt, The first 5,000 Years*, Brooklyn, New York: Melville House.

Jackson, T. H. (2009). "Chapter 11F: A proposal for the use of bankruptcy to resolve financial institutions," in *Ending Government Bailouts as We Know Them*, K. E. Scott, G. P. Shultz and J. B. Taylor (eds.), Hoover Press.

Kaufman, G. G. (2004). "Depositor liquidity and loss-sharing in bank failure resolutions," *Contemporary Economic Policy*, Vol. 22, No. 2, pp. 237–249.

Kaufman, G. G. and K. E. Scott (2003). "What is systemic risk, and do bank regulators retard or contribute to it?" *The Independent Review*, Vol. 7, No. 3, pp. 371–391.

Krishnamurthy, A., S. Nagel and D. Orlov (2011). "Sizing up repo," Northwestern University Working Paper.

Miller, H. (2009). "Too big to fail: The role of bankruptcy and antitrust law in financial regulation reform," Testimony before the Subcommittee on Commercial and Administrative Law of the House of Representatives Committee on the Judiciary, October 22.

Olson, J. S. (1988). *Saving Capitalism*, Princeton University Press, Princeton, New Jersey.

Perotti, E. (2010). "Systemic liquidity risk and bankruptcy exceptions," Center for Economic Policy Research, Policy Insight No. 52, October.

Reinhart, C. M. and K. S. Rogoff (2009). *This Time is Different, Eight Centuries of Financial Folly*, Princeton University Press, Princeton and Oxford.

Roe, M. J. (2009). "End bankruptcy priority for derivatives, repos and swaps," *Financial Times*, December 16.

Roe, M. J. (2010). "Bankruptcy's financial crisis accelerator: The derivatives players' priorities in Chapter 11," Harvard Public Law Working Paper No. 10-17.

Tuckman, B. (2010). "Amending safe harbors to reduce systemic risk in OTC derivative markets," CFS Policy Paper.

Tuckman, B. (2012a). "Flash: Tri-party repo infrastructure reform," CFS Policy Paper.

Tuckman, B. (2012b). "How to contain a financial crisis without bailouts," Forbes.com, March 22.

Upham, C. and E. Lamke (1934). *Closed and Distressed Banks*, Brookings Institution, Washington, D.C.

Willis, H. P. and J. M. Chapman (1934). *The Banking Situation*, New York: Columbia University Press.

Reexamining Financial Innovation after the Global Financial Crisis*

W. Scott Frame
University of North Carolina at Charlotte
and
Federal Reserve Bank of Atlanta

Lawrence J. White
New York University

> The innovations of recent years — the alphabet soup of CDOs and SIVs, RMBS, and ABCP — were sold on false pretenses. They were promoted as ways to spread risk, making investment safer. What they did instead — aside from making their creators a lot of money, which they didn't have to repay when it all went bust — was to spread confusion, luring investors into taking on more risk than they realized.
>
> Paul Krugman (2007)

Introduction

Krugman's colorful commentary reflects a narrative that has led many to cast doubt on the usefulness of most financial innovation, as such activity is viewed as having caused the recent global financial crisis. Interestingly, this view contrasts with that provided by academic economists in recent

*W. Scott Frame is a Professor of Finance at the University of North Carolina at Charlotte's Belk College of Business and is currently on leave from the Federal Reserve Bank of Atlanta, where he is a financial economist and senior policy advisor. Lawrence J. White is affiliated with New York University's Stern School of Business. The views expressed do not necessarily reflect those of the Federal Reserve Bank of Atlanta or the Federal Reserve System. The authors thank participants at the Federal Reserve Bank of Chicago's 2012 International Banking Conference for comments.

decades (e.g., Miller, 1986, 1992; Merton, 1992; Tufano, 2003; Frame and White, 2004, 2010; Allen, 2012). The more positive view is that since finance facilitates such a large share of economic activity, any improvements in the financial sector should have direct positive ramifications throughout an economy. While a reevaluation of financial innovation is natural in light of the most recent financial crisis, we do need to keep in mind that not every innovation will be successful or represent an improvement. By its nature, innovation involves trial and error, and failures can sometimes be costly.

In a recent paper, Beck *et al.* (2012) empirically explore the two different views of financial innovation: The first is the "innovation-growth" view under which financial innovations help to reduce transaction costs, agency costs, facilitate risk-sharing, and ultimately improve allocative efficiency and economic growth. The second is the "innovation-fragility" view that posits that financial innovations are the root cause of the recent global financial crisis (and several previous ones). The authors present cross-country evidence that is consistent with both views. Financial innovation is associated with a stronger relationship between a country's growth opportunities and actual growth, but also with higher growth volatility and higher bank fragility. While these findings are interesting and intuitive, they do not speak to the net welfare implications of financial innovations (individually or collectively).

A significant amount of recent research describes the roles that were played by relatively new financial technologies in the propagation of the global financial crisis. This paper will synthesize this work as it applies to three of the "usual suspects:" credit default swaps, off-balance sheet conduits, and securitization (and the structured finance that has followed from it). The goal is to shed light on why these innovations appeared, as well as on their prospective social value. Before doing so, however, we provide some background on financial innovation.

Background[1]

According to Merton (1992), the primary function of a financial system is to facilitate the allocation and deployment of economic resources, both

[1] This section draws heavily on Frame and White (2004).

spatially and across time, in an uncertain environment. This function, in turn, encompasses a payments system with a medium of exchange; the transfer of resources from savers to investor-users of the resources (and the eventual repayment to the savers); the gathering of savings for the purposes of pure time transformation (i.e., deferral/smoothing of consumption); and the reduction of risk through insurance and diversification.

The operation of a financial system involves real resource costs, such as labor, materials, and capital employed by financial intermediaries (e.g., banks, insurance companies, etc.) and by financial facilitators (e.g., stock brokers, market makers, etc.). Much of these resources are expended in the data gathering and analyses in which financial market participants engage so as to deal with problems of asymmetric information. Further, since multiple time periods are an inherent characteristic of finance, there are also uncertainties about future states of the world that generate risks. For risk-averse individuals, these risks represent costs.

Viewed in this context, Frame and White (2004) define a financial innovation as a new or improved product/service/instrument that lowers costs, reduces risks, or otherwise better satisfies the demands of financial system participants. Financial innovations can be grouped as new products (e.g., exchange-traded index funds); new services (e.g., online securities trading); new "production" processes (e.g., electronic record keeping for securities); or new organizational forms (e.g., a new type of electronic exchange for trading securities).

Campbell (1988, Chapter 16) lists several key environmental factors that encourage financial innovation: (1) underlying technologies; (2) macroeconomic conditions; (3) regulation; and (4) taxes. We discuss each below and where applicable tie them to the recent crisis. However, it is worth noting that Campbell largely focuses on the levels of these environmental factors and neglects the possibility that *changes* in the levels may also induce innovation.[2] We adopt the broader perspective.

[2]When changes occur, we expect an initial wave or flurry of financial innovations that represent an initial response; the flow of innovations will then, over time, settle to a new equilibrium flow that is appropriate to the new environmental conditions. Thus a significant change in any of the major environmental categories would likely induce (with some lag) its own initial wave of innovations that would eventually settle to a lower equilibrium rate.

1. Underlying technologies. The basic underlying "physical" technologies of finance are those of telecommunications and data processing, which permit the gathering of information, its transmission, and its analysis. Increasingly, these technologies allow financial market participants to measure and manage their risk exposures more efficiently and effectively using applied statistics. For example, with respect to lending, asymmetric information problems imply that lenders have difficulties determining who is a creditworthy borrower (adverse selection) and also have difficulties monitoring borrowers after a loan has been made (moral hazard). Accordingly, better (more advanced, faster, lower cost) physical technologies have permitted more innovations (e.g., credit and behavioral scoring) that allow lenders better to overcome those asymmetric information problems. Similarly, in terms of market risk, the use of value-at-risk and portfolio stress testing provide useful risk measures that can be used internally to set risk tolerance levels or allocate capital and externally to provide investors with a sense of overall exposure. Better physical technologies may also permit organizational innovations (e.g., electronic securities exchanges) that would not be possible with less advanced technologies.[3]

Rapid technological advancement has also presented new challenges. First, as the ability to measure and manage risks rapidly improved during the 1990s and 2000s, financial institutions and their regulators increasingly relied on analytical and statistical models. However, when unusual events unfolded and historical data relationships changed, many such models broke down and left their users vulnerable. Second, much of technological advancement is also associated with scalability and resulted in a much more concentrated and globally interconnected banking sector. While there are almost assuredly private (and some social) benefits to this trend, it does lead to greater concerns about contagion and systemic risk that can result in social costs.

[3] In addition to physical technologies, the state of progress in the understanding of financial theory might also be described as a "technology" that can underlie and encourage financial innovation. For example, it may well be the case that the development of the Black and Scholes (1973) and Merton (1973) models of option pricing helped encourage the widespread innovation of financial options and futures instruments in the 1970s and 1980s; and similarly the development of the "capital asset pricing model" (CAPM) in the 1960s (Sharpe, 1964; Lintner, 1965; Mossin, 1966) helped pave the way for the innovation of the stock index fund in 1976.

2. *Macroeconomic conditions.* Unstable macroeconomic conditions — as evidenced in fluctuating equity prices, interest rates, or exchange rates — create uncertainties and risks that are likely to spur innovations to alleviate those risks (relative to what otherwise would be true in a stable macroeconomic environment).

During the housing boom of the mid-2000s, there was a substantial increase in what had previously been niche mortgage products (e.g., low documentation loans and interest-only or negatively amortizing loans). There was also tremendous growth in the securitization of mortgages and the further securitization of mortgage-backed securities (e.g., into collateralized debt obligations, or CDOs) and the emergence of derivative securities tied to home prices and subprime mortgage-backed securities. Some of these phenomena are discussed below.

3. *Regulation.* Regulation is a two-edged sword when it comes to financial innovation.[4] On the one hand, some forms of regulation must inhibit innovation. For example, if regulation prevents commercial banks from owning insurance companies (and vice versa), then whatever innovations might arise from joint ownership and operation will not occur. On the other hand, it is also clear that innovation can arise from efforts to circumvent regulation. To continue with the bank/insurance example, if cross-ownership is prevented, then banks will have the incentive to create insurance-like products and services (but, of course, will avoid labeling them as insurance), while insurance companies will have an incentive to create bank-like products. Further, the innovation that arises as a consequence of regulation may be a socially positive or negative phenomenon. This depends on whether one sees the regulation itself as socially worthwhile (so that innovative evasion is a waste of resources or may even have socially deleterious consequences) or as a social waste (in which case the innovative evasion is a second-best improvement).

One important regulatory issue discussed below is "regulatory capital arbitrage," or the ability to hold a particular risk in a different form and receive regulatory capital relief for doing so. Specifically, it appears that this practice distorted risk management and risk-sharing incentives in the

[4]See White (2000) for a more extensive discussion of the interaction between regulation and financial innovation.

years leading up to the crisis — and in a way that was ultimately systemically destabilizing. In essence, our view is that minimum capital requirements for prudentially regulated institutions are socially worthwhile — indeed, capital requirements that were too low, badly measured, and/or poorly enforced were the root cause of much of the financial crisis — and that innovations that allowed financial institutions to evade these capital minimums were largely antisocial.

4. *Taxes.* To the extent that a tax system levies differential taxes on different streams of income or on different categories of assets, the higher-taxed parties will seek ways of reducing their taxes. Financial innovation will follow. Higher levels of taxation will likely yield a larger flow of innovation. Again, whether one sees this innovation as a socially positive or negative phenomenon will depend on the social interpretation that one puts on the differential taxation scheme.

Building on Campbell's list, Frame and White (2004) also add appropriability (and the intellectual property considerations that are associated with appropriability) and the Schumpeter-inspired hypotheses relating to firm size and market power. Traditionally, the intellectual property protection system (i.e., patent, copyright, trademark) has not been considered important for financial innovation; patents for financial innovations were a rare phenomenon before 1980 and only became noticeable and significant in the late 1990s (Lerner, 2002, 2006; Hunt, 2010). Since Tufano (1989) shows that imitation of some innovations is rapid, a regime of intellectual property protection could encourage greater innovation.[5] As for the Schumpeterian hypotheses, the absence of formal R&D facilities in financial services firms has probably been a significant factor in the relative neglect of the size and market-power considerations with respect to financial innovation.

Three Usual Suspects

Many commentators have blamed financial innovations for the recent financial crisis. Three of these have garnered special attention: credit default

[5]It is also possible, however, that excessively broad protection for ideas could discourage follow-on innovation, because of the transaction costs of negotiations between the original innovator and the follow-on innovators.

swaps, off-balance sheet conduits, and securitization (structured finance). Below, we synthesize some recent research about each technology in an attempt to shed light on why these innovations appeared as well as on their prospective social value.

Credit Default Swaps

Credit default swaps (CDS) are effectively insurance contracts that pay off in the event that a firm or country defaults on its bond obligations over some fixed period of time in exchange for a premium. CDS originally emerged as a way for financial institutions to hedge/transfer some amount of credit risk of certain bond holdings to other market participants. However, some market participants also trade CDS to express views (long or short) on the credit quality of individual firms on an unfunded basis. Data from the Bank for International Settlements show that the total notional (insured) amount of CDS outstanding grew from $6.4 trillion to $57.9 trillion between 2004 and 2007 and stood at $25.0 trillion at the end of 2012. Stulz (2010) provides a nice overview of the economics of the CDS market and its role in the credit crisis.

CDS were most likely vilified because of their central role in the failure of AIG, as well as the introduction of the so-called ABX-HE index that allowed market participants synthetically to trade exposure to subprime mortgage credit. In the case of AIG, the institution sold CDS contracts that insured against the default of a large quantity of AAA-rated structured finance securities for which it was insufficiently capitalized. While there were clearly risk-management and regulatory failures associated with AIG, the case is very similar to those for monoline bond insurers, mortgage insurance companies, and the US government-sponsored secondary mortgage market conduits (Fannie Mae and Freddie Mac).

In all of these instances of failure, the true source of the failure of the institution was an inadequate amount of capital (in essence, net worth) to protect the institution's solvency against the risks that the institution had taken on. Financial innovations, such as CDS in the case of AIG, may have made it easier for the institutions to take on new (and sometimes poorly understood) risks. But these institutions were all subject to prudential regulation that involved minimum capital requirements that were supposed to be risk sensitive. Hence, inadequate prudential regulation surely must bear some of the blame.

The ABX-HE is an index that was introduced by a financial market information services firm (Markit Group Limited) and is based on the value of baskets (i.e., cross-sectional average values) of subprime mortgage-backed securities of a given original rating.[6] The demand-side of this credit derivative market arose because of a strong desire by some market participants to hedge their exposures to US house prices in general and subprime mortgage credit in particular. On the supply-side were many investors who wanted exposure to the same risks without having to hold/fund the underlying assets.

While CDS outstanding has declined from its peak, it has been relatively stable in the past few years. The rapid increase in the market leading into the financial crisis and decrease thereafter should not be surprising given the default risk concerns at large financial institutions and sovereigns. Given the remaining depth of the market, one can infer that it provides value by providing hedging opportunities (on the buy-side) and more liquid exposure to credit risk than bonds (on the sell-side). But, again, for prudentially regulated financial institutions, their capital levels should be commensurate with the risks that the institutions incur in the CDS market.

Structured Investment Vehicles

Structured investment vehicles (SIVs) were off-balance sheet entities that were created by banks to hold highly rated, long-term assets (often, AAA-rated asset-backed securities) and that were typically funded with very short-term debt (asset-backed commercial paper, or ABCP). Furthermore, in order to calm ABCP investors, the sponsor generally provided a backup liquidity guarantee to the SIV. Such guarantees markedly reduced regulatory capital requirements to a small fraction of what would otherwise have been required if the assets remained on-balance sheet.

As described and analyzed in Acharya, Schnabl, and Suarez (2013), prior to the financial crisis banks moved $1.3 trillion in financial assets to SIVs — primarily to engage in regulatory capital arbitrage. When the asset values of

[6] For example, the ABX.HE.BBB 07–01 index captures the average value of 20 BBB-rated mortgage-backed securities issued during the first two quarters of 2007.

many conduits plummeted in 2007, ABCP investors retreated, and sponsors repatriated the assets onto their balance sheets. This had the effect of reducing sponsor capital-to-asset ratios. Thankfully, this organizational innovation has disappeared as a result of changes in accounting rules.

Securitization

Securitization, or the process of pooling loans and selling shares of the underlying cash flows, has been with us for a long time. (This is the devilish "originate-to-distribute" model of financial intermediation.) Securitization was originally designed and principally used for residential mortgages — first through US government agency Ginnie Mae in 1970 and then subsequently by two US government-sponsored enterprises (GSEs) — Fannie Mae and Freddie Mac.[7] In these cases, the US government was explicitly or implicitly guaranteeing the timely payment of principal and interest on the securities.

These "Agency" mortgage securitizations initially involved a simple "pass-through" structure whereby securities were *pari passu* (i.e., of equal priority) and investors each received monthly principal and interest payments in relation to their investment. However, in the 1980s, collateralized mortgage obligations, or CMOs, were introduced that allowed for priority structuring (tranching) for prepayments. This allowed for the tailoring of security payoffs based on investors' appetite for interest rate risk exposure.

The "pooling and tranching" of cash flows was extended in the 1990s and applied to credit risk — effectively creating a "capital structure." This approach was initially largely used to create "non-Agency" mortgage-backed securities (jumbo and subprime), but was later extended to many other types of loans and financial assets. Such structured finance meant that credit risks were repackaged in a way to create a large volume of highly rated "safe assets" from otherwise risky collateral; however, this structuring depended heavily on the rating agencies' perceived ability to estimate underlying default risks and their correlation. This relates to the earlier discussion about market participants' heavy reliance on risk measurement models. See Coval, Jurek, and Stafford (2009) for a review of structured finance.

[7]However, Goetzmann and Newman (2010) show that the securitization of commercial real estate mortgages dates back at least to the 1920s.

Data from the Securities Industry and Financial Markets Association, or SIFMA, indicates that asset-backed securities issuance will exceed $200 billion in 2012 — something that has not occurred since 2007 when issuance topped $500 billion. (The two largest issuance years on record were 2005 and 2006 at around $750 billion in each year.) Almost all of the reduction in asset-backed securities issuance can be attributed to the virtual elimination of the market for new "private-label" residential mortgage-backed securities. This market is unlikely to return (even in modest amounts) until US home prices stabilize, new mortgage underwriting regulations are finalized, legal ambiguity is resolved, and the breadth and depth of government-sponsored programs recede.

The pooling and tranching of cash flows (through securitization and subsequent structuring) can serve to match investor demands better with the supply of securities (e.g., DeMarzo, 2005) and allow greater specialization of functions. And by doing so, securitization can reduce borrowing costs. But securitization has also meant the replacement of the vertically integrated lending model with a vertically disintegrated model. This, in turn, has created greater possibilities for adverse selection and moral hazard (principal-agent) problems.

Moreover, a great deal of securitization activity was driven by regulatory capital arbitrage. As noted by Frame and White (2005), this trend first became apparent after the introduction of the Basel I capital standards for banks and statutory capital requirements for Fannie Mae and Freddie Mac. Banks that were bound by the regulatory leverage requirement typically securitized and sold Agency mortgage-backed securities to Fannie Mae and Freddie Mac. The reason was that GSE funding costs were lower as a bank would have to hold 8% total capital to total risk-weighted assets (as well as 4% "Tier 1" capital to total assets) versus only 2.5% total capital to total assets that had to be held by a GSE. On the other hand, banks bound by the risk-based capital requirement securitized and held Agency mortgage-backed securities. In this case, the bank faced a 4% risk-based capital charge for whole mortgage loans (50% risk weight), but only a 1.6% charge for holding the assets in securitized form (20% risk weight).

Other types of securitization became advantaged under the Basel II risk-based capital standards. US investment banks and European banks were both subject to Basel II — but without facing any minimum leverage capital requirements. AAA-rated asset-backed securities became popular holdings as they were subject to extremely low Basel II capital charges (0.56%). For related discussions, see Frame and White (2007), Acharya and Richardson (2009), and Nadauld and Sherlund (2009).

Besides being thinly capitalized, structured finance transactions had become increasingly complex during the mid-2000s boom — more complicated capital structures and cash flow waterfalls, and the pooling of securitized assets into collateral pools (CDOs). The valuation of asset-backed securities relies on statistical models to predict the behavior of borrowers on underlying loans. However, such models are often built on incomplete or insufficient data and are subject to misspecification and error. The Basel II "internal ratings-based approach" for setting required risk-based capital for such assets was built upon the same models and data.

Securitization will surely remain as part of the government-supported route for mortgage finance and guarantees: the mortgages that are insured by the Federal Housing Administration (FHA), the Department of Veterans Affairs (VA), and the US Department of Agriculture (USDA), and that are securitized by Ginnie Mae. The future of quasi-governmental support for mortgage securitization, as historically occurred for Fannie Mae and Freddie Mac, is still uncertain, as of year-end 2012.[8] However, the advantages of securitization in opening privately financed residential mortgages to a wider group of investors, rather than restricting the sources of finance to the deposits that can be gathered by banks and other depository institutions, appear to us to be strong. We believe that investors, chastened by the experiences of 2007–2008, will insist on simpler and more transparent structures that will better deal with the inherent problems of asymmetric information in finance (and which are potentially exacerbated by securitization) and that will thereby allocate risks and returns appropriately.

Conclusions

Economists have generally viewed financial innovation as welfare enhancing on net. However, in light of the recent global financial crisis, financial

[8]For a review and critique of the various proposals that have been offered with respect to mortgage securitization, see Frame, Wall, and White (2013, forthcoming).

innovation has come under greater scrutiny. While research is ongoing as to the role of specific financial innovations in the financial crisis, we have here briefly discussed three of the often-cited culprits: credit default swaps, off-balance sheet conduits, and securitization.

We have two principal (and related) conclusions. First, regulatory capital arbitrage appears to have played a central role in the crisis as many tarnished innovations were those that were principally designed to lower regulatory capital for a given risk. Second, financial firms and regulators appear to have over-relied on applied statistics for risk measurement and management. While intellectually appealing and promising, there was perhaps too little appreciation for the limitations of data inputs and model misspecification.

Finally, it is worth remembering that finance is inherently laden with potential problems of asymmetric information. It is the recognition of these potential problems that underlies the extensive regulation of the financial sector: prudential regulation of important categories of financial institutions; restrictions on the types of financial products and services that can be offered in the marketplace; and requirements that extensive amounts of information accompany many financial transactions. In this context, financial innovations certainly have the potential to reduce costs, reduce risks, and/or better satisfy the demands of financial system participants, as we stated earlier; but, as the financial crisis has revealed, financial innovations also have the potential to exacerbate those problems of asymmetric information. In a sector that is already heavily regulated, financial regulators must take a clear-eyed approach to financial innovation: to try to encourage and approve the former and restrain the latter. This is surely not an easy task, but there is no avoiding it.

References

Acharya, V. V. and M. Richardson (2009). "Causes of the financial crisis," *Critical Review*, Vol. 21, No. 2–3, pp. 195–210.

Acharya, V. V., P. Schnabl and G. Suarez (2013). "Securitization without risk transfer," *Journal of Financial Economics*, Vol. 107, No. 3, pp. 515–536.

Allen, F. (2012). "Trends in financial innovation and their welfare impact: An overview," *European Financial Management*, Vol. 18, No. 4, pp. 493–514.

Beck, T., T. Chen, C. Lin and F. M. Song (2012). "Financial innovation: The bright and dark sides." Available at: http://papers.ssrn.com/sol3/papers.cfm?abstract_id=1991216, Accessed July 20, 2013.

Black, F. and M. Scholes (1973). "The pricing of options and corporate liabilities," *Journal of Political Economy*, Vol. 81, No. 3, pp. 637–654.

Campbell, T. S. (1988). *Money and Capital Markets*, Scott Foresman, Glenview, IL.

Coval, J., J. Jurek and E. Stafford (2009). "The economics of structured finance," *Journal of Economic Perspectives*, Vol. 23, No. 1, pp. 3–25.

DeMarzo, P. M. (2005). "The pooling and tranching of securities: A model of informed intermediation," *Review of Financial Studies*, Vol. 18, No. 1, pp. 1–36.

Frame, W. S. and L. J. White (2004). "Empirical studies of financial innovation: Lots of talk, little action?," *Journal of Economic Literature*, Vol. 42, No. 1, pp. 116–144.

Frame, W. S. and L. J. White (2005). "Fussing and fuming over Fannie and Freddie: How much smoke, how much fire?," *Journal of Economic Perspectives*, Vol. 19, No. 2, pp. 159–184.

Frame, W. S. and L. J. White (2007). "Charter value, risk-taking incentives, and emerging competition at Fannie Mae and Freddie Mac," *Journal of Money, Credit and Banking*, Vol. 39, No. 1, pp. 83–104.

Frame, W. S. and L. J. White (2010). "Technological change, financial innovation, and diffusion in banking," in *The Oxford Handbook of Banking*, Allen N. Berger, Phillip Molyneux, and John O.S. Wilson (eds.), Oxford, UK: Oxford University Press.

Frame, W. S., L. Wall and L. J. White (2013). "The devil's in the tail: Residential mortgage finance and the U.S. Treasury," *Journal of Applied Finance*, forthcoming.

Goetzmann, W. N. and F. Newman (2010). "Securitization in the 1920s," National Bureau of Economic Research, working paper, No. 15650. Available at: http://cid.bcrp.gob.pe/biblio/Papers/NBER/2010/enero/w15650.pdf. [Accessed on July 20, 2013].

Hunt, R. M. (2010). "Business method patents and U.S. financial services," *Contemporary Economic Policy*, Vol. 28, No. 3, pp. 322–352.

Krugman, P. (2007). "Innovating our way to financial crisis," *New York Times*, December 3.

Lerner, J. (2002). "Where does State Street lead? A first look at finance patents, 1971–2000," *Journal of Finance*, Vol. 57(2), pp. 901–930.

Lerner, J. (2006). "The new new financial thing: Innovation before and after State Street," *Journal of Financial Economics*, Vol. 79, No. 2, pp. 223–255.

Lintner, J. V., Jr. (1965). "The valuation of risk assets and the selection of risky investments in stock portfolios and capital budgets," *Review of Economics and Statistics*, Vol. 47, No. 1, pp. 13–37.

Merton, R. C. (1973). "Theory of rational option pricing," *Bell Journal of Economics and Management Science*, Vol. 4, No. 1, pp. 141–183.
Merton, R. C. (1992). "Financial innovation and economic performance," *Journal of Applied Corporate Finance*, Vol. 4, pp. 12–22.
Miller, M. H. (1992). "Financial innovation: Achievements and prospects," *Journal of Applied Corporate Finance*, Vol. 4, pp. 4–12.
Miller, M. H. (1986). "Financial innovation: The last twenty years and the next," *Journal of Financial and Quantitative Analysis*, Vol. 21, No. 4, pp. 459–471.
Mossin, J. (1966). "Equilibrium in a capital asset market," *Econometrica*, Vol. 34, No. 4, pp. 768–783.
Nadauld, T. D. and S. M. Sherlund (2009). "The role of the securitization process in the expansion of subprime credit," Finance and Economics Discussion Series, Board of Governors of the Federal Reserve System, Divisions of Research and Statistics and Monetary Affairs, No. 2009-28, Washington, DC. Available at www.federalreserve.gov/pubs/feds/2009/200928/200928-pap.pdf [accessed on July 20, 2013].
Sharpe, W. F. (1964). "Capital asset prices: A theory of market equilibrium under conditions of risk," *Journal of Finance*, Vol. 19, No. 3, pp. 425–442.
Stulz, R. M. (2010). "Credit default swaps and the credit crisis," *Journal of Economic Perspectives*, Vol. 24, No. 1, pp. 73–92.
Tufano, P. (2003). "Financial innovation," in *Handbook of the Economics of Finance*, George M. Constantinides, Milton Harris, and René M. Stulz (eds.), Vol. 1A, Amsterdam: Elsevier/North Holland.
Tufano, P. (1989). "Financial innovation and first mover advantages," *Journal of Financial Economics*, Vol. 25, No. 2, pp. 213–240.
White, L. J. (2000). "Technological change, financial innovation, and financial regulation in the US: The challenges for public policy," in *Performance of Financial Institutions: Efficiency, Innovation, Regulation*, P. Harker and S. Zenios (eds.), New York: Cambridge University Press, pp. 388–415.

Financial Innovation and Shadow Banking

Luc Laeven*
International Monetary Fund
and
Centre for Economic Policy Research (CEPR)

There are bright and dark sides to financial innovation. On the bright side, financial innovations that improve screening and monitoring can facilitate the allocation of resources by financial intermediaries to their most productive use (Greenwood, Sanchez, and Wang, 2010; Laeven, Levine, and Michalopoulos, 2012). Notable examples of such productive forms of financial innovation in the past include credit bureaus and venture capital. Financial innovations that improve risk-sharing can, in principle, also be welfare enhancing. A good example is derivatives in their various forms and colors. However, financial innovations can be "deadly weapons" if abused, allowing financial institutions to further boost excessive leverage and contributing to systemic risk. The same derivatives that can improve risk-sharing can also harbor very large tail risks that can jeopardize individual financial intermediaries that engage in ill-managed derivatives trades and with it the entire financial system.

Much of financial innovation has occurred in what has come to be known as the shadow banking system, consisting of a broad range of activities, including asset securitization, collateral intermediation (such as repos), and regulatory arbitrage through special investment vehicles, conduits, and

---

*Luc Laeven is Deputy Division Chief in the Research Department of the International Monetary Fund (IMF) and a Research Fellow at the Centre for Economic Policy Research. The views expressed herein are those of the author and should not be interpreted as those of the IMF or IMF Board.

other off-balance sheet items (Claessens *et al.*, 2012). The key distinction between the shadow and traditional banking systems is that the former is more lightly regulated (or even unregulated). However, there is much overlap between the two because banks are counterparties to many shadow banking institutions and because much of the shadow banking activity takes place in subsidiaries of existing bank holding companies.

In this short piece, I will review three papers that look at various aspects of financial innovation and the shadow banking system, and that I discussed at this year's International Banking Conference at the Federal Reserve Bank of Chicago.

The three papers were presented by professors Robert Vishny, Viral Acharya, and Scott Frame. Vishny's paper focuses on securitization, Acharya's paper on repos, and Frame's paper on all of the above with the exception of repos. Each of these financial instruments offers ways for financial intermediaries to boost value by increasing leverage. The markets for most of these financial instruments are highly concentrated, being dominated by a few players, most of which are systemically important financial institutions. This implies that any failure in the delivery of these instruments or a mispricing of risk embedded in these instruments can pose systemic threats to the financial system.

The growth in these instruments and associated boom in shadow banking prior to the recent global financial crisis was in part driven by a demand for safe assets and regulatory arbitrage but was also very much associated with financial innovation. For example, innovations in securitization methods, including the tranching of assets, enabled risk-sharing through securitization at unprecedented levels.

Given the interplay between financial innovation and regulatory arbitrage in the lightly regulated shadow banking, and the associated shifting of risks and other unintended consequences, this has raised important questions about the boundaries of regulation, including: What is the key driver of systemic risk in the shadow banking system? Should shadow banking be regulated more? Would it be better to regulate specific assets or markets? But at what cost to the financial system and society?

The papers that I will discuss touch upon these issues, although more work is needed to strike the right balance between safeguarding the financial system through regulation and enabling the financial system to perform its function of spreading risks and financing productive growth.

The paper by Gennaioli, Shleifer, and Vishny (2012) presents a theoretical model of the shadow banking system. The starting point of the model is that, by enabling the diversification of idiosyncratic risk, securitization promotes the expansion of balance sheets of banks and increases financial links among them. Under rational expectations, securitization facilitates a better allocation of risks (eliminates idiosyncratic risk and concentrates systematic risk in risk-neutral financial intermediaries), boosts leverage and productive investment, and improves welfare. However, they then add a twist in the form of bounded rationality. Specifically, under what they label as "local thinking," securitization magnifies exposure to unrecognized aggregate risks, creating excessive leverage and financial fragility. The nice feature of the model is that it delivers the main features of shadow banking (asset securitization) and associated financial fragility in a novel and plausible way, including the role of the demand for safe debt in driving securitization, the co-movement of bank assets and leverage, and the rising interdependence of banks and associated exposure to unrecognized aggregated risks as a byproduct of securitization. These results also fit nicely with the historical pattern of decreasing idiosyncratic risk and increasing correlated risk observed in US banks prior to the crisis (see Fig. 1).

The model rests on two key assumptions. First is the neglect of tail risk (labeled as "local thinking"), which means that investors do not attend to certain improbable risks. Local thinking is a useful new concept; a form of bounded rationality that captures well neglect of tail risks in crisis (examples abound, including the underestimated default risk of AAA-rated securities, money market funds, CDOs, etc.), but likely has broader applications. But the empirical basis for it needs to be established. Perhaps behavioral experiments could be helpful in this regard.

The second assumption is investor preference for safe assets ("preferred habitat"). This captures well the notion of global imbalances and (Chinese) demand for safe assets (US Treasuries). But where did demand for safe assets come from? Has there been a shift in demand for safe assets? We know that the fraction of safe assets in GDP has been relatively constant over time (see Gorton *et al.*, 2012); but there may have been compositional shifts.

Moreover, the model predicts an overproduction of certain assets, until the market for such assets collapses (akin to a "sudden-stop"). However, it is not clear whether this is consistent with observed patterns of boom-bust

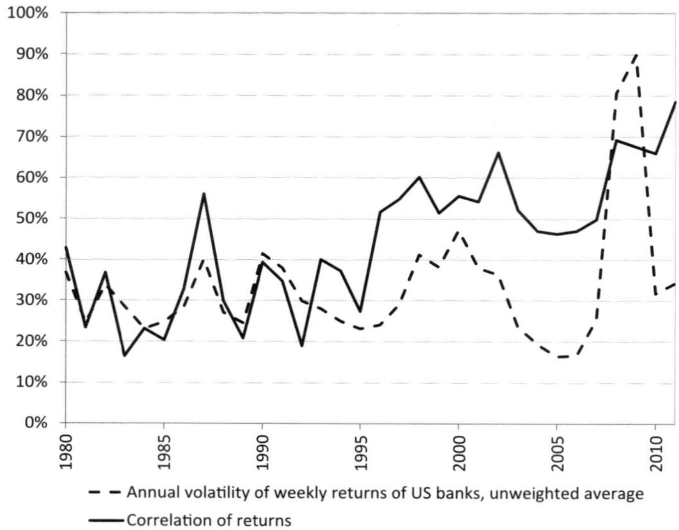

Fig. 1. Idiosyncratic and correlated risks in large US financial institutions. Based on weekly stock returns, 1980–2011.

Source: Datastream based on weekly stock returns. Sample of large and complex US financial institutions as defined in Stern and Feldman (2004, Box 4.1, p. 39).

cycles where markets collapse and revive? Do we expect memory or learning in local thinking? If so, this could alter the dynamics.

Additionally, we know with benefit of hindsight that not everyone neglected risks. There was a market for catastrophe bonds and CDS contracts, including by some banks and investors that neglected tail risks!

More generally, it would be very useful going forward to contrast the model with other models of the crisis, including explanations relying on systemic bailouts (including the models by Farhi and Tirole (2012), and Rancière and Tornell (2012) — the latter presented also at the conference). In these models there is extreme attention to low probability aggregate risks!

The presentation by Acharya covered much ground and ended with a proposal on reviving the repo market, as summarized in Acharya and Öncü (2012).

A repo contract is financing the purchase of securities with short-term repurchase agreements. Importantly, repos are exempt from automatic stay at bankruptcy. A key concern from a systemic risk point of view is, therefore, that runs by repo counterparties on broker–dealers can trigger fire sales with negative impact on market prices and investor portfolios. During the recent crisis, this risk was dealt with through LOLR financing from central banks and capital injections into broker–dealers by government. These solutions are potentially costly to taxpayers and increase moral hazard. Acharya's proposal of a repo "utility" strikes a nice balance between making repo subject to automatic stay while preserving necessary liquidity in the market without the use of LOLR financing or taxpayer money, at least in normal circumstances.

However, under the proposal, one may still need LOLR financing from the central bank in a systemic crisis. Moreover, from a systemic risk perspective it is important to consider that the market for (tri-partite) repos is very concentrated (J P Morgan Chase and Bank of New York dominate the market), raising the likelihood of a systemic event in which LOLR financing is needed. From this perspective, one question is whether concentration limits are desirable. It would also be useful to contrast the proposal with other existing proposals on repos, including central bank insurance of repo transactions or a market-financed emergency bank that would have access to central bank financing.

Finally, it is important to emphasize in the context of the discussion that the securitization and repo markets were linked in the sense that many banks used AAA tranches of (safe, long-term) securitized assets to attract repo funding from institutional investors or money market funds. Spillovers from one market to the other were, therefore, a major contributor to systemic risk.

Going forward, the question remains how to prevent excess leverage by financial institutions engaged in shadow banking activities, such as asset securitization and repo transactions. Gennaioli, Shleifer, and Vishny (2012) propose to increase capital requirements in the context of securitization. Would this also apply to repos, or are collateral requirements a more efficient way to curtail risks?

The third paper, by Frame and White (2012), offers a useful reevaluation of the merits of financial innovation, paying more attention to the dark side of financial innovation unlike their earlier review on the topic. They explain how financial innovations enabled and regulatory arbitrage encouraged excessive risk-taking by financial intermediaries, and claim that financial innovation and regulatory arbitrage together are seen as main culprit of the recent crisis. They conclude that there is a need to reduce capital arbitrage and improve risk management going forward.

The literature on financial innovation primarily focuses on the good and dark sides of innovation but not on the incentives that the owners of financial institutions have to exploit such innovation. There is a need to recognize that financial intermediaries subject to limited liability and deposit insurance will take excessive risks beyond those that are socially optimal, and in particular that they will abuse existing innovation or develop new financial instruments to achieve their risk objectives. The financial sector not only faces a market failure from not internalizing these social costs of bank failures, but also a regulatory failure to prevent regulatory arbitrage (with some exceptions). Regulators find it hard to play catch-up with markets and at times find it difficult to enforce existing regulations. For example, while regulatory arbitrage in ABCP markets has already largely been addressed by aligning capital requirements for off-balance sheet conduits investing in such markets with those of on-balance sheet exposures, financial intermediaries are likely to find other ways to take on comparable exposures. The solution to the problem cannot be to improve internal governance and risk management alone, because even if the interests of shareholders and managers are aligned, financial intermediaries will boost shareholder value including through raising leverage and asset risk. And putting limits on financial innovation risks "throwing the baby out with the bath water," stifling financial deepening and growth.

There is a need to address systemic risk directly by curtailing the desire of banks to take excessive risk. This requires a strong regulatory response, such as raising capital requirements, creditor bail-ins, strict macroprudential regulation, and a strengthening of supervisory and resolution frameworks.

References

Acharya, V. V. and S. Öncü (2012). "A proposal for the resolution of systemically important assets and liabilities: The case of the repo market," New York University mimeo, (the Acharaya article cited is Chapter 10 in this volume).

Claessens, S., Z. Pozsar, L. Ratnovski and M. Singh (2012). "Shadow banking: Economics and policy," IMF Staff Discussion, Note SDN/12/12, International Monetary Fund, Washington, DC.

Farhi, E. and J. Tirole (2012). "Collective moral hazard, maturity mismatch, and systemic bailouts," *American Economic Review*, Vol. 102, No. 1, pp. 60–93.

Frame, W. S. and L. J. White (2012). "Reexamining financial innovation after the global financial crisis," University of North Carolina at Charlotte mimeo, this volume.

Gennaioli, N., A. Shleifer and R. W. Vishny (2012). "A model of shadow banking," *Journal of Finance*, Vol. 68, No. 4, pp. 1331–1363.

Greenwood, J., J. M. Sanchez and C. Wang (2010). "Financing development: The role of information costs," *American Economic Review*, Vol. 100, No. 4, pp. 1875–1891.

Laeven, L., R. Levine and S. Michalopoulos (2012). "Financial innovation and endogenous growth," Berkeley and Brown University mimeo.

Rancière, R. and A. Tornell (2012). "Systemic bailout and the welfare gains of financial liberalization," International Monetary Fund mimeo.

Stern, G. H. and R. J. Feldman (2004). *Too Big to Fail: The Hazards of Bank Bailouts*, Washington, DC: Brookings Institution Press.

PART V

EFFECTS OF REGULATION, THE SAFETY NET AND OTHER GOVERNMENT GUARANTEES

Evolving Intermediation

Nicola Cetorelli*

Federal Reserve Bank of New York

While the term "the Great Recession" has been loosely applied to almost every economic downturn in the past 20 years, the crisis of 2007–2009 has lived up to that name.[1] The crisis has been felt across virtually all economic sectors and in all parts of the world. Yet the consensus is that it had roots in the financial sector and, more precisely, manifested itself through disruptions in the system of financial intermediation.

This story is in itself not new. Many economic crises in history have been the result of financial crises, and many financial crises in turn originated as failures of financial intermediaries. And in every instance the reference has been to *banks*, in their essential role as deposit-taking entities involved primarily in the business of lending. For example, Reinhart and Rogoff (2008) identify some 30 separate instances of banking crises across many countries and at different points in time during the last 100 years.

Indeed, the terms *bank* and *financial intermediary* have normally been used interchangeably. However, what was new in this last crisis is that we witnessed many instances of financial intermediation failure that did not necessarily, or at least not directly, result from bank failures. To be sure, many banks did indeed fail during the crisis and many more were left with impaired operations — outcomes that certainly exacerbated the scale and scope of the crisis. Nevertheless, major disruptions occurred among

*Nicola Cetorelli is a Research Officer at the Federal Reserve Bank of New York. This article draws from material published as: Cetorelli, Nicola, Benjamin H. Mandel, and Lindsay Mollineaux (2012). "The evolution of banks and financial intermediation," *Economic Policy Review*, Federal Reserve Bank of New York, July, pp. 1–12.

[1] The term "Great Recession," in reference to the 2007–2009 crisis, is commonly attributed to Paul Volcker, who used it in a speech in April 2009 (http://news.vanderbilt.edu/).

segments of financial intermediation activity that had grown at a fast pace in previous years and that did not seem to revolve around the activity and operations of banks.

For instance, we have learned that the crisis originated as a run on the liabilities of issuers of asset-backed commercial paper (ABCP), a short-term funding instrument used to finance asset portfolios of long-term maturities (see, for example, Gorton, 2008; Covitz, Liang, and Suarez, 2009; Acharya, Schnabl, and Suarez, 2013; and Kacperczyk and Schnabl, 2010). In this sense, ABCP issuers (conduits) perform typical financial intermediation functions, but they are not banks. Certainly, in many instances, banks were the driving force behind ABCP funding growth, sponsoring conduit activity and providing the needed liquidity and credit enhancements. But the main point is that ABCP financing shifts a component of financial intermediation away from the traditional location — the bank's own balance sheet. Similarly, and concurrently with the ABCP disruptions, financial markets also witnessed a bank-like run on investors that funded their balance sheet through repurchase agreement (repo) transactions, another form of financial intermediation that grew rapidly but did not take place on bank balance sheets (Gorton, 2008; Gorton and Metrick, 2010). Additionally, in the aftermath of Lehman Brothers' default, money market mutual funds, yet another class of nonbank entities that serve as financial intermediaries, experienced a run on their liabilities, an event that triggered in turn an even bigger run on ABCP issuers (Acharya, Schnabl, and Suarez, 2013).

The crisis has therefore exposed significant instances of financial intermediation failure but also an apparent disconnect between financial intermediation activity and banks. A new narrative has emerged, describing intermediation as a decentralized rather than a bank-centered system, one in which the matching of the supply of and demand for funds occurs along an extended *credit intermediation chain*, with specialized markets and nonbank institutions playing a part along the way.

This is the so-called shadow banking model of financial intermediation, as described, for instance, in Pozsar *et al.* (2010).[2] Pozsar *et al.* characterize the transition from a bank-centered to a decentralized model in this

[2]The term *shadow banking* was apparently coined in McCulley (2007).

way: "In essence, the shadow banking system decomposes the simple process of deposit-funded, hold-to-maturity lending conducted by banks into a more complex, wholesale-funded, securitization-based lending process that involves a range of shadow banks" (p. 13). As the authors explain, the "backbone" of the new system is the credit intermediation chain. Loans are originated, but with a funding approach that involves a precise sequence of steps, during which they are removed from the balance sheet of the originator (warehousing), and then packaged into securities (asset-backed security [ABS] issuance). This last step could expand into additional steps that may involve warehousing of the asset-backed securities themselves and further repackaging into more complex securities (for instance, collateralized debt obligations, or ABS CDO issuances).

This decentralization of activities opens up significant opportunities for economies of specialization, in which nonbank firms emerge as organizations that have a narrower scope than banks but perform an important function in finalizing securitization activity.

In this alternative model, traditional banks may have a diminished role. Understanding the extent to which this is the case is important in and of itself, but it also raises key normative questions. Namely, what are the consequences of the new reality for the monitoring and regulation of financial intermediation? The system of controls that has been in place over time, certainly until the crisis erupted, assumes that risks, especially in their systemic component, are mainly concentrated on the balance sheet of banks. If financial intermediation now occurs somewhere else, should we rethink the "boundaries" of regulatory control? To what extent will the new model of financial intermediation and its associated risks be subject to review and intervention with a bank-based regulatory approach?

These questions have motivated a broad research undertaking at the Federal Reserve Bank of New York, which resulted in the production of 7 articles, for a total of 13 individual authors, published in a special issue of the *Economic Policy Review* in July 2012.[3] The thesis that unites all of the contributions in the volume is that banks — i.e., regulated banking institutions — have in fact *not* been bypassed in the modern process of financial intermediation. Indeed, we argue that banks have shown a remarkable

[3] See www.newyorkfed.org/research/epr/index.html.

capacity to adapt to the evolving system of intermediation, continuing to provide, albeit in new ways, those services needed to facilitate the matching of fund supply and demand. Moreover, we contend that when nonbank intermediation has come into play, banks have actually supported its growth.

Our thesis unfolds through two complementary approaches. First, we provide an in-depth analysis of the credit intermediation chain, focusing on the roles needed for a dollar of funding to be successfully intermediated through the new model, centered on asset securitization. Because each role is performed by a specific entity, this *role-based* approach allows us to assess the scale and scope of participation by banks — and nonbanks — in the process. The approach confirms that banks have indeed adapted naturally to the changing model of intermediation, redefining their "production function" while continuing to provide the type of services needed for intermediation to occur.

Second, we look at the same issues from the perspective of the organizational form of the banking firm itself. In particular, we posit that banks have adapted through a significant transformation of their organizational structure. If financial intermediation entails increasing participation by nonbank entities, then banks can adapt by integrating those nonbank entities in the same bank holding company structure. This second approach, focusing on *entity type*, confirms that BHCs have allotted nonbank subsidiaries an increasingly important role in their activities, consistent with the view of adaptation through organizational changes. Significantly, the structural changes initiated by banks have clear normative implications, since bank and financial holding companies (BHCs) are regulated by the Federal Reserve. If entities active in the credit intermediation chain have in fact been incorporated in BHCs, then we may need to reassess how much of modern financial intermediation has been overtaken by "shadow banking" and how much remains open to regulatory scrutiny.

From Bank-Based to Securitization-Based Intermediation

As any textbook on money and banking would explain, the standard problem of external financing — that is, the matching of agents in possession of funds with those in need of funds — is resolved in one of two ways: (1) with *direct finance*, where fund suppliers support demand through ownership participation (acquisition of equity positions) and/or with the acquisition of debt instruments (for example, bonds) directly issued by the agents demanding the funds; or (2) with *indirect finance*, where fund supply is funneled to "in-between" agents, the financial intermediaries, which are then responsible for the allocation to demand.

Direct finance grants agents an immediate participation in, and control over, investment activities, but it also entails dealing with a number of well-known informational and liquidity frictions. For instance, unless the agent seeking funds has an established track record of performance, *selection* requires learning about the agent and its intended use of funds. But even when a record of satisfactory performance exists, a supplier still needs to follow the investment project, *monitoring* activities throughout its life cycle. Moreover, before the supplier selects a specific investment opportunity, it must employ resources to *screen* available alternatives, evaluating the many dimensions of risk, return, business, scale, scope, and geography before making an informed decision. And because of these informational costs, funding constraints may still limit the ability of the supplier to *diversify* risks across a suitably large portfolio of alternative investment opportunities. Finally, even if the informational issues are successfully resolved, the fund supplier still needs to factor in its own *liquidity* preferences, that is, the need to have funds available before the investment matures.

The wide range of costs associated with direct finance justifies the existence of financial intermediaries, traditionally understood to be *centralized agents* performing under one roof the roles of screening, selection, monitoring, and diversification of risk while simultaneously providing credit and liquidity services to fund suppliers. These services — the *credit, maturity, and liquidity transformations* of financial claims — presuppose all of the roles just described and show the intrinsic fragility of the intermediary's activity: Given the nature of its operations, the financial intermediary never holds sufficient balances to guarantee full withdrawals, a condition that exposes it to potential "runs." And because the investments of intermediaries are naturally opaque, it is difficult to distinguish the problems specific to one intermediary from problems affecting the industry as a whole, with the result that the observation of distress at one entity could lead to runs on others as well. Hence, financial intermediation activity carries a significant social risk — the potential for systemic disruptions.[4]

The existence of this risk is one rationale, and perhaps the major one, for the fact that financial intermediation activity in modern history has been closely governed by laws and regulations and, more specifically, restricted to entities that are able to obtain explicit authorization in the form of a charter. In the US, a charter permitting the taking of deposits is granted exclusively to entities organized as *commercial banks* (and similarly to thrifts and credit unions as well).[5] Moreover, because of the potential for systemic risk, the restricted bank charter also comes with exclusive access to liquidity and credit support by the taxpayer — made available, in the US, through access to the Federal Reserve's discount window and the insurance of deposit accounts by the Federal Deposit Insurance Corporation (FDIC), respectively. The existence of these official backstops is a significant factor strengthening investors' confidence in banks.[6]

Hence, both the chartering restrictions and the official liquidity and credit guarantees have been key in making the traditional system of financial intermediation a *bank-centered* system. In this framework, risks reside on banks' balance sheets, which is the main justification for a system of regulation and supervision that is likewise focused on banks.

The left side of Fig. 1 describes in a stylized fashion the traditional model of financial intermediation, with banks as central brokers between supply and demand.

A Role-Based Approach to Understanding Bank Evolution

As suggested earlier, however, the advent of asset securitization has broken down the traditional system of intermediation. The right side of Fig. 1

[4]See, for example, Ennis and Keister (2010) for a survey of the theoretical arguments on financial intermediation fragility.

[5]The first bank charter in US history is probably that granted by the Continental Congress to the Bank of North America in 1781 (Knox, 1900), although some earlier contenders for this distinction exist (for example, the Massachusetts Land Bank in 1739).

[6]"FDIC insurance is backed by the full faith and credit of the US government. Since the FDIC was established in 1933, no depositor has ever lost a single penny of FDIC-insured funds." See www.fdic.gov/deposit/deposits/dis/index.html.

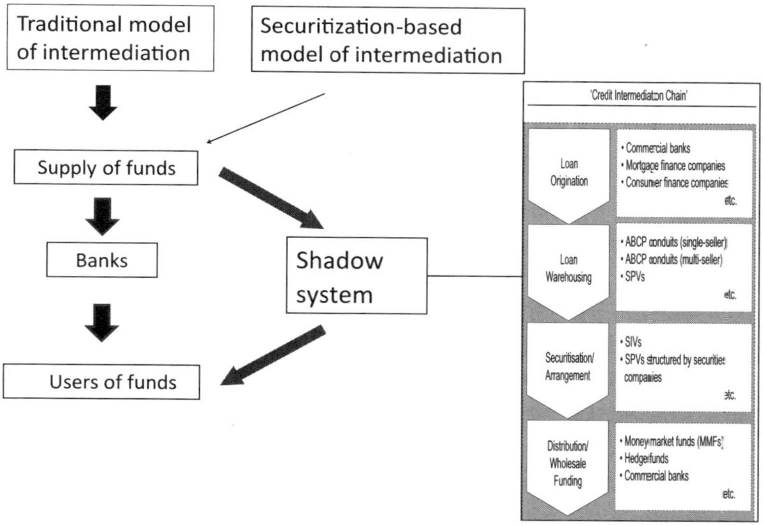

Fig. 1. Schematic description of traditional and securitization-based models of financial intermedation.

depicts the basic steps in the longer credit intermediation chain according to the securitization-based model of intermediation.

The origination of loans is now just the first step in a longer sequence, and in every subsequent step, specialized entities now perform specific roles. For instance, warehousing in step 2 is done through dedicated entities (for instance, the ABCP conduits mentioned earlier) that finance the acquisition of the long-term assets through the issuance of shorter-term liabilities. Because of the implied maturity transformation that this role involves, this stage would typically require the provision of some form of liquidity and credit enhancement — for the same reason that banks' traditional activity requires both liquidity and credit guarantees. Following warehousing, the assembly of the loans into securities and the related sale to investors require the services of several parties: an *issuer*, that is, a company that acquires the assets to be transformed into securities; an *underwriter*, the entity in charge of the packaging and sale of the securities; a *trustee*, an agent that acts on behalf of and looks after the interests of the securities buyers; and a *servicer*, a party that manages the income streams from the underlying assets and the related payments to the investors. Finally, along the whole chain, the process may also require further liquidity and credit enhancement to boost the quality of the issuances.

Although these roles are now typically played by separate specialized entities, *they are the same roles performed simultaneously, albeit in implicit form, by a bank in the traditional centralized model of intermediation*: The bank is the loan originator, but it is also the implicit issuer and underwriter of the loan portfolio to its own investors, depositors, and equity holders. Likewise, the bank performs the role of trustee, as the delegated agent for its investors, and that of servicer, as it collects the revenue stream from the loan contracts. Finally, it provides credit enhancement to debt holders, represented by the existence of equity held on the balance sheet, and liquidity services, in fact on both sides of the balance sheet, to firms and depositors.

This continuity in roles is an important qualification, showing clearly that while the system has become decentralized and complex, it is still plainly financial intermediation at its core. Consequently, we can more clearly assess whether banks have in fact been eclipsed by other players by analyzing who performs each role along the credit intermediation chain.

Hence, if funds are intermediated on a longer credit intermediation chain, then we ought to really see how it is done — that is, who does what and when at every step — in order to establish whether banks are still active players or whether other entities have eclipsed them. More specifically, we propose a different map (see Fig. 2), morphologically equivalent to the one above but highlighting, instead of the steps in the chain, the *roles* needed at every step in order for a dollar of funding to go through from beginning to end. And so, a map that highlights the importance of the *issuer*, the *underwriter*, the *servicer*, and parties providing liquidity and credit *enhancement*. All these roles are essential to the modern process of securitization, and understanding who plays these roles should tell us how far intermediation has moved away from the realm of banks.

Organizational Adaptation: An Entity-Based View

The second element in our framework of analysis places the focus directly on organizational adaptation. We have suggested that banks have adapted to the modern decentralized system of intermediation by engaging, to varying

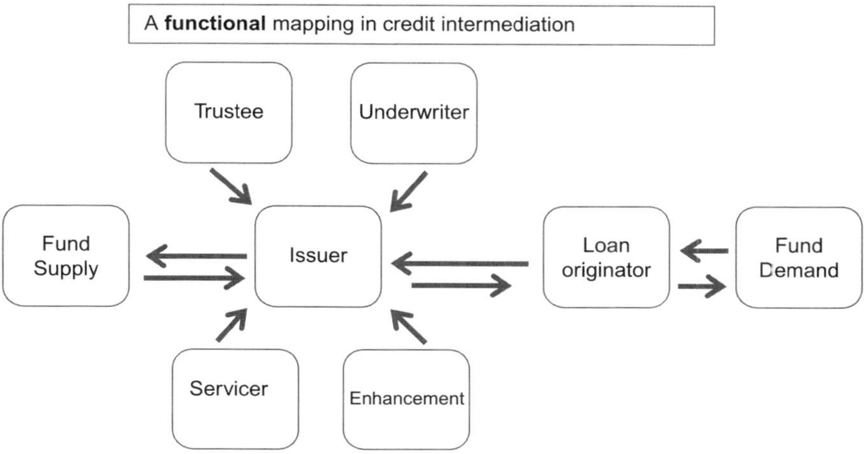

Fig. 2. The essential roles in the process of asset securitization.

degrees, in the roles that have emerged along the new credit intermediation chain. This adaptation should then be evident in the changes made by banks to their organizational structure. With intermediation services provided in a decentralized fashion and increasingly by nonbank entities, banking firms may have responded by integrating such entities under common ownership and control. This potential expansion of the *boundaries of the banking firm*, in the sense articulated by Coase (1937), thus suggests shifting the focus of observation from commercial banks to bank holding companies. Banks' organizational adaptation occurred somewhat organically over time, even in the presence of the strict regulatory restrictions imposed by the Banking Act of 1933 (Glass–Steagall) on the type of activities allowed by chartered banking institutions, but it was then officially sanctioned with the passage of the Financial Modernization Act of 1999 (Gramm–Leach–Bliley) and the constitution of the Financial Holding Company as the legal entity allowed to own and control both bank and nonbank financial entities.

What does financial intermediation look like once we broaden our scope to consider bank and financial holding companies as the unit of observation (for brevity, we refer to both as BHCs)? Figure 3 compares the asset growth rates of regulated bank entities with those of "other" financial

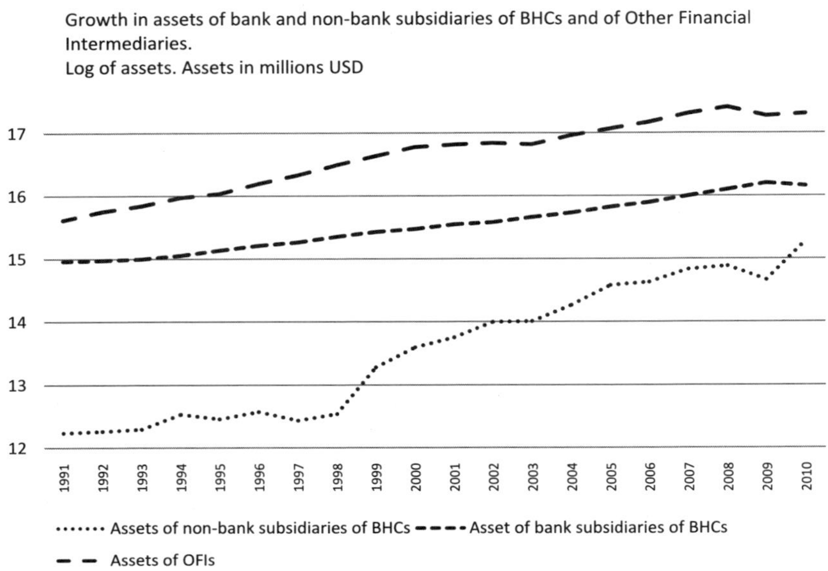

Fig. 3. Comparison in growth over time of OFIs, bank and non-bank subsidiaries of BHCs.

intermediaries (OFIs), an aggregate aimed at capturing the evolution outside the world of banks. The OFIs aggregate is constructed from the Federal Reserve's Flow of Funds data as the sum of total assets of funding corporations, insurance companies, finance companies, closed-end funds, exchange-traded funds, pension funds, mutual funds, real estate investment trusts, money market mutual funds, brokers and dealers, and issuers of asset-backed securities. The total for commercial banks is from call report data. The aggregate numbers are expressed in natural logarithms, so that the line trend visualizes the growth rate of each series.

As the chart clearly shows, nonbank entities have grown substantially over the last 30 years and, most importantly, at a faster pace than commercial banks. It is also clear, however, that a significant chunk of the growth in the BHCs actually came from the nonbank subsidiaries that are consolidated on the balance sheet of the holding companies. Not surprisingly, the growth of these subsidiaries picked up in the late 1990s, with the process of deregulation mentioned earlier. The growth comparison across categories is also quite remarkable: OFI assets grew about 1.7 times from 1990 to 2010.

Over the same period, commercial bank assets grew 1.2 times, while assets of nonbank subsidiaries grew more than 3.0 times.

Results

Figure 4 summarizes the results from some of the articles in the special issue of the *Economic Policy Review*. The chart depicts again the functional mapping of the securitization-based model of intermediation, this time indicating to what extent bank holding companies were involved in the different roles. And so, for instance, in "The Rise of the Originate-to-Distribute Model and the Role of Banks in Financial Intermediation," Vitaly Bord and João Santos focus on the role of loan origination by banks. Using supervisory data on corporate loans, the authors are able to track the life of a loan from origination to subsequent sales. Equipped with information on the identity of the originator and the entities that acquire the loan at later stages, Bord and Santos can nail down the actual role of banks in origination at the start of the modern credit intermediation chain. Their results confirm that banks play a much more important part in lending than what the balance sheet suggests. In addition, the results indicate that bank actions

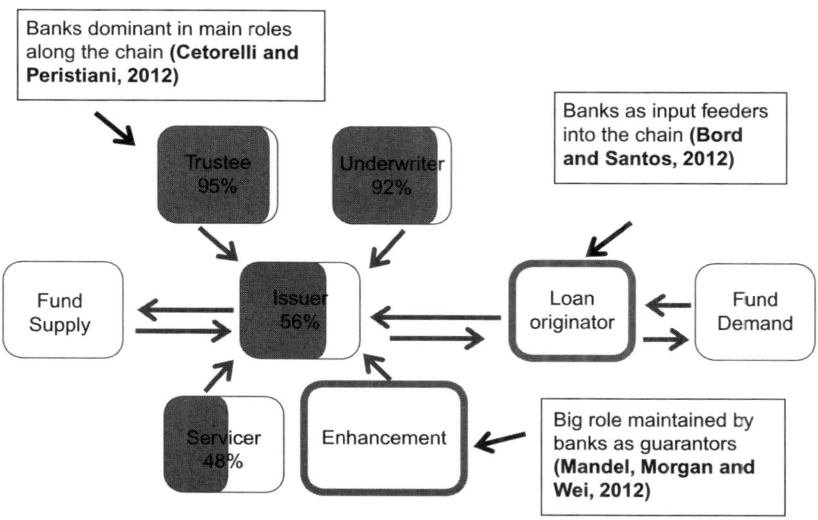

Fig. 4. Role played by BHC subsidiaries in the process of asset securitization.

have actually fed the growth of the shadow bank entities involved in the subsequent steps of the credit intermediation chain.

The importance of banks in providing credit enhancements is taken as the topic of analysis in "The Role of Bank Credit Enhancements in Securitization," by Benjamin Mandel, Donald Morgan, and Jason Wei (2012). The authors focus on the economics of credit enhancement: Why is it provided and what functions does it play? One argument, probably the most natural, is that the extension of such guarantees is a way to buffer investors — the buyers of loans repackaged as securities — to reduce their credit risk exposure. At the same time, enhancement may resolve some of the informational frictions discussed earlier by providing a signal of the quality of the underlying security. The two hypotheses imply a specific relationship between the amount of enhancement afforded and the ex post performance of the security. Namely, buffering would lead one to expect higher enhancements among more poorly performing securities, while the signaling hypothesis would imply instead that high enhancements are associated with high performance. The authors' econometric analysis suggests that buffering investors is, in fact, the main motivation behind the provision of enhancement in asset securitization, thus corroborating the underlying argument that banks have played a fundamental role in supporting the modern intermediation process.

Hence, banks seem to have been "private central bankers" to important components of shadow banking activity throughout the years of its growth. This is another way in which banks have asserted their renewed importance in the transformed mode of intermediation: If intermediation has migrated away from bank balance sheets, its growth still seems largely dependent on banks' support.

The article by Nicola Cetorelli and Stavros Peristiani, "Mapping the Role of Banks in Asset Securitization" completes the analysis of the roles implicit in the credit intermediation chain. Parsing a Bloomberg database that includes virtually the universe of asset-backed securities issued over time, and drawing on supplementary information from Moody's, the authors are able to identify the entities that play the roles of issuer, underwriter, trustee, and servicer. This "bean-counting" approach is necessary to establish the extent to which financial intermediation is now occurring "in the shadow" — that is, outside the realm of banks and beyond the scrutiny of regulators. As the chart shows, the evidence suggests that very little securitization-based intermediation is actually in the shadow, with much of it remaining within the scope of regulated bank entities.

The evidence also shows support to the idea that banks have increasingly become complex and that the organizational boundaries have expanded considerably. In "A Structural View of US Bank Holding Companies," Dafna Avraham, Patricia Selvaggi and James Vickery describe the organizational structure and history of US bank holding companies. While the literature on this subject draws heavily on aggregate data on bank holding companies (obtained from the Federal Reserve's publically available FR Y-9C regulatory reports), the authors of this article merge information from a number of more-obscure regulatory sources to obtain a very detailed set of stylized facts that document changes in the size and complexity of BHCs over time. In particular, the authors demonstrate that while the number of nonbank subsidiaries is an order of magnitude larger than in the 1990s, most of the structural expansion beyond the traditional boundaries of commercial banking has been limited to the largest organizations — a development that signifies the existence of important economies of scale with this form of adaptation. Figure 5 describes the snapshot in terms of numbers of banks and nonbank subsidiaries for the top BHCs, while Fig. 6 shows the comparison with 1990. Both figures confirm the point that nonbank subsidiaries have grown substantially over time.

In the final article in the volume, "Evolution and Heterogeneity among Large Bank Holding Companies 1994 to 2010," Adam Copeland tracks the changing activities of bank holding companies by analyzing data on BHC income streams. Copeland shows the rising importance of fee-based income across the largest BHCs, and — consistent with our thesis — the increasing importance of nonbank subsidiaries as a source of income for the larger organization. Figure 7 documents the increasing importance of nonbank subsidiaries as a source of income for the entire BHC organization.

Summary and Normative Suggestions

Financial intermediation has become very complex, and banks' balance sheets are now less reflective of actual intermediation activity. However, when intermediation is distilled down to its basic components, it is still

BHCs organizational structure in 2012

BHC rank	BHC Name	Number				Asset value	
		Domestic					
		Commercial bank	Other	Foreign	Total	Domestic Commercial bank (% of Y-9C Assets)	Consolidated Total Assets (Y-9C) (in billions USD)
1	Jpmorgan Chase & Co.	4	2,936	451	3,391	86.1%	2,265.8
2	Bank Of America Corporation	5	1,541	473	2,019	77.9%	2,136.6
3	Citigroup Inc.	2	935	708	1,645	68.8%	1,873.9
4	Wells Fargo & Company	5	1,270	91	1,366	92.5%	1,313.9
5	Goldman Sachs Group, Inc., The	1	1,444	1,670	3,115	11.2%	923.7
6	Metlife, Inc.	1	39	123	163	3.2%	799.6
7	Morgan Stanley	2	1,593	1,289	2,884	10.5%	749.9
10	Bank Of New York Mellon Corporation, The	3	211	146	360	83.2%	325.8
20	Regions Financial Corporation	1	35	4	40	97.1%	127.0
30	Comerica Incorporated	2	72	2	76	99.8%	61.1
40	First Horizon National Corporation	1	35	1	37	99.1%	24.8
50	Webster Financial Corporation	1	21	0	22	99.8%	18.7
Total		86	13,670	5,847	19,603	70.4%	14,359.1

Fig. 5. Number and distribution of subsidiaries in selected top 50 US Bank Holding Companies.

Source: Avraham, Selvaggi and Vickery (2012).

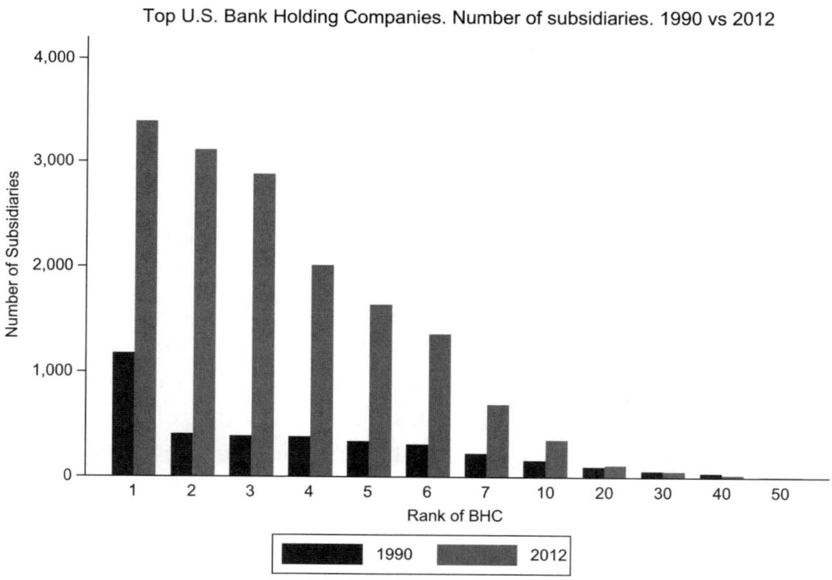

Fig. 6. Evolution in orginizational structure in US BHCs.

Source: Avraham, Selvaggi and Vickery (2012).

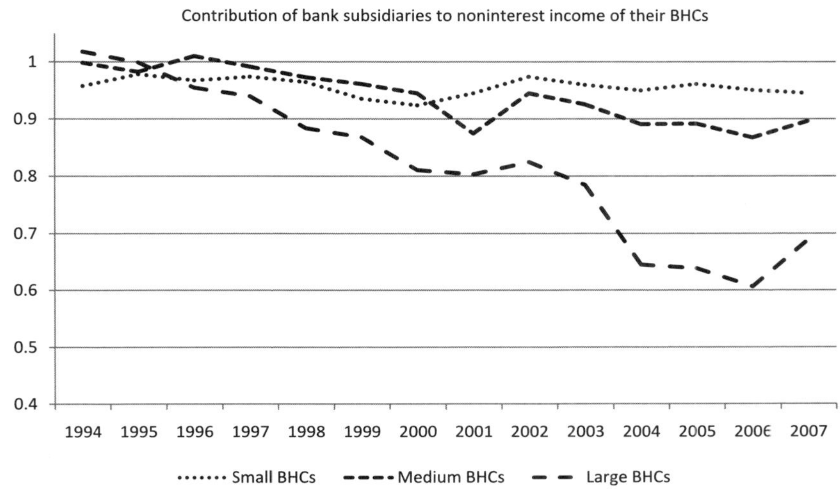

Fig. 7. Increasing role of non-bank subsidiaries.

Source: Copeland (2012).

the same system, with the same roles needed so that funding can be successfully matched with demand. The crucial difference is that these roles are performed in a new way, such that it becomes economically viable, and perhaps more efficient, for different entities to specialize in providing different services.[7]

This observation is important, since it has provided a key to analyze the evolution of banks. We have shown, through both a role-based and an entity-based approach, that regulated banking institutions have remained crucially involved in every step of the credit intermediation chain. This ability to adapt has occurred in large part through a significant expansion of the boundaries of the banking firm, with bank holding companies becoming increasingly broad in the number of their subsidiaries and the type of activities they have been engaged in.

Our findings take us back to the policy questions we raised earlier: With so many nonbanks involved in modern intermediation, and with systemic

[7]We are aware, however, that this decentralization of roles brings with it new layers of agency/informational friction (see, for example, Ashcraft and Schuermann, 2008).

risk now spread along the chain, regulatory agencies around the globe are currently considering reforms to the principles governing the regulation and monitoring of financial intermediation.[8] These efforts are likely to lead to an expansion of the boundaries of prudential-based regulation and supervision to include entities and activities that contributed heavily to systemic events during the crisis.

However, the biggest challenge facing regulators is not redesigning current regulatory boundaries but delineating principles and guidelines for monitoring and identifying *future* mutations in the system of intermediation — mutations that, if history has taught us anything, will at least in part be the result of the battery of regulatory fixes on the table now.

We believe that the results of our analysis can offer insights on this issue. The demonstrated ability of regulated banking institutions to adapt to the changing environment suggests that there may be much to learn about the future evolution of intermediation directly from the observation of banks. Risks are still likely to be concentrated in other parts of the system — that is, outside of banks' balance sheets — but there is a good chance a bank will be involved in new mutations of the intermediation system, either directly or indirectly. This observation thus suggests a new role for bank supervisors: In addition to carrying out their main mandate of monitoring the health of banking firms, supervisors could contribute to a dynamic and forward-looking oversight of the whole system of financial intermediation as it continues to evolve.

References

Acharya, V., P. Schnabl and G. Suarez, "Securitization without risk transfer," *Journal of Financial Economics*, Vol. 107, No. 3, pp. 515–536.

Ashcraft, A. and T. Schuermann (2008). "Understanding the securitization of subprime mortgage credit," *Foundations and Trends in Finance*, Vol. 2, No. 3, July, pp. 191–309.

[8]For example, in response to an explicit mandate by the Group of Twenty, the Financial Stability Board (2011) is conducting a cross-jurisdiction exercise (still in process at the time of this article's publication) aimed at providing both monitoring and regulatory recommendations to pursue better governance of financial intermediation activities (see www.financialstabilityboard.org/publications/r_120420c.pdf).

Coase, R. H. (1937). "The nature of the firm," *Economica*, Vol. 4, No. 16, November, pp. 386–405.

Covitz, D. M., N. Liang and G. A. Suarez (2009). "The evolution of a financial crisis: Panic in the asset-backed commercial paper market," Finance and Economics Discussion Series, Board of Governors of the Federal Reserve System, No. 2009-26.

Ennis, H. M. and T. Keister (2010). "On the fundamental reasons for bank fragility," *Economic Quarterly*, Federal Reserve Bank of Richmond, Vol. 96, No. 1, First Quarter, pp. 33–58.

Financial Stability Board (2011). "Progress report to the G20 on strengthening the oversight and regulation of shadow banking." Available at: www.financialstabilityboard.org/publications/r_120420c.pdf.

Gorton, G. B. (2008). "The panic of 2007," NBER Working Paper No. 14358.

Gorton, G. B. and A. Metrick (2010). "Securitized banking and the run on repo," Yale ICF Working Paper No. 09–14.

Kacperczyk, M. and P. Schnabl (2010). "When safe proved risky: Commercial paper during the financial crisis of 2007–2009," *Journal of Economic Perspectives*, Vol. 24, No. 1, Winter, pp. 29–50.

Knox, J. J. (1900). *A History of Banking in the United States*, New York: Rhodes and Company.

McCulley, P. (2007). "Teton reflections," PIMCO Global Central Bank Focus.

Pozsar, Z., T. Adrian, A. Ashcraft and H. Boesky (2010). "Shadow banking," Federal Reserve Bank of New York, staff report, No. 458, July.

Reinhart, C. M. and K. S. Rogoff (2008). "This time is different: A panoramic view of eight centuries of financial crises," NBER Working Paper No. 13882.

The Socially Optimal Level of Capital Requirements: A View from Two Papers

Javier Suarez*
Centro de Estudios Monetarios y Financieros (CEMFI)
Casado del Alisal 5, 28014 Madrid, Spain

Introduction

Capital regulation remains the centerpiece of banks' micro- and macro-prudential regulation. Basel III (Basel Committee on Banking Supervision, 2010) has opted for increasing the quality and quantity of the capital required to banks. Basel III also promotes the maintenance of new regulatory buffers (the so-called capital preservation buffer and countercyclical buffer) with the purpose of adhering to the seemingly good principles of accumulating loss absorption capacity in good times and having the effective ability to off-loading the buffers in bad times.

In theory, the reforms on this front are intended to make banks more individually and systematically resilient. One goal is that the contribution of the banking system to future business or credit cycles becomes less pro-cyclical than what we have witnessed in the recent crisis (Hanson *et al.*, 2011).

In the discussions about the pros and cons of this reform, we find two polar views (and of course many in the middle). The first polar view is sustained by academics such as Admati *et al.* (2011), who have reminded everyone about the contents of the Modigliani–Miller theorem and its implications for the discussion about the optimal level of bank capital

*Javier Suarez is a Professor of Finance at CEMFI, Madrid, and a Research Fellow of the CEPR. This article summarizes the author's presentation at the 2012 International Banking Conference at the Federal Reserve Bank of Chicago, November 15–16, 2012. It builds extensively on joint work with David Martinez-Miera (Universidad Carlos III) and Rafael Repullo (CEMFI), but responsibility for its contents corresponds solely to the author. Financial support from Spanish government grant ECO 2011–26308 is gratefully acknowledged.

requirements. They argue that if the perfect conditions under which capital structure decisions are irrelevant hold for banks, then the claims about the presumably large costs of increasing their capital requirements are unwarranted.

They also argue that if, more plausibly, the main reasons why this irrelevance does not hold in practice are the coexistence of financial distress costs and ex post debt overhang problems, then increasing the capital requirements would certainly be a good idea. With tax distortions and improperly priced safety net guarantees, (i) it would not destroy much total value from an individual bank perspective (but rather redistribute value between shareholders, debtholders, and the taxpayers) and (ii) it would yield a positive reward from an overall social welfare perspective (in the form financial stability gains, a lower subsidization of banks' risky activities, and better-aligned risk-taking incentives).

The other polar view is sustained by the banks and their lobbies. In the documents produced to assess the reforms (e.g., Institute for International Finance, 2010), they work on very different premises. They do not deny the systemic externalities that banks produce when their solvency deteriorates, but they argue that equity-like financing is really more costly (or less easily accessible on short notice) for banks than debt-like financing, especially short-term debt. And, they claim that banks (and bank lending in particular) play an important role in the financing of growth, and growth is a risky process that makes banking risky and yet a socially valuable activity. They argue that, with these considerations in mind, imposing higher capital requirements might have a significant contractive effect on the supply of credit and, thereby, on economic activity and growth.

With somewhat oversimplifying reduced-form calculations, the Institute for International Finance (2010) estimates that the effects of the new requirements on credit supply and overall economic activity will be contractive. These estimates suggest, although without explicit or detailed welfare calculations, that our societies might significantly suffer from the full implementation of Basel III (and, of course, even more from more radical proposals such those of Admati *et al.*, 2011).

Against this background, my intention in this brief note is to summarize the basic ingredients and main policy implications of two recent research papers written by me with two different coauthors. The analytical frameworks considered in such papers capture some of the frictions emphasized by the bank lobbies. In both papers, we consider equity financing relatively more costly than debt financing and, more importantly, we take dynamic issues regarding its "availability" seriously into account. Specifically, we explicitly consider the process whereby banks (and their inside equity contributors) accumulate equity capital (own funds) through earnings retention. We also consider economic fluctuations and systemic shocks that impair banks' solvency or increase the regulatory capital requirements at specific points in time, originating possible procyclical effects.

Capturing these frictions involves taking a few shortcuts. In particular, it requires deviating from the ideal conditions under which the Modigliani–Miller results hold and entering a terrain in which providing convincing micro-foundations for each of the frictions would require theoretical and empirical work that either does not exist or is very dispersed in the microeconomics of banking literature (which means that it may be enunciated in very different modeling setups which are hard to integrate in a single macroeconomic model).

In the two papers that I will summarize below, we definitely adopt some shortcuts. But we adopt them pretty much within the canons of two increasingly connected literatures. First, a long tradition in the microeconomics of banking that has looked at risk choices and the rationale and effects of capital requirements (for an overview, see Freixas and Rochet, 2008). Second, the incipient literature on the macroeconomic implications of bank capital dynamics (e.g., Gertler and Kiyotaki, 2010, Brunnermeier and Sannikov, 2013).

The common conclusions that we get from our two (otherwise very different) studies are the following. First, the socially optimal level of the capital requirements is possibly higher than the levels observed prior to this crisis (which is in line with Admati *et al.*, 2011, and the move taken by Basel III). Second, the positive welfare effects of introducing higher capital requirements are compatible with the prediction that their introduction may imply losses in aggregate credit (or in the overall level of economic activity), as frequently claimed by the bank lobbies. In fact, according to some of our results, the socially optimal design of capital requirements would involve a lower degree of countercyclical adjustment than that expected before formally modeling and quantifying the underlying trade-offs. Additionally, the piece that considers banks' ex ante risk-taking decisions calls for the increase in capital requirements to be gradual because otherwise the costs of the implied transitional credit crunch would offset part of the long term financial stability gains.

The Procyclical Effects of Bank Capital Regulation

The basic argument about the procyclical effects of bank capital requirements is well known (Blum and Hellwig, 1995; Kashyap and Stein, 2004). In recessions, losses erode banks' capital, while risk-based capital requirements, such as those in Basel II (Basel Committee on Banking Supervision, 2004), become higher. If banks cannot quickly raise sufficient new capital, their lending capacity falls and a credit crunch may follow. Yet, correcting the potential contractionary effect on credit supply by relaxing capital requirements in bad times may increase bank failure probabilities precisely when, because of high loan defaults, they are largest.

Given the conflicting goals at stake, some observers think that procyclicality is a necessary evil, whereas others think that procyclicality should be explicitly corrected. Basel III (Basel Committee on Banking Supervision, 2010) is a compromise between these two views. It not only reinforces the quality and quantity of the minimum capital required to banks but also establishes that part of the increased requirements be in terms of mandatory buffers — a capital preservation buffer and a countercyclical buffer — that are intended to be built up in good times and released in bad times.

Repullo and Suarez (2013) develop a model that captures the key trade-offs in the debate. The model is constructed to highlight the primary micro-prudential role of capital requirements (containing banks' risk of failure and, thus, deposit insurance payouts and other social costs due to bank failures) as well as their potential procyclical effect on the supply of bank credit.

Bank borrowers in the model are overlapping generations of entrepreneurs who demand loans for two consecutive periods. Consistent with the view that relationship banking makes banks privately informed about their borrowers, the paper assumes that borrowers become dependent on the banks with whom they first start a lending relationship, and banks with ongoing relationships have no access to the equity market. These assumptions capture the lock-in effects caused by the potential *lemons problem* faced by banks when a borrower switches from another bank (like in Sharpe, 1990) and the implications of these informational asymmetries for the market for seasoned equity offerings (like in Myers and Majluf, 1984). And they provide a micro-foundation for the connection between the capital shortages experienced by some banks and the credit rationing of some potential borrowers.

Different from many papers in the literature, the model allows banks in their first lending period to raise more capital than needed to just satisfy the capital requirement. This addresses the concerns about the limitations of analyses based on static models that predict that capital requirements are always binding and, in particular, about the fact that voluntary capital buffers might partly mitigate the procyclical effects of capital requirements.

For simplicity, the model formalizes the market for loans to newly born entrepreneurs as perfectly competitive and free from capital constraints. Also, it captures the business cycle as a Markov process with two states, expansion and recession, which affect the probability of default of all loans (lower in expansions than in recessions). The model is calibrated with US data for the period prior to the financial crisis that started in 2007, and is used to compare a *laissez-faire* regime with no capital requirements, Basel I, Basel II, and the regime in which capital requirements maximize a social welfare function that incorporates a social cost of bank failure.

One key finding of the paper is that the equilibrium buffers, in spite of being quite sizable (of up to 3.8% in the expansion state under Basel II), are not sufficient to neutralize the effects of the arrival of a recession on the supply of credit to bank-dependent borrowers (which falls by 12.6% on average in the baseline Basel II scenario). Moreover, despite Basel II inducing banks to hold larger buffers during expansions (in order to prepare for the rise in capital requirements when entering a recession), the cyclical swings in the supply of credit (in the form of credit rationing suffered by the borrowers dependent on capital constrained banks) are more pronounced under the risk-based requirements of Basel II than under the flat requirement of Basel I.

However, bank failure probabilities are also related to the state of the business cycle and risk-based requirements, such as those of Basel II, are more effective in bringing them down during recessions, when they are larger. This means that the welfare comparison between the two Basel regimes, as well as the design of socially optimal capital requirements, involves nontrivial trade-offs. In fact, the paper shows that Basel II dominates Basel I in welfare terms, except for very low values of the social cost of bank failure. It also shows that the optimal capital requirements are lower and more cyclically varying than the requirements of Basel II if the social cost of bank failure is low, and they are higher and less cyclically varying if it is large.

The paper states that, conditional on assessing that the social cost of bank failure is large (as the recent crisis appears to confirm), Basel III may be considered a move in the right direction: The new capital conservation and countercyclical buffers would assume the role of making the effective capital requirements faced by banks less sensitive to the cycle (in particular, less prone to produce credit rationing at the arrival of recessions) than the Basel II requirements.

The analysis in the paper also uncovers the limits of the one-size-fits-all principle. Economies with larger social costs of bank failure (e.g., with a banking sector whose size implies a larger systemic threat) should face larger but less cyclically varying capital requirements than economies at the other side of the spectrum.

A Macroeconomic Model of Endogenous Systemic Risk-Taking

Martinez-Miera and Suarez (2012) analyze the role of banks in generating endogenous systemic risk. They consider a canonical problem of excessive risk-taking by banks in a dynamic general equilibrium setup where banks are subject to capital requirements and the supply of equity funding to them is limited by the wealth endogenously accumulated by bank owners. They find that systemic risk-taking, which can lead some banks to fail in equilibrium, is reduced by increasing capital requirements. Yet doing so has negative implications for the levels of credit and output, producing trade-offs relevant for determining the socially optimal level of the capital requirements.

Systemic shocks in the model are small probability events in which certain investments fail in a highly correlated manner, provoking the default of the loans financing them. Importantly, banks make an unobservable decision on their degree of exposure to these shocks, i.e., the extent to which loans in their portfolio tend to default in a correlated manner. Banks' temptation to undertake highly correlated investments is due to the risk-shifting incentives that limited liability provides to the owners of highly levered firms (Jensen and Meckling, 1976) and that in banks is reinforced by their ability to issue liabilities protected by safety net guarantees (Kareken and Wallace, 1978).

Banks collect deposits from savers and are the exclusive providers of loans to perfectly competitive firms, which need to pay for physical capital and labor in advance. Firms' production processes are subject to failure risk and, depending on the degree of exposure to systemic shocks, may be systemic or nonsystemic. Nonsystemic production processes feature stochastically independent failures, whereas systemic production processes fail simultaneously if the negative systemic shock occurs (and independently otherwise). Importantly, following the literature on risk-shifting, systemic firms are assumed to have probabilities of failure that, conditional on not suffering the systemic shock, are lower than those of nonsystemic firms, but unconditionally systemic firms are more likely to fail and, thus, generate lower expected net present value.

This paper models the dynamics of bank capital along the same lines as Gertler and Kiyotaki (2010), among others. This implies thinking of bank capital as the funds provided by the special class of agents who own and manage the bank (the *bankers*). The maximum available amount of this funding is determined by bankers' wealth, whose endogenous dynamics is affected by the profits and losses made by the banks in each period. Bank capital requirements influence bankers' incentives in regard to the adoption of systemic risk in two ways. First, the conventional leverage-reduction effect diminishes the static gains from risk-taking. Second, higher capital requirements increase the relative scarcity of bank capital in each state of the economy, altering bankers' dynamic incentives in an interesting manner.

Indeed, Martinez-Miera and Suarez (2012) show that the anticipated value of a unit of bank capital in the future is key to systemic risk-taking decisions. When a banker's capital is devoted to make systemic loans, the banker obtains higher returns insofar as the systemic shock does not occur. But if the systemic shock occurs, the invested equity is lost. In contrast, if the banker invests in nonsystemic loans, he receives a lower return in *normal times* (i.e., if the systemic shock does not realize), but preserves his capital when the systemic shock occurs. The destruction of bank capital after a shock allows surviving capital to earn higher scarcity rents and produces a *last bank standing effect* like in Perotti and Suarez (2002). This effect reduces bankers' inclination for systemic lending.

Strengthening capital requirements reduces bankers' systemic risk-taking through the two channels mentioned above. Higher capital requirements reduce the proportion of resources going into inefficient systemic investments, which in turn reduces the loss of bank capital and the contraction in credit supply produced by the possible realization of the systemic shock. However, these gains come at the cost of reducing credit and output in *normal times*. Measuring welfare as the expected present value of total net consumption flows in the economy, the paper finds that there is a unique interior social welfare maximizing level of capital requirements.

Under the current calibration of the model, social welfare is maximized under a positive and relatively large capital requirement: 14%. The paper compares the scenario with a 14% capital requirement with another with a 7% capital requirement. The unconditional mean of the fraction of bank equity devoted to support systemic lending is 71% under the low capital requirement and 24% under the optimal capital requirement. And, the social welfare gain from having the requirement of 14% rather than 7% is equivalent to a perpetual increase of 0.9% in aggregate net consumption.

Importantly, common macroeconomic aggregates such as GDP and bank credit have lower unconditional expected values (6.5% and 21% lower, respectively) under a capital requirement of 14% than under one of 7%. However, the fall in aggregate net consumption, GDP, and bank credit in the year that follows a systemic shock is much lower with the 14% capital requirement.

The model is suitable for the analysis of the transition from a regime with a low capital requirement (say, 7%) to another with a higher capital requirement. It allows to explicitly take into account transitional dynamics and the welfare losses implied by the credit crunch suffered when the requirements are raised but the economy has not yet accumulated the levels of bank capital that will characterize the new regime. The paper finds that it is socially optimal to implement the higher requirements in a gradual way (over 7 to 10 years under our calibration) and to establish a more modest long-term goal than if transitional costs were neglected (12% or 13%, depending on the desired speed of convergence to the target, rather than 14%).

Conclusions

The explicit normative analysis of bank regulation can yield surprising results. One does not need to minimize the importance of frictions affecting the cost (or the raising) of equity financing to find significant welfare gains associated with the reinforcement of capital requirements. As representatives of the banking industry tend to emphasize, higher capital requirements are likely to reduce credit and GDP. However, this might well be a price worth paying (in social welfare terms) in order to reduce bank failure probabilities and to induce better ex ante risk taking decisions.

The socially optimal design of capital regulation calls for an explicit recognition of complex trade-offs, the adoption of a proper social risk management perspective, and the full consideration of dynamic issues that may be of relevance to establish the right time for the adoption of higher requirements, the extent to which such adoption must be made gradual over time, and the possible need for countercyclical adjustments.

References

Admati, A., P. DeMarzo, M. Hellwig and P. Pfleiderer (2011). "Fallacies, irrelevant facts, and myths in the discussion of capital regulation: Why bank equity is *not* expensive," Stanford University, Graduate School of Business Research Paper No. 2063.

Bank for International Settlements, Basel Committee on Banking Supervision (2004). "International convergence of capital measurement and capital standards: A revised framework," report, Basel, Switzerland.

Bank for International Settlements, Basel Committee on Banking Supervision (2010). Basel III, "A global regulatory framework for more resilient banks and banking systems," report, Basel, Switzerland.

Blum, J. and M. Hellwig (1995). "The macroeconomic implications of capital adequacy requirements for banks," *European Economic Review*, Vol. 39, No. 3–4, April, pp. 739–749.

Brunnermeier, M. and Y. Sannikov (2013). "A macroeconomic model with a financial sector," *American Economic Review*, forthcoming.

Freixas, X. and J.-C. Rochet (2008). *Microeconomics of Banking*, 2nd ed., Cambridge, MIT Press, MA.

Gertler, M. and N. Kiyotaki (2010). "Financial intermediation and credit policy in business cycle analysis," in *Handbook of Monetary Economics*, B. Friedman and M. Woodford (eds.), Vol. 3A, Amsterdam: Elsevier/North-Holland, pp. 547–599.

Hanson, S., A. Kashyap and J. Stein (2011). "A macroprudential approach to financial regulation," *Journal of Economic Perspectives*, Vol. 25, No. 1, Winter, pp. 3–28.

Institute for International Finance (2010). "Interim report on the cumulative impact on the global economy of proposed changes in banking regulatory framework," report, June.

Jensen, M. and W. Meckling (1976). "Theory of the firm: Managerial behavior, agency costs and ownership structure," *Journal of Financial Economics*, Vol. 3, No. 4, October, pp. 305–360.

Kareken, J. and N. Wallace (1978). "Deposit insurance and bank regulation: A partial equilibrium exposition," *Journal of Business*, Vol. 51, No. 3, July, pp. 413–438.

Kashyap, A. and J. Stein (2004). "Cyclical implications of the Basel II capital standards," *Economic Perspectives*, Federal Reserve Bank of Chicago, Vol. 28, First Quarter, pp. 18–31.

Martinez-Miera, D. and J. Suarez (2012). "A macroeconomic model of endogenous systemic risk taking," Centre for Economic Policy Research, No. DP9134, September.

Myers, S. and N. Majluf (1984). "Corporate financing and investment decisions when firms have information that investors do not have," *Journal of Financial Economics*, Vol. 13, No. 2, June, pp. 187–221.

Perotti, E. and J. Suarez (2002). "Last bank standing: What do I gain if you fail?" *European Economic Review*, Vol. 46, No. 9, October, pp. 1599–1622.

Repullo, R. and J. Suarez (2013). "The procyclical effects of bank capital regulation," *Review of Financial Studies*, Vol. 26, No. 2, pp. 425–490.

Sharpe, S. (1990). "Asymmetric information, bank lending, and implicit contracts: A stylized model of customer relationships," *Journal of Finance*, Vol. 45, No. 4, September, pp. 1069–1087.

Effects of Regulation, the Safety Net, and Other Government Guarantees

Mathias Dewatripont*
National Bank of Belgium
and
Université Libre de Bruxelles
(ECARES and Solvay Brussels School)

In these comments, I will mostly focus on the presentations by Nicola Cetorelli and Javier Suarez, since I only learned yesterday evening that Ed Kane was going to be part of the session. At the end, I will say a couple of words about Ed's presentation. Let me start with Javier's presentation, which he has used to present analysis from two interesting papers.

As he stressed, both papers take as a given the scarcity of bank equity, a feature often stressed by the banking industry. And interestingly, both papers take a general equilibrium perspective, with calibration. I will not comment very much on the quantitative results, which only represent a first attempt at doing such an exercise.

The papers show that capital requirements can be helpful even if they are costly for lending. Of course the devil is in the details as far as quantitative results are concerned; here, the social welfare function. Specifically, one does need a high enough social cost of bankruptcy to have action, given the strong assumption about the cost or unavailability of equity, and there are big effects on the loss of GDP due to higher capital ratios.

In order for Basel-style ratios to emerge as the optimal ones, one does need these high social costs of bankruptcy of banks and one could ask whether these numbers make sense, given that if one bank goes bankrupt,

*Mathias Dewatripont is Executive Director at the National Bank of Belgium and Professor of Economics at the Université Libre de Bruxelles.

borrowers can always go to another bank. In an interesting empirical paper about the Spanish dynamic provisioning experiment, Jimenez *et al.* (2012) show that the increase in dynamic provisions on the upside of the bubble have constrained lending by individual banks, but the aggregate effect was roughly zero because borrowers switched to another bank that was not constrained. So I think we need more work on the social impact of restricted bank lending.

Both papers show that capital requirements can be helpful even if equity is costly. Instead, on procyclicality, the two papers have different results. Repullo paper argues that a Basel III-style counter cyclical capital buffer can be helpful because the scarcity of equity is particularly costly in recessions. On the other hand, Martinez-Miera paper stresses the cost of (ill-designed) counter cyclical policies in reducing the cost of investing in riskier inefficient "systemic lending," since it reduces the cost of being insolvent in a recession.

Let me say a couple of words about the (hotly debated) assumption that equity is costly. We can all agree that there is a private cost of equity, given that the tax system subsidizes leverage. Added to the "too-big-to-fail" premium, these are ways in which leverage is being subsidized in so many countries. It is in fact pretty strange that we are all the time complaining about excessive leverage and discussing ways to limit it while at the same time having a tax system that subsidizes it. This lack of consistency in fact makes supervisors' lives extremely hard because, since there is obviously a private cost of equity at least, banks spend much time and energy trying to get around capital requirements through financial innovation, so-called "risk-weighted asset optimization," and through "ingenious" asset valuations.

Clearly, it would be very helpful to reconsider our tax system so as to address this inconsistency. Of course, another way to tackle the relative cost of debt versus equity, which is in vogue these days, is bail-in. We should, however, not get carried away here. Asking for all debt to be bail-inable is a bit of a paradox: Everybody agrees that bankruptcies are very costly (think Lehman) because they create much financial instability. But what exactly is the difference between regular bankruptcy and a resolution where everybody is bail-inable? Yes, resolution must of course guarantee that the essential functions of a bank are preserved. And yes, it is good for resolution to ascertain without much delay the losses creditors will face. But this will *not* prevent creditors from a neighboring bank from running if they fear that their bank runs the risk of being resolved, too, and they can face losses.

So I think it is worth thinking of designing a bail-in system that will foster financial stability and not financial instability. And in that sense, targeting it to longer-term creditors, possibly junior ones, and making sure such creditors provide enough of a buffer (next to shareholders) for the other creditors would make a lot of sense.

Beyond the tax system and bail-in, there is a third way one can impact the relative cost of debt versus equity: forced recapitalization, with a threat of nationalization. This was done in the US in 2009, and, in a softer version, in Europe more recently.

The point of the above discussion is that there are several ways to impose limits to this cost of equity. Therefore, when it comes to empirical estimates of the cost of equity, I think these kinds of considerations could naturally enrich Javier's interesting analysis, which right now implies an effect of bank capital on lending and GDP which is probably on the high side.

Let me now turn to procyclicality. Both papers make the very useful point that banks do adapt to capital regimes (adaptations known in regulatory circles as "unintended consequences"). Regulators should think harder at the many ways in which bankers quickly adapt to new regulations. In Repullo's paper, if a regime is more procyclical, like in Basel II as compared with Basel I, banks build their own additional buffers.

In Martinez-Miera's paper, when one introduces a safety net element to reduce procyclicality, this induces banks to lend in a way which will induce more systemic risk. This is a classic moral hazard effect but it will occur only if the counter cyclical mechanism is imperfectly designed. If it is possible to fully target it only to exogenous risk, this problem will not occur. In this sense, I would very much subscribe to this idea of capital insurance pioneered by Kashyap, Rajan, and Stein (2008) if it can be targeted solely to exogenous macrovariables (in fact, in Dewatripont and Tirole, 2012, we elaborate on these kinds of issues).

Let me turn now to Nicola's very interesting presentation on shadow banking and the complexity of the regulated banking sector. It documents very nicely the important role of the regulated banking sector in shadow banking activities and also stresses the dramatic increase in complexity in the last 20 years, due to the activity of bank holding companies.

For example, I found it striking that J.P. Morgan owns four commercial banks in the US but almost three thousand other entities, and that this complexity has increased tremendously in the last 20 years.

One question I would have is: What has happened since 2007? Has this increase in complexity continued even after the crisis, or has it stopped and even reversed? Also, has some of it been due to increased concentration, or has it been complexity for complexity's sake? Finally, how will these trends be impacted by evolving regulation?

Indeed, right now we have a very busy regulatory agenda. First, Basel III stresses the need for more and better capital, for liquidity ratios, and macro-prudential instruments (and in particular the counter cyclical buffer). Note that the view that "big is beautiful" has been somewhat altered, with the introduction of "global SIFI surcharges."

Second, more and more people are asking for a simplification of the Basel framework. One can argue that Basel III already goes part of the way, insisting on higher-quality (and thus simpler) capital, and on the leverage ratio as an additional simple constraint. But more and more voices ask to go further, for example, in limiting model complexity when computing risk weights.

Third, there is all the action on recovery and resolution plans with bail-in as one instrument.

Fourth, there is the discussion on how to deal with shadow banking.

Fifth, there is the issue of structural reforms, e.g., Vickers in the UK, Volcker in the US, and Liikanen in Europe.

And sixth, there are voices calling for more regulation of governance and remuneration.

What can we say about this busy agenda?

First, that it is important to keep in mind the risk of inconsistency and to ask the question: How will each reform impact behavior? For example, some people argue that if one wants bail-in not to promote instability, it should be limited to debt with a maturity of more than one month; but note that the LCR aims at inducing banks to hold debt ... with a maturity of more than one month! So, there is a need for an aggregate assessment of the various reforms (my take would be to stick to the LCR and focus on requiring sufficient loss absorbency by equity and junior, long-term debt).

A second comment on this regulatory agenda is prompted by Nicola's presentation and concerns the simplification debate, and in particular the question: Should we simplify Basel or should we simplify banks?

As far as simplifying Basel is concerned, clearly there is a lot of worry about internal models, and I think I tend to agree with the idea that introducing these internal models into the regulation was looking for trouble. Indeed, we always talk about the fact that rating agencies have conflict of interest, but in a sense, the conflict of interest is much worse when you ask a bank to have a model that will at the same time be good for risk management and be good for computing how much capital you need to have, given that capital is so expensive for them. So the idea that we should simplify this system using a variety of backstops, extending in this way the idea of the leverage ratio, is a natural way to go.

If we now turn to bank complexity, Nicola's numbers on the number of subsidiaries suggest that maybe the efforts on recovery and resolution plans and living wills may run into the same difficulties as with internal models. I am worried that these recovery plans that banks have to draw up themselves may face serious credibility issues that will be challenging in crisis time. So, I wonder whether we should not put the burden of proof on banks, i.e., forcing them to explain the social usefulness of the kind of complexity that Nicola has shown us.

Finally, on shadow banking, the evidence presented by Nicola is interesting when we think about the two approaches suggested by the FSB to deal with shadow banking: (i) regulate it directly; and (ii) regulate the link between banks and shadow banks.

Clearly, as shown by Nicola, these links are really important. Interestingly, one can interpret Vickers and Liikanen as trying to contribute to limiting them, which I think makes a lot of sense: Let's indeed try and limit the ability of using insured deposits to fund these kinds of risky/shadowy activities.

But I think it is also important to think about extending the perimeter of regulation to include more shadow banking activities. Analyzing the impact of such policies could be facilitated by the fact that there are significant differences among countries on this. For example, France and Germany seem to define banking in a way that is so broad that basically everything ends up being regulated.

Let me finish with a couple of words on Ed's interesting presentation. I fully agree that in the last years big banks have been able to take advantage of the implicit subsidy from taxpayers. Clearly, this should be limited. I'm not a lawyer and definitely have limited knowledge about common law systems, so I will not comment on the exact feasibility of what is being proposed, but it does look like a promising avenue.

Other interesting avenues are, as we talked about, bail-in, or a somewhat similar idea, granting priority to the deposit insurance fund in resolution. Indeed, this is another way to move taxpayers higher up in the queue and I do think that is a natural idea. Let's face it, however: A number of big lenders will not like being "downgraded" in the queue, and they will ask for collateral, which will be a way to get back up again in the queue, in front of the other depositors, and so this kind of race will occur especially if you do not have enough people "firmly" at the bottom of the queue, namely shareholders and long-term junior debtholders, which can "reassure" senior creditors. My feeling is that one cannot afford not to have enough of such a buffer of equity and long-term junior debt.

References

Dewatripont, M. and J. Tirole (2012). "Macroeconomic shocks and banking regulation," *Journal of Money, Credit and Banking*, Vol. 44, Supplement S2, pp. 237–254.

Jiménez, G., S. Ongena, J.-L. Peydró and J. Saurina (2012). "Macroprudential policy, counter cyclical bank capital buffers and credit supply: Evidence from the Spanish dynamic provisioning experiments," Barcelona Graduate School of Economics Working Paper No. 628.

Kashyap, A., R. Rajan and J. Stein (2008). "Rethinking capital regulation," Federal Reserve Bank of Kansas City, 2008 Economic Symposium, Maintaining Stability in a Changing Financial System.

PART VI

FINANCE AND ECONOMIC ACTIVITY: VARIATIONS ACROSS EMERGING AND DEVELOPED MARKETS

Legal and Alternative Institutions in Finance and Commerce*

Franklin Allen
The Wharton School
University of Pennsylvania

Jun "QJ" Qian
Carroll School of Management
Boston College

Introduction

Transiting from a central-planning to a market-based economy, China's economic achievements in the past three decades have been remarkable. Its economic growth, lifting hundreds of millions of people out of poverty in the process, represents one of the greatest economic transformations in history. India is also successful in terms of economic growth during the past two decades. At the end of 2011, China and India together accounted for 40% of the world population and more than 20% of the world GDP in purchasing power parity terms. With growth rates among the highest of all countries, these two countries will play an increasingly important role in the world economy for years to come.

The conventional wisdom is that, to be successful in terms of long-run economic growth, a country needs good institutions. In particular, it needs

---

*Franklin Allen is the Nippon Life Professor of Finance and Professor of Economics at the Wharton School of Business, and Co-Director of the Wharton Financial Institutions Center. Jun "QJ" Qian is Associate Professor of Finance and Haub Family Fellow at the Carroll School of Management, Boston College. The authors appreciate helpful comments from participants at the Federal Reserve Bank of Chicago–CEPR International Banking Conference. Research assistance by Lin Shen and Chenying Zhang, as well as financial support from Boston College and the Wharton Financial Institutions Center, are gratefully acknowledged. The authors are responsible for all remaining errors.

a good legal system that enforces contracts and resolves disputes and a good financial system, including financial markets and a banking sector, to fund firm growth. In earlier work (Allen, Qian, and Qian [AQQ], 2005, 2008; Allen *et al.* [ACDQQ], 2012), we have documented that China and India do not have these. In fact, the governments of these countries are notoriously corrupt, the legal systems are ineffective, and the financial markets and banks are small relative to their economies and inefficient.

Most observers would characterize the economic performance in China as "successful *despite* the lack of Western-style institutions." By contrast, we argue in this paper that China has done well *because of* this lack of Western-style institutions — in that conducting business outside the legal system in fast-growing economies, such as China and India, can actually be superior to using the law as the basis for business transactions. We develop our main theses by comparing and contrasting two different sets of systems, with the focus on dispute resolution and contract enforcement mechanisms. In one system, observed in developed and democratic countries such as the United States, there is a commitment to use the law as the basis for finance and commerce, with legal institutions serving as the ultimate source for resolving disputes and enforcing contracts. Moreover, any fundamental changes to the law must be approved by the legislature and electorate. In the other system, with China providing the primary example, there is no clear definition of private property rights at the highest level and, in place of the law, nonlegal mechanisms based on reputation, relationships, and trust rather are the norm for conducting business.[1]

We first present a number of examples on how alternative mechanisms work. The practice of corporate sectors in China and India shows alternative mechanisms can substitute for legal mechanisms. Based on earlier work, we show that despite the differences in their history of developing laws and formal institutions, the legal environment for business is characterized by an underdeveloped legal system (China), or a sophisticated legal system on paper but of limited use in practice (India). In another set of examples we show that alternative mechanisms can handle disputes that arise from

[1] These classifications are made to facilitate the comparisons between legal and alternative mechanisms and not meant to be mutually exclusive when studying a given country. Indeed, in many countries, a combination of the two systems could be working in practice.

complicated transactions. The diamond industry has historically operated outside the legal system of any one country and flourished worldwide despite the lack of transparency of most of its dispute resolutions.

Next, we focus on examples in developed countries, such as the United States, to highlight the problems of using the law and legal system as the basis for finance and commerce. The reason for this choice is obvious. If there are significant deficiencies in using the legal system in countries with the most developed institutions, these deficiencies are likely to be magnified in developing countries with poor institutions.

A central concept in the legal paradigm and institutions is (private) property rights. One of the intensely debated topics on property rights is intellectual property rights, including patents and copyrights. The practice of enforcing intellectual property rights by courts is much more vigilant and prevalent in developed countries than in developing countries. An extensive literature in industrial organization in economics has found mixed results on the relationship between patent/copyright protection and the pace of innovations. On one hand, exclusive property rights provide strong incentives for innovations and do lead to more innovations in some industries such as chemicals and pharmaceuticals. On the other hand, such a positive relationship between protection and pace of innovations is not observed in many other industries; instead, excessive protection deters competition, which is another important factor in spurring innovations. One of the problems with the patent/copyright and litigation systems is that they induce rent-seeking behaviors by vested interest groups and individuals. With abundant resources they can undertake various measures and use the legal system to block competition and innovations from other individuals or smaller companies, and this type of behavior reduces social welfare.

Another potential problem of using the law lies in the legal system capacity and fixed costs associated with revising the law as may be required by changes in the economic environment. In democracies, the legislature must approve any revisions in the law before corporations and investors can freely implement new techniques in their activities and transactions in practice. However, in any given period politicians have limited time and effort to devote to one area of the law, implying a fixed cost in revising the law. An example illustrating such limited capacity and fixed costs is the US payments system. At the beginning of the 21st century, the US had a 19th-century payments system, relying mostly on paper checks and the mail, and significantly lagging behind other developed nations. Checks had to be physically transported from where they were deposited to a central operations center, then to the clearer, and then back to the banks they were drawn on. This process significantly delayed business transactions as compared to electronic methods.

Despite repeated calls for changes from the banks and businesses, it appeared that the US Congress was not interested in solving this seemingly simple yet costly problem, until September 11, 2001. After the terrorist attack, all commercial flights in the US were grounded for several days, completely halting the check clearing process. The Check Clearing for the 21st Century Act was signed in October 2003, allowing electronic images to be a substitute for the original checks, thereby offering the clearing process a means to circumvent the mail and transportation system.

These examples motivate our analysis on the advantages and disadvantages of a system based on rule of law and legal institutions versus a system relying on alternative, nonlegal institutions. Using the law and the legal system as the basis of finance and commerce has many well-known advantages. The legal system of a democracy ideally allows equal and full access by all and fairness in trials and settlements. With powerful enforcement mechanisms including civil and criminal penalties, disputing individuals, firms, and organizations have strong incentives to follow the resolutions backed by courts and the government. This in turn provides long-term stability on how things should be done in practice. By using the entire legal operator and system, the marginal enforcement costs for an additional case can be low and this improves overall efficiency.

However, there are also disadvantages in using the law and legal institutions. First, recent research on political economy factors — in particular, work by Rajan and Zingales (2003a, 2003b) — argues that rent-seeking behaviors by vested interest groups can turn legal institutions into barriers to changes. We expect these problems to be much more severe in developing countries, where the costs of building good institutions can be enormous. We argue that one way to solve this problem is not to use the law as the basis for finance and commerce but instead to use alternative mechanisms. Second, as shown by the example of US payment system reform, the capacity of the legal system and legislature can impose significant fixed costs in revising the law and thus delaying the pace of innovations. These fixed costs can further increase if the people in charge of revising the law (e.g., politicians and judges) lack expertise in business transactions. In addition, interest groups with more resources may receive more protection than individuals, and this asymmetric protection system induces more rent-seeking behaviors and further deters innovations.

In the context of a fast-growing economy, such as that of China or India, characterized by frequent, fundamental changes in the economic environment, the disadvantages of using the legal system can overshadow its advantages, and it may be better to conduct business without using the law and legal system. In addition to minimizing the political economy costs associated with legal institutions, using alternative mechanisms is advantageous in that such mechanisms can adapt and change much more quickly than the law. In particular, competition among different networks and institutions can ensure the most efficient prevails, and it is not necessary to persuade the legislature and the electorate that the law needs to be revised when circumstances change.

There are also limitations to alternative mechanisms. By design, these mechanisms often exist within a network (or networks) of firms and investors and may be inaccessible to outsiders. The limited access can come with the price of biases favoring insiders. With frequent changes and limited enforcement (since penalties cannot be imposed with authority), these systems generate instability and hence weak long-term incentives. While in a fast-growing economy profit-sharing in the long run and reputation-based mechanisms can ensure "good" (cooperative) behavior, these mechanisms may be insufficient to induce such behavior in environments with limited long-term profits. On the other hand, in such static environments with infrequent changes to the fundamentals (e.g., a developed economy with low growth rates), the fixed costs of using the legal system are relatively small (especially in large transactions); hence the law and legal system become superior to the alternative mechanisms.

Overall, we conclude that while legal mechanisms are an important part of developed economies' institutions, alternative mechanisms play a much more prominent role in emerging economies and can be superior to legal mechanisms in supporting business transactions in certain industries or entire economies. Therefore, our main policy implication is that in emerging economies, alternative dispute resolution and contract enforcement mechanisms should be encouraged and developed alongside the development of legal and other formal institutions. The coexistence of alternative and legal mechanisms can also foster competition among (legal and nonlegal) institutions, which, in our view, is essential for creating an environment conducive for innovations. Competition from alternative institutions can also exert positive impact on the development of legal institutions, so that they are less likely to be captured by interest groups and become more efficient in adapting to changes.

The rest of the paper is organized as follows. In Sec. 2, we present a series of examples demonstrating how alternative mechanisms work and illustrating the problems with using the law and legal system as the basis for commerce. In Sec. 3, we compare and contrast the advantages and disadvantages of alternative and legal mechanisms and discuss policy implications. Finally, Sec. 4 concludes.

Examples of Alternative Mechanisms and Problems with the Legal System

In this section, we first provide examples on how alternative mechanisms work and substitute for legal mechanisms in different industries and countries. We then present examples that illustrate potential problems with using the law and legal system as the basis for finance and commerce.

Alternative Mechanisms in China and India

In the first set of examples, we describe how alternative mechanisms substitute for legal mechanisms in China and India. Using information from the IMF, Table 1 presents GDPs based on simple exchange rates and purchasing power parity (PPP) and the growth rates in GDPs and per capita GDP (both in constant prices) during 1990–2011 for the top 15 countries in *each* category. China is leading the world in terms of growth rates of both GDP and per capita GDP over this period. At the end of 2011, China's PPP-adjusted GDP is the second largest in the world. In PPP terms, China's economy will surpass the US and become the largest in the world in 2016 according to IMF's World Economic Outlook, and will have *double* the US GDP

Table 1. The Largest 15 Economies in the World: GDP and Growth.

	GDP in 2011 (simple exchange rates)		GDP in 2011 (PPP)		GDP growth: 1990–2011* (constant prices)		GDP per capita in 2011 (PPP)		Per capita GDP growth 1990–2011* (constant prices)	
Rank	Country/ Region	US$ Billion	Country/ Region	Int'l $ billion	Country/ Region	Annual growth	Country/ Region	Int'l $ unit	Country/ Region	Annual growth
1	United States	15,094	United States	15,094	China	10.4%	United States	48,387	China	9.5%
2	China	7,298	China	11,300	Vietnam	7.3%	Netherlands	42,183	Vietnam	5.8%
3	Japan	5,869	India	4,458	India	6.5%	Canada	40,541	India	4.7%
4	Germany	3,577	Japan	4,440	Angola	6.0%	Australia	40,234	Korea	4.6%
5	France	2,776	Germany	3,099	Malaysia	5.8%	Germany	37,897	Taiwan	4.3%
6	Brazil	2,493	Russia	2,383	Bangladesh	5.4%	Taiwan	37,720	Sri Lanka	4.2%
7	U.K.	2,418	Brazil	2,294	Nigeria	5.4%	U.K.	36,090	Sudan	4.1%
8	Italy	2,199	U.K.	2,261	Sri Lanka	5.3%	France	35,156	Poland	3.9%
9	Russia	1,850	France	2,218	Sudan	5.3%	Japan	34,740	Chile	3.9%
10	Canada	1,737	Italy	1,847	Chile	5.3%	Korea	31,714	Bangladesh	3.6%
11	India	1,676	Mexico	1,662	Korea	5.3%	Spain	30,626	Thailand	3.5%
12	Spain	1,494	Korea	1,554	Taiwan	5.0%	Italy	30,464	Malaysia	3.5%
13	Australia	1,488	Spain	1,413	Peru	4.9%	Greece	26,294	Argentina	3.4%
14	Mexico	1,155	Canada	1,396	Indonesia	4.7%	Saudi Arabia	24,237	Peru	3.3%
15	Korea	1,116	Indonesia	1,125	Egypt	4.5%	Poland	20,334	Indonesia	3.2%

*Countries with population fewer than 11 million or GDP less than US$50 billion in 2011, or less than 15 years' of GDP observations, are excluded from the rankings.

Source: International Monetary Fund (2012).

around 2035 as long as it maintains an average growth rate that is at least twice as high as that of the US. While economic growth has widened the income and wealth gap in China as compared to the pre-reform period, it has elevated hundreds of millions of people from absolute poverty.[2] India's records in economic growth are not as impressive as those of China, but its growth rates in GDP and per capita GDP are the third highest in the world during 1990–2011. At the end of 2011, India's PPP-adjusted GDP is the third largest in the world. With 40% of the world's population and the two largest emerging markets in the world, China and India are expected to play an increasingly important role in the global economy for years to come.

The remarkable economic performances of China and India also present significant counterexamples to existing literature on law, institutions, finance, and growth. The conventional wisdom is that a necessary condition for long-run economic growth is good (Western-style) institutions, including laws that protect small investors, a legal system that enforces contracts and resolves disputes, a financial system with efficient financial markets and a banking sector, and a democratic and benign government. However, AQQ (2005) and ACDQQ (2012) document that both China and India have ineffective legal systems, banks, and markets that are small relative to the economies and have played a limited role in allocating resources to most efficient uses, and governments that are among the most corrupt in the world.

While there are many factors that have contributed to the economic growth in these two countries, we want to emphasize the role of financial systems in funding the growth of different corporate sectors.[3] In our earlier work (AQQ 2005, 2008 [on China]; ACDQQ, 2012 [on India]), we document that state-owned enterprises and publicly listed firms in these countries have much easier access to the legal system and banks and financial markets than nonstate, nonlisted firms. Most of the nonstate, nonlisted firms are small and medium firms, and to a large extent, conduct business outside the legal system and rely on nonlegal methods based on reputation, relationships, and trust to settle disputes and enforce contracts; most of

[2]For example, using different metrics, Ravallion and Chen (2004) report steep declines in the proportion of rural Chinese living in absolute poverty over the period 1980–2001.

[3]For an excellent review of China's economic growth during the past thirty years, see the book, *China's Great Economic Transformation*, edited by Brandt and Rawski (2008).

these firms' financing comes from alternative channels such as trade credits and funds from family and friends. Interestingly, the growth of nonstate, nonlisted firms has been much faster than listed and state-owned firms and provides most of the economic growth, and these firms also employ most of the labor forces in both countries. The dominance of this sector over state and listed sectors is especially pronounced in China. These findings suggest that alternative financing channels, along with nonlegal mechanisms, might be superior to bank and market finance, along with the legal and other formal institutions. We formalize and discuss this argument below.

These two countries also present distinctly different cases in their histories of developing Western-style legal and other formal institutions. Transiting from a socialist system to a market-based system, China had no formal commercial legal system and associated institutions in place when its economy began to take off in the 1980s. However, historically China had highly commercialized societies without the development of Western institutions. India, on the other hand, has a long history of Western legal institutions and financial systems due to its colonial ties to the UK. Based on the British judicial system, India's formal legal system dates back more than two centuries. The State Bank of India, the largest commercial bank in the country in terms of deposits as well as assets, is over 200 years old and thriving. The Bombay Stock Exchange (BSE), at 130 years, is the oldest in Asia. Yet, Indian firms, like Chinese firms, generally conduct business with little reliance on the legal system.

What economic lessons can be learned from the remarkable performance of China and India? In the West, we take it for granted that finance and commerce should be undertaken using the law as the basis for contracts. Many would agree that the same should be applied for China:

> "The modern corporation based on a Western model would be the essential vehicle for private economic development" (China, 1904).

Interestingly, this statement was not written today but was the view of China's first Company Law in 1904 (*Gongsilü*), drafted by the then newly created Ministry of Commerce (*Shangbu*) of the waning Qing government and aimed at promoting China's industrial development. Several subsequent versions of the Company Law (1904–1946) tried to promote the development of share holding corporations with limited liabilities, but despite these attempts the model of Western-style corporations was never taken up in China. An important factor is that the philosophy of having a disperse ownership that included outsiders ran directly against the traditional Chinese model of keeping business within the family. Indeed, most firms' fear of incorporation stemmed from their distrust of government and unwillingness to let strangers gain partial control of the firm.[4]

Despite the lack of rule of law in finance and commerce and their separation from the legal system, China had a highly commercialized society. The earliest form of capitalism can be traced back to the late Ming Dynasty (17th century), with commerce initiated in the Zhejiang–Jiangsu area and further developed during the Qing Dynasty (17th to early 20th century). The Opium War (in the 1840s) between China and Great Britain destroyed China's sovereignty, but it brought Western-style legal and capital systems into China's coastal areas (until 1949). During this period, foreign systems and the Chinese system co-existed and commerce boomed. Yet, despite the entrance and development of numerous Western-style courts in Shanghai and other major coastal cities, most business-related disputes were resolved outside courts. Since the Qing Dynasty, dispute resolution by guilds (merchant coalitions), families, and local notables based on explicit and implicit regulations of guilds, family traditions, and social norms was commonplace. Chinese firms on the mainland (pre-1949) and later in Taiwan (after 1949) did not use the provisions of the law but again conducted commerce outside the formal legal system. Modern equivalents of these dispute and contract-enforcing mechanisms are arguably behind the success of Chinese firms since 1979.

The development of China's financial system from the late 19th century to the early 20th century was highlighted by the emergence of Shanghai as the financial center of China and Asia. With thriving entrepreneurial and trading activities, financial institutions proliferated and financial innovations surged. Merchants used up to 11 currencies in their transactions, some of which were printed by local banks. The exchange rates of local currency saw wide fluctuations; many unregistered local banks (*diaotang*) engaged in

[4]For more descriptions of China's current financial system see AQQ (2005, 2008). For more anecdotal evidence on the development of China's financial system in the period discussed, see, for example, Kirby (1995) and Lee (1993).

high-leverage credit transactions with little capital reserves and defaulted frequently. At the same time, merchants' fear of risk spawned an active insurance industry, which was first introduced by the British. Insurance on real estate, ships, and goods became routine, with collateral and personal guarantors accompanying large transactions to reduce the risk of non-payments. To alleviate the problems of asymmetric information, foreign merchants hired Chinese middlemen (and guarantors) to select Chinese merchants. Chinese and foreign merchants also devised the "commission indent system," an early form of trade credit allowing firms and institutions to operate with minimum financial resources. The stock exchange in Shanghai was the largest in Asia for most of the 1920s and 1930s.

To summarize, relying on alternative mechanisms, China has a long history of developing finance and commerce outside the legal system. In fact, most of the development of the sophisticated financial system prior to 1949 coincided with one of the most volatile periods in Chinese history characterized by political turmoil and (civil and foreign) wars.

A review and comparison of India's corporate sectors also provide an example of the effectiveness of alternative mechanisms and problems with legal institutions. The Indian economy is unbalanced relative to other large economies, in that 52% of output is from services, 26% is from manufacturing, and 22% is from agriculture (67% of workforce). Manufacturing industries have not done well, and a widely accepted reason is that they are constrained by unions and traditional political economy factors, including corruption and bureaucracy in the government and legal system. New industries like software have done much better because they are not constrained by political economy factors as much and rely more on alternative mechanisms.

ACDQQ (2012) have conducted detailed surveys of more than 200 firms from the small and medium enterprises (SMEs) sector in India, and the results clearly favor the use of alternative mechanisms over the law and legal system. For example, when asked about their preferred actions following defaults, breaches of contract and disputes initiated by their business partners, over 80% of surveyed firms say they do not use the legal system at all. Out-of-courts channels of dispute resolution play a far more important role for these firms. About 50% of the firms surveyed do *not* have a regular legal advisor. When pressed for a reason, 63% of respondents who did not have legal advisors claimed they did not need lawyers as they knew all their business partners and could deal with them fairly. Clearly, the formal legal system takes a back seat while reputation, trust, and informal personal relationships are the driving factors in screening potential business opportunities.

The survey responses further indicate that the law not only is a disfavored means to resolve a breach that has already occurred or a dispute that has already arisen but also plays a weak role in dissuading future breaches and disputes. To this end, the survey findings indicate that legal sanctions are far less important than the demands and responsibilities of the networks within which they exist and function. For instance, in the case of default, late payment, and a breach of contract, the primary concern is loss of future business opportunities or reputation; the fear of legal consequences (adverse court sentence or jail term) is the *least* important concern, below even threat to personal safety.

Overall, the picture that emerges of the SME sector in India clearly indicates that the sector has little confidence in the legal system. It relies little on the courts in settling disputes and enforcing contracts and is minimally concerned about legal consequences of infractions. Nonlegal sanctions, on the other hand, are far more effective. This is also the finding of the Chinese corporate sectors today.

The limited role played by the law and legal system in the economic growth of China and India has been found in other East Asian economies. Upham (2002) shows that Japan had developed economic and political systems operating outside the formal legal system before World War II (WWII). After WWII, despite the influence of the US, Japan's formal legal system actually shrunk during the high economic growth period, and alternative mechanisms, similar to those in China and India, were the main force in finance and commerce. In addition, some researchers argue that during early stages of development, it was informal relationships of trust, rather than law as commonly believed, that promoted the development of the financial systems in western European countries.[5]

[5]Greif (1989, 1993) documents the important role of reputation, trust, and implicit contractual relations in the growth of Mediterranean traders' organizations in the 11th century. Mayer (2008) offers a review of how similar mechanisms were behind the development of financial markets in the UK and the banking sector in Germany in the early 20th century.

Alternative Mechanisms Can Work in Complicated Transactions

One may wonder if the limited role of the legal system documented above is limited to simple financial and business transactions and a few developing countries. We next provide two examples to demonstrate that nonlegal mechanisms can deal with complicated, international transactions. First, the global diamond industry has historically operated outside the legal systems and systematically ignored state-created laws (e.g., Bernstein, 1992). This is in part due to the fact that legal contracts cannot be enforced since the value of each transaction (a particular diamond) is highly idiosyncratic, and most diamond traders do not have access to capital markets, and hence calculated damages based on "what if" contingencies are not applicable. Moreover, it generally takes too long for courts to issue their decisions. In its place, the sophisticated diamond traders (belonging to trading clubs or bourses) who dominate the global industry have developed an elaborate internal set of rules, complete with distinctive institutions and sanctions, to handle disputes. The arbitration process within the DDC (diamond dealers club) based on the rules is usually straightforward and quick, with rulings often involving parties simply splitting the differences in estimated damages. Typically, the private arbitration system keeps all judgments secret as long as payments are promptly paid. Given the long-term relationship of members and their interest in preserving their reputations, these simple rules work much better in the long run (even though they may not be fair in individual cases) and save costs. In recent years, the World Association of Diamond Bourses (WADB) has successfully shifted from the traditional relationship-based DDCs to a worldwide information technology-based regime (a database containing reports of arbitrations from 20 plus member countries, many of which are in Asia). Only rarely do a state's laws enter the discussions about the reform.[6]

Another industry that has relied on out-of-court mediations and arbitrations to settle disputes is reinsurance. Reinsurance is the practice where

[6]There is the argument that the bypassing of the national legal systems by the diamond industry has led to lack of accountability and transparency in diamond-producing countries, especially concerning miners in Africa (see, e.g., the Smillie *et al.* (2000) report on Sierra Leone). However, the expansion of WADB has actually restricted the monopoly power of the DeBeers Cartel, the largest supplier of diamond worldwide, which has its own dealers (Bernstein, 1992).

an original insurer, for a definite premium, contracts with another insurer or insurers, to carry a part or the whole of a risk assumed by the original insurer. While the earliest reinsurance contract can be traced to 14th-century Italy (e.g., Kopf, 1929), the first use of an arbitration clause in an insurance contract was, by most accounts, the one in the Insurance Company of North America in 1793 (e.g., Winn and Davis, 2004). The original arbitration system requires each party to appoint their own arbitrator and typically requires the two party-appointed arbitrators to appoint a third arbitrator referred to as an "umpire." In practice, however, it is the parties and their outside counsel who play a large role in the selection of the umpire. This often results in disagreements, especially in large transactions, which delay the appointment and hence the arbitration process as a whole.

In recent years the industry has been revising the traditional procedure in order to expedite the process while still preserving its fairness. Industry experts have turned to other industries where arbitration has been used most successfully, such as securities arbitration, where the New York Stock Exchange and the National Association of Securities Dealers disseminate and continually refine and improve a set of rules (e.g., Kondo, 2007). The Dispute Resolution Protocol, developed by the Conflict Prevention and Resolution International Industry for the reinsurance business, reflects these new ideas and changes. It is nonlegally binding for members. Based on best practices from the field, the Protocol, among other things, simplifies and standardizes the process of selecting neutral arbitrators and has been endorsed by leading companies such as Lloyd's. This example demonstrates the importance of adapting to changes quickly as a main condition for the long-term viability of a dispute resolution mechanism.

Intellectual Property Rights and Innovations

As discussed earlier, one of the cornerstones of Western law and institutions is property rights. A "hot-button" issue in property rights is the protection of intellectual property rights and their role in economic growth, which is also at the center of our comparisons between the two different systems of finance and commerce. Due to space limitations we cannot review all the evidence on intellectual property rights (see, e.g., the OECD (2004) report and the Bessen and Meurer [2008] book for excellent reviews). We focus on two aspects of intellectual property rights. First, whether the protection of exclusive rights (through patents, copyrights, trade secrets, trademarks, etc.) has a positive impact on the pace of innovations, and second, the problems of using the law and legal institutions as the basis for disputes related to intellectual property rights.

In almost all the countries with laws on intellectual property rights, the scope of patentable subject matter has traditionally *not* included fundamental scientific discoveries. A frequently mentioned rationale for this omission is that, given the far-reaching impact in many fields of these discoveries, it would be impossible to outline the boundaries of the patent protection. In fact, whether the boundary of a patent can be precisely defined is an important determinant of effective enforcement of the patent law (e.g., Bessen and Meurer, 2008). Once the patent is approved and issued, the primary forum for resolving disputes is the (federal) courts, which have exclusive jurisdiction over disputes involving the infringement of patents and appeals of court decisions.

There is an extensive literature in industrial organization in economics examining the relationship between the protection of intellectual property rights and the pace of innovations during the past three decades, and the research yields mixed findings. In the chemicals and pharmaceuticals industries, stronger and more effective protection has been found to lead to more R&D spending and innovations in developed countries. This positive relation is attributed to the fact that most patents are valuable with clearly defined boundaries. This, in turn, helps keep litigation costs (of alleged infringers) low. However, it is unclear whether the most important inventions and discoveries in the chemicals and pharmaceuticals industries were made under the protection of property rights (see, for example, Allen and Qian, 2010, for more details).

Outside the chemical and pharmaceutical industries, prior economic research finds, that in many developed countries, there is no positive relation between the protection of intellectual property rights and the pace of innovations. Instead, excessive protection deters competition, which is another important factor in spurring innovations, and small inventors do not benefit from the laws on intellectual property as much as large corporations. In addition, based on changes in patent laws and enforcement regulations, Lerner (2002, 2005), among others, finds only weak or no evidence that *strengthening* patent rights and the enforcement of patent laws spur the pace of innovations across developed countries.

Research in developing countries also generally fails to establish a positive relationship between the protection of intellectual property rights and the pace of innovations. This is due to weak enforcement of such rights and the lack of other relevant institutions.[7] China is often singled out as notoriously bad in protecting intellectual property rights, as copying and imitation via reverse engineering is a prevalent strategy across industries. Legal actions by foreign firms have been nearly useless in preventing these activities. As argued above, despite efforts by the government to pass new laws and strengthen existing ones, including those on intellectual property rights, in part as a response to mounting international pressure, it is doubtful that these efforts will have any system-wide impact. First, there is no systematic statement of the law of property or clear definitions of private property rights. Second, law enforcement is likely to be ineffective due to the intrinsic conflict of interest between fair play in practicing law and the monopoly power of the single ruling party, especially in cases in which government officials or their affiliates are involved (e.g., Clarke *et al.*, 2008). Notably, though, while the protection of intellectual rights in China has been poor, the pace of innovations has been furious due to the pressure of competition.

One of the main problems of the patent system based on the law is that it motivates rent-seeking behaviors by interest groups. An example to illustrate such behavior is that companies, especially large corporations with abundant resources, come up with numerous *non essential* inventions to pad the one significant (patented) invention or establish a new standard in production (e.g., Dewatripont and Legros, 2007). The creation of such a standard can impact the use of many different technologies — in the case of mobile technology, for instance, a production standard on a new handset requires the use of more than 1000 technologies protected by patents. By jamming the patent system with extra patents or standards, the patent holders can essentially block or delay innovations by competitors. This is

[7] See, for example, Djankov and Murrell (2002) for a review on the obstacles in the development of commercial laws and legal system in the economies of transition in Eastern Europe and Vietnam.

what has led to the FRAND concept — "fair, reasonable, and nondiscriminatory royalties."

Another form of rent-seeking behavior is that patent holders, especially those with more resources, seek the best possible legal venue to maximize the likelihood of winning a lawsuit against patent or copyright infringements. This type of behavior runs against the principle that the legal system within a democracy should be based on fair procedures and should allow equal access to all. In our final set of examples illustrating problems of intellectual property rights, we examine recent innovations in communications and knowledge industries based on Internet revolutions. Some of these inventions are free of charge and are not protected by patents or copyrights, while others do charge and are protected. As discussed above, when it is difficult to determine whether an invention has broached the boundary of a patent, as is often the case for Internet-related innovations, enforcement efforts become ineffective and may cause rent-seeking behaviors to escalate.

On the knowledge front, SSRN (Social Science Research Network) and JSTOR are great academic inventions that bring new working papers and published articles, in electronic format, to individual researchers worldwide essentially free of charge (based on institutional subscriptions). For the general public, Wikipedia, a multilingual, web-based platform with free content, is quickly becoming the most useful encyclopedia. Written collaboratively by volunteers from around the world, the Wikipedia articles provide links to guide users to related pages with additional information and offer a useful point to begin research on almost any subject (including some of the topics discussed in this chapter). Since its creation in 2001, it has grown rapidly into one of the largest reference websites, attracting over 600 million visitors annually by 2008.

While the growth of Wikipedia has met with little resistance from the traditional media companies, it is a totally different situation with Google's equally ambitious "Print and Library Project." Under the "fair use doctrine" of the US Copyright Law, Google's plan has two components, Google Publisher Program, in which a publisher holding copyrights to a book can authorize Google to scan the entire book into Google's search database, and Google Library Project, where some of the largest libraries (Harvard, Oxford, and Stanford Universities; University of Michigan; and the New York Public Library) allow Google to scan materials. According to Google, for books/print materials in the public domain (not subject to copyright) from the libraries, Google will display the full text of the book with the search result; for those that are still covered by copyrights, readers can only see a few sentences of the text around the search item; copyright holders can also exclude selected books from Google Print. Ever since the initial idea of the Project floated around, it was met with disdain from publishing companies. The Association of American Publishers, including well-known companies such as Penguin, McGraw-Hill, Pearson Education, Simon & Schuster and John Wiley & Sons, and the Authors Guild, the nation's largest organization of book authors, filed suits against Google in the second half of 2005.

After several years of painstaking negotiations, Google finally worked out a $125 million legal settlement with groups representing authors and publishers. However, on March 22, 2011, a federal judge in New York rejected the legal settlement (see *New York Times*, March 22, 2011). While Judge Denny Chin acknowledges that "the creation of a universal digital library would benefit many," he said it would have granted Google a "*de facto* monopoly" and the right to profit from books without the permission of copyright owners. Regardless of whether Google will gain monopolist status in the new realm of digital library, a project that clearly benefits societies worldwide must be put off indefinitely due to the legal process — first the lawsuits filed by the publishers, followed by the lengthy negotiations, and now the new court ruling.

Limited Capacity of the Legislature

Another potential problem of using the legal system in a democracy is that when there are fundamental changes in an economy so that the law and/or regulation must be revised, the legislature must approve any revisions before corporations and investors can freely implement new techniques in their transactions and interactions (without worrying about breaking the law). However, politicians have limited time and effort that can be devoted to any given area of the law, and hence there is a legislature capacity and a fixed cost in revising the law. The following example illustrates that such limited capacity and fixed costs can single-handedly slow down the pace of financial and business transactions in practice.

Figure 1 compares payments systems in major developed economies. At the start of the 21st century, the US had a 19th century payments system,

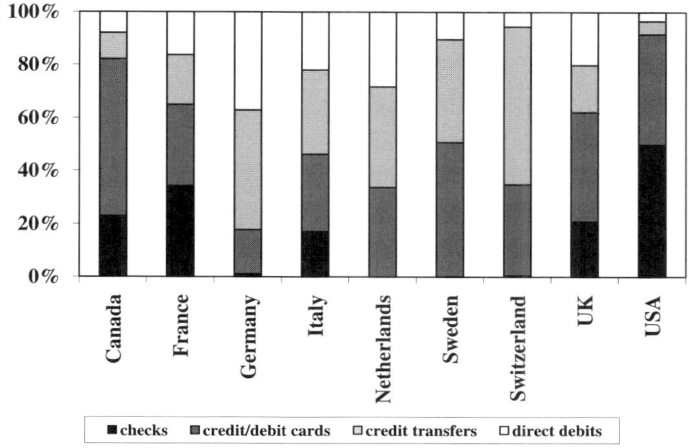

Fig. 1. Comparing payments systems in developed countries.

Source: Bank for International Settlements (2008).

relying mostly on checks and the mail, and significantly lagging behind other developed nations. While countries like Germany, the Netherlands, Sweden, and Switzerland had almost completely abandoned checks (and relied instead on electronic payments systems), about half of all the payments in the US were still in the form of paper checks. Under the old Uniform Commercial Code, the only legally acceptable proof of payment was cancelled checks, or checks processed by both the deposited and paying financial institutions. Hence, checks had to be physically transported from where they were deposited to a central operations center, then to the clearer, and then back to the banks they were drawn on. This check-and-clearing process significantly delayed business transactions as compared to electronic methods.

How costly was this backward payment system? Using information from Humphrey *et al.* (1996) and Bolt *et al.* (2005), we can conduct a back-of-the-envelope calculation. From cross-country comparisons and analysis, these researchers suggest that there are savings of about 1–2% of GDP when a country moves away from paper checks (e.g., the US) and toward electronic-based methods. The US 2007 GDP was $13,543 billion, which indicates the magnitude of savings from reforming the payment system to be $135 billion to $270 billion per year. With a 5% discount rate (roughly the risk-free rate in the US), the discounted present value of this savings (assuming a 10-year growing annuity of 2% per year to control for inflation) is between $1.1 trillion to $2.2 trillion; in other words, the magnitude of the savings is comparable or higher than the total cost of the most recent Iraqi war.

Despite years of calls for changes from the banks and businesses, the US Congress appeared not in a hurry to solve this seemingly simple yet costly problem. Without the approval of the legislature, banks cannot expedite the payment process due to the fear of lawsuits. Then, the tragic events of September 11, 2001, occurred and served as a catalyst for change. After the terrorist attack, all commercial flights in the US were grounded for several days, completely halting the check clearing process. After the flights resumed, the call for change in the payments system finally resonated with Congress. The Check Clearing for the 21st Century Act ("Check 21 Act") was signed in October 2003 and became effective one year later. The Check 21 Act allows electronic images of both sides of paper checks to be a "legally equivalent" substitute for the original checks, and these "substitute checks" can be exchanged among financial institutions including banks, clearing houses, and the Federal Reserve Bank (see, e.g., Board of Governors of the Federal Reserve System [2008] for more details). Therefore, the clearing process is no longer dependent on the mail and transportation system.

To summarize, in this section, we presented examples to highlight two potential problems of relying on the law as the basis for finance and commerce: rent-seeking behaviors by vested interest groups and limited capacity of the legislature in approving changes to the law. We also argue that these problems are likely to be worsened in developing countries until they can develop sound legal and other related institutions. We also present examples to illustrate that alternative systems can work well outside the legal system in both developing and developed countries.

Legal Institutions versus Alternative Mechanisms: Comparisons and Policy Implications

The above examples motivate our comparisons of two different sets of systems. The first system, employed by developed and democratic countries such as the US, commits to use the law as the basis for finance and commerce and legal institutions as the ultimate source for resolving disputes and enforcing contracts; further, changes to the law must be approved by the legislature and electorate. In the second system, symbolized by countries such as China, there is no systematic definition of private property rights or property law, and, in practice, nonlegal mechanisms are the norm for conducting business; the process of change in finance and commerce is often bottom up rather than top down.[8]

There are well-known advantages of using the law and legal system as the basis for finance and commerce. The legal system of a democratic society allows equal and full access by all and promises fairness in trials and settlements. Backed by the government and legislature, the legal system also has the ultimate authority in its decisions on any and all disputes. The legal system is endowed with powerful enforcement mechanisms, including criminal penalties, such as imprisonment, as well as civil laws and financial penalties to affect people's behaviors. These enforcement mechanisms and penalties provide strong incentives for individuals and organizations to follow the resolutions endorsed by the legal system, which in turn provides long-term stability in the economy. The legal process, including resolution and enforcement, can be anonymous (e.g., details of a settlement of a dispute may not be disclosed) or transparent (the entire procedure of a high-profile trial may be covered by media). By using the entire legal system, the marginal costs for resolving an additional dispute and enforcing an additional contract can be reduced, and this improves overall efficiency.

However, there are also disadvantages in using the law and legal institutions. First, recent research on political economy factors suggests that rent-seeking behaviors by vested interest groups can turn legal institutions into barriers to changes. For example, Rajan and Zingales (2003a, 2003b) suggest that the development of a formal financial system may trigger political economy costs, causing a disconnection between the level of

[8]We make these classifications to better differentiate these two systems and facilitate the comparisons, but they may not be mutually exclusive when we look at a particular country. In fact, as the literature on legal pluralism (see, e.g., Merry, 1988. for a review) shows, in many countries these two systems can coexist but do not necessarily work to improve each other.

financial market activity and economic development. Similarly, Acemoglu and Johnson (2005) find that while "contracting institutions," or laws protecting contracts between individual parties, do not affect long-term growth, "property rights institutions," or laws and regulations restraining powerful elites and the government, do affect economic growth. We expect these problems to be much more severe in developing countries, where the costs of building good institutions can be enormous. We argue that one way to solve this problem is not to use the law as the basis for finance and commerce but instead to use alternative mechanisms, as the experience in China and India documented earlier.

Second, in democracies, there can be a lengthy political process before significant changes can be approved (by the majority of the electorate or legislature), and the people in charge of approving or disapproving changes (e.g., politicians and judges) may lack expertise in the business transactions under scrutiny and have limited capacity (time and effort) to study the proposed changes. The process of passing the Check 21 Act epitomizes this capacity issue. In addition, as demonstrated in examples in the previous section, interest groups with more resources may receive more protection than individuals and organizations with fewer resources. This asymmetry in protection induces more rent-seeking behaviors and further deters innovations.

Unlike the legislature, which has monopoly power and authority in revising the law, one of the main advantages for alternative mechanisms, along with the bottom-up process for changes, is that such mechanisms are more likely to foster competition among different mediation/resolution agencies/organizations. Competition can ensure that the most efficient mechanism prevails — for example, only experts are involved in the rule-changing process. Competition can also limit rent-seeking behaviors by one or more groups. Clearly, alternative mechanisms as described can be much faster in adopting new rules to deal with changes in finance commerce since these changes do not require the permission from the legislature or electorate.

One of the main disadvantages of the alternative mechanisms is the lack of enforcement power and authority. Without the backing of the government and judicial system, alternative mechanisms can only rely on reputation along with economic and financial incentives (e.g., avoiding future losses due to sanctions by other members of the network or coalition) and mutual monitoring to enforce contractual agreements. These methods may be insufficient to ensure good behavior if future losses are not substantial relative to the gains that can be made today, or if these losses can be recuperated by entering other lines of business or networks. Another negative for alternative mechanisms is that, by design, they exist among a network and thus may be inaccessible to outsiders; partial access by outsiders may come with the price of biased outcomes in dispute resolution favoring insiders. In addition, frequent changes adopted by a network (or networks) create instability in the entire economy and hence weak long-term incentives.

These advantages and disadvantages lead to the tradeoffs of the two systems in different economic environments. In *static* environments with infrequent and predictable changes (i.e., mature and slow-growing economies and industries), the advantages of the legal mechanisms dominate the disadvantages. First, the strong incentives provided by the enforcement mechanisms of the legal system imply that efficient systems can be designed that do not rely solely on positive monetary incentives. Second, the fixed costs of using the legal system when changes occur can be negated by the infrequent revisions of the law and by a few large-scale transactions; the legislature and the judicial system can appoint experts to be involved with the process of changing the law and grant them the authority in decision making. The combination of effective enforcement and infrequent changes also implies that there is stability in the system, which in turn creates strong long-term incentives for economic agents to play by the (universal) rule.

In *dynamic* environments with frequent and unforeseen shocks (i.e., new industries and/or emerging, fast-growing economies such as China and India), however, the disadvantages of legal mechanisms are magnified and can outweigh their advantages. The lengthy approval process by the legislature and electorate of any change to the law, along with the limited capacity and possible lack of expertise by the judges and politicians, means that the legal system is slow in reacting to changes. Moreover, a legal system captured by interest groups can in fact oppose changes, and with its monopoly power, it can become a barrier to competition and innovations. On the other hand, alternative mechanisms can adapt to changes much more quickly, since competition ensures that the most efficient mechanism will be implemented quickly, and this process does not require the approval of the legislature. Weak enforcement power and long-term incentives of the alternative mechanisms can be significantly strengthened by effective reputation mechanisms as long as there are long-term profits to be made and shared by participating individuals and organizations.

The interaction between legal and alternative mechanisms is another reason why alternative mechanisms can promote economic growth and improve social welfare. Since most of the laws are adopted from best practices, having a viable system of alternatives can thus improve the efficiency of legal institutions, especially in dynamic environments. Competition among formal and alternative mechanisms can also ensure that the best mechanism will be eventually adopted in the entire economy, and this is especially important in environments where special interest groups can easily capture the legal system. A fair and functional legal system can also improve the effectiveness of alternative mechanisms by adopting the best rules and enforcing the changes in the entire economy and by instilling stability amid frequent changes.

We conclude that legal mechanisms are an important part of developed economies' institutions, providing stability and strong long-term incentives. This conclusion is based on the premise that there are infrequent shocks to the economy that cause fundamental changes in ways that business is conducted, that the legal system allows full access by all and promises fair resolution of disputes and enforces the rules uniformly.

However, the assumptions making legal institutions the optimal system in developed countries are unlikely to hold in many emerging economies. A fast-growing economy, such as that of China and India, is often characterized by frequent shocks to the fundamentals of the economy, which make repeated changes to the practice of finance and commerce a requirement, not a choice. Given that it typically takes years to build a well-functioning legal system and other formal institutions, the fixed costs of using the legal system can be quite high in a dynamic economy, even if the system provides fairness and expertise when dealing with changes in the law.

A much more severe problem with the legal system, perhaps, is the political economy factor. It would be much easier for interest groups to capture the legal system and government in a country with underdeveloped institutions than in a country with developed institutions. As a result, an economy relying on law and legal institutions as the sole basis for commerce may find that such reliance is, in fact, a barrier to change and innovation.

Therefore, we argue that alternative mechanisms play a much more prominent role in emerging economies and can actually be superior to legal mechanisms in supporting business transactions in certain industries or entire economies. Our main policy implication is that, in emerging economies, alternative dispute resolution and contract enforcement mechanisms should be encouraged and developed alongside the development of legal and other formal institutions. In particular, measures that help foster competition and reduce entry barriers are welfare enhancing. The coexistence of and competition between alternative and legal mechanisms can also exert positive impact on the development of legal institutions, so that they are less likely to be captured by interest groups and become more efficient in adapting to changes.[9] Whether and how a transition from a system dominated by alternative mechanisms to one using the law and legal institutions as the focal point depends on the country's economic history and growth potential, as well as the workings of many other social and cultural factors that help build the social norms in the society and business communities.

Concluding Remarks

In our view, China and India's economic success contains important lessons. While using the law in finance and commerce has become a widely accepted idea, it is based on the history of institutional development in the West. We have argued that it can be optimal in static environments with infrequent changes. In dynamic environments such as China and India, it may be better to use other mechanisms that do not rely on the law because this reduces the inefficiencies associated with political economy factors. Designing economic institutions that minimize political economy problems by not relying on the legal system is one of the keys to fast economic growth.

[9] Qian and Weingast (1997) argue that government decentralization since 1979 has helped foster competition among local officials and preserve market incentives in China. Allen and Qian (2008) argue that competition among officials from different regions curtails the negative impact of corruption on economic growth in China.

References

Acemoglu, D. and S. Johnson (2005). "Unbundling institutions," *Journal of Political Economy*, Vol. 113, No. 5, pp. 949–995.

Allen, F. and J. Qian (2008). "Corruption and competition," Boston College Working Paper.

Allen, F. and J. Qian (2010). "Comparing legal and alternative institutions in finance and commerce," Chapter 6 in *Global Perspectives of Rule of Law*, J. Heckman and R. Nelson (eds.), Oxon, OX, UK: Routledge, pp. 118–144.

Allen, F., J. Qian and M. Qian (2005). "Law, finance, and economic growth in China," *Journal of Financial Economics*, Vol. 77, No. 1, pp. 57–116.

Allen, F., J. Qian and M. Qian (2008). "China's financial system: Past, present and future," in *China's Great Economic Transformation*, L. Brandt and T. Rawski (eds.), Cambridge, UK: Cambridge University Press, pp. 506–568.

Allen, F., R. Chakrabarti, S. De, J. Qian and M. Qian (2012). "Financing firms in India," *Journal of Financial Intermediation*, Vol. 21, pp. 409–445.

Bank for International Settlements (2008). "Statistics on payment and settlement systems in selected countries: Figures for 2006." Available at: www.bis.org/publ/cpss82.pdf. Accessed 23 November 2008.

Bernstein, L. (1992). "Opting out of the legal system: Extralegal contractual relations in the diamond industry," *Journal of Legal Studies*, Vol. 21, pp. 115–157.

Bessen, J. and M. J. Meurer (2008). *Patent Failure: How Judges, Bureaucrats, and Lawyers Put Innovators at Risk*, Princeton, NJ: Princeton University Press.

Board of Governors of the Federal Reserve System (2008). 94th Annual Report 2007, Washington, DC.

Bolt, W., D. Humphrey and R. Uittenbogaard (2005). "The effects of transaction pricing on the adoption of electronic payments: A cross-country comparison," Federal Reserve Bank of Philadelphia Working Paper.

Brandt, L. and T. Rawski (2008). *China's Great Economic Transformation*, Cambridge, UK: Cambridge University Press.

Clarke, D., P. Murrell and S. Whiting (2008). "The role of law in China's economic development," in *China's Great Economic Transformation*, L. Brandt and T. Rawski (eds.), Cambridge, UK: Cambridge University Press, pp. 375–428.

Dewatripont, M. and P. Legros (2007). "Essential patents, FRAND royalties and technological standards," European Center for Advanced Research in Economics and Statistics Working Paper.

Djankov, S. and P. Murrell (2002). "Enterprise restructuring in transition: A quantitative survey," *Journal of Economic Literature*, Vol. 40, pp. 739–792.

Fisher, M. (2007). "Download uproar: Record industry goes after personal use," *Washington Post*, Sunday Arts, December 30, p. M5.

Government of China (1904). "Company law."

Government of China (People's Republic) (2007). "Enterprise Bankruptcy Law," effective June 1, 2006 (official Chinese version). Available at: www.gov.cn/ziliao/flfg/2006-08/28/content_371296.htm.

Government of United States (2003). "Check Clearing for the 21st Century Act," Washington, DC.

Greif, A. (1989). "Reputation and coalitions in medieval trade: Evidence on the Maghribi traders," *Journal of Economic History*, Vol. 49, pp. 857–882.

Greif, A. (1993). "Contract enforceability and economic institutions in early trade: The Maghribi traders' coalition," *American Economic Review*, Vol. 83, pp. 525–548.

Humphrey, D., L. Pulley and J. Vesala (1996). "Cash, paper, and electronic payments: A cross-country analysis," *Journal of Money, Credit and Banking*, Vol. 28, pp. 914–939.

International Monetary Fund (2012). "World Economic Outlook Database." Available at: www.imf.org/external/pubs/ft/weo/2012/01/weodata/index.aspx/. Accessed April 2012.

Kirby, W. (1995). "China unincorporated: Company law and business enterprise in twentieth-century China," *Journal of Asian Studies*, Vol. 54, pp. 43–63.

Kondo, J. (2007). "Self-regulation and enforcement: Evidence from investor-broker disputes at NASD," MIT Working Paper.

Kopf, E. (1929). "Notes on the origin and development of reinsurance," *Proceedings of the Casualty Actuarial Society*, Vol. XVI, No. 33/34, pp. 22–91.

Lee, T. V. (1993). "Risky business: Courts, culture, and the marketplace," *University of Miami Law Review*, Vol. 47, pp. 1335–1414.

LegalMetric (2008). "Eastern District of Texas patent litigation study." Available at: www.legalmetric.com/studies/txed_pat_study.html [accessed on November 23, 2008].

Lerner, J. (2002). "150 years of patent protection," *American Economic Review Papers and Proceedings*, Vol. 92, pp. 221–225.

Lerner, J. (2005). "150 years of patent office practice," *American Law and Economics Review*, Vol. 7, pp. 112–143.

Mayer, C. (2008). "Trust in financial markets," *European Financial Management*, Vol. 14, pp. 617–32.

Merry, S. E. (1988). "Legal pluralism," *Law & Society Review*, Vol. 22, No. 5, pp. 869–896.

Organization for Economic Co-operation and Development (OECD), Directorate for Financial and Enterprise Affairs of the Competition Committee (2005). Policy Roundtables: Intellectual Property Rights 2004. Available at www.oecd.org/dataoecd/61/48/34306055.pdf [accessed on November 23, 2008].

Qian, Y. and B. Weingast (1997). "Federalism as a commitment to preserving market incentives," *Journal of Economic Perspectives*, Vol. 11, pp. 83–92.

Rajan, R. and L. Zingales (2003a). "The great reversals: The politics of financial development in the twentieth century," *Journal of Financial Economics*, Vol. 69, pp. 5–50.

Rajan, R. and L. Zingales (2003b). *Saving Capitalism from Capitalists: Unleashing the Power of Financial Markets to Create Wealth and Spread Opportunity*, New York: Random House.

Ravallion, M. and S. Chen (2004). "China's (uneven) progress against poverty," World Bank Policy Research Working Paper No. 3408, Washington, DC.

Smillie, I., L. Gberie and R. Hazleton (2000). "The heart of the matter: Sierra Leone, diamonds, and human security," Partnership Africa Canada, Ontario. Available at: http://pacweb.org/e/index.php?option=content&task=view&id=42&Itemid=65> [accessed on November 23, 2008].

Upham, F. (2002). "Mythmaking in the rule of law orthodoxy," Carnegie Endowment for International Peace, Democracy and Rule of Law Project Working Paper, Washington, DC.

Winn, B. and E. Davis (2004). "Arbitration of reinsurance disputes: Is there a better way?" *Dispute Resolution Journal*, Vol. 59, pp. 22–25.

Finance in the Tropics: Understanding Structural Gaps and Policy Challenges

Thorsten Beck*
Tilburg University
and
CEPR

Introduction

Ample empirical evidence has shown a positive though nonlinear relationship between financial depth and economic growth. Specifically, cross-country, within-country, industry-level, and firm-level studies have shown a positive relationship between finance and growth. While recent evidence has pointed to decreasing benefits of financial deepening at higher levels of financial development in high-income countries, there is strong evidence that low-, and especially middle-income, countries benefit significantly from financial deepening.

At the same time, a rapid increase in credit has been associated with higher bank fragility and the likelihood that a country suffers a systemic banking crisis. The history of finance is full of boom-and-bust cycles, bank failures, and systemic bank and currency crises (Reinhart and Rogoff, 2009). Just as there is a comprehensive literature on the impact of finance on growth, there is an equally important literature that has explored the causes and socioeconomic costs of financial fragility, including systemic banking crises (see Demirgüç-Kunt and Detragiache, 2005, for a survey). This ambiguous empirical association of financial deepening is consistent with theory. The same mechanism through which finance helps growth also

*Thorsten Beck is Professor of Economics at Tilburg University and Chairman of the European Banking Center. He is also affiliated with the Centre for Economic Policy Research. This paper builds partly on joint work with Adolfo Barajas, Era Dabla-Norris, and Reza Yousefi.

makes finance susceptible to shocks and, ultimately, fragility. Specifically, the maturity and liquidity transformation from short-term savings and deposit facilities into long-term investments is not only at the core of the positive impact of a financial system on the real economy but also renders the system susceptible to shocks, with the possibilities of bank and liquidity runs. The information asymmetries and ensuing agency problems between savers and entrepreneurs that banks help to alleviate also can turn into a source of fragility given agency conflicts between depositors/creditors and banks.

The importance of the financial sector for the overall economy, while at the same time being a source of volatility, raises the question of the "optimal" or "Goldilocks" level of financial depth and the question of policies to reach this optimum. Building on Barajas *et al.* (2013), this paper presents the concept of the financial possibility frontier as gauge of the relative position of a financial system. I use this concept for a taxonomy of different challenges that financial sector authorities can face and discuss several policy areas that might help financial systems in developing countries move toward the frontier and push out the frontier. Specifically, I will discuss the roles of competition, financial innovation, and globalization in the financial deepening process in developing countries. In the context of these challenges, I will also point to the changing role of government both in developing but also harnessing financial markets.

This paper is related to several literatures. Specifically, it is related to the finance and growth literature, the financial crisis literature, and the literature on policies for a sound and effective financial system (see Beck, 2012, for a critical survey of these three literatures and their links). The finance and growth literature, as surveyed by Levine (2005), among others, has shown a positive relationship between financial deepening and growth. More recent work, however, has shown nonlinearities in this relationship. There is evidence that the effect of financial development is strongest among middle-income countries, whereas other work finds a declining effect of finance and growth as countries grow richer.[1] More recently, Arcand, Berkes, and Panizza (2012) find that the finance and growth relationship turns negative for high-income countries, identifying a value of

[1] Rioja and Valev (2004a, 2004b) and Aghion, Howitt, and Mayer-Foulkes (2005).

110% private credit to GDP as approximate turning point, with the negative relationship between finance and growth turning significant at around 150% private credit to GDP, levels reached by some high-income countries in the 2000s. This paper is also related to a growing literature exploring the anatomy of financial crises.[2] This literature has pointed to macroeconomic, bank-level, and regulatory policy factors in causing and exacerbating financial fragility. It has also shown trade-offs of financial deepening in terms of long-term higher growth but short-term higher fragility (Loayza and Rancière, 2006; Rancière, Tornell, and Westermann, 2006). Finally, this paper is related to a diverse literature exploring macroeconomic and institutional determinants of sound and efficient financial deepening.[3]

The remainder of the paper is structured as follows. I will first develop the idea of the financial possibility frontier and derive a taxonomy of financial sector policies. I will use this concept to discuss the roles of competition, financial innovation and globalization in financial deepening in developing countries. Finally, I will discuss the role of government in these three policy areas and point to the importance of political economy considerations.

The Financial Possibility Frontier

Financial systems are constrained by two major market frictions, transaction costs and risks, which can constrain the deepening and broadening of financial systems in developing countries.[4] As I will discuss in the following, financial intermediaries and markets arise exactly because these market frictions prevent direct intermediation between savers and borrowers. However, their efficient operation is limited by the same market frictions.

Fixed transaction costs in financial service provision result in decreasing unit costs as the number or size of transactions increases. These fixed costs exist at the level of the transaction, client, institution, and even financial system. Processing an individual payment or savings transaction entails

[2]See Detragiache and Demirgüç-Kunt (2005) and Claessens *et al.* (2011)

[3]See, for example, Boyd *et al.* (2001) and Djankov *et al.* (2007).

[4]For the following, see a similar discussion in Beck and de la Torre (2007) and Barajas *et al.* (2013).

costs that are, at least in part, independent of the value of the transaction. Maintaining an account for an individual client also implies costs that are largely independent of the number and size of the transactions the client makes. At the level of a financial institution, fixed costs span a wide range — from the brick-and-mortar branch network to computer systems, legal and accounting services, and security arrangements — and are independent of the number of clients served. Fixed costs also arise at the level of the financial system, including regulatory costs and the costs of payment, clearing, and settlement infrastructure, which are, up to a point, independent of the number of institutions regulated or participating in the payment system. The resulting economies of scale at all levels explain why financial intermediation costs are typically higher in smaller financial systems and why smaller economies can typically only sustain small financial systems, even in relation to economic activity. They also explain the limited capacity of small financial systems to broaden their financial systems toward clients with need for smaller transactions.

In addition to costs, the depth and outreach of financial systems, especially in credit and insurance services, is constrained by risks, particularly default risk. The risks can be either contract specific or systemic. Systemic risk typically stems from high macroeconomic uncertainty and volatility, weaknesses in the contractual and informational environment, or geographical limitations. It hinders the supply of financial services because it raises the default probability or the loss given default for all contingent contracts written in a given jurisdiction. This leads to a higher cost for funds and, hence, a higher floor for lending interest rates, shorter maturities as risk increases with the loan horizon, or higher premiums to write insurance policies. As systemic risk increases, it enlarges the set of borrowers and projects that are effectively priced out of the credit market. Similarly, it makes insurance policies unaffordable for larger segments of the population. While idiosyncratic risks are specific to individual borrowers, projects, or policy holders, their management is influenced by the systemic risk environment. High macroeconomic uncertainty and deficient contract enforcement institutions exacerbate the agency problems, while the lack of diversification possibilities can hinder the ability of financial institutions to diversify nonagency risks. The lack of agricultural lending in many developing countries has often been explained by the inability of financial institutions to diversify the high risk stemming from agricultural activity and therefore agricultural lending. Similarly, limited lending to SMEs is often related to the deficient contractual and information framework in many developing countries. At the same time, the easing of agency frictions in the absence of adequate oversight can create incentives for excessive risk-taking by market participants (by failing to internalize externalities), fueling financial instability.

While financial institutions can influence their costs and risks to a certain degree, they are constrained by state variables, that is, factors that do not change in the short run and affect all financial institutions and markets in a given country. State variables are either directly related to the financial sector (including macroeconomic fundamentals, the available technology, contractual, and information frameworks underpinning the financial system) or the broader socio-political environment the financial system operates in. Such factors might include the average level and distribution of per capita income, and the system-wide costs of doing business determined by, among others, the quality of the transportation and communication infrastructure and the degree of general insecurity associated with crime, violence, and terrorism. Among the state variables is also the size of the market, related to the oft-found triple problem of smallness — small transactions, small financial institutions, and small market size — which reduces the possibilities to diversify and hedge risks, while at the same time increasing concentration risks. This is notable when comparing small and larger low-income countries, with the latter having typically more diversified and larger financial systems. State variables are hard to change in the short term and might be even outside the purview of policymakers. It is important to stress that state variables comprise a large number of factors and are defined relative to a specific time horizon.

Using the concept of state variables allows us to define the financial possibility frontier as a rationed equilibrium, that is, the maximum sustainable depth and breadth of a financial system. This frontier looks different for payment and savings services, for which transaction costs are the decisive friction, and credit and insurance services, for which risk is an additional important friction. Such frontiers can be designed for different services, products, and markets, and they can focus either on depth (credit, contract, transaction, or deposit volume) or outreach (share of population that uses a specific financial service). The financial possibility frontier can move over time, as income levels change, the international environment adjusts, new technologies arise, and — most importantly — the overall socio-political environment in which financial institutions work changes. Critically, policy levers, including the macroeconomic environment and contractual and information frameworks, can be used to push out the frontier, although such benefits are rarely to be reaped in the short term.

The financial possibility frontier also allows us to distinguish between several challenges to deepen and broaden financial systems in developing countries and the corresponding policies. Depending on where a financial system stands relative to the frontier and where the frontier stands in comparison to other countries with similar characteristics, different policy priorities apply and thus different functions for government. In the following, we will discuss situations, where (i) a financial system is below the frontier, (ii) is above the frontier, and (iii) the frontier is too low.

First, there is the possibility that a financial system is below the frontier, i.e., below the constrained maximum defined by state variables. This would imply that the financial system is not exploiting its possibilities to the best extent, due to either demand and/or supply-side constraints. Demand-side constraints can arise because the number of loan applicants is too low simply because of the self-exclusion resulting from cultural barriers or financial illiteracy. Similarly, there might be a lack of demand for payment and savings services because these products may be accessed indirectly through family and friends or avoided for cultural or religious reasons. However, there may also be a lack of knowledge about the advantages of certain financial products or a general adversity against formal institutions. Critically, there might be a lack of investment projects in the economy. Supply constraints might hold the financial system below the frontier, with existing financial institutions and markets not exploiting all possibilities or a lack of new entrants that could push the system to the frontier. Lack of competition or regulatory restrictions might prevent financial institutions and players to exploit possibilities offered by the constrained maximum. Lack of competition might prevent financial institutions to reach out to new clientele or introduce new products or services. Similarly, regulator restrictions or high regulatory costs might prevent enterprises' access to financial markets. Limited access to reliable financial information and weak corporate disclosure practices can also create obstacles for the functioning of securities markets.

Second, there is the possibility that a financial system moves beyond the frontier, which indicates an unsustainable expansion of the financial system beyond its fundamentals. Lending binges can arise in credit markets moving to an equilibrium above the financial possibilities frontier, whereby loans are granted to a larger share of loan applicants than is prudent based on the lending interest rate and the state variables. It is important to note that fragility in low-income countries is often linked to governance problems, so that an overshooting of the financial possibilities frontier can also be related to limited supervisory and market discipline.

A final problem of deepening and broadening involves a financial possibilities frontier that is too low relative to countries at similar levels of economic development, due to deficiencies in state variables. We are able to distinguish here among the role of technology, the general socio-economic environment in expanding the frontier outward, and the role of government policies. First, technology can push out the frontier, as the example of cell phone-based banking in several developing countries has shown, by reducing cost of financial service provision substantially. Similarly, technology can improve risk management, as the example of agricultural insurance based on objective rainfall data has shown. Second, the general socio-economic environment is critical for financial depth, as it influences the costs of financial service provision, but is mostly outside the perimeter of financial sector policies. Low income levels imply a lower bankable clientele, increasing the costs and risks for financial institutions and excluding large segments of the population from formal financial services. The fixed costs of payments and settlement infrastructure and regulation (and network effects) tend to be even higher in the case of capital markets, suggesting that not all developing countries will find it possible to develop local capital markets. In addition, economic concentration, low savings rates, and economic informality of large parts of the population are relevant as well. Economic concentration limits diversification of risks needed for domestic market development, while high informality also limits the bankable clientele. Third, macroeconomic policies and the contractual and institutional environment can explain a low frontier. Greater macroeconomic stability can allow for deepening of long-term financing markets, while fiscal dominance can lead to bond issuance volumes in excess of the absorption capacity of the existing investor base, which can stunt local bond market development. The capacity to enforce contracts and — more generally — the protection of property rights will encourage long-term investments and arms-length financial contracting.

Taxonomy of Financial Sector Challenges

Identifying a financial system's position relative to the financial possibility frontier is a first step toward defining an adequate policy mix to achieve an optimum, long-term sustainable level of financial sector development. We can distinguish between policies that (i) push the frontier outward (market-developing policies), (ii) push the system toward the frontier (market-enabling policies), and (iii) prevent the financial system from moving beyond the frontier (market-harnessing policies). It is important to stress that all these policy areas focus on overcoming market frictions and market failures and aim at better-functioning markets. They stand in contrast to market-replacing policies that aim to replace market mechanisms with government mechanisms. In the overwhelming majority of cases, such mechanisms have not worked.

Market-developing policies aim at pushing out the financial possibility frontier by improving macroeconomic and institutional state variables. Such policies, however, are long-term processes as they not only involve deep and often drawn-out political processes, but their benefits also take a long time to materialize. *Market-enabling* policies help push a financial system closer to the frontier and include more short- to medium-term policy and regulatory reforms that can aim both at supply and demand-side deficiencies. A final set of policies aims at preventing the financial system from moving beyond the frontier, i.e., the sustainable long-term equilibrium. This set of policies, *market-harnessing or market-stabilizing*, refers to risk oversight and management and includes the regulatory framework, macroeconomic, and macro prudential management.

In the following, I will discuss three policy areas that can help push financial systems toward the frontier and help push out the frontier:

competition, financial innovation, and globalization.[5] Across these three areas, however, there is also the risk of overreaching and moving toward a point beyond a sustainable equilibrium. And across these three areas, the role of government is critical.

The Role of Competition in Financial Deepening

Competition can have a critical role in moving a financial system toward the frontier, especially in smaller economies where there is limited scale to sustain a large number of banks. It is important to stress that this competition does not necessarily have to come from incumbent financial institutions, but can also come from new providers. In this context, it is important to focus on financial service delivery rather than incumbent financial institutions or service providers. Banks are an important component of every financial system, but if nonbanks are better in providing certain financial services, they should be allowed to do so. If small financial systems cannot sustain organized exchanges, the emphasis should be rather on alternative sources of equity finance, such as private equity funds. If the local economy is not large enough to sustain certain segments of a financial system, then import of such services should be considered.

Empirical evidence has shown the critical role that competition can play in deepening and broadening financial systems in developing countries. Beck, Demirgüç-Kunt, and Maksimovic (2004) and Love and Martínez Pería (2012) show that less-concentrated and more-competitive banking systems are associated with better access to finance by firms, while Claessens and Laeven (2005) show that financially dependent industries grow faster in more competitive banking systems.

Fostering competition is more than a simple *laissez-faire* approach enabling entry into the financial system by sound and trustworthy players. It also implies ensuring equal and broad access by sound financial institutions to critical elements of the financial infrastructure, including payment systems and credit registries. Too often, incumbent banks restrict access to new players in and outside the banking system. Competition is thus as much a political economy concern as it is a policy issue.

[5] Some of this discussion is based on Beck *et al.* (2011).

In this context, there is also a need for increased attention toward the users of financial services. Turning unbanked enterprises and households into bankable and ultimately banked customers involves more than pushing financial institutions down-market. Achieving such change requires financial literacy, i.e., knowledge about products and capability to make good financial decisions, both for households and enterprises. It also implies addressing nonfinancial constraints, such as most prominently in the area of agriculture. It includes a stronger emphasis on equity financing for often over leveraged enterprises.

In summary, competition is a critical element of the market-enabling policy tool box. It is a multifaceted phenomenon, which requires fine-tuning with respect to country circumstances. And, as I will discuss below, it might require some counter-weighing market-harnessing policies to limit excesses that might also come out of competition.

The Role of Financial Innovation

Financial innovation can play an important role in financial deepening in developing countries in spite of the bad reputation it has gained in many developed countries. It can help push out the frontier across the developing world, allowing the establishment of new markets and broadening the share of population with access to formal financial services.[6]

Financial innovation comprises a variety of new products, new processes, and new organizational forms that can help reduce transaction costs, provide better risk-management tools, and overcome information frictions. Recent examples across the developing world include (i) mobile banking, i.e., access to basic payment services through mobile phones, even without having to have a bank account, in Kenya and the Philippines; (ii) the use of psychometric assessments as a viable low-cost, automated screening tool to identify high-potential entrepreneurs in South Africa; (iii) agricultural insurance based on objective rainfall data in India; (iv) new players in the financial systems, such as microdeposit-taking institutions in Uganda; and (v) agency agreements between banks and nonfinancial corporations

[6] See Beck *et al.* (2012) for some recent evidence on both bright and dark sides of financial innovation in developed economies.

(supermarkets, post offices, etc.) to deliver financial services to remote and low-income areas in many Latin American countries.

Financial innovation can be critical in overcoming the two main challenges that financial intermediation faces in developing countries: the high costs and the high risks. Take the example of mobile banking. First, it relies to a greater extent on variable rather than fixed costs, which implies that even customers who undertake small and few transactions are viable or bankable relative to banking through conventional channels. Second, trust can be built much more easily by reducing the risk from the customer's and the provider's viewpoint. Financial innovation can thus be critical in helping reduce the large share of population that is currently unbanked across the developing world.

How does financial innovation come about? How do financial systems move to the new expanded frontier? First of all, incumbent financial institutions are rarely interested in innovating unless forced to do so by competitive pressure. Second, financial innovation cannot be introduced per regulation. It is introduced by market players — mostly private, though not always profit oriented. Third, such innovation often comes from unexpected quarters. In Kenya, Equity Bank transformed itself from an under performing building society into an innovative bank and is now the largest bank in the country in terms of clientele. It did this by offering new delivery channels, such as mobile branches, by targeting a new clientele, and by focusing on the quality of service delivery (Allen *et al.*, 2012). These experiences suggest that an open, contestable banking system is needed and that new providers might come from outside the established market.

Globalization

Integration into international financial markets has been an important but controversial aspect of financial sector policy throughout the world in the past decades and even more so after the recent crisis. It can help move the frontier outward by overcoming the problem of scale economies and risk diversification, but can also push a financial system toward the frontier through stronger competition.

While many developing countries have opened up their financial systems to foreign bank entry, regional patterns are uneven (Claessens and van Horen, 2014). Sub-Saharan Africa has always had high levels of foreign bank participation, increasing further over recent years, while Eastern Europe and Central Asia have seen a rapid increase during the transition process of the late 1990s and early 2000s. Latin America has also seen high foreign bank entry, while South Asia is still relatively closed. However, the population of foreign banks has changed over recent years, with regional banks taking a stronger role at the expense of European and North American banks.

Foreign bank entry has been controversial among academics and policymakers alike. On the one hand, international banks can help foster governance: They can bring in much-needed technology and experience from their home countries or other host countries, which should translate into increased efficiency of financial intermediation; and they can help exploit scale economies in small host countries. On the other hand, it is especially in low-income countries, with their many small, risky, and opaque enterprises, that the dark side of foreign bank entry can become obvious, even more so in countries where foreign banks have captured almost 100% of the banking market. Specifically, the larger reliance of foreign banks on hard information about borrowers as opposed to relying on soft information can have negative repercussions for riskier and more opaque borrowers if foreign banks crowd out domestic banks.[7]

Evidence on the effect of foreign bank entry has been mixed and has shown important interactions with other elements of the financial infrastructure. On the one hand, firm-level survey evidence suggests that firms report lower financing obstacles in countries with a higher share of foreign banks, a finding that holds across different-sized groups of firms (Clarke, Cull, and Martínez Pería, 2006). This positive effect can be a direct or an indirect one. Foreign banks can bring the necessary know-how and scale to introduce new transaction lending techniques. By competing with domestic banks for large corporate clients, they can also force domestic banks to go down-market to cater to SMEs (de Haas and Naaborg, 2006). On the other hand, bank-level information from specific countries suggests that foreign banks are less likely to lend to small and opaque companies than domestic banks (Mian, 2006).

[7] See, for example, Sengupta (2007) and Detragiache, Gupta, and Tressel (2008).

Recent evidence, however, has questioned that domestic banks are better in catering to SMEs. Rather, the more nuanced view has been put forward that large and foreign banks, relative to other institutions, can have a comparative advantage at financing SMEs through arms-length lending technologies, such as asset-based lending, factoring, leasing, fixed-asset lending, credit scoring, and centralized organizational structures (see Berger and Udell, 2006, and de la Torre, Martínez Pería, and Schmukler, 2010). Using data for 91 banks across 45 countries, Beck, Demirgüç-Kunt, and Martínez Pería (2011) find that foreign banks are more likely to use transaction-based lending techniques and more centralized business models than domestic banks. However, they also show that foreign banks do not tend to lend less to SMEs than other banks. Beck, Ioannidou, and Schäfer (2012) show for Bolivia that foreign and domestic do indeed cater partly to the same clientele, but with different lending techniques; foreign banks' lending depends, however, on the existence of credit registries and effective collateral protection, an observation confirmed on the cross-country basis (Claessens and van Horen, 2013).

What Role for Government?

The different policy areas discussed in the previous section seem to call for an important role of government in the deepening and broadening of financial systems. But the exact role of government is still subject to discussion. Least controversial is the role of government in providing the contractual and informational framework and ensuring a stable macroeconomic environment. Government is the natural provider of key institutions such as legislation and court systems. Similarly, given the government's monopoly over the issue of monetary instruments, ensuring macroeconomic stability is a natural government task. However, governments in most developed and developing countries have taken a much more active approach to financial sector policies over the past 50 years, going beyond the provision of basic "institutional infrastructure."

As discussed above, competition is an important area for government action that has to balance (i) the need for innovation, (ii) avoiding market dominance of new players that rapidly gain market share in new products, and (iii) reducing risks of fragility. In certain instances, authorities might have to force financial service providers to cooperate rather than compete with each other, especially in financial sector infrastructure such as payment systems. Another lever to increase competition is transparency, which can be created by, for example, forcing financial institutions to publish their service fees in major newspapers (Beck *et al.*, 2008, find a strong effect of media freedom on barriers to bank access).

The role of the government might have to go beyond competition and regulatory policies in order to create competitive and inclusive financial systems. The setting up of credit reference bureaus, for example, often requires involvement of the government to overcome resistance by financial institutions as especially the sharing of positive information can diminish information rents of incumbent banks. Avoiding segmentation in the financial sector through expanding access to the payment system or the credit information sharing system beyond the commercial banks to bank-like institutions, such as cooperatives or regulated microfinance institutions, can help the financial system cater to marginal customers in all financial services. Sometimes, government action takes the form of "affirmative regulatory" policy, such as the moral suasion exercised by authorities to make South African banks introduce the Mzansi (basic transaction) account or make British banks introduce the Basic Bank Account (BBA). Government authorities might also have an important role in defining the border between cooperation and competition across financial institutions: Inducing banks to share or ensure interoperability of payments infrastructures (including ATM networks) can help avoid undesirable competition on access to infrastructure while enhancing desirable competition on price and quality of service.

Governments can also try to move the financial system to be more inclusive by addressing hindrances such as coordination failures, first mover disincentives, and obstacles to risk distribution and sharing. While not easy to define in general terms, given their variety, these government interventions tend to share a common feature in creating incentives for private lenders and investors to step in, without unduly shifting risks and costs to the government (de la Torre, Gozzi, and Schmukler, 2006). Three examples illustrate this approach. One is the creation by NAFIN (a Mexican development bank) of an Internet-based market, which allows small suppliers to use their receivable from large creditworthy buyers to receive working capital financing (Klapper, 2006). Another example is the Chilean program (FOGAPE) to promote lending to SMEs via the auctioning of partial government guarantees (Benavente, Galetovic and Sanhueza, 2006). In general, partial credit guarantees have become very popular policy tools as they require little upfront funding, though they can result in large liabilities for taxpayers if not carefully designed to balance sustainability and additionality. Finally, the Mexican development fund FIRA has brokered a variety of structured finance packages to finance agricultural production (e.g., shrimp and corn) to realign credit risks with the pattern of information between financial institutions and different participants in the supply chains of these agricultural products. While intriguing examples, it is not for sure whether risk is really not being shifted to government and taxpayers through such interventions and whether these interventions have sunset clauses that will allow the government to withdraw once its engagement is not needed anymore. There are also governance concerns stemming from a government intervention in a private market. Finally, from political economy viewpoint, such schemes might take away the pressure to implement the long-term institution building to create effective contractual and informational frameworks.

Fostering competition, financial innovation, and opening up of financial systems to globalization pose new challenges for regulators and supervisors. The same competitive forces that can increase efficiency and help deepen and broaden financial systems can also result in lending binges and boom-and-bust cycles. A prominent strand of the literature has shown that higher bank competition can result in higher bank fragility (see, for instance, Allen and Gale, 2004; Boot and Thakor, 1993), while more recent empirical evidence has shown that a properly designed regulatory framework can reduce risks stemming from higher competition (Beck, de Jonghe, and Schepens, 2013). Similarly, new financial products can help open the financial system for previously unbanked parts of the population, but can also result in over-indebtedness and socio-economic stress, as the recent subprime mortgage crisis in the US and several European countries has shown. Both competition and financial innovation require a permanent process of regulatory updating and a more risk-based rather than institution-focused supervisory approach.

Foreign banks can help stabilize host economies, especially in the case of local shocks; however, they also expose host countries to spillover effects from crises in home countries, as shown during the recent global financial crisis (de Haas and van Lelyveld, 2014). This requires not just adjustment in macroeconomic management, but also in the regulatory structure, including in the cooperation with home country supervisors. The crisis has shown that colleges of supervisors and nonbinding memorandums of understanding might not be enough and stronger forms of cooperation are needed, including ex ante burden-sharing agreements.

Beyond Policies — All Financial Sector Policy is Local

While a large literature discussed above has pointed to specific policy areas to deepen and broaden financial systems, the politics of financial sector reform is difficult. An extensive literature has pointed to the political economy of financial sector policies and reforms (see Haber and Perotti, 2008, for an overview). Recent work by Quintyn and Verdier (2010) has shown that an accountable political environment with checks and balances is the strongest predictor for sustainable financial deepening without a subsequent bust period.

While a competitive and accountable political system is thus critical for financial sector reform, there are important feedback loops. One important effect of financial sector deepening and broadening is the increase in competition and contestability throughout the economy. New players, new markets, and new products undermine the rents of the incumbents, not only in the financial sector but also throughout the economy. Pushing a financial system beyond banks toward new providers and products will also generate resistance from incumbent financial institutions, most prominently from banks. A critical role has to be played by a constituency for financial sector reform. Small enterprises and previously unbanked segments of the population constitute the potential beneficiaries. In the long term it is thus critical to create a constituency for financial sector reform, which comprises the beneficiaries of further broadening financial services.

References

Aghion, P., P. Howitt and D. Mayer-Foulkes (2005). "The effect of financial development on convergence: Theory and evidence," *Quarterly Journal of Economics*, Vol. 120, No. 1, February, pp. 173–222.

Allen, F., E. Carletti, R. Cull, J. Qian, L. Senbet and P. Valenzuela (2012). "Improving access to banking: Evidence from Kenya," University of Pennsylvania, Wharton Financial Institutions Center Working Paper No. 12-11.

Allen, F. and D. Gale (2004). "Competition and financial stability," *Journal of Money, Credit and Banking*, Vol. 36, No. 3, June, pp. 453–480.

Arcand, J. -L., E. Berkes and U. Panizza (2012). "Too much finance?" International Monetary Fund Working Paper No. WP/12/161.

Barajas, A., T. Beck, E. Dabla-Norris and R. Yousefi (2013). "Too cold? Too hot? Or just right? Assessing financial sector development across the globe," International Monetary Fund Working Paper, forthcoming.

Beck, T. (2012). "The role of finance in economic development: Benefits, risks, and politics," in *Oxford Handbook of Capitalism*, D. Mueller (ed.), New York: Oxford University Press, pp. 161–203.

Beck, T., T. Chen, C. Lin and F. Song (2012). "Financial innovation: The bright and the dark sides," Tilburg University Working Paper [Unpublished].

Beck, T., A. Demirgüç-Kunt and V. Maksimovic (2004). "Bank competition and access to finance: International evidence," *Journal of Money, Credit and Banking*, Vol. 36, No. 3, June, pp. 627–648.

Beck, T. and A. de la Torre (2007). "The basic analytics of access to financial service," *Financial Markets, Institutions and Instruments*, Vol. 16, No. 2, pp. 79–117.

Beck, T., A. Demirgüç-Kunt and M. Soledad Martínez Pería (2011). "Bank financing for SMEs: Evidence across countries and bank ownership types," *Journal of Financial Services Research*, Vol. 39, No. 1, April, pp. 35–54.

Beck, T., A. Demirgüç-Kunt and M. Soledad Martínez Pería (2008). "Banking services for everyone? Barriers to bank access and use around the world," *World Bank Economic Review*, Vol. 22, No. 3, pp. 397–430.

Beck, T., V. Ioannidou and L. Schäfer (2012). "Foreigners vs. natives: Bank lending technologies and loan pricing," Tilburg University, Center for Research in Economics and Business Discussion Paper No. 2012–055.

Beck, T., O. de Jonghe and G. Schepens (2013). "Bank competition and stability: Cross-country heterogeneity," *Journal of Financial Intermediation*, Vol. 22, pp. 218–244.

Beck, T., S. Munzele Maimbo, I. Faye and T. Triki (2011). *Financing Africa: Through the Crisis and Beyond*, Washington, DC: The World Bank.

Benavente, J. M., A. Galetovic and R. Sanhueza (2006). "Fogape: An economic analysis," University of Chile, Department of Economics Working Paper No. WP222.

Berger, A. N. and G. F. Udell (2006). "A more complete conceptual framework for SME financing," *Journal of Banking and Finance*, Vol. 30, No. 11, November, pp. 2945–2966.

Boot, A. and A. Thakor (1993). "Self-interested bank regulation," *American Economic Review*, Vol. 83, No. 2, May, pp. 206–212.

Boyd, J., R. Levine and B. D. Smith (2001). "The impact of inflation on financial sector performance," *Journal of Monetary Economics*, Vol. 47, No. 2, April, pp. 221–248.

Claessens, S., A. Kose and M. Terrones (2011). "Financial cycles: What? How? When?" International Monetary Fund Working Paper No. WP/11/76.

Claessens, S. and N. van Horen (2014). "Foreign banks: Trends and impact," *Journal of Money, Credit and Banking*, forthcoming.

Claessens, S. and L. Laeven (2005). "Financial sector competition, financial dependence, and growth," *Journal of the European Economic Association*, Vol. 3, No. 1, March, pp. 179–207.

Clarke, G., R. Cull, and M. S. Martínez Pería (2006). "Foreign bank participation and access to credit across firms in developing countries," *Journal of Comparative Economics*, Vol. 34, pp. 774–95.

de Haas, R. and I. Naaborg (2006). "Foreign banks in transition countries: To whom do they lend and how are they financed?" *Financial Markets, Institutions & Instruments*, Vol. 15, pp. 159–199.

de Haas, R. and I. van Lelyveld (2014). "Multinational banks and the global financial crisis," *Journal of Money, Credit and Banking*, forthcoming.

de la Torre, A., J. C. Gozzi and S. Schmukler (2006). *Innovative Experiences in Access to Finance: Market Friendly Roles for the Visible Hand*, World Bank, Latin America Regional Study. Washington, DC.

de la Torre, A., M. S. Martínez Pería, and S. Schmukler (2010). "Bank involvement with SMEs: beyond relationship lending," *Journal of Banking and Finance*, Vol. 34, No. 9, September, pp. 2280–2293.

Demirgüç-Kunt, A. and E. Detragiache (2005). "Cross-country empirical studies of systemic banking distress: A survey," in *Financial Instability, Asset Prices and Credit*, P. Davis (ed.), *National Institute Economic Review*, Vol. 192, pp. 68–83.

Detragiache, E., P. Gupta and T. Tressel (2008). "Foreign banks in poor countries: Theory and evidence," *Journal of Finance*, Vol. 63, No. 5, October, pp. 2123–2160.

Djankov, S., C. McLiesh and A. Shleifer (2007). "Private credit in 129 countries," *Journal of Financial Economics*, Vol. 84, No. 2, May, pp. 299–329.

Haber, S. and E. Perotti (2008). "The political economy of financial systems," Tinbergen Institute Discussion Paper No. 2008-045/2, Amsterdam.

Klapper, L. (2006). "The role of factoring for financing small and medium enterprises," *Journal of Banking and Finance*, Vol. 30, No. 11, November, pp. 3111–3130.

Levine, R. (2005). "Finance and growth: Theory and evidence," in *Handbook of Economic Growth*, Vol. 1B, P. Aghion and S. Durlauf (eds.), Amsterdam: Elsevier Science, pp. 865–934.

Loayza, N. V. and R. Rancière (2006). "Financial development, financial fragility, and growth," *Journal of Money, Credit and Banking*, Vol. 38, No. 4, June, pp. 1051–1076.

Love, I. and M. S. Martínez Pería (2012). "How bank competition affects firms' access to finance," World Bank, policy research working paper, No. 6163.

Mian, A. (2006). "Distance constraints: The limits of foreign lending in poor economies," *Journal of Finance*, Vol. 61, No. 3, June, pp. 1465–1505.

Quintyn, M. and G. Verdier (2010). "Mother, can I trust the government? Sustained financial deepening — a political institutions view," International Monetary Fund Working Paper No. WP/10/210, September 1.

Reinhart, C. and K. Rogoff (2009). *This Time is Different: Eight Centuries of Financial Folly*, Princeton, NJ: Princeton University Press.

Rancière, R., A. Tornell and F. Westermann (2006). "Decomposing the effects of financial liberalization: Crises vs. growth," *Journal of Banking and Finance*, Vol. 30, No. 12, December, pp. 3331–3348.

Rioja, F. and N. Valev (2004a). "Finance and the sources of growth at various stages of economic development," *Economic Inquiry*, Vol. 42, No. 1, January, pp. 127–140.

Rioja, F. and N. Valev (2004b). "Does one size fit all?: A reexamination of the finance and growth relationship," *Journal of Development Economics*, Vol. 74, No. 2, August, pp. 429–447.

Sengupta, R. (2007). "Foreign entry and bank competition," *Journal of Financial Economics*, Vol. 84, No. 2, May, pp. 502–528.

Foreign Banks: Access to Finance and Financial Stability

Neeltje van Horen*

De Nederlandsche Bank

Introduction

In the past two decades, the world has become increasingly more integrated, not just through trade but also through financial flows. Financial integration offers many benefits, but the global financial crisis has shown that it also poses important risks. As a result, a question high on the policy agenda is how to best benefit from greater financial integration while limiting its adverse effects.

The benefits of financial integration are straightforward. International financial flows provide financing for investment and consumption in capital-scarce economies, where returns should be higher. This reduces cost of capital in these countries, thus boosting investment and growth. Furthermore, financial integration can help cushion the impact of adverse shocks, as external borrowing can help smooth out domestic business cycle movements. Finally, it can provide risk diversification by allowing residents to transfer domestic risks to foreign investors while gaining exposure to foreign investment opportunities. But financial flows can also be a source of risk and international financial contagion. Not only in emerging and developing countries with relatively weak institutions but, as became apparent during the global financial crisis, also in advanced economies where markets are deep and the absorptive capacity of the economy is much larger.

---

*Neeltje van Horen is with De Nederlandsche Bank (DNB). She would like to thank Stijn Claessens for many valuable comments. The views expressed in this paper are those of the author and do not necessarily represent those of the institutions with which she is or has been affiliated.

Although there are several other types of international capital flows, such as foreign direct investment, portfolio equity, and debt securities, capital flows related to banks have been at the forefront of the policy debate. This is not surprising, given that these capital flows have proven to be especially procyclical and volatile. Furthermore, they provide an important channel through which financial conditions can be transmitted from one country to another.

Banks have expanded their global activities over the past two decades using two avenues. On one hand, they increased the provision of cross-border credit to other banks as well as to corporates. On the other hand, they expanded their global reach by establishing a presence abroad through a branch or a subsidiary. This allowed them to lend locally to firms and households financed either through local liabilities or through international capital, including funding from the parent. While direct cross-border credit in general has been the most volatile component of international bank lending, also local affiliates of foreign banks can be a source of instability (Kamil and Rai, 2010; Cetorelli and Goldberg, 2011).

The fact that affiliates of foreign banks functioned, at least to some extent, as a channel through which the global financial crisis could spread has reignited the debate on the costs and benefits of foreign bank ownership. In this note I will give an overview of this debate, where we stand, and what we know and do not know. I will start with an overview of the growth in foreign bank presence over the past two decades, highlighting differences across countries and highlighting heterogeneity within the group of foreign banks. Then, in the following section I will discuss the impact of foreign banks on financial development and access to credit. The paper continues with a critical assessment on how foreign banks affect financial stability. I will finish with some final remarks on policy.

Foreign bank presence

In a recent paper, Stijn Claessens and I, using a unique database of bank ownership, document a number of trends related to foreign bank ownership (Claessens and Van Horen, 2012a). As is evident from Fig. 1, foreign banks have become increasingly more important in the period analyzed. In fact, the relative importance of foreign banks in terms of numbers increased from a share of 20% in 1995 to 34% in 2009.

(A)

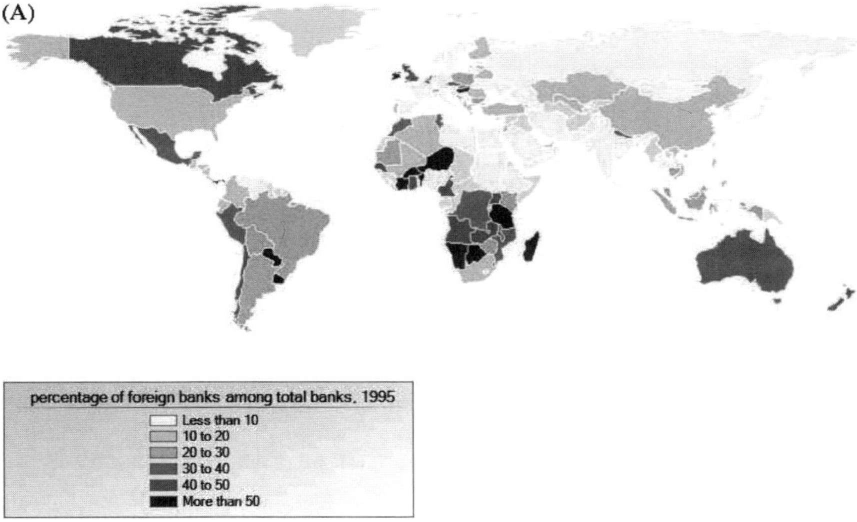

(B)

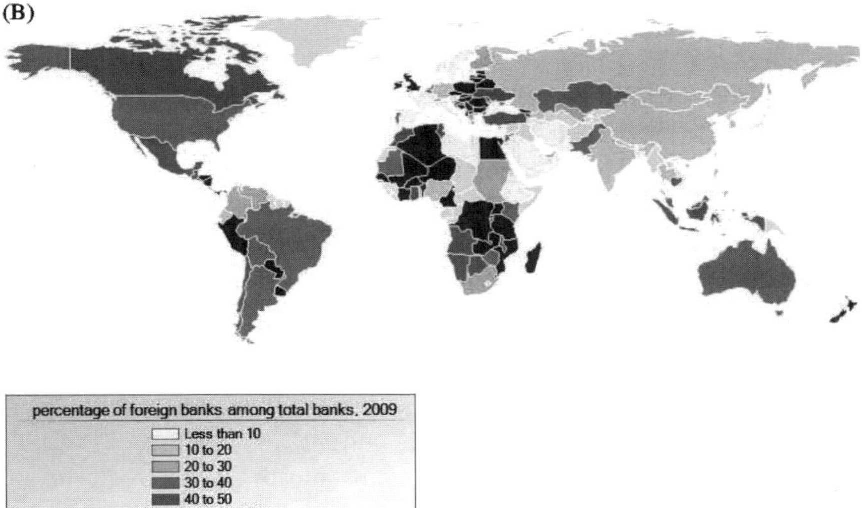

Fig. 1. Foreign bank presence, 1995 and 2009.

Source: Claessens and Van Horen (2012a).

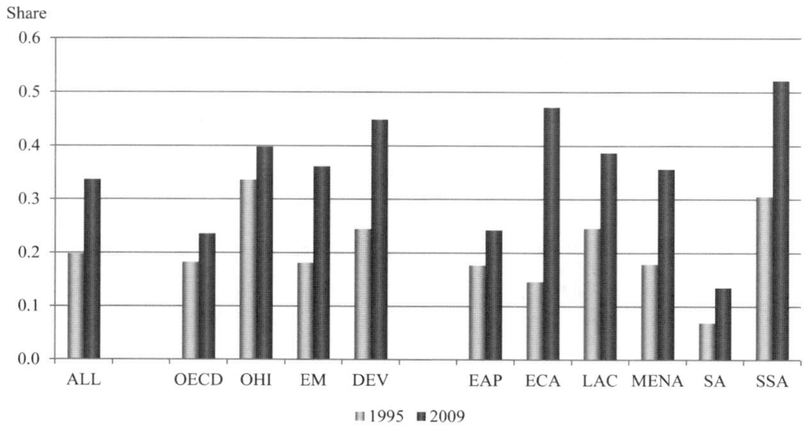

Fig. 2. Share of foreign banks by income level and region, 1995 and 2009.

Note: OECD includes all core OECD countries. Other high-income countries include all countries classified as high income by the World Bank in 2000 but not belonging to the OECD. Emerging markets includes all countries that are included in the Standard and Poor's Emerging Market and Frontier Markets indexes and that were not high-income countries in 2000. Developing countries includes all other countries. The regions represent the regional classifications as used by the World Bank.
Source: Claessens and van Horen (2012a).

While foreign bank presence increased in general, the trends and current penetrations differ greatly across host countries. Figure 2 indicates that especially in emerging markets and developing countries foreign banks presence grew sharply, with market shares of 36% and 45% in 2009, up from 18% and 24% in 1995. In many of these countries, foreign banks now play important roles in financial intermediation, with average loan, deposit, and profit shares between 42% and 50%. In contrast, in OECD countries financial intermediation remains mostly the prerequisite of domestic banks, with average foreign bank loan, deposit, and profit shares of around 20%.

Within the emerging market and developing country group, substantial regional differences exist, though. Growth rates over this period were by far the highest in Eastern Europe and Central Asia (225%), and foreign bank penetration in this region is now the second largest at 47%. Increases were also large in South Asia (120%), but as the base was very low, penetration in this region remains relatively limited: Only 14% of the banks active in this region are foreign owned. Latin America saw very strong growth early in the period, but after 1999, in the aftermath of the Brazilian and Argentine crises, many foreign banks exited the region and new entries remained limited until investment picked up again in 2006. Still, in Latin America shares went up considerably over the sample period, from 25% to 39%. Foreign bank penetration in Sub-Saharan Africa, already high in 1995 at 31%, in part due to colonial links, rose further over the sample period, and in 2009 over 50% of the banks active in the region were foreign owned.

Foreign bank ownership importantly also varies by home country as some countries export (many) more banks than others do (Fig. 3). Not surprisingly, OECD countries export the largest number of foreign banks — 883 in 2009. The biggest investors are banks from the UK (10%), the US (9%), and France (7%). Emerging markets and developing countries export much fewer banks, 268 and 97, respectively. However, this still implies that banking groups headquartered in emerging markets or developing countries own close to 30% of all foreign banks, a non-negligible share.

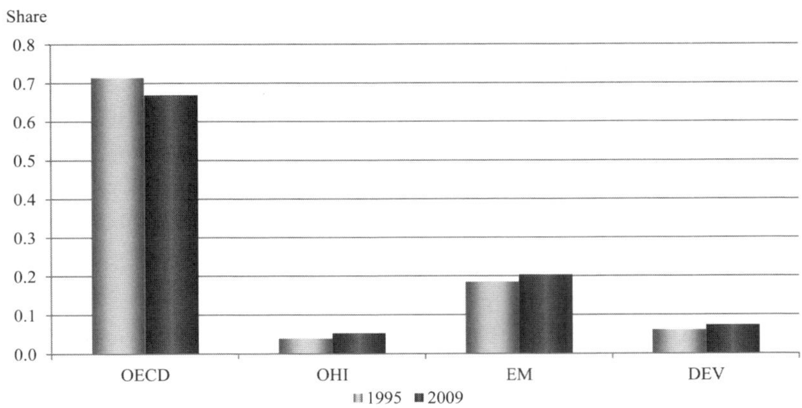

Fig. 3. Share of foreign banks by home country income group, 1995 and 2009.

Note: OECD includes all core OECD countries. Other high-income countries include all countries classified as high income by the World Bank in 2000 but not belonging to the OECD. Emerging markets includes all countries that are included in the Standard and Poor's Emerging Market and Frontier Markets indexes and that were not high-income countries in 2000. Developing countries includes all other countries.
Source: Claessens and Van Horen (2012a).

Global banks from OECD countries tend to invest mostly in emerging markets or in other OECD countries. Banks from emerging markets tend to invest in emerging markets and developing countries, and those from developing countries tend to invest mostly within their own income group. So banks, taking into account competition and growth opportunities, seem to seek out those host countries that are relatively similar in income levels to their home market. Among developing countries and emerging markets these patterns have strengthened over time, highlighting the increasing role of South–South investment in foreign bank ownership, as analyzed by Van Horen (2006).

Furthermore, banks tend to invest within their own geographical region (Fig. 4). Splitting countries in four broad geographical regions that cut across income groups (America, Asia, Europe, and the Middle East and Africa), we see that both in 1995 and 2009 the share of foreign banks coming from countries within the region is always more than 50%. In all regions except America, the intraregional share has increased over time, which mirrors the trend toward greater intraregional activity found in trade.[1] This pattern may not surprise, since research has shown that foreign banks tend to follow their customers and therefore tend to enter countries with strong trade linkages (e.g., Goldberg and Grosse, 1991). In addition, studies have found that banks tend to invest in countries that are (geographically and/or institutionally) close (e.g., Buch and De Long, 2004; Galindo, Micco, and Serra, 2003) or, as Stijn Claessens and I show, are further away from competitor home countries (Claessens and Van Horen, 2012b).

However, some difference exists among banks from different income groups. While almost 50% of banks from advanced countries venture outside their region (reflecting past colonial linkages or desires to operate globally), the vast majority of investments done by banks from emerging markets and developing countries are within their own region. A possible explanation for this difference is the fact that both distance and competitor remoteness concerns seem to be more important drivers behind foreign entry decisions of these banks (Claessens and Van Horen, 2012b).

[1]As shown by Whalley and Xin (2007), trade has become increasingly more regional over the last three decades, which they explain by the proliferation of regional free trade agreements.

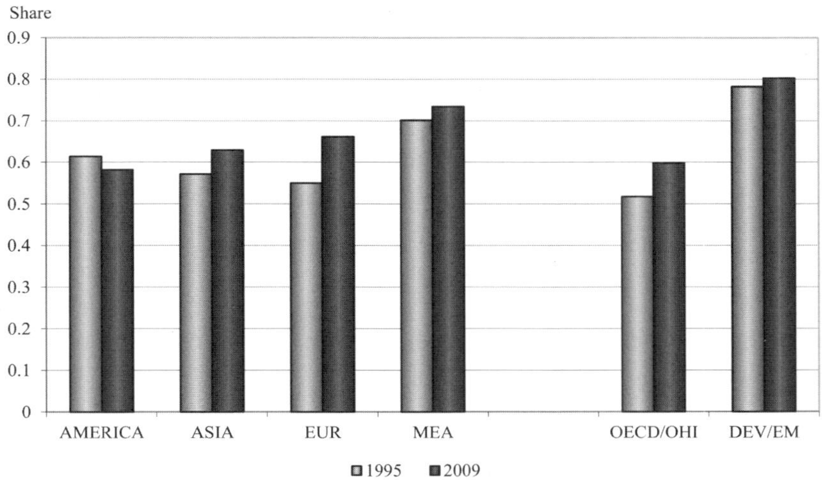

Fig. 4. Share of foreign banks investing in own region, 1995 and 2009.

Note: The first four column pairs show for each of the four regions the share of foreign banks from the region investing in host countries located in that same region (e.g., banks from the US investing in Canada or any Latin American country). Countries are grouped in four geographical regions irrespective of the income level of the countries. "America" includes Canada, the US, and all countries in Latin America and the Caribbean. "Asia" includes all countries in Central, East, and South Asia, and the Pacific countries, including Japan, Australia, and New Zealand. "Europe" includes all western and eastern European countries. "MEA" includes all countries in the Middle East and North and Sub-Saharan Africa. In the last two column pairs, we first grouped the foreign banks according to the income level of the home country (OECD/OHI or DEV/EM), and then determined for each of the banks whether it invested in its own region or not (e.g., an American-owned foreign bank is included in the group OECD/OHI; if it has invested in one of the countries included in the region "America," the investment is considered regional).
Source: Claessens and Van Horen (2012a).

Finally, it is important to realize that foreign banks differ substantially with respect to their business models, size, and profitability. Some banks are important players in the domestic financial system, while others are just niche players. This difference tends to be closely related to the form of entry — through a greenfield investment or by taking over a domestic bank including its local branch network. Importantly, funding structures differ a lot as well. While all foreign banks to some extent rely on funding by their parent, some of them generate a large part of their funding locally by accessing the local deposit market. As I will argue in Sec. 4, these differences in funding models have important implications for the stability of credit provision by a foreign bank during a financial crisis.

Summarizing, the data that Stijn Claessens and I collected show not only that foreign banks have become much more important over the last two decades in many countries' banking systems, but also that there is much heterogeneity among foreign banks' investment patterns. In the next sections, I will have a closer look at how foreign banks affect the provision of credit during tranquil and crisis times and argue that it is important to take this heterogeneity into account when rethinking the costs and benefits involved with foreign bank ownership.

Impact of Foreign Banks on Domestic Credit

In general, studies have found that foreign banks have a positive impact on the domestic financial system as they lower the overall costs and increase the quality of financial intermediation, increase access to financial services, and enhance financial and economic performance of their borrowers (Claessens, Demirgüç-Kunt, and Huizinga, 2001; Clarke *et al.*, 2003; Martínez-Pería and Mody, 2004; Claessens, 2006). Therefore, before the crisis the general consensus was that the benefits of foreign banks greatly outweighed their costs.

Likely a number of factors are behind these effects. First, foreign bank presence can increase competition within the host country. Second, the entry of foreign banks can lead to the introduction of new, more diverse products, greater use of up-to-date technologies, and know-how spillovers (e.g., as people learn skills at foreign banks, they may move to domestic banks). Third, foreign banks likely pressure governments to improve regulation and supervision, increase transparency, and more generally catalyze domestic reform (Levine, 1996).

However, the literature also shows that these effects of foreign bank presence tend to depend on some conditions. For example, limited general development and entry barriers seem to hinder the effectiveness of foreign banks and can lead to "cream skimming" (Garcia-Herrero and Martínez Pería, 2005; Demirgüç-Kunt, Laeven, and Levine, 2004; Detragiache, Gupta, and Tressel, 2008; Beck and Martínez Pería, 2007). Also, the relative size of foreign banks' presence appears to matter: With more limited entry (as a share of the total host banking system), fewer spillovers seem to arise, suggesting the existence of some threshold effect (Claessens and Lee, 2003). Furthermore, Stijn Claessens and I found that an important interplay exists between (cultural and institutional) distance of foreign banks to their host country and their performance in the local economy (Claessens and Van Horen, 2012c).

In terms of access to financial services, greater foreign bank presence seems to help, although here results depend (even) more on individual bank characteristics. Clarke, Cull, and Martínez Pería (2001) find that foreign bank entry improves financing conditions for enterprises of all sizes, although larger firms benefit more. Beck, Demirgüç-Kunt, and Maksimovic (2004) and Berger, Hasan, and Klapper (2004) instead conclude that a larger presence of foreign banks leads to a greater availability of credit to SMEs. Brown *et al.* (2011) find, on the other hand, evidence of greater access to finance for more transparent firms when more foreign banks are present in a country. Gianetti and Ongena (2012) show that large and foreign firms are more likely to have a relationship with a foreign bank, while small firms tend to be served by private domestic banks. In addition, they find that an increase in foreign bank presence increases the probability that a firm gets access to bank loans and that this holds for all types of firms.

The extent to which foreign banks contribute on net to financial sector development and, related, to access to financial services remains one of the most controversial aspects of foreign bank entry. Although some studies have looked at the relationship between private credit and foreign bank ownership (most notably Detragiache, Gupta, and Tressel 2008, and Cull and Martínez Pería 2011), surprisingly little is known under what conditions foreign ownership positively relates to private credit and when negatively.

In a recent paper, Stijn Claessens and I therefore explore in more detail under what conditions foreign ownership positively relates to private credit extension and when negatively (Claessens and Van Horen, 2012a). In particular, we examine the relationship between foreign bank presence and levels of private credit to GDP for 111 countries representing all levels of development. Figure 5 shows a simple correlation between foreign bank

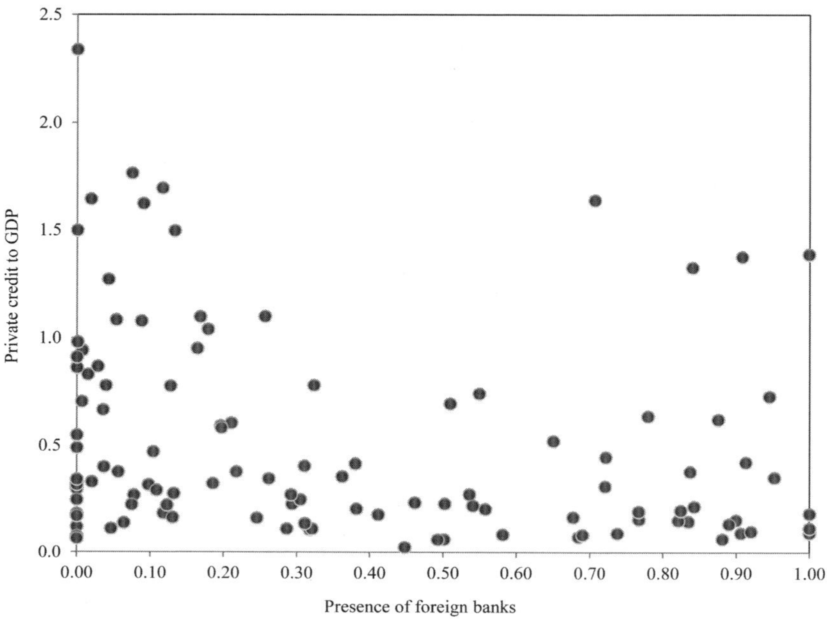

Fig. 5. Relation between private credit/GDP and presence of foreign banks.

Note: The graph shows the simple correlation between private credit and the presence of foreign banks in 111 countries. The horizontal axis depicts the share of foreign bank assets in total bank assets in 2004; the vertical axis shows private credit relative to GDP averaged over 2005–2007.

Source: Claessens and Van Horen (2012a) and IMF International Financial Statistics.

presence and the level of private credit in 111 countries. It shows that although there seems to exist a negative relationship, it is not very strong as there are quite a few outliers. This raises the question: What role do home and host country characteristics play?

To get a better sense of the interplay between foreign bank heterogeneity and the relationship between the presence of foreign banks and private credit to GDP, we run cross-country regressions. The dependent variable is the ratio of private credit to GDP (average over 2005–2007 to smooth out business cycle fluctuations), and the variable of interest captures foreign presence as measured by the ratio of foreign bank assets to total bank assets in the country (in 2004 to limit as much as possible joint endogeneity concerns). In addition, we include a number of standard control variables known to affect the level of private credit in an economy: GDP per capita, inflation, availability of information to creditors, and the cost of enforcing contracts.

We find strong evidence that results very much depend on host country characteristics. While on average we find a negative relationship between foreign bank presence and private credit, once we split the sample into developing countries, emerging markets, and advanced economies, this negative relationship is only apparent for the first group (which is in line with the findings of Detragiache, Gupta, and Tressel, 2008). Furthermore, when splitting the sample across other dimensions, we find that this negative relationship between private credit and foreign bank presence only seems to occur in countries where banks have a limited market share, when enforcing contracts is costly, and when credit information is only available to a limited extent.

In addition, we examine whether distance between the home country of the foreign bank and the host country matters. We find for our sample of emerging markets and developing countries that foreign bank presence is only statistically significant negatively related to private credit when foreign banks are relatively distant. This is in line with theoretical and empirical evidence that suggests that distance makes it harder for foreign banks to extend credit (see, for example, Hauswald and Marquez, 2006; Mian, 2006). Although one has to be careful to make any inferences about the direction of causality, these results suggest that it is not so much the level of development (or the institutional environment) of the host country that matters, but rather the fact that foreign banks that are more remote tend to enter countries with such characteristics. This large distance between home and host country in turn might make foreign banks engage in cream-skimming, which in turn negatively affects credit.

While these findings are only suggestive, they do point toward the importance of considering bank, home, and host country characteristics when studying the impact of foreign banks on domestic financial sector development. In the next section I will show that this is also the case when examining the impact of foreign banks on financial stability.

Foreign Banks and Financial Stability

While it is realized that foreign banks can offer valuable diversification services (especially recently) concerns have been raised on the risks to financial stability that foreign banks may introduce. So, what do we know about the impact of foreign bank ownership on credit supply during times of crisis?

Currently the debate mostly focuses on the impact that funding shocks to the parent have on credit provided by their affiliates. For example, the IMF has pointed to the presence of foreign banks in developing countries as a key mechanism through which the 2008–2009 crisis was transmitted from advanced to developing countries (IMF, 2009). Policy initiatives like the Vienna Initiative have been specifically aimed to avoid this type of transmission.[2] Some earlier empirical studies indeed show that (funding) shocks to parent banks can be transmitted to their foreign subsidiaries with negative consequences for their lending (Peek and Rosengren, 1997, 2000). And more recent evidence also indicates that, during the global financial crisis, global banks were transmitting shocks across borders via their affiliates. Specifically, Cetorelli and Goldberg (2012) show that global banks actively manage their interoffice positions: When faced with a funding shock, they tend to reallocate capital within the holding toward "important" subsidiaries.

Using the global financial crisis as an event study, several papers have compared credit supply of foreign banks with that of domestic banks during the global financial crisis. de Haas and van Lelyveld (2012), for example, compare foreign banks with large domestic banks and find that the former group on average contract more. de Haas *et al.* (2011) and Mihaljek (2010) find similar results for a sample of Eastern European countries.

Stijn Claessens and I performed a similar exercise using our database, which covers almost the universe of banks, focusing especially on heterogeneity within the group of foreign banks (Claessens and Van Horen, 2013).

[2]The Vienna Initiative is a public–private partnership among European governments, multinational banks, and international financial institutions, in which foreign banks were eligible for financial support in return for commitments that they would maintain their exposures and keep subsidiaries adequately capitalized in affected host countries.

We find that, while on average foreign banks reduced lending more compared to domestic banks, there was a clear difference between countries where foreign banks control more than half the market and those in which they do not. Only in the second group did foreign banks contract lending more compared to domestic banks. Furthermore, our results show that while both domestic as well as foreign banks that were importantly funded with local deposits were more likely to continue lending during the crisis, this was especially important for foreign banks.

The importance of accounting for these differences is also confirmed by a recent paper by Cull and Martínez Pería (2012), who show that in Eastern Europe, loan growth by foreign banks fell more than that of domestic private banks during the crisis, but that in Latin America foreign banks did not contract their loans at a faster pace. The distinction between the two continents seems to be driven by differences in business models due to differences in regulation. For example, foreign banks in Latin America were, forced by regulatory requirements, mostly funded through a domestic deposit base with most of the lending denominated in domestic currency. In Eastern Europe, on the other hand, many foreign affiliates resorted to wholesale funding from nonlocal sources (including their parent) and denominated (at least in some countries) a substantial part of their loans in foreign currencies (Kamil and Rai, 2010).

While providing interesting insights in the behavior of foreign banks, studies using aggregate bank balance sheet data have two important weaknesses. First, they cannot fully control for demand shocks if domestic and foreign banks have different clients that are differently affected by the crisis. Second, they cannot say anything about whether there is a pass-through to firms, i.e., whether there truly are real effects resulting from the credit contraction of foreign banks. Related, given that the data are aggregate, they can potentially hide the fact that maybe small firms are affected while large firms are not.

While not studying the global financial crisis but the 1998 Russian default, Schnabl (2012) circumvents some of these problems by using data on exact lending by banks to firms. This allows him to control for changes in demand at the firm level. He shows that the negative liquidity shock resulting from the Russian default led international banks to reduce lending to domestic and foreign-owned Peruvian banks. These banks in turn reduced lending to Peruvian firms. Therefore, Schnabl (2012) provides strong evidence of a transmission mechanism of parent-funding shocks to their foreign affiliates, which impacts the credit provision to firms. However, it is hard to tell whether these results can be generalized. It is possible that features that are specific to Peru exist that explain why shocks were transmitted in this case, but might not in other situations.

Popov and Udell (2012) take a different approach and use a survey conducted on a group of SMEs in a number of Eastern European countries. This allows them to differentiate between firms that want credit but cannot get it, firms that get a loan, and firms that do not want a loan. They show that if banks in the vicinity of the firm are in distress, the likelihood of a firm being credit constrained increases. In other words, they find evidence that negative shocks to bank's balance sheets are transmitted to firms (especially those that are high-risk and have fewer tangible assets), and that this also holds for shocks to the balance sheet of the parents of the foreign-owned subsidiaries. In other words, they also find evidence of a transmission channel through foreign-bank ownership.

In a recent paper that I wrote with Steven Ongena and José Luis Peydró, we link banks to firms in a number of Eastern European countries (Ongena, Peydró, and van Horen 2012). This allows us to examine whether firms linked to foreign-owned banks experience a stronger reduction in their profitability, sales, or operational revenue compared to firms linked to domestic banks during the global financial crisis. We find that foreign-owned banks reduce credit more compared to domestic banks (albeit not compared to domestic banks that received a lot of funding from the international capital market in the years leading up to the global financial crisis). This reduction in credit was mirrored by a reduction in borrowing by firms linked to foreign banks, and subsequently had a negative impact on these firms' profitability, sales, and operational revenue. However, only smaller firms and firms with less-tangible assets were affected.

An important difference between the global financial crisis and previous crises is that the recent crisis episode erupted in foreign banks' parent countries, while previous crises were endemic to developing countries and emerging markets. Therefore, it is not surprising that the debate almost exclusively focuses on the impact of parent funding shocks on the lending by their affiliates. However, when thinking about the impact of foreign banks on financial stability, it is important to not lose sight of the positive impact that research has found foreign banks to have on financial stability as well.

Crisis episodes that originated in a number of emerging markets and developing countries in the early and late 1990s have fueled a substantial literature examining the role of foreign banks when a host country is hit by an adverse shock. In general, these studies find that, under these circumstances, foreign banks actually behave as a stabilizing force in terms of credit supply. For example, in Eastern Europe, domestic banks contracted their credit base during crises between 1993 and 2000, whereas greenfield foreign banks did not (de Haas and van Lelyveld, 2006). In addition, foreign banks in Latin American countries showed more robust loan growth, a more aggressive response to asset deterioration, and greater ability to absorb losses than domestic banks did in the mid- and late 1990s (Crystal, Dages, and Goldberg, 2001, 2002). More generally, for a sample of 45 large multinational bank holdings, de Haas and van Lelyveld (2010) find that due to support by the parent bank, foreign affiliates did not need to rein in their credit supply during a financial crisis in the host country, while domestic banks had to contract their lending.

In addition, foreign ownership also is found to have another positive effect on financial stability, this time related to the stability of cross-border lending. In two recent papers written with Ralph de Haas, we find that banks when faced with a funding shock reduce their cross-border lending (de Haas and van Horen, 2012). However, we also find that they are more likely to stay committed to countries in which they have a subsidiary (de Haas and van Horen, 2013). This is especially important in countries with weak institutions. Therefore, the existence of foreign affiliates can stabilize cross-border flows to a country during crisis times.

Concluding, foreign ownership can have a positive impact on financial stability as cross-border lending is more stable during a crisis when global banks make a commitment to the country in terms of bricks and mortar. Furthermore, parents can and do support their affiliates in times of stress. What is less clear is under what circumstances foreign banks transmit shocks that parent banks are faced with and how this affects the real economy. This is an area that could benefit from more extensive analyses.

Final Remarks

The policymaker's goal is to reap the benefits from international capital flows while guarding against costs from potential financial instability. By bringing about greater international financial integration, globally operating banks have provided many benefits. But at the same time, they have also proven to be important factors behind the buildup and transmission of imbalances. As such, the behavior and effects of these banks should require careful regulatory and policymakers' attention.

A lesson from the experience of different countries during the global financial crisis is that banks that are funded by deposits tend to pose fewer risks, while banks that rely on short-term wholesale funding represent a greater risk. This holds for both domestic as well as foreign-owned banks. Therefore, there could be a case for requiring foreign-owned banks to hold more deposits, as is already mandatory for subsidiaries operating in many Latin American countries. In fact, a number of large European banking groups are already focusing on increasing the local deposit base of their Eastern European subsidiaries.

Another important lesson is that having banks operating across national borders can be incompatible with national supervision. The scope for externalities and spillovers, already large at the national level, are even greater globally. As outlined by CIEPR (2012), without global rules and shared responsibilities for regulation and supervision there is a clear danger that measures that might be in a nation's (short-term) interest take priority over what is optimal on a supranational level. Therefore, common ground rules are needed to prevent spillovers, including those arising from bank failures, to be imposed on other countries. This requires common rules and shared mechanisms for burden sharing. Making this the goal is especially important as the alternative could be that national regulators start to enforce banks active in their jurisdiction to ring-fence their local operations. This could undermine international financial integration. While establishing a global supervisor is not feasible at this stage, the establishment of the European banking union with integrated regulation and supervision, and hopefully also common resolution frameworks and burden sharing to deal with weak financial institutions, is an important step in the right direction. This can create an institutional structure that matches the current state of high regional and global financial integration. However, it is important to realize that the banking union does not include Eastern European countries. Therefore, these countries will still be faced with possible misaligned incentives at the home and host country in case of failure of one of the European banking groups with a large presence in that region.

Whether from efficiency or financial stability perspectives, foreign banks should establish a presence in a host country as a branch or subsidiary is not directly clear. From the perspective of host countries where foreign banks play an important role in financial intermediation, subsidiaries are likely to be preferred as these are regulated and supervised by the host country. This can allow host country supervisors to force foreign banks operating in their jurisdiction to rely more on local deposit funding and to ring-fence their capital and liquidity. However, this at the same time hinders capital to move freely within the holding company and is therefore synonymous with more financial market segmentation. Branches allow a smoother and potentially more efficient allocation of liquidity internationally and might therefore in the long run be socially more optimal.

Finally, in order to understand the implications of international capital flows intermediated by banks in general and foreign bank ownership in particular, having good data to monitor trends and conduct empirical analyses with is paramount. As I have shown, foreign banks are a heterogeneous group and accounting for this heterogeneity is important when trying to understand their impact on access to finance and financial stability. The database on bank ownership collected by Stijn Claessens and myself can hopefully provide a contribution to a better understanding. In addition, the extensive new data collection effort on international bank lending implemented jointly by the BIS, central banks, and international financial institutions, is extremely valuable as it will provide a much better overview of the cross-border interconnectedness of national banking systems.

References

Beck, T., A. Demirgüç-Kunt, and V. Maksimovic (2004). "Bank competition and access to finance: International evidence," *Journal of Money, Credit and Banking*, Vol. 36, No. 3, pp. 627–648.

Berger, A. N., I. Hasan and L. F. Klapper (2004). "Further evidence on the link between finance and growth: An international analysis of community banking and economic performance," *Journal of Financial Services Research*, Vol. 25, No. 2–3, pp. 169–202.

Beck, T. and M. S. Martínez Pería (2007). "Foreign bank acquisitions and outreach: Evidence from Mexico," World Bank Working Paper No. 4467.

Brown, M., S. Ongena, A. Popov and P. Yeşin (2011). "Who needs credit and who gets credit in Eastern Europe?," *Economic Policy*, Vol. 26, No. 65, pp. 93–130.

Buch, C. M. and G. DeLong (2004). "Cross-border bank mergers: What lures the rare animal?" *Journal of Banking and Finance*, Vol. 28, No. 9, pp. 2077–2102.

Cetorelli, N. and L. S. Goldberg (2011). "Global banks and international shock transmission: Evidence from the crisis," *IMF Economic Review*, Vol. 59, No. 1, pp. 41–76.

Cetorelli, N. and L. S. Goldberg (2012). "Liquidity management of U.S. global banks: Internal capital markets in the great recession," *Journal of International Economics*, Vol. 88, No. 2, pp. 299–311.

Claessens, S. (2006). "Competitive implications of cross-border banking," in *Cross-Border Banking: Regulatory Challenges*, G. Caprio, Jr., D. D. Evanoff and G. G. Kaufman (eds.), Singapore: World Scientific Publishing, pp. 151–182.

Claessens, S., A. Demirgüç-Kunt and H. Huizinga (2001). "How does foreign entry affect the domestic banking market?," *Journal of Banking and Finance*, Vol. 25, No. 5, pp. 891–911.

Claessens, S. and J.-K. Lee (2003). "Foreign banks in low-income countries: Recent developments and impacts," in *Globalization and National Financial Systems*, J. A. Hanson, P. Honohan and G. Majnoni (eds.), Washington, DC: World Bank, pp. 109–141.

Claessens, S. and N. van Horen (2012a). "Foreign banks: Trends and impact," *Journal of Money, Credit and Banking*, forthcoming.

Claessens, S. and N. van Horen (2012b). "Location decisions of foreign banks and competitor remoteness," *Journal of Money, Credit and Banking*, forthcoming.

Claessens, S. and N. van Horen (2012c). "Being a foreigner among domestic banks: Asset or liability?" *Journal of Banking and Finance*, Vol. 36, No. 5, pp. 1276–1290.

Claessens, S. and N. van Horen (2013). "Impact of foreign banks," *Journal of Financial Perspectives*, Vol. 1, No. 1, pp. 1–18.

Clarke, G. R. G., R. Cull and M. S. Martínez Pería (2001). "Does foreign bank penetration reduce access to credit in developing countries? Evidence from asking borrowers," World Bank Working Paper, No. 2716.

Clarke, G., R. Cull, M. S. Martínez Pería and S. Sánchez (2003). "Foreign bank entry: Experience, implications for developing countries, and agenda for further research," *World Bank Research Observer*, Vol. 18, No. 1, pp. 25–40.

Crystal, J. B., G. Dages and L. S. Goldberg (2001). "Does foreign ownership contribute to sounder banks in emerging markets? The Latin American experience," in *Open Doors: Foreign Participation in Financial Systems in Developing Countries*, April 19–21.

Crystal, J. B., G. Dages and L. S. Goldberg (2002). "Has foreign bank entry led to sounder banks in Latin America?," *Current Issues in Economic and Finance*, Federal Reserve Bank of New York, Vol. 8, No. 1.

Committee on International Economic Policy and Reform (2012). "Banks and cross-border capital flows: Policy challenges and regulatory responses," September.

Cull, R. and M. S. Martínez Pería (2011). "Foreign bank participation in developing countries: What do we know about the drivers and consequences of this phenomenon?" in *Encyclopedia of Financial Globalization*, Gerard Caprio, Jr. (ed.), Elsevier, Amsterdam.

Cull, R. and M. S. Martínez Pería (2012). "Bank ownership and lending patterns during the 2008–2009 financial crisis: Evidence from Latin America and Eastern Europe," World Bank Working Paper No. 6195.

de Haas, R., Y. Korniyenko, E. Loukoianova and A. Pivovarsky (2011). "Foreign banks and the Vienna Initiative: Turning sinners to saints?" European Bank for Reconstruction and Development Working Paper No. 143.

de Haas, R. and N. van Horen (2012). "International shock transmission after the Lehman Brothers collapse: Evidence from syndicated lending," *American Economic Review: Papers & Proceedings*, Vol. 102, No. 3, pp. 231–237.

de Haas, R. and N. van Horen (2013). "Running for the exit? International banks and crisis transmission," *Review of Financial Studies*, Vol. 26, No. 1, pp. 244–285.

de Haas, R. and I. van Lelyveld (2006). "Foreign banks and credit stability in Central and Eastern Europe: A panel data analysis," *Journal of Banking and Finance*, Vol. 30, No. 7, pp. 1927–1952.

de Haas, R. and I. van Lelyveld (2010). "Internal capital markets and lending by multinational bank subsidiaries," *Journal of Financial Intermediation*, Vol. 19, No. 1, pp. 1–25.

de Haas, R. and I. van Lelyveld (2012). "Multinational banks and the global financial crisis: Weathering the perfect storm?," *Journal of Money, Credit and Banking*, forthcoming.

Demirgüç-Kunt, A., L. Laeven and R. Levine (2004). "Regulations, market structure, institutions, and the cost of financial intermediation," *Journal of Money, Credit and Banking*, Vol. 36, No. 3, pp. 593–622.

Detragiache, E., P. Gupta and T. Tressel (2008). "Foreign banks in poor countries: Theory and evidence," *Journal of Finance*, Vol. 63, No. 5, pp. 2123–2160.

Galindo, A., A. Micco and C. Serra (2003). "Better the devil that you know: Evidence on entry costs faced by foreign banks," Inter-American Development Bank Working Paper No. 477.

Garcia-Herrero, A. and M. S. Martínez Pería (2005). "The mix of international banks' foreign claims: Determinants and implications," World Bank Working Paper No. 3755.

Giannetti, M. and S. Ongena (2012). "Lending by example: Direct and indirect effects of foreign banks in emerging markets," *Journal of International Economics*, Vol. 86, No. 1, pp. 167–180.

Goldberg, L. and R. Grosse (1991). "Foreign bank activity in the United States: An analysis by country of origin," *Journal of Banking and Finance*, Vol. 15, No. 6, pp. 1092–1112.

Hauswald, R. and R. Marquez (2006). "Competition and strategic information acquisition in credit markets," *Review of Financial Studies*, Vol. 19, No. 3, pp. 967–1000.

International Monetary Fund (2009). "World economic outlook," April.

Kamil, H. and K. Rai (2010). "The global credit crunch and foreign banks' lending to emerging markets: Why did Latin America fare better?," International Monetary Fund Working Paper No. 10/102.

Martínez Pería, M. S. and A. Mody (2004). "How foreign participation and market concentration impact bank spreads: Evidence from Latin America," *Journal of Money, Credit and Banking*, Vol. 36, No. 3, pp. 511–537.

Levine, R. (1996). "Foreign banks, financial development, and economic growth," in *International Financial Markets*, C. E. Barfield (ed.), Washington, DC: AEI Institute Press, pp. 224–254.

Mian, A. (2006). "Distance constraints: The limits of foreign lending in poor countries," *Journal of Finance*, Vol. 61, No. 3, pp. 1465–1505.

Mihaljek, D. (2010). "Domestic bank intermediation in emerging market economies during the crisis: Locally owned versus foreign-owned banks," Bank for International Settlements Working Paper No. 54.

Ongena, S., J. L. Peydró and N. van Horen (2012). "Shocks abroad, pain at home? Bank-firm level evidence on the international transmission of financial shocks." DNB Working Paper No. 385.

Peek, J. and E. Rosengren (1997). "The international transmission of financial shocks: The case of Japan," *American Economic Review*, Vol. 87, No. 4, pp. 495–505.

Peek, J. and E. Rosengren (2000). "Collateral damage: Effects of the Japanese bank crisis on the United States," *American Economic Review*, Vol. 90, No. 1, pp. 30–45.

Popov, A. and G. Udell (2012). "Cross-border banking, credit access, and the financial crisis," *Journal of International Economics*, Vol. 87, No. 1, pp. 147–161.

Schnabl, P. (2012). "The international transmission of bank liquidity shocks: Evidence from an emerging market," *Journal of Finance*, Vol. 67, No. 3, pp. 897–932.

Van Horen, N. (2006). "Foreign banking in developing countries: Origin matters," *Emerging Market Review*, Vol. 8, No. 2, pp. 81–105.

Whalley, J. and X. Xin (2007). "Regionalization, changes in home bias, and the growth of world trade," National Bureau of Economic Research Working Paper No. 13023.

Institutions, Finance, and Economic Activity: Views and Agenda

Elias Papaioannou*
London Business School, NBER
and
CEPR

Introduction

Finance, legal institutions, and economic development are closely interlinked. Not only proxies of financial depth and measures of the efficiency of financial intermediation correlate strongly with both economic development and various indicators of property rights institutions, but the process of industrialization and the spur of commerce during the Enlightenment and the Industrial Revolution coincided with the emergence of legal institutions that protected investors from expropriation and the spread of financial instruments, such as letters of credit, bank loans, and derivative instruments.

Yet in spite of the evident cross-country and the historical associations among financial efficiency, legal institutions, and economic well-being, many issues are open. First, does finance lead to growth or does it just emerge in regions and periods where investment prospects are favorable? Moreover, there is always a possibility that both financial efficiency/development and economic well-being are outcomes of deeply rooted factors, related, for example, to trade and the spread of commerce

* Elias Papaioannou is Associate Professor of Economics at the London Business School; he is also a Research Affiliate of the Centre for Economic Policy Research and the National Bureau of Economic Research. The author would like to thank Viral Acharya, Thorsten Beck, Doug Evanoff, George Kaufman, and Richard Portes for inviting him to the participate in the session on "Finance and Economic Activity: Variations across Emerging and Developed Markets." All errors are his sole responsibility.

(that may itself be driven by geography), or particular cultural traits, such as trust, the ethos of Protestantism, family values, and civic-mindedness. Second, how do contractual and property rights institutions shape financial and economic development? Do they help, for example, capital-scarce countries attract foreign lending and investment (as the baseline neoclassical growth paradigm suggests), or do they spur growth by enabling the efficient allocation of capital across and within sectors (as Walter Bagehot and Joseph Schumpeter famously hypothesized 100 years ago)? Third, can financial and economic development emerge in the absence of sound legal and property rights institutions or is institutional capacity a *sine qua non* condition for growth? While economic (financial) and institutional development go in tandem, many countries, such as China and other East Asian countries, have grown fast in recent decades under autocratic regimes without well-defined legal institutions.

Summary

The three presentations — and the associated background papers — in this session on *Finance and Economic Activity* explore the interlinkages among legal institutions, financial structure, and economic development, and therefore naturally touch upon these key issues. Thorsten Beck, Neeltje van Horen, and Franklin Allen (and their collaborators) have made significant contributions to the exciting research agenda that tries to (a) measure the degree of financial structure and the efficiency of financial intermediation (and to some extent legal quality) across countries over time[1]; (b) isolate the one-way effect of financial size and structure on various aspects of economic performance (such as income, growth, entry, firm size)[2]; (c) explore the role of legal institutions and other factors — related to the role of

[1]For example, Beck *et al.* (2000, 2012) construct detailed indicators of the structure and size of the financial system for more than 100 countries; Claessens and van Horen (2012a, 2012b) have compiled an impressive dataset of foreign banks' presence around the world; and Allen *et al.* (2007, 2010, 2011) provide a thorough mapping of the financial system in Africa and East Asia (see Van Horen, 2013, for a review).

[2]See for example Levine, Loyaza and Beck (2000a, 2000b).

culture and politics — in shaping financial patterns around the world[3]; and (d) understand how finance, legal institutions, and development interact.

Thanks to laborious data collection efforts and ingenious theoretical advances and econometric approaches, our understanding of the links between legal institutions, financial structure, and economic performance has increased significantly over the past decade. In a nutshell, the key lesson from the voluminous body of research is that institutional, financial, and economic development are strongly correlated across countries, within countries over time, across regions within countries, and across industries within countries. Yet, correlation does not imply causation, and given the forward-looking aspect of both bank and stock market financing, it is inherently hard to identify causal effects. Another lesson from this body of work is the presence of significant — and not well understood — heterogeneity. For example, Claessens and van Horen (2012a, 2012b) show that foreign bank investment across the world is quite heterogeneous, as foreign banks' operations differ considerably even across nearby countries. While few doubt the importance of a competitive, efficient, and liquid financial system and the need for a legal system that protects investors for development, in many instances, growth take-offs and industrialization took place in nondemocratic countries that offered minimal legal protection to shareholders and creditors (e.g., East Asia); similarly in many countries that have experienced sizable improvements in well-being (such as China), financial intermediation is problematic and inefficient while legal rights against expropriation are weak.

Structure

In the next section, I review the main lessons stemming from the research agenda on finance and growth (that mostly touches Thorsten Beck's

---

[3] See, for example, Claessens and van Horen (2012a) and Papaioannou (2009) for the role of legal institutions in attracting foreign bank investment and Allen *et al.* (2007, 2010, 2011) on the role of other-than-the-law institutions in shaping financial patterns in China, India, and Sub-Saharan African countries. Beck *et al.* (2011) provide a synopsis on the African financial system.

contributions) and on law and finance (that Neeltje van Horen and Franklin Allen's research focuses upon). Then I discuss the main econometric and theoretical issues that remain open. In the last section, I discuss the role of other-than-the-law institutions in shaping financial (and economic) development, such as informal (cultural and institutional) traits and politics (issues that are raised by all three presenters).

Legal Institutions, Finance, and Development

Finance and Economic Performance

In a series of papers co-authored with Ross Levine and other collaborators from the World Bank, Thorsten Beck has constructed detailed measures of the size, structure, and efficiency of the financial system across the world (Financial Structure Database) over the post-World War II period (Beck *et al.*, 2000, 2012). The compilation of these databases has spurred a wave of research that explored the origins and consequences of the significant heterogeneity in financial patterns around the world.[4]

Figure 1 plots two proxies of the size of the financial system by continent using data from the latest update of World Bank's Financial Structure Database. As commonly done in the empirical literature, to smooth cyclical fluctuations I use the average of the two series over the period 2000–2009. North America (NA) and Western Europe (WE) have quite large and liquid markets; in contrast, private credit provided by banks and other financial institutions is quite low in Sub-Saharan African countries (SSA), South Asia (SA), and the Latin American and Caribbean (LAC) region.

A vast literature on finance and growth shows that there is a strong positive correlation between such proxies of financial size ("financial development") and various measures of economic development, such as GDP growth, income per capita, entry of new firms, labor productivity (see, for example, King and Levine, 1993; Levine and Zervos, 1998; Wurgler, 2000; Levine, Loyaza, and Beck, 2000a; and Beck and Levine; 2004).

[4]Since my objective is not to discuss this huge amount of research, I refer the reader to the exhaustive surveys of the finance and growth literature by Levine (2005) and Papaioannou (2009) and on law and finance by Beck (2003, 2011) and La Porta, López-de-Silanes, and Shleifer (2008).

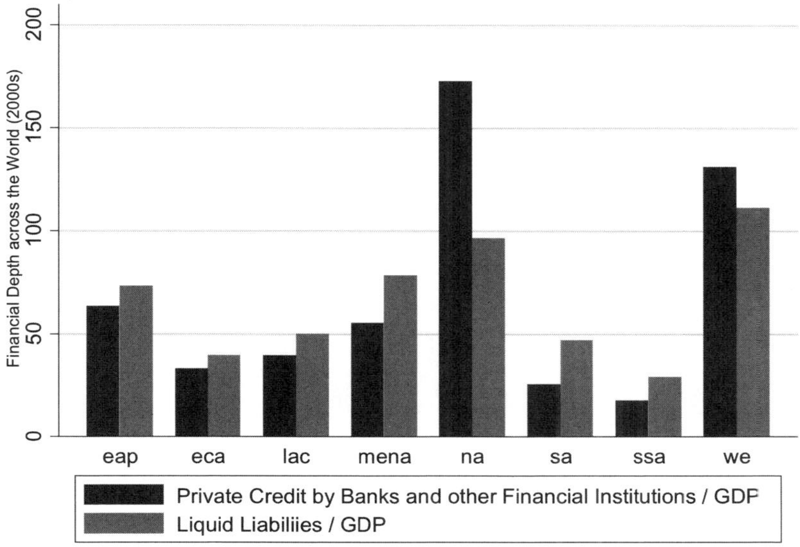

Fig. 1.

Figures 2(a) and 2(b) illustrate the strong cross-country correlation between private credit to GDP (averaged over the period 1991–2010) and the log or real PPP-adjusted GDP per capita in 2010 (using data from the latest vintage of the Penn World Tables).[5]

The literature provides similar evidence of a strong positive correlation between financial depth and economic performance across regions within countries (e.g., Guiso, Sapienza, and Zingales, 2004, in Italy; Bertrand *et al.*, 2007, in France; and Jayaratne and Strahan, 1996, and numerous subsequent works across US states). Likewise, studies that examine the evolution of growth and investment before and after financial liberalization policies (such as relaxing capital account controls) show that such reforms are followed by higher growth rates (Henry, 2001; Bekaert *et al.*, 2005). Finally, following the seminal contribution of Rajan and Zingales (1998), who showed that financial development is associated with fast growth of sectors that for

[5]An interesting outlier in the scatter-plot is China, which although still underdeveloped, has grown quite fast over the past two decades in spite of a small and in general inefficient (government-controlled) financial system.

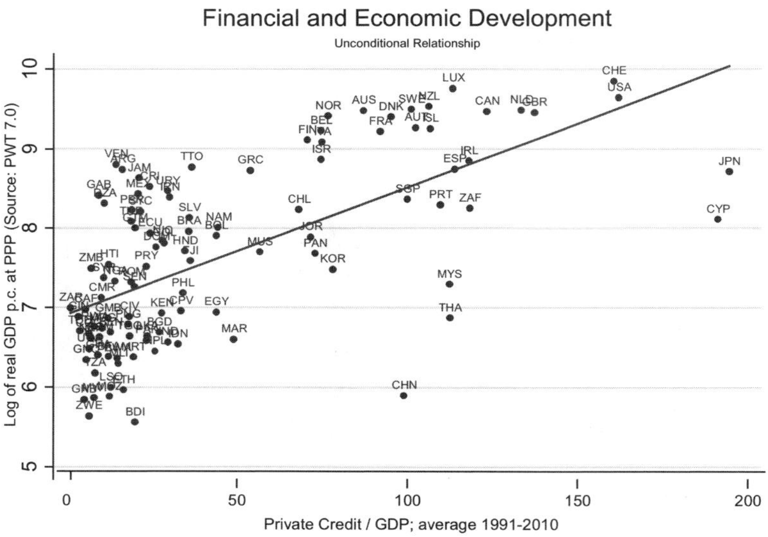
Financial and Economic Development
Unconditional Relationship
Log of real GDP p.c. at PPP (Source: PWT 7.0)
Private Credit / GDP; average 1991-2010
5
6
7
8
9
10
0
50
100
150
200
CHE
USA
LUX
CAN
JPN
CYP
CHN
MYS
THA
KOR
MAR
BDI

(a)

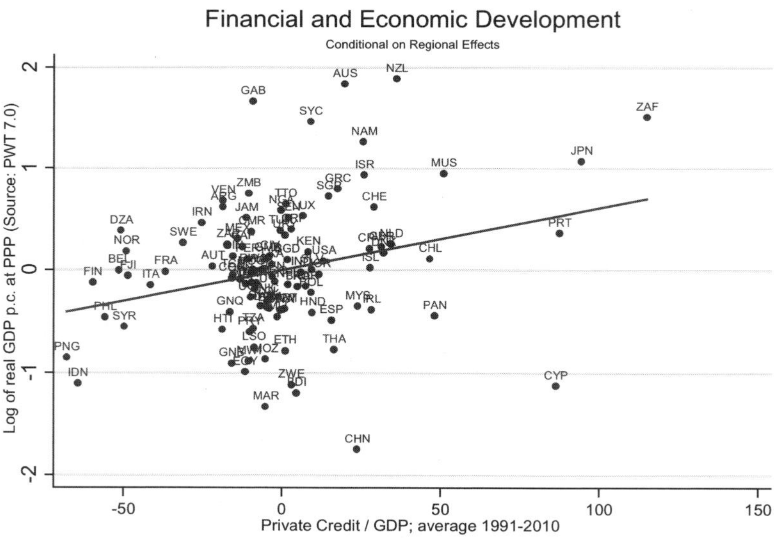
Financial and Economic Development
Conditional on Regional Effects
Log of real GDP p.c. at PPP (Source: PWT 7.0)
Private Credit / GDP; average 1991-2010
-2
-1
0
1
2
-50
0
50
100
150
AUS
NZL
GAB
ZAF
JPN
PRT
CYP
CHN
PNG
IDN
MAR

(b)

Fig. 2.

inherent technological reasons rely heavily on external finance (because of good prospects or because of high physical capital intensity), many cross-country cross-industry works have established a strong positive association between financial development and growth within countries across industrial sectors (see, among others, Beck and Levine, 2002; Fisman and Love, 2004, 2007; Ciccone and Papaioannou, 2006).

Law and Finance

In a series of influential works, La Porta *et al.* (1997, 1998, 1999) did what legal scholars were avoiding doing for many years: measure the efficiency, speed, and formalism of the legal system across a large number of countries (see for a review, La Porta, López-de-Silanes, and Shleifer, 2008). Figure 3 plots the continental average of a 0–6 shareholder's protection index and a 0–4 creditor's rights index that reflect how well the civil code, corporate law, and bankruptcy procedures protect outside investors from managerial misuse of a firm's funds. An interesting pattern is evident. While there is some heterogeneity, there is not much variation between industrial (rich) and developing or even underdeveloped regions. For example, on average Sub-Saharan African countries tend to protect shareholders better than Western European countries — where "insiders," managers, and large stakeholders are shielded from outside checks. Similarly in the US, creditors are only modestly protected in bankruptcy as quite often Chapter 11 procedures result in sizable changes of the pecking order of the capital structure.

Following the seminal contributions of La Porta, López-de-Silanes, and Shleifer (1997, 1998), subsequent works have constructed refined measures of the quality of various aspects of the legal system, such as securities legislation (La Porta, López-de-Silanes, and Shleifer, 2006), bankruptcy code (Djankov *et al.*, 2008), judicial checks and balances (La Porta *et al.*, 2004), among others. Moreover, research by World Bank's *Doing Business* project and others have compiled *de facto* (rather than *de jure*) proxies of legal quality, based on the days and procedures it takes to resolve some simple disputes in court and the formalism of the court system. At the same time, the World Bank, through its *Governance Matters* project, has aggregated various measures of institutional quality across the world producing indicators of the quality of government, the rule of law, and the control for corruption and regulatory quality, among others.

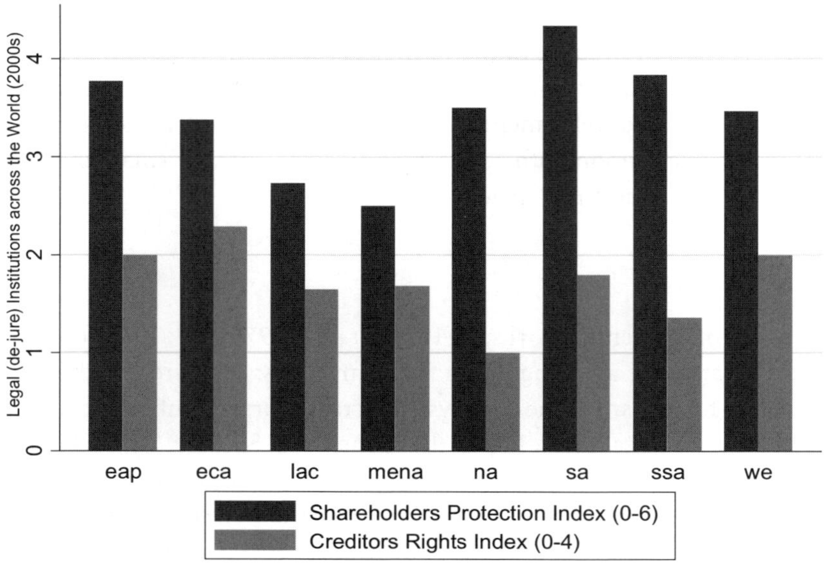

Fig. 3.

The law and finance literature provides compelling evidence that those differences in legal protection of investors and court formalism map to proxies of financial markets depth (see Beck and Levine, 2005, for a review). Figures 4(a) and 4(b) show that private credit is, on average, higher in countries that better protect creditors and shareholders from managerial entrenchment. Yet the correlation is far from perfect, suggesting that other factors may also be at play.

Figures 5(a) and 5(b) show the cross-country association between financial development (again as reflected by private credit to GDP) and an anti-self-dealing index that measures the measures the actual (de facto) efficiency of the legal system in protecting shareholders from tunneling activities by managers and other corporate insiders. There is a positive, though not particularly strong, correlation.

The correlation between legal quality and financial depth turns significantly stronger when instead of using *de jure* measures of investor protection that are based on how well the law safeguards shareholders and creditors, one uses indicators of legal formalism, based on the number of

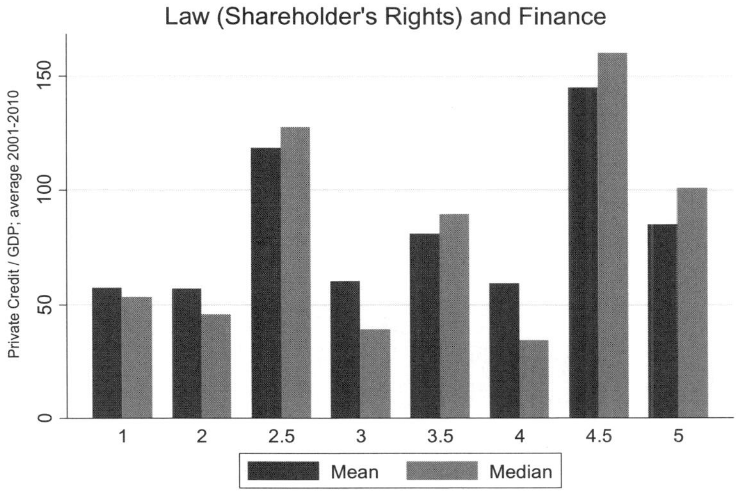
Law (Shareholder's Rights) and Finance
Private Credit / GDP; average 2001-2010
0
50
100
150
1
2
2.5
3
3.5
4
4.5
5
Mean
Median

(a)

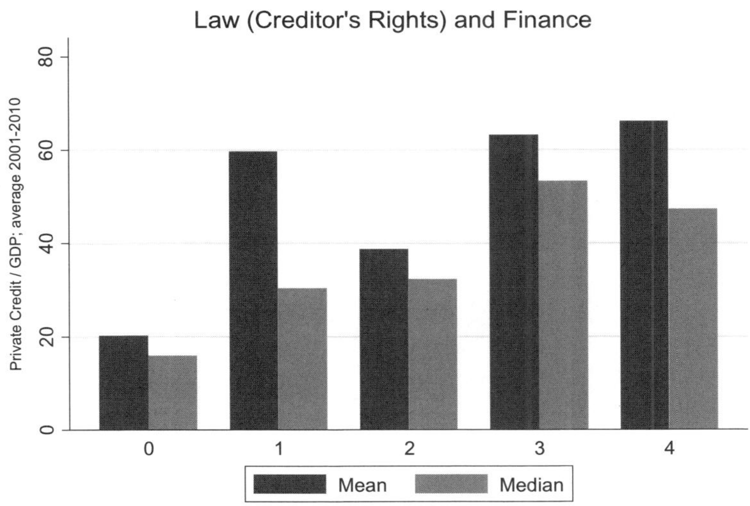
Law (Creditor's Rights) and Finance
Private Credit / GDP; average 2001-2010
0
20
40
60
80
0
1
2
3
4
Mean
Median

(b)

Fig. 4.

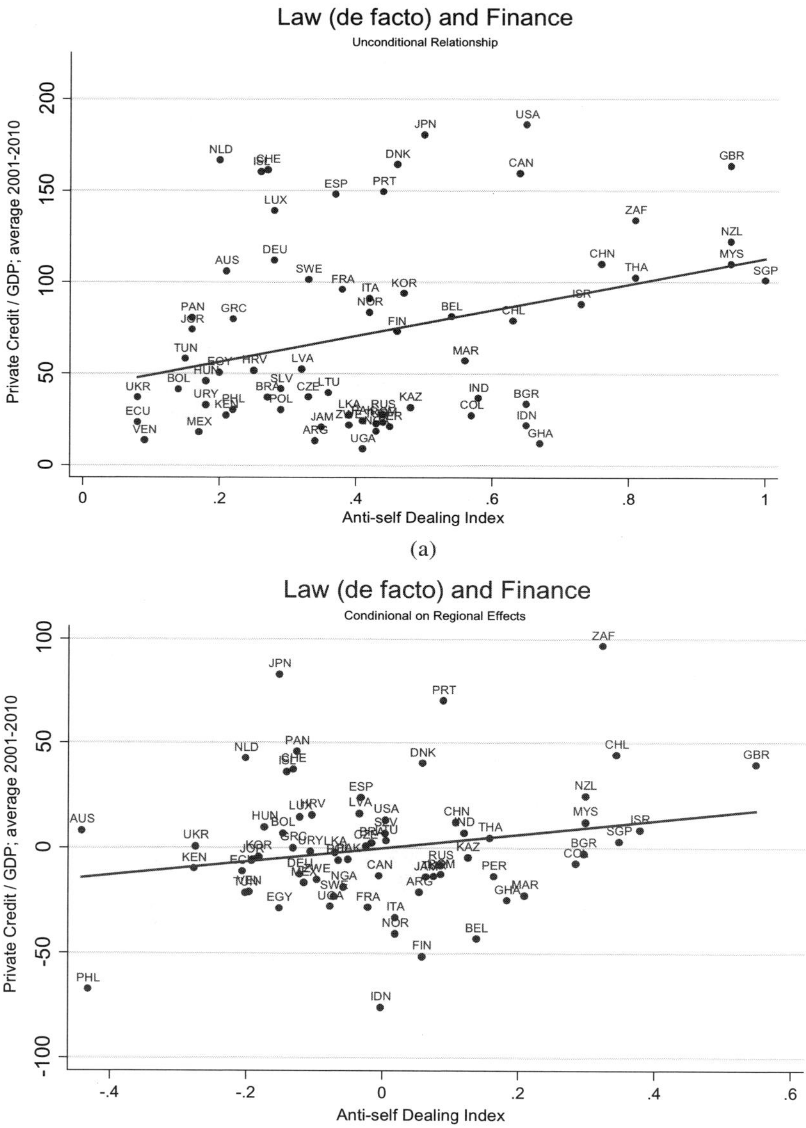
Law (de facto) and Finance
Unconditional Relationship
Private Credit / GDP; average 2001-2010
Anti-self Dealing Index

(a)

Law (de facto) and Finance
Condinional on Regional Effects
Private Credit / GDP; average 2001-2010
Anti-self Dealing Index

(b)

Fig. 5.

procedures and the time it takes to resolve through courts some simple disputes. Figures 6(a) and 6(b) illustrate the strong negative association between financial development and a proxy of legal formalism (using data from Djankov *et al.*, 2003).

The correlation between financial (as well as economic) development and legal institutions turns even stronger when one uses broader measures of institutional capacity that besides legal quality also capture corruption, the efficiency of the bureaucracy, and the political risk. Figures 7(a) and 7(b) show the almost perfect association between financial development and World Bank's composite rule of law index.

Summary: There are four broad patterns on the link between legal quality and financial structure (and efficiency). First, there is significant regional variation, both in financial patterns (private credit, role of equity markets), the structure of financial intermediation (such as state ownership of banks, competition), financial regulation, and features of the legal system. This hints that geography, culture, and other features may be important drivers of both legal infrastructure and financial structure. Second, the association between financial development and legal efficiency strengthens considerably when one uses *de facto* rather than *de jure* measures of legal quality; this suggests that (quite reasonably) foreign and local investors focus on the actual enforcement of their legal rights rather than on the exact provision of commercial law. Similarly, the correlation between law and finance strengthens further when one uses broad objective measures of institutional quality that besides legal quality also capture investors' perceptions on the efficiency of the administration, corruption, regulatory features, and the quality of government. This implies that other than strictly legal features may be important factors shaping financial patterns. Fourth, the correlation between measures of legal quality and financial depth strengthens further when ones uses long-run averages; this implies that cyclical fluctuations in financial depth (related to boom/busts and financial crises) may have different effects on economic performance as compared to the trend.

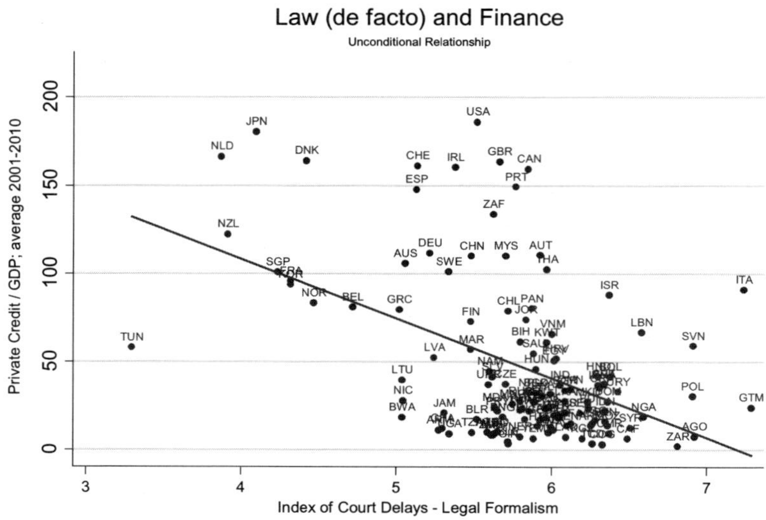
Law (de facto) and Finance
Unconditional Relationship
Private Credit / GDP; average 2001-2010
0
50
100
150
200
3
4
5
6
7
Index of Court Delays - Legal Formalism
JPN
NLD
DNK
USA
CHE
IRL
GBR
CAN
ESP
PRT
ZAF
NZL
DEU
AUS
CHN
MYS
AUT
SWE
SGP
THA
ISR
ITA
NOR
BEL
GRC
CHL
PAN
FIN
VNM
LBN
TUN
MAR
SVN
LVA
HUN
LTU
NIC
POL
GTM
BWA
JAM
BLR
NGA
AGO
ZAR

(a)

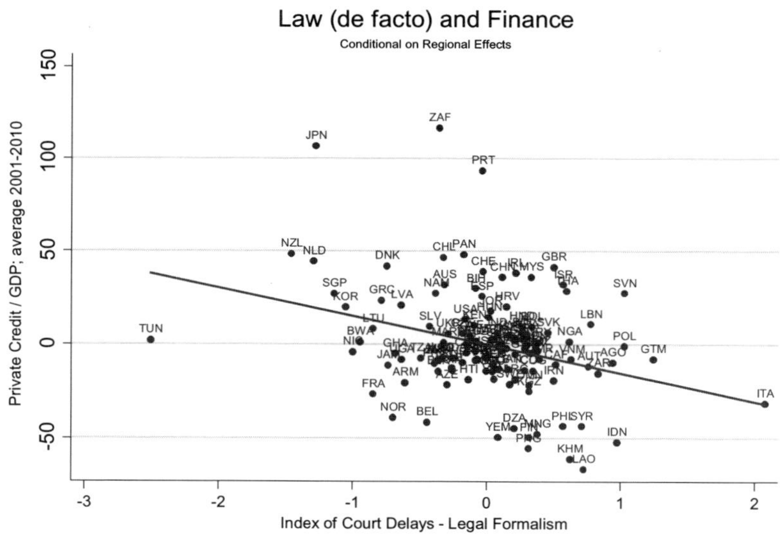
Law (de facto) and Finance
Conditional on Regional Effects
Private Credit / GDP; average 2001-2010
-50
0
50
100
150
-3
-2
-1
0
1
2
Index of Court Delays - Legal Formalism
ZAF
JPN
PRT
NZL
NLD
DNK
PAN
GBR
SGP
KOR
SVN
TUN
LBN
POL
GTM
NGA
ITA
ARM
FRA
NOR
BEL
IRN
IDN
KHM
LAO

(b)

Fig. 6.

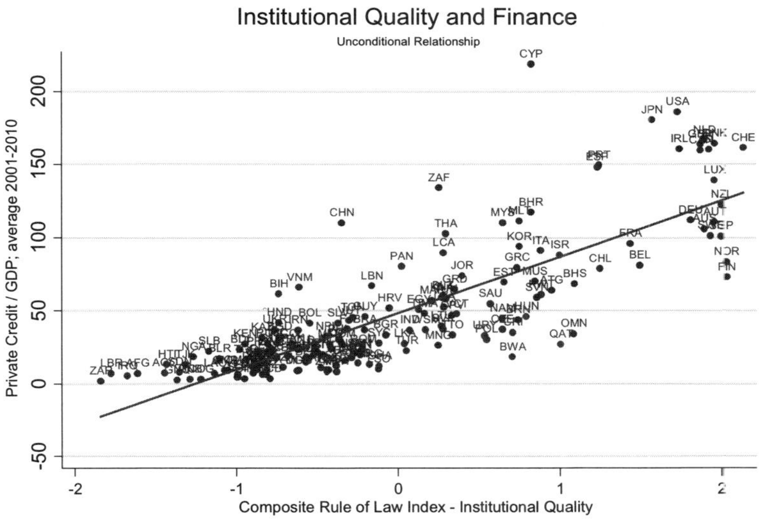
Institutional Quality and Finance
Unconditional Relationship
Private Credit / GDP; average 2001-2010
Composite Rule of Law Index - Institutional Quality
-50
0
50
100
150
200
-2
-1
0
1
2

(a)

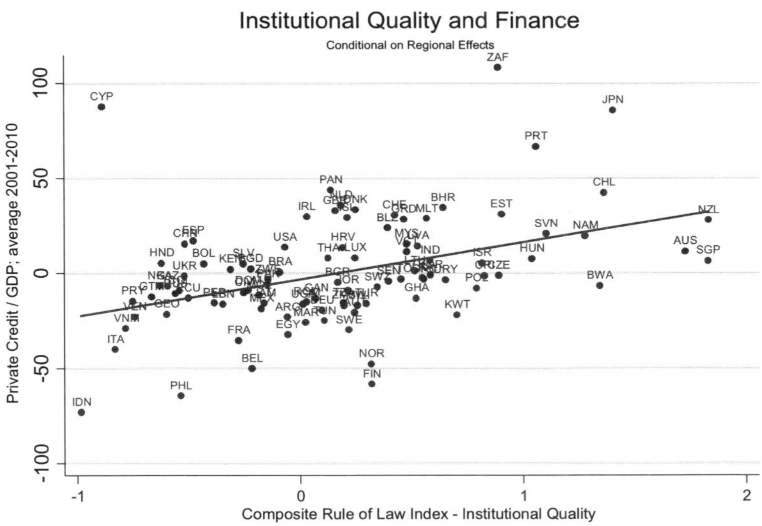
Institutional Quality and Finance
Conditional on Regional Effects
Private Credit / GDP; average 2001-2010
Composite Rule of Law Index - Institutional Quality
-100
-50
0
50
100
-1
0
1
2

(b)

Fig. 7.

The Issues

There are two broad set of issues related to the correlation between (a) financial structure and economic development and (b) law and finance (and also on the correlation between legal institutions and development).[6] On the empirical side, the key consideration is moving beyond correlations and identifying causal effects. On the theoretical side, the key consideration is to understand how and through which channels law and financial structure affect economic performance.

Econometric Considerations — Identification

Clearly the correlations between law and finance or finance and development do not imply causal relationships for a variety of reasons. First is the issue of reverse causation. Since countries with more-developed capital markets and financial intermediaries are richer, they can invest more in legal infrastructure. Similarly, governments of countries with good growth prospects have a higher incentive to invest in legal capacity so as to attract foreign capital and channel local savings to investment. The second issue is omitted variables. Hard-to-account-for factors related to geography (the disease environment, land quality, terrain ruggedness); cultural traits related to religion, trust, and the societal structure; and history may affect both legal capacity and financial (and economic) development. Third, multicollinearity and the limited degrees of freedom are important issues in most cross-sectional data. Since data is available for around 100–150 countries (or regions within countries) and since countries (regions) with well-developed capital markets are also richer, with better-functioning governments, high levels of human capital and trust, low degrees of ethnic fragmentation, etc., it is almost impossible to isolate the impact of legal quality on financial (or economic) development (Mankiw, 1995). The problem gets magnified because the available data do not map well to the theoretical concepts and because of error-in-variables; as the literature on the stability of cross-country regressions shows, the interaction

[6]See Acemoglu *et al.* (2005) for a review of the literature on institutions and long-run development.

of multicollinearity and measurement error results in significant instability even to small model permutations or data revisions (e.g., Ciccone and Jarocinski, 2010).

The literature has tried to account for these issues with various methods in an effort to push on identification.

Within Country: First, some studies explore within country over time variation, as this allows accounting for time-invariant country factors related to geography, culture, and history. Beck and Levine (2004) show that changes in financial market size are correlated with changes in income growth, while Djankov, McLiesh, and Shleifer (2007) show that legal reforms that improve creditors' protection are followed by increases in financial depth. Similarly, other works explore regional (within-country) variation in an effort to account for country-specific features related to macroeconomic policies, leadership, political risk, etc. (e.g., Laeven and Woodruff, 2007). Focusing on developed countries, Christensen, Hail, and Leunz (2011) show that improvements in financial regulation across EU countries are correlated with a drop in the cost of capital. Exploiting (bilateral) country-pair over time-data variation, Kalemli-Ozcan, Papaioannou, and Peydró (2011, 2013) show that legal harmonization policies in financial services across EU member countries are associated with an increased degree of cross-border financial linkages. Yet, while panel studies have straightforward merits, they are not a panacea; in this context, the within-country (or even country-pair) correlation is much weaker as compared to the cross-sectional correlation and the economic significance of the estimates much smaller. Moreover, theoretically the impact of financial depth on growth may differ in the short run as compared to the long run; and of course panel studies (and regional studies) do not account for reverse causation.

Instrumental variable (IV) approaches. Second, following La Porta, López-de-Silanes, and Shleifer (1997, 1998) many scholars have used the legal origin of a country's legal system — that was exogenously imposed by colonizers — as an "instrument" for the degree of legal quality and financial development. La Porta, López-de-Silanes, and Shleifer (1997, 1998) and subsequent works show that there are large differences in investors' rights, court efficiency, and financial structure across countries based on the legal tradition. At the one extreme, common-law countries offer on average superior protection to investors as compared to countries whose corporate law is based on the Napoleonic civil law of 1804 (and to some lesser extent to Otto von Bismarck's German civil code). Instrumental-variable estimates show that the (exogenously imposed by colonization) component of investor protection rights explained by legal origin correlates strongly with financial depth, such as private credit to GDP, bank credit, number of IPOs, etc. Beck *et al.* (2000) further show that the component of financial depth explained by legal origin also correlates positively and significantly with economic development. Yet while these results show that historical traits related to the identity of colonizer and the policies of European colonizers have long-lasting effects, they do not necessarily show that legal institutions exert a causal effect on financial (or economic) development, as legal origin has shaped numerous other-than-the-law features, such as the regulation of labor, bureaucratic procedures on firm entry, the role of state in the economy, conscription, etc. Figure 8, reproduced from La Porta, López-de-Silanes, and Shleifer (2008), illustrates the multidimensional long-run effects of legal origin and transplantation on contemporary institutions and economic outcomes.

Thus, in spite of these valuable contributions, we need more research, most likely exploiting random or quasi-random (experimental) variation, establishing the one-way effect of legal institutions on financial and economic development as well as on identifying the effect of financial structure and depth on economic performance.

Theoretical — Channels

Given the impressive data construction that followed the work of La Porta, López-de-Silanes, and Shleifer (1997, 1998), Djankov *et al.* (2003, 2006) and the development of the financial structure database (Beck *et al.*, 2000, 2012), it comes as no surprise that most research in the past decade was empirical trying mostly to identify causal relationships. Yet there is a sizable gap between theory and empirics, both because financial structure features are not explicitly modeled in most growth theories and because the data do not map well to the theoretical concepts. For example, in the workhorse neoclassical (Solow–Swan–Ramsey) growth model finance is absent, as the

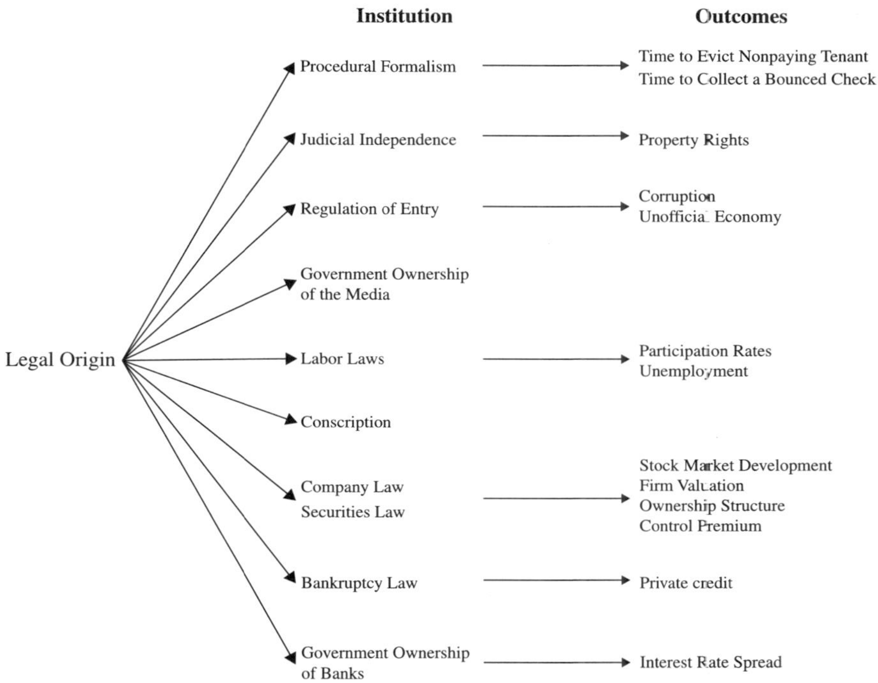

Fig. 8.

model assumes that savings are channeled without any frictions or costs to investment. And, while in the Schumpeterian growth models financial intermediation is present as it identifies promising entrepreneurs with good projects (facilitating endogenous growth via creative destruction), the commonly used proxies of financial development do not measure this "selection" aspect.[7] Another theoretical channel linking finance with growth emerges in "poverty trap" models; in this set-up, the financing of big (mostly infrastructure) projects, especially in sectors with strong linkages, is particularly useful as it can move the economy from the poverty-trap equilibrium to a new one with sustained growth.

[7] See, for example, Aghion *et al.* (2005) and Levine, Laeven, and Michalopoulos (2012), among others.

One approach in shedding light on the theoretical mechanism with cross-country data is to examine the role of legal institutions and financial structure on the main components of growth within a growth-accounting framework that decomposes growth on physical capital accumulation (across various vintages of physical capital), employment (labor force participation), human capital accumulation, and total-factor-productivity (the so-called Solow residual). Existing works provide mixed results showing that financial depth is associated with both capital deepening and TFP growth (Levine, Loyaza, and Beck, 2000b; La Porta, López-de-Silanes, and Shleifer, 2002). Yet such growth decompositions are just the first step. Clearly, only with detailed micro studies and case studies can one uncover the exact mechanisms via which finance and legal institutions shape economic performance.

Following the important contribution of Rajan and Zingales (1998), one fruitful avenue is to explore not only country-level variation on financial development but also sector-level variation on industrial needs for external finance. This cross-country cross-industry approach is not only useful because it allows conditioning on country-fixed effects, but mostly because it sheds light on how does finance affect economic performance. For example, research shows that financial development is especially beneficial for capital-intensive sectors with good investment opportunities that rely intensively on intangible assets (like R&D) and use many differentiated intermediate goods as inputs. In the same vein, Ciccone and Papaioannou (2006) and Fisman and Love (2007) show that in countries with well-functioning legal institutions and deep capital markets capital is reallocated quickly from (relatively) declining sectors to industries with good growth opportunities (see also Wurgler, 2000; Ciccone and Papaioannou, 2006; and Bekaert *et al.*, 2008).[8]

Another approach is focusing on a particular aspect of financing and explore its role on economic performance. Neeltje van Horen's work focuses on one channel of law's influence on financial and economic development, that of foreign bank presence and lending. The authors have compiled an

[8]However, as Ciccone and Papaioannou (2010) show, the cross-country cross-industry approach is not problem free, as the reliance of data from a benchmark country (usually the US) to proxy latent global industry characteristics, may yield to (hard-to-sign) econometric biases.

impressive dataset of foreign bank presence around the world and document that sound property rights and legal institutions tend to attract foreign banks (see also Alfaro, Kalemli-Ozcan, and Volosovych, 2008, and Papaioannou, 2009). Yet their research reveals high heterogeneity both in the factors that attract foreign banks and on the type of lending that foreign banks do (van Horen, 2013).

Future Research: Understanding Heterogeneity and the Role of Other-than-Law Factors

In this last section, I will use the provocative thesis of Allen *et al.* (2011) that examines in detail economic performance, financing, and legal institutions in China (but also in India and Sub-Saharan African countries) to briefly discuss the importance of other-than-the-law institutions and traits on the development path. Their paper touches what is perhaps the most fascinating — and hard to address — inquiry of economics: Why some countries manage to grow out of poverty, such as East Asian countries after the 1950s, while some others, such as Sub-Saharan African countries after independence in the early 1960s, have not managed to do so?

Allen *et al.* (2011) start with the observation that that legal and property rights institutions are not well developed in China, nor are local financial intermediaries. Yet somehow China has managed to experience steady growth since the late 1970s (see Fig. 9). Similarly, other East Asian economies have experienced the most remarkable growth rates since the end of World War II, although again the protection of shareholders and creditors was minimal, corruption was high, and the government was autocratic.

So how can we reconcile growth with the weak legal institutions and inefficient — government-controlled — financial intermediaries?[9]

One explanation is that financial efficiency and sound legal institutions are particularly important for innovation and technological progress (total-factor-productivity) while governments have alternative means to channel

[9] On the role of state ownership and control of banks on lending and economic performance, see, among others, La Porta, López-de-Silanes, and Shleifer (2002), Sapienza (2004), Dinç (2006), and Khwaja and Mian (2005).

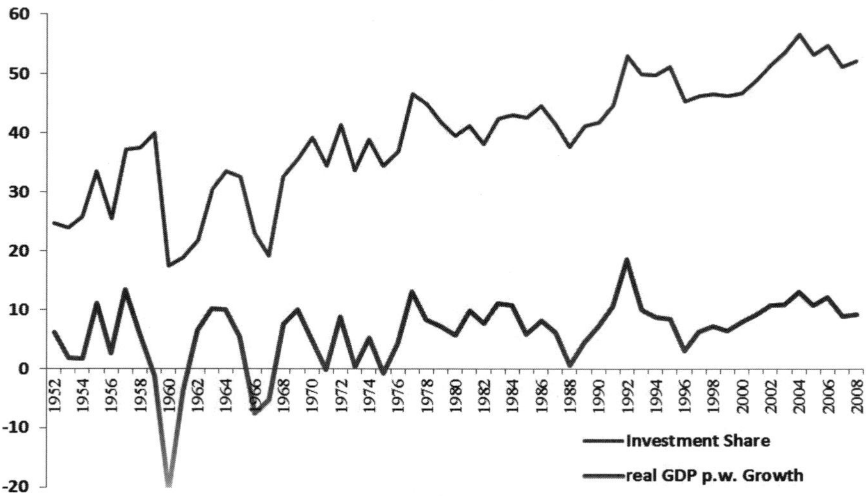

Fig. 9.

savings to investment and thus initiate growth via (physical capital) accumulation. In influential work, Young (1995) showed that most — if not all — of the remarkable growth of Singapore, Hong Kong, South Korea, and Thailand in the 1960s, 1970s, and 1980s was driven by investment (in physical and human capital), while TFP growth played a minimal role (see also Krugman, 1994). So, if indeed efficient legal and financial institutions are important mostly for technological advancement, then the prospects for China are not particularly optimistic, unless of course the Chinese government modernizes legal infrastructure, privatizes banks, and implements deep structural reforms on product markets.

A second explanation — which touches upon Thorsten Beck's recent work — is that sound policies, rather than well-defined property rights institutions, are key for development. In line with this idea, the autocratic regimes of many East Asian countries implemented sound economic policies and thus managed to attract foreign investment. And of course the openness and liberalization policies of Deng Xiaoping in the late 1970s and the 1980s initiated the remarkable transformation of the Chinese economy. A merit of focusing on politics is that it can shed light on how legal institutions emerge and consolidate (see, for example, Pagano and Volpin, 2005).

Yet a problem, however, with the "good policies" explanation is that policies (as well as institutions) are themselves outcomes, driven by the stance of the economy, history, geography, culture, and other factors. Moreover, good (or bad) policies may be reversed, while stable legal institutions have long-lasting effects.

Third, many scholars downplay the role of institutions, stressing instead the importance of cultural features, historical traits, and the societal structure in shaping economic (and financial) development (see Landes, 1998).[10] Allen *et al.* (2011) follow this line of thought and argue that the clan structure of the Chinese society and the history of its evolution have offered alternatives to formal institutions' devices to monitor economic transactions and enforce penalties (see also Greif, 2006, and Tabellini and Greif, 2010, for a comparative analysis of the evolution of informal cultural norms in Europe and China). This approach fits a growing research agenda that examines the role of social features, such as trust and civic capital, on various aspects of finance (e.g., Guiso, Sapienza, and Zingales 2009, 2011) and growth (Algan and Cahuc, 2011). Figures 10(a) and 10(b) illustrate the strong cross-country association between trust and financial depth using data from the World Value Surveys. I believe that future research should try to dig deeper and shed light on the exact mechanisms linking trust, finance, and economic development. Understating the interlinkages between trust and financial patterns is quite important because almost certainly trust and social capital more generally shape also contractual and legal institutions (see Aghion *et al.*, 2010) for a theoretical exposition and cross-country evidence linking distrust with administrative-bureaucratic procedures/barriers to entry and Alesina *et al.* (2011) for a model linking family values with the regulation of labor).

Fourth, in many countries other-than-the-law — informal — institutions play an important role in settling disputes, assigning legal rights, and enforcing contracts. Allen *et al.* (2011) emphasize the role of the family and the clan structure of the Chinese society on commerce, financial structure, and development more generally (see Greif, 2006, and Greif and Tabellini,

[10]Fernadez (2011) and Guiso *et al.* (2011) review the literature on the role of social-civic capital on economic performance. See also Spolaore and Wacziarg (2012) for a thorough overview of the literature linking cultural and epidemiological features with economic development.

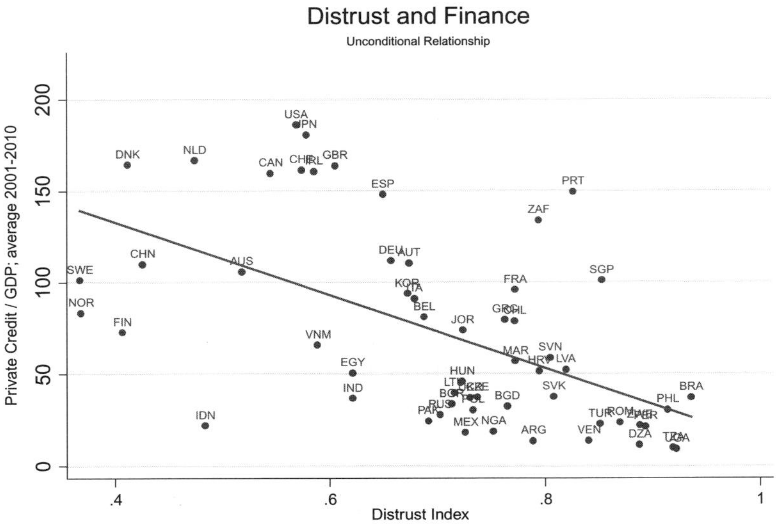
Distrust and Finance
Unconditional Relationship
Private Credit / GDP; average 2001-2010
0
50
100
150
200
.4
.6
.8
1
Distrust Index
USA
JPN
DNK
NLD
CAN
GBR
ESP
PRT
ZAF
DEU
AUT
CHN
SWE
AUS
SGP
FRA
NOR
FIN
BEL
JOR
VNM
MAR
SVN
LVA
EGY
HUN
IND
SVK
BGD
BRA
PHL
IDN
MEX
NGA
ARG
VEN
DZA

(a)

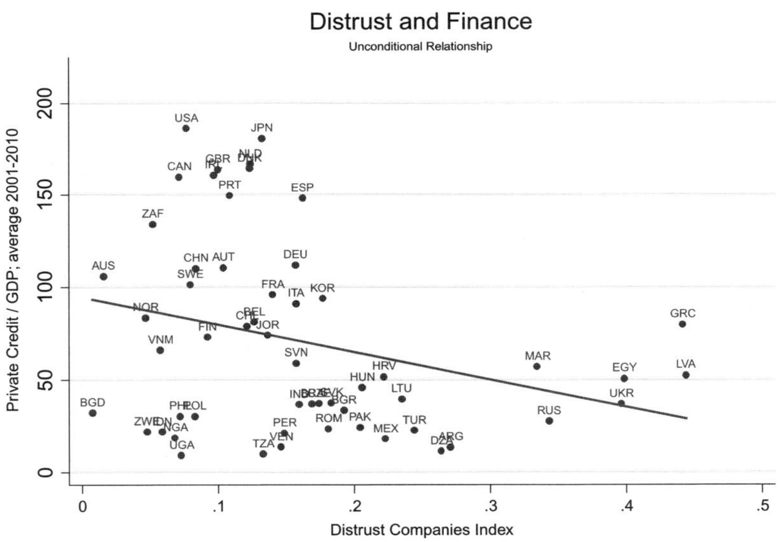
Distrust and Finance
Unconditional Relationship
Private Credit / GDP; average 2001-2010
0
50
100
150
200
0
.1
.2
.3
.4
.5
Distrust Companies Index
USA
JPN
CAN
PRT
ESP
ZAF
CHN
AUT
DEU
AUS
SWE
FRA
ITA
KOR
NOR
GRC
FIN
JOR
VNM
SVN
MAR
HRV
EGY
LVA
HUN
LTU
UKR
BGD
BGR
RUS
NGA
PER
ROM
PAK
MEX
TUR
UGA
TZA

(b)

Fig. 10.

2010). I believe that we need more research to understand how informal cultural and institutional factors shape financial structure and economic development. A new wave of research documents and tries to understand the role of deeply rooted social, cultural, historical, and informal institutional traits on long-run development (see Spolaore and Wacziarg, 2012, for a review). For example, in recent work with Stelios Michalopoulos, we document that in Africa deeply rooted pre-colonial ethnic institutions correlate much more strongly with contemporary economic development at the ethnic homeland level (as reflected in satellite images on light density at night) rather than national "formal" institutions (Michalopoulos and Papaioannou, 2012, 2013a). While these findings may contradict the findings of the "institutions" and development literature (see Acemoglu *et al.*, 2005, for a review), they are in line with both the African historiography — that downplays the role of colonial and national institutions, especially in areas far from African capitals — and the evidence from the ground that suggests that ethnic norms and traditional leaders exert considerably de facto political and legal power. For example, data from the *Afrobarometer Surveys* covering 18 Sub-Saharan African countries reveal that traditional leaders ("chiefs") have significant power in allocating land and settling disputes (see Figs. 11(a) and 11(b)).[11] Moreover, as Figs. 12(a) and 12(b) show, traditional leaders are perceived as being less corrupt compared to government officials and elected politicians, and people — especially in rural areas — tend to trust local ethnic chiefs much more than politicians.

Concluding Remarks

The law and finance literature and the finance and growth literature have produced important insights over the past decade(s). Yet, the key issues of identification and understanding the theoretical channels linking legal institutions, financial structure, and economic development remain open. Among others, future research needs to shed light on (i) the role of informal cultural and institutional traits on financial and economic development; (ii) understand the role of politics and the social equilibrium in shaping

[11]See Michalopoulos and Papaioannou (2013b) for a review of the available evidence and Acemoglu, Reed, and Robinson (2012) for a case study on the role of chiefs in Sierra Leone.

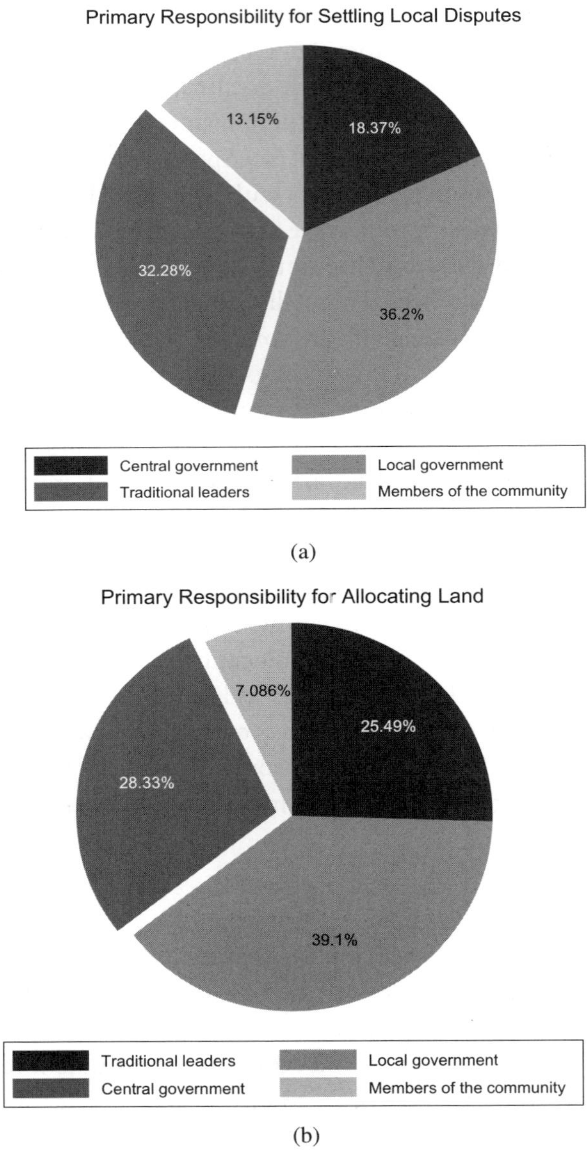

Fig. 11.

Source: Atrobarometer Surveys 4th Round.

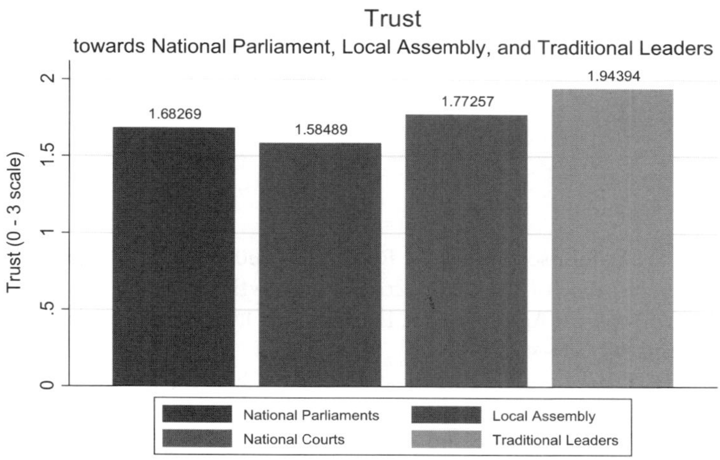

(a)

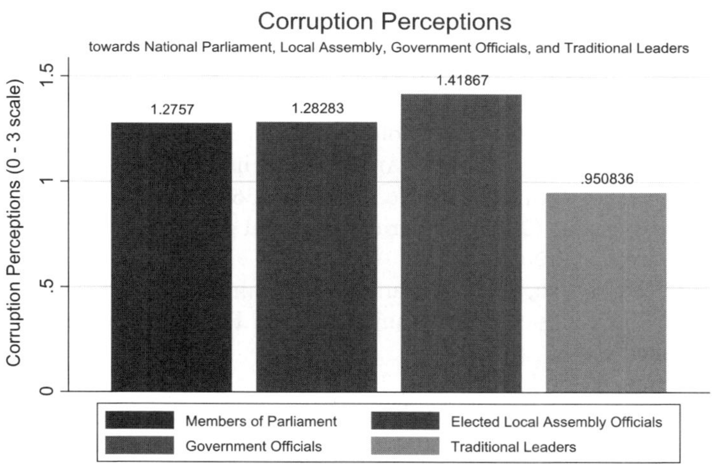

(b)

Fig. 12.

Source: Atrobarometer Surveys 4th Round.

the law and the way financial intermediation operates; and (iii) exploiting (quasi)-random variation and randomized experiments push on identification, shedding light on the channels.

References

Acemoglu, D., S. Johnson and J. A. Robinson (2005). "Institutions as the fundamental cause of long-run economic growth," in *The Handbook of Economic Growth*, P. Aghion and S. Durlauf (eds.), Amsterdam: Elsevier/North-Holland, pp. 386–472.

Acemoglu, D., T. Reed and J. A. Robinson (2012). "Chiefs," Harvard University and Massachusetts Institute of Technology mimeo.

Aghion, P., Y. Algan, P. Caluc and A. Shleifer (2010). "Regulation and distrust," *Quarterly Journal of Economics*, Vol. 125, No. 3, pp. 1015–1049.

Aghion, P., P. Howitt and D. Mayer-Foulkes (2005). "The effect of financial development on convergence: Theory and evidence," *Quarterly Journal of Economics*, Vol. 120, No. 1, pp. 173–222.

Alesina, A., Y. Algan, P. Cahuc and P. Giuliano (2011). "Family values and the regulation of labor," Harvard University mimeo.

Alfaro, L., S. Kalemli-Ozcan and V. Volosovych (2008). "Why doesn't capital flow from rich to poor countries? An empirical investigation," *Review of Economics and Statistics*, Vol. 90, No. 2, pp. 347–368.

Algan, Y. and P. Cahuc (2011). "Inherited trust and growth," *American Economic Review*, Vol. 100, No. 5, pp. 2060–2092.

Allen, F., R. Chakrabarti, S. De, J. Qian and M. Qian (2007). "Financing firms in India," University of Pennsylvania, Wharton Financial Institutions Center Working Paper.

Allen, F., I. Otchere and L. W. Senbet (2010). "African financial systems: A review," University of Pennsylvania, Wharton School mimeo.

Allen, F., J. Qian and C. Zhang (2011). "An alternative view on law, institutions, finance, and growth," University of Pennsylvania, Wharton School mimeo.

Beck, T., A. Demirgüç-Kunt, L. Laeven and R. Levine (2004). "Finance, firm size, and growth," National Bureau of Economic Research Working Paper No. 10983.

Beck, T., A. Demirgüç-Kunt and R. Levine (2000). "A new database on financial development and structure," *World Bank Economic Review*, Vol. 14, No. 2, pp. 597–605.

Beck, T., A. Demirgüç-Kunt, R. E. Levine, M. Cihák and E. H. B. Feyen (2012). "A database on financial development and structure; update September 2012," World Bank Policy Research Paper No. 2146.

Beck, T. and R. Levine (2002). "Industry growth and capital allocation: Does having a market- or bank-based system matter?" *Journal of Financial Economics*, Vol. 64, No. 2, pp. 147–180.

Beck, T. and R. Levine (2004). "Stock markets, banks, and growth: Panel evidence," *Journal of Banking and Finance*, Vol. 28, No. 3, pp. 423–442.

Beck, T. and R. Levine (2005). "Legal institutions and financial development," in *The Handbook for New Institutional Economics*, Claude Menard and Mary M. Shirley (eds.), Norwell, MA: Kluwer Academic Publishers.

Beck, T., R. Levine and N. Loyaza (2000). "Finance and the sources of growth," *Journal of Economic Literature*, Vol. 58, No. 1–2, pp. 261–300.

Beck, T., S. Munzele Maimbo, I. Faye and T. Triki (2011). "Financing Africa: Through the crisis and beyond," International Bank for Reconstruction and Development/World Bank.

Bekaert, G., C. R. Harvey and C. Lundblad (2005). "Does financial liberalization spur growth?" *Journal of Financial Economics*, Vol. 7, No. 1, pp. 3–55.

Bekaert, G., C. R. Harvey and C. Lundblad (2008). "Global growth opportunities and market integration," *Journal of Finance*, Vol. 62, No. 3, pp. 1081–1137.

Bertrand, M., A. Schoar and D. Thesmar (2007). "Banking deregulation and industry structure: Evidence from the French banking reforms of 1985," *Journal of Finance*, Vol. 62, No. 2, pp. 597–628.

Christensen, H. B., L. Hail and C. Leunz (2011). "Capital-market effects of securities regulation: Hysteresis, implementation, and enforcement," National Bureau of Economic Research Working Paper No. 16737.

Ciccone, A. and M. Jarocinski (2010). "Determinants of economic growth: Will data tell?" *American Economic Journal: Macroeconomics*, Vol. 2, No. 4, pp. 222–246.

Ciccone, A. and E. Papaioannou (2006). "Adjustment to target capital, finance, and growth," Centre for Economic Policy Research Discussion Paper, No. 5969.

Ciccone, A. and E. Papaioannou (2008). "Financial development and inter-sectoral investment," *Moneda y Credito: Revista de Economia.*

Ciccone, A. and E. Papaioannou (2010). "Estimating cross-industry cross-country models using benchmark industry characteristics," Centre for Economic Policy Research Discussion Paper No. 8056.

Claessens, S. and N. van Horen (2012a). "Foreign banks: Trends and impact," *Journal of Money, Credit and Banking*, forthcoming.

Claessens, S. and N. van Horen (2012b). "Location decisions of foreign banks and competitor remoteness," *Journal of Money, Credit and Banking*, forthcoming.

Dinç, S. (2006). "Politicians and banks: Political influences on government-owned banks in emerging countries," *Journal of Financial Economics*, Vol. 77, No. 2, pp. 453–479.

Djankov, S., O. Hart, C. Mc Liesh and A. Shleifer (2008). "Debt enforcement around the world," *Journal of Political Economy*, Vol. 116, No. 6, pp. 1105–1149.

Djankov, S., R. La Porta, F. López-de-Silanes and A. Shleifer (2003). "Courts," *Quarterly Journal of Economics*, Vol. 118, No. 2, pp. 453–517.

Djankov, S., C. McLiesh and A. Shleifer (2007). "Private credit in 129 countries," *Journal of Financial Economics*, Vol. 84, No. 1, pp. 299–329.

Fernández, R. (2011). "Does culture matter?" in *The Handbook of Social Economics*, Jess Benhabib, Alberto Bisin and Matthew O. Jackson (eds.), Amsterdam: Elsevier/North-Holland.

Fisman, R. and I. Love (2004). "Financial development and inter-sectoral allocation: A new approach," *Journal of Finance*, Vol. 54, No. 6, pp. 2785–2805.

Fisman, R. and I. Love (2007). "Financial development and growth in the short and long run," *Journal of the European Economic Association.*

Greif, A. (2006). *Institutions and the Path to the Modern Economy: Lessons from Medieval Trade*, Cambridge University Press, Cambridge, UK.

Greif, A. and G. Tabellini (2010). "Cultural and institutional bifurcation: China and Europe compared," *American Economic Review: Papers and Proceedings*, Vol. 100, No. 2, pp. 1–10.

Guiso, L., P. Sapienza and L. Zingales (2004). "Does local financial development matter?" *Quarterly Journal of Economics*, Vol. 119, No. 3, pp. 929–969.

Guiso, L., P. Sapienza and L. Zingales (2008). "Trusting the stock market," *Journal of Finance*, Vol. 63, No. 6, pp. 2557–2600.

Guiso, L., P. Sapienza and L. Zingales (2009). "Cultural biases in economic exchange?," *Quarterly Journal of Economics*, Vol. 124, No. 3.

Guiso, L., P. Sapienza and L. Zingales (2011). "Civic capital as the missing link," in *The Handbook of Social Economics*, J. Benhabib, A. Bisin and M. O. Jackson (eds.), Elsevier/North-Holland, Amsterdam.

Henry, P. B. (2001). "Do stock market liberalizations cause investment booms?" *Journal of Financial Economics*, Vol. 58, No. 1–2, pp. 301–334.

Jayaratne, J. and P. E. Strahan (1996). "The finance-growth nexus: Evidence from bank branch deregulation," *Quarterly Journal of Economics*, Vol. 113, No. 3, pp. 39–670.

Kalemli-Ozcan, S., E. Papaioannou and J.-L. Peydró (2010). "What lies beneath the euro's effect on financial integration? Currency risk, legal harmonization, or trade?" *Journal of International Economics*, Vol. 81, No. 1, pp. 75–88.

Kalemli-Ozcan, S., E. Papaioannou and J.-L. Peydró (2013). "Financial regulation, financial globalization, and the synchronization of economic activity," *Journal of Finance*, Vol. 68, No. 3, pp. 1179–1220..

Khwaja, A. and A. Mian (2005). "Do lenders favor politically connected firms? Rent provision in an emerging financial market," *Quarterly Journal of Economics*, Vol. 120, No. 4.

King, R. and R. E. Levine, (1993). "Finance and growth: Schumpeter might be right," *Quarterly Journal of Economics*, Vol. 153, No. 2, pp. 717–738.

Krugman, P. (1994). "The myth of Asia's miracle," *Foreign Affairs*, Vol. 73, No. 6, pp. 62–79.

Laeven, L. and C. Woodruff (2007). "The quality of legal system, firm ownership, and firm size," *Review of Economics and Statistics*, Vol. 89, No. 4, pp. 601–614.

Landes, D. S. (1998). *The Wealth and Poverty of Nations: Why Some Are So Rich and Some So Poor*, New York: W.W. Norton & Company.

La Porta, R., F. López-de-Silanes and A. Shleifer (2002). "Government ownership of banks," *Journal of Finance*, Vol. 57, No. 1, pp. 256–301.

La Porta, R., F. López-de-Silanes and A. Shleifer (2004). "Judicial checks and balances," *Journal of Political Economy*, Vol. 112, No. 2, pp. 446–470.

La Porta, R., F. López-de-Silanes and A. Shleifer (2006). "What works in securities laws," *Journal of Finance*, Vol. 61, No. 1, pp. 1–31.

La Porta, R., F. López-de-Silanes and A. Shleifer (2008). "The economic consequences of legal origins," *Journal of Economic Literature*, Vol. 46, No. 2, pp. 285–332.

La Porta, R., F. López-de-Silanes, A. Shleifer and R. Vishny (1997). "Legal determinants of external finance," *Journal of Finance*, Vol. 53, No. 1, pp. 1131–1150.

La Porta, R., F. López-de-Silanes, A. Shleifer and R. Vishny (1998). "Law and finance," *Journal of Political Economy*, Vol. 106, No. 6, pp. 1113–1155.

La Porta, R., F. López-de-Silanes, A. Shleifer and R. Vishny (1999). "The quality of government," *Journal of Law, Economics, and Organization*, Vol. 15, No. 1, pp. 222–279.

Levine, R. E. (2005). "Finance and growth: Theory, evidence, and mechanisms," in *The Handbook of Economic Growth*, P. Aghion and S. Durlauf (eds.), Amsterdam: Elsevier/North-Holland.

Levine, R. E., L. Laeven and S. Michalopoulos (2012). "Financial innovation and endogenous growth," National Bureau of Economic Research Working Paper No. 15356.

Levine, R. E., N. Loyaza and T. Beck (2000a). "Financial intermediation and growth: Causality and causes," *Journal of Monetary Economics*, Vol. 46, No. 1, pp. 31–77.

Levine, R. E., N. Loyaza and T. Beck (2000b). "Finance and the sources of growth," *Journal of Financial Economics*, Vol. 58, No. 1–2, pp. 261–300.

Levine, R. E. and S. Zervos (1998). "Stock markets, banks, and economic growth," *American Economic Review*, Vol. 88, No. 3, pp. 559–586.

Mankiw, G. (1995). "The growth of nations," *Brookings Papers on Economic Activity*, No. 1, pp. 275–326.

Michalopoulos, S. and E. Papaioannou (2012). "National institutions and development: Evidence from partitioned ethnicities," National Bureau of Economic Research Working Paper No. 18275.

Michalopoulos, S. and E. Papaioannou (2013a). "Pre-colonial ethnic institutions and contemporary African development," *Econometrica*, Vol. 81, No. 1, pp. 113–152.

Michalopoulos, S. and E. Papaioannou (2013b). "On the ethnic origins of African development: Traditional chiefs and pre-colonial political centralization," *Mimeo London Business School and Brown University.*

Pagano, M. and P. Volpin (2005). "The political economy of corporate governance," *American Economic Review*, Vol. 95, No. 4, pp. 1005–1030.

Papaioannou, E. (2009). "What drives international bank flows? Politics, institutions and other determinants," *Journal of Development Economics*, Vol. 88, No. 2, pp. 269–281.

Rajan, R. G. and L. Zingales (1998). "Financial dependence and growth," *American Economic Review*, Vol. 88, No. 3, pp. 559–586.

Sapienza, P. (2004). "The effects of government ownership on bank lending," *Journal of Financial Economics*, Vol. 72, No. 2, pp. 357–384.

Spolaore, E. and R. Wacziarg, (2012). "How deep are the roots of economic development?," *Journal of Economic Literature*, Vol. 51, No. 2, pp. 325–369.

Van Horen, N. (2013). "Foreign banks: Access to finance and financial stability," in *The Social Value of the Financial Sector: Too Big to Fail or Just Too Big? Proceedings of the 15th Annual International Banking Conference, Federal Reserve Bank of Chicago* World Scientific, Singapore.

Wurgler, J. (2000). "Financial markets and the allocation of capital," *Journal of Financial Economics*, Vol. 58, No. 1, pp. 187–124.

Young, A. (1995). "The tyranny of numbers: Confronting the statistical realities of the East Asian growth miracle," *Quarterly Journal of Economics*, Vol. 110, No. 3, pp. 641–680.

PART VII

BREAK UP THE BIG BANKS?

Breaking (Banks) Up Is Hard to Do: New Perspective on Too Big to Fail

James R. Barth*
Auburn University, Milken Institute
and
Wharton Financial Institutions Center

Apanard (Penny) Prabha
Milken Institute

Big is bad. At least that has become the view of many individuals about big banks ever since the financial crisis of 2007–2009. The fear is that, if a big bank gets into trouble, its problems will infect other financial institutions and threaten the entire economy. In theory, of course, regulators have long been expected to prevent banks from reckless behavior and to shut down failing banks in a timely, orderly, and cost-effective manner. Historically, however, big banks in the US and in many other countries have been implicitly treated as "too big to fail." In the US, the practice of treating troubled big banks differently from troubled small ones dates back to the 1984 bailout of Continental Illinois Corporation. That taxpayer-funded rescue was based on fears that a bank collapse of Continental's magnitude would destabilize the entire financial system (see Kaufmann, 2002; Shull, 2010; and Barth, Prabha, and Swagel, 2012). Those same fears prompted far bigger bank bailouts, both in the US and abroad, during the recent

*James R. Barth is the Lowder Eminent Scholar in Finance at Auburn University, Senior Finance Fellow at the Milken Institute, and Fellow at the Wharton Financial Institutions Center. Apanard (Penny) Prabha is an economist at the Milken Institute. The authors are grateful to Tong (Cindy) Li, Clas Wihlborg, and Thomas D. Willet for helpful comments and Nan (Annie) Zhang and Stephen Lin for excellent research assistance.

global financial crisis. In the wake of that experience, regulators and banking experts almost unanimously agree that regulatory reform is essential to ensuring that no bank is ever again too big to fail.

Unfortunately, there is far less agreement about the best approach for ending too big to fail. In the US, some believe that the Dodd–Frank Act — the sweeping overhaul of financial regulation in 2010 — will solve the problem. Dodd–Frank limits the growth of major banks by prohibiting mergers or acquisitions if the resulting bank would have more than 10% of aggregate consolidated liabilities of all financial companies nationwide. It also requires the Federal Reserve to impose stricter prudential oversight on bank holding companies with assets of more than $50 billion. In the event that a major bank holding company encounters financial difficulty and early remediation efforts fail, the Federal Reserve is to recommend to the Treasury Department and the Federal Deposit Insurance Corporation (FDIC) that the company be "resolved" under the FDIC's new orderly liquidation authority.

Despite all this effort, it is far from clear that any of the new regulatory approaches will end too big to fail. As a result, a number of prominent bank regulators and industry experts recommend a more drastic change: simply breaking up the biggest banks. There is no question that too big to fail is an urgent problem in need of a solution. But there are huge complexities at almost every level. What is "big?" How big is too big? What is a "bank?" What kinds of risk-taking are appropriate for a bank — and why? What do we know about the costs and benefits of different strategies?

In the next section, we examine a basic but important question: How do you measure "big," and how do policy makers distinguish between banks that are merely big and banks that are too big to fail? The simplest and most straightforward approach is to rank banks by asset size. As we shall see, however, such rankings fail to take into account differences in accounting practices of different countries. We also examine a number of measures of "bigness" in addition to asset size. We present these and other measures for the world's 100 biggest publicly traded banks.

The third section discusses the difficulty of another basic and seemingly simple question: What is a "bank?" Big banks come in wildly different shapes and colors, mainly because of differences in regulations and organizational structures between countries. In some countries, "banks" are bank holding companies that own an umbrella of separate subsidiaries for traditional banking and a host of other financial services. In both of these cases, moreover, the scope of financial services that are allowed differs across countries. Other countries allow universal banks, which provide a wide range of financial services through a single entity. Likewise, some countries allow nonfinancial firms to own banks while others do not. As a result, the actual business of a "bank," and the kind of risk it takes on, varies between and sometimes within countries.

The fourth section of this paper describes various actual or proposed regulatory reforms to end too big to fail. The goal of all the reforms is to promote a safer and sounder banking system and to ensure that taxpayers never have to bail out another big bank. The reforms range from relying on more stringent capital requirements to regulations limiting the size and activities of banks to enhanced resolution authority, and to breaking up big banks.

The fifth and last section summarizes our conclusions. There are two major and legitimate concerns about big banks. The first is that big banks, through a concentration of power, will successfully lobby regulators for leniency and effectively receive greater leeway for excessive risk-taking. The second concern is that the failure of a big bank can radiate instability throughout the financial system, forcing policymakers to bail out troubled big banks for the sake of the overall economy.

Just How Big are the World's Biggest Banks?

There are several different ways to measure "big." We start by ranking the 100 biggest publicly traded banks in the world by their total assets. This enables us to work with a large but not unmanageable sample of banks. It also enables us to obtain information about market assessments on the value of banks as well as other relevant information. The banks are headquartered in 26 different countries and show a wide range in the asset size. The biggest is Deutsche Bank of Germany, with $2,822 billion in assets, while the smallest is American Express of the US, with $148 billion in assets. The biggest bank is therefore 20 times the size of the 100th biggest bank in the world. There are 24 "trillion dollar banks" in the world, of which four are US banks, according to our list.

Ranking total assets, however, does not produce an apples-to-apples comparison. There is no uniform worldwide accounting standard for measuring assets. Most of the home countries for banks in this table reply on International Financial Reporting Standards (IFRS), but others rely on their own Generally Accepted Accounting Principles (GAAP). That leads to big differences. For example, countries that use IFRS, and some that use GAAP, report derivatives on a gross rather than a net basis. In Switzerland, banks are allowed to choose between the two accounting standards. When an adjustment is made to measure total assets on a comparable basis, the result is a significant change for several of the world's biggest banks. In particular, JPMorgan Chase reports total assets of $2.3 trillion under US GAAP, in which case derivatives are measured on a net basis. When derivatives are calculated on a gross basis, JPMorgan's assets almost double to $4 trillion and the bank jumps from third place to first place among the world's largest. Likewise, Bank of America leaps from tenth place to second.

It is useful to explain more fully the impact on total assets of the treatment of derivatives under different accounting standards. Figure 1 shows what happens to the total assets of the 15 US banks if derivatives are measured under the IFRS rules rather than under US GAAP. The most dramatic changes occur at the biggest of the big US banks, which carry out a disproportionate share of trading in derivatives. As a result, several of

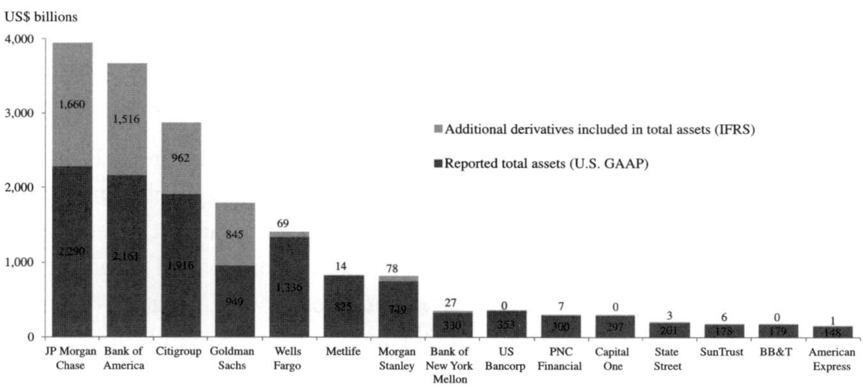

Fig. 1. Differences in total assets of big US banks due to differences in the accounting treatment of derivatives, Q2:2012.

Source: BankScope, Bloomberg, annual reports, and Milken Institute.

those institutions suddenly appear to eclipse competitors in other countries if they are measured on the same basis. Indeed, US GAAP treatment may be understating the assets of all US banks on our list by a total of $5 trillion.

As already noted, the world's 100 biggest publicly traded banks are headquartered in 26 countries. There are a total of 1,074 publicly traded banks in these countries, with total assets of $93 trillion. The 100 biggest banks account only for 9% of all the banks, but 84% of the total assets. The US has the most publicly traded banks of any nation, with 681 banks. Japan and Russia rank second and third with 93 and 25 banks, respectively. The US is also the country whose publicly traded banks collectively have the most total assets — $15.5 trillion. The publicly traded banks in Japan and China are ranked second and third in terms of total assets at $12.5 trillion and $12.4 trillion, respectively. The total assets of the banks in these three countries total $40.4 trillion, or 42% of assets at all of the banks on our list.

Another way to view the world's 100 biggest banks is not simply in terms of total assets, but their total assets relative to the total assets of all banks. In terms of individual countries, the ratio of the total assets of the biggest banks to total bank assets ranges from a low of 17% in Taiwan to a high of 100% in Ireland and the UK. In the case of the US, the comparable ratio is 78%.

Still another way to view the world's 100 biggest banks is by measuring total assets as a share of GDP. By that measure, Swiss banks are by far the world's "biggest," with assets equal to 458% of Switzerland's GDP. Russia's banks would be the "smallest," with assets equal to only 43% of GDP. The 15 biggest US banks are at the lower end of the range, with assets equal to 99% of US GDP.

Figure 2 shows the distribution of the world's 100 biggest banks by number and total assets across the 26 countries. The US, with 15, has more banks than any other nation on the list. China ranks second and Japan third, with 12 and 10 banks, respectively. The remaining 23 countries account for 63 banks. Measured by total banking assets, however, China's big banks lead the world with $12.3 trillion. The US banks come in second, with combined assets of $12.1 trillion, and the UK ranks third with $9.5 trillion. Banks in the remaining countries have $44.3 trillion in assets, or 57% of the worldwide total.

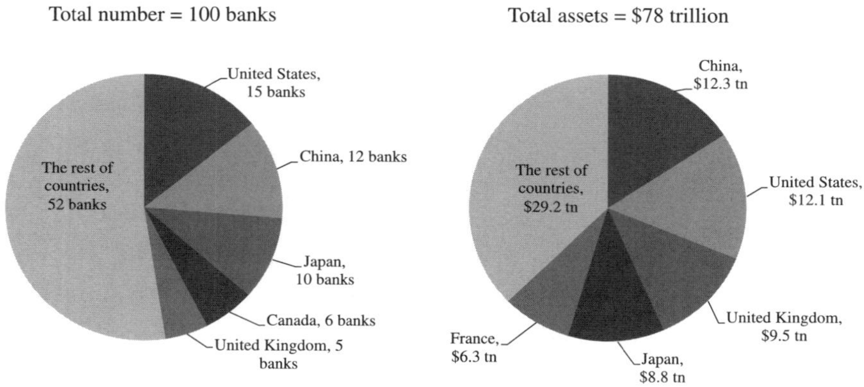

Fig. 2. Number and assets of the world's 100 biggest banks by country, Q2:2012.

Sources: BankScope, Milken Institute.

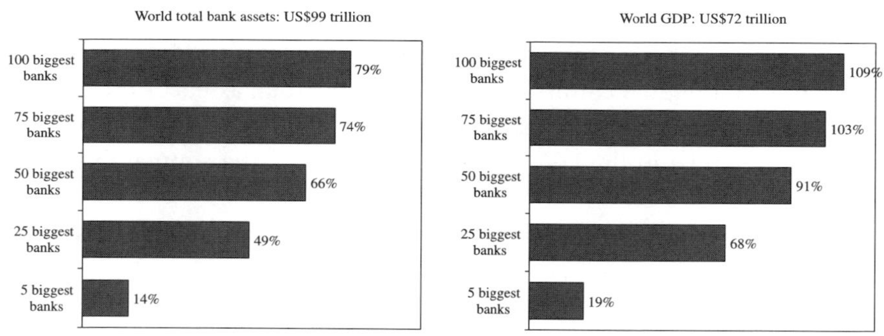

Fig. 3. Combined assets of the world's biggest banks, Q2: 2012.

Note: The 100 biggest publicly traded banks in the world ranked by total assets. World GDP is a 2012 IMF estimate. World total bank assets are based on all publicly traded banks worldwide, which include commercial banks, savings banks, cooperative banks, and bank holding companies.

Source: Bloomberg, International Monetary Fund, Milken Institute.

Figure 3 provides a breakdown of the relative importance of different subsets of the world's 100 biggest banks. The largest 25 banks account for about half of the total assets of all banks worldwide. The assets of the same banks are slightly more than two-thirds of world GDP. As may be seen, only a few of world's 1,470 publicly traded banks are big in terms of either their share of the global bank assets or global GDP. The list of big banks would be even smaller if US banks accounted for their derivatives under IFRS rather than US GAAP rules.

There are still other ways in which to rank the size of banks. Two of these ways are to measure individual banks by their assets as a share of either total banking assets in their home countries or as a share of their home-country GDP. As regards the first way, Danske Bank in Denmark tops the list, with 84% of Denmark's total banking assets. American Express in the US accounts for the smallest share, at 1% US banking assets. The median share is 17%. Among US banks, JPMorgan Chase was in first place with 14.8% of the total. In the global context, however, JPMorgan Chase ranks only 58th among the world's biggest 100 banks. This means that the biggest US banks are relatively small when compared to the world's other 100 biggest banks on the basis of the share of an individual bank's total assets relative to the all banking assets of the bank's home country.

The other way to compare individual banks is by their total assets relative to the home country's GDP. In this case, UBS ranks number 1 with assets equal to 238% of Switzerland's GDP. Once again, American Express is at the bottom of the list with total assets equal to a mere 0.9% of US GDP. The median ratio is 25%. JPMorgan Chase, with total assets equal to 17.4% of US GDP, ranks 64th worldwide. In short: The biggest US banks are relatively small players in their own country when compared to many of their counterparts elsewhere in the world.

What Is a Bank?

It is important to digress for a moment and define the term "bank." Under US law, a bank is a firm that offers demand deposits, makes commercial and industrial loans, and has its deposits insured by the FDIC. The "biggest banks" are typically holding companies, which conduct banking and certain other financial activities, such as securities and insurance activities, through separate subsidiaries. All 15 US banks on our list are bank holding companies, and it is the total assets of the holding companies, not simply of their banking subsidiaries, that appear in the many of the tables and figures. In some countries, however, the biggest banks are universal banks in which banking and other financial activities are conducted in the same entity. In order to make apple-to-apple comparisons, we include US bank holding companies rather than simply the bank subsidiaries.

Even then, however, "big banks" come in different shapes and sizes. Table 1 shows that the total assets of the 15 bank holding companies are $12 trillion, while the total assets of all their FDIC-insured bank subsidiaries are $8 trillion. It's clearly more accurate to compare the assets of a US bank holding company with those of a universal bank such as Deutsche Bank. But that doesn't mean the comparisons are strictly accurate. Regardless of how they are organized, most of the world's big banks have a mix of businesses with very different kinds of assets. Indeed, some bank holding companies are primarily in nonbank businesses, such as insurance. The distinction is especially dramatic for Metlife, which is overwhelmingly an insurance provider. The assets of its FDIC-insured subsidiaries account for only 1.1% of its total assets and only 2.3% of total equity capital.

That makes cross-border comparisons difficult at either the individual or aggregate bank level. Largely because of differences in regulation between countries, the assets of big banks can include different mixtures of bank loans, securities, insurance policies, and other products (see Barth, Caprio, and Levine, 2006). This diversity is wide even among US bank holding companies.

Not surprisingly, financial markets assess the value of big banks in very different ways. In the US, for example, the ratio of market value to book value for the banks listed in Table 1 ranges from a high of 3.44 for American Express to a low of 0.41 for Bank of America, as of the end of the second quarter, 2012. In addition to American Express, four other banks have market-to-book ratios of greater than 1.0: US Bancorp (1.84), Wells Fargo (1.29), BB&T (1.18), and State Street (1.10). In addition to Bank of America, the other banks with ratios of less than 1.0 include PNC Financial (0.95), Capital One (0.85), Bank of New York Mellon (0.76), JPMorgan Chase (0.74), Goldman Sachs (0.70), SunTrust (0.64), Metlife (0.54), Morgan Stanley (0.47), and Citigroup (0.44). The markets clearly recognize that the 15 big US banks represent a range of different business models, which suggests that they should not be viewed as the same when it comes to tackling the problem of too big to fail, especially any proposals to break them up.

The US contains yet another major variant among banks: industrial loan companies, or ILCs. These are FDIC-insured depository institutions,

Table 1. **Total assets and equity of the US biggest bank holding companies and their FDIC-insured subsidiaries, Q2:2012.**

	Holding company		FDIC-insured subsidiaries			% holding company	
	Total assets ($ billions)	Total equity capital ($ billions)	No. of insured subsidiaries	Combined total assets ($ billions)	Combined total bank equity capital ($ billions)	Total assets	Total equity capital
JP Morgan Chase & Co.	2,290	184	4	1,944	160	84.9	87.0
Bank of America Corp.	2,161	217	5	1,652	207	76.5	95.1
Citigroup	1,916	186	3	1,350	156	70.4	83.9
Wells Fargo & Co.	1,336	138	5	1,236	133	92.5	96.3
Goldman Sachs	949	68	1	115	20	12.1	29.1
Metlife	825	61	1	9	1	1.1	2.3
Morgan Stanley	749	70	2	91	11	12.2	15.7
US Bancorp	353	34	2	349	38	98.9	112.5
Bank of New York Mellon Corp.	330	35	4	275	24	83.3	67.5
PNC Financial Services Group	300	37	1	292	39	97.4	106.0
Capital One Financial Corp.	297	37	3	332	47	112.1	125.6
State Street Corp.	201	19	1	197	19	98.1	97.7
BB&T Corp.	179	18	2	176	22	98.8	118.2
SunTrust Bank	178	20	1	172	21	96.5	104.3
American Express	148	19	2	69	13	46.6	68.4
Total	12,211	1,143	37	8,260	910		

Note: Financial data for bank holding companies represent the summation of FFIEC Call Reports or OTS Thrift Financial Reports (TFR) filed by all FDIC-insured bank and thrift subsidiaries held by a bank holding company, and do not reflect nondeposit subsidiaries or parent companies. Data values have not been adjusted for intracompany transactions, which mean that some percentages for some holding companies can exceed 100 percent.

Source: National Information Center, Federal Reserve, FDIC, Bloomberg, and Milken Institute.

but some are owned by nonfinancial corporations.[1] Table 2 shows nine such institutions currently operating in the US. The largest nonfinancial company that owns one is General Electric (GE), with $694 billion in assets. Toyota is the second-largest owner with $376 billion in assets, while BMW is third with $160 billion in assets. Under US law, these corporate parents are not currently considered to be financial services or bank holding companies even though they own FDIC-insured depository institutions (see Barth, *et al.*, 2012). For that reason, we do not include the corporate parents in any of the earlier tables and figures, even though all of them could qualify as one of the world's 100 biggest banks. In practice, the ILCs have very different business models from both bank holding companies and financial services companies. As Table 2 indicates, moreover, the ILCs are relatively unimportant in terms of their shares of the total assets and total equity of their parent companies.

What Should Be Done to Resolve the Too-Big-to-Fail Problem?

The purpose of the regulatory reforms being proposed or already being carried out is to prevent future banking crises whenever possible and to lessen the severity of those that do occur.[2]

The reforms attempt to tackle too big to fail in roughly five ways: (1) restricting the size of banks; (2) restricting the scope of bank activities; (3) requiring higher capital levels for systemically important institutions; (4) providing an orderly framework for shutting down troubled banks, including through requirements that banks prepare "living wills" and through an expansion of the government's "resolution" authority; and (5) various combinations of these approaches.

The first type of reform involves restricting the size of banks. The Dodd–Frank Act limits the size of banks by prohibiting bank mergers or acquisitions if the resulting bank would hold more than 10% of total nationwide bank deposits or more than 10% of the aggregate consolidated liabilities

[1]The US, with the exception of existing ILCs, is only one of two countries, the other being Namibia, that currently prohibit nonfinancial companies from owning banks based on information from World Bank Survey IV.

[2]This section draws upon Barth, Prabha, and Swagel (2012).

Table 2. Importance of corporate parents to commercially owned industrial loan companies, Q2:2012.

	Parent company							ILC				
Parent company	Total assets ($ billions)	Total equity capital ($ billions)	Equity capital to total assets (%)	ROA (%)	ROE (%)	Commercially owned ILC	State	ILC assets as % of its parent's assets	ILC equity as % of its parent's equity	Equity capital to total assets (%)	ROA (%)	ROE (%)
BMW	160.2	34.8	21.7	1.0	4.7	BMW Bank of North America	UT	5.8	3.2	11.9	1.1	9.6
Harley-Davidson	9.3	2.7	28.6	2.7	9.3	Eaglemark Savings Bank	NV	0.3	0.3	23.1	6.9	29.8
CMS Energy	16.3	3.2	19.3	0.6	3.2	EnerBank USA	UT	3.2	1.8	11.0	1.5	13.2
Fry's Electronics	n.a.	n.a.	n.a.	n.a.	n.a.	First Electronic Bank	UT	n.a.	n.a.	86.4	4.8	5.5
General Electric	694.1	123.9	17.8	0.4	2.5	GE Capital Financial Inc.	UT	1.8	1.7	17.0	1.2	7.3

(*Continued*)

Table 2. (*Continued*)

Parent company	Parent company: Total assets ($ billions)	Parent company: Total equity capital ($ billions)	Parent company: Equity capital to total assets (%)	Parent company: ROA (%)	Parent company: ROE (%)	Commercially owned ILC	State	ILC: ILC assets as % of its parent's assets	ILC: ILC equity as % of its parent's equity	ILC: Equity capital to total assets (%)	ILC: ROA (%)	ILC: ROE (%)
Pitney Bowes	8.1	0.3	3.2	4.8	152.1	The Pitney Bowes Bank Inc.	UT	9.1	20.6	7.1	5.4	75.3
Target Corp.	46.6	15.8	33.9	6.6	19.6	Target Bank	UT	0.1	0.1	35.6	9.6	27.0
Toyota	376.3	138.2	36.7	0.6	1.7	Toyota Financial Savings Bank	NV	0.2	0.1	18.6	1.3	6.8
Flying J*	1.8	0.5	29.7	18.9	63.5	TAB Bank*	UT	29.1	13.5	13.2	1.8	13.2
						All FDIC-insured institutions				11.46	0.99	8.84

Total assets of US nonfinancial corporate business (Q2: 2012): $31 trillion.
Total net worth of US nonfinancial corporate business (Q2: 2012): $17 trillion.

*As of Q2: 2010. The owner of Transportation Alliance Bank Inc. changed from Flying J to FJ Management Inc. in July 2010. TAB Bank, Inc. was formerly named as Transportation Alliance Bank, Inc.

Source: "Flow of Funds," Federal Reserve, FDIC, Bloomberg, and Milken Institute.

of all financial companies. These limits could impede future mergers and acquisitions in the banking industry.

Johnson and Kwak (2010, pp. 214–215) state that "[t]he simplest solution [to the TBTF problem] is a hard cap on size: no financial institution would be allowed to control or have an ownership interest in assets worth more than a fixed percentage of U.S. GDP." They add that "[a]s a first proposal, this limit should be *no more than 4 percent of* GDP, or roughly $570 billion in assets today." For investment banks, they state that "[a]s an initial guideline, an investment bank (such as Goldman Sachs) should be effectively limited in size to *2 percent of GDP*, or roughly $285 billion today." Based upon GDP in the second quarter of 2012, 4% amounts to $624 billion. JP Morgan Chase, Bank of America, Citigroup, and Wells Fargo all have assets that exceed this amount. Moreover, Goldman Sachs and Morgan Stanley both have assets that exceed 2% of GDP, or $311 billion.[3]

The problem, of course, is that there is no bright line that enables one to easily distinguish between big banks that are or will become a systemic risk versus those big banks that are or will not become such a risk. To the extent that the demarcation line is adjusted for individual banks of different degrees of bigness, the end result might once again lead back to a TBTF problem. Indeed, the globally systemically important banks (G-SIBs) identified by the Financial Stability Board are of different asset sizes and some of these banks are smaller than other banks not so identified. Moreover, some of the US banks are identified G-SIBs even though their asset size is substantially less than 4% or even 2% of US GDP.

A potential weakness with such limits on size such is that they could reduce economies of scale, not to mention economies of scope, in banking. That could increase the cost of banking services. In this regard, Wheelock and Wilson (2012, p. 171) found that "... as recently as 2006, most US banks faced *increasing* returns to scale, suggesting that scale economies are a plausible (but not necessarily only) reason for the growth in average bank size." In addition, Hughes and Mester (2011, p. 23) found that "... evidence of large scale economies at smaller banks and even larger economies at large banks..." They added that these measured economies of scale did not result from cost advantages that large banks may derive from being considered

[3]Metlife is excluded for purposes of these calculations.

"too big to fail." To the extent that US banks are limited in size, they may also be at a competitive disadvantage to the big banks in other countries that don't impose such limits. The implication is clear: One should not rush to limit bank size unless one can be more certain that the benefits outweigh the costs.[4]

The second type of reform involves requiring banks to legally separate certain particularly risky activities or simply barring banks from those activities altogether. The Liikanen report proposes separating proprietary trading of securities and derivatives, and certain other activities linked to those markets, from deposit-taking banks within a banking organization. Similarly, the Vickers report proposes a structural, but not legal, separation between retail banking and wholesale/investment banking. The "ring-fenced" banks would take retail deposits, provide payments and services, and supply credit to households and businesses. In the US, the Volcker rule under Dodd–Frank goes further by prohibiting an insured depository institution or its affiliates from engaging in "proprietary trading." It also prohibits insured institutions from sponsoring or acquiring ownership interests in hedge funds or private equity funds. The theory is that simpler banks pose less risk to the financial system and the broader economy, because some activities are inherently more risky and because simpler organizations are easier to manage and regulate.

An important concern with the Volcker rule is that it is difficult to evaluate the costs and benefits. It is not clear, for example, that proprietary trading was a significant factor in the recent financial crisis. The losses that led to problems at Lehman Brothers, Bear Stearns, IndyMac, Washington Mutual, and other failed institutions were mainly connected to mortgage-backed securities and real estate, rather than to losses from the kind of trading that would be targeted by the Volcker rule.[5] Nor is there clear evidence that separating commercial banking from investment banking would increase safety. Despite strong separation between the two businesses in the 1980s under the Glass–Steagall Act, several big banks nevertheless almost failed because of bad loans in Latin America. Likewise, legions of savings-and-loans failed due to real estate loans. This suggests it is unlikely

[4]See Saunders and Walter (2010) for a more general discussion on this issue.
[5]See Barth *et al.* (2009).

that by simply reinstating Glass–Steagall problems at big banks in the future would not occur. In a sense, it is not even easy to pinpoint the problem that the Volcker rule would solve. This is not to say that there will be no benefits from it. It may be true that simpler institutions are less prone to excess and less likely to contribute to a future crisis. But without evidence that this is the case it seems difficult to justify reorganizing the banking industry.

Some evidence regarding trading losses might be helpful in this regard (see Barth and McCarthy, 2012). Since 1990, there have been 15 instances when traders at different firms lost at least $1 billion (in 2011 dollars). The losses totaled nearly $60 billion and ranged from a low of S1.1 billion on ill-fated foreign exchange derivatives at a Japanese subsidiary of Shell Oil to a high of $9 billion on credit default swaps at Morgan Stanley. Four of the firms were banks, two were investment banks, two were hedge funds, one was a local government, and six were manufacturing or petrochemical firms. In other words, almost half the losses were not at financial services firms but at institutions that typically use financial products for hedging purposes. A total of 26% of the losses occurred at manufacturing, petrochemical firms, and local governments. The remaining 74% occurred at financial services firms — 33% at banks, 21% at hedge funds, and 20% at investment banks. It is quite clear that the proprietary trading problem is not limited to banks.

While the magnitude of these losses was staggering, that was only a small part of the story. A smaller trading loss that jeopardizes a firm's entire equity capital poses a greater threat — to the institution itself, to other market participants, and (in the case of banks) to the federal deposit insurance fund and to taxpayers — than a bigger trading loss at a larger and better-capitalized firm. The latter firms are better able to sustain trading losses, and thus less likely to fail and present costs to counterparties.

Look at the same 15 losses above in relation to the equity those institutions had at the time. The losses at the banks were less threatening to financial stability than those at the nonbank firms. Relative to equity, the largest losses were at nonbanks. Thus, the Volcker rule may be targeting the wrong firms. Moreover, the more regulators limit banking activities, the more they are likely to create incentives for those same activities to take place at nonbanking firms or offshore firms. Already there have been indications that proprietary traders are moving from banks to nonbanks.

Given that the hedge funds suffering major losses over the past 20 years either failed or required bailouts, this may not be a good thing for financial stability. More generally, the so-called shadow banking system may more than benefit by gaining additional business from banks as more stringent regulations curtail their size and scope of activities. In the process, however, risks may also shift from the banking industry to the shadow banking system.

Furthermore, as noted in Swagel (2011), the Volcker rule is likely to both reduce liquidity and increase transactions costs. That would translate into less investment, slower economic growth, and less job creation. This concern is implicit in the exemption with respect to trading in Treasury securities. It is also implicit in the entreaties of domestic state and local borrowers, and of foreign governments, for similar treatment. There may be benefits to separating certain derivatives activities from bank holding companies, but there is no evidence yet. Indeed, regulators have found it difficult to implement these provisions of the Dodd–Frank Act, in part because of concerns about both the costs and benefits.

The post-crisis regulatory regime embodied in Dodd–Frank does not seek to break up big banks or to reinstitute Glass–Steagall barriers between commercial and investment banking. This perhaps reflects the observation that the failures of banks in the crisis are not well correlated with the end of the Glass–Steagall restrictions. Bear Stearns and Lehman Brothers both suffered failures, but both were essentially pure investment banks. By contrast, JPMorgan Chase combined investment and commercial banking, but weathered the crisis well. An alternative to Glass–Steagall-like restrictions would be for regulators to focus on activities that appear to pose particular risks, and to act more pre-emptively to head off systemic problems. This approach is embodied in the creation of the Financial Stability Oversight Council (FSOC), an umbrella group of federal regulators that is meant to watch over the entire financial system. One, however, is right to question whether this new approach will indeed be successful.[6]

The third type of reform involves requiring banks to hold additional equity capital. This is meant to ensure that firms have a bigger buffer against losses and a greater ability to survive a crisis. More equity capital

---

[6]For further discussion of this and related issues, see Barth, Caprio, and Levine (2012).

would also provide more protection for taxpayers against future bailouts. Under Basel III there are new and more stringent capital requirements. The guidelines for globally systemically important banks (G-SIBs) call for additional requirements. The identification of the G-SIBs banks is based upon a variety of factors. In addition, the Dodd–Frank Act subjects the largest banks, defined as those with assets of $50 billion or more, to an enhanced supervisory regime. That enhanced regime includes additional capital requirements and heightened regulatory scrutiny.

In a first, the Basel III agreement among international bank regulators calls for a minimum leverage ratio. This ratio is not risk-based, like the other capital guidelines. According to Haldane (2012, p. 19), "... the leverage ratio [should play] the frontstop role [in Basel III] given its simplicity and superior predictive performance." He adds that "[t]he more complex the bank, the stronger is this case." Furthermore, we concur with Hoenig (2012), who states that "[a]n effective capital rule should result in a bank having capital that approximates what the market would require without the safety net in place. The measure that best achieves these goals is what I have been calling the tangible equity to tangible assets ratio." During the US financial crisis, this seemed to be the only ratio that anyone paid attention to insofar as banks in general were amply capitalized by nearly all the other capital ratios.

Additional capital requirements for big or systemically important banks provide an incentive against size (and perhaps also against complexity or interconnectedness). These might also be seen as an "incentive" that offsets the possible funding advantages of big banks — a disincentive for size, but not a blunt restriction along the lines of the Volcker rule.

As already noted, it should be kept in mind that big banks provide benefits as well as costs to society, a point discussed by the Clearing House Association (2011) and Swagel (2011). Moreover, the capital charge, as usual with a tax, results in a deadweight loss in the form of reduced lending and economic activity. The quantitative importance of this impact remains a subject of considerable debate. Admati *et al.* (2010) see little negative impact of higher capital requirements. But Kashyap, Stein, and Hanson (2010) see a meaningful impact on bank funding costs during the transition period as banks raise additional equity capital, and then a modest ongoing impact. Research by regulators points to modest impacts, while banks and their associations point to greater impacts. In the wake of the recent crisis, it is certain that big banks will hold more capital, both at the insistence of regulators and of their own volition. Given the considerable changes in the banking industry and its more stringent regulation, the ongoing impacts of higher capital standards will be understood only over time.

The fourth type of reform involves changes to the framework for dealing with the collapse of big or systemically important banks. There are two motivations behind such policies: first, to better ensure the stability of the system; second, to alert market participants that banks are more likely to be allowed to fail and that creditors will be forced to take losses. That awareness may help remove advantages that big banks have previously enjoyed by being perceived as too big to fail.

The Dodd–Frank Act requires banks to devise their own "living wills," or plans for and orderly shutdown if they begin to fail. This could prove to be a symbolic step, because no one knows how or if the plans will work in the event of an actual crisis. Even so, however, the preparation of a living will may provide an additional signal that regulators will let banks collapse rather than bail them out in the future.

The new orderly liquidation authority in the Dodd–Frank Act could fundamentally change the way in which failures at big banks are resolved.[7] As noted earlier, it could also have profound impacts on the cost of funding for big, complex banks. Bondholders and other creditors are now more likely to incur losses if a bank fails, even though the act allows for the deployment of government resources to support a bank and slow its demise through the Orderly Liquidation Fund. Absent additional congressional action (which is now hard to imagine, given the unpopularity of the Troubled Asset Relief Program, TARP), in the case of a future failure of a big bank that involves the resolution of the holding company beyond simply the insured depository institutions, bondholders will incur losses.

While it is difficult to predict how the new resolution authority will be used, it seems likely that FDIC would initially deploy public funds to prevent a repeat of the crisis that followed the collapse of Lehman Brothers. The FDIC might then use its new authority to arrange a debt-for-equity swap that recapitalizes the failing bank, turning the former bondholders

[7] For a discussion of resolution procedures in other countries, see Wihlborg (2012).

into the new owners. Such a debt-for-equity recapitalization would be similar to a prepackaged Chapter 11 reorganization under the bankruptcy code, but the new authority would allow this to be done faster and with government providing the equivalent of debtor-in-possession financing. Losses to the government would be borne by bondholders. The resolution authority provides government officials with an open checkbook to act through the troubled bank, with bondholders picking up the tab. It seeks to narrow the FDIC's scope of action by guaranteeing bondholders that they will receive as much through the resolution as they would have through a bankruptcy.

The possibility of having such a swap imposed on them should affect the terms under which potential creditors, such as bond buyers, are willing to provide funding to banks that might be put through a resolution. One risk is that the new resolution authority could give providers of funding an incentive to flee at first hint of trouble. The threat of such bank runs is an important disciplining device, but it could also lead to more hair-trigger responses and inadvertently prove destabilizing.

Either way, however, the resolution authority will be incomplete and perhaps unworkable until there is more international coordination of bankruptcy regimes. In the case of Lehman's failure, for example, the UK bankruptcy regime disrupted the operations of many US-based firms when it froze their overseas assets.

International coordination of regulatory regimes for both normal times and during resolution or bankruptcy procedures will be crucial for the continued evolution of the global financial system.[8] As Brummer (2012, p. 250) points out, "In the absence of detailed, prescriptive global standards, national regulators enjoy considerable discretion with regard to their local approaches. In practice, such flexibility means any one country's efforts to deal with the problem can potentially be undercut by another country's inaction."

The fifth type of reform is a combination of the first four approaches as well as other factors. This includes a provision of the Dodd–Frank Act requiring the Federal Reserve to impose more stringent liquidity standards

[8] See, for example, Prabha and Wihlborg (forthcoming) for a discussion of this issue as it relates to global bank organizational structure.

on the largest bank holding companies. It also includes the use of regular stress tests with the goal to provide better information for regulators and market participants, which in turn will have an impact on bank behavior. While this will not directly address the potential for banks to become too big to fail, such information and the resulting incentives could help affect behavior in a way that makes it less likely that future failures will transpire. Unfortunately, there is no uniformity among the countries. Some supervise systemically important institutions differently from nonsystemic ones, and the countries rely on different factors to assess systemic risks. Some countries have established a specialized department to deal with financial stability and systemic supervision, while others have not. Not all countries have the same tools to oversee and/or limit the activities of large, interconnected institutions. Tracking these differences will provide valuable information about which approaches work best in preventing and mitigating future crises. Unfortunately, it will take a future crisis to make a real assessment.

It's important to note, however, that some regulators and experts would take a much more direct approach on too big to fail: simply break up the big banks.[9] Johnson and Kwak (2010, p. 208), for example, state that "... do not allow financial institutions to be too big to fail; break up the ones that are." However, others disagree. For example, Krugman (2010) states that:

> Breaking up big banks wouldn't really solve our problems, because it's perfectly possible to have a financial crisis that mainly takes the form of a run on smaller institutions. In fact, that's precisely what happened in the 1930s, when most of the banks that collapsed were relatively small — small enough that the Federal Reserve believed that it was O.K. to let them fail. As it turned out, the Fed was dead wrong: the wave of small-bank failures was a catastrophe for the wider economy. The same would be true today. Breaking up big financial institutions wouldn't prevent future crises, nor would it eliminate the need for bailouts when those crises happen. The next bailout wouldn't be concentrated on a few big companies — but it would be a bailout all the same. I don't have any love for financial giants, but I just don't believe that breaking them up solves the key problem.

[9]This is not a replacement for other reforms discussed earlier, but in addition to these reforms.

The fact that these and other distinguished individuals do not agree on whether the TBTF problem can be solved by breaking up the big banks suggests that one should be cautious about adopting such an approach without evidence regarding its benefits and costs. In this regard, Scott (2010, p. 20) states that "... the surprising fact is that we do not know whether larger institutions pose greater systemic risk and, if so, whether that increase is significant".[10] Moreover, breaking up big banks seems to be based on the assumption that such banks per se caused the financial crises in the US and other countries, and therefore will cause future crises, despite other reforms being implemented. Yet, in the case of the US, Gorton and Metrick (2012, p. 150) point out that:

> One strong similarity to history comes in the acceleration of system-wide leverage just before the crisis, the strongest predictor of crises in the past two centuries. Furthermore, the recent crisis was preceded by rapid increases in housing prices, also a feature of all major crises since World War II. At this macro level, the pattern (but not the scale) of our crisis is very ordinary.

The crisis was exacerbated by panics in the banking system, where various types of short-term debt suddenly became subject to runs. This, also, was a typical part of historical crises. The novelty here was in the location of runs, which took place mostly in the new evolving 'shadow banking' system, including money-market mutual funds, commercial paper, securitized bonds, and repurchase agreements. This new source of systemic vulnerability came as a surprise to policymakers and economists, and some knowledge of its details is necessary for understanding the contagion that eventually spread to the real economy.

Summary and Conclusion

That some banks are too big to fail is not new. Neither is the challenge for policymakers to implement reforms that eliminate the need to bail out big banks. The regulatory regimes for big banks in many countries are undergoing changes from those that prevailed before the global financial crisis.

[10] Also, see the discussion by Calomiris (2009) and Wallison (2012).

Banks will now be required to hold more capital, have more robust access to liquidity, undergo increased regulatory scrutiny, and face restrictions on certain activities. In the US and in other countries, many of these changes are still evolving as some reforms are being implemented and proposals for additional reforms are still being evaluated.

We share the concern of individuals who believe that these reform efforts may fall short of solving the too big to fail problem. Some, therefore, recommend that the most definitive solution to the problem is to break up the big banks. However, there does not appear to be any agreement on how big is too big or how big banks should be broken up. Big banks do possess considerable power that may be used to influence the regulatory authorities to pursue policies that increase the risk of a systemic crisis. The regulatory authorities, moreover, may also pursue such policies based upon a bias in favor of banks. Yet, despite these legitimate concerns, there is far too little evidence on the costs and benefits of breaking up big banks. In the absence of that evidence, policymakers may simply have to monitor the incremental reforms they have already begun to implement and make adjustments as the results come in. Barth, Caprio, and Levine (2012) point out that given the poor past performance of the regulatory authorities, it may also be prudent to establish procedures to hold them more accountable for achieving stability in the future.

References

Admati, A. R., P. M. DeMarzo, M. F. Hellwig and P. Pfleiderer (2010). "Fallacies, irrelevant facts, and myths in the discussion of capital regulation: Why bank equity is not expensive," Stanford University, Graduate School of Business Research Paper No. 2063, September.

Barth, J. R., G. Caprio, Jr. and R. Levine (2006). *Rethinking Bank Regulation: Till Angels Govern*, Cambridge, UK: Cambridge University Press.

Barth, J. R., G. Caprio, Jr. and R. Levine (2012). *Guardians of Finance: Making Regulators Work for Us*, Cambridge, MA: MIT Press.

Barth, J. R., T. Li, W. Lu, T. Phumiwasana and G. Yago (2009). *The Rise and Fall of the U.S. Mortgage and Credit Markets: A Comprehensive Analysis of the Meltdown*, Hoboken, NJ: John Wiley & Sons.

Barth, J. R., A. Prabha and P. Swagel (2012). "Just how big is the too-big-to-fail problem?" *Journal of Banking Regulation*, Vol. 13, pp. 265–299.

Barth, J. R., T. Li, A. Angkinand, Y.-H. Chiang, L. Li (2012). "Industrial loan companies: Where banking and commerce meet," *Financial Markets, Institutions & Instruments*, Vol. 21, No. 1, pp. 1–69.

Barth, J. R. and D. McCarthy (2012). "Trading losses: A little perspective on a large problem," Milken Institute Research Reports, October 24.

Brummer, C. (2012). *Soft Law and the Global Financial System: Rule Making in the 21st Century*, Cambridge, UK: Cambridge University Press.

Calomiris, C. (2009). "In the world of banks, bigger can be better," *Wall Street Journal*, October 19.

Clearing House Association (2011). "Understanding the economics of large banks," November.

Gorton, G. and A. Metrick (2012). "Getting up to speed on the financial crisis: A one-weekend-reader's guide," *Journal of Economic Literature*, Vol. 50, No. 1, pp. 128–150.

Haldane, A. G. (2012). "The dog and the frisbee," Bank of England, August 31.

High-level Expert Group on Reforming the Structure of the EU Banking Sector (Liikanen report), 2012, Brussels, October 2.

Hoenig, T. M. (2012). "Back to basics: A better alternative to Basel capital rules." Speech to the American Banker Regulatory Symposium, Washington, DC, September 14.

Hughes, J. P. and L. J. Mester (2011). "Who said large banks don't experience scale economies? Evidence from a risk-return-driven cost function," Federal Reserve Bank of Philadelphia, Working Paper No. 11–27.

Independent Commission on Banking, Final Report Recommendations (Vickers report), 2011, September.

Johnson, S. and J. Kwak (2010). *13 Bankers: The Wall Street Takeover and the Next Financial Meltdown*, New York: Pantheon.

Kashyap, A., J. C. Stein and S. G. Hanson (2010). "An analysis of the impact of 'substantially heightened' capital requirements on large financial institutions," Harvard University mimeo, May.

Kaufman, G. G. (2002). "Too big to fail in banking: What remains?" *Quarterly Review of Economics and Finance*, Vol. 42, pp. 423–436.

Krugman, P. (2010). "Financial reform 101," *New York Times*, April 1.

Prabha, A. and C. Wihlborg (2012). "Cross-border banking in subsidiaries and branches: Organization, supervision and resolution," in *Handbook of Safeguarding Global Financial Stability*, G. Caprio, Jr. (ed.), London, UK: Elsevier, pp. 285–296.

Saunders, A. and I. Walter (2010). "Financial architecture, systemic risk, and universal banking," *Financial Markets and Portfolio Management*, Vol. 26, No. 1, pp. 39–59.

Scott, H. (2010). "Implications of the 'Volcker rules' for financial stability," Committee on Banking, Housing and Urban Affairs, US Senate, Washington, D.C., February 4.

Shull, B. (2010). "Too big to fail in financial crisis: Motives, countermeasures, and prospects," Bard College, Levy Economics Institute Working Paper No. 601, Annandale-on-Hudson, New York.

Swagel, P. L. (2011). "Enhanced supervision: A new regime for regulating large, complex financial institutions," testimony on large complex financial institutions, U.S. Senate, Committee on Banking, Housing, and Urban Affairs, Subcommittee on Financial Institutions and Consumer Protection, Washington, DC, December 7.

Wallison, P. J. (2012). "Breaking up the big banks: Is anybody thinking?" American Enterprise Institute for Public Policy Research, August–September.

Wheelock, D. C. and P. W. Wilson (2012). "Do large banks have lower costs? New estimates of returns to scale for U.S. banks," *Journal of Money, Credit and Banking*, Vol. 44, No. 1, pp. 171–199.

Wihlborg, C. "Developing distress resolution procedures for financial institution," *SUERF Studies*, The European Money and Finance Forum, forthcoming.

Restructuring the Banking System to Improve Safety and Soundness

Thomas M. Hoenig*
Federal Deposit Insurance Corporation

Charles S. Morris
Federal Reserve Bank of Kansas City

Executive Summary

Proposal

This paper provides a specific proposal to limit the financial activities that are covered, and thus subsidized by, the government safety net in order to protect the financial system and the economy. The US safety net, which consists of central bank loans to solvent but liquidity strained banks and federal deposit insurance, was developed in the early 1900s to protect commercial banks.

The safety net originally was limited to commercial banks because they are critical to an economy's overall health and growth. Their core activities of making loans funded by short-term deposits provide essential payment, liquidity, and credit intermediation services. But banks also are inherently unstable because depositors will "run" if they believe their bank is in financial trouble.

*Thomas M. Hoenig is the Vice Chairman of the Federal Deposit Insurance Corporation. Charles S. Morris is a Vice President and Economist at the Federal Bank of Kansas City. This is a revised version of a paper originally issued in May 2011. The views in this paper are those of the authors and not those of the Federal Deposit Insurance Corporation, the Board of Governors of the Federal Reserve, the Federal Reserve System, or the Federal Reserve Bank of Kansas City. Michal Kowalik, an economist in the Banking Research Department at the Bank, contributed substantially to the proposal. The authors would like to thank Viral Acharya, Matt Richardson, Larry White, Richard Sylla, Thomas Philippon, Lasse Pedersen, Jacob Goldfield, and Nada Mora for helpful comments and suggestions.

While the safety net solves the instability problem, it also creates incentives to take excessive risk because it subsidizes banks. With safety net protection, depositors and other protected creditors are willing to lend to banks at lower interest rates, given the amount of risk. This cheaper funding and reduced market discipline creates incentives for banks to make riskier investments and increase leverage. The subsidy and associated incentive to take greater risks have grown substantially over the past 30 years because the activities the safety net supports have expanded beyond the core banking activities considered necessary to protect.

The recommendation in this paper is to limit the safety net — and thus its subsidy — to what the safety net should protect by restricting banking organization activities by business line. Under the proposal, banking organizations would continue to provide the core services of commercial banks — making loans and taking deposits to provide payment and settlement, liquidity, and credit intermediation services. Other allowable services would be securities underwriting, merger and acquisition advice, trust, and wealth and asset management. Banking companies would not be allowed to conduct broker–dealer activities, make markets in derivatives or securities, trade securities or derivatives for either their own account or customers, or sponsor hedge or private equity funds.

The difference between what banks would and would not be allowed to do is based on the principle that beyond their core services, they should not conduct activities that create such complexity that their management, the market, and regulators are unable to adequately assess, monitor, and control bank risk-taking. Current activities conducted by banks that would be prohibited for them, such as trading and market-making, are important to the economy. But they should not be subsidized by the safety net because it causes their overproduction, and therefore imposes unnecessary risks and costs on the financial system and economy. In fact, by removing the safety net's protection for activities such as securities and derivatives market-making, the market for these services should become more competitive and less dominated by the largest investment banks, which currently are all affiliated with commercial banks.

The benefits of prohibiting banks from conducting high-risk activities outside of their core business, however, would be limited if those activities continue to threaten stability by migrating to the "shadow" banking system. Shadow banks are financial companies not subject to prudential supervision and regulation that use short-term or near-demandable debt to fund longer-term assets. In other words, shadow banks essentially perform the same critical, core functions as traditional banks, but without an explicit safety net or prudential regulation. As a result, the shadow banking system is susceptible to disruptions that threaten financial and economic stability and lead to additional implicit government guarantees and the associated incentive to take excessive risks.

To mitigate the incentive for shadow banks and other financial companies to take excessive risk and the associated potential systemic effects, this paper makes two additional recommendations. First, money market mutual funds and other investment funds that are allowed to maintain a fixed net asset value (NAV) of $1 should be required to have floating net asset values. Second, bankruptcy law for repurchase agreement collateral should be rolled back to the pre-2005 rules, which would eliminate mortgage-related assets from being exempt from the automatic stay in bankruptcy when a borrower defaults on its repurchase obligation.

The problem with fixed NAVs and current bankruptcy law is they provide special treatment — that is, they essentially subsidize — short-term funding. As with the safety net for banks, the subsidy leads to the overproduction of risky shadow banking activities. By reining in this subsidy, these two recommendations should greatly curtail shadow banking activities by exposing shadow bank creditors to the true costs of their investments.

Why Restricting Activities Is the Solution

The reduced market discipline and incentive to take excessive risk caused by the safety net has long been recognized, which is one of the major reasons for the prudential supervision of banks. The incentive to take *excessive* risk traditionally has been contained through strong onsite examinations and minimum capital requirements that were supplemented as appropriate based on the exam results. This does not mean that banks do not take risks, nor that they do not make mistakes that cause them to fail. Banking is a business of risk-taking, and when they do make bad decisions that lead to insolvency or liquidity problems, they should fail and be resolved. Thus, it is the prevention of excessive risk-taking arising from the safety net subsidy that prudential supervision is supposed to stop.

This traditional financial structure and regulatory framework worked well for many years, and it still does for those banks that still operate within the framework, which includes all but the largest universal banks. That framework has three components. First, it limits bank activities to those essential to the economy but inherently unstable. Second, it provides a safety net for banks and their limited activities, which prevents the instability but has undesirable side effects. Third, it includes strong supervision to control the side effects.

The current financial structure, however, is vastly different. Leading up to the financial crisis, the financial system became dominated by a handful of large *and* complex financial organizations, and these companies have become even more dominant. These complex universal banking companies combine traditional banking activities with a variety of investment banking and insurance activities.

The problem with this change in structure is not that banks are larger, but that the scope of the safety net and its subsidy — and therefore their sizes — has expanded beyond the traditional bank activities that provide external social benefits. The subsidy is provided, either explicitly or implicitly, to the organization as a whole and not limited to the specific activities for which it was intended. The riskiness of banks can be reduced by the additional activities, for example, if they increase the diversification of bank assets and revenue streams. However, the riskiness of banks also can be increased by the additional activities because they not only are subsidized by the safety net, but also because they create complexity that makes it more difficult for bank management, the market, and regulators to assess, monitor, and contain the excessive risk-taking induced by the safety net. Moreover, the large size of the universal banks — both individually and collectively given the increased interconnections among them — further endangers the stability of the financial system and the overall economy. Thus, the social costs of extending the safety net to large, complex universal banks that cannot be sufficiently monitored by their own management, the market, or regulators greatly exceeds the private benefits to an individual bank.

Evolution of Current Financial Structure

Over the past 30 years, the US banking system has changed dramatically from the stylized view of banking that arose from the banking panics of the early 1930s. The structure of the banking industry that emerged from the 1930s separated investment banking and other financial services from "traditional" commercial banking — making loans and taking deposits to provide payment, liquidity, and credit intermediation services. These core banking services are the foundation of the financial infrastructure that is critical for the overall health of an economy and its growth.

Regulation

The 1930s financial structure that lasted largely until the end of the century was shaped by three major legislative and regulatory changes: the Glass–Steagall Act, creation of federal deposit insurance, and the Federal Reserve's Regulation Q.

The Glass–Steagall Act typically refers to four provisions of the Banking Act of 1933 that separated commercial and investment banking. Deposit (i.e., commercial) banks were prohibited from conducting securities activities (underwriting and dealing) or affiliating with companies that conducted securities activities. The rationale was that banks are crucial for a well-functioning economy because they settle payments, provide deposits that are available at par value on demand, and are the primary source of credit for the vast majority of businesses and individuals. These functions are a critical part of the economy's financial infrastructure.

Banks are provided access to a public safety net because of their importance and susceptibility to runs from using demand deposits to fund longer-term, illiquid loans. Prior to the 1930s, the Federal Reserve's discount window provided a limited safety net for solvent banks.[1] The public safety net was significantly enhanced in 1933 by passage of the Federal Deposit Insurance Act and the associated provision of limited deposit insurance because it protected depositors of banks that failed.

Access to a safety net, however, increases the incentive for banks to take excessive risks. Given the importance of a stable banking system, the

[1] Also, only members of the Federal Reserve could borrow from the discount window until the Monetary Control and Depository Institutions Deregulation Act of 1980.

necessity of a public safety net to provide the stability, and the resulting incentive to take greater risk, a mechanism is needed to prevent banks from taking excessive risks and endangering the safety net. The market cannot be solely relied upon to prevent the risk-taking because some deposits are insured and banks are inherently opaque. As a result, prudential supervision and regulation must be used to prevent excessive risk-taking.

One of the key regulations of the Banking Act of 1933 was the prohibition of paying interest on demand deposits and the authority to impose ceilings on savings deposit rates, which was implemented through the Federal Reserve's Regulation Q. The rationale for Regulation Q was to prevent competition for deposits from causing instability in the banking system.

The combined effect of the Glass–Steagall Act, bank access to a government safety net, prudential supervision and regulation, and deposit rate ceilings was a fairly stable, profitable banking industry with a positive franchise value for many years. The franchise value was protected to the extent banks were protected from outside competition and competition among themselves.

Increased Competition

Over time, banks faced increasing competition on both the liability and asset sides of the balance sheet. The increase in competition was spurred by advancements in portfolio theory, investment and money management techniques, and information technology combined with greater volatility of the economic environment.

On the liability side, banks had to compete with money market mutual funds (MMMFs) and savings association NOW accounts that paid interest on close substitutes for bank demand deposits. They also faced greater competition for household savings from mutual funds, pension funds, and insurance companies.

MMMFs started in 1971 as a competitive alternative to bank deposits because they paid a market interest rate and were allowed to maintain a net asset value (NAV) of $1 a share as long as their actual NAV is greater than 99.5 cents (i.e., they do not "break the buck") and not too far above $1, and they met certain investment (quality and maturity) requirements. They allow investors to withdraw funds on demand and have limited check-writing privileges. MMMF shares are held by individuals, institutional investors, and corporate and noncorporate businesses as an alternative to bank deposits for cash management and payments purposes. MMMFs started out investing in highly rated financial and nonfinancial company commercial paper (CP) and short-term Treasury securities, and then over the years expanded to other money market instruments (MMIs), such as asset-backed commercial paper (ABCP), and short-term repurchase agreements (repos).

It is important to note that although an MMMF investor technically owns equity shares of the fund — that is, there is *no leverage* — the investor is more like a depositor because the expectation is that funds can be withdrawn at a par value of $1 a share — that is, there is no equity and *leverage is infinite.* As a result, MMMF investors act more like depositors and will run whenever they are concerned about a fund's safety so they can redeem their shares for $1 before the fund "breaks the buck" and reduces the value of the shares.

NOW accounts were developed by savings and loans in the early 1980s as a competitive alternative to demand deposits that paid interest. NOW accounts essentially were just like demand deposits — funds were available upon demand and had unlimited check-writing privileges — but they could pay interest because the depository institution reserved the right to require notice before allowing funds to be withdrawn or transferred by check.

On the asset side, banks faced competition in making loans from investment banks (junk bonds, securitization, and nonfinancial commercial paper), mortgage brokers, and specialty lenders such as unaffiliated finance companies (primarily consumer lending), captive lenders (auto financing, retailers), and factors (trade receivable lending).

Banks have long faced competition in making loans from unaffiliated and captive finance companies and factors. Commercial paper became a competitive alternative to bank operating loans for large, highly-rated nonfinancial companies in the late 1960s and early 1970s.

Competition for bank loans increased substantially beginning in the 1980s with the growth of junk bonds and an ability to originate and distribute loans through the development of mortgage-backed securities (MBS), followed by other types of asset-backed securities (ABS), which are typically backed by consumer loans (credit cards, auto, student).

Shadow Banking

The combination of alternatives to bank deposits and loans created an alternative system for providing complete end-to-end banking — from gathering funds to making loans — which collectively comprises the so-called shadow banking system.[2] In contrast to a typical bank that conducts the entire process of borrowing funds from savers, making loans to ultimate borrowers, and holding the loans to maturity, credit intermediation through the shadow banking system is a vertical process that takes place through a series of entities — collectively called shadow banks — similar to a supply-chain manufacturing process.

Funding for each of the entities takes place in wholesale markets. Money market instruments — specifically CP, ABCP, and short-term repos — are a major source of funds at virtually each step in the process.[3] The major investors in the MMIs are MMMFs and other short-term investment funds that have a fixed NAV of $1.[4] At some steps of the process, major funding sources also include medium-term notes and ABS that are purchased by long-term investors, such as mutual funds, pension funds, and insurance companies. A typical example of the shadow banking intermediation process is as follows:

1. A loan is made by either a nonbank financial company or a bank. The nonbank companies finance the initial loans with CP or medium-term notes (MTN).
2. The loan is sold to a bank or broker–dealer conduit, which is an intermediate entity that temporarily warehouses the individual loans until it has enough to package together as an MBS or ABS. The conduits are funded with ABCP.
3. The loan warehouse sells the package of loans to a securitization sponsor that sets up a trust to hold the loans, which is financed by selling MBS/ABS backed by the loans. This is the only step in the process not financed by MMIs.

[2] The description of the shadow banking system and the process described below is largely from Pozar *et al.* (2010).

[3] The one exception is the step that actually securitizes loans into MBS/ABS.

[4] There are also direct investors in these money market instruments, such as securities lenders.

4. The ABS are purchased by a variety of entities that are funded by a variety of sources.
    a. Entities that purchase ABS and tend to fund them with longer-term sources of funds include mutual funds, pension funds, and insurance companies.
    b. BHCs may purchase ABS and hold them on bank balance sheets funded by deposits. However, prior to the financial crisis, they generally held them in off-balance-sheet entities, such as structured investment vehicles (SIVs) or other conduits, that were funded by CP or ABCP. The CP or ABCP, in turn, was typically purchased by MMMFs and other MMI funds with fixed $1 NAVs.
    c. Investment banks and BHCs purchase ABS for a variety of reasons. They may be held by a securities subsidiary as a proprietary trading asset, in inventory for filling customer trades, or warehoused for creating collateralized debt obligations (CDOs). The ABS are typically funded with repos and sometimes ABCP, which again are funded by MMMFs and other MMI funds with fixed $1 NAVs.

Expansion of Bank Activities

Increased competition for banks from the shadow banking organizations combined with regulatory capital requirements (stemming from the Basel I Accord) that were higher than for their competitors led to reduced profits and declining franchise values. As a result, banking organizations looked for alternative activities, revenue streams, and business models, which included the originate-to-distribute shadow banking business model. Whereas the traditional banking model of making loans and holding them to maturity earned profits from loan-deposit rate spreads, the shadow banking model earned profits from fees and trading gains.

Some banks responded to the increased competition by focusing first on being able to engage in traditional investment banking and securities activities and later more broadly on broker–dealer and shadow banking activities. Banks were able to whittle away at the Glass–Steagall Act restriction on investment banking activities in the 1990s by creating Section 20 securities subsidiaries that were supported by Federal Reserve Board approvals of higher thresholds for being "principally engaged" in securities activities.[5]

To fully participate, however, banks needed the Glass–Steagall Act prohibition on affiliation with securities companies to be repealed, which was achieved with the passage of the Gramm–Leach–Bliley Act (GLBA) in 1999. The GLBA allowed the formation of financial holding companies (FHCs), which were BHCs engaged in certain nonbanking activities, such as securities underwriting, broker–dealer activities, and insurance underwriting, not permitted for BHCs.

Significant changes in the investment banking industry also occurred to take full advantage of the opportunities of the shadow banking industry. With the growth of bond markets and the development of MBS securities in the 1980s, investment banks moved from partnership structures to public corporate structures. The corporate structures essentially allowed the investment banks to engage in riskier activities that put the firm's capital at risk, such as proprietary trading, leveraged lending, and hedge fund sponsorship, that the partners were much less willing to do when their own money was at risk. The risks were exacerbated by relying on debt financing, i.e., leverage, much of which was short-term repos. In fact, it became much easier to use debt after 2004 when the SEC allowed broker–dealers to use their internal risk management models to compute the haircuts for calculating their net capital.[6]

[5]One of the Glass–Steagall Act provisions was Section 20 of the Banking Act of 1933, which prohibited Federal Reserve member banks from affiliating with organizations that "engaged principally in the issue, floatation, underwriting, public sale, or distribution of stocks, bonds, debentures, notes, or other securities." For many years, the administrative limit for not being "principally engaged" was that underwriting and dealing accounted for 5% or less of a subsidiary's gross revenue. As banks became larger, underwriting and dealing became cost effective even with the 5% revenue limit. Over time, banking organizations began petitioning for larger limits, which the Federal Reserve agreed to based on assessments of the risks and benefits to the economy, with the limit eventually rising to 25% in 1997.

[6]Prior to the 2004 SEC ruling, the SEC determined the haircuts used to calculate the leverage ratios of broker–dealers. The 2004 ruling allowed the broker–dealers to use their internal risk management models to compute these haircuts. The ruling followed a similar change to the Basel I Accord in 1996, under which commercial banks could compute their capital requirements for trading positions using their own models.

Implications for Financial Structure, Stability, and Risk

Changes in Financial Structure and Stability

The sharp line between commercial and investment banks is significantly blurred as each has engaged in shadow banking activities. The larger banking organizations engage in activities that were traditionally limited to investment banks, which exposes them to investment bank risks. Traditional banks that take in deposits and make and hold loans to maturity have to manage credit and interest rate risk. As FHCs have expanded activities to earning fees from trading and ABS underwriting, their risk exposures expanded to include market risk from trading and the risk from having to roll over uninsured wholesale money market funding risks.

Similarly, the larger investment banks now engage in activities that were traditionally limited to commercial banks, which exposes them to commercial bank risks. By switching from partnerships to public corporate structures, taking on leverage, and making direct investments and loans that are held on the balance sheet, investment banks expanded their risk exposures beyond market risk to credit and funding risk.

With the largest financial companies — both banking and investment banking organizations — being the key players in shadow banking activities, both types of organizations play a special role in the economy that once was limited to commercial banks. Through shadow banking activities, both types of organizations ultimately provide the same credit intermediation function of traditional banks — lending long term using short-term funds available upon demand.

The expansion of activities by commercial and investment banks has led to a less stable financial system because it is dependent on wholesale, money market funding without an explicit safety net of insurance and access to central bank lender-of-last-resort facilities. Just like banks were subject to depositor runs that created liquidity crises before deposit insurance was available, virtually every step of the shadow banking process is dependent on uninsured investments in MMMFs and other MMI funds with fixed NAVs of $1. Investors in these money market funds have full access to their money as long as the underlying NAV is $1 or more, so once concerns arise about the quality of the underlying assets, i.e., that the underlying NAV will drop below $1, investors have an incentive to withdraw their funds before others. A loss in funding at any step of the process will cause the system to break down just like a loss in funding at a traditional commercial bank.

The heavy involvement of large banking organizations (in the form of FHCs) and investment banks in shadow banking activities exposes them to similar risks that previously had been eliminated by deposit insurance in retail banking. Bank subsidiaries are still protected from insured depositor runs, but the holding companies and banks are now exposed to money market fund runs.

The bank subsidiaries also are exposed to money market runs because the banks often provide credit lines on the ABCP that fund ABS held by affiliated holding company subsidiaries, such as off-balance-sheet conduits and SIVs. The ABCP often needs a credit line or guarantee so that it has the AAA rating needed to make it an eligible investment for MMMFs. So if MMMFs decide not to roll over their ABCP investments in a SIV and the value of the underlying ABS is below par, the SIV would sell the ABS to the bank guarantor at par, which means the bank takes the loss and has to fund the ABS on balance sheet. In other words, the credit and funding risk to the bank from guaranteeing the off-balance-sheet funding of ABS with ABCP is the same as if it held the underlying ABS on its own balance sheet.

To make matters worse, even though the risks to the bank of holding assets on balance sheet or guaranteeing them off balance sheet are the same, FHCs had an incentive to move the assets off balance sheet because it can fund those assets with much less capital.[7] Specifically, the risk-based capital requirements of FHCs had a much higher risk weight for holding the loans or ABS on balance sheet than for guaranteeing the ABCP funding of an off-balance-sheet entity. As a result of this arbitrage of regulatory

[7]Acharya, Schnabl, and Suarez (2011) provide evidence consistent with regulatory arbitrage being a reason for the use of ABCP programs by banks. They also document changes in regulatory rules that enabled banks to perform this type of regulatory arbitrage. In July 2004, the OCC, Federal Reserve, FDIC, and OTS exempted assets in ABCP programs from the calculation of risk-weighted assets. As a result, assets moved from banks' balance sheets to ABCP programs did not have to be considered when calculating risk-weighted assets for capital requirements. Moreover, under the Basel I and Basel II Accords, assets placed in ABCP programs carried lower capital charges than the same assets carried on balance sheets.

capital requirements, FHCs became much riskier because they could fund the credit risk with much higher leverage.

FHCs also are exposed to runs by money market investors even if the MMIs are not fully guaranteed because of reputational risk. Although subsidiary conduits and SIVs that hold ABS are technically bankruptcy remote, FHCs either purchase assets and bring them on balance sheet or provide capital support to avoid the negative reputational effects of defaulting on the securities funding the subsidiaries.

Finally, the broker–dealer subsidiaries of investment banks and FHCs also are exposed to MMI runs. As already noted, broker–dealers use repos and ABCP to fund ABS held as part of their proprietary trading business, as inventory for filling customer trades, and for creating CDOs.

New Activities Make It More Difficult to Manage and Monitor Risk

Overall, the largest financial companies conduct a variety of traditional and nontraditional banking activities, many of which have increased the complexity of their operations and portfolios. The potential problem is not that the new activities are risky — all financial activities are inherently risky, even traditional banking activities. These companies may even benefit from additional activities, for example, if they increase the diversification of their assets and revenue streams. However, it is more likely that these benefits are outweighed by the significant complications the activities pose for bank management, the market, and regulators to assess, monitor, and contain risk-taking that is ultimately borne by the public safety net and endangers financial stability. Specifically, as explained below, combining banking and nonbanking activities makes it more difficult for bank management to manage risk, for the market to monitor and effectively discipline banks, and for regulatory authorities to supervise and regulate banks and price deposit insurance.

Risk management complexity. Complexity makes risk management much more difficult.[8] Risk management is particularly difficult when a banking organization has many different operational divisions and activities.

---

[8]All aspects of managing a large, complex financial company is difficult, but given the context of this paper, the focus is on risk management.

Examples include understanding all of the different business lines and their interactions, having appropriate management information systems, and appropriately allocating and pricing capital across activities. Such difficulties and shortcomings in risk management practices and effectiveness at several US and foreign global banking organizations leading up to and during the recent financial crisis are highlighted in two reports by the Senior Supervisors Group (2008, 2009).

The risk management of a complex institution can also vary with the background of its senior leadership. For example, trading is risky in the short term, so it attracts people predisposed to taking risks. In contrast, lenders tend to have a longer term perspective. As a result, an organization's risk culture and appetite is likely to be lower if its senior leadership has a commercial banking background rather than a trading background.

To the extent that a bank's senior management has difficulty understanding and managing its risks, it is even more difficult for supervisors to scrutinize and monitor a banking organization's risks.

Reduced transparency reduces market discipline. Banking organizations with a variety of nontraditional activities tend to be less transparent than others, which makes it difficult for the market to discipline their risk-taking. Relative to nonfinancial companies, it is difficult for investors to evaluate the condition of traditional banks and their riskiness because their balance sheet assets and activities are opaque and easily changed.[9] Traditional banking is opaque because banks have more information than investors about the quality and risk of their loans. Banks that engage in nontraditional activities, such as trading, hedge funds, private equity, and market-making are even less transparent because the success of these strategies depends on the confidentiality of their positions and speed at which their exposures can be changed. Given the lack of transparency, regulators must play a larger role relative to the market in monitoring and disciplining banks, but as discussed below, regulators also are at a disadvantage when dealing with banks that are engaging in nontraditional activities.

[9]Morgan provides evidence on the increased opacity of banks from combining lending and trading activities.

Some activities make bank supervision more difficult. The goal of prudential supervision is to control excessive risk-taking by banks so that they are safe and sound and do not endanger the safety net. Supervision includes reviewing a bank's operations and risk management policies; monitoring its financial condition, lending, operations, risk management, and other practices; and enforcing regulatory rules. Because of the periodic nature of bank supervision, supervisors get only a snapshot of bank processes, risk exposures, and capital positions at a given time. Even for the largest complex banking organizations, at which supervisory staff work on site and are continuously looking at some part of the organization and its operations, supervisors still only have snapshots of various operations, albeit at higher frequencies. These snapshots are limited in their ability to predict the safety of a bank's processes, its risk exposures, and its capital positions between supervisory examinations. The flexibility to adjust risk profiles between exams depends, to some extent, on a banking organization's activities and the nature of the risks.

Many of the nontraditional activities that the large, complex banking organizations engage in are difficult to supervise effectively because they are very risky in the short term, which can quickly change a bank's risk profile. For example, trading and market-making are high frequency activities that result in thousands of daily transactions. As a result, snapshots of the positions of these activities may have limited predicative value for future positions. Continuous supervision at the largest banking organizations clearly provides a better understanding of their risks than the traditional approach of periodic exams. Nevertheless, understanding and monitoring the risks still can be difficult, especially when management itself has difficulties in understanding and monitoring risk. Thus, while bank supervision is not meant to prevent risk-taking, and is subject to errors regardless of a bank's activities, effective supervision of complex organizations that engage in many nontraditional banking activities is even more difficult.

Regulation complexity. Banks with a variety of activities require much more complex regulations, which can be difficult for management, the market, and regulators to monitor and understand. The history of the Basel capital requirements provides a good example of the difficulty in effectively regulating complex financial companies. The increased variety and complexity of bank activities required much more complex capital standards, which the financial crisis showed were not very effective in adequately aligning bank risks with capital levels.

One problem is that the various capital requirements under Basel are essentially relative prices, and they are set either administratively through regulation or using the banks' own internal models. Administratively setting risk weights generally will misprice risks. In addition, allowing banks to set risk weights with their own risk models can systematically under price risk. In fact, news articles (Braithwaite, 2011; Vaughan, 2011) cite several examples of US and foreign banks that plan on "managing" risk weights or are engaging in "risk-weighted asset optimization" to lower their risk-weighted assets and increase their risk-based capital ratios. Thus, it should not be surprising that leading up to the financial crisis the regulatory capital requirements did not adequately align bank capital levels with their risk.

The Basel requirements also created opportunities for regulatory arbitrage that was a major contributor to the risk-taking of the large, complex banking companies and the financial crisis. For example, the capital charge for an MBS based on a pool of subprime loans was lower than that for a portfolio of mortgages held on the balance sheet. Capital charges were also lower for an MBS held in off-balance-sheet conduits than on the balance sheet.

Deposit insurance pricing. Complexity of activities makes it difficult to price deposit insurance. Deposit insurance would not lead to excessive risk-taking if the premiums were priced appropriately to reflect a bank's risk. However, pricing deposit premiums correctly is difficult for the same reasons that it is difficult to determine capital requirements.

Resolution complexity. To the extent it is possible, resolving large, complex banks is much more difficult and costly. Even with the FDIC's new authority under the Dodd–Frank Act to liquidate a failed complex banking organization, doing so in a quick and orderly manner will be difficult.

The Lehman Brothers failure in 2008 is a good example of the difficulty in resolving a complex company. The number of transactions and complexity of interconnections made it very difficult to determine the company's value quickly enough to find a buyer and have it reopened the following Monday morning. Moreover, Lehman Brothers was a relatively simple company compared to some of the largest BHCs. Some of these BHCs have a thousand or more majority-owned subsidiaries, several of which could be as large and complex as Lehman Brothers. It would be much harder to wind down or find enough buyers to transfer the critical operations necessary for an orderly resolution.

In summary, the financial system has become less stable over the past 30 years as banks and other financial companies have expanded into more complicated activities. The root of the problem is that large, complex financial companies are funding long-term, illiquid assets with liabilities available upon demand. In addition, after the crisis, the concentration of the industry and complexity of activities at the largest banks increased. The industry is dominated by a handful of companies that combined are half as large as annual US economic output, and the failure of any of them could cause financial instability. Finally, because these companies are so large and complex, they and other institutions that are viewed as systemically important receive an implicit government guarantee on their debt and sometimes on their equity, which creates the incentive to take excessive risk, thereby further increasing systemic risk (the too-big-to-fail problem).

Proposal to Reduce Costs and Risks to the Safety Net and Financial System

This proposal to reduce costs and risks to the safety net and financial system has two parts. The first part proposes to restrict bank activities to the core activities of making loans and taking deposits and to other activities that do not significantly impede bank management, the market, and regulators in assessing, monitoring, and controlling risk. However, prohibiting banks from engaging in activities that do not meet these criteria and that threaten financial stability would provide limited benefits if those activities migrate to shadow banks. The second part proposes changes to the shadow banking system by making recommendations to reform money market funds and the repo market.

Restricting Activities of Banking Organizations

The financial activities of commercial, investment, and shadow banks can be categorized in the following six groups (Richardson, Smith, and Walter, 2010):

— Commercial banking — deposit taking and lending to individuals and businesses.
— Investment banking — underwriting securities (stocks and bonds) and providing advisory services.
— Asset and wealth management services — managing assets for individuals and institutions.
— Dealing and market-making — securities, repos, over-the-counter (OTC) derivatives.
— Brokerage services — retail, professional, and institutional investors, and hedge funds (prime brokerage).
— Proprietary trading — trading for own account and owning hedge and private equity funds.

Using the criterion for permissible activities stated above, banking organizations would be able to conduct the following activities: commercial banking, investment banking, and asset and wealth management services. Investment banking and asset and wealth management services are mostly fee-based services that do not put much of a firm's capital at risk. In addition, asset and wealth management services are similar to the trust services that always have been allowed for banks.

In contrast, the other three categories of activities — dealing and market-making, brokerage, and proprietary trading — have little in common with core banking services and create risks that are difficult to assess, monitor, and control. Banking organizations would not be allowed to do any trading, either proprietary or for customers, or make markets because it requires the ability to do trading.[10] In addition, allowing customer but not proprietary trading would be difficult to enforce because the securities inventory used to facilitate customer trading cannot be easily distinguished

[10]Banking organizations would be allowed to purchase and sell derivatives to hedge their assets and liabilities.

from proprietary assets. Prime brokerage services not only require the ability to conduct trading activities, but also allow companies to finance their activities with "free balances," which can be highly unstable funds.[11]

Other potential restrictions include limits on bank investments. Historically, bank investments were restricted to loans and investments in investment-grade securities. As demonstrated in the financial crisis, the complexity of many asset-backed securities made it very difficult to determine their credit quality. As a result, consideration should be given to restrictions on investing in "complicated" securities, such as multilayer structured securities (e.g., CDOs) that are difficult to value, and to determine and monitor credit quality.

Off-balance-sheet holdings and exposures should be supervised and regulated as if they were on-balance-sheet because, as was also demonstrated in the crisis, they ultimately put a bank's capital at risk.

The recommended activity restrictions would make banks more transparent and would enable better risk management, market discipline, supervision, regulation, and resolution. Specifically, the proposed activity restrictions will improve the risk management of banks by focusing their activities solely on the traditional banking business with exposure only to risks inherent in these activities.

The underlying factors that make commercial banking successful are inherently different from those that make securities firms successful. Banking is based on a long-term customer relationship where the interests of the bank and customer are the same. Both the bank and loan customers benefit if borrowers do well and are able to pay off their loans. In contrast, trading is an adversarial zero-sum game — the trader's gains are the customer's losses. Thus, restricting these activities removes a conflict of interest between a bank and its counterparty customers, which could produce a more stable, less risky company.

The inherent riskiness of securities trading, dealing, and market-making attracts, and in fact requires, people who are predisposed to taking short-term risks rather than lenders with a long-term perspective. The

[11]Hedge funds hold cash balances with their prime brokers to finance and facilitate transactions. "Free balances" is the cash a hedge fund client has a right to demand on short notice.

combination of securities with commercial banking activities in a single organization provides opportunities for the senior management and boards of directors to be increasingly influenced by individuals with a short-term perspective. As a result, the increased propensity of these corporate leaders to take risk leads to more of a short-term-returns culture throughout the organization.

Prohibiting the activities mentioned above would allow capital regulation to be simplified and improved. Capital regulation would be simpler and more effective because there would be less need for complicated risk-based requirements if the balance sheet is largely limited to loans and investment-grade securities. For example, capital regulation could be structured as a relatively high, simple leverage ratio combined with supervision.[12] Moreover, regulatory arbitrage between balance-sheet and off-balance-sheet activities and between banking and trading books is difficult to prevent with regulation.

Critics of restricting bank activities argue it would reduce the economies of scale and scope that are critical for the largest banks to be successful in global markets and that large corporations want one-stop shopping for their financial services. These arguments, however, are not persuasive.

First, there is no strong evidence of economies of scale at the sizes of the largest banking companies. There are many conceptual and empirical problems with studies of economies of scale.[13] Nevertheless, older studies from the 1990s show that there are no economies of scale when banks are larger than about $250 million in assets, although the threshold is likely to be higher in today's economy because of inflation and advancements in information technology. Although a more recent study from the mid-2000s suggests there are economies of scale for the largest banking organizations, the results are highly questionable because there are so few banks at the sizes in question and the study uses data prior to the problems that banks had during the financial crisis.

[12]Admati *et al.* (2011) provide an excellent discussion of the reasons for substantially increasing bank capital requirements. Hellwig (2010) provides arguments for abandoning risk-sensitive capital requirements.

[13]DeYoung (2010) comments that it is not really possible to provide empirical evidence for or against existence of economies of scale in large and complex financial institutions because there are too few of them for a meaningful statistical analysis to be conducted.

Second, there is even less evidence of economies of scope.[14] In fact, there is evidence that multiple functions of large, complex banks actually increase systemic risk and anecdotal evidence that if bank activities are restricted as suggested here, a more competitive nonbank financial industry would emerge and thrive.

Third, large corporations would still be able to do one-stop shopping for commercial and traditional investment banking services, although they would have to go to securities dealers to purchase swaps and other derivatives for hedging purposes.

Finally, even if there are economies of scale or scope, it does not necessarily mean that banks should be allowed to continue to conduct all of their current activities. Whether they should depends on comparing the marginal benefits from the reduced private costs of operation to the social costs associated with financial crises. Given the large costs of the 2007–2009 crisis and the continued weakness of the economic recovery five years after the crisis began, the efficiencies and cost benefits of size and scope would need to be extremely large.

Critics of restricting activities also question how we would go about divesting the prohibited activities. The divestitures that were required by the Glass–Steagall Act and the breakup of AT&T in the 1980s suggest that divestitures can be conducted in an orderly manner in a relatively short period of time.

Critics of restricting activities also are concerned that it would cause two major problems for US banks because they would face a competitive disadvantage relative to universal banks, mostly from Europe, that are allowed to conduct the full range of activities. One problem is it would drive US banks to move to other countries. However, it seems highly improbable that any other country would be willing or able to expand its safety net to new large and complex banking organizations. Second, the competitive disadvantage of US banks would lower their franchise values, which would provide an incentive to take even greater risks to raise lost revenues and maintain ROEs. However, the virtue of restricting activities is that it is

[14] Richardson, Smith, and Walter (2010) provide a survey of empirical studies on economies of scale.

easier for the supervisors and the market to detect, prevent, and if necessary punish excessive risk-taking.

Reforming the Shadow Banking System

Restricting the activities of banking organizations alone, however, does not completely address the stability of the financial system. In fact, it could worsen the risk of financial instability by pushing even more activities from the regulated banking sector to large, interconnected securities firms, which would expand the sector that was an integral part of the financial crisis.

As previously discussed, the source of this instability is the use of short-term funding for longer-term investment in the shadow banking market, i.e., the maturity and liquidity transformation conducted by a lightly regulated/unregulated sector of the financial system. We believe this source of systemic risk can be significantly reduced by making two changes to the money market.

The first recommendation addresses potential disruptions coming from money market funding of shadow banks — money market mutual funds and other investment funds that are allowed to maintain a fixed \$1 NAV should be required to have floating net asset values. The primary MMIs today are MMMFs and repos. Individuals, institutional investors, and non-financial companies are the primary holders of MMMF and other MMI funds with a fixed \$1 NAV, which in turn are major investors in repos along with other financial companies.

Some have suggested that MMMFs should be backed by government guarantees. We see no reason why the safety net should be extended and the taxpayer put at risk when other solutions are feasible. In addition, providing government guarantees would require prudential supervision to prevent excessive risk-taking, but it would not be effective because of the ability of funds to rapidly shift their risk profiles.

The runs during the crisis on MMMFs occurred because of concerns about the quality of their investments and because of the promise to maintain a \$1 NAV. MMMF investment rules have been strengthened by increasing the minimum average quality and decreasing the maximum average maturity of their investments.[15] However, because of the difficulty in calibrating these requirements, it is not clear that the vulnerability of MMMFs to runs in a systemic event would be significantly reduced as long as the fixed $1 NAV is maintained. We believe reliance on this source of short-term funding and the threat of disruptive runs would be greatly reduced by eliminating the fixed $1 NAV and requiring MMMFs to have floating NAVs.

Critics of eliminating a $1 NAV for MMMFs argue that this limits cash management options for large corporations. However, MMMFs were first introduced to evade interest rate ceilings on deposits, and the only remaining Regulation Q deposit rate ceiling — the prohibition of paying interest on business transactions deposits — was eliminated by the Dodd–Frank Act. Some may be concerned that their deposits will be largely uninsured, but they are uninsured when invested in MMMFs. In addition, European MMMFs historically have mostly used floating NAVs. Although the percentage of fixed NAV European MMMFs has increased in recent years, the majority still have floating NAVs.

The second recommendation addresses potential disruptions stemming from the repo financing of shadow banks — the bankruptcy law for repurchase agreement collateral should be rolled back to the pre-2005 rules. By making this change, mortgage-related assets would no longer be exempt from the automatic stay in bankruptcy when a repo borrower defaults on its repurchase obligation.

One reason for the runs on repos during the crisis was because of the prevalence of repo borrowers using subprime mortgage-related assets as collateral. Essentially, these borrowers funded long-term assets of relatively low quality with very short-term liabilities. The price volatility of subprime MBS rose sharply when subprime defaults started reducing MBS income flows. As a result, haircuts on subprime repos rose sharply or the repos were not rolled over.

[15] Some of the new rules for MMMFs are: 30% of assets must be liquid within one week, no more than 3% of assets can be invested in second-tier securities, the maximum weighted-average maturity of a fund's portfolio is 60 days, and MMMFs have to report their holdings every month.

The eligibility of mortgage-related assets as collateral exempt from the automatic stay in bankruptcy in case of default by the borrower is relatively recent. The automatic stay exemption allows the lender to liquidate the collateral upon default as opposed to having to wait for the bankruptcy court to determine payouts to secured creditors.

Prior to 2005, collateral in repo transactions eligible for the automatic stay exemption was limited to US government and agency securities, bank certificates of deposits, and bankers' acceptances. The Bankruptcy Abuse Prevention and Consumer Protection Act of 2005 expanded the definition of repurchase agreements to include mortgage loans, mortgage-related securities, and interest from mortgage loans and mortgage-related securities. This meant that repos collateralized by MBS, CMOs, CMBS, and CDOs backed by mortgage-related assets became exempt from the automatic stay.

We believe the problem of runs by repo lenders would be significantly reduced by rolling back the bankruptcy law for repurchase agreement collateral to the pre-2005 rules. The problem with the current bankruptcy law for repos is it provides special treatment — that is, it essentially subsidizes — short-term funding with mortgage-related collateral relative to other longer-term repo collateral or securities-based lending. As with the safety net for banks, the subsidy leads to the overuse of short-term repo funding, and therefore the overproduction of risky shadow banking activities.

Overall, these two changes to the rules for money market funds and repo would increase the stability of the shadow banking system because term lending would be less dependent on "demandable" wholesale funding and more reliant on term funding. Fixed NAVs, like the just-noted problem with current repo bankruptcy law, provide special treatment and therefore subsidize short-term funding. These subsidies lead to an overreliance on short-term funding and excessive risk in shadow banking activities. With the recommended changes, shadow banks would rely less on short-term wholesale funding and more on term funding, which would continue to be provided by institutional investors such as mutual funds, pension funds, and life insurance companies. While this might increase the cost of funds and, therefore, the cost of mortgages and other consumer loans, it would be less risky and more reflective of the true costs.

References

Acharya, V., P. Schnabl and G. Suarez (2011). "Securitization without risk transfer," Social Science Research Network Working Paper, August.

Admati, A. R., P. M. DeMarzo, M. F. Hellwig and P. Pfleiderer (2011). "Fallacies, irrelevant facts, and myths in the discussion of capital regulation: Why bank equity is *Not* expensive," Rock Center for Corporate Governance, Stanford University Working Paper No. 86, Stanford University, Graduate School of Business Research Paper No. 2065, March.

Braithwaite, T. (2011). "Banks turn to financial alchemy in search for capital," *Financial Times*, October 24.

DeYoung, R. (2010). "Scale economies are a distraction," *The Region*, Federal Reserve Bank of Minneapolis, Vol. 24, No. 3, September, pp. 14–16.

Hellwig, M. (2010). "Capital regulation after the crisis: Business as usual?" Max Planck Institute for Research on Collective Goods, reprint 2010/31.

Morgan, D. (2002). "Rating banks: Risk and uncertainty in an opaque industry," *American Economic Review*, Vol. 92, No. 4, September, pp. 874–888.

Pozsar, Z., T. Adrian, A. Ashcraft and H. Boesky (2010). "Shadow banking," Federal Reserve Bank of New York Staff Report No. 458, July.

Richardson, M., R. Smith and I. Walter (2010). "Large banks and the Volcker rule," Chapter 7 in *Regulating Wall Street: The Dodd-Frank Act and the New Architecture of Global Finance*, V. V. Acharya *et al.* (eds.), Hoboken, NJ: New York University Stern School of Business, John Wiley & Sons Inc., pp. 181–212.

Senior Supervisors Group (2008). "Observations on risk management practices during the recent market turbulence," Report, March 6.

Senior Supervisors Group (2009). "Risk management lessons from the global banking crisis of 2008," Report, October 21.

Vaughan, L. (2011). "Financial alchemy foils capital rules as banks redefine risk," Bloomberg, November 9.

Ending Too Big to Fail: A Proposal for Reform

Richard W. Fisher and Harvey Rosenblum*

Federal Reserve Bank of Dallas

The US economy, along with much of the global economy, is still struggling with weak economic growth some five years since the last official recession began in December 2007. The long and deep recession, in combination with tepid growth that has been unresponsive to monetary and fiscal policy stimulus, has produced a growing burden of government debt — a so-called fiscal cliff — that has compromised the federal government's and the Federal Reserve's ability to respond to future shocks.

Financial institutions deemed to be "Too Big to Fail" (TBTF) were at the epicenter of the 2007–2009 financial crisis and have been a key source of the failure of government policies to gain the necessary traction to return the US economy to its long-term growth trajectory of just under 3% annually. We contend that the Dodd–Frank Wall Street Reform and Consumer Protection Act ("Dodd–Frank") has, in the short run, exacerbated weak economic growth by increasing regulatory uncertainty in key sectors of the US economy. In the long run, Dodd–Frank will not live up to its promise of ending TBTF, but will, instead, entrench TBTF firms, thereby guaranteeing another financial crisis, likely bigger than the last one.

---

*Richard Fisher is President and Chief Executive Officer, and Harvey Rosenblum is Executive Vice President and Director of Research, at the Federal Reserve Bank of Dallas. The views expressed are those of the Federal Reserve Bank of Dallas and not necessarily those of others in the Federal Reserve System. The authors thank David Luttrell for his excellent assistance throughout this project.

To reduce the likelihood of such a catastrophic outcome, we recommend that TBTF financial institutions be restructured into multiple business entities, each of which will have a safety net — federal deposit insurance and access to the Federal Reserve's discount window — available only to its downsized commercial banking entity, but totally unavailable to its shadow banking affiliates.

Costs of the Financial Crisis

Putting a price tag on the 2007–2009 financial crisis is a daunting task. The costs of crippled consumer and business confidence, lost educational and job opportunities, increased uncertainties, not to mention human misery and suffering, are not easily amenable to conventional measurement. Estimates of lost output and income, reduced wealth, extended unemployment claims and other safety net programs, and the costs of extraordinary government interventions in support of the financial service industry and other corporations can be compiled. For example, output per capita in the US is 1.3% below its prior peak attained in the fourth quarter of 2007. Had this recession been more like the average of the last six recessions, per capita output would have returned to prior peak levels by year-end 2009. As it stands, given the current economic growth trajectory, per capita output will likely not return to its prior peak until late 2013, and will likely not attain its prior projected trend for at least another decade! Our back-of-the-envelope estimate is that costs like these aggregate to as much as $10–20 trillion, with the wide range due in part to the uncertain time frame over which the recovery-to-trend trajectory will occur. To put this estimate in perspective, annual output in the US, that is, GDP, is about $15 trillion. Adding to this cost burden is the fact that these adverse impacts will likely endure for years to come and will reduce the capacity of the US government — ultimately the insurer of last resort — to respond to the next crisis, whatever its source.

Clearly, the benefits of avoiding such catastrophic outcomes in the future warrant a search for solutions that will truly reduce the likelihood and costs of another financial crisis and not place excessive reliance on a vague promise of reform.

Earlier Statements on the Need to End TBTF

Over the last several years, we have written extensively on the need to quickly and meaningfully address policies that perpetuate the belief that some financial institutions, and their customers and creditors, are TBTF (see references section). The consistent bottom line of our analysis has been, and continues to be: "Though it sounds radical, restructuring is a far less drastic solution than quasi-nationalization, as happened in 2008–2009" (Fisher and Rosenblum, 2012). Responses to this viewpoint have been extensive, both in agreement and disagreement, with many suggestions for refinement having been offered. Until now, we have purposely refrained from saying how banking institutions should be restructured or what the acceptable limits are for size, product, and geographic diversity; complexity; and interconnectedness. Our goal has been to stimulate input from a wide variety of experts, especially business and banking practitioners. A selection of these responses has been compiled and published by the Dallas Fed (*Summer Reader 2012* and *Holiday Reader 2012*).

Defining and Reducing the Impact of TBTF

What does TBTF mean in practice? Our definition is firms whose owners, managers, and customers believe them to be exempt from the *processes* of bankruptcy and creative destruction. Such firms capture the financial upside of their actions, but largely avoid much of the downside, thereby violating one of the basic tenets of market capitalism (at least as it is supposed to be practiced in the US). Such firms enjoy subsidies relative to their non-TBTF competitors and are likely to grow faster and take greater risks in search for profits, especially because bankruptcy is a highly unlikely outcome.

As practiced in the 21st century, TBTF is the result of an implicit (but widely understood) government-sanctioned policy of coming to the aid of the owners, managers, and creditors of a financial institution deemed to be so large, interconnected, and/or complex that its demise could substantially damage the financial system and the economy if the institution were allowed to fail. By reducing a TBTF firm's exposure to losses from excessive risk-taking, such policies undermine the discipline that market forces normally provide to management decision-making. This reduction of market discipline has been further eroded by implicit extensions of the federal safety net beyond commercial banks to their nonbank affiliates. Moreover, industry consolidation, fostered by subsidized growth of the shadow banking portion of banking companies, further perpetuates and enlarges the list of financial firms deemed TBTF, promoting "survival of the fattest rather than . . . survival of the fittest" (Fisher).[1]

The stated goal of the Dodd–Frank Act is "an Act to End Too Big to Fail." Dodd–Frank is long on promise and process, but will likely be short on results. The statute itself is 849 pages, with more than 8,800 pages of proposed regulations having been written, and only about one-third of the required regulations having been finalized as of year-end 2012. To effectively end TBTF, Rosenblum (2012) recommended that those writing the regulations implementing Dodd–Frank should "simplify and codify quickly." The opposite has been done, with the result that Dodd–Frank contributes complexity and confusion to regulatory and supervisory discipline in the financial arena, thereby increasing economic uncertainty and stifling economic growth.

Dodd–Frank has undermined the ability of banking regulators and supervisors, as well as bankers, to follow the new law. It is difficult, if not impossible, to enforce, let alone comply with, rules that are not easily and generally understood.

The Role of Market and Regulatory Discipline

Market and regulatory discipline play important roles in restraining excessive risk-taking by banks, at least for more than 99% of all US banking institutions. Unfortunately, neither market nor regulatory discipline has much influence on the 0.2% of banking firms that could be clearly labeled TBTF.

As of third quarter 2012, there were nearly 5,600 banking organizations in the US. The bulk of these, roughly 5,500 in number, were community

[1] For further discussion of the macroeconomic threat posed by the largest financial institutions, see Fisher and Rosenblum (2009).

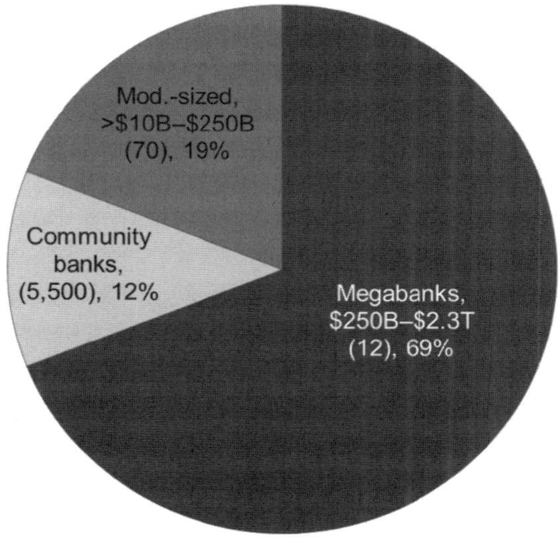

Fig. 1. The US banking industry concentration conundrum.

Note: Data for commercial banks and bank holding companies as of September 30, 2012. Asset size is based on the total assets of a US banking organization (holding company, when applicable).

Source: Call Report, Federal Financial Institutions Examination Council; Consolidated Financial Statements for Bank Holding Companies (FR Y-9C), National Information Center data, Federal Reserve System; authors' calculations.

banking organizations with assets less than $10 billion (Fig. 1). These community bank-focused organizations comprised 98.6% of all banking organizations but only 12% of industry assets. Another group comprises roughly 70 banking organizations with assets between $10 billion and $250 billion. This group of moderate-sized BHCs controls 19% of industry assets, while accounting for 1.2% of the number of organizations. The remaining group, the megabanks —- those with assets between $250 billion and $2.3 trillion — are composed of a mere 12 institutions, roughly 0.2% of all banking organizations, but with 69% of industry assets. The dozen institutions that presently account for 69% of total industry assets are among the few candidates to be considered TBTF because of the threat they could pose to the financial system and the economy should one or more of them get into trouble. By contrast, should any of the other 99.8%

	Can Fail Outright?	Speed of Resolution	Regulatory Discipline	Market Discipline from: Shareholders	Market Discipline from: Unsecured Creditors
Community Banks (5,500)	Yes	Weekend	Often significant	Some, often considerable	Too few to matter
Regional / Moderate-Sized Banks (70)	Yes	Few weeks to 18 months	Significant, but slow	Significant, but lagged	Some, possibly significant
Megabanks (12)	No	Never closed	Insufficient, may be ineffective	Limited	Perverse

Fig. 2. Bank size and Complexity versus impact of external discipline.

of banking institutions get into trouble, they most likely could be handled with private sector ownership changes and minimal governmental intervention. How and why does this work for 99.8% but not the other 0.2%?

To answer this question, we analyze the sources of regulatory and market discipline imposed on each of the three groups of banks (Fig. 2). We examine two dimensions of regulatory discipline:

- Potential closure of the institution; and
- The effectiveness of supervisory pressure on bank management practices.

In short, do the owners and managers of a banking institution operate with the belief that their institution is subject to a type of bankruptcy process that works reasonably quickly to transfer ownership and control to another banking entity? Can management be replaced and ownership value wiped out? In addition, is there a group of interested and involved shareholders who can exert a restraining force on risk-taking by the bank's top management team? Would we determine that the firm is controlled by its owners, or would we call it, effectively management-controlled?[2] In addition, we examine the extent to which uninsured creditors of the banking entity, knowing that the entity might be subject to

[2]The distinction between owner-controlled versus management-controlled firms goes back to Berle and Means (1932).

a bankruptcy process, impose risk-management discipline on the firm's management.

Community banks (Fig. 2, line 1) are subject to considerable external discipline. Community banks can and do fail. In the last few years, the FDIC has built a reputation for carrying out Joseph Schumpeter's concept of creative destruction for small banks, with a bank being taken over by FDIC staff on a Friday evening, but reopening on Monday morning under new ownership and with a new management team. The entire process, requiring preparation and planning that extends beyond a single weekend, comes down to "in on Friday and out on Monday," the antithesis of TBTF. Knowing the power of their banking supervisors to close the institution, owners and managers of community banks must pay some heed to supervisory suggestions to limit risk. Community banks often have a few significant shareholders who have a considerable portion of their wealth tied to the fate of the bank; risk and potential closure matter to them. Community banks, however, derive the bulk of their funding from federally insured deposits, so uninsured and unsecured creditors provide limited, if any, market discipline. For community banks, shareholder and regulatory discipline matter most.

Of the three size-groups, the roughly 70 regional and moderate-sized BHCs are subject to the most market discipline. Like community banks, these institutions are not exempt from the bankruptcy process; they can and do fail, but given their size, complexity, and generally larger geographic footprint, the failure resolution and ownership transfer process cannot be accomplished over a weekend. Nonetheless, the failure process is definite and unequivocal. Owners and managers of mid-sized institutions should be aware of the downside consequences of the risks taken by the institution. Uninsured depositors and unsecured creditors should also be aware of their unprotected status in the event the institution were to experience financial difficulties. However, the financial information they do receive is often incomplete and delayed — that's why we see large market reactions to what may appear to be small restatements of earnings or announced losses. Mid-sized banking institutions receive considerable external discipline from both supervisors and market-based signals.

On the other hand, TBTF megabanks receive far too little regulatory and market discipline. This is unfortunate given that such discipline has to be focused on so few institutions, each of which, if it were allowed to fail, could be disruptive to important segments of financial markets and the economy. For all intents and purposes, we believe that TBTF banks have not been allowed to fail outright.[3] Knowing that, the management of TBTF banks can, with impunity, choose to ignore the recommendations and guidance of their bank supervisors' efforts to impose regulatory discipline.

For TBTF banks, the forces of market discipline are limited. Having millions of stockholders leaves management of TBTF banks considerable freedom to pursue corporate strategies that are profitable for management, not necessarily shareholders. As is the case with mid-sized banking institutions, adverse information on poor financial performance generally becomes available with a long lag, often when it is too late for shareholder reactions to have a significant impact on management behavior. Shareholders do participate in the institution's poor financial performance. During the financial crisis, the stock of two of the largest BHCs showed declines of more than 95% from their prior peak price.[4] But the damage from excessive risk-taking had already been done. After the crisis, efforts by shareholders of many of the largest institutions to meaningfully influence management compensation practices were rebuffed. So much for stockholder-imposed market discipline for TBTF banking institutions.

Another important facet of TBTF is that the funding sources for megabanks extend far beyond insured deposits. The largest banks, not just the TBTF banks, fund themselves with a wide range of liabilities including, to name just a few: (1) large, negotiable CDs, much of which exceeds the FDIC insurance limit; (2) federal funds purchased from other banks (all uninsured); and (3) subordinated notes and bonds, generally unsecured. It is

[3]Two banking institutions, Citigroup and Bank America Corp., received massive and extraordinary government assistance in 2009, but were never listed as failures in the FDIC database, nor were they ever included on the list of "problem banks." Discipline without teeth probably leads the management of such institutions to "turn a deaf ear" to their supervisors. Rod Stewart said it well in his song "Young Turks": "But there ain't no point in talking, when there's nobody listening."

[4]See Rosenblum, Renier, and Alm (2010), Chart 1, p. 6. More specifically, Citigroup and Bank America Corp. experienced peak-to-trough declines in their common stock prices of over 96%.

not unusual for such uninsured/unsecured liabilities to comprise well over half the liabilities of TBTF institutions. If market discipline were to be imposed on TBTF institutions, one would expect it to come from uninsured/unsecured depositors, creditors, and debt holders. But the TBTF status exerts a *perverse market discipline* on the risk-taking activities of these banks. Recognizing the implicit government guarantee of the liabilities of TBTF financial institutions, including those issued by the parent company and nonbank subsidiaries, depositors and creditors offer their funds at a discount relative to the rates demanded from mid-size and regional banks. This TBTF subsidy is quite large, and has risen during and following the financial crisis.

Recent estimates by the Bank for International Settlements suggest that the implicit government guarantee provides the largest US BHCs with an average credit rating uplift of more than two notches, thereby lowering their average funding costs by *a full percentage point* relative to their smaller competitors (BIS, 2012). Andrew Haldane (2012), with the Bank of England, estimates the current implicit TBTF global subsidy to be roughly $300 billion per year for the 29 global institutions identified by the Financial Stability Board (2011) as "systemically important." To put that $300 billion estimated subsidy in perspective, *all US BHCs* reported aggregate 2011 earnings of $108 billion.

To recap, TBTF banking institutions operate with very limited and even perverse regulatory and market discipline. The implicit subsidy provided by government policy enables TBTF banking institutions to:

- Grow more rapidly than their smaller competitors;
- Take excessive risks, with seeming impunity;
- Undermine the stability of the financial system; and
- Impose trillions of dollars of costs on the economy and taxpayers.

Furthermore, these perverse outcomes seem to be continuing in spite of, or perhaps reinforced by, Dodd–Frank.

Is this what we want as a nation? What steps can be taken to remediate this issue? If nothing is done to address the unintended impacts of TBTF policies, how might the next financial crisis play out? The answer could conceivably be that the largest BHCs would consolidate even more, with perhaps two megabanks ending up with 75% of banking industry assets. Surely, this is *not* the intended goal of public policy.

A Proposal for Reform

In keeping with the spirit of our past recommendations to address the issue of TBTF, we believe strongly in the principle that market forces, perhaps aided and prodded by government policy, should reshape and restructure the TBTF banking institutions into smaller, less complex institutions that are:

- Economically viable;
- Profitable;
- Competitively able to attract financial capital, talented personnel, and management; and
- Of a size, complexity and scope where both regulatory and market discipline will restrain excessive risk-taking.

As demonstrated in the previous section, mid-sized and regional BHCs, and community banks as well, satisfy these four characteristics.

In guiding the changes that need to be undertaken, four additional principles should be followed. Changes to the financial system should be:

- Simple;
- Easy to understand;
- Accomplished with minimal statutory modifications; and
- With as little government intervention as possible.

We believe these principles can be adhered to with TBTF policies being reversed through a three-part plan:

(1) Roll back the federal safety net to apply only to basic, traditional commercial banking.
(2) Clarify through simple, understandable disclosures that the federal safety net applies only to the commercial bank and its customers, and never ever to the customers of any other affiliated subsidiary or the parent holding company.

We believe that parts (1) and (2) of our plan would, over a long time span, begin to impose market discipline on the nonbank affiliates of TBTF institutions, eventually removing the TBTF subsidy. However, undoing customer inertia and management habits at TBTF banking institutions would take too many years, during which the subsidies and perverse incentives of TBTF banks will maintain or increase their size and risk profile, thereby sowing the seeds for another financial crisis, likely worse than the last one, a few years down the road. To reduce the severity and immediacy of another crisis, and to put the financial system in a more stable equilibrium, a third step is necessary:

(3a) Downsize and restructure the TBTF BHCs to the point where the safety net-supported commercial banking part of the BHC is appropriately sized such that both regulatory and market discipline will work effectively; and,
(3b) Restrict (or possibly prohibit) the ability to move assets or liabilities from a shadow banking affiliate to a banking affiliate within the BHC.

In essence, we advocate that 100% of banking institutions should become Too Small to Save (TSTS) and that none should remain TBTF. Treat the largest 0.2% of institutions the same way as the other 99.8%. This can happen only if the very largest banking institutions are restructured into drastically smaller, separately owned and competing entities. In short, we need a single, uniform policy for all financial institutions: **Every institution should be TSTS. No institution should be TBTF.**

To illustrate how the first two points in our plan would work, we show the hypothetical structure of a financial holding company (Fig. 3). The financial holding company has a commercial bank subsidiary and several

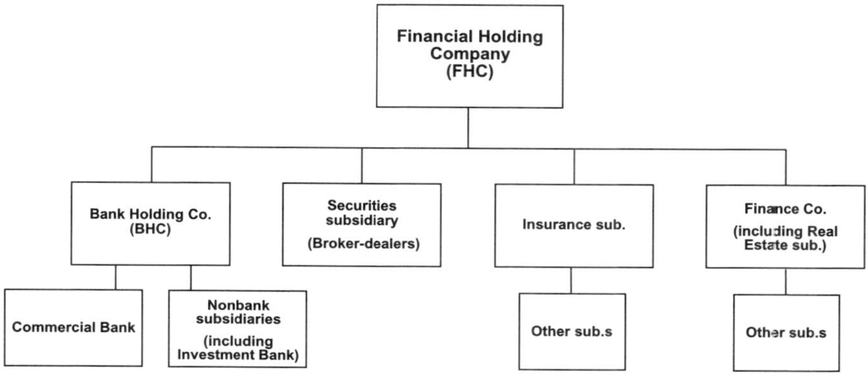

Fig. 3. Typical financial holding company structure.

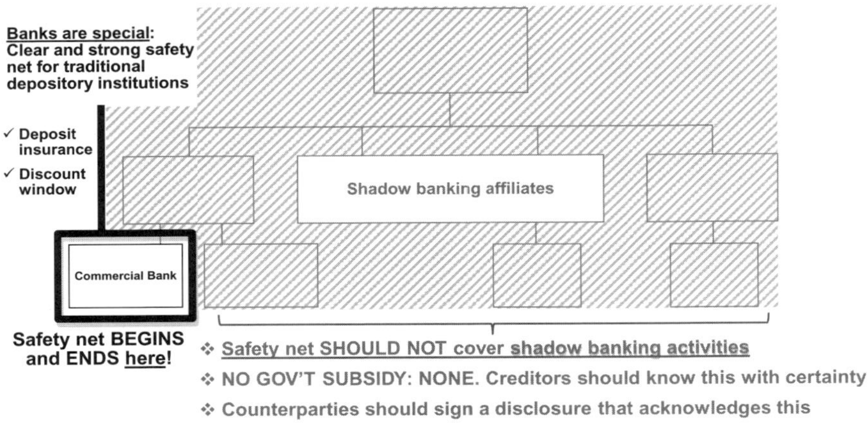

Fig. 4. Clearly define where the safety net begins and ends.

subsidiaries that are not traditional commercial banks. Such a holding company would likely include insurance, securities underwriting and brokerage, and finance company operations.

For simplicity, we can label all the operations, other than the commercial banking operation, as *shadow banking affiliates* (Fig. 4).[5] The commercial bank has access to deposit insurance provided by the FDIC and discount window loans provided by the Federal Reserve. These two features of the safety net begin and end with the commercial bank. They would explicitly, by statute, become unavailable to any shadow banking affiliate.[6]

To reinforce the statute and add to its credibility, every customer, creditor, and counterparty of every shadow banking affiliate, including the parent BHC and financial holding company, would be required to agree to and sign a simple disclosure statement that acknowledges their unprotected status. A sample disclosure can be seen in Fig. 5. This last step should begin to remove the implicit TBTF subsidy provided to shadow banking operations of BHC affiliates, thereby slowing down the growth of shadow

[5]For a review of shadow banking, see Luttrell, Rosenblum, and Thies (2012).

[6]The Federal Reserve Board could make an emergency exception to its discount window policy by offering support to preserve the functioning of markets for high-quality assets, rather than support for a nonbank institution. An example from the 2007–2009 financial crisis is the Commercial Paper Funding Facility (CPFF).

A disclaimer, such as:
"WARNING: Conducting business with this banking affiliate
carries NO federal deposit insurance or other
federal government protection or guarantees."

A signed disclosure, such as:
"I, ______, fully understand that in conducting business with ______ banking affiliate,
I have NO federal deposit insurance or other federal government protection or guarantees.
None."

Fig. 5. Simple sample disclaimer and disclosure.

banking operations that have benefited from an implicit safety net, thereby leveling the playing field with competitors who face market and regulatory discipline.

As indicated earlier, some government intervention may be necessary to accelerate the imposition of effective market discipline. We believe that market forces should be relied upon as much as practicable, but that entrenched oligopoly forces, in combination with customer inertia (or perceived high switching costs relative to the benefits of changing established bank relationships), will likely only be overcome through government-sanctioned reorganization and restructuring of the TBTF BHCs. In doing so, as little government intervention as necessary should be used to reestablish a competitive landscape and level playing field.

The irony is that roughly 99.8% of all banking institutions are not, by any stretch of the imagination, likely to fall into the TBTF category. Less than 0.5% of all US BHCs, less than 25 and more likely as few as 10, *might* be considered TBTF. Part of the reluctance to support a breakup or restructuring of the TBTF BHCs owes to the uncertainty of knowing where to draw the line. How big is too big? Why subject the owners, managers, employees, and customers of a clearly TBTF bank to a restructuring if there is no single, clearly identifiable size that delineates TBTF from not-TBTF? But absent an externally imposed mandate to break up the existing TBTF institutions, banking industry consolidation will continue as more financial institutions seek to merge to take advantage of the TBTF subsidy. Thus, if we do nothing, an ever-expanding list of TBTF institutions seems to be an inevitable outcome. This is a far more unpalatable outcome than the breakup solution, and provides a compelling argument for acting sooner, not later.

It's Not Just Size — Complexity Matters Too

We have argued that breaking up and restructuring the megabanks is a far less radical plan of action than the quasi-nationalization of several financial institutions as happened in 2008–2009. In the next financial crisis, nationalization of several TBTF banks could become a distinct possibility. Under the Orderly Liquidation Authority provisions of Dodd–Frank, a systemically important financial institution would receive debtor-in-possession financing from the US Treasury over the period during which its operations needed to be stabilized. This is quasi-nationalization, just in a new, and untested, format. Government ownership of our financial institutions, even on a "temporary" basis, is a clear perversion of our capitalist principles.

The equity market, too, has been sending signals on the need to restructure several of the biggest and most complex BHCs (Fig. 6). The recent stock

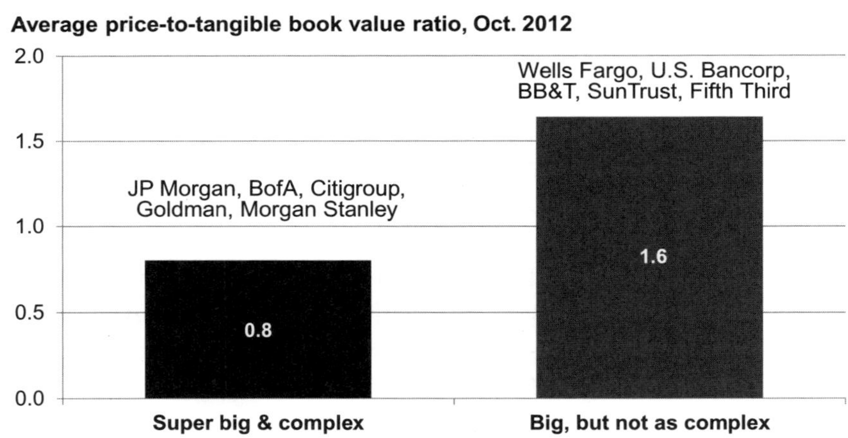

Fig. 6. Equity market rewards reduced complexity.

Note: The "big, but not as complex" group includes banks larger than $100 billion in assets and predominately driven by commercial/retail banking activities rather than "global banking" or investment services and management.
Source: Bloomberg: author's calculations.

market performance of the five "super big and complex BHCs" (JPMorgan Chase, Bank of America, Citigroup, Goldman Sachs, and Morgan Stanley) demonstrates that their shareholders value these companies at less than their accounting value if they were to be liquidated. In October 2012, these behemoth banks traded at 80% of tangible book value, a 20% discount, due at least in part to the fact that investors have trouble comprehending what these companies do, and estimating the risks embedded in their balance sheets. The stock market performance of five of their largest US competitors (Wells Fargo, US Bancorp, BB&T, SunTrust, and Fifth Third) reveals that the stock of these BHCs sells at a 60% *premium* to tangible book value. A common characteristic of these five "big, but not as complex BHCs" is the dominance of traditional banking activities in their corporate structures, and therefore, a much smaller involvement in shadow banking activities. Given that shareholders value the assets of the less complex, banking-focused BHCs at *double* their tangible book value *relative* to the super big/complex five BHCs, the message seems clear: Shareholders of the Big 5 are telling management that their companies should be broken up and sold off; *the sum of the parts is worth more than the whole.*

Unfortunately for these shareholders, the market for corporate control of large banking companies is highly restricted by statute and regulation. A group of hedge funds, private equity companies, and/or wealthy investors cannot buy up a controlling interest in these BHCs and then sell off the parts to maximize shareholder value, as would be done in the case of, say, a manufacturer, or a restaurant or retail chain. This markdown of shareholder value reinforces the point made above that shareholders seem powerless in comparison to the bargaining strength of entrenched management, not only with respect to compensation practices but also with the underlying business models and focus of the companies. As long as management can continue to participate in garnering some portion of the TBTF subsidy, they have little incentive to alter their business model. Were the TBTF subsidy to accrue to shareholders, the shares would likely sell at a premium to tangible book value, instead of the significant discount that prevails.

In a recent speech, Fed Governor Daniel Tarullo (2012) suggested that consideration be given to capping the size of the largest financial institutions. Rather than use assets as a measure of size, Governor Tarullo suggested using nondeposit liabilities, scaled by percentage of US GDP (seen

	Total Non-Deposit Liabilities ($B)	Non-Deposit Liabilities as a % of GDP	Total Subsidiaries	Countries of Operation
J.P. Morgan Chase	$983	6.3%	5,183	72
Bank of America	890	5.7	4,647	56
Goldman Sachs	817	5.2	3,550	53
Citigroup	816	5.2	3,556	93
Morgan Stanley	609	3.9	2,718	64
Wells Fargo	258	1.7		
Bank of NY Mellon	74	0.5		
U.S. Bancorp	73	0.5		
PNC Financial	52	0.3		

Fig. 7. How big is "too big"?

Note: Bank data and calculations as of June 30, 2012.
Source: See McGrane (2012) and Financial Stability Oversight Council (2012).

in Fig. 7, columns 2 and 3). The Big 5 have a scale that is roughly 10 times larger than that of other BHCs, excluding Wells Fargo, which is very large but not nearly as complex.

Another distinguishing feature of the Big 5 is their complexity, as measured by the total number of subsidiaries and the number of countries in which each BHC operates. Is a financial institution TBTF by definition if it has 3,500 to 5,000 subsidiaries in 50 to 90 countries? Can there be any real regulatory discipline imposed on any institution that is too big and complex to close? And can shareholders or unsecured creditors impose any market discipline on such an institution? Are such institutions too big and complex to manage effectively, or have they simply grown this big and complex through TBTF subsidies?

To add a degree of perspective to the matter of size and complexity, the geographic reach of Lehman Brothers should be reviewed for comparison. Lehman Brothers declared bankruptcy in September 2008, the largest bankruptcy in US history, with total liabilities of $619 billion. More than four years later, the Lehman bankruptcy is still not completely resolved.

Following Lehman's Chapter 11 filing, global money and capital markets seized up, and only began to function more normally a few months later, after the Federal Reserve initiated extraordinary special credit facilities to jump-start US and global financial markets. As of its 10K regulatory filing in 2007, Lehman operated a *mere* 209 subsidiaries across *only* 21 countries. Lehman was a small player compared to any of the Big 5. If Lehman Brothers was too big for a private sector solution to be found for its resolution while still a going concern, what can we infer about members of the Big 5?

Concluding Comments

How "big" is "too big?" Our answer: small enough and noncomplex enough for regulatory and market discipline to work effectively, just as it does for 99.8% of all banking institutions. Our solution: restructure the dozen or so TBTF BHCs into whatever number of institutions such that every last one of them is Too Small to Save (TSTS), just like the rest of the industry.

The full range of financial services desired by the public will still be provided, but by refocused and unsubsidized financial institutions. This should put an end to the decision-making paradigm of the 2008–2009 Financial Crisis that remains embedded in Dodd–Frank: "I'm TBTF, so bail me out or the world will end!" The means to achieving this goal is to **Put the Discipline Back in Market Discipline and Restore Market Discipline to Market Capitalism.**

References

Bank for International Settlements (2012). *82nd Annual Report: 1 April 2011–31 March 2012,* Basel, Switzerland, June 24, pp. 75–76.

Berle, A. A. and G. C. Means (1932). *The Modern Corporation and Private Property,* Macmillan, New York.

Federal Reserve Bank of Dallas (2012). *Holiday Reader 2012.* Available at: www.dallasfed.org/assets/documents/fed/annual/2012winter.pdf.

Federal Reserve Bank of Dallas (2012). *Summer Reader 2012.* Available at www.dallasfed.org/assets/documents/fed/annual/2012summer.pdf.

Financial Stability Board (2011). "Policy measures to address systemically important financial institutions," Report, Basel, Switzerland, November 4.

Financial Stability Oversight Council (2012). *2012 Annual Report*, Washington, DC, July, pp. 141–143.

Fisher, R. W. (2011). "Taming the too-big-to-fails: Will Dodd–Frank be the ticket or is lap-band surgery required?" Remarks before Columbia University's Politics and Business Club, New York, November 15. Available at: www.dallasfed.org/news/speeches/fisher/2011/fs111115.cfm.

Fisher, R. W. and H. Rosenblum (2012). "How huge banks threaten the economy," *Wall Street Journal*, April 4. Available at: http://online.wsj.com/article/SB10001424052702303816504577312110821340648.html.

Fisher, R. W. and H. Rosenblum (2009)."The blob that ate monetary policy," *Wall Street Journal*, September 27. Available at: http://online.wsj.com/article/SB10001424052748704471504574438650557408142.html.

Haldane, A. G. (2012). "On being the right size." Speech at the 2012 Beesley Lectures, Institute of Economic Affairs' 22nd Annual Series, London, October 25.

Luttrell, D., H. Rosenblum and J. Thies (2012). "Understanding the risks inherent in shadow banking: A primer and practical lessons learned," Federal Reserve Bank of Dallas, *Staff Papers*, No. 18, November. Available at: www.dallasfed.org/assets/documents/research/staff/staff1203.pdf.

McGrane, V. (2012). "Which banks could face cap on size?" *Wall Street Journal*, October 11.

Rosenblum, H. (2012). *Choosing the Road to Prosperity: Why We Must End Too Big to Fail — Now*, 2011 Annual Report, Federal Reserve Bank of Dallas, 19. Available at: www.dallasfed.org/assets/documents/fed/annual/2011/ar11.pdf.

Rosenblum, H., J. J. Renier and R. Alm (2010). "Regulatory and monetary policies meet 'too big to fail'," Federal Reserve Bank of Dallas, *Economic Letter*, Vol. 5, No. 3. Available at: www.dallasfed.org/assets/documents/research/eclett/2010/el1003.pdf.

Tarullo, D. (2012). "Financial stability regulation." Speech at the Distinguished Jurist Lecture, University of Pennsylvania Law School, Philadelphia, October 10.

PART VIII

WHERE TO FROM HERE? THE IMPLICATIONS FOR FINANCIAL REGULATORY POLICY

Where to from Here? Implementation, Implementation, Implementation

Claudio Borio*

Bank for International Settlements

Introduction

The question posed to this policy panel is: "Where to from here?" There are times to imagine new buildings and times to complete those already started. This is a time to complete the regulatory building that has been taking shape in response to the Great Financial Crisis. To be sure, this building is far from perfect. But it is a major improvement over what we had before. In his book, *A Theory of Justice*, in which he criticizes much of the preceding philosophical literature on the subject, Amartya Sen rightly notes that it is better to strive for an unambiguous incremental improvement than to shoot for an illusory first best. This is very much where regulatory efforts stand. I will illustrate the point with reference to Basel III, and to its systemic orientation in particular.

I would like to highlight three messages. First, post-crisis, international initiatives have fully recognized the need to strengthen the *systemic orientation* of prudential arrangements — what has come to be known as their "macroprudential" orientation. This has been reflected most clearly in G20 calls to put in place fully fledged macroprudential frameworks in national jurisdictions; indeed, many countries have taken major steps in this direction. Second, Basel III represents the very core of such frameworks; it is a solid foundation on which to build Caruana (2010a). Finally, the shift has

*Claudio Borio is the Deputy Head of the Monetary and Economic Department and Director of Research and Statistics at the Bank for International Settlements. The views are the author's and not necessarily those of the Bank for international settlements.

gone hand-in-hand with useful steps to strengthen international coordination, not just in the design of the standards but, for the first time, in their implementation.

So, in one word, what is the priority going forward? Implementation, implementation, implementation.

Recognition of the Systemic Dimension of Regulation and Supervision

One important lesson from the crisis is that prudential arrangements heavily focused on ensuring the safety and soundness of *individual institutions* are inadequate. It is not reasonable to assess risk and calibrate standards for each institution on a stand-alone basis, as if it operated in splendid isolation from the rest.

Such a microprudential orientation has two drawbacks. It sets the same standards regardless of the impact of the failure of the institution on the financial system. It is as if the same speed limit applied to both trucks and cars. And it sets the same standards regardless of the condition of the system as a whole. It is as if the same speed limit applied irrespective of traffic conditions. In effect, it assumes that the sources of risk, such as asset prices, credit conditions, and the macroeconomy, are independent of what financial institutions collectively do — that is, they are "exogenous."

The macroprudential approach addresses the two drawbacks head-on by focusing on the system as a whole rather than on individual institutions (Borio, 2003, 2011). That is, it focuses on the wood rather than the trees. Such an approach has two key features. It calibrates standards with respect to individual institutions' contribution to systemic risk (the so-called cross-sectional dimension). And it calibrates them taking into account the evolution of risk in the system as a whole (the so-called time dimension). Therefore, it addresses what has come to be known as the "procyclicality" of the financial system — those self-reinforcing processes operating within the financial system and between the financial system and the macroeconomy that tend to amplify financial and real economic fluctuations and that are at the root of financial crises.

In passing, it is worth asking: what is the ultimate source of systemic risk? Put differently: What distinguishes the financial sector from other sectors? To my mind, it is not asymmetric information: This is pervasive elsewhere too. Nor is it safety nets. Admittedly, ill-designed safety nets can make matters worse: The expectation of support in times of stress numbs market discipline. But, analytically, financial crises can occur even without safety nets. And, historically, safety nets were actually put in place precisely in response to crises; they did not precede them.

Rather, I believe that there are two deeper factors at work. The first has to do with the *causes* of crises. In contrast to what occurs in other sectors, in the financial industry supply tends to create its own demand. Elsewhere, an increase in supply reduces the equilibrium price and is stabilizing. If, say, more cars are produced, their price will fall as higher supply meets a given demand. By contrast, in the financial industry, for long phases, an increase in supply actually tends to increase demand — i.e., shift the demand curve outward. What I have in mind is the powerful positive feedback between credit creation — a key output of the industry — asset prices, and the macroeconomy — the main source of procyclicality. Put differently, finance has a certain "bootstrap" element to it that can be destabilizing. The second factor has to do with the *consequences* of crises. Simply put, their damage can be devastating. Here again, the role of credit is critical. As a result, dealing with the time dimension of systemic risk, i.e., with procyclicality, is of paramount importance.

Basel III and Systemic Resilience

Basel III is the very foundation of macroprudential frameworks. It is so in three particular respects:

First, the calibration of higher and better quality capital and, for the first time, liquidity standards was informed by a top-down analysis of what was appropriate for the financial system as a whole; i.e., by an assessment of the costs and benefits in terms of the macroeconomy. The assessment considered both the long term, or steady state, and the transition to it, taking initial conditions into account (BCBS, 2010a; MAG, 2010).

Second, Basel III puts in place tougher solvency standards — higher loss absorbency, including through higher capital — for banks whose failure causes greater damage to the system, so-called systemically important banks (SIBs) (BCBS, 2012a, 2012b). It does so to reduce the likelihood of their failure. This has been complemented by efforts, under the aegis of the

Financial Stability Board, to improve resolution regimes so as to reduce the impact of the failure on the system and also its likelihood, to the extent that the regimes reinforce market discipline by limiting perceptions of official support (the "too-big-to-fail" subsidy).

Finally, Basel III seeks to reduce the procyclicality of financial system. For first time, it puts in place true buffers, not only minimum requirements, which can be drawn down at times of stress (BCBS, 2010a). This can cushion the blow to the system, by avoiding the risk that retrenchment caused by fear of breaching the minimums actually exacerbates systemic stress. And it is true of both capital and liquidity, as the Governors and Heads of Supervision — the governing body of the Basel Committee of Banking Supervision — has made clear (GGHOS, 2012).

More specifically, Basel III has put in place the countercyclical capital buffer (BCBS, 2010b, 2010c; Drehmann *et al.*, 2010; Drehmann, Borio, and Tsatsaronis, 2011). The idea is to have tougher capital standards as risks build up in the system and allow the accumulated capital to be drawn down as problems emerge. It is to build up the defenses of the system when it is cheapest and easiest to do so in order to cushion the blow if strains subsequently materialize. The objective is first and foremost to protect the banks from the financial cycle. But it may also have the collateral benefit of protecting the cycle from the banks, if it succeeds to restrain the financial boom itself. The scheme sets as common reference to guide the build-up of the buffer an indicator of unusually strong and prolonged credit growth — the "credit gap," tracing deviations of the credit-to-GDP ratio from a long-term trend. But this is just a starting point for the richer analysis of vulnerabilities that the authorities are encouraged to do.

International Coordination

It goes without saying: international coordination is necessary in regulation and supervision. The financial system is global. And avoiding regulatory arbitrage is critical.

Basel III addresses this problem head-on and takes coordination to a new level. Let me illustrate the point with the countercyclical capital buffer and with the latest steps to monitor and promote the full, timely, and consistent implementation of Basel III more generally.

The cross-border dimension introduces two problems for the countercyclical capital buffer. There is an indicator problem: What happens if losses are incurred on foreign, rather than domestic, exposures? The credit gap works well to guide the build-up of the buffer if the losses are linked to domestic exposures, such as in the case of the US, UK, or Spain. The reason is that, in this case, a domestic financial boom tends to precede the subsequent bust. But the indicator would have missed completely crises originating from cross-border exposures, such as those in Germany or Switzerland. In this case, the losses were incurred on financial booms elsewhere, notably in the US. Then there is a control problem: How can a national supervisory authority offset the impact of international lending, either granted from outside the country or through local branches, on which supervisors often have less leverage? International lending is a typical way of circumventing domestic regulation.

The countercyclical capital buffer addresses both problems. It addresses the indicator problem by basing the buffer on a weighted average of exposures of individual banks to the various jurisdictions. This makes a major difference for banking systems such as those in Germany and Spain ahead of the crisis: It would have called for an increase in the buffer during the build-up of vulnerabilities (BCBS, 2010b; Drehmann *et al.*, 2010; Drehmann, Borio, and Tsatsaronis, 2011). And it addresses the control problem by putting in place cooperative arrangements based on reciprocity. Specifically, it is the host authority that activates the buffer when it sees signs of build-up of risks in its own jurisdiction; the home authority can require more, but never less, from its own banks on their corresponding exposures. This arrangement represents a major, badly under appreciated shift in responsibility to host authorities, which is fully consistent with the systemic orientation of the scheme. In addition, there will be a supervisory group tasked with monitoring correct implementation of the system. Such a mechanism could be a model of cross-border cooperation for a broader set of instruments.

More generally, as recognized and endorsed by the G20, it is essential to go beyond pure standard setting and to closely monitor and promote the full, timely, and consistent implementation of the standards. This is precisely what the Basel Committee is doing with respect to Basel III. As Stefan Ingves (2011), chairman of the Committee, has aptly put it, "Setting rules without ensuring their implementation is akin to building a lighthouse without ever switching the light on." This is a major new priority of the Committee. The first such reports to the G20 ministers and governors were released in October 2012 and covered the US, the European Union, and Japan. The fact that the reports did not prove uncontroversial indicates that the process is far from toothless.

These examples suggest a broader reflection: In a world in which calls for international macroeconomic cooperation grow louder and are repeatedly disappointed, despite *all* its limitations — and there are many — cooperation in regulation and supervision sets an example for other policy areas to follow.

Conclusion

In my remarks, I have argued that it is now time to move decisively to implement the international regulatory reform agenda that has taken shape in response to the Great Financial Crisis. And I have illustrated the importance of such steps with reference to Basel III, highlighting in particular the aspects of the framework that strengthen its macroprudential orientation. The reforms are far from ideal, but they represent a major improvement compared with what existed before. To oppose them risks throwing away the baby with the bathwater. The best should not be allowed to be the enemy of the good.

That said, let me conclude with a note of caution. It would be illusory to think that better regulation and supervision, by itself, can ensure financial stability. This is true regardless of how macroprudential its orientation is. Ensuring financial stability is far too big a task to rest on the shoulders of regulation and supervision alone. Other policies, especially monetary and fiscal policies, also have a critical role to play (see Caruana, 2010b; Borio, 2012). And much still needs to be done there. But this, as they say, is another story!

References

Basel Committee for Banking Supervision (2010a). "Basel III: A global regulatory framework for more resilient banks and banking systems," Report, Basel, Switzerland, December.

Basel Committee for Banking Supervision (2010b). "An assessment of the long-term economic impact of stronger capital and liquidity requirements," Report, Basel, Switzerland, August.
Basel Committee for Banking Supervision (2010c). "Countercyclical capital buffer proposal — consultative document," Report, Basel, Switzerland, July.
Basel Committee for Banking Supervision (2010d). "Guidance for national authorities operating the countercyclical capital buffer," Report, Basel, Switzerland, December.
Basel Committee for Banking Supervision (2012a). "A framework for dealing with domestic systemically important banks — final document," Report, Basel, Switzerland, October.
Basel Committee for Banking Supervision (2012b). "Global systemically important banks: Assessment methodology and the additional loss absorbency requirement," Report, Basel, Switzerland, November.
Borio, C. (2003). "Towards a macroprudential framework for financial supervision and regulation?," *CESifo Economic Studies*, Vol. 49, No. 2, pp. 181–216. Also available as Bank for International Settlements, Working paper, No. 128, February.
Borio, C. (2011). "Implementing a macroprudential framework: Blending boldness and realism," *Capitalism and Society*, Vol. 6, No. 1.
Borio, C. (2012). "The financial cycle and macroeconomics: What have we learnt?," Bank for International Settlements, Working paper, No. 395, December. Forthcoming in the Journal of Banking and Finance.
Caruana, J. (2010a). "Macroprudential policy: Could it have been different this time?," keynote speech at the People's Bank of China seminar on macroprudential policy, organised in cooperation with the International Monetary Fund, Shanghai, October 18.
Caruana, J. (2010). "Macroprudential policy: What we have learned and where we are going," keynote speech at the Second Financial Stability Conference of the International Journal of Central Banking, Bank of Spain, Madrid, June 17.
Drehmann, M., C. Borio, L. Gambacorta, G. Jimenez and C. Trucharte (2010). "Countercyclical capital buffers: Exploring options," Bank for International Settlements Working Paper No. 317, July.
Drehmann, M., C. Borio and K. Tsatsaronis (2011). "Anchoring countercyclical capital buffers: The role of credit aggregates," *International Journal of Central Banking*, Vol. 7, No. 4, pp. 189–240. Also available as Bank for International Settlements Working Paper No. 355, November.
Group of Governors and Heads of Supervision (GGHOS) (2012). "Basel III liquidity standard and strategy for assessing implementation of standards

endorsed by Group of Governors and Heads of Supervision." Press release, Basel, Switzerland, January 8.

Ingves, S. (2011). "Talk is cheap — putting policies into practice." Remarks at the FSI-ASBA sixth high-level meeting, Strengthening Financial Sector Supervision and Regulatory Priorities in the Americas, San Francisco, CA, November 16.

Macroeconomic Assessment Group (MAG) (2010). "Assessing the macroeconomic impact of the transition to stronger capital and liquidity requirements — final report." Group established by the Financial Stability Board and the Basel Committee on Banking Supervision, December.

Complexity in Financial Regulation

Andrew G. Haldane and Vasileios Madouros*

Bank of England

The regulatory infrastructure supporting the financial system is tremendously complex. It is not difficult to see why: Complex regulation has been the natural regulatory response to an increasingly complex financial system. The public policy question is whether this has been the best response to the evolution of the financial system. We suspect not.

The right response to uncertainties about the environment is more often found in simple, rather than complex, control rules. To explain why, we first set out the conceptual and empirical arguments and then outline some policy options for streamlining the financial regulatory infrastructure to make it more robust to such uncertainty.

Complexity, Comparability, and Credibility

The original Basel Accord — the first truly international capital standard for banks agreed in the 1980s — was relatively simple. It only defined five distinct risk weights, determined entirely by regulators, at the level of broad asset classes. This enabled Basel I to come in at a modest 30 pages.

By the time Basel II was agreed in 2004, the Accord had grown tenfold to 347 pages. Why? Because Basel II, and the Market Risk Amendment that preceded it, allowed banks to use their own risk models to

*Andrew Haldane is Executive Director for Financial Stability at the Bank of England. He is a member of the newly established Financial Policy Committee as well as several senior management committees of the Bank. He is also a member of the Basel Committee on Banking Supervision. Vasileios Madouros is an Economist in the Financial Stability area of the Bank of England. His work focuses on prudential policy issues. The views presented in this paper are not necessarily those of the Bank of England or the Financial Policy Committee.

Table 1. Approximate number of estimated parameters for a typical large international bank

	Probability of Default	Loss Given Default	Number of Models	Range of Parameters
Retail Mortgages	10–15	10–15	40	400–600
Credit Cards	10–15	3	15	100–140
SME Retail	10–15	3	6	40–50
Wholesale	5–15	5–15	100	500–1500
SME Corporate	5–15	5–15	2	10–30

Note: Number of parameters used to determine credit risk capital requirements under the internal ratings-based approach. Number of parameters used to determine PD and LGD, as well as the number of models used for each portfolio, have been estimated based on a large representative UK bank, so they are a broad approximation only. To calculate the range of total parameters, we have assumed that half the models are used to estimate PD and the other half are used to estimate LGD.

determine regulatory capital requirements. The result was a step increase in the complexity of the framework for calculating risk-weighted assets (RWAs). For a large, internationally-active bank, the number of models used to determine capital requirements runs into the hundreds (Table 1). The number of estimated parameters runs into the thousands, perhaps tens of thousands.

Most recently, the Basel III package of reforms has been agreed. This increased overall capital ratios, simplified the definition of capital, added a nonrisk–based leverage constraint as a backstop to risk-based requirements, and — for the first time — introduced internationally-consistent liquidity standards.

For those reasons, Basel III is an important improvement over Basel II — especially in simplifying and strengthening the definition of capital (the "numerator" problem). But Basel III did nothing to improve the greater source of regulatory complexity and inconsistency — the calculation of RWAs (the "denominator" problem). That is why the Basel III rule book now adds up to over 600 pages.[1]

[1]This refers to the sum of Basel II, Basel II.5, and Basel III and covers liquidity, leverage, and risk-based capital requirements.

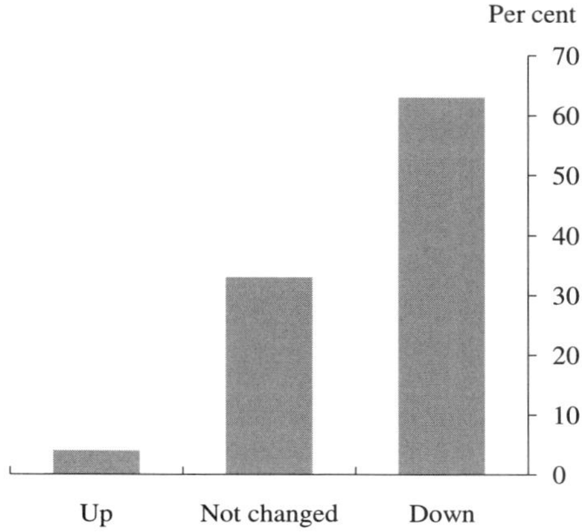

Fig. 1. Investor perceptions — "Has your confidence in RWAs gone up or down?"

Note: Based on survey responses of over 130 investors carried out in 2012 H1 (of perceptions over the previous year).
Source: Barclays Capital.

Increasingly over the past 12 months, market participants have begun to recognize the scale of this denominator problem. They have started to lose faith in the reliability of the risk-weighting regime (Fig. 1). Investors appear to find risk-weight calculations simply too complex and too opaque. This opacity has real costs, weakening market discipline in the upswing and increasing uncertainty about solvency in the downswing. The latter is a particular problem for global banks today.

The introduction of internal models was motivated by a desire to increase risk sensitivity. But, in doing so, it introduced a new source of variation in regulatory capital ratios: Differences in banks' own modeled estimates of risk. The variation in risk weights due to differences in models — rather than true portfolio risk — appears, on the basis of evidence to date, to be very large.

For example, supervisors in the UK have recently undertaken a number of benchmarking exercises where banks are asked to use their own models to estimate risk weights for a *common* hypothetical portfolio. Figure 2 shows the headline results of the latest exercise. The cross-bank ranges are huge, with estimated risk weights varying by a factor of 3 or more across

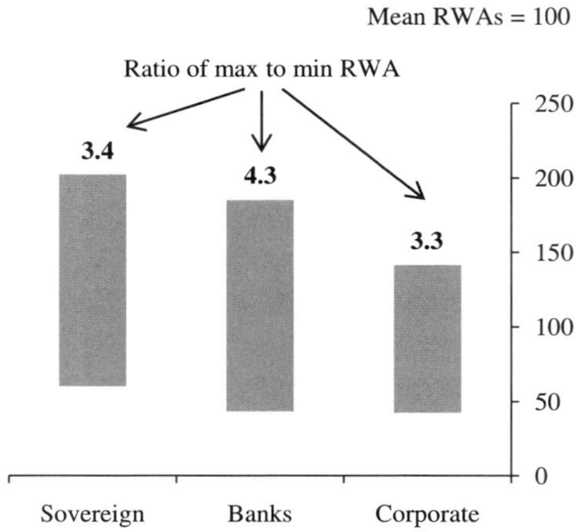

Fig. 2. Variability of risk-weighted assets for a common, hypothetical portfolio.

Note: Based on the results of the FSA's hypothetical portfolio exercise for 2011. Portfolios for each metric in each category comprise only co-rated assets. Results have been normalized to mean = 100. Figure shows minimum–maximum ranges.
Source: FSA Hypothetical Portfolio Analysis 2011 (www.fsa.gov.uk/static/pubs/international/2011hpe.pdf) and authors' calculations.

different asset classes. This suggests that banks might be financing the same portfolios with vastly different amounts of capital.

Differences on this scale are not helpful system-wide diversity; they reflect unhelpful system-wide inconsistency. Similar exercises for a wider set of international banks suggest similar degrees of RWA inconsistency. In other words, the quest for risk sensitivity has injected a large dose of model risk into the capital equation. The public policy question is whether the benefits of such granularity outweigh these costs — for example, by improving regulators' ability to spot and avert crises.

Can Less Be More in Finance?

In a recent paper, we tried to shed some light on this question.[2] It began with a conundrum. Catching a frisbee can be difficult. In principle, one

[2]See Haldane and Madouros (2012).

might wish to weigh a range of different factors when frisbee-catching — such as wind speed and frisbee rotation — using the laws of physics as a guide. Yet catching a frisbee in practice is surprisingly common, including among dogs without PhDs in physics. On the face of it, that is puzzling.

So what is the secret of the dog's success? It turns out that it follows a simple rule of thumb: run at a speed such that the angle of gaze to the frisbee remains roughly constant. This is called the "gaze heuristic." Humans tend to follow an identical rule of thumb when catching balls in sport.

The typical explanation for the use of such simple heuristics is that collecting and processing the necessary information is costly. So people deviate from rational, complex decision-making and instead rely on simple rules of thumb. But there is another, quite different rationale for simple rules. Under certain circumstances, simple solutions are, in fact, the best response to such uncertainty, in the sense that they are more robust to model error. When uncertainty about the environment is great, less can be more.[3] Put differently, the greater the complexity and uncertainty in the world, the stronger the case for simple control rules.

This has been shown in a number of practical settings, including predictions of sports events, doctors diagnosing heart attacks, and investors picking stocks. We investigated whether this "less is more" effect carried across to modern finance in general, and to banking crises in particular. To do so, we conducted a small number of analytical experiments.

Leverage versus Risk-Based Capital

The first experiment was a horse race between two measures of bank solvency — one complex (a Basel risk-weighted capital ratio), the other simple (an unweighted leverage ratio). We assessed which of these ratios did a better job at differentiating banks that would subsequently fail. This experiment covered about 100 of the world's largest and most complex banks. Visually, Fig. 3 suggests that the leverage ratio outperformed the risk-based ratio in differentiating ex ante between banks that failed and those that

[3] For a review of the literature on how less information, computation, and time can improve accuracy, see Gigerenzer and Brighton (2009).

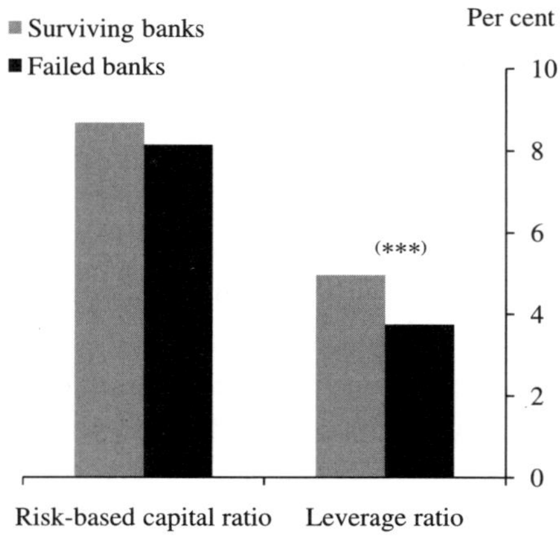

Fig. 3. Average solvency ratios of major global banks, end–2006.

Note: The classification of bank distress is based on Laeven and Valencia (2010), updated to reflect failure or government intervention since August 2009. For the purposes of the leverage ratio calculation, total assets have been adjusted on a best-efforts basis to achieve comparability between institutions reporting under US GAAP and IFRS.
Source: Capital IQ, SNL Financial, published accounts, Laeven and Valencia (2010), and authors' calculations.
***Denotes null hypothesis of mean equality rejected at the 1% significance level.

did not. Formal econometric evidence supported this visual impression. The simpler metric outperformed the more complex one in predicting bank distress. Less was more.

Modelling the Risk of Small Bank Default

In a second experiment, we looked at a much larger sample of small US banks. Here, we compared the performance of a set of models of bank failure, some complex (based on a range of right-hand side variables — covering the full set of CAMEL indicators), some simple (for example, based on a single right-hand side variable, like liquidity). In-sample, complex models always did better. But when predicting bank failure out of sample, the story was reversed. Figure 4 shows that when samples sizes were small, the complex model was outperformed by the simple ones. Less was more. Why? Because, in the language of econometrics, complex models suffer from an "over-fitting" problem. This increases their fragility and reduces

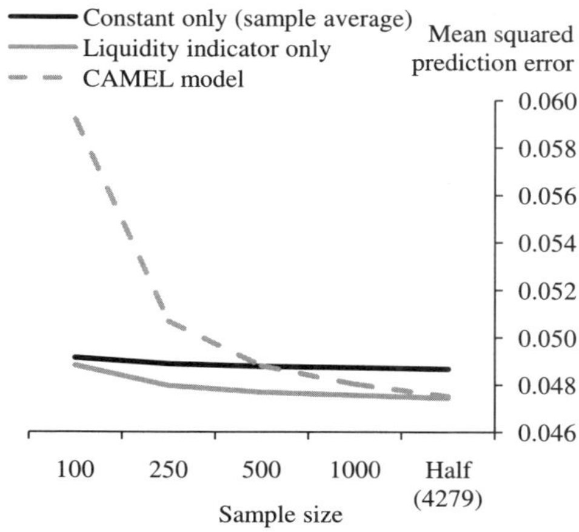

Fig. 4. Summary of out-of-sample model performance.

Note: Different models estimated using 10,000 random samples of different size. Samples are rejected if there are no observations of bank failure. The different models are used to predict bank failure for approximately 4,500 banks out-of-sample. Out-of-sample performance is measured by the mean square prediction error. A lower number implies better performance.
Source: Federal Deposit Insurance Corporation and authors' calculations.

their robustness out of sample. This robustness problem is more acute the smaller the sample.

Modeling Financial Risk

The final experiment looked at modelling risk in financial markets. Assuming the price of a hypothetical financial asset followed a well-defined stochastic process, we compared different time series models for forecasting asset return volatility. When sample sizes were small, simpler models were unambiguously superior. With highly imperfect information, adding model complexity simply increased prediction errors. Less was more. As the sample size expanded, model uncertainty decreased and prediction errors fell. But the threshold sample size at which this occurred was often very large indeed, requiring perhaps hundreds of years of data in our hypothetical experiment.

The message from these financial experiments was consistent with that found by physicians, sports predictors and stock pickers. Complex control rules generate robustness problems, especially when the financial environment is uncertain (as it is) and samples sizes are small (as they almost always are). In financial environments, simple rules may offer a more robust policy yardstick.

Public Policy Implications

So where does all of this leave us from a public policy perspective? From a potentially long list, here are a few regulatory options for the future.

First, with the benefit of hindsight, there is a real question whether the regulatory community took a false turn in the 1990s by relying on banks' own models to determine risk weights. Not only did this spawn hypercomplexity; it also passed the keys to the regulatory kingdom to the banks themselves. This is not something tackled by Basel III. Going forward, a useful starting point might be to take a more sceptical view of both the robustness of such models and their role in the regulatory framework. This may call, for example, for a greater use of simple, standardized approaches to setting risk weights, as a robust backstop or floor to banks' complex, over-fitted models.

Second, our analysis suggests that, at least for the world's largest, most complex banks, a simple leverage ratio would have performed better as a predictor of failure. This underlines the importance of introducing a leverage ratio as an additional constraint. Basel III did deliver this — though only as a backstop measure. While it may not make sense to place all eggs in the leverage ratio basket, empirical evidence would suggest leverage ratios might be placed on a more equal footing relative to risk-based ratios when seeking to detect big bank weakness.

Third, the drive to more complex regulatory rules (so-called Pillar 1 of the Basel framework) has over the course of the past few decades distracted attention from the other Basel pillars — Pillar 2 (the supervisory review process) and Pillar 3 (market discipline). Simplifying Pillar 1 could provide greater scope for supervisory judgment; for example, by freeing up resources and allowing supervisors to focus on an assessment of the big risks facing firms. Simplifying Pillar 1 would also allow investors to better understand the drivers of risk-based capital ratios. In other words, greater simplicity and consistency of the regulatory framework would help restore market confidence and — with it — market discipline.

Conclusion

Modern finance is complex. The regulatory response for the past 30 years has been to fight such complexity with regulatory complexity. That is precisely the wrong response from a public policy perspective. A regulatory response grounded in simplicity offers greater hope of a regulatory regime that is robust to the inevitable uncertainties of today's complex financial network.

References

Gigerenzer, G. and H. Brighton (2009). "Homo heuristicus: Why biased minds make better inferences," *Topics in Cognitive Science*, Vol. 1, pp. 107–143.

Haldane, A. and V. Madouros (2012). "The dog and the Frisbee." Paper presented at the Federal Reserve Bank of Kansas City's 36th Economic Policy Symposium, The Changing Policy Landscape, Jackson Hole, WY, USA.

Financial Reform: On the Right Road, at the Right Pace?

Thomas F. Huertas*

Ernst & Young LLP

Where should we be headed in financial reform? Are we on the right road and are we getting there at the right pace?

There seems broad agreement that we have the right destination in mind. In response to the financial crisis, policymakers have fundamentally restructured financial regulation. The G-20 leaders have mandated the Financial Stability Board FSB (2012) to oversee the development and implementation of an agenda to:

- Strengthen the resilience of financial institutions so that they are less likely to fail;
- Make financial institutions "safe to fail" so that they can be resolved without cost to the taxpayer and without significant disruption to the economy;
- Strengthen financial infrastructures and channel all significant trading activity through such infrastructures; and
- Assure that all significant financial institutions and financial activities are subject to appropriate regulation and supervision, including activities in the so-called shadow banking sector.

There is also broad consensus that we have the right route map to take us to this destination. Specifically, Basel III proposes a very substantial

*Thomas Huertas is a Partner in the risk advisory practice at Ernst & Young LLP. This paper is an updated (to December 17, 2012) version of remarks prepared for the Fifteenth Annual International Banking Conference at the Federal Reserve Bank of Chicago, held on November 16, 2012. The opinions expressed here are the author's own personal views.

increase in the amount and quality of capital that banks will be required to hold. This will strengthen the resilience of banks, especially the systemically important banks that are at the heart of the financial system. Although some (Haldane, 2012) question whether capital regulation should be so complex and suggest that simpler measures such as control over leverage might be more effective, the consensus remains that the leverage ratio should be a backstop to the risk-based capital measure rather than a substitute.

This, in my view, makes sense. As Bagehot (1873, p. 319) remarked,

> The practical difficulties of life often cannot be met by very simple rules; those dangers being complex and many, the rules for encountering them cannot well be single or simple.

Risk in banking is indeed complex and multifaceted and one wants to assure that capital regulation is taking all risk into account. Reliance on a simple leverage ratio would be an open invitation for banks to increase the risk of assets that count toward the ratio and to take risk in forms that do not result in assets included in the ratio.

Strengthening capital is only the first step toward improving resiliency. Strengthening liquidity is just as important, and Basel III takes the first steps toward developing a global liquidity standard. This starts with a requirement that banks actually measure and report on the liquidity risks that they run. It further requires banks to hold a buffer of liquid assets against the possibility that outflows from the bank will be greater than expected. It also proposes to set limits on the extent to which banks can rely on unstable sources of funding. These measures are long overdue. Indeed, considerable progress will, in my view, result from the introduction of the measuring and reporting requirement and this should be implemented as soon as possible, even if agreement cannot immediately be reached on what assets should count toward the liquidity buffer or what sources of funding are or are not stable.

With respect to resolution, policymakers have taken the first steps to make banks "safe to fail." They have introduced legislation to align resolution regimes to the Key Attributes developed by the FSB (2011), and they are aiming to develop institution-specific resolution plans that will allow the authorities to resolve a systemically important bank without cost to the taxpayer and without significant disruption to the economy at large.

With respect to financial market infrastructures policymakers (CPSS IOSCO 2012) have mandated the use of central counterparties (CCPs) and highlighted the steps that will need to be taken to assure that such CCPs are robust, i.e., able to withstand the simultaneous failure of their two largest participants.

Finally, policymakers (FSB, 2012a) have taken steps to identify systemically important nonbanking institutions and to outline steps needed to protect the financial system and economy at large from so-called shadow banks, such as money market mutual funds (FSB, 2012c).

That's the good news. Where's the catch?

Although the destination is desirable and route map is correct, we haven't gone very far down the road. Most jurisdictions, including the US and the European Union, did not implement Basel III so that it could take effect as planned on January 1, 2013, and some, notably the European Union, are planning to do so in a manner that the Basel Committee considers to be deficient (BCBS, 2012). This delay threatens to slow the rate at which banks are improving their capital positions and strengthening their resiliency. Similarly, the ongoing dispute as to which assets should count toward the liquidity buffer may be delaying the implementation of the fundamental requirement that banks measure, report and manage their liquidity risk.[1]

As for resolution, this is still at the design stage. We have recognized that banks need to be made "safe to fail" but we are in my view still a long way away from saying with confidence that we can resolve a global systemically important bank without cost to the taxpayer and without disruption to the economy. Although the FSB has filled in further details on how jurisdictions might implement the Key Attributes (FSB, 2012b) and the FDIC and the Bank of England (2012) have sketched out how they might cooperate to resolve a G-SIFI, much still needs to be done to transform resolution plans into "presumptive paths" that the authorities could follow

[1] It should be noted, however, that some jurisdictions have already implemented extensive liquidity regulation and supervision. In the UK, this extends not only to UK-headquartered banks, but to UK subsidiaries and branches of foreign banks (Financial Services Authority, 2009). In the US, the Federal Reserve has initiated liquidity stress testing for major banks (Nasiripour, 2012).

if a G-SIFI required resolution. Key issues to be addressed include strengthening statutory resolution regimes to include bail-in, devising measures to provide liquidity to the bank in resolution, handling derivative contracts (specifically avoiding closeout), assuring continued access of the bank in resolution to financial market infrastructures, and assuring appropriate cooperation and coordination among home and host authorities around the world. Only then can one say with some assurance that a G-SIFI can be resolved without cost to the taxpayer and without significant disruption to financial markets or the economy at large.

With respect to financial market infrastructures, there is a risk that we are putting the cart before the horse. We have mandated a vast shift of transactions to CCPs without assuring that those CCPs are in fact robust. We need to urgently assure that they become robust lest CCPs become what might be called "Fukushimas of finance."

As to shadow banking, it seems that we are stalled at the first tollgate. The SEC correctly identified money market mutual funds as systemically important and suggested various means to control that risk, including shifting to a floating net asset value or imposing of capital requirements on the fund and/or their sponsors for funds that continued to promise "not to break the buck." However, the SEC failed to adopt these measures and it remains to be seen whether or not the Financial Stability Oversight Committee will impose the change as the Financial Stability Board is urging it to do.

So what needs to be done? In my view, implementation holds the key to building a more resilient and more stable financial system. We have to get on with strengthening capital and liquidity and we have to make resolution workable both for SIFIs and for CCPs. We have to tackle shadow banking. We have to continue to improve supervision. We have to make microsupervision more forward looking and more proactive, and we have to turn macroprudential supervision from a theoretical concept into a practical and effective tool kit.

And, we have to do all that at the same time that we guide the economy past the fiscal cliff in the US and past the euro crisis in the European Union. This is a tall order, but one that supervisors and financial firms will find easier to meet if G20 leaders reconfirm that they want the world to stay the course toward financial reform.

References

Bagehot, W. (1873, reprint 1999). *Lombard Street: A Description of the Money Market*, John Wiley & Sons, London.

Bank for International Settlements, Basel Committee on Banking Supervision (2012a). "Report to G20 finance ministers and central bank governors on Basel III implementation," October. Available at: www.bis.org/publ/bcbs234.pdf. Accessed November 12, 2012.

Bank for International Settlements, Committee on Payment and Settlement Systems and Board of the International Organization of Securities Commissions (2012b). "Recovery and resolution of financial market infrastructures: Consultative report," July. Available at: www.bis.org/publ/cpss103.pdf. Accessed November 12, 2012.

Committee on Payment and Settlement Systems and Board of the International Organisation of Securities Commissions (2012). Recovery and resolution of financial market infrastructers: consultative report. Available at http://www.bis.org/publ/cpss103.pdf. Retrieved November 12, 2012.

Federal Deposit Insurance Corporation and Bank of England (2012c). "Resolving globally active, systemically important, financial institutions," report, December 10. Available at: http://www.bankofengland.co.uk/ publications/Documents/news/2012/nr156.pdf. Accessed December 17, 2012.

Financial Services Authority (2009). "Strengthening liquidity standards: Including feedback on CP08/22, CP09/13, CP09/14," October. Available at: www.fsa.gov.uk/pubs/policy/ps09_16.pdf. Accessed December 17, 2012.

Financial Stability Board (2011)."Key attributes of effective resolution regimes for financial institutions," November 4. Available at: www.financialstabilityboard.org/publications/r_111104cc.pdf. Accessed May 31, 2012.

Financial Stability Board (2012a). "Progress of financial regulatory reforms," October 31. Available at: www.financialstabilityboard.org/publications/r_121105.pdf. Accessed November 12, 2012.

Financial Stability Board (2012b)."Recovery and resolution planning: Making the key attributes requirements operational," November. Available at: https://www.financialstabilityboard.org/publications/r_121102.pdf. Accessed December 17, 2012.

Financial Stability Board (2012c)."Consultative document: Strengthening oversight and regulation of shadow banking: An integrated overview of policy recommendations," November 18. Available at: www.financialstabilityboard.org/publications/r_121118.pdf. Accessed December 17, 2012.

Haldane, A. (2012). "The dog and the frisbee," August 31. Available at: www.kansascityfed.org/publicat/sympos/2012/ah.pdf. Accessed November 12, 2012.

Nasiripour, S. (2012)."Fed begins stress tests on bank liquidity," December 10. Available by subscription at: www.ft.com/intl/cms/s/0/6e276c62-4545-11e2-858f-00144feabdc0.html#axzz2FK2qx5vn. Accessed December 17, 2012.

Banking Regulation and Supervision in the Next 10 Years and Their Unintended Consequences

Danièle Nouy*

Autorité de Contrôle Prudentiel

Politicians, policymakers, and supervisors have responded to the current crisis by introducing tighter legislation and regulations. The new rules will shape the future banking system. However, the new rules and laws will also be evaded. Indeed the creativity that financial institutions demonstrate in such circumstances can even increase the risks that the new rules were designed to manage. Should we therefore be seeking solutions to crises in the form of new legislation and regulations? What are the limitations and unintended consequences of such an approach? And what can supervisors themselves do to ensure that these "unintended consequences" are recognized and managed? In addition, from a European perspective, what will be the impact of the banking union in this process?

Introduction

The Global Financial Crisis has amply demonstrated the limitations of self-regulation and market discipline. Besides the strengthening of the resilience of financial institutions, the new regulations also call for an intensification of supervision. Supervisors are to be entrusted with new

---

*Danièle Nouy is Secretary General of the Autorité de Contrôle Prudentiel, the French Prudential Supervision Authority. Contributions by Boubacar Camara, Jean-Baptiste Haquin, Laurent Mercier Emmanuel Point and Martin Rose from ACP are gratefully acknowledged.

powers, as was the *Autorité de Contrôle Prudentiel* at its birth. This comes with stronger responsibilities. But, after the irrational exuberance that intoxicated economic agents before the financial crisis, has the pendulum not swung too far in the opposite direction leading to an excessive reliance on supervisors?

The new regulations address major weaknesses that the crisis has revealed: stronger solvency ratios, capital of a better quality, and risks better accounted for. The French supervisor strongly supports these invaluable improvements that will result in much more robust financial institutions and a more resilient financial system. Nevertheless, supervisors have to anticipate changes in the environment as a response and to manage unintended consequences that may emerge from these new regulations. This is notably the case for the liquidity coverage ratio and the leverage ratio for which some technical aspects require caution and some further improvements.

Beside new regulations, banking supervision is also evolving toward more stress test practices and macroprudential supervision. The supervisor is also adopting a more intrusive approach. The French supervisory authority is used to relying on intrusive off-site and on-site supervision, to get an in-depth as well as an updated understanding of risks incurred by banks and to monitor any undesired evolution before it becomes out of control. The crisis confirmed that this supervisory approach was well founded. But it has also dramatically increased the issues at stake and has been extremely demanding on supervisors in terms of speed of reaction, resources, and ability to deal with increased complexity.

In the remainder of the paper, Sec. 2 discusses the possible unintended consequences of the new regulation framework introduced in response to the financial crisis and suggests ways to address them. Section 3 presents the challenges associated with the new forms of supervision and the future European Banking Union, which would increase the effectiveness of the banking supervision in the European Union, involving a strengthened financial system. Section 4 concludes.

Unintended Consequences of New Regulation

Basel III was introduced to strengthen the banking system by notably increasing solvency and liquidity requirements. However, these new regulations have to be closely monitored to avoid the unintended consequences that may emerge from their implementation. In fact, more capital requirements may lead to an uncontrolled process of deleveraging, which may threaten the lending activity. They can also introduce regulatory arbitrage leading to less regulatory effectiveness. The contraction of the phase in period due to the pressure exerted by the financial crisis and market expectation on banks to comply with the new regulations in a much shorter time frame may also have several unintended and adverse consequences. We first present the possible unintended consequences of regulations regarding deleveraging. We then analyze concerns associated with the implementation of the Basel III regulation. We finally deal with the question of the development of the shadow banking sector.

Recapitalization, Deleveraging, and Lending Activity

One of the main reasons why the economic and financial crisis became so severe was that the banking sectors in many countries had built up excessive on and off-balance sheet leverage. This was accompanied by a loss of confidence by market participants in the level and quality of the capital base. To address these failures, the BCBS introduced a number of fundamental reforms to the international regulatory framework,[1] including raising the quality, consistency, and transparency of capital while enhancing the coverage of risks.

Deleveraging is part of a necessary adjustment in response to the crisis to restructure banks' balance sheets and restore the conditions of a sound banking sector. In the wake of the crisis, market participants have been exerting a strong pressure on banks to deleverage and to target higher capital ratios.

While supervisory authorities have to monitor that this deleveraging process is effectively implemented, an obvious unintended consequence that they have to prevent relates to the possible procyclicality of the process from a system-wide perspective. Excessive deleveraging that would disrupt lending to the real economy and further amplify the crisis must be avoided.

[1] See BCBS (2010).

The evolution of cross-border exposures has been an area of concern for European supervisory authorities. Chief among them has been the risk of reduction in lending from foreign banks to southern Europe and emerging market economies.[2] Lending cuts by European banks also focused on dollar-denominated loans. European banks, especially French groups, reduced their US dollar activities in project finance or the financing of trade, aircraft, and ships. This did not appear to weigh too heavily on these types of credit, because other lenders abroad took over. However, this may call for supervisory attention because of potential unintended consequences. As a matter of fact, according to article 481 of the CRR under consideration, the European Banking Authority (EBA) will report to the European Commission whether the specifications of the new regulations are likely to have a material detrimental impact on the business and risk profile of credit institutions or on lending to the real economy, with a particular focus on lending to SMEs and on trade financing.

In a market environment, with pressures on banks, deleveraging could lead to forced sales, contraction of credit, and weaker economic activity. Against this background, the 2011 EU capital exercise demanded especially careful and tactful handling. Recommendations[3] for major European banks to raise their Core Tier 1 capital ratios to 9% by mid-2012 had the potential to increase these fears and had to be closely supervised ex ante to prevent unintended behavioral responses by individual banks. The recapitalization plan evaluated the capital needs at EUR 114.7 billion, after including sovereign capital buffer. The EBA stated that these buffers were explicitly not designed to cover losses in sovereigns but to provide a reassurance to markets about the banks' ability to withstand a range of shocks and still maintain adequate capital. The amount of any capital shortfall identified was based on September 2011 figures. However, it was decided that the amount of the sovereign capital buffer would not be revised so that sales of

---

[2]See BIS (2012).

[3]On December 8, 2011, the European Banking Authority (EBA) published a recommendation stating that national supervisory authorities should require the banks in the sample to strengthen their capital positions by building up an exceptional and temporary capital buffer against sovereign debt exposures to reflect market prices as of the end of September. In addition, banks were required to establish an exceptional and temporary buffer such that the Core Tier 1 capital ratio reaches a level of 9% by the end of June 2012.

sovereign bonds would not alleviate the buffer requirement to be achieved by June 2012; the sales of selected assets could be accepted provided that they did not lead to a reduced flow of lending to the real economy, in particular in the EU. It was clearly stated that banks should first use private sources of funding to strengthen their capital position to meet the required target, including retained earnings, reduced bonus payments, new issuances of common equity, and suitably strong contingent capital as well as other liability management measures.

So far, this recapitalization plan has not lead to a significant reduction in lending into the European real economy according to the EBA. The deleveraging process, which started before this capital exercise, has been implemented in an orderly fashion. French and German banks decreased their exposure to Greece, Ireland, Italy, Portugal, and Spain (GIIPS) but stabilized their total exposures to the foreign public sector between December 2010 and June 2012 (see Fig. 1(a) and 1(b)).

Besides other European supervisors, the French authorities have been closely monitoring this risk. The attention has been mainly focusing on small and medium-sized enterprises (SMEs) and local public authorities. In Europe, SMEs, contrary to large companies, have more limited access

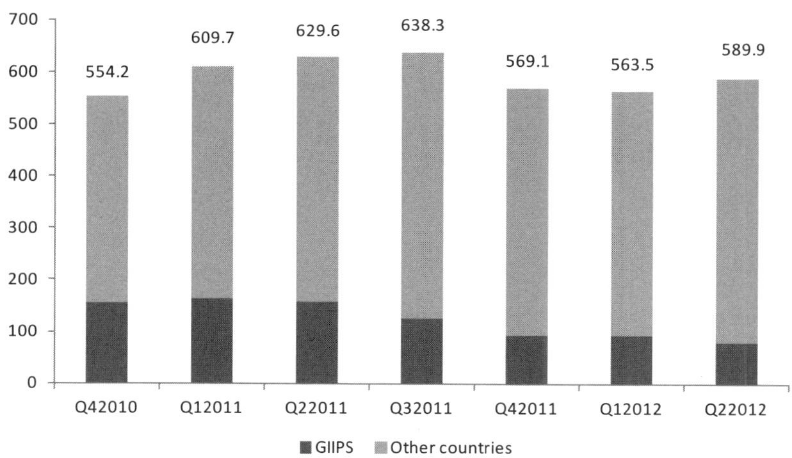

Fig. 1(a). French bank's exposures to foreign public sector (bn. USD).

Source: Bank for International Settlement and author's calculations.

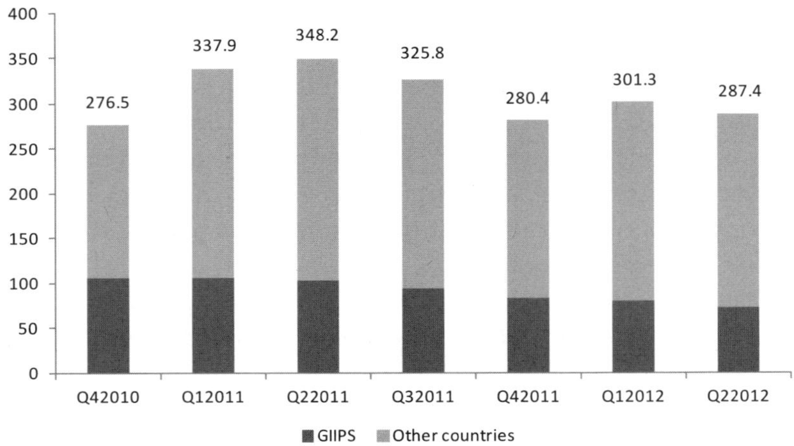

Fig. 1(b). German bank's exposures to foreign public sector (bn. USD).

Source: Bank for International Settlement and author's calculations.

to alternative funding sources in case of a banking credit squeeze. Local public authorities face growing financing needs in a context of increased decentralization in France and seem to experience funding strains as a consequence of the restructuring of the banking market.

In the French domestic markets, despite the tighter standards used by banks when granting credit since 2008, French SMEs do not appear to have been strongly affected by credit rationing.[4] Indeed, French banks have been focusing their business models on core activities, i.e., retail and corporate banking. They have reduced their market operations and are disposing of legacy assets. This is an intended consequence of the new framework.

Concerns Associated with the Implementation of Basel III Regulation

Basel III capital and liquidity requirements constitute major improvement in banking regulation. However, these new rules could have unintended consequences, especially on banks' business models and the development of the shadow banking sector, which have to be addressed.

[4]See Kremp and Sevestre (2011).

Liquidity and Long-Term Funding Needs

In December 2010, the BCBS published the Basel III international framework for liquidity risk measurement, standards, and monitoring. It came as reaction to the major vulnerabilities that were revealed during the financial crisis that began in 2007, when many banks experienced difficulties because they had not managed their liquidity in a prudent manner. The BCBS developed two minimum standards for funding liquidity. The first requirement on the Liquidity Coverage Ratio (LCR) aims to ensure that banks maintain an adequate level of unencumbered, high-quality liquid assets that can be converted into cash to meet their liquidity needs for a 30-calendar-day time horizon under a significantly severe liquidity stress scenario specified by supervisors. The Net Stable Funding Ratio (NSFR), with a one-year time horizon, was developed to provide a sustainable maturity structure of assets and liabilities.

An internationally harmonized liquidity ratio will be a major improvement. However, this new regulation has system-wide implications that are difficult to fully identify and anticipate. Assessing the impacts of the LCR calibration and monitoring the adjustments of financial institutions during the transition period are key areas of attention for regulatory and supervisory authorities. Implications of the standard for financial markets, credit extension, and economic growth have to be closely monitored so as to address unintended consequences as necessary.

According to the results of the Basel III monitoring exercise of the BCBS as of December 31, 2011,[5] the aggregate LCR shortfall was €1.8 trillion in the sample of 209 banks in the liquidity monitoring exercise. For the European banks in the sample, the shortfall was €1.17 trillion.[6] This is a source of supervisory concern since many banks simultaneously have to change in depth their funding structure that could, if unchecked, increase systemic risk. Competition among banks to secure long-term funding may come on top of the competition from other economic agents (sovereigns, public administrations, and private corporations) experiencing strong refinancing needs and who might also find it more difficult to borrow long term

[5] Basel Committee on Banking Supervision (2012).
[6] European Banking Authority (2012).

from banks. The ability of the long-term debt market to increase correspondingly remains an open issue, especially in the market conditions that have been prevailing since the beginning of the financial crisis. The rise in sovereign risk in Europe has adversely affected banks' funding conditions, thus delaying their adaptation to the future regulatory framework.[7] Regulatory proposals in relation to the bail-in of unsecured debt have also been weighing on the unsecured funding markets.

Supervisors have an important role to play to prevent unintended consequences stemming from the calibration of new regulations. In this regard, it would be hard to disentangle the responsibility of the supervisor from that of the regulator. Despite its strengths, the LCR required adjustments that were introduced in January 2013. One example can illustrate some of the concerns of the French supervisor.

Regarding the definition of High-Quality Liquid Assets (HQLA), too narrow a definition of HQLA would have several drawbacks, mainly cliff effects and concentration risk. Any event that would cause previously eligible assets to become ineligible would have market-wide consequences, for both debt issuers and banks, particularly those that had relied on the excluded assets and would have to adjust their balance sheet to comply with the LCR. For these reasons, the strong demand for HQLA assets would drive up their prices, leading to market distortions. The current definition of HQLA would give banks a strong incentive to increase their sovereign risk exposures, despite the experience of the negative consequences of market concerns about the sovereign risk exposures of banks, and despite the fact that it is not obvious that government bonds are always more liquid than other securities. An unfavorable treatment of certain types of privately issued collateral would weaken incentives for the financial industry to improve the market liquidity of these assets. Furthermore, for those central banks that rely on a larger set of eligible collateral for their refinancing operations, too narrow a definition of HQLA would raise the incentives for banks to pledge their less liquid assets at the central bank, thereby inducing a detrimental regulatory arbitrage.

Stressed conditions embedded in the definition of the ratio may be viewed as too stringent, in particular, regarding the treatment of interbank

[7] Committee on the Global Financial System (2011).

lending. This leads to an asymmetric treatment of the interbank debt: Banks as borrowers are assumed not to be able to draw facilities provided by other banks, but banks as lenders are required to assume in their LCR calculations that facilities extended to other banks would be fully drawn upon. Obviously, this may have strongly negative effects on activity in the interbank market.

The LCR aims at being applied internationally and has to encompass very different banking activities, legal, and structural frameworks. The impacts of this new regulation on the national banking systems differ. In its supervisory work, the ACP has to deal with intended and unintended consequences of the future regulation on French banks. Although a regulatory liquidity ratio — sharing many traits with the LCR — has been in force in France since 1988,[8] French banking groups are strongly impacted by the new regulation and lag behind some of their peers. There are several reasons for that.

First, the major French banking groups have historically developed according to the model of universal banking,[9] with significant business lines in asset management and insurance. This model showed its resilience during the crisis. Diversification of sources of income and risks proved to be strength. But this model has also some drawbacks, one of them being that a significant portion of savings was not intermediated through the balance sheets of French banks,[10] but was directed toward off-balance-sheet products: mutual funds and life insurance. In turn, these vehicles were investing part of their funds in bank debts.

Second, regulated tax-exempt savings accounts (*Livret A*, *Livret de Développement Durable*, and *Livret d'Epargne Populaire*) are another feature of the French financial system. For households, they combine several advantages. They are notably highly liquid and represent an important

[8]The French regulation relating to liquidity was reviewed in 2009, introducing a standard and an advanced approach for liquidity risk.

[9]The second banking coordination directive of 1999 made universal banking the norm in the European Union by introducing a single banking license valid throughout the European Union, and limiting product-mix restrictions to those imposed by home regulators (see Morrison, 2010).

[10]French banks were previously banned from paying interest on sight deposits.

asset class, therefore influencing the market of short-term as well as long-term savings products. The funds are collected by banking networks, but a major part is then centralized at the *Caisse des Dépôts* in order to finance a substantial portion of the construction and renovation of social housing through long-term loans granted at attractive rates. At the end of 2011, outstanding regulated savings totaled €337 bn.[11] (of which tax-exempt *Livrets A* amounted to €215 bn.). More structural shifts in the allocation of household savings are therefore dependent on tax incentives benefiting regulated savings products and long-term savings instruments, notably life insurance.

Third, unlike their US peers, French banks cannot rely on government-sponsored entities (GSEs) and keep large amounts of originated housing loans[12] on their balance sheets. This is a good illustration of the impact of international structural differences on the funding structure of banks.

French banks are reacting to the new regulatory framework by actively seeking retail deposits, which is obviously a long-term effort but could possibly trigger a deposit war. The ACP and the Banque de France have been closely monitoring the market and have issued preventive warnings in order for deposits-gathering to be achieved at a reasonable cost. This has been the case so far.

The LCR must be implemented rigorously and consistently across jurisdictions to achieve a level playing field.[13] The BCBS proposed that the LCR be introduced on January 1, 2015. The European Union includes liquidity requirements in the regulation implementing Basel III. However, there are major uncertainties regarding whether this regulation will be effectively implemented on the same scope and in a similar time frame in other areas, possibly leading to an uneven playing field. The level of application of the European capital requirement regulation and capital requirement directive (CRR–CRD IV) is very stringent because it covers credit institutions and investment firms, while Basel III applies, as a minimum, to internationally active banks.

[11] See Observatoire de l'épargne réglementée (2011).
[12] French housing loans are a low-risk asset class (see ACP, 2012).
[13] For a progress report, see BCBS (2012).

Leverage Ratio Requirement and Regulatory Arbitrage

Another important concern about new regulations is the possibility for banks to evade them by shifting their business to less-regulated markets. Shortcomings in the solvency regulation have been pointed out, among several other important factors,[14] as playing a major role in allowing banks to take advantage of regulatory arbitrage opportunities on a large scale. It has been generally claimed that banks had developed securitization activities without increasing their regulatory capital accordingly (Acharya and Schnabl, 2012). For the period between 2002 and 2005, Mian and Sufi (2009) find that the expansion in mortgage credit in US geographical areas characterized by a disproportionately large share of subprime borrowers — despite a sharp decrease in income growth — and the increase in securitization of subprime mortgage was closely correlated. This was all the more worrisome, given the poor quality of the assets involved in securitization and the substantial degree of risks that turned out to remain in banks' balance sheets through credit lines either explicitly or implicitly due to reputational factors.

Regulatory arbitrage has always been a major concern for regulatory authorities. For example, in a theoretical setting, if a bank exhibits low risk aversion, its reaction to the introduction of a minimum capital to asset ratio might be a larger shift toward riskier assets to offset the decrease of its return (Kim and Santomero, 1980). To avoid this unintended effect, regulators have to set a capital requirement taking account of the quality of bank assets and the off-balance sheet risk exposures. This risk-based capital ratio requires to optimally weight bank assets and off-balance-sheet exposures to avoid possibilities of regulatory arbitrage. However, in the recent past, the low weighting assigned to some bank activities under Basel II, such as securitization, introduced regulatory arbitrage opportunities. The banking sector of many countries built up excessive on- and off-balance sheet leverage, contributing to the worsening of the financial and economic crisis that started in 2007.

[14]The conjunction of several factors has contributed to the emergence of the financial crisis: overreliance on external ratings flawed rating models, insufficient investors diligence, moral hazard, inadequate accounting methods, etc.

There is a broad agreement that among securitization activities, asset-backed commercial paper (ABCP) significantly contributed to the breakout of the financial crisis, especially in the US. Banks engaging in ABCP transactions sold securitized assets to conduits, which financed their investment by issuing commercial paper. Banks also played the role of sponsor by providing guarantees to outside investors. By selling part of their assets to conduits and providing liquidity guarantees, commercial banks reduced their capital requirement without transferring risk to outside investors (Acharya and Schnabl, 2012). Figure 2 shows that ABCP outstanding highly increased between 2001 and 2007. During this period, bank sponsors' total exposures to ABCP increased by 121%. After 2007, sponsors significantly decreased their ABCP exposures.

An answer to the insufficiencies of Basel II risk-based capital requirement has been the proposal to introduce a leverage requirement at the international level. This raises the question of whether there is a trade-off between the simplicity of the regulation and the comprehensiveness of risk assessment. A minimum leverage ratio is aimed at acting as a backstop to risk-based capital requirements. If risk-sensitive capital requirements rely

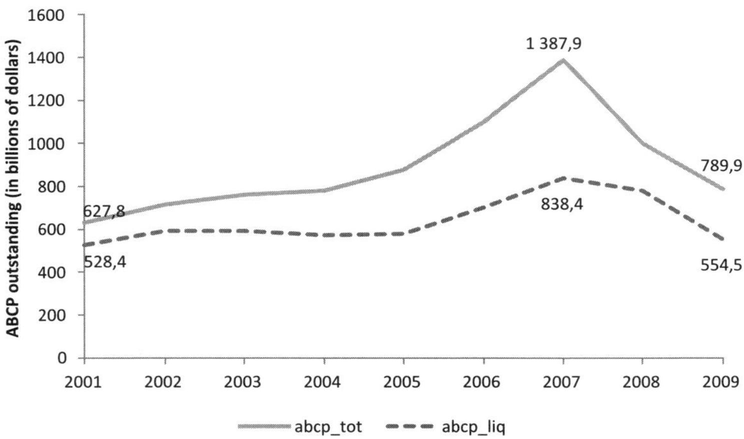

Fig. 2. Evolution of bank sponsors' total exposures to ABCP (abcp_tot) and exposures with a liquidity guarantee (abcp_liq) from 2001 to 2009.

Note: Data are from Moody's and used in Acharya and Schnabl (2012). abcp_tot and abcp_liq respectively represent the total amount of sponsor's exposures to ABCP and the amount of ABCP for which sponsors provided a liquidity guarantee.
Source: Acharya and Schnabl (2012) and author's calculations.

on banks' voluntary disclosure of their risk profiles, it can be useful to introduce a leverage ratio requirement to avoid that some banks understate their risk (Blum, 2008). Moreover, leverage ratio is a simple tool that may also be used as a counter cyclical instrument for macroprudential regulation.

However, the introduction of a leverage ratio requirement may, in turn, have unintended effects on banks' soundness. There are strong reservations *vis-à-vis* such a ratio that failed to prevent the emergence of the crisis in countries where it was implemented. A leverage ratio requirement may introduce wrong incentives in terms of bank risk-taking behavior. In fact, because it does not distinguish assets according to their riskiness, it may encourage banks to hold the riskier assets on their balance sheet and to develop their off-balance-sheet activities. A leverage ratio could also negatively impact some banks' business model, such as banks principally exercising retail activity, or at least the segments facing the higher risk weights, hence adversely affecting credit supply. A leverage ratio requirement could also discourage banks from developing robust internal models and managing their assets in a prudent manner. Prudent banks holding in their portfolios a greater part of liquid and high-quality assets may be penalized by the introduction of such a requirement. Furthermore, the dynamic effect of the leverage ratio among the package of reforms is difficult to anticipate. The Basel Committee has been assessing these unintended effects through quantitative impact studies. The results of the Basel III implementation monitoring exercise as of December 31, 2011, notably show that 56 out of 212 banks failed to meet the 3% Basel III Tier 1 minimum leverage ratio.

Great care is absolutely necessary when introducing new requirements or tightening existing ones since they may generate regulatory arbitrages. The leverage ratio should complement other prudential tools, such as risk-based capital and liquidity requirements. It should be used as a supplemental tool for supervisors in order to implement an efficient micro- and macroprudential regulation.

Regulatory Arbitrage, Risks Associated with the Development of the Shadow Banking Sector, and the Scope of Banking Activities

Stronger regulation in a given country could not only lead to massive transfers of assets to less-regulated ones via regulatory arbitrage, but also trigger a shift in favor of the shadow banking system, which may represent a systemic threat that the regulators and the supervisors need to address properly.

At the November 2010 Seoul Summit, in view of the completion of the new capital standards for banks (Basel III), the G20 leaders highlighted the need for strengthening regulation and supervision of the shadow banking sector as one of the remaining issues of financial sector regulation that warranted attention.[15] The Financial Stability Board issued recommendations as to the measures regulators should take and the way they could reincorporate the shadow business into the regulated one.[16] Risks associated with shadow banking have been intensely scrutinized in the US[17] and in the European Union, which has shown global leadership in implementing its G20 commitments.[18] In 2011, the total assets of the shadow banking sector was slightly greater than the total assets of banks in the United States, despite a decrease since 2007. It represented roughly 40% of the total assets of banks in Europe, with lower growth since 2008.[19] The risk is that the importance of the shadow banking sector increases as regulatory constraints pile up. In that respect, the ACP strongly supports initiatives aiming at addressing areas for possible further regulatory recommendations.

One major concern relates to credit operations that could be increasingly undertaken by nonbanks, be it unregulated entities, such as hedge funds, or entities subject to different regulatory requirements, such as insurance companies. Those entities could take advantage of their nonbank status in order to enter in credit-like operations, having the same features as bank credit — liquidity or maturity transformation — but without being regulated as such, and falling outside the scope of banking supervision. Adrian and Shin (2009) showed that, in the US, a sharp increase in "market based" credit (i.e., from nonregulated institutions) occurred during the pre-crisis period and that it exhibited the most dramatic contraction in the current financial crisis, hence propagating the subprime crisis.

More generally, the transfer of risks out of the banking sector requires special attention. For instance, the emerging and still small market for

[15] See G20 (2010).
[16] Financial Supervisory Board (2012).
[17] Pozsar *et al.* (2012).
[18] European Commission (2012).
[19] See Bakk-Simon *et al.* (2012).

liquidity swaps, whereby insurance companies lend liquid and high-graded securities to banks in exchange for assets with lesser liquidity or quality, has been a scrutinized concern in Europe lately. It demonstrated that the supervisor must be reactive to emerging trends and keep in touch with financial innovation induced by regulatory changes, and which is often designed to circumvent regulation. The role of the supervisory authority on this issue is pivotal, in particular when these new categories of transactions are apt to increase interconnectedness between institutions and to foster the transfer of systemic risks outside the regulated sectors. The ACP shares the view that these operations have to be closely monitored and that strict limits have to be applied when appropriate.

In addition, the increasing interconnectedness between various institutions within the financial system, with potential consequences on regulatory imbalances, reinforces the relevance of ACP's extensive approach of supervision, which encompasses banks and insurance companies under the same authority. It is our belief that all institutions that play the same economic role should be ruled by the same regulations and supervised in a coordinated manner.

As a result, the supervisor must be careful about the side effects of any new regulation on credit institutions and foresee the implications of a regulatory regime shift. Discussions relating to the European legislative package CRR–CRD IV — which transposes into European law the recommendations of the BCBS — show policymakers' willingness and determination to set stringent rules that will apply equally to all European countries. This unified approach, across the whole banking sector, covering all credit institutions and also investment firms, contrasts with the choice that could be made elsewhere to adopt a differentiated treatment according to the entities' size. The idea prevailing in Europe was to apply identical rules to all credit institutions, irrespective of their country of establishment, with little leeway for national regulators to set different standards, in order to preserve comparability and avoid regulatory arbitrage within the European Union. With such an approach, however, it appears that the narrow definition of credit institutions[20] in CRR–CRD IV, which would

[20]Article 4 of CRR under consideration states that "credit institution" means an undertaking, the business of which is to receive deposits or other repayable funds from the public *and* to grant credits for its own account.

exclude all the institutions that do not collect deposits, reshapes the regulatory environment. For instance, institutions specialized in mortgages or consumer loans could fall outside the banking sector.

This might be a source for concern as notably mortgages regularly experience credit bubbles and affect conditions in the real estate market. What is more, mortgages entail clear transformation risks. Therefore, unless all institutions granting mortgages are captured under the same rules, there is a potential risk that more lending of mortgages will be done through noncredit institutions. A possible solution could be to broaden the scope of the CRR–CRD IV package to those entities providing credit to the economy. Alternatively, the definition of an *ad hoc* status would be appropriate for those institutions no longer covered by the new regulation. This issue is also of importance for these institutions that would otherwise no longer have access to central bank funding.

In France, such companies are currently standing at a crossroads: Should they change their business model and start collecting deposits so as to be considered as credit institutions and have access to the central bank — at the cost of implementing Basel III requirements — or not? This also applies to other categories of institutions labeled as "financial companies" (*sociétés financières*), 277 in total as of 2011, which operate in such segments as leasing, factoring, consumer credit, or equipment finance (see Figs. 3(a) and 3(b)). In order to avoid loopholes and preserve financial stability, the French regulator is considering designing a regulatory framework that would converge toward the CRR–CRD IV requirements, so as to promote a level playing field and encourage best practices.

Regulation is now defining the scope of banking activity. Different projects have been put forward: Vickers in the UK, Volcker in the US, and Liikanen in Europe. The Liikanen report proposes a mandatory separation of trading activities when the trading portfolio and available for sale (AFS) is greater than 100 billion or when the proportion of this portfolio in the total assets exceeds a threshold included between 15% and 25%. A "trading entity" should also be created when specific assets are greater than a certain percentage (to be determined) of total assets. Assets such as proprietary trading and market-making, loans and commitments to hedge funds, and private equity investments should be transferred to the "trading entity." However, the implementation of these reforms requires resolving

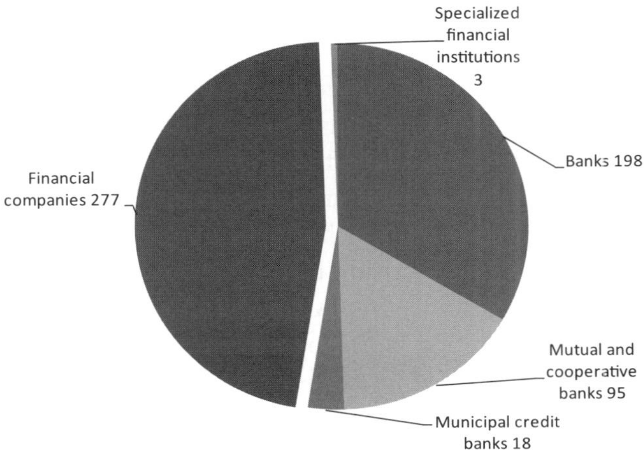

Fig. 3(a). Number of credit institutions authorized in France (2011).

Source: SGACP

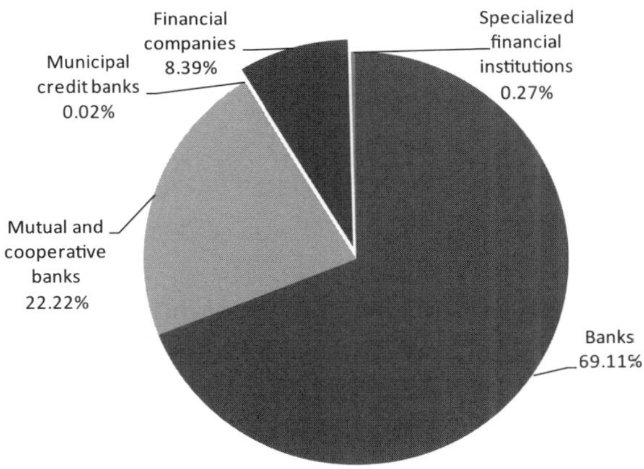

Fig. 3(b). Different types of French credit institutions by total assets (2011).

Source: SGACP

issues relative to the level playing field and the regulation of the shadow banking sector. It also requires preserving the advantage of the universal bank model. In the French case, universal banks contributed to reduce financial fragility and to dampen the macroeconomic consequences of the financial crisis. This can be notably explained by the diversified business mix of the banking groups, retail banking representing the lion's share of their activities. The structural characteristics of the domestic credit market, such as fixed rates for mortgage loans, reasonable loan-to-value and debt-to-income ratios, and the overall relatively risk-adverse culture also explain the resilience of French universal banks.

All in all, Basel III is essential in supporting financial stability, but some undesired effects can already be perceived, e.g., between banking and insurance companies: new types of transactions arising from regulation, increased competition between banks and life insurers for households' savings, higher cost of financing to the economy, etc. This shows that, facing globalized markets and interconnected financial institutions, supervisors must more than ever pay attention to the consequences of new regulation on financial stability and actively seek the suppression of any regulatory arbitrage opportunity. The question of the shadow banking regulation needs also to be addressed at the international level in order to resolve the issue concerning the externalization of risky activities outside of the regulated scope. European countries intend to adopt a unified approach across the whole banking sector, covering all credit institutions and also investment firms, which may contrast with the choice that could be made elsewhere to adopt a differentiated treatment according to the entities size.

Challenges Associated with the New Forms of Supervision

Beside new regulations and their unintended consequences, supervision is evolving in the post-crisis world. Supervisors are developing new methods and practices. In return, they raise new and higher expectations from banks and the general public. Communication by supervisors needs therefore to adapt, overcome the effects of asymmetric information, and remedy the increase in risk aversion. Indeed, badly managed communication may, in certain circumstances, precisely precipitate the financial distress that supervisors try to prevent. This is particularly the case for stress tests that have experienced a significant development in the recent past. Supervisors also need to carefully monitor the consequences on banks' behavior, hence on financial stability, from implementing a more intrusive supervision approach, and from adopting a macroprudential perspective. This implies addressing possible tradeoffs regarding the current increase in banks' reporting burden, which has dramatically developed since the crisis. To address these challenges, European authorities initiated the creation of a Banking Union aiming to ensure the financial stability.

New Supervision Methods

The Growing Importance of Stress Tests

Stress tests can be used as a tool for micro- as well as macroprudential concerns. In the microprudential approach, it provides information on the ability of individual banks to face potential losses. From the macroprudential point of view, stress tests give information on the resilience of the whole banking system. However, the micro- and macroprudential objectives of stress tests may sometimes conflict, leading to potential unintended effects of the disclosure of stress test results. In particular, the disclosure of the stress test results may sometimes adversely affect incentives and create inefficiencies at the individual bank level. There is a risk of self-fulfilling prophecies at the individual level that the supervisors have to prevent. Furthermore, a bank can make ex ante suboptimal portfolios choices (e.g., large scale of sovereign asset sales) to avoid a possible market overreaction. Supervisors have therefore to determine which information on individual banks is relevant to disclose in order to limit markets' overreaction.

Stress test exercises have been one response to the financial crisis. Arguably, national supervisory authorities have been carrying out stress tests for quite some time, but they were exceptionally published.[21] The situation changed in 2010. Indeed, since 2009, European authorities have conducted three coordinated stress test exercises on European banks. The Committee of European Banking Supervisors (CEBS) conducted the first exercise in 2009 without any disclosure of participant banks' results. The individual simulation results of the second European stress test were published on July 23, 2010. In 2011, the EBA and the national supervisors carried out the third stress test exercise and the simulation results were disclosed on July 15, 2011. Twenty banks fell below the 5% Core Tier 1

[21] The publication of bank stress tests was usually limited to IMF FSAP exercises.

threshold under the adverse scenario for 2012. In 2011, more comprehensive public disclosure of credit risk exposures was made mandatory. The aim was to provide relevant information to market participants to enable them to conduct their own stress test. However, disclosing stress tests results can have an unintended effect on bank as well as market participants' behavior since new information can be misinterpreted: Figures 4(a) and 4(b) shows a fall in the European banks' stock market prices and an increase in the price of their credit default swap around the July 15, 2011, disclosure. Nonetheless, it is important to mention that the evolution of banks' stock market and credit default swap prices around the publication of stress test results is widely explained by the worsening of the European sovereign debt crisis.

The main argument in favor of public disclosure of stress test results is that it enhances market discipline by allowing investors and counter parties to better understand the risk profiles of each institution. Market discipline based on timely and accurate information should contribute to the optimal allocation of capital and provide incentives for banks to operate efficiently and to manage and control their risk exposures prudently (Flannery and Sorescu, 1996). The disclosure of the results of stress tests is intended to restore investors' confidence in the banking system and ultimately sustain

Fig. 4(a). Evolution of the European banks' stock prices around the European stress test disclosures.

Source: Bloomberg and author's calculations.

Fig. 4(b). Evolution of the European banks' CDS prices around the European stress test disclosures.

Source: Bloomberg and author's calculations.

activity in the real economy. During the crisis it has become a piece of information strongly awaited from the supervisors, subject to great scrutiny.

However, such disclosures may have unintended consequences. They may involve inefficiencies at the individual bank level in an environment characterized by market and informational frictions. In such cases, more disclosure may reduce welfare. Indeed, if investors and other counter parties do not correctly understand a bank's operations due to previous opacity and complexity, market discipline may force this bank to make suboptimal portfolios choices or to decide inefficient asset sales. To avoid market overreactions and their destabilizing effects, the bank may be willing to take suboptimal decisions in order to pass the stress tests. A supervisor, disclosing detailed information on the results of the stress test, gives market participants a larger set of information on the underlying risk exposures of the banks, but this information reflects the change in bank's ex ante behavior, consisting of a sub-optimal portfolios choice and a window-dressing behavior (inefficient asset sales), in order to pass the stress test. The bank is considered as healthy by the market although its actions were not efficient. As a consequence, in a second-best environment with market and informational frictions, it is important to take account of possible ex ante inefficiencies. Furthermore, it is highly desirable that remedial measures be published at the same time as bad news (Himino, 2012).

A compromise to this inefficient ex ante reaction of banks may be to disclose aggregate results of the stress test, which may be useful for financial stability as a whole. However, this supervisory choice in term of disclosure may in turn not be sufficient to discipline individual banks' behavior. Supervisors may then complement these aggregated results with a detailed description of the exposures of the individual banks.

An additional and important concern about the disclosure of the results of stress tests is that the ex post reaction of market participants may be inefficient. The decisions of market participants are made in an incomplete informational environment. The decision of each market participant takes the expectation of others' actions into account. This may lead to overreactions. The extent of these over reactions may depend on banks' specificities. Market over reactions may particularly be severe for banks that are relatively less liquid that exhibit significant maturity mismatches and whose creditors are of small size, as they are less likely to take externalities into account. Moreover, greater supervisor information disclosure may reduce the incentives of market participants to find and exploit their own information. So, market prices may become less informative. This can lead to a situation in which supervisory information disclosure involves less market discipline. Supervisors have to pay attention to externalities between market participants when disclosing stress test results.

Another dimension is the credibility of the supervisor when implementing stress tests. This requires expert knowledge of banks' operations, designing the most relevant scenarios, processing optimally the information from banks using state-of-the art techniques. Credibility can only be achieved in the medium run, but appears to be crucial in crisis periods.

Overall, one may conclude that stress testing is helpful for financial stability. It can help the supervisor to identify weak institutions and to require them to take corrective actions such as raising additional capital. Solving properly these individual problems prevents contagion within the banking system and the market's deficiency. An international harmonization of stress test practices can be useful since a possible loss of credibility of one supervisor may affect the others. Methodological improvements for correctly capturing nonlinearities and feedback effects, both within the financial system and between the financial system and the macroeconomy, should enhance the effectiveness of stress tests.

A More Intrusive Approach to Supervision

Before the financial crisis, there was a clear distinction between supervisors favoring off-site analysis and those favoring a more intrusive approach. The French approach has always been intrusive with the supplemental feature that on-site inspections are allowed to be carried out over an extended period of time when it is required by the size or the complexity of the mission. Some other supervisors have been changing their supervisory approach from the so-called "light touch" to a more intrusive approach. The supervisory model of some countries was characterized by a larger amount of data reporting. Others may rely on less-intrusive controls but impose very severe sanctions when a regulated institution does not comply with regulatory requirements. Nowadays, a consensus seems to emerge on the necessity to adopt a more intrusive approach in banking supervision. More frequent and more stringent audits should discipline banks in their risk-taking behavior since they have more incentives for truthfully reporting their risks. On-site audits can also contribute to the production of more accurate financial reports by banks. However, the advantages of increasing on-site audits are not unlimited. The question of the efficient intensity of supervisor internal audits is of major interest.

Until a certain threshold, increasing the number of supervisory audits contributes to strengthening the solidity of banks. However, beyond this efficient level, more on-site audits may become counterproductive. The reason is that banks may interpret this intensification of scrutiny as a signal of a higher probability of becoming subject to supervisory enforcement action. As a consequence, they may be inclined to postpone certain projects and wait for the supervisor to give her/his views. The second explanation is that the higher frequency of audits may render the market more suspicious if it happens to notice this higher frequency. Market reactions may then exercise a negative impact on bank stock price and financing conditions. This can destabilize the institution even if it does not present major weaknesses. Delis and Staikouras (2009) provide evidence of an inverted U-shaped relationship between the frequency of on-site audits and bank soundness.

Adopting a more intrusive approach in banking supervision also raises the problem of how supervisors should allocate their limited resources when examining banks. Obviously, it must not be to the detriment of the efficiency of off-site supervision.

This evolution in banking supervision requires the disclosure of a lot of information to the supervisory authorities as well as to the market. On the one hand, new reporting is indispensable when new risks emerge; on the other hand, the accumulation of requirements from different parts could provide diminishing returns in terms of true information and effectiveness of the supervisor's action. Therefore regulators and supervisors have to carefully assess the costs and benefits of new reporting and data collections, which may otherwise turn out to be counterproductive.

Integrating Further Micro and Macro Supervision

The financial crisis highlighted the limits of relying only on microprudential regulation. There is now a large consensus on the need for increasing the role of macroprudential regulation in order to manage systemic risk, which does not focus on individual failures but rather on contagion effects and correlated shocks/exposures (see the contribution of Houben in this volume). However, discrepancies may emerge between the objectives of micro- and macroprudential regulation. In particular, some microprudential measures can lead to a reduction of lending activity and thus to a deterioration of economic conditions. The challenge is to take advantage of both micro and macro approaches.

Some microprudential regulation measures may amplify problems in the banking system. For example, if a bank experiences solvency problems, the microprudential supervisor will require that this entity restore its capital ratio. A weak bank maximizing the shareholder value may choose to shrink its assets, leaving its capital unchanged. A supervisor with a narrow microprudential mandate would not necessarily have the ability to enforce a capital increase instead of an asset reduction (Hanson, Kashyap, and Stein, 2011). However, this choice is not neutral from a macroprudential standpoint. Indeed, if the main banks are in trouble and decide simultaneously to shrink their assets by reducing their lending activity, this behavior may badly affect economic activity.

Conversely, macroprudential concerns may introduce regulatory forbearance *vis-à-vis* important banking institutions. In fact, it may be difficult for weak institutions to increase equity. So, in order to avoid a credit crunch and fire sales, a macroprudential supervisor could be reluctant to take prompt corrective action against the institutions in difficulty. In the extreme case, if macroprudential concerns may lead public authorities to bail out insolvent institutions, this can be perceived as a signal that too-big-to-fail institutions will always be supported. This situation may encourage excessive risk-taking by important institutions and reduce the efficiency of market discipline. Setting clearly the conditions of public authorities' intervention may help to solve this moral hazard problem.

On top of capital surcharges on systemically important financial institutions (SIFIs) that were introduced by the Financial Stability Board in response to requests by the G20 leaders, Basel III tries to set up a macroprudential regulation framework through the countercyclical capital buffer (CCB) that would apply to all banks covered by Basel III (or the CRD4/CRR in Europe). The implementation of a countercyclical capital buffer may introduce a substitution in loan supply between regulated institutions and local intermediaries that are not subject to domestic capital regulation. Aiyar, Calomiris, and Wieladek (2012) recently highlighted the existence of this substitution effect for the UK banking system. This situation may influence the effectiveness of this macroprudential measure. International coordination of macroprudential regulation is needed to prevent regulatory arbitrage by banks not subject to domestic bank regulation. Besides these measures, the European CRD4/CRR allows national authorities in Europe to temporarily strengthen its regulatory requirements in order to address systemic risk.

Considering this new framework, another major concern is to set up an institutional arrangement to solve the discrepancies between the objectives of micro- and macroprudential regulation. Indeed, except for the CCB and the SIFIs capital surcharge, the same tools (e.g., capital and liquidity requirements, risk-weighted assets) will be used at the macro and the micro level. Therefore, in most of the cases the same instrument could be used to solve a common issue at the micro and macro level. But there is a risk that a tool is used differently at both levels for different and inconsistent purposes. Thus either a single institution should be responsible for the whole supervision, or there has to be a very close coordination between the different bodies. Presently, the French Systemic Risk Board (the CoReFRiS, which stands for *Conseil de régulation financière et du risque systémique*) is a council chaired by the Ministry of Finance that gathers the heads of supervision and the Central Bank. It is not a macroprudential authority in itself, but its role is to ensure the coordination of the policies in the field of financial stability. One recent example is the implementation of a specific reporting on mortgage loans to better assess risks on the real estate market. In the 2013 French banking law, the COREFRIS is replaced by the Haut Conseil de Stabilité Financière, with a rather similar composition, which will become the national macroprudential authority, consistently wih CRDIV-CRR.

Efforts must be pursued to adequately define and measure systemic risk. More research is needed to improve and find efficient tools that can be used at micro- and macroprudential levels, without introducing unintended negative effects. This also includes the use of system-wide stress tests taking into account the spillover effects through bilateral financial exposures.[22] These instruments must provide the right incentives so that financial institutions internalize the externalities associated with their use. More theoretical work could be useful to efficiently use strict macroprudential tools as complements to microeconomic instruments for macroprudential supervision. Furthermore, macroprudential regulation has to be coordinated at the international level to avoid regulatory arbitrage. This will preserve the level playing field.

Coordinating Banking Supervision across the EU: The European Banking Union

One possible response to these new challenges to supervision in the EU is the future European Banking Union, which aims to coordinate and improve the effectiveness of the European banking supervision. The future Banking Union would lead to more effectiveness in the application of prudential regulation and supervisory intervention. This would create a more resilient banking system. It would allow direct recapitalization of banks

[22] See Gouriéroux, Heam, and Monfort (2012).

through the European Stability Mechanism (ESM). It would also protect deposits and avoid bank runs in periods of stress and break the vicious circle between banks and sovereigns. More generally, the Banking Union would contribute to the effectiveness of the European single monetary policy. It will be based on three pillars: a single supervisory mechanism, a single resolution mechanism, and a single deposit insurance scheme. For the time being EU countries have agreed on the first pillar, which already complements and deepens the current national supervisory regimes, but the other two pillars are expected to take place at a later stage.

Building on the model of Freixas (2003), Schoenmaker (2011) points out a "financial trilemma" leading to the impossibility to reach the three objectives of financial stability, financial integration, and maintaining national financial policies in an environment with globalized financial markets. This result is explained by the fact that in financial integration frameworks national policies alone do not take into account the externalities associated with the decisions of the national supervisor *vis-a-vis* other supervisors. This is the case when a failing cross-border bank has to be refunded. In the absence of sufficient cooperation, supervisors of the countries that will be less affected by the failure of the bank may be reluctant to participate to the operation. In fact, at the individual level, the benefit of the intervention will be lower than the costs of the rescue for a given country. In this situation, the supervisor of the home country, which is presumed to support the larger costs of the failure, may be conducted to take inefficient measure consisting in imposing asset sales to the weak institution.

The creation of the Banking Union would allow to quickly and efficiently resolve problems in the banking sector, avoiding propagation to the entire euro area banking system. The risk that problems in the banking sector of a given country affect the rest of the monetary union is exacerbated by high degree of interconnectedness between the financial sectors of the different countries. In this regard, Ongena, Peydró, and van Horen (2012) notably analyze the international contagion through cross-border lending, liquidity shocks, and foreign ownership and find that Eastern European and Middle Eastern countries were affected by a larger contraction in lending by international and foreign banks compared to local banks. Reliance on the Banking Union when a weak bank requires an intervention would break the vicious circle between banks and sovereigns. With the European Banking Union, bank resolution schemes will be unified with a unique legal framework that clearly specifies rules and procedures when resolution is required for a given bank. This is of large importance in the European banking sector characterized by the existence of large and complex cross-border banking groups. The European Banking Union would also allow implementing a deposit insurance scheme. This would preserve the level playing field in the Union since depositors of the different countries would be treated at the same way. However, in a context of financial instability, it could be more difficult to quickly proceed to the deposit insurance reform. In fact, the rationale of deposit insurance schemes is associated with the capacity of deposit insurance to have sufficient resources. This requires few banks failures.

The future Banking Union should apply at least to all Euro area member states with a close cooperation with other EU countries that can "opt-in" the new system. In this future architecture of the European supervision, national supervisors would play a major role. They would prepare and implement the ECB acts under its oversight. This would consist, for example, of day-to-day assessment of a bank's situation and related on-site verifications. National authorities have crucial local expertise, daily monitoring experience, and qualified resources. They would also conserve their responsibility in the area of anti-money laundering and terrorism, consumer protection, and supervision of third-country branches and investment firms. Moreover, the tasks and prerogatives of the European Banking Authority (EBA), notably the regulatory and coordination role would also be maintained.

The implementation of the European Banking Union constitutes a major progress in the European Banking supervision, while at the same time preserving the single European market for financial services. In coordination with national supervisors, it would largely contribute to the strengthening of the financial stability by breaking the close link between banks and sovereigns. Beyond this current concern, the Banking Union would globally help to ensure a healthy banking sector and improve the efficiency of monetary policy.

Conclusions

New regulations aim at changing behaviors from market participants. Some reactions are intended, while others are not, as supervised institutions react strategically and opportunistically. Innovation, in turn, requires new regulatory adaptations. Although this feedback process entail new risks when institutions try to circumvent regulation by developing risky and convoluted alternatives, this dialectical process of regulatory response remains the best answer to the dynamic nature of risk.

We have touched upon the important topic of the unintended consequences of supervision. The attention was first drawn to the undesirable effects that may emerge from new regulation and that have to be managed by the supervisor. The deleveraging process implemented by banks has particularly been closely followed by European supervisors, notably the ACP, to avoid its negative impact on the credit supply, in particular for SMEs that cannot rely on alternative sources of funding. The implementation of the liquidity requirements also requires particular attention in order to achieve a level playing field and to prevent excess competition for long-term funding. Regulatory arbitrage, which can emerge from the implementation of a leverage ratio, is also a major concern. Moreover, higher regulatory requirements could lead to a transfer of certain risky assets to a less-regulated shadow banking sector that may threaten the financial stability. Reflections have to be pursued to determine the best way to address this problem.

Nevertheless, the new Basel III regulation and the measures adopted by the European national supervisors have largely contributed to a significant increase in banking solvency and liquidity, and this tendency should continue. However, efforts have to be pursued to minimize the regulatory arbitrages. The new requirements should also penalize size and complexity, leading banks to focus on their core business.

Besides changes in regulatory requirements, there is a growing demand for more supervisory action and communication. In this framework, stress tests can be helpful for financial stability. However, disclosing their results requires special care to avoid banks' ex ante inefficient behavior and the market's overreaction. Furthermore, integrating the objectives of micro and macroeconomic supervision has been growing in importance and will certainly remain a flourishing field for further studies. Finally, the coordination of stress test practices as well as macroprudential supervision under the stimulating influence of peer supervisory pressure will improve supervisory practices. Besides, the future European Banking Union will significantly contribute to the financial stability.

Providing the right incentives to institutions in order to preserve financial stability is the core objective of supervision. The new regulatory landscape after the financial crisis has changed the perspectives and may introduce further unintended consequences of supervision. They create new challenges for supervision. We are confident that we will collectively be able to address them properly in order to offer still more effective supervision.

References

Acharya, V. and P. Schnabl (2012). "Securitization without risk transfer," *Journal of Financial Economics*, Vol. 107, pp. 515–536.

Adrian, T. and H. S. Shin (2009). "Money, liquidity and monetary policy," *American Economic Review*, Vol. 99, No. 2, pp. 600–605.

Aiyar, S., C. W. Calomiris and T. Wieladek (2012). "Does macro-pru leak? Evidence from a UK policy experiment," National Bureau of Economic Research Working Paper No. 17822.

Autorité de Contrôle Prudentiel (2012). "Analyses et synthèse: Enquête annuelle sur le financement de l'habitat en 2011."

Bakk-Simon, K., S. Borgioli, C. Giron, H. Hempell, A. Maddaloni, F. Recine and S. Rosati (2012). "Shadow banking in the euro area: An overview," European Central Bank Occasional Paper.

Bank for International Settlements (2012a). *Quarterly Review*, March.

Bank for International Settlements (2012b). *Quarterly Review*, June.

Basel Committee on Banking Supervision (2009). "Strengthening the resilience of the banking sector."

Basel Committee on Banking Supervision (2010). "Basel III: A global regulatory framework for more resilient banks and banking systems."

Basel Committee on Banking Supervision (2012). "Results of the Basel III implementation monitoring exercise as of 30 June 2011."

Basel Committee on Banking Supervision (2012). "Report to G20 leaders on Basel III implementation," June.

Blum, J. M. (2008). "Why 'Basel II' may need a leverage ratio restriction," *Journal of Banking & Finance*, Vol. 32, pp. 1699–1707.

Committee on the Global Financial System (2011). "The impact of sovereign credit risk on bank funding conditions," CGFS Papers No. 43.

Delis, M. D. and P. Staikouras (2009). "On-site audits, sanctions, and bank risk-taking: An empirical overture towards a novel regulatory and supervisory philosophy," Munich Personal RePEc Archive Paper No. 16836.

European Banking Authority (2012). "Results of the Basel III monitoring exercise as of 31 December 2011."

European Central Bank (2010). "Recent developments in supervisory structures in the EU member states," October.

European Commission (2012). "Shadow banking," Green Paper.

Financial Supervisory Board (2012). "Strengthening the oversight and regulation of shadow banking." Progress report to G20 ministers and governors," April 16.

Flannery, M. J. and S. M. Sorescu (1996). "Evidence of bank market discipline in subordinated debenture yields," *Journal of Finance*, Vol. 51, pp. 1347–1377.

Freixas, X. (2003). "Crisis management in Europe," in *Financial Supervision in Europe*, J. Kremers, D. Schoenmaker, and P. Wierts (eds.), Cheltenham, UK: Edward Elgar Publishing, pp. 102–119.

G20 (2010). "G20 Seoul Summit leaders' declaration," November 11–12.

Gouriéroux, C., J. C. Heam and A. Monfort (2012). "Bilateral exposures and solvency systemic risk," *Canadian Journal of Economics*, Vol. 45(4), pp. 1273–1309.

Hanson, S., A. K. Kashyap and J. C. Stein (2011). "A macroprudential approach to financial regulation," *Journal of Economic Perspectives*, Vol. 25, pp. 3–28.

Himino, R. (2012). "Rethinking banking supervision," *Risk*, March.

Kim, D. and A. M. Santomero (1980). "Risk in banking and capital regulation," *Journal of Finance*, Vol. 35, pp. 1235–1244.

Kremp, E. and P. Sevestre (2011). "Did the crisis induce credit rationing for French SMEs?" Banque de France.

Morrison, A. (2010). "Universal Banks," in *Oxford Handbook of Banking*, A. N. Berger, P. Molyneux and J. S. Wilson (eds.), Oxford: Oxford University Press.

Mian, A. and A. Sufi (2009). "The consequences of mortgage credit expansion: Evidence from the U.S. mortgage default crisis," *Quarterly Journal of Economics*, Vol. 124, pp. 1449–1496.

Observatoire de l'épargne réglementée Annual Report (2011). Banque de France. Available at http://www.banque-france.fr/fileadmin/user-upload/banque_de_france/Economic_et_Statistiques/Titres_Credits_Depots/oer-rapport-2011.pdf.

Ongena, S., J.-L. Peydró and N. van Horen (2012). "Shocks abroad, pain at home? Bank-firm level evidence on financial contagion during the recent financial crisis," European Central Bank.

Pozsar, Z., T. Adrian, A. Ashcraft and H. Boesky (2012). "Shadow banking," Federal Reserve Bank of New York.

Schoenmaker, D. (2011). "The financial trilemma," *Economics Letters*, Vol. 111, pp. 57–59.

The Social Value of the Financial Sector: Where to from Here?

Barbara A. Rehm*

American Banker

Where to from here? Such a great question and obviously none of us has the answer, in fact there is no single answer. But I have been watching financial services policy being formulated for 25 years, and I truly don't have a dog in this fight, so let me take a stab at an answer.

Actually before I go there I'd like to spend a few minutes on what isn't or shouldn't be the answer. We cannot continue on the path we're on. Regulators from five separate agencies simply can't keep their heads down and keep trying to crank out rules required by the Dodd–Frank Act or the Basel Committee. It isn't getting us where we need to be. The end result of numerous agencies pumping out massive rules to meet statutory deadlines will be a tangle of contradictory mandates that will be tough to enforce and impossible to comply with.

More is not better. Only better is actually better. We are simply on a mission impossible right now and the sooner policymakers acknowledge this, the better.

And that brings me to the tip of my answer — we need someone in the federal government to LEAD — to tell Congress that it asked for too much, too soon, and for too many things that have nothing to do with the crisis. This brave soul needs to stand up and say doing all these rules together will not solve the problem and in fact will tie our financial system in knots, which in turn will continue to be a drag on economic growth.

---

*Barbara Rehm is *American Banker*'s editor at large.

We need to identify the most-necessary rules, prioritize them, and then focus on getting those things accomplished. We need to do it with the least amount of complexity possible, with a bias toward relying on clear principles and better supervision (remember Pillar 2?).

It will take courage and a whole lot of energy to be that voice. And once he or she gets everyone's attention, it will be difficult to get agreement on the priorities and then to get the agencies to get the work done. The person perhaps best positioned to be this voice is the next Treasury Secretary because he or she will come to the debate as an honest broker — not someone who's been in the trenches for the past two-plus years.

But I don't think we can wait for that person to be nominated and confirmed, so as naïve as I know this will sound to many of you, I honestly believe the only person to do so is President Obama. He is the only person who can truly stand up to Congress and simultaneously give the regulators some cover.

Now before you dismiss this as impossible, arguing in your head that the President is much too busy: Think of the role financial services plays in our economy? The President could easily combine this with his campaign to fix the debt and deficit and create more jobs.

So just imagine for a moment if President Obama took half a day, and held a public meeting in a big auditorium and invited all the federal regulators to attend — the principals, the rule writers, the examiners — and he said something like this:

> *Dodd–Frank is important. The American people are counting on you to get it done.*
>
> *But I understand that a lot is being asked of you and that some of it is even contradictory. I realize you are being criticized from many quarters, that you are overworked and in some cases under budgeted.*
>
> *But your work is important and I need to you come together and make some tough decisions. Every decision won't be right, but that's OK. We don't expect you to be infallible.*
>
> *I am asking Treasury Secretary Tim Geithner to convene a meeting tomorrow and I'd like each agency head to be in the room and brainstorm a list of priorities — the things we most need to ensure a stable financial system that can still fuel a growing economy.*
>
> *I can't force independent agencies to do anything, but I do hope you will rally together in a common direction for the common good.*

Do you realize how powerful that would be? Lawmakers would complain, but they always do. So let them. But I really think this would let us hit a reset on Dodd–Frank that will allow the law's potential to be realized. Dodd–Frank took us in the right direction. I just think it stuffed too many things in and required them to be done all at once.

So what needs to be on that priority list?

Number one on the list has to be "Too Big To Fail " (TBTF). I do believe Dodd–Frank does end TBTF and the FDIC and the Fed have done a solid job writing the Orderly Liquidation Authority and living wills rules. But this part of the law is less about writing an effective rule and more about enforcing it. It's about demanding living wills that can work and forcing companies to divest risky affiliates if they don't have enough capital or enough management talent. It's about actually using the Orderly Liquidation Authority when the time comes. Simply put: the regulators have to get better at early intervention — identify problems early and then demand institutions actually fix them. The living wills cannot just be a blizzard of paper. They have to be an effective means of understanding our largest banks and forcing change when necessary.

Systemically important financial institutions are my next priority. Let's name the nonbank SIFIs. Which financial companies that aren't banks are so big or interconnected that their failure could cause a systemic threat? What's taking so long to answer that? We are the only country to actually legislate a plan for overseeing nonbank financial firms and yet we can't get it off the ground. I'd cast the net wide at first and at least give the Fed a chance to get in and really assess the risks posed by each firm. The FSOC can knock a company off the list if supervisors decide it is not truly systemic.

Capital is next on my priority list. I am all for more and better capital. But for the love of somebody, let's simplify these rules. We are wasting so much time and energy trying to put square pegs in round holes. Come up with something simpler and then enforce it and don't forget regulators have the power to require any institution to hold more than the required minimum.

I would table Basel III. Our regulators know what those rules require and they can simply work to move our banks to those capital levels, but stop wasting so much time and angst over implementing a global agreement that will never be adopted in any sort of unified and consistent manner. I am not worried about disappointing foreign supervisors. They'll get over it.

Liquidity is another worthy goal, but I am okay with pushing those complex rules off until we get some of the core Dodd–Frank rules nailed down. Liquidity has improved a lot already and I think, considering how complicated that rule is, we can push it to Round Two but still have close supervisory review of the liquidity positions of major institutions.

I'm going to take a moment here to list some of the other things I think could wait until Round Two — after some fundamental regulations are in place and we have a chance to see how they are working:

— Do we need three different capital surcharges?
— Do we need two sets of counterparty limits?
— Do we need everything in Sec. 165 proposal considering we already have the stress tests?

OK — so beyond that core group of priorities — TBTF, SIFIs, and capital — I would tack on two more: derivatives and proprietary trading. If the system is really still so fragile and still so interconnected (and I for one think it is), then we need to get the Dodd–Frank rules designed to bring more transparency and stability to the derivatives market and we need to get a Volcker rule in place that can work.

Everyone from regulators to bankers has to realize that not all financial activity is beneficial. Some of it is just plain speculative and a way to shift money around for financial gain. Regulators and bankers have to agree on what activities fall in this bucket and cut them out.

I am no expert on the derivatives provisions in Dodd–Frank, but we need to pin down those rules and start enforcing them. Again we can't let perfect be the enemy of the good. While not ideal, if the CFTC and SEC can't agree, then let them both issue rules and eventually it will become clear which one is more effective and we can move toward that rule for the entire market. But doing something is better than doing nothing.

Ditto the Volcker rule. Let's get a simple rule out and start enforcing it. It can be refined if it's too tough or not tough enough. But regulators could simply tell banks — making markets and meeting customer needs is OK as Dodd–Frank says — but no proprietary trading and then examine for compliance. The bank would have the burden of proving it was making a market or meeting some other exception.

The sixth thing on my priority list is getting the Office of Financial Research (OFR) up and really running. In my view, Dodd–Frank should have made the office independent from the Treasury Department, but it didn't. I really don't understand Treasury on this one. The OFR was supposed to be our avenue for finally quantifying the relationships among banks, to track the complex interconnections. What we don't know here can kill us and yet the government is not putting enough effort into figuring out how all these giant firms are linked to each other.

Ok, that's my initial priority list. I realize I have not mentioned housing, which is obviously a huge hole in our public policy right now. But I only have 12 minutes so I decided to talk solely about rules relating to safety and soundness though I could easily argue that the underwriting rules for mortgages fall into this category. I had to draw the line somewhere.

So to summarize my argument so far: We need to pick our spots and follow through. Measure our progress and figure out what else needs doing. Spinning our wheels trying to do 5,000 things at once is a sure way to do nothing well. What is critical to the well-being of the financial system is the faith and confidence that individuals, market makers, and liquidity providers have in the system. And having too many complicated and potentially contradictory rules that nobody truly understands doesn't add to that faith. It detracts from it.

I have a separate shorter priority list for industry executives. Two related things bank executives can and should do on their own — improve corporate governance and culture. My point about corporate governance relates back to my first point about TBTF and examiners holding senior management's feet to the fire. If executives don't act fast enough, examiners should take the concerns to the board of directors. If a company is taking too much risk, or worse doesn't understand the risks it's taking, examiners need to force some changes. But wouldn't it be better for all involved if bankers and their boards tackled this themselves?

Banks know (or should) where their weak spots are, who their weak players are, what processes need improving. Instead of ignoring problems, or hiding them, go after them ahead of examiners. If your compensation policies are still encouraging risk-taking, fix them. If a business line has a predatory bent to it, get out of the business or reform the practices.

I would start this sort of change at the board level. Too many bank boards just follow the CEO blindly, packed with people who are loyal to the CEO. The board has to be independent. Directors have to raise questions. Directors have to really understand the bank's risk appetite and whether it's operating within that range. One simple way to ensure this: Require every board member to invest in the bank's stock, maybe a certain percentage of their net worth. That would go a long way toward ensuring an engaged board.

Culture is a close cousin to governance. Bankers have got to find a way to convince employees that doing the right thing will be rewarded. You can't just talk about it. You have to show people by doing things like killing a product that may be profitable, but just isn't "right."

I'd also love to hear a large bank CEO talk about "Too Big To Manage." You get an occasional comment about why we need big banks, but you rarely hear them talk about the challenges of managing a company with assets in the 13 digits. Tone at the top matters — to customers, to employees, to shareholders, and to regulators.

If banks don't do this on their own, then the remedy forced upon them will be harsh ... It will be some sort of "structural reform" where the largest banks are busted up or retail banking will be separated from investment banking. This might even happen without government action — shareholders already discount bank stocks below book value and it's not hard to envision a day when investors force a large bank to break itself up to unlock value.

That's where I would go in the near term.

I do have some ideas for longer-term reforms and the number 1 thing I would do is create a single federal agency for financial supervision. We have too many cooks in that kitchen. I hear the concern about not having the checks and balances we have today and I don't find them convincing. We aren't balancing anything. We are just taking forever to write rules because agencies can't agree.

I would create an elite corps of large bank examiners and house them inside this single federal agency. All the supervisors from the Fed, the OCC, and the FDIC would be moved to this agency. I'd combine the CFTC and the SEC and make that a bureau within this agency. The Fed would do monetary policy and the FDIC would be the insurer. They could get any data they want about individual banks from this consolidated supervisor.

The Financial Stability Oversight Council could serve as a counterweight to this new agency. In my ideal world, the FSOC has 5 members: Treasury, the leader of the new federal agency for supervision, the Fed, FDIC, and the independent OFR director. It would operate as a commission and need a majority vote to approve actions.

The one piece of the pie that I am not addressing is the shadow system ... Actually, I am not sure what's left of it once the nonbank SIFI net is cast. But bankers tell me they are really worried about it from both a business and a talent perspective. Clearly it's a chunk of the financial world that needs monitoring and FSOC should be on top of it.

Finally, I'd get the scores of researchers working for the government try to answer some basic questions — the answers to which we could base future policy decisions. We really don't have answers to some fundamental questions like:

— Does our economy need big banks?
— How big is "too big?"
— Is proprietary trading really bad?
— Does enterprise risk management really work?

I think if we had some of these answers we could make better policy decisions.

Thank you.

Public Policy Options

Jürgen Stark*

University of Tübingen, Germany

My remarks are based on the experience in the run-up to the crisis until 2007 and during the crisis since 2008. In my comments I will discuss the following issues:

1. The G20 financial sector reform agenda;
2. Progress made in implementing reforms;
3. Is the financial system safer today?;
4. Is there "too much finance?"; and
5. Has the financial sector stepped out of its role of serving the real economy?

It is very likely that I will raise more questions than I provide answers.

Nobody can argue today that there were no early warnings or serious questions raised before 2007–2008 about the risks in the global financial system and whether these risks were appropriately priced and managed. What did we know about the allocation of risks? It was assumed that unregulated new risk transfer instruments and new financial institutions would create a safer financial system by distributing the risks more evenly across the system, including the shadow banking system. In the end, it was the financial crisis that made the allocation of risks more transparent — in a very dramatic and costly way. It was obvious that the global financial system — markets, institutions, and instruments — had become too

*Jürgen Stark is affiliated with the University of Tübingen, Germany, and is also an independent economist. He is a former Member of the European Central Bank's Executive Board and Governing Council (2006–2011) and former Deputy Governor of Deutsche Bundesbank (1998–2006).

sophisticated and too complex and was understood and managed solely by highly remunerated specialists. Risk-taking was separated from risk-bearing through securitization.

1. Four years ago the G20 leaders recognized that "*the global economy is facing its most serious financial crisis and economic slowdown in decades.*" In November 2008 the G20 finance ministers and Central Bank governors pointed to the root causes that have led to the crisis: "*...the current financial crisis is largely a result of excessive risk taking and faulty risk management practices in financial markets, inconsistent macroeconomic policies, which gave rise to domestic and external imbalances, as well as deficiencies in financial regulation and supervision in some advanced economies.*"

The G20 members drew the conclusion that "*all countries (...) must improve their regulatory and supervisory regimes.*" The G20 meetings in Washington, DC, in November 2008 and in Pittsburgh in the fall of 2009, generated an agenda for putting financial regulation on a stronger footing. The declaration of the Washington Summit already established the major principles that should henceforth guide the reform of financial markets. These principles are still valid: (i) strengthening transparency and accountability; (ii) enhancing sound regulation; (iii) promoting integrity in financial markets; (iv) reinforcing international cooperation; and (v) reforming international financial institutions.

Regarding the call for better regulation, the declaration pledged "*to strengthen our regulatory regimes, prudential oversight, and risk management, and ensure that all financial markets, products and participants are regulated or subject to oversight ....*" This call was amended by an important political escape clause: "*...as appropriate to their circumstances.*"

2. The G20 leaders' statement of Pittsburgh in 2009 foresaw "*strict and precise timetables*" for the implementation of the reforms. However, after the initial impetus under the impact of the culminating financial crisis, the steps toward reform have frequently been criticized as having lost momentum. In fact, the Financial Stability Board has put in place a framework to monitor the progress made in implementing the G20 financial reforms. This shows that, for some of the identified priority areas, the advances have not gone beyond agreeing some general pronouncements. Important reforms are expected to be finalized only in the years to come. This is

true, for instance, of the key task of regulating and supervising the shadow banking system, which is at the stage of spelling out the respective policies.

Some progress has been made. In particular, the necessary regulations or legislation aimed at implementing the Basel III framework — especially strengthening banks' capital and liquidity standards — will start to be put in place as of January 2013. The full set of regulations will only be phased in by 2019, more than 10 years after the recent financial crisis peaked. Unfortunately, it is very likely that Basel III will not be implemented in all G20 jurisdictions within the agreed time frame. If this turns out to be the case, this would set a bad precedent for other G20 reform agenda items. In case anyone forgets, Basel III was endorsed by all G20 leaders in spring 2011 at their meeting in Seoul. However, there is a valid criticism of the Basel III rules, which relates to their complexity. The new framework regarding banks' capital and liquidity standards is indeed very comprehensive and detailed. But do complex rules merely reflect a complex system? Or should the system itself become simpler to allow for simpler rules as well? All in all, we are still in the early stages of financial reform.

The G20 Leaders warned at their Pittsburgh meeting that "*a sense of normalcy should not lead to complacency.*" Indeed, the first signs of a re-stabilizing global economy eased the necessary pressure behind the process of reforming financial regulation. While regulators have correctly adopted the view that it is more important to get the regulations right and make them waterproof, we have to ensure that the financial market reform is put in place not just rigorously, but also rapidly, in order to make the global financial system safer.

3. There is a broad political consensus that we do need a safer financial system. However, vested interests have come into play, linked to the fear of possible negative growth effects of a more appropriate regulation and supervision regime. But these fears represent a short-term view. Perhaps the most important benefits of a safer financial system are those stemming from effective prevention and mitigation of banking crises, which cause enormous economic and social costs. Indeed, as history shows, systemic banking crises can produce losses that are multiples of annual GDP, which undoubtedly makes the benefits of reducing the likelihood of costly financial crises very high.

The costs of the recent crisis were in fact sizable. For the OECD countries, a loss of about 4% of GDP was recorded in 2009. Added to this is the likelihood of a permanent dampening of medium-term potential output. Governments and central banks took unprecedented action globally in response to the perils originating from the financial market turmoil. Euro-area governments, for instance, increased their deficits on average by more than 5% points of GDP in 2010. This was the combined consequence of rescue packages for financial institutions, cyclical stimulus packages, and the operation of automatic stabilizers. Debt-to-GDP ratios in advanced economies have increased on average by about 25% points since 2007. Central banks around the world have expanded their balance sheets, though to different extents and with different asset–liability structures.

It is clear that, in our democracies, such measures taken by fiscal and monetary authorities can only be an exception to the rule. They are in no way repeatable, either in nature or in scale. The disasters that we have witnessed in the financial system must not be allowed to recur. All the evidence points to one conclusion: More radical reforms of the financial system are urgently required.

Recently, the International Monetary Fund raised the question of whether the financial system is safer today than it was on the eve of the crisis. According to the chairman of the Financial Stability Board, the answer is "yes." The IMF, however, provides a more differentiated and ambiguous answer: Financial systems are still overly complex; banking assets are concentrated; the *too-important-to-fail* issues are unresolved; new products are being developed, circumventing new regulations. This assessment reflects the limited progress that has been made in financial market regulation, despite some improvement in increasing capital and liquidity and more proactive risk management at the level of individual banks.

4. For all these reasons — and also for as long as the focus of reform and regulation is on individual banks rather than on the system as a whole — we have to dig deeper into the causes of the crisis by asking more searching questions: (i) Is the G20 regulation approach credible, or is it just about curing the symptoms? (ii) Do we need much more radical reforms of the system, because the root causes of the financial crisis are not being addressed? (iii) Has the massive bailout of the financial system created

moral hazard? (iv) In more general terms: What kind of financial system is required to properly and adequately fulfill its economic and social role?

As the reform process has not gone far enough and has additionally lost steam over time, there is still the perception in the market that governments and central banks will intervene again when faced with a failing bank which is considered to be systemically important. As a consequence, the expectation of a bailout may lead to a financial sector that is "*too large*" with respect to the "*social optimum.*" In order to avoid taxpayers being taken hostage again by banks (...by the system...?), more resolute measures are needed to make the system less complex, less leveraged, more transparent, and the risks better managed. Ultimately, a safer system should be more narrowly focused and, as mentioned by Hal Scott, should provide less short-term funding, which is a deeply rooted problem of today's capital markets.

The two or three decades preceding the crisis saw a large expansion of the financial sector in many advanced economies. Viewed together with the negative experiences of the recent financial crisis, it is thus tempting to assert that the financial sector has in fact grown out of proportion.

The idea that "too much finance" can be detrimental to economic growth has found some empirical and theoretical confirmation. It evidences a nonmonotonic relation between the size of the financial sector and economic growth: If the size of the financial system exceeds a certain threshold, it may have a negative growth impact. One mechanism behind such a pattern may be that a larger financial sector could contribute to exacerbating the positive relation between average growth and the probability of sizeable economic downturns. Another explanation could be that even in tranquil times, an oversized financial sector may represent a misallocation of financial and human resources that could be better utilized elsewhere in the economy. According to recent BIS research, once bank assets exceed annual GDP in size, they start to act as a drag on economic growth.

5. Nevertheless, it should be clear that the sheer scale of financial sector activity per se is not the only relevant factor for growth and economic welfare, but rather the types and qualities of financial sector activity as well. This applies, in particular, to the assessment of the years preceding the crisis. Beyond merely stating that "*the financial sector has become too big,*"

a more specific conclusion can be drawn: "*The financial sector had stepped out of its role of serving the real economy.*"

It has long been recognized that the financial sector does not exist in the economy for its own sake. Its role is that of serving the real economy. Or, as Joseph Schumpeter put it in 1934: "*He* (the banker) *stands between those who wish to form new combinations and the possessors of productive means...He is the ephor* (the overseer) *of the exchange economy.*"

In fact, all the elements that have been identified in financial and economics literature as the key functions of the financial sector are ultimately directed at supporting the real economy. In providing these well-known functions, the financial industry plays its role in contributing to sustainable economic growth. In recent years, however, the financial sector has allowed its focus to wander from this central role. In a period characterized by the search for yield — featuring inadequate risk assessment and pricing, weak underwriting standards, inadequate risk management practices, fragile short-term funding of long-term assets, a proliferation of opaque financial products, and excessive leverage — the financial sector has become to some extent self-referential.

These failures were undoubtedly attributable partly to deficiencies in financial regulation and supervision. The regulatory overhaul of the financial sector is intended to correct this. But will it help the financial sector to refocus on its service role? Looking forward, a system serving the real economy requires a safer and more narrowly focused banking system, equipped with sufficiently high capital. In fact, a sounder and more role-focused financial system has to be smaller than the one before the crisis started. In this respect, some progress has been made on this side of the Atlantic, less so in Europe, where in the fall of 2008 all banks were considered to be systemically important and the possibility of banks exiting the market became a taboo.

6. To conclude, recent years have seen a financial system that has outgrown its proper size, lost track of its core functions and become a major source of risk itself. Overall, the financial sector has veered away from its genuine role of serving the real economy and thereby society as a whole. The current overhaul of financial regulation is a key element in helping the financial sector to become safer and thus eventually to once again contribute toward

sustainable economic growth. At present, the system is not as safe as it needs to be and as it could be. It is now vital to regain the necessary momentum and to strictly follow the implementation schedules. At the same time, the adequacy of the regulatory system needs to be assessed on a regular basis. This will help to avoid the past mistake of regulators failing to spot new sources of risk arising in the financial sector. The guiding principles of all regulatory measures and any redimensioning of the financial sector must be: simplicity, transparency, and the avoidance of short-termism. Finance must resume its core role of serving both society and the real economy without becoming a source of risk itself.

Finally, let me raise an issue which is not the subject of this conference: Whatever impact any new and more adequate regulation has on the soundness of the financial system and on sustainable economic growth, we should not forget the macroeconomic environment in which financial institutions operate. We have been living for a very long time already in an era of "*ultra-cheap money*," with de facto zero-interest rates (negative interest rates in real terms), and "*ultra-cheap credit*" globally. Major central banks have already signaled that they will maintain their zero-rate policy for at least three more years. The key question in this context is: How would the financial system operate in this environment of very low interest rates if it is maintained too long? The most likely result is: inadequate pricing of risks, market distortions, and misallocation of resources — thus sowing the seeds of the next crisis.

Agenda

Thursday, November 15, 2013

9:00 AM REGISTRATION AND CONTINENTAL BREAKFAST

9:40 AM WELCOMING REMARKS
Charles L. Evans, President and Chief Executive Officer, Federal Reserve Bank of Chicago
Richard Portes, London Business School and Founder and President, Centre for Economic Policy Research (CEPR) — London

10:00 AM SESSION I: DESCRIPTION AND MEASUREMENT OF THE FINANCIAL SYSTEM
Moderator: Douglas D. Evanoff, Federal Reserve Bank of Chicago
Charles W. Calomiris, Columbia University
Alan M. Taylor, University of Virginia
Enrico Berkes, Northwestern University
Ugo Panizza, University of Geneva
Commentator: Eugene N. White, Rutgers University

11:45 AM LUNCHEON AND KEYNOTE ADDRESS
Introduction: Charles L. Evans, President and Chief Executive Officer, Federal Reserve Bank of Chicago
Charles Goodhart, Emeritus Professor of Banking and Finance, Financial Markets Group, London School of Economics

1:45 PM SESSION II: SOCIAL BENEFITS AND COSTS OF THE CURRENT FINANCIAL SYSTEM
Moderator: Richard Portes, London Business School and CEPR
Ross Levine, University of California, Berkeley
Marco Pagano, University of Naples Federico II
Commentator: Gerard Caprio, Jr., Williams College

3:30 PM BREAK

3:45 PM SESSION III: FINANCIAL INDUSTRY INNOVATION
Moderator: Daniel G. Sullivan, Executive Vice President and Director of Research, Federal Reserve Bank of Chicago
Viral V. Acharya, New York University
W. Scott Frame, University of North Carolina at Charlotte
Luc Laeven, International Monetary Fund

5:50 PM RECEPTION

6:45 PM DINNER AND KEYNOTE ADDRESS
Introduction: Charles L. Evans, President and Chief Executive Officer, Federal Reserve Bank of Chicago
Raghuram Rajan, Eric J. Gleacher Distinguished Service Professor of Finance, University of Chicago

Friday, November 16, 2013

7:30 AM REGISTRATION AND CONTINENTAL BREAKFAST

8:15 AM SESSION IV: EFFECTS OF REGULATION, THE SAFETY NET, AND OTHER GOVERNMENT GUARANTEES
Moderator: Bethany McLean, Vanity Fair
Edward Kane, Boston College
Nicola Cetorelli, Federal Reserve Bank of New York
Javier Suarez, Center for Monetary and Financial Studies (CEFMI), Madrid
Commentator: Mathias Dewatripont, National Bank of Belgium

10:00 AM BREAK

10:15 AM SESSION V: FINANCE AND ECONOMIC ACTIVITY: VARIATIONS ACROSS EMERGING AND DEVELOPED MARKETS
Moderator: María J. Nieto, Banco de España
Franklin Allen, University of Pennsylvania

Thorsten Beck, Tilburg University, The Netherlands
Neeltje van Horen, De Nederlandsche Bank
Commentator: Elias Papaioannou, London Business School

12:00 PM LUNCHEON AND KEYNOTE ADDRESS
Introduction: David Marshall, Senior Vice President, Associate Director of Research and Director of Financial Markets, Federal Reserve Bank of Chicago
Mary John Miller, Under Secretary for Domestic Finance, U.S. Treasury Department

2:00 PM SESSION VI: BREAK UP THE BIG BANKS?
Moderator: David Marshall, Federal Reserve Bank of Chicago
James R. Barth, Auburn University and Milken Institute
Thomas M. Hoenig and Charles S. Morris, Federal Deposit Insurance Corporation
Harvey Rosenblum, Federal Reserve Bank of Dallas
Hal S. Scott, Harvard University Law School

3:45 PM BREAK

4:00 PM SESSION VII: WHERE TO FROM HERE? WHAT DOES ALL OF THIS MEAN FOR FINANCIAL REGULATORY POLICY?
Moderator: George G. Kaufman, Loyola University Chicago
Claudio Borio, Bank for International Settlements
Thomas Huertas, Ernst & Young, London
Vasileios Madouros, Bank of England
Danièle Nouy, Banque de France
Barbara A. Rehm, American Banker
Jürgen Stark, Formerly European Central Bank Executive Board

6:00 PM RECEPTION

Index